Olga Bertelsen (ed.)

# REVOLUTION AND WAR IN CONTEMPORARY UKRAINE

The Challenge of Change

*ibidem*-Verlag
Stuttgart

**Bibliografische Information der Deutschen Nationalbibliothek**
Die Deutsche Nationalbibliothek verzeichnet diese Publikation in der Deutschen Nationalbibliografie; detaillierte bibliografische Daten sind im Internet über http://dnb.d-nb.de abrufbar.

**Bibliographic information published by the Deutsche Nationalbibliothek**
Die Deutsche Nationalbibliothek lists this publication in the Deutsche Nationalbibliografie; detailed bibliographic data are available in the Internet at http://dnb.d-nb.de.

∞

Gedruckt auf alterungsbeständigem, säurefreien Papier
Printed on acid-free paper

ISSN: 1614-3515

ISBN-13: 978-3-8382-1016-2

© *ibidem*-Verlag
Stuttgart 2016

Alle Rechte vorbehalten

Das Werk einschließlich aller seiner Teile ist urheberrechtlich geschützt. Jede Verwertung außerhalb der engen Grenzen des Urheberrechtsgesetzes ist ohne Zustimmung des Verlages unzulässig und strafbar. Dies gilt insbesondere für Vervielfältigungen, Übersetzungen, Mikroverfilmungen und elektronische Speicherformen sowie die Einspeicherung und Verarbeitung in elektronischen Systemen.

All rights part of this publication may be reproduced, stored in or introduced into a retrieval system, or transmitted, in any form, or by any means (electronical, mechanical, photocopying, recording or otherwise) without the prior written permission of the publisher. Any person who does any unauthorized act in relation to this publication may be liable to criminal prosecution and civil claims for damages.

Printed in the EU

# Soviet and Post-Soviet Politics and Society (SPPS) Vol. 161
ISSN 1614-3515

**General Editor:** Andreas Umland,
*Institute for Euro-Atlantic Cooperation, Kyiv,* umland@stanfordalumni.org

**Commissioning Editor:** Max Jakob Horstmann,
London, mjh@ibidem.eu

## EDITORIAL COMMITTEE*

### DOMESTIC & COMPARATIVE POLITICS
Prof. **Ellen Bos**, *Andrássy University of Budapest*
Dr. **Ingmar Bredies**, *FH Bund, Brühl*
Dr. **Andrey Kazantsev**, *MGIMO (U) MID RF, Moscow*
Prof. **Heiko Pleines**, *University of Bremen*
Prof. **Richard Sakwa**, *University of Kent at Canterbury*
Dr. **Sarah Whitmore**, *Oxford Brookes University*
Dr. **Harald Wydra**, *University of Cambridge*

### SOCIETY, CLASS & ETHNICITY
Col. **David Glantz**, *"Journal of Slavic Military Studies"*
Dr. **Marlène Laruelle**, *George Washington University*
Dr. **Stephen Shulman**, *Southern Illinois University*
Prof. **Stefan Troebst**, *University of Leipzig*

### POLITICAL ECONOMY & PUBLIC POLICY
Prof. em. **Marshall Goldman**, *Wellesley College, Mass.*
Dr. **Andreas Goldthau**, *Central European University*
Dr. **Robert Kravchuk**, *University of North Carolina*
Dr. **David Lane**, *University of Cambridge*
Dr. **Carol Leonard**, *Higher School of Economics, Moscow*
Dr. **Maria Popova**, *McGill University, Montreal*

### FOREIGN POLICY & INTERNATIONAL AFFAIRS
Dr. **Peter Duncan**, *University College London*
Prof. **Andreas Heinemann-Grüder**, *University of Bonn*
Dr. **Taras Kuzio**, *Johns Hopkins University*
Prof. **Gerhard Mangott**, *University of Innsbruck*
Dr. **Diana Schmidt-Pfister**, *University of Konstanz*
Dr. **Lisbeth Tarlow**, *Harvard University, Cambridge*
Dr. **Christian Wipperfürth**, *N-Ost Network, Berlin*
Prof. **William Zimmerman**, *University of Michigan*

### HISTORY, CULTURE & THOUGHT
Dr. **Catherine Andreyev**, *University of Oxford*
Prof. **Mark Bassin**, *Södertörn University*
Prof. **Karsten Brüggemann**, *Tallinn University*
Dr. **Alexander Etkind**, *University of Cambridge*
Dr. **Gasan Gusejnov**, *Moscow State University*
Prof. em. **Walter Laqueur**, *Georgetown University*
Prof. **Leonid Luks**, *Catholic University of Eichstaett*
Dr. **Olga Malinova**, *Russian Academy of Sciences*
Prof. **Andrei Rogatchevski**, *University of Tromsø*
Dr. **Mark Tauger**, *West Virginia University*

## ADVISORY BOARD*

Prof. **Dominique Arel**, *University of Ottawa*
Prof. **Jörg Baberowski**, *Humboldt University of Berlin*
Prof. **Margarita Balmaceda**, *Seton Hall University*
Dr. **John Barber**, *University of Cambridge*
Prof. **Timm Beichelt**, *European University Viadrina*
Dr. **Katrin Boeckh**, *University of Munich*
Prof. em. **Archie Brown**, *University of Oxford*
Dr. **Vyacheslav Bryukhovetsky**, *Kyiv-Mohyla Academy*
Prof. **Timothy Colton**, *Harvard University, Cambridge*
Prof. **Paul D'Anieri**, *University of Florida*
Dr. **Heike Dörrenbächer**, *Friedrich Naumann Foundation*
Dr. **John Dunlop**, *Hoover Institution, Stanford, California*
Dr. **Sabine Fischer**, *SWP, Berlin*
Dr. **Geir Flikke**, *NUPI, Oslo*
Prof. **David Galbreath**, *University of Aberdeen*
Prof. **Alexander Galkin**, *Russian Academy of Sciences*
Prof. **Frank Golczewski**, *University of Hamburg*
Dr. **Nikolas Gvosdev**, *Naval War College, Newport, RI*
Prof. **Mark von Hagen**, *Arizona State University*
Dr. **Guido Hausmann**, *University of Munich*
Prof. **Dale Herspring**, *Kansas State University*
Dr. **Stefani Hoffman**, *Hebrew University of Jerusalem*
Prof. **Mikhail Ilyin**, *MGIMO (U) MID RF, Moscow*
Prof. **Vladimir Kantor**, *Higher School of Economics*
Dr. **Ivan Katchanovski**, *University of Ottawa*
Prof. em. **Andrzej Korbonski**, *University of California*
Dr. **Iris Kempe**, *"Caucasus Analytical Digest"*
Prof. **Herbert Küpper**, *Institut für Ostrecht Regensburg*
Dr. **Rainer Lindner**, *CEEER, Berlin*
Dr. **Vladimir Malakhov**, *Russian Academy of Sciences*

Dr. **Luke March**, *University of Edinburgh*
Prof. **Michael McFaul**, *Stanford University, Palo Alto*
Prof. **Birgit Menzel**, *University of Mainz-Germersheim*
Prof. **Valery Mikhailenko**, *The Urals State University*
Prof. **Emil Pain**, *Higher School of Economics, Moscow*
Dr. **Oleg Podvintsev**, *Russian Academy of Sciences*
Prof. **Olga Popova**, *St. Petersburg State University*
Dr. **Alex Pravda**, *University of Oxford*
Dr. **Erik van Ree**, *University of Amsterdam*
Dr. **Joachim Rogall**, *Robert Bosch Foundation Stuttgart*
Prof. **Peter Rutland**, *Wesleyan University, Middletown*
Prof. em. **Marat Salikov**, *The Urals State Law Academy*
Dr. **Gwendolyn Sasse**, *University of Oxford*
Prof. **Jutta Scherrer**, *EHESS, Paris*
Prof. **Robert Service**, *University of Oxford*
Mr. **James Sherr**, *RIIA Chatham House London*
Dr. **Oxana Shevel**, *Tufts University, Medford*
Prof. **Eberhard Schneider**, *University of Siegen*
Prof. **Olexander Shnyrkov**, *Shevchenko University, Kyiv*
Prof. **Hans-Henning Schröder**, *SWP, Berlin*
Prof. **Yuri Shapoval**, *Ukrainian Academy of Sciences*
Prof. **Viktor Shnirelman**, *Russian Academy of Sciences*
Dr. **Lisa Sundstrom**, *University of British Columbia*
Dr. **Philip Walters**, *"Religion, State and Society"*, *Oxford*
Prof. **Zenon Wasyliw**, *Ithaca College, New York State*
Dr. **Lucan Way**, *University of Toronto*
Dr. **Markus Wehner**, *"Frankfurter Allgemeine Zeitung"*
Dr. **Andrew Wilson**, *University College London*
Prof. **Jan Zielonka**, *University of Oxford*
Prof. **Andrei Zorin**, *University of Oxford*

\* While the Editorial Committee and Advisory Board support the General Editor in the choice and improvement of manuscripts for publication, responsibility for remaining errors and misinterpretations in the series' volumes lies with the books' authors.

# Soviet and Post-Soviet Politics and Society (SPPS)
ISSN 1614-3515

Founded in 2004 and refereed since 2007, SPPS makes available affordable English-, German-, and Russian-language studies on the history of the countries of the former Soviet bloc from the late Tsarist period to today. It publishes between 5 and 20 volumes per year and focuses on issues in transitions to and from democracy such as economic crisis, identity formation, civil society development, and constitutional reform in CEE and the NIS. SPPS also aims to highlight so far understudied themes in East European studies such as right-wing radicalism, religious life, higher education, or human rights protection. The authors and titles of all previously published volumes are listed at the end of this book. For a full description of the series and reviews of its books, see www.ibidem-verlag.de/red/spps.

**Editorial correspondence & manuscripts** should be sent to: Dr. Andreas Umland, c/o DAAD, German Embassy, vul. Bohdana Khmelnitskoho 25, UA-01901 Kyiv, Ukraine. e-mail: umland@stanfordalumni.org

**Business correspondence & review copy requests** should be sent to: *ibidem* Press, Leuschnerstr. 40, 30457 Hannover, Germany; tel.: +49 511 2622200; fax: +49 511 2622201; spps@ibidem.eu.

**Authors, reviewers, referees, and editors** for (as well as all other persons sympathetic to) SPPS are invited to join its networks at
www.facebook.com/group.php?gid=52638198614
www.linkedin.com/groups?about=&gid=103012
www.xing.com/net/spps-ibidem-verlag/

## Recent Volumes

153 Duncan Leitch
Assisting Reform in Post-Communist Ukraine 2000–2012
The Illusions of Donors and the Disillusion of Beneficiaries
With a foreword by Kataryna Wolczuk
ISBN 978-3-8382-0844-2

154 Abel Polese
Limits of a Post-Soviet State
How Informality Replaces, Renegotiates, and Reshapes Governance in Contemporary Ukraine
With a foreword by Colin Williams
ISBN 978-3-8382-0845-9

155 Mikhail Suslov (ed.)
Digital Orthodoxy in the Post-Soviet World
The Russian Orthodox Church and Web 2.0
With a foreword by Father Cyril Hovorum
ISBN 978-3-8382-0871-8

156 Leonid Luks
Zwei „Sonderwege"? Russisch-deutsche Parallelen und Kontraste (1917-2014)
Vergleichende Essays
ISBN 978-3-8382-0823-7

157 Vladimir V. Karacharovskiy, Ovsey I. Shkaratan, Gordey A. Yastrebov
Towards a New Russian Work Culture
Can Western Companies and Expatriates Change Russian Society?
With a foreword by Elena N. Danilova
Translated by Julia Kazantseva
ISBN 978-3-8382-0902-9

158 Edmund Griffiths
Aleksandr Prokhanov and Post-Soviet Esotericism
ISBN 978-3-8382-0903-6

159 Timm Beichelt, Susann Worschech (eds.)
Transnational Ukraine?
Networks and Ties that Influence(d) Contemporary Ukraine
ISBN 978-3-8382-0944-9

160 Mieste Hotopp-Riecke
Die Tataren der Krim zwischen Assimilation und Selbstbehauptung
Der Aufbau des krimtatarischen Bildungswesens nach Deportation und Heimkehr (1990-2005)
Mit einem Vorwort von Swetlana Czerwonnaja
ISBN 978-3-89821-940-2

# Contents

Acknowledgements ............................................................................. 7

Note on Spelling and Transliteration ................................................. 8

About the Editor and Contributors ...................................................... 9

Introduction by Olga Bertelsen ............................................................. 15

## I  Ukraine: Sources of Destabilization

1  The Ukrainian Revolution of 2013–2014 and the Sources of Russia's Response by George O. Liber ................................................. 41

2  Ukraine is the Epicenter of the "World Hurricane" by Yurii Scherbak ............................................................................... 69

## II  War of Narratives

3  Ukraine and Russia: Entangled Histories, Contested Identities, and a War of Narratives by Igor Torbakov ........................... 89

4  Living with Ambiguities: Meanings of Nationalism in the Russian-Ukrainian War by Myroslav Shkandrij ............................. 121

## III  The Euromaidan, War, and Cultural Change in Ukraine

5  Ideologies of Language in Wartime by Laada Bilaniuk ..................... 139

6  Ukrainian Euromaidan as Social and Cultural Performance by Tamara Hundorova .......................................................................... 161

## IV Crimea, the Black Sea, and the Straits

7 The Annexation of Crimea: Russia's Response to
Ukraine's Revolution by Nedim Useinov ............................................. 183

8 Russian Hegemony in the Black Sea Basin: The "Third Rome"
in Contemporary Geopolitics by Dale A. Bertelsen and Olga Bertelsen .... 213

## V Information and Religious Wars

9 The Invisible Front: Russia, Trolls, and the Information War
against Ukraine by Peter N. Tanchak ................................................... 253

10 The Impact of Russia's Intervention in Ukraine on Muslim,
Jewish and Baptist Communities by Andrii Krawchuk ......................... 283

## VI Reforming Ukraine

11 The Perpetual Cycle of Political Corruption in Ukraine and
Post-Revolutionary Attempts to Break Through It by Oksana Huss .. 317

12 Police Reform: Challenges and Prospects by Bohdan Harasymiw ...... 353

Epilogue by Olga Bertelsen ................................................................. 377

Dictionary of Abbreviations ................................................................. 413

Index ..................................................................................................... 417

# Acknowledgements

I would like to thank all the contributors for their insightful analyses about contemporary Ukraine's realities, a colorful mosaic of perspectives that help us better understand a new Ukraine that emerged as a result of the 2013–2014 revolution and Russia's invasion of Ukrainian territories in 2014. Considering the contemporary nature of the topic, some information included in various chapters had to be updated several times in the process of editing the manuscript. I appreciate the patience of the authors who kept up with my pace and the pace of Ukrainian history, going through several drafts of their manuscripts.

I am grateful to the Petro Jacyk Program for the Study of Ukraine, the Munk School of Global Affairs, and the Centre of European, Russian, and Eurasian Studies at the University of Toronto for their support. Special thanks to Peter H. Solomon, Jr., Olga Kesarchuk, and Romana M. Bahry who contributed greatly to the idea of this publication. The Harriman Institute and the Ukrainian Studies Program at Columbia University that hosted many talks and discussions on Ukrainian and Russian politics served as an inspiration and enthusiastic supporter for this project.

I am indebted to George O. Liber, Lynne Viola, Alexander J. Motyl, Serhy Yekelchyk, Sergei I. Zhuk, Michael C. Hickey, Myroslav Shkandrij, Andrii Krawchuk, Bohdan Harasymiw, Mark von Hagen, Igor Torbakov, and Dale A. Bertelsen who read various chapters and the entire manuscript for their thoughtful and enlightening suggestions. I owe a great deal to my students at Columbia University and the University of Toronto whose diligence and interest in Russian–Ukrainian relations made our intellectual exchange lively and vigorous, and made me explore several ideas that would not otherwise find their way into this volume.

# Note on Spelling and Transliteration

In this volume we employed a slightly modified Library of Congress version for Ukrainian or Russian languages. Ukrainian personal and place names have been transliterated from Ukrainian: for example, Hrushevskyi instead of Grushevskii, Kyiv instead of Kiev, Odesa instead of Odessa, Donbas instead of Donbass. To make it easier for English-speaking readers, we avoided diacritical marks in names and other words: for instance, Glaziev instead of Glaz'iev, Silantiev instead of Silant'iev, Korchynska instead of Korchyns'ka, Kyivan Rus or Kyiv Rus instead of Kyivan Rus'. We preserved them only in quotations. Russian personal names and places were transliterated from Russian: for example, Danilevskii instead of Danylevskyi, Aleksandr instead of Oleksandr, Tsargrad instead of Tsarhrad, Vladivostok instead of Vladyvostok. The occupied territories of Crimea and the Donbas are treated as Ukrainian, and thus names of places have been transliterated from Ukrainian: for example, Simferopil instead of Simferopol. The "English" spelling is preserved in names that gained international fame, such as Alexander Solzhenitsyn. For letters "й" and "я" we used "i" and "ia" respectively: for example, Iegor instead of Egor, Ianukovych instead of Yanukovych, Iatseniuk instead of Yatseniuk, Ieltsyn instead of Yeltsin, Iuliia instead of Yuliya. Yalta constitutes an exception. For the ending "ii" or "ei" in Russian or "yi" or "ii" in Ukrainian in first or last names, we preserved "y" only for names that have been consistently used with "y" in the West, or in cases when we mention a certain publication in English written by a person with this type of name: for instance, Andrey Makarychev instead of Andrei Makarychev, Dostoevsky instead of Dostoevskii, Brudny instead of Brudnyi, Kuchabsky instead of Kuchabskyi, Rudnytsky instead of Rudnytskyi.

# About the Editor and Contributors

**Dale A. Bertelsen** (Ph.D., Pennsylvania State University) is Professor of Communication Studies at Bloomsburg University, Bloomsburg, Pennsylvania served as President of the Eastern Communication Association (1995–1996), President of the Speech Communication Association of Pennsylvania (1991–1992), Editor of Publications for the Kenneth Burke Society (1991–1993), Book Review Editor for *Critical Studies in Media Communication* (1999–2001), Editor of *Communication Quarterly* (2001–2003). He is co-author of *Analyzing Media: Communication Technologies as Symbolic and Cognitive Systems* (Guilford, 1996) and *Introduction to Communication Criticism: Methods, Systems, Analysis and Societal Transformations* (Kendall-Hunt, forthcoming), and has published in journals such as *Communication Education, Philosophy and Rhetoric, Communication Quarterly, Qualitative Research Reports in Communication, Journal of Computer-Mediated Communication, Russian Journal of Communication* and *The Speech Communication Teacher*. He was a Fulbright scholar to Ukraine in 2004. His current research focuses on leadership and public advocacy, strategic communication, the rhetoric of genocide, and the intrusion and implications of violence in cross-generational cultural transmission.

**Olga Bertelsen** (Ph.D., University of Nottingham) is a writer in residence at New York University and research fellow of the Harvard Ukrainian Research Institute. She held fellowships at the Harriman Institute (Columbia University) and the Munk School of Global Affairs (University of Toronto), and has published monographs on the Ukrainian theatre "Berezil" (Smoloskyp, 2016) and Ukraine's House of Writers in the 1930s (Pittsburgh, 2013), as well as translated documents in two volumes on the persecution of Zionists in Ukraine (*On the Jewish Street*, 2011). She is currently preparing books for publication on Stalin's terror in Ukraine, post-Soviet imperial consciousness among Russian writers, and the social history of Ukraine's 1932–1933 famine.

**Laada Bilaniuk** is Associate Professor of Anthropology at the University of Washington. She completed her PhD in anthropology at the University of Michigan. Her main fields of research are language ideology, identity politics, popular culture, and nation building in Ukraine. She is author of the book, *Contested Tongues: Language Politics and Cultural Correction in Ukraine* (Cornell University Press 2005), and she is currently working on a book on popular culture in Ukraine. She has also published articles on changing language ideologies in Ukraine, language and gender, education, and the politics of language on Ukrainian television.

**Bohdan Harasymiw** is Professor Emeritus of Political Science at the University of Calgary, Canada, and in 2013–16 was Acting Coordinator of the Contemporary Ukraine Studies Program at the Canadian Institute of Ukrainian Studies, University of Alberta, Edmonton. Born in Saskatchewan, he studied at the Royal Military College and at Queen's University (both in Kingston, Ontario) as well as at the University of Alberta, before completing his doctorate at the University of Toronto. He joined the University of Calgary in 1969, where he continued teaching until his retirement in 2005. He is the author of *Post-Communist Ukraine* published by the CIUS Press (2002). His most recently published article "Alberta's Premier Ed Stelmach: The Anomalous Case of Leadership Selection and Removal in a Canadian Province" appeared in the *American Review of Canadian Studies*. Since retirement, he has participated as an election observer with the Canadian mission in Ukraine in 2006, 2007, and 2010. In 1989–91, he was seconded to the federal government in Ottawa as a Strategic Analyst with the Canadian Security Intelligence Service. A lifelong member and former President of the Canadian Association of Slavists, he served as Program Chair for its 2016 conference in Calgary.

**Tamara Hundorova** (Ph.D. in Philology) is a Corresponding member of the National Academy of Sciences of Ukraine (NAN Ukrainy), professor and chair of the Department of Literary Theory and Comparative Studies in the Shevchenko Institute of Literature (NAN Ukrainy), the Executive Director of the Institute of Krytyka, professor and dean of the Ukrainian Free University (Munich), and an Associate of the Harvard Ukrainian Research Institute. She has published extensively on Ukrainian literature, modernism, postmodernism, postcolonial criticism, kitsch, feminism and Chornobyl. She is the author of books *Transit Culture. The Symptoms of Postcolonial Trauma* (2013), *Post-Chornobyl Library. Ukrainian Literary Postmodernism* (2005, 2013), *The Emerging Word. The Discourse of Early Ukrainian Modernism* (1997, 2009), *Kitsch and Literature. Travesty*

(2008), *Franko and/not Kameniar* (2006), *Femina melancholica. Sex and Culture in Gender Utopia of Olha Kobylianska* (2002) and others. She is a recipient of various fellowships at Columbia University (USA), Harvard University (USA), University of Hokkaido (Japan), and Monash University (Australia). She is a Fulbright scholar, the editor of several journals, and she taught at American, Canadian, European and Ukrainian universities.

**Oksana Huss** is a Ph.D. candidate of Political Science at the Institute for Development and Peace, University of Duisburg-Essen (Germany), and is working for the Ukrainian Think Tanks Liaison Office in Brussels. She graduated from Ludwig-Maximilians-University, where she has been awarded a scholarship from the Hanns-Seidel-Foundation. She was a Petro Jacyk visiting fellow at the University of Toronto (Munk School of Global Affairs), and gave numerous talks on the mechanisms of corruption in Ukraine. She is co-founder of the Interdisciplinary Corruption Research Network and project supervisor of the young researcher's network "Ukraine in Transition," supported by the Institute for Advanced Study in the Humanities (Essen). Her main area of expertise is corruption and corruptive schemes in hybrid regimes.

**Andrii Krawchuk** is Professor of Religious Studies and past President (2004–2009) of the University of Sudbury, Canada. He is the author of *Christian Social Ethics in Ukraine: the Legacy of Andrei Sheptytsky* (Canadian Institute of Ukrainian Studies Press, 1997), and a co-editor, with Thomas Bremer, of *Eastern Orthodox Encounters of Identity and Otherness: Values, Self-Reflection, Dialogue* (Palgrave Macmillan, 2014) and of the forthcoming *Churches in the Ukrainian Crisis* (Palgrave Macmillan, 2016). He has also edited numerous documentary collections on religion, society and ethics in Eastern Europe. Vice-President of the International Council for Central and East European Studies, he is also a member of the Religion in Europe Group (American Academy of Religion), and of the Executive of the Canadian Association of Slavists. His current research is on interreligious dialogue and intercultural ethics in the wake of the Russian-Ukrainian conflict.

**George O. Liber** is Professor of History at the University of Alabama at Birmingham. He is the author of: *Soviet Nationality Policy, Urban Growth, and Identity Change in the Ukrainian SSR, 1923–1934* (Cambridge University Press, 1992); *Alexander Dovzhenko: A Life in Soviet Film* (British Film Institute, 2002); and *Total Wars and the Making of Modern Ukraine, 1914–1954* (University of Toronto Press, 2016). With Anna Mostovych, he compiled and edited *Nonconformity and Dissent in the Ukrainian SSR, 1955–1975: An Annotated Bibliography* (Harvard Ukrainian Research Institute, 1978). He also served as a Short-Term Observer to the Organization for Security and Cooperation in Europe (OSCE) for the 2010 Presidential Elections in Ukraine, the 2011 Presidential Elections in Kazakhstan, and the 2012 parliamentary elections in Ukraine.

**Yurii Scherbak** is a Ukrainian writer, doctor of medicine, politician, diplomat, and environmental activist. He is a laureate of prestigious literary awards, and currently chairs the Committee of the Shevchenko Literary Award in Ukraine. He is a co-founder and Chairman of the Ukrainian Environmental Association "Green World", and the first leader of the Green Party of Ukraine. First environment Minister of independent Ukraine and Member of the National Security Council of Ukraine in (1991–1992), he served as the Extraordinary and Plenipotentiary Ambassador of Ukraine to Israel (1992–1994), to the USA (1994–1998, also to Mexico since 1997), and to Canada (2000–2003). Scherbak was an Advisor to the President of Ukraine (1998–2000) and Advisor to the Chairman of the Verkhovna Rada of Ukraine (2004–2006). In 2006 he became President of the Vernadsky Institute for Sustainable Development in Ukraine, and in 2009—a co-founder and a member of the Council on Foreign and Security Policy. In 2013 he was elected a member of the World Academy of Art and Science. He is a recipient of many national and international awards and honors, and the author of numerous books which became international bestsellers and prominent studies on geopolitics and environmental issues, including Chornobyl.

**Myroslav Shkandrij** is Professor of Slavic Studies at the University of Manitoba, and has published on modern Ukrainian and Russian literature, art and cultural politics, the avant-garde, and nationalism. He is the author of *Ukrainian Nationalism: Politics, Ideology and Literature, 1929–1956*

(Yale University Press, 2015), *Jews in Ukrainian Literature: Representation and Identity* (Yale University Press, 2009), *Russia and Ukraine: Literature and the Discourse of Empire from Napoleonic to Postcolonial Times* (McGill-Queens University Press, 2001), and *Modernists, Marxists and the Nation: The Ukrainian Literary Discussion of the 1920s* (Canadian Institute of Ukrainian Studies Press, 1992). Exhibitions curated by him include: *Futurism and After: David Burliuk, 1882–1967* (Winnipeg Art Gallery, 2008) and *The Phenomenon of the Ukrainian Avant-Garde, 1910–35* (Winnipeg Art Gallery, 2001). He is also the translator of Serhiy Zhadan's *Depeche Mode* (Glagoslav Publications, 2013) and Mykola Khvylovy's *Cultural Renaissance in Ukraine. Polemical Pamphlets, 1925–26* (Canadian Institute of Ukrainian Studies, University of Alberta, 1986).

**Peter N. Tanchak** is a Research Fellow at the Citizen Lab, the University of Toronto's preeminent cyber security research institution, studying cyber operations involving Russia and Ukraine. He holds his Master's from the Centre for European, Russian and Eurasian Studies (CERES) at the Munk School of Global Affairs, University of Toronto. He has previously held positions with the Canadian public service, and interned as an analyst with the Polish Institute of International Affairs (Polski Instytut Spraw Międzynarodowych), where he conducted policy work and was a contributing author with the European Union Evolving Concepts of Security Project (EvoCS, 2015). He also co-authored *Nie tylko dla orłów. Czy terroryści sięgają po hybrydowość?* (PISM, 2015).

**Igor Torbakov** is a Senior Fellow at the Center for Russian and Eurasian Studies at Uppsala University, Sweden. He holds an MA in History from Moscow State University and a PhD from the Ukrainian Academy of Sciences, and specializes in Russian and Eurasian history and politics. He was a Research Scholar at the Institute of Russian History (Russian Academy of Sciences in Moscow); a Visiting Scholar at the Kennan Institute (Woodrow Wilson International Center for Scholars, Washington, DC); a Fulbright Scholar at Columbia University; a Visiting Fellow at Harvard University; a Fellow at the Swedish Collegium for Advanced Study; a Senior Fellow at the Finnish Institute of International Affairs in Helsinki; and a Visiting Fellow at the German Council on Foreign Relations in Berlin. His recent publications discuss the history of Russian nationalism, the links between Russia's domestic politics and foreign policy, Russian-

Ukrainian relations, and the politics of history and memory wars in Eastern Europe.

**Nedim Useinov** is a Ph.D. candidate of Political Science at the University of Gdansk, Poland, and also works for the Solidarity Fund PL in Warsaw, contributing to the program aimed at supporting political reforms in post-Maidan Ukraine. He is the author of a number of publications on the Crimean Tatars political movement in the 20th century. His most recent publication is a chapter on Crimea in *The Maidan Uprising, Separatism and Foreign Intervention*, edited by Klaus Bachmann and Igor Lyubashenko (Peter Lang, 2014).

# Introduction

*Olga Bertelsen*

In late March of 2015, a Kyiv pensioner, a volunteer who makes camouflage nets, socks, and underwear for the Ukrainian army, asked a soldier who had just returned to Kyiv from the war in eastern Ukraine, whether the army needed more white camouflage nets to cover their equipment. "We've made plenty of them," she said. The young man replied: "It is warmer now. There is no snow there. We now need green nets. But no worries... We'll need the white ones next winter..." Fighting in Donetsk and Luhansk for nearly a year, the soldier perceived the Russian-Ukrainian war as a long-term conflict which was not going to end any time soon. His certainty and casual fatalism appeared striking and disturbing to the woman. This conversation exacerbated her uncertainties about the future of her country.[1] There are innumerable stories like this one about Ukraine, illuminating a popular feeling of instability and collective insecurity.

Observers have argued that Ukraine's transitional period has been "one of the most difficult and prolonged" because the country was hesitant to break from the Soviet traditions of corruption and political passivity.[2] By late 2013, governed by the Ianukovych regime, the Ukrainians felt that their country no longer belonged to them. The revolution of 2013–2014, known as the Euromaidan, was an attempt to discontinue the vicious cycle of the state's failures and its inability to function within the rule of law, especially after Viktor Ianukovych's election to the presidency in February 2010.[3] Indeed, the Euromaidan Revolution broke the monotony of Ukraine's transition and slow progress. The loss of more than one hundred human lives, people who were shot by snipers in broad daylight in the center of Kyiv in February 2014, triggered a far-reaching national

---

1    Private conversation with Liudmyla Shalaieva, a resident of Kyiv, May 9, 2015.
2    Anders Aslund, *Ukraine: What Went Wrong and How to Fix It* (Washington, DC: Peterson Institute for International Economics, 2015), xi.
3    Igor Lyubashenko, "Euromaidan: From the Students' Protest to Mass Uprising," in *The Maidan Uprising, Separatism and Foreign Intervention: Ukraine's Complex Transition*, eds. Klaus Bachmann and Igor Lyubashenko (Frankfurt am Main: Peter Lang, 2014), 61–85.

awakening and accelerated the tempo of change in Ukraine. The victory of the revolution and people's subsequent optimism, however, were marred by the separatist movement in eastern Ukraine, backed by the Russian Federation. Russia's annexation of Crimea and its hybrid war in the Donbas fundamentally changed Ukraine's priorities in modernizing its economic sector, legal and political system, and jeopardized the implementation of social reforms, so desperately needed in Ukraine.[4]

Despite the fact that Ukraine has been a center of world attention on several occasions over the course of the last century and new millennium, many in the West are still uncertain about where Ukraine is located. The closest approximation they often offer is "somewhere in Europe." Over the years, Ukrainian news that made the cover pages of the international press was uplifting, most was tragic. For example, in the late twenties the West was shocked by scattered reports about the scale of Soviet terror. The cultural renaissance of the mid-1920s made many Ukrainian poets, writers, and theatre directors internationally recognized celebrities who contributed to European and world culture. For the first time, speaking Ukrainian became stylish and fashionable, and the Ukrainian diaspora began to return to Soviet Ukraine to help build a new Ukrainian culture. Yet, in the late twenties newspaper accounts about Soviet show trials against Ukrainian intellectuals proliferated in the United States, Canada, and Great Britain. Unprecedented state violence in Ukraine in the early thirties claimed the lives of millions of Ukrainian peasants during the man-made famine (the Holodomor) and thousands among the intelligentsia, which provoked deep concerns around the world.[5]

---

[4] For a discussion about Russia's annexation of Crimea in 2014 and the role of Crimea in Ukraine-Russia relations, see Nedim Useinov, "Crimea: From Annexation to Annexation, or How History Has Come Full Circle," 207–26; and Natalia Shapovalova, "The Role of Crimea in Ukraine-Russia Relations," 227–65, both in *The Maidan Uprising, Separatism and Foreign Intervention: Ukraine's Complex Transition*, eds. Klaus Bachmann and Igor Lyubashenko (Frankfurt am Main: Peter Lang, 2014).

[5] William Henry Chamberlain, *Russia's Iron Age* (Boston: Little, Brown, and Company, 1935); Anonymous author, *Experiences in Russia-1931: A Diary* (Pittsburgh: The Alton Press, Inc., 1932); Marco Carynnyk, Lubomyr Y. Luciuk, and Bohdan S. Kordan, eds., *The Foreign Office and the Famine: British Documents on Ukraine and the Great Famine of 1932–1933* (Ontario-Vestal, New York: The Limestone Press Kingstone, 1988); Margaret Siriol Colley, *More Than a Grain of Truth: The Biography of Gareth Richard Vaughan Jones* (Newark,

During the Second World War Ukraine, together with other states, became the bloodlands where mass killings occurred that resulted in tremendous losses of human life. Millions of Jews, Ukrainians, Russians, Belorussians, and Poles were exterminated by Hitler and Stalin in the territories of Poland, Estonia, Lithuania, Latvia, Soviet Ukraine, Soviet Belarus, and RSFSR. The world observed in trepidation the unmatched mass violence that transformed the war into "the most lethal conflict" in human history.[6]

The period of late socialism in the 1970s and 1980s made human rights activists in the West anxious. They alerted the international community about Moscow's prosecution of Ukrainian dissidents and the use of punitive psychiatry against them. After prolonged pharmaceutical torture by administering haloperidol and sulphazine in psychiatric clinics, the Ukrainian intellectual Leonid Pliushch and the Ukrainian student Viktor Borovskii made their way to Europe and the United States. Their revelations about the psychiatric abuse of dissidents resulted in heated public discussions about human rights violations in Ukraine and in the Soviet Union.[7]

---

Nottinghamshire, UK: AlphaGraphics, 2005). For more details on the Holodomor, see Bohdan Klid and Alexander J. Motyl, eds., *The Holodomor Reader: A Sourcebook on the Famine of 1923–1933 in Ukraine* (Edmonton, Toronto: Canadian Institute of Ukrainian Studies Press, 2012); Stanislav Kulchytskyi, *Holodomor 1932–1933 rr. iak henotsyd: Trudnoshchi usvidomlennia* (Kyiv: Nash chas, 2008); on Stalin's repressions of the Ukrainian intelligentsia, see Olga Bertelsen and Myroslav Shkandrij, "The Secret Police and the Campaign against Galicians in Soviet Ukraine, 1929–34," *Nationalities Papers: The Journal of Nationalism and Ethnicity* 42, no. 1 (2014): 37–62; Myroslav Shkandrij and Olga Bertelsen, "The Soviet Regime's National Operations in Ukraine, 1929–1934," *Canadian Slavonic Papers* LV.3–4 (2013): 417–47.

6 Timothy Snyder, *Bloodlands: Europe between Hitler and Stalin* (New York: Basic Books, 2010), viii.

7 Leonid Pliushch, *History's Carnival: A Dissident's Autobiography*, ed. and trans. Marco Carynnyk (New York: Harcourt Brace Jovanovich, 1979); Victor Borovsky, *Potsilunok satany* (New York: Meta Publishing Company, 1981); Petro G. Grigorenko, *Memoirs*, trans. Thomas P. Whitney (New York & London: W.W. Norton and Company, 1982); Sidney Bloch and Peter Reddaway, *Soviet Psychiatric Abuse: The Shadow over World Psychiatry* (Boulder, Colorado: Westview Press, 1985); Robert van Voren, *Cold War in Psychiatry: Human Factors, Secret Actors* (Amsterdam and New York: Rodopi, 2010); Olga Bertelsen, "Rethinking Psychiatric Terror against Nationalists in Ukraine," *Kyiv-Mohyla Arts and Humanities* no. 1 (2014): 27–76.

The devastating news about the Chernobyl nuclear disaster in 1986 once again made Ukraine the epicenter of concerns that were overwhelmed by more striking news—the collapse of the Soviet Union in 1991.[8] Even then, Ukraine was on the pages of all leading international newspapers that considered the newly created independent state of Ukraine a key player in the politics of destruction of the "evil empire."[9]

Since its independence in 1991, Ukraine did not follow in the political and economic footsteps of Poland, Estonia, Latvia, or Lithuania. The post-Soviet political order resembled in many ways the Soviet one. Despite the Orange Revolution, which astounded the world with its innovative techniques, the bravery, and sacrifice of the demonstrators, little changed in post-Soviet Ukraine.[10] Only the Euromaidan fundamentally restructured Ukrainian political life,[11] awakened patriotic feelings and sharpened national consciousness among the majority of Ukraine's citizens. A deep re-evaluation of identities and cultural realignment occurred on individual and collective levels, a dramatic cultural change that propelled the state's nearly dormant transition toward a more unified nation and civil society.

Our hope is that this book will help our readers understand what important changes occurred after the revolution of 2013–2014 in Ukraine, and why they took place. We believe that our analyses will facilitate their discovery or rediscovery of Ukraine, a state whose historical flow has

---

[8] For more details about the Chernobyl disaster, see David R. Marples, *Chernobyl and Nuclear Power in the USSR* (New York: St. Martin's Press, 1986); Zhores A. Medvedev, *The Legacy of Chernobyl* (New York and London: W. W. Norton & Company, 1992); Svetlana Alexievich, *Voices from Chernobyl: The Oral History of a Nuclear Disaster*, trans. Keith Gessen (New York: Picador, 2006); Adriana Petryna, *Life Exposed: Biological Citizens After Chernobyl* (Princeton, NJ: Princeton University Press, 2013).

[9] The first recorded use of this expression in reference to the USSR belongs to Ronald Reagan. See the transcript of Ronald Reagan's speech "Evil Empire," an address to the National Association of Evangelicals in Orlando, Florida (March 8, 1983), *Miller Center (University of Virginia)*, accessed June 18, 2016, http://millercenter.org/president/speeches/speech-3409; on the role of Ukraine in the collapse of the Soviet Union, see Serhii Plokhy, *The Last Empire: The Final Days of the Soviet Union* (New York: Basic Books, 2014).

[10] For a discussion about the Orange revolution, see Andrew Wilson, *Ukraine's Orange Revolution* (New Haven and London: Yale University Press, 2005).

[11] Serhiy Kvit, "The Euromaidan Revolution and the Struggle for Ukraine's Place in Europe," in *Jews, Ukrainians, and the Euromaidan*, ed. Lubomyr Y. Luciuk (Toronto: Kashtan Press, 2014), i.

been at times dynamic, at times stagnant but whose future means a great deal to global security.

We also hope that this book will help more people to see Ukraine as an important counterbalance to Russia's aggression and militant ideology, rather than a region fated to remain in Russia's shadow or as a permanent borderland between East and West. The manifesto of the Russian youth organization "Rossiia-3," founded by Aleksandr Dugin, a Russian ideologue whose ideas inspire Putin, reads:

> We are imperial builders of the newest kind and will not agree to less than governing the world, because we are the masters of the Earth, we are the children and grandchildren of the masters of the Earth. Peoples and countries worshiped us and were subservient to us, we governed half of the world, and our feet trampled the mountains and valleys of all continents of the Earth. We will recover everything.[12]

This manifesto suggests an ideological imperative for new generations of Russian citizens, an immediate tenuous future for Ukraine and other former Soviet republics, as well as a possible long-term threat to global peace and security. Importantly, the events in Ukraine, the focus of this anthology, seem to align with the dynamics in other parts of eastern Europe, which reveal the uneven relations between Russia and its neighboring states.

This volume invites readers to revisit conceptions about the immense power of human agency, the ethics of politics, and the morality of human choice. As events of the last two years in Ukraine and Russia have demonstrated, the activities and behavior of a single individual driven by his or her identities, values, and beliefs, have a broader impact, going beyond this individual's village, city, or state: these activities ultimately change patterns and procedures of global security and political behavior.

The discussion of cultural change in Ukraine, provoked by the Euromaidan, and Russia's cultural realignment and motivation for invading the Ukrainian territories allows us to contextualize newly occurring events and, most importantly, to introduce historical, moral, and aesthetic analyses of individuals' actions which shape others people's behaviors, perceptions, and lives. These analyses help us employ history, facts,

---

12  See "The Catechesis of a Member of the Eurasian Union of Youth," *Rossiia-3, Ievraziiskii soiuz molodiozhi*, accessed June 18, 2016, http://www.rossia3.ru/katehizis.html.

imagination, intellect, and common sense to establish patterns of politics and human behavior, which have always been "the ultimate criterion of reality as against illusion, incoherence, fiction," and fabrication.[13]

Some scholars argue that Ukraine's history runs in certain temporal rhythms or cycles.[14] Others identify it as "repeated patterns inimical to the consolidation of democratic norms and the creation of a vibrant civil society."[15] No matter how Ukrainian history is defined, the Euromaidan created a paradigm shift in Ukraine's development, a shift which suggests rapid change, and illustrates the contingent nature of history, affirming the paramount role of human agency in history.

Although all authors traverse their topics in their own unique ways, there are several common themes that explicitly shape the leitmotif and the thesis of this collection.

Contemporary Ukrainian history and culture serves as a starting point for our inquiry and as the conceptual thread of this book, which helps us grasp, among other things, the deep connection between culture and the degree of coherence in Ukrainian society. Language, art, literature, and religion are the integral assets of a people with a common identity. In Ukraine, cultural construction, destruction, and reconstruction are associated with Stalinism, mass killings, and an enormous loss of cultural artifacts, and this legacy of a disrupted and distorted national narrative and identity haunts the Ukrainians in their struggle to rejuvenate their traditions, the core of social cohesiveness and civilized political culture. The analyses of cultural trends in contemporary Ukraine help us better understand Ukraine's self-destructive paroxysms and, most importantly, the evolution of national sensibilities provoked by the Euromaidan and Russia's invasion.

---

13  See, for instance, Isaiah Berlin's discussion about the possibilities such analyses grant in his essay "The Concept of Scientific History," in *The Proper Study of Mankind: An Anthology of Essays* by Isaiah Berlin, eds. Henry Hardy and Roger Hausheer (New York: Farrar, Straus and Giroux, 1998), 48–49.
14  Taras Kuzio, "University of Toronto Censors Book on Corruption in Ukraine," *YouTube*, July 3, 2015, https://www.youtube.com/watch?v=2mCSORPNBh8, and his book *Ukraine: Democratization, Corruption, and the New Russian Imperialism* (Santa Barbara, California: Praeger Security International, 2015).
15  George Liber, private e-mail conversation, July 13, 2015.

The Euromaidan and its grounding in dignity, humanity, and resilience are the recurrent themes that inform this discussion.[16] The revolution is viewed as a historical event, a tradition, and a philosophical metaphor of freedom that cemented a common, multi-national narrative in Ukraine. The events of January–February 2014 appeared to many insiders and outsiders no more than a surrealistic staged spectacle,[17] a splash of human emotions, and a revolution without any prospect of political victory. As the essays in this collection demonstrate, the Euromaidan instead seems to have been a historical turning point, "the beginning of a new history,"[18] yet with dramatic consequences. The revolution that became known as the Revolution of Dignity was saved through the sheer critical mass of people who stayed and visited Independence Square in Kyiv during several critical months in 2013 and 2014 and through human sacrifice. The studies included in this collection implicitly divide Ukraine's history into pre-, mid-, and post-Maidan, a phenomenon that led to global changes, rearranging political alliances in the world. In anthropological terms, this division is of course relative. History constitutes itself through human communication and individual and collective experiences,[19] and changes in such day-to-day exchanges are often gradual and even blurred. Yet in political terms, as the Euromaidan has demonstrated, this conceptual framework is justifiable and even necessary. Tectonic shifts in Ukraine's political culture, social arrangements, and people's mentality have occurred, which revived the ferment of resistance that for centuries has kept Ukraine from disappearing into the vortex of imperial abuse.[20]

---

16  For a discussion about the Ukrainian "psyche," see Alexander J. Motyl, "Here's Why More Ukrainians Admire Nationalists, and Why the West Shouldn't Freak Out," *Atlantic Council*, July 8, 2015, http://www.atlanticcouncil.org/blogs/new-atlanticist/understanding-contemporary-ukraine.

17  Vladyslav Kyrychenko, "Black Side of the Maidan," in *Maidan. (R)evoliutsiia dukhu*, ed. Antin Mukharskyi (Kyiv: Nash format, 2014), 54.

18  Iurii Andrukhovych, "Simsot liutykh dniv, abo rol kontrabasa v revoliutsii," in *Maidan. (R)evoliutsiia dukhu*, ed. Antin Mukharskyi (Kyiv: Nash format, 2014), 146.

19  Reinhart Koselleck, *The Practice of Conceptual History: Timing History, Spacing Concepts*, trans. Todd Samuel Presner and others (Stanford, CA: Stanford University Press, 2002), 27.

20  Ukrainian intellectuals have written a great deal about the imperishability of the Ukrainian "ferment." See Michael Browne, ed., *Ferment in the Ukraine* (New York: Praeger Publishers, 1971); Kenneth C. Farmer, *Ukrainian Nationalism in the Post-Stalin Era: Myth, Symbols and Ideology in Soviet Nationalities Policy* (The

But what reignited world interest in Ukraine in 2013 was not this prolonged struggle for its independence and nationhood but rather people's willingness to sacrifice their lives for freedom and moral values in the digital age, where relative comfort, consumerism, and pragmatism prevail. Many felt that the Ukrainian revolution emerged from a parallel world, an anti-world, as the Russian poet Andrei Voznesenskii would characterize it,[21] where human gallantry and the pursuit of the ideal exist, but not in our world. The Euromaidan has demonstrated that human sacrifice for the common good and the desire to create a better world—free, happy, just— is not an anachronism or a utopian romantic concept.[22] These Enlightenment ideas and beliefs are vivid and quite modern. Commentators on Ukraine around the world found this particular phenomenon astounding when the imagined ideal and the reality had collided, reestablishing and reaffirming people's beliefs in the possibility of human altruism and resourcefulness. Once again, the world was inspired to rethink the nature of state violence and the danger of total liberty which are not simply dangerous—they are fraught with mass death and destruction. "Total liberty for wolves is death to the lambs," Isaiah Berlin reminded us.[23] Are people able to remain human during violent revolutions, and is there a compromise when moral and cultural values clash? Should people resist an atrocious tyranny at all costs, even at the expense of their own lives or the lives of their loved ones? These torturous and at the same time vital questions became an underlying motif of this book.

By March of 2015, when this book was conceived, the separatists backed by the Russian army had occupied a significant portion of Ukrainian territories and war had become a frightening reality.[24] For the

---

Hague, Boston, London: Martinus Nijhoff Publishers, 1980); Mykola Zhulynskyi, *Natsiia. Kultura. Literatura: Natsionalno-kulturni mify ta ideino-estetychni poshuky Ukrainskoi literatury* (Kyiv: Naukova dumka, 2011).

21  Andrei Voznesenskii, *Antimiry* (Moscow: Molodaia Gvardiia, 1964).
22  On people's pursuit of the ideal, see Isaiah Berlin, "The Pursuit of the Ideal," in *The Proper Study of Mankind: An Anthology of Essays*, eds. Henry Hardy and Roger Hausheer (New York: Farrar, Straus and Giroux, 2000), 1–16.
23  Berlin, "The Pursuit of the Ideal," 10.
24  By late March 2015, reports by the National Security and Defense Council of Ukraine (RNBO) such as this one became quite typical: "Kremlin-backed terrorists attacked Ukrainian forces and shelled Ukrainian positions a dozen times overnight using weapons that [were] inside the 25 kilometer buffer zone that militants should have cleared by early March in violation of the Minsk 2 agreement. The Ukrainian army did not return fire." See "Crisis in Ukraine: Daily

first time during its years of independence, military issues, such as weapons, ammunition, and conscription, became the primary concern for a post-Maidan Ukraine. According to Ukraine's Defense Minister Stepan Poltorak, by late March 2015, 230,000 people were serving in the Ukrainian armed forces, fighting against an army of "rebels" that employed the most modern Russian guns, rockets, and heavy equipment.[25] In many Ukrainian cities, towns, and villages people have been mourning over the dead and missing soldiers. Commemorative events to honor the dead have become common place. Mutilated combatants fill Ukrainian hospitals and rehabilitation centers. In contrast, Moscow conceals its war casualties, and dead Russian soldiers are buried secretly or cremated in the Donbas by mobile crematoriums.[26]

This volume offers a discussion of external and internal factors that contribute to the fragility and instability of the situation in Ukraine, and its general difficulties in reforming the country. Although Ukraine's domestic problems, such as massive corruption, account for this, the major destabilizing factors are Russia's annexation of Crimea, its war in the Donbas, and Russian propaganda. Putin's "geopolitical project" has been discussed in several essays of this anthology, and his efforts at destabilizing Russia's "near abroad" seem to be quite successful despite the western sanctions imposed on Russia. It has become quite apparent that they do not constrain Russia's aggression in Ukraine or elsewhere. Explanations for that lay beyond the scope of this volume. However, one view seems particularly relevant here to contextualize Russia's protracted war in Ukraine and the findings of some of the essays of this collection.

According to various sources, the range of Russian President Vladimir Putin's wealth has been calculated between $79.2 and $200 billion.

---

Briefing—20 March 2015, 6 PM Kyiv time," *Ukrainian Canadian Congress* (the official website), March 20, 2015, http://www.ucc.ca/2015/03/20/crisis-in-ukraine-daily-briefing-20-march-2015-6-pm-kyiv-time/.

25 "Crisis in Ukraine: Daily Briefing—18 March 2015, 6 PM Kyiv time," *Ukrainian Canadian Congress* (the official website), March 18, 2015, http://www.ucc.ca/2015/03/18/crisis-in-ukraine-daily-briefing-18-march-2015-6-pm-kyiv-time/.

26 "They Were Never There: Russia's Silence for Families of Troops Killed in Ukraine," *The Guardian*, January 19, 2015, http://www.theguardian.com/world/2015/jan/19/russia-official-silence-for-families-troops-killed-in-ukraine; Douglas Ernst, "Russia Using Mobile Crematoriums to Hide Dead Troops in Ukraine, U.S. lawmakers Say," *The Washington Times*, May 26, 2015, http://www.washingtontimes.com/news/2015/may/26/russia-using-mobile-crematoriums-hide-dead-soldier/.

Some argue that he runs the country as his own household, financing it from his own pocket. The former Vice-Prime Minister of the Russian Federation Alfred Kokh posits that Putin controls an enormous machine of illegal businesses in Russia such as drug trafficking, shielding a network of brothels and casinos, and a lucrative arms trade, a claim that was also confirmed by other accounts, including one by Aleksandr Litvinenko, who was allegedly assassinated by Russian secret services in London in 2006. The annual income from these businesses has been estimated to be tens of billions of dollars. Kokh insists that these funds are controlled by Russian secret services and Putin personally, and that is how he finances their special operations in "near abroad" and runs his "Komintern" in Europe and the United States. Everyone who is significant is paid: the agents of influence, journalists, deputies, radical parties, and politicians.[27]

The analysts of the Polish business channel "TVN24 Biznes i Swiat" hold that over the last six months Russia's currency reserves decreased by approximately $130 billion. They presume that if this tempo continues, by 2017 Russia should be bankrupt. However, according to Kokh, Putin's private funds are non-exhaustible: low oil prices, the sanctions, and other cataclysms of mammoth proportions will not lead to the collapse of the Russian government. Kokh and other commentators believe that Putin's financial power makes his shadow economy stable and indestructible, and thus, his short-term goals (individual power, personal enrichment, and support of his inner circle), and long-term-goals (destabilization of Europe and NATO) are potentially possible and even likely. Moreover, there are also grounds to suggest that Putin controls many politicians in Kyiv and elsewhere, who are positioned at the very top of the political hierarchy: Ukraine's own sanctions against Russia have not been seriously considered even two years after Russia's invasion, and the war in eastern Ukraine is still identified as an ATO (anti-terrorist operation).[28]

If this is true, analyses of Putin's military doctrine, its geopolitical implications, and practical application make perfect sense at least from a

---

[27] "Kokh rasskazal, kak finansiruietsia putinskii 'Komintern' v Ievrope i SShA," *Khartyia'97*, March 5, 2016, https://www.charter97.org/ru/news/2016/3/5/193904/.

[28] Iurii Pryhornytskyi, "Fistashka miliard berezhe, abo Haman presydenta i hamanets RF," *Literaturna Ukraina*, March 17, 2016, p. 5.

financial standpoint: Russia manages to support considerable military maneuvers and maintain multiple theatres of war, which require huge financial investments. Its grandiose plans in the Middle East, the Caucasus, and in the Black Sea region seem to suggest the availability of routinely replenished, and thus unlimited, resources, a serious problem for the West in general, and Europe in particular. More immediately, the dilemma to be solved in Ukraine focuses on how the country should reform while being continuously destabilized economically and politically by its powerful neighbor. Putin has created a situation in which future relations between Russia and Ukraine will be difficult for generations to come, and where peace seems to be possible only when subversion is a key element of the political landscape in the region. Crucially, chronic political instability in eastern Europe and its vulnerable balance between war and peace may have disastrous global ramifications, as the history of this region has demonstrated.[29]

Russia's propaganda efforts to portray the new Ukrainian government as fascist and the power of words are prominent themes in this anthology. Indeed, the information war became an inseparable part of Russia's expansion in Crimea and its incursions in other parts of the region. On March 18, 2014 Putin recognized Crimea's "independence" and signed the treaty of accession in Moscow. Almost immediately, the new authorities distributed guns to residents of the peninsula to protect them

---

29  As Iurii Shcherbak persuasively showed in 2006, Russia's "games" in Ukraine began much earlier than 2013–2014. The new global energy empire chose Ukraine for economic, geopolitical and ideological reasons. Yet Putin's plans are not limited to Ukraine. Today, without fully completing its plans in Ukraine, Russia prepares to move westward, testing the defense systems of European states and the United States by probing their airspace and territorial waters. The danger to global peace is real, especially given the murky and unpredictable nature of Russian politics. For a discussion about Russia's attempts at ideological subversion in Ukraine, see Iurii Shcherbak, "Pro natsionalnu hordist Ukraintsiv," in *Ukraina v zoni turbulentnosti: Demony mynuloho i tryvohy XXI stolittia* (Kyiv: Ukrainskyi pysmennyk, 2010), 305–15. See also Nolan Peterson, "Why Putin's Warplanes Are Penetrating European Airspace," *Newsweek*, March 27, 2015, http://www.newsweek.com/why-putins-warplanes-are-penetrating-european-airspace-317255; and the expert evaluation of US President Obama's choice to chair the Joint Chiefs of Staff, Marine Corps Commandant Joseph F. Dunford, about Vladimir Putin's Russia as the most significant military threat to the United States in Rob Garver, "A New Warning About Putin's Russia from a Top U.S. General," *The Fiscal Times*, July 9, 2015, http://finance.yahoo.com/news/warning-putin-russia-top-u-172100437.html.

against "Ukrainian fascists," and this narrative was firmly imbedded in the psyche of the Crimeans by its routine reiteration in the mass media. The Kremlin's extraordinarily strong presence and dominance in the media's narrative have been studied extensively.[30] Pro-Kremlin narratives are systematically reinforced through television channels such as *Sputnik* and *RT* (Russia Today), which are generously supported by a variety of agencies favoring Putin's regime. The idea of fascists in Kyiv was amplified and expanded by Putin who on March 18, 2015 at a concert in the center of Moscow, dedicated to the one-year anniversary of the takeover of Crimea, addressed thousands and praised the Russian people's "amazing patriotism" by supporting the annexation of Crimea and its people who fought against fascist Kyiv.[31]

Defining democratic transformations in Ukraine as fascism was and still remains crucial for Russia, and was designed for domestic and foreign consumption. Truly, whoever defines the situation has power over people and their perceptions. "The very concept of 'fact' becomes irrelevant because every meaningful political object and person is an interpretation that reflects and perpetuates an ideology," as Murray Edelman has suggested.[32] Guns as a defensive tool and measures against the "fascists" in Kyiv became a powerful argument and "evidence" of "defenseless" Crimean citizens who needed help. Interestingly, in order to receive a Kalashnikov at the local military commissariat, it was sufficient to show a passport with local *propiska* (registration) at one of the locations provided by the new authorities and to swear allegiance to Russia, expressing simultaneously hatred toward Kyiv.[33]

---

30  On the suppression of the media in Russia, see, for instance, Yuri Felshtinsky and Vladimir Pribylovsky, *The Corporation: Russia and the KGB in the Age of President Putin* (New York: Encounter Books, 2008), 355–428.
31  "Russia Celebrates Anniversary of Crimea Takeover—and Eyes Second Annexation," *The Guardian*, March 18, 2015, http://www.theguardian.com/world/2015/mar/18/russia-celebrates-anniversary-crimea-takeover-eyes-second-annexation; see also Andrea Chalupa, "Putin's Fabricated Claim Of A Fascist Threat In Ukraine," *Forbes*, April 4, 2014, http://www.forbes.com/sites/realspin/2014/04/04/putins-fabricated-claim-of-a-fascist-threat-in-ukraine/#cc97c6a1782e.
32  Murray Edelman, *Constructing the Political Spectacle* (Chicago and London: The University of Chicago Press, 1988), 10
33  Andrey Kurkov, *Ukraine Diaries: Dispatches from Kiev*, trans. Sam Taylor (London: Harvill Secker, 2014), 160.

Students of KGB methods and practices, contemporary Russian propagandists employ repetition as a powerful tool capable of transforming people's beliefs, views, and perceptions. The language and words matter, as several essays in this anthology demonstrate. Russia's use of definitions, such as the "Ukrainian crisis" and the "conflict in Ukraine," repeated over and over again, transcended the space of journalism, encouraging scholars and politicians to refer to Russia's aggression in Ukraine in these terms and entitle their books, speeches, and articles using the same concepts. The examples are numerous: the "conflict in Ukraine," the "crisis in Ukraine," "the Ukraine crisis of 2014," "the civil war and crisis in Ukraine," and the like.[34] These concepts reinforce the idea of "locality" and an isolated conflict that is not contingent on external factors. Repeatedly employed, these terms shape a certain perception of reality in Ukraine, and have helped the Russians position themselves as outsiders and neutral observers of the "crisis" in Ukraine. The use of this term may have been accurate until late December 2013, when the first victims of protests began to die in the streets of Kyiv. But after many, potentially hundreds of protesters in various cities of Ukraine disappeared and were murdered, after the Ukrainian parliament stripped Ianukovych of his presidential powers, and after Russia's invasion of Crimea and eastern Ukraine, this intellectual short-cut, a bastardized notion of Ukraine's purely domestic affair, which has become a "convenient truth," is a distraction from the larger political reality. "Language games…construct alternative realities."[35] They truly do.

Interestingly, Reinhart Koselleck[36] has reminded us that the notion of "crisis" is associated with the pressure of time, uncertainty, a desperate need to prevent disaster and to find a solution and salvation.[37] However,

---

34   See, for instance, Andrew Wilson, *Ukraine Crisis: What it Means for the West* (New Haven and London: Yale University Press, 2014); Rajan Menon and Eugene Rumer, *Conflict in Ukraine: The Unwinding of the Post-Cold War Order* (Cambridge, MA; London: The MIT Press, 2015).
35   Edelman, 103.
36   Reinhart Koselleck (1923–2006) was a German historian whose specialty was conceptual history. He contributed greatly to our understandings of epistemological, linguistic and anthropological issues related to history. He was one of the most influential historians of the twentieth century.
37   Reinhart Koselleck, "Some Questions Regarding the Conceptual History of 'Crisis,'" in *The Practice of Conceptual History: Timing History, Spacing Concepts*, trans. Todd Samuel Presner and others (Stanford, CA: Stanford University Press, 2002), 238.

he has also argued that crisis is a philosophical and historical term which can identify a "singular, accelerating process," or an intersection of an "epochal threshold," or can be understood as a permanent crisis in world history, or more broadly, as a "final crisis of all history"—self-destruction. Koselleck has theorized about the possible meanings of the term "crisis," including the economic concept of crisis. All those meanings are theoretically demanding, and are grounded in certain historical and intellectual traditions. The term "crisis" was also applied to the American and French revolutions, and Karl Marx tended to believe that the final crisis of the capitalist system would lead to tectonic social changes, such as the disappearance of the state and class differences. Koselleck has disputed the teleology of this notion, suggesting that it has always been human nature to exaggerate a particular situation and identify it as an apocalyptic one. Moreover, the misuse of this term, he believed, obscures its initial theological meaning (apocalypse; the end of the world), a semantic model of crisis as final decision for human civilization.[38] In her essay, Tamara Hundorova has shown that the apocalyptic myth constitutes an important dimension in the rhetoric of the Maidan; it also embraces an eschatological meaning. Yet, when used habitually in political and historical contexts, the term "crisis" overdramatizes and often distorts reality—sometimes innocently, often deliberately.

Many commentators on the Russian-Ukrainian war fall into the same semantic trap, describing the Russians' concealed aggression in Ukraine as Ukraine's crisis. Our preference is to omit the term from our writings altogether, and to identify the realities in Ukraine for what they are. We follow the road paved by the senior fellow at the Cato Institute's Center for Global Liberty and Prosperity, economist and former advisor to the Putin administration, Andrei Illarionov, who on June 16, 2014 at the NATO Parliamentary Assembly session in Vilnius stated:

> You may hear statements that this is 'the Ukrainian crisis' or that this is 'the crisis in Ukraine'. It is incorrect. It is neither 'the crisis in Ukraine', nor 'the Ukrainian crisis'. This is not an internal affair of Ukraine. This is a war. This is the Russian-Ukrainian war. To be correct, this is Mr Putin's war against Ukraine. And this war is only an introductory chapter of a much larger event which can

---

38  Koselleck, "Some Questions Regarding the Conceptual History of 'Crisis,'" 240–47.

be called and actually has already been called 'War', 'World War', 'the Fourth World War'.³⁹

In our view, the conflict perpetuated by the Russian Federation in Ukraine should be defined as "Russia's war in Ukraine" or "the Russian-Ukrainian war" that began, formally, with the occupation of Crimea in February 2014.

Significantly, this book illuminates how the meanings of words can be transformed and how words can lose their meaning during wars, how their "weaponization" occurs and how arguments shift to the contrary over the course of 24 hours. In turn, transformed meanings and words are employed for rewriting histories, which leads to information wars and the politicization of popular memory, realities that can be observed both in Russia and Ukraine today.⁴⁰ The theme of memory politics and competing national historical narratives consistently appears in several chapters, an issue that complicates the relations between Ukraine and Russia, thwarts their peaceful coexistence and undermines their potential rapprochement. This book avoids casting rosy scenarios and is restrained in terms of offering solutions. Instead, it interrogates the procedures and complex mechanisms of constructing national historical memories, institutionalizing their premises, and defending them through legal means. This discourse demonstrates an uneasy equilibrium of national narratives, which is vulnerable, routinely threatened and in constant need of restoration to prevent the escalation of information wars that are often transformed into serious collisions, such as terrorist activities and conventional warfare.

In this anthology, special attention is paid to a fascinating aspect of Russia's propaganda machine—the work of social network "trolls," whose goal is to discredit news stories critical of Russia while promoting those

---

39  "Speech by Andrei Illarionov at NATO PA in Vilnius," *The Lithuania Tribune: News and Views from Lithuania*, June 16, 2014, http://www.lithuaniatribune.com/69155/speech-by-andrei-illarionov-at-nato-pa-session-in-vilnius-201469155/; also see https://charter97.org/en/news/2014/11/21/127194/.

40  For a broader discussion about memory politics, see Jie-Hyun Lim, Barbara Walker, and Peter Lambert, eds., *Mass Dictatorship and Memory as Ever Present Past* (New York: Palgrave Macmillan, 2014); on the politics of the Russian language from Gorbachev to Putin, and the deep connection between language and politics, see Michael S. Gorham, *After Newspeak: Language Culture and Politics in Russia from Gorbachev to Putin* (Ithaca and London: Cornell University Press, 2014).

presenting pro-Russian narratives.[41] These trolls efficiently curtail reasonable online debate and contribute to the publics' uncertainty about the realities in the region that are difficult to decipher even without their immense efforts to sow confusion. Ultimately, the discussion concentrates on unofficial government tools that play a crucial role in Russia's politics of ideological subversion designed to confuse the international community about the Kremlin's real goals in Ukraine. The process of ideological subversion and constant attempts to keep Ukraine in the orbit of Russia's influence has a long history.[42] Over the last two decades Russia perfected its strategies and the mechanisms of undeclared hybrid wars, modernizing and swiftly adapting to changing political, social and cultural circumstances in Ukraine and elsewhere.[43]

The Russian presence in Crimea and Russia's increasing control of the Black Sea basin serve as an example of such adaptations. Two essays in this anthology disentangle chronological and tactical complexities of Russia's secret operation in the peninsula in January and February 2014,[44] provide an overview of the post-annexation situation in Crimea, and analyze Russia's geopolitical project through the lens of the discursive myth of the "Third Rome," a project that considers territories far beyond Ukraine—Turkey, Romania, Bulgaria, and the Middle East. This discussion explores the degree to which the "Third Rome" myth acts as a powerful discursive formation, infiltrating and informing Russian foreign and domestic policy. This myth is often offered directly and indirectly as a

---

41  For more details on the work, tasks, and functions of Russian trolls and the headquarters of the Internet Research Agency in St. Petersburg (Russia), see Adrian Chen, "The Agency," *The New York Times Magazine*, June 2, 2015, http://www.nytimes.com/2015/06/07/magazine/the-agency.html.

42  For a discussion about the Russian secret service's tactics, including ideological subversion, see Christopher Andrew and Vasili Mitrokhin, *The World Was Going Our Way: The KGB and the Battle for the Third World* (New York: Basic Books, 2005); Christopher Andrew and Vasili Mitrokhin, *The Sword and the Shield: The Mitrokhin Archive and the Secret History of the KGB* (New York: Basic Books, 1999).

43  Edward Lucas, *The New Cold War: Putin's Russia and the Threat to the West* (New York: Palgrave Macmillan, 2008); Karen Dawisha, *Putin's Kleptocracy: Who Owns Russia?* (New York: Simon & Schuster, 2014).

44  A year later, in a documentary, Putin admitted that the Russian soldiers were involved in a well-planned operation to take Crimea, and that the Kremlin was behind this operation. See "Putin Reveals Secrets of Russia's Crimea Takeover Plot," *BBC News*, March 9, 2015, http://www.bbc.com/news/world-europe-31796226.

rationale for Russian incursions into a host of Black Sea basin states. In this context, this discussion provides an explanation of how the Third Rome myth facilitates political concealment at home and abroad for destabilizing Turkey as a means of acquiring control over the Turkish Straits, and considers the myth's predictive value when examining future Russian actions in and around the Black Sea basin.

Furthermore, Russia's military solutions in Ukraine and its war in the Donbas bring to light one of the most tragic aspects of war—its divisiveness. We now live in a world where such a notion as "occupied territories" has become a routine description of reality. Wars divide and destroy families, organizations, unions, alliances, and religious institutions. The religious dimension of the Russian-Ukrainian war, an undeservedly underrepresented topic in scholarship on Russian-Ukrainian relations, is discussed in this anthology through the prism of new policies introduced by occupation authorities in Crimea and the Donbas. Faith communities in these territories (the focus of scrutiny is Muslims, Jews, and Baptists) are polarized for a number of reasons, among which are political loyalties, refugee displacement, and the regimentation of religious practices and organizations. However, religious communities are viewed here not only as passive observers but also as pro-active agencies, actors who creatively adjust themselves to the conditions of war, developing new survival skills and remaining socially engaged and spiritually focused. A narrative that analyzes these men's and women's difficult personal (and collective) choice, whether to remain under Russian occupation or to become refugees, invites readers to revisit complex notions, such as self-identification, moral responsibility, and faith, that are inevitably threatened and reshaped by war and violence.

We also believe that there is a pressing need to discuss the paramount issue of corruption, an intrinsic feature of most political and social operations in Ukraine. The book delivers a nuanced understanding of pervasive corruption and examines this phenomenon from theoretical and practical perspectives. In addition, it offers insight into the multifaceted interdependence of political traditions and practices, the loopholes in the legislature, and family and business connections among the political elites, factors that perpetuate the cycle of corruption which remains robust and resilient in Ukraine.[45] Perspectives and challenges of anti-corruption policies are examined through the lens of the National Anti-Corruption Bureau's activities and other initiatives that emanate from civil society.

Another salient element of Ukraine's challenges that has been discussed in this book is the reform of the police (*militsia*). This issue has been on the Ukrainian government's agenda for so long that the current effort provoked pessimism and a storm of sarcastic comments and questions from the Ukrainian public and professionals. What is different this time? For one, it is part of an ambitious and wide-ranging program of reform of governance as a whole. For another, it is directed in part by outsiders (Georgians) who have some track record of success in reforming the police. Will this be adequate in making a wholesale transformation to democratic and European Union standards, or at least a reasonable facsimile thereof? Looking at past and present reform efforts in Ukraine, as well as comparing experiences in other post-communist states, a fairly confident assessment can be made as to the prospect of significant and fundamental change. Individual and collective identity and political will in Ukraine, as well as its sovereignty and stability, seem to endorse the effectiveness of democratic reforms.

In all, the contributors to this book engage in a shared effort to identify and analyze the challenges, problems, and difficulties that Ukraine faced in the past and continues to experience today, obstacles that impede democratic changes and the formation of mature civil society. We explore the reasons for why the difficulties of the transitional period culminated in the Euromaidan and consequent state violence, and examine the multifaceted roles of people, organizations, and governments in the dynamic Ukrainian political, social and cultural landscape from historical and legal perspectives. This endeavor helps us better understand not only the underlying currents of Ukrainian politics and change in Ukraine's and Russia's culture and society, but also provides insight into the future of the Ukrainian national project and its chances for survival in a state of war. Revolutions and wars destroy, create, and restructure states. In this context, this anthology invites readers to consider several scenarios, among

---

45    For an interesting discussion about corruption in Ukraine, see also Bohdan Vitvitsky, "Corruption in Ukraine: What Needs to Be Understood, and What Needs to Be Done?" *VoxUkraine,* June 5, 2015, http://voxukraine.org/2015/06/05/corruption-in-ukraine-what-needs-to-be-understood-and-what-needs-to-be-done/.

which at least two deserve public attention and provoke crucial questions: should the world community yield to Russia's military and ideological supremacy in the region, allowing further "restructuring" of geographic and political borders through erasing an independent state "at the edge of Europe," or should it protect the "gates of Europe"[46] and the nascent democratic society in Ukraine?

Ukraine, a constrained and contested space and place, is a zone of death, displacement, and suffering today, but it is also a place of hopes and dreams that are nurtured by millions of its citizens, regardless of their nationality, ethnicity, or religious affiliation. Ukraine may be associated with the place Andrei Tarkovskii portrayed in his 1979 film *Stalker*, the Zone that had a special room where people's dreams could be consummated.[47] The road leading to this room was hazardous and dangerous. The detours along the way brought people there faster than direct pathways. The film's main character, the Stalker, led people through the Zone to this special room for a modest fee under one condition—they had to strictly follow the Zone's rules and his instructions. Otherwise, the Zone would fail them. A member of the group, the Writer, violated the established rules. He refused to follow the Stalker and suggested that there was a shortcut which would allow them to reach the Zone's room faster. In frustration, the Stalker yelled at him:

> Don't you understand? . . . this is the Zone . . . This is a complex system of traps . . . Everything is changing here every minute . . . safe traps become mortal and vice versa . . . The Zone is treacherous and vindictive. It cannot forgive. But it is such because we made it behave like this. Everything that is happening here depends not on the Zone but on us.[48]

*In actu*, we rarely find places and times as we imagined them, and the seemingly fastest routes only delay the day of achievement. Going back in time, so that we could better understand what is happening now, is necessary, even if this pathway appears to be long and challenging. We

---

46   Serhii Plokhy, *The Gates of Europe: A History of Ukraine* (New York: Basic Books, 2015).
47   Tarkovskii's 1979 film *Stalker* is based on Boris and Arkadii Strugatskii's novel *The Roadside Picnic*.
48   Andrei Tarkovskii, *Stalker* (1979), *YouTube*, Part 1, 59:00, June 20, 2011, https://www.youtube.com/watch?v=JYEfJhkPK7o.

are stepping back and revisiting Ukraine's past and the entangled histories of Ukraine and Russia to identify the pathway to the present, and to construct a more precise narrative of today's events in Ukraine. Understanding the Euromaidan, people's identities in Russia and Ukraine, the Russian-Ukrainian war, and its geopolitical consequences without contextualizing them in the history of Russian-Ukrainian relations seems neither possible nor conceivable.

Some observers have suggested that Ukraine is a state born to struggle and lose, to struggle again and to lose once again.[49] Others have defined Ukraine's transitional experiences along the road toward a modern European state as complex, difficult, and chaotic. We characterize it as persistent, suggesting the continuity of the process, in which events such as the revolution of 2013–2014 and Russia's invasion, take Ukraine to another level, this time rather rapidly, further from corruption and chaos toward meaningful and honorable existence. We identify the hindrances that have been conditioned by internal and, most importantly, external pressures, and share our view about transnational dangers and the potential political ramifications of Russia's expansion. The ritualization and institutionalization of oligarchs' illegal activities when the Firtashs and the Akhmetovs [50] continue to drain the nation's resources constitute only a part of the problem for Ukraine. Russia's invasion of Ukraine and Putin's insatiable neo-imperial appetite that grows daily present the principal threat to international security and to Ukraine's independence, dragging it

---

49   I am grateful to George O. Liber for reminding me about the myth of Sisyphus which would exemplify this definition. Sisyphus, a hero of Greek mythology, was condemned to repeat forever the same meaningless task of pushing a boulder up a mountain, only to see it roll down again. This myth inspired Albert Camus to ruminate about the absurdity of life, which is filled with meaningless tasks and struggles, in his essay "The Myth of Sisyphus."

50   *Rinat Akhmetov* is a Ukrainian businessman and oligarch. One of the wealthiest man in Ukraine and a member of Ukraine's parliament, he is the founder and President of System Capital Management (SMC), the owner and President of the Ukrainian football club Shakhtar Donets, and the sponsor of the Party of Regions in Ukraine. *Dmytro Firtash* is a Ukrainian businessman and oligarch. He is head of the board of directors of Group DF, President of the Federation of Employers of Ukraine (FEU), Chairman of the National Tripartite Social and Economic Council (NTSEC), Co-Chairman of the Domestic and Foreign Investors Advisory Council under the Ministry of Education, Science, Youth and Sports of Ukraine, and a member of the Committee for Economic Reforms under the President of Ukraine.

into another cycle of tortuous struggle for its independence. A challenge of change and the restoration of stability in this region are indeed a global concern.

## Bibliography

Alexievich, Svetlana. *Voices from Chernobyl: The Oral History of a Nuclear Disaster.* Translated by Keith Gessen. New York: Picador, 2006.

Andrew, Christopher, and Vasili Mitrokhin. *The Sword and the Shield: The Mitrokhin Archive and the Secret History of the KGB.* New York: Basic Books, 1999.

_____. *The World Was Going Our Way: The KGB and the Battle for the Third World.* New York: Basic Books, 2005.

Andrukhovych, Iurii. "Simsot liutykh dniv, abo rol kontrabasa v revoliutsii." In *Maidan. (R)evoliutsiia dukhu,* edited by Antin Mukharskyi, 158–64. Kyiv: Nash format, 2014.

Anonymous author. *Experiences in Russia—1931: A Diary.* Pittsburgh: The Alton Press, Inc., 1932.

Aslund, Anders. *Ukraine: What Went Wrong and How to Fix It.* Washington, DC: Peterson Institute for International Economics.

Berlin, Isaiah. "The Concept of Scientific History." In *The Proper Study of Mankind: An Anthology of Essays* by Isaiah Berlin, edited by Henry Hardy and Roger Hausheer, 17–58. New York: Farrar, Straus and Giroux, 1998.

_____. "The Pursuit of the Ideal." In *The Proper Study of Mankind: An Anthology of Essays* by Isaiah Berlin, edited by Henry Hardy and Roger Hausheer, 1–16. New York: Farrar, Straus and Giroux, 2000.

Bertelsen, Olga, and Myroslav Shkandrij. "The Secret Police and the Campaign against Galicians in Soviet Ukraine, 1929–34." *Nationalities Papers: The Journal of Nationalism and Ethnicity* 42, no. 1 (2014): 37–62.

Bertelsen, Olga. "Rethinking Psychiatric Terror against Nationalists in Ukraine." *Kyiv-Mohyla Arts and Humanities* no. 1 (2014): 27–76.

Bloch, Sidney, and Peter Reddaway. *Soviet Psychiatric Abuse: The Shadow over World Psychiatry.* Boulder, Colorado: Westview Press, 1985.

Borovsky, Victor. *Potsilunok satany.* New York: Meta Publishing Company, 1981.

Browne, Michael, ed. *Ferment in the Ukraine.* New York: Praeger Publishers, 1971.

Carynnyk, Marco, Lubomyr Y. Luciuk, and Bohdan S. Kordan, eds. *The Foreign Office and the Famine: British Documents on Ukraine and the Great Famine of 1932–1933.* Ontario-Vestal, New York: The Limestone Press Kingstone, 1988.

Chalupa, Andrea. "Putin's Fabricated Claim Of A Fascist Threat In Ukraine." *Forbes.* April 4, 2014. http://www.forbes.com/sites/realspin/2014/04/04/putins-fabricated-claim-of-a-fascist-threat-in-ukraine/#cc97c6a1782e.

Chamberlain, William Henry. *Russia's Iron Age.* Boston: Little, Brown, and Company, 1935.

Chen, Adrian. "The Agency." *The New York Times Magazine.* June 2, 2015. http://www.nytimes.com/2015/06/07/magazine/the-agency.html.

Colley, Margaret Siriol. *More Than a Grain of Truth: The Biography of Gareth Richard Vaughan Jones*. Newark, Nottinghamshire, UK: AlphaGraphics, 2005.

"Crisis in Ukraine: Daily Briefing—18 March 2015, 6 PM Kyiv time." *Ukrainian Canadian Congress* (the official website). March 20, 2015. http://www.ucc.ca/2015/03/18/crisis-in-ukraine-daily-briefing-18-march-2015-6-pm-kyiv-time/.

"Crisis in Ukraine: Daily Briefing—20 March 2015, 6 PM Kyiv time." *Ukrainian Canadian Congress* (the official website). March 20, 2015. http://www.ucc.ca/2015/03/20/crisis-in-ukraine-daily-briefing-20-march-2015-6-pm-kyiv-time/.

Dawisha, Karen. *Putin's Kleptocracy: Who Owns Russia?* New York: Simon & Schuster, 2014.

Edelman, Murray. *Constructing the Political Spectacle*. Chicago and London: The University of Chicago Press, 1988.

Ernst, Douglas. "Russia Using Mobile Crematoriums to Hide Dead Troops in Ukraine, U.S. lawmakers Say." *The Washington Times*. May 26, 2015. http://www.washingtontimes.com/news/2015/may/26/russia-using-mobile-crematoriums-hide-dead-soldier/.

Farmer, Kenneth C. *Ukrainian Nationalism in the Post-Stalin Era: Myth, Symbols and Ideology in Soviet Nationalities Policy*. The Hague, Boston, London: Martinus Nijhoff Publishers, 1980.

Felshtinsky, Yuri, and Vladimir Pribylovsky. *The Corporation: Russia and the KGB in the Age of President Putin*. New York: Encounter Books, 2008.

Garver, Rob. "A New Warning About Putin's Russia from a Top U.S. General." *The Fiscal Times*. July 9, 2015. http://finance.yahoo.com/news/warning-putin-russiatop-u-172100437.html.

Gorham, Michael S. *After Newspeak: Language Culture and Politics in Russia from Gorbachev to Putin*. Ithaca and London: Cornell University Press, 2014.

Grigorenko, Petro G. *Memoirs*. Translated by Thomas P. Whitney. New York & London: W.W. Norton and Company, 1982.

Klid, Bohdan, and Alexander J. Motyl, eds. *The Holodomor Reader: A Sourcebook on the Famine of 1923-1933 in Ukraine*. Edmonton, Toronto: Canadian Institute of Ukrainian Studies Press, 2012.

"Kokh rasskazal, kak finansiruietsia putinskii 'Komintern' v Ievrope i SShA." *Khartyia'97*. March 5, 2016. https://www.charter97.org/ru/news/2016/3/5/193904/.

Koselleck, Reinhart. "Some Questions Regarding the Conceptual History of 'Crisis'." In *The Practice of Conceptual History: Timing History, Spacing Concepts* by Reinhart Koselleck, 240–47. Translated by Todd Samuel Presner and others. Stanford, CA: Stanford University Press, 2002.

⸺. *The Practice of Conceptual History: Timing History, Spacing Concepts*. Translated by Todd Samuel Presner and others. Stanford, CA: Stanford University Press, 2002.

Kulchytskyi, Stanislav. *Holodomor 1932–1933 rr. iak henotsyd: Trudnoshchi usvidomlennia*. Kyiv: Nash chas, 2008.

Kurkov, Andrey. *Ukraine Diaries: Dispatches from Kiev*. Translated by Sam Taylor. London: Harvill Secker, 2014.

Kuzio, Taras. *Ukraine: Democratization, Corruption, and the New Russian Imperialism.* Santa Barbara, California: Praeger Security International, 2015.

_____. "University of Toronto Censors Book on Corruption in Ukraine." *YouTube.* July 3, 2015. https://www.youtube.com/watch?v=2mCSORPNBh8.

Kvit, Serhiy. "The Euromaidan Revolution and the Struggle for Ukraine's Place in Europe." In *Jews, Ukrainians, and the Euromaidan,* edited by Lubomyr Y. Luciuk, i-xvi. Toronto: Kashtan Press, 2014.

Kyrychenko, Vladyslav. "Black Side of the Maidan." In *Maidan. (R)evoliutsiia dukhu,* edited by Antin Mukharskyi, 60–64. Kyiv: Nash format, 2014.

Lim, Jie-Hyun, Barbara Walker, and Peter Lambert, eds. *Mass Dictatorship and Memory as Ever Present Past.* New York: Palgrave Macmillan, 2014.

Lucas, Edward. *The New Cold War: Putin's Russia and the Threat to the West.* New York: Palgrave Macmillan, 2008.

Lyubashenko, Igor. "Euromaidan: From the Students' Protest to Mass Uprising." In *The Maidan Uprising, Separatism and Foreign Intervention: Ukraine's Complex Transition,* edited by Klaus Bachmann and Igor Lyubashenko, 61–85. Frankfurt am Main: Peter Lang, 2014.

Marples, David R. *Chernobyl and Nuclear Power in the USSR.* New York: St. Martin's Press, 1986.

Medvedev, Zhores A. *The Legacy of Chernobyl.* New York and London: W. W. Norton & Company, 1992.

Menon, Rajan, and Eugene Rumer. *Conflict in Ukraine: The Unwinding of the Post-Cold War Order.* Cambridge, MA; London: The MIT Press, 2015.

Motyl, Alexander J. "Here's Why More Ukrainians Admire Nationalists, and Why the West Shouldn't Freak Out." *Atlantic Council.* July 8, 2015. http://www.atlanticcouncil.org/blogs/new-atlanticist/understanding-contemporary-ukraine.

Peterson, Nolan. "Why Putin's Warplanes Are Penetrating European Airspace." *Newsweek.* March 27, 2015. http://www.newsweek.com/why-putins-warplanes-are-penetrating-european-airspace-317255.

Petryna, Adriana. *Life Exposed: Biological Citizens After Chernobyl.* Princeton, NJ: Princeton University Press, 2013.

Pliushch, Leonid. *History's Carnival: A Dissident's Autobiography.* Edited and translated by Marco Carynnyk. New York: Harcourt Brace Jovanovich, 1979.

Plokhy, Serhii. *The Gates of Europe: A History of Ukraine.* New York: Basic Books, 2015.

_____. *The Last Empire: The Final Days of the Soviet Union.* New York: Basic Books, 2014.

Pryhornytskyi, Iurii. "Fistashka miliard berezhe, abo Haman presydenta i hamanets RF." *Literaturna Ukraina,* March 17, 2016, p. 5.

"Putin Reveals Secrets of Russia's Crimea Takeover Plot." *BBC News.* March 9, 2015. http://www.bbc.com/news/world-europe-31796226.

Reagan, Ronald. "Evil Empire" Speech (March 8, 1983) [transcript]. *Miller Center (University of Virginia).* Accessed June 18, 2016. http://millercenter.org/president/speeches/speech-3409.

"Russia Celebrates Anniversary of Crimea Takeover—and Eyes Second Annexation." *The Guardian*. March 18, 2015. http://www.theguardian.com/world/2015/mar/18/russia-celebrates-anniversary-crimea-takeover-eyes-second-annexation.

Shapovalova, Natalia. "The Role of Crimea in Ukraine-Russia Relations." In *The Maidan Uprising, Separatism and Foreign Intervention: Ukraine's Complex Transition*, edited by Klaus Bachmann and Igor Lyubashenko, 227–65. Frankfurt am Main: Peter Lang, 2014.

Shcherbak, Iurii. "Pro natsionalnu hordist Ukraintsiv." In *Ukraina v zoni turbulentnosti: Demony mynuloho i tryvohy XXI stolittia*, 305–15. Kyiv: Ukrainskyi pysmennyk, 2010.

Shkandrij, Myroslav, and Olga Bertelsen. "The Soviet Regime's National Operations in Ukraine, 1929–1934." *Canadian Slavonic Papers* LV.3–4 (2013): 417–47.

Snyder, Timothy. *Bloodlands: Europe between Hitler and Stalin*. New York: Basic Books, 2010.

"Speech by Andrei Illarionov at NATO PA in Vilnius." *The Lithuania Tribune: News and Views from Lithuania*. June 16, 2014. http://www.lithuaniatribune.com/69155/speech-by-andrei-illarionov-at-nato-pa-session-in-vilnius-201469155/.

Tarkovskii, Andrei. *Stalker* (1979). *YouTube*. Part 1, 59:00. June 20, 2011. https://www.youtube.com/watch?v=JYEfJhkPK7o.

"The Catechesis of a Member of the Eurasian Union of Youth." *Rossiia-3, Ievraziiskii soiuz molodiozhi*. Accessed June 18, 2016. http://www.rossia3.ru/katehizis.html.

"They Were Never There: Russia's Silence for Families of Troops Killed in Ukraine." *The Guardian*. January 19, 2015. http://www.theguardian.com/world/2015/jan/19/russia-official-silence-for-families-troops-killed-in-ukraine.

Useinov, Nedim. "Crimea: From Annexation to Annexation, or How History Has Come Full Circle." In *The Maidan Uprising, Separatism and Foreign Intervention: Ukraine's Complex Transition*, edited by Klaus Bachmann and Igor Lyubashenko, 207–26. Frankfurt am Main: Peter Lang, 2014.

Vitvitsky, Bohdan. "Corruption in Ukraine: What Needs to Be Understood, and What Needs to Be Done?" *VoxUkraine*. June 5, 2015. http://voxukraine.org/2015/06/05/corruption-in-ukraine-what-needs-to-be-understood-and-what-needs-to-be-done/.

Voren, Robert van. *Cold War in Psychiatry: Human Factors, Secret Actors*. Amsterdam and New York: Rodopi, 2010.

Voznesenskii, Andrei. *Antimiry*. Moscow: Molodaia Gvardiia, 1964.

Wilson, Andrew. *Ukraine Crisis: What it Means for the West*. New Haven and London: Yale University Press, 2014.

Wilson, Andrew. *Ukraine's Orange Revolution*. New Haven and London: Yale University Press, 2005.

Zhulynskyi, Mykola. *Natsiia. Kultura. Literatura: Natsionalno-kulturni mify ta ideino-estetychni poshuky Ukrainskoi literatury*. Kyiv: Naukova dumka, 2011.

# Part One

# Ukraine: Sources of Destabilization

# 1
# The Ukrainian Revolution of 2013–2014 and the Sources of Russia's Response

George O. Liber

In February 2013, after several frustrating years negotiating with Ukraine, the European Union (EU) gave Ukraine a November 2013 deadline to sign an Association Agreement with the world's largest economy. President Viktor Ianukovych, the country's most pro-Russian president since independence since 1991, agreed to do so, despite the EU's insistence that his government free Iuliia Tymoshenko, Ianukovych's most popular political opponent, from prison.

In October 2013, Leonid Kozhara, Ukraine's Foreign Minister, asserted that

> European integration is not an end in itself but a tool. We want to modernize our country, adopt European standards, enhance our citizens' living standards. In other words, we want to build a Europe inside Ukraine, and we sincerely believe that Russia will only benefit from that.[1]

But Russia vehemently disagreed with Ukraine's European choice. The Russian government, which had long planned to bring Ukraine into the Eurasian Customs Union of Russia, Belarus, and Kazakhstan, sought to overturn this decision. In addition to critical articles in the Russian press and the media, Russia launched a brief customs war with Ukraine in August 2013, then threatened to introduce a visa regime for Ukrainians travelling to Russia. In response to these overt interventions, the citizens of Ukraine became "more sympathetic to European integration."[2] But after several visits by President Vladimir Putin to Kyiv and President Ianukovych to Moscow, Ukraine's president announced on November 21—one

---

[1]  Quoted in Yelena Chernenko, "Even Pork Fat Threat Will Not Stop Ukraine," *Kommersant*, Oct. 29, 2013; cited in *The Current Digest of the Russian Press* (*CDRP*) 65, no. 44–45 (2013): 3.
[2]  Tatyana Ivzhenko, "Kyiv Heads West," *Nezavisimaia gazeta*, Sept. 19, 2013; cited in *CDRP* 65, no. 38 (2013): 19.

week before the scheduled EU Summit Meeting in Vilnius—that Ukraine would not sign the agreement.

Pro-EU demonstrations started the next day, leading to the overthrow of the Ianukovych government on February 21–22, 2014, to the Russian invasion of the Crimea, to a separatist upsurge abetted by Russia in eastern Ukraine, and to increased tensions between the EU and the United States, on one hand, and the Russian Federation—on the other. As of early March 2016, the United Nations' High Commissioner for Human Rights announced that his office recorded more than 30,000 casualties (at least 9,160 killed and 21,000 injured) in eastern Ukraine since April 2014. These figures included Ukrainian military personnel, members of armed groups, and civilians.[3]

Over the past two years, Russia's power elite, those men and women closely associated with President Putin, have vehemently opposed the idea of Ukraine signing the EU agreement, which would have precluded its joining the Eurasian Customs Union, and the efforts of its citizens to determine their own political future in a globalized world. Russian state-controlled television stations and media networks, the main source of information for the residents of the Russian Federation, have disseminated and amplified their views. The Russian press is also highly critical of Ukraine's pro-EU orientation, but somewhat more nuanced.

The sources of this Russian hostility are not a recent phenomenon, but a product of long-term attitudes. The end of the Cold War, the collapse of the USSR in 1991, and the subsequent search for stability and order shifted these mental tectonic plates and made them buckle and rub against each other.

**Tectonic Plate A: Ukraine as an Existential Threat**

For most members of the Russian political elite, the idea of Ukraine as an independent nation-state is perceived as an existential threat to the Russian identity. In their view of the world, Ukraine cannot exist without Russia or Russian "tutelage," however one defines the term.

---

3   Nick Cumming-Bruce, "Death Toll in Ukraine Conflict Hits 9,160, U.N. Says," *The New York Times*, March 3, 2016, http://www.nytimes.com/2016/03/04/world/europe/ukraine-death-toll-civilians.html?_r=0; and Radina Gigova, "Ukraine Crisis: Growing Sense of Despair," *CNN*, March 4, 2016, http://www.cnn.com/2016/03/03/world/ukraine-un-report/index.html.

With the development of the Ukrainian national movement in the Russian and Austrian Empires in the late eighteenth and nineteenth century, Ukraine as an actual or potential incubator of cultural and political separatism from Russia remained an important unspoken assumption of its elites.[4] According to official tsarist imperial interpretations, Ukrainians formed the Little Russian part of the all-Russian, Orthodox nation, which possessed three branches (the Velikorusski [Great Russian], Malorusski [Little Russian], and Belorusski [White Russian]). Members of these groups spoke East Slavic languages, which possessed many common features, and shared the Orthodox Christian faith (even the Ukrainian-speaking Greek Catholics in the Habsburg Monarchy adhered to a similar liturgy).[5]

Tsarist authorities did not discriminate against men and women of Little Russian origin who did not attempt to politicize their identity and who recognized their role within the "all-Russian" political landscape. Russian officials, historians, and public commentators interpreted the history of "Little Russia" as an integral part of mainstream Russian history; they perceived the "Little Russians" as "nashi" (ours). In contrast, the government repressed all individuals who demonstrated a distinct Ukrainian identity "in the political or in the cultural sphere."[6] The authorities considered the act of identifying oneself as a Ukrainian (instead of a Little Russian) as a political and anti-governmental act.

The tsars feared the subversion of the empire's Little Russian community by outside powers and sought "to stamp out the proto-nationalist activities of a handful of ethnically conscious Ukrainian intellectuals."[7] In light of the constant competition among the European

---

4  See Vera Tolz, *Russia: Inventing the Nation* (London: Arnold, 2001).
5  By the end of the nineteenth century, many tsarist officials recognized that the Ukrainian-speaking populations of the Habsburg and Romanov Empires were related, but considered the Greek Catholics religious renegades. In their view of the world, the Ukrainian-speaking population left the Orthodox Church in 1596 under Polish pressure and began to consider themselves separate from the Russians only then.
6  Bohdan Krawchenko, *Social Change and National Consciousness in Twentieth Century Ukraine* (New York: St. Martin's Press, 1985), 31.
7  David Saunders, "Russia's Nationality Policy: The Case of Ukraine (1847–1941)," in Serhii Plokhy and Frank E. Sysyn, eds., *Synopsis: A Collection of Essays in Honour of Zenon E. Kohut* (Edmonton, Alberta: Canadian Institute of Ukrainian Studies Press, 2005), 408.

powers in the nineteenth century and Russia's seemingly permanent internal insecurity, the empire's political elite aspired to keep the Great Russians, the Little Russians, and the Belarusians together, by force if necessary.

Ukraine's geographic location influenced these Russian anxieties. Located at the Western borderlands, Little Russians constituted the second largest East Slavic group and the second largest Orthodox population within the empire. Primarily a peasant group, they possessed nearly half of the total non-Russian peasants in the empire. Most importantly, from the perspective of those always concerned about the prospect of a peasant uprising, the empire's Ukrainian-speaking provinces experienced disturbing changes in the second half of the nineteenth century.

Following the same post-1861 trends within the empire, which produced one of the highest rates of growth in the world, the population in the Ukrainian-speaking provinces nearly doubled between 1870 and 1914. By 1897 these provinces possessed the highest population density (at 55 per square kilometer) in European Russia.[8] The Little Russians steadily increased their share of the total population in the empire's nine south-western provinces. By 1897, most Ukrainian-speakers in these provinces were under twenty years of age, and this cohort represented nearly forty percent of the *entire* population. At the turn of the century, this youth bulge grew rapidly, strengthening the Ukrainian-speaking majority in Russia's south-western provinces.[9] Most precariously, almost all of these men and women engaged in agricultural pursuits. In 1861 the amount of land per peasant averaged 2.9 desiatiny; by 1906, it had declined to 1.4. Peasant holdings in Kyiv, Podillia, and Volhynia comprised the smallest in the Russian Empire.[10]

As the Ukrainian-speaking provinces industrialized in the late nineteenth century, they attracted literate men from Central Russia to the new

---

8 Frank Lorimer, *Population of the Soviet Union: History and Prospects* (Geneva: League of Nations, 1946), 13, 67.
9 Olga Andriewsky, "The Making of the Generation of 1917: Towards a Collective Biography," in Plokhy and Sysyn, *Synopsis,* 22.
10 Robert Edelman, *Proletarian Peasants: The Revolution of 1905 in Russia's Southwest* (Ithaca, NY: Cornell University Press, 1987), 63–65. Also see H. R. Weinstein, "Land Hunger and Nationalism in the Ukraine, 1905–1917," *Journal of Economic History* 2, no. 1 (1942): 24–35.

industrial centers but only a small number of Ukrainian-speaking peasants. This migration of Russian workers reinforced Russian as the language of work and of the cities. Industrialization, in effect, produced an overwhelmingly Russian urban environment. The countryside remained a universe of spoken, but illiterate, Ukrainian. If these trends continued, the Ukrainian-speaking provinces would become a very crowded social and political tinderbox.

The end of serfdom and the beginning of industrialization intensified the competition between Russian and Ukrainian. As the officially sanctioned language and as the language of modernization, Russian experienced an upsurge; Ukrainian—a decline. Industrialization and Russification, then, tilted the urban language competition towards Russian. Migration and Russification re-oriented the migrants' "culturally defined need to read and write."[11] Migration into the cities made literacy a necessity and literacy in Russian essential. Learning to read and write in Russian made this national identity and culture attractive to those who already possessed the predisposition to change their social status. The mass illiteracy of the peasants who spoke Ukrainian and the nineteenth century governmental bans on Ukrainian-language schools and books hampered the Ukrainophile intelligentsia's efforts in primary "nation-building."[12]

In order to establish an imagined community of Ukrainians, members of this group had to agree on a common set of characteristics that constituted their identity and its boundaries.[13] Not only did the Ukrainian-speakers need to clarify their own identity, they also had to define the "other," especially the Russians, who remained culturally close to them. But in a hostile political environment and without Ukrainian-language schools, a mass-based literacy in Ukrainian, or Ukrainian publications, a mass dialogue on these critical issues could not develop. Without this vital discussion, the Ukrainian national movement could not attract the masses necessary to move from Miroslav Hroch's academic stage to his cultural

---

11   The phrase comes from Thomas W. Laqueur, "Toward a Cultural Ecology of Literacy in England, 1600–1850," in Daniel P. Resnick, ed., *Literacy in Historical Perspective* (Washington, DC: The Library of Congress, 1983), 55.
12   Ivan L. Rudnytsky, *Essays in Modern Ukrainian History* (Edmonton, AL: Canadian Institute of Ukrainian Studies, 1987), 377.
13   Benedict Anderson, *Imagined Communities: Reflections on the Origins and Spread of Nationalism* (London and New York: Verso, 1991).

and political stages.[14] Without this exchange, members of the Ukrainian national movement could not form a consensus defining themselves and their compatriots.

The long brutal First World War destroyed the imperial control of the Ukrainian-speaking provinces of the Russian and Austro-Hungarian Empires. Battlefield losses, enormous casualties, and the widespread destruction of villages and towns on the ever-shifting front disillusioned millions of soldiers, refugees, and civilians, even those far from the zones of engagement. By mobilizing "official" mass national identities and by forcibly evicting hundreds of thousands from their homes, these governments undermined the old prewar imperial and dynastic loyalties. Radical, anti-imperial, and nationalist allegiances replaced them.[15]

The resentments and frustrations of the Ruthenians in the Habsburg armies and the Little Russians in the tsarist armies prompted many to think of themselves as Ukrainians and to question their loyalty to their respective imperial structures. In an age of popular sovereignty and national self-determination, why not demand home rule or autonomy, even independence for the downtrodden Ukrainian masses? Surely, such a brave new world could be no worse than the old one.

## Tectonic Plate B: The Ukrainian SSR as an Integral Part of the USSR

The cumulative repercussions of World War One, Russia's February Revolution, the Bolshevik Revolution, German occupation, the disintegration of the Russian, Ottoman, German, and Austro-Hungarian Empires, and the emergence of new nation-states from this political debris "radically dislocated existing social organization(s), strengthening old

---

14 Miroslav Hroch, *Social Preconditions of National Revival in Europe: A Comparative Analysis of the Social Composition of Patriotic Groups Among the Smaller European Nations* (Cambridge, UK, and New York: Cambridge University Press, 1985), 22–23. Hroch defined these three stages as Phase A, B, and C. Roman Szporluk re-named these phases as the academic, cultural, and political stages of all national movements. See Roman Szporluk, *Ukraine: A Brief History* (Detroit: Ukrainian Festival Committee, 1979), 41–54.

15 Eric Lohr, *Nationalizing the Russian Empire: The Campaign Against Enemy Aliens During World War I* (Cambridge, MA: Harvard University Press, 2003), 69.

antagonisms between groups and inaugurating new ones."[16] Each of these convulsive events comprised a small, but integral part of the Great War and its post-war consequences.[17]

Ten years of mass violence destroyed the old social order and launched an unprecedented era of revolutionary upheaval. In the course of the war, revolutions, and social upheavals, Ukraine evolved from a territorial designation to the officially recognized homeland of Ukrainians, who differed from the Russians and the Poles. In response to the fierce resistance the Bolsheviks encountered in the Ukrainian provinces, the Russian Communist Party's leadership approved the establishment of the Soviet Ukrainian state, possessing clear borders (separating it from the Russian and Belarusan republics) and claiming control over a well-defined, contiguous territory. This new political entity included the nine (not five, as the Provisional Government claimed in August 1917) former tsarist provinces where Ukrainians constituted the majority of the population.[18] The Ukrainian SSR emerged as an interactive compromise on the shoals of social antagonisms, nationalist aspirations, Bolshevik visions, and political realities. It included both the overwhelming populous agricultural regions as well as the less populous smaller, industrial regions, including the breakaway Kryvyi Rih-Donetsk and Soviet Odesa Republics.

---

16  Geoff Eley, "Remapping the Nation: War, Revolutionary Upheaval and State Formation in Eastern Europe, 1914–1923," in Peter J. Potichnyj and Howard Aster, eds., *Ukrainian-Jewish Relations in Historical Perspective* (Edmonton, AL: Canadian Institute of Ukrainian Studies, 1988), 207.

17  Peter Holquist, *Making War, Forging Revolution: Russia's Continuum of Crisis, 1914–1921* (Cambridge, MA: Harvard University Press, 2002).

18  These territories included the provinces of Kyiv, Volhynia, Podillia, Chernihiv, Poltava, Kharkiv, Katerynoslav, Kherson, and Taurida (without the Crimean peninsula). In the ceremony marking Crimea's annexation by the Russian Federation on March 18, 2014, President Putin falsely claimed that Ukraine's southeastern provinces did not possess a Ukrainian majority population when the Bolsheviks established the Ukrainian SSR. See "Address by the President of Russia at Crimea's Annexation," *Prezident Rossii* (official site), March 18, 2014, http://en.kremlin.ru/events/president/news/20603. Compare Putin's assertion with the statistics in Imperial Russia's first census (1897) and in the USSR's first census (1926): N. A. Troinitskii, ed., *Pervaia vseobshchaia perepis naseleniia Rossiiskoi Imperii 1897 g.* (Saint Petersburg: Izd. Tsentralnogo statisticheskogo komiteta Ministerstva vnutrennikh del, 1899–1905), Table xiii, vols. 8, 13, 16, 32, 33, 41, 46, 47, and 48; Tsentralnoe statisticheskoe upravlenie SSSR, otdel perepisi, *Vsesoiuznaia perepis naseleniia 1926 goda* (Moscow, 1928–29), Table vi, vols. 11, 12, and 13.

Bolshevik leaders in effect created the Ukrainian SSR within the parameters declared by the Ukrainian National Republic's Third Universal in November 1917. They reluctantly recognized this territory with its agricultural and industrial regions as the homeland of the Ukrainians and implicitly acknowledged the leading role of Ukrainians in it. At the same time, they also granted the equality of all nations within the borders of Soviet Ukraine.

Despite the outward appearance of a state, the Ukrainian SSR (like the other republics) remained more of a quasi-state rather than a true "sovereign" one. Soviet Ukraine's communist party and government did not completely control those who lived within the newly-delineated entity, which possessed one primary and unspoken mission: to win over the Ukrainian peasants to the Bolshevik cause. Lenin's ideas prevailed; the communist leadership recognized the legitimacy of a separate Ukrainian identity (which the tsarist government had never done) and institutionalized it within the framework of a Soviet republic, a constituent member of the federated Union of Soviet Socialist Republics. In spite of "the suspicious attitude of the significant majority . . . the working class and, at the beginning, even of part of the peasantry," the Ukrainian SSR emerged, but with many political, national, and social contradictions.[19] These shortcomings would haunt the Ukrainian Soviet Socialist Republic (and independent Ukraine) over the next century.

Under Lenin's leadership, the Bolsheviks created the Soviet Union and the Ukrainian SSR, and in the 1920s obliged all officials dealing with the public to learn Ukrainian and created a policy giving preference to Ukrainians entering the party, the government, and other public organizations.[20] This policy of indigenization strengthened the Ukrainian national identity in the 1920s, especially in the urban centers.

---

19 The quote comes from *Budivnytstvo Radianskoi Ukrainy: Zbirnyk, no. 1* (Kharkiv: Derzhavne vyd. Ukrainy, s.a.); cited in George Y. Shevelov, *The Ukrainian Language in the First Half of the Twentieth Century (1900–1941): Its State and Status* (Cambridge, MA: Harvard Ukrainian Research Institute, 1989), 87.

20 "Pro zakhody zabezpechennia rivnopravnosty mov i pro dopomohu rozvytkovi ukrainskoi movy," in *Kulturne budivnytstvo v Ukrainskii RSR: Naivazhlyvishi rishennia komunistychnoi partii i radianskoho uriadu: Zbirnyk dokumentiv*, vol. 1 (Kyiv: Derzhavne vyd. politychnoi literatury URSR, 1959), 242–47; Basil Dmytryshyn, *Moscow and the Ukraine, 1918–1953: A Study of Russian Bolshevik Nationality Policy* (New York: Bookman Associates, 1956); George S. N. Luckyj,

But by 1933, the Kremlin's party leaders felt that the compromises on the national question hammered out in the early 1920s no longer addressed the new political realities. With forced collectivization, the removal of the kulaks in 1930–31, the "minor" famines of 1928–29 and 1932, ignited by the heavy-handed grain collections, and the "major" famine of 1933 (the Holodomor), which killed millions, the party gained unprecedented control over the countryside and over the wayward Ukrainian peasantry.[21] With the purges of the Communist Party of Ukraine and the decimation of the Ukrainian intelligentsia in the 1930s, the All-Union Communist Party abandoned its political overtures to the peasants and to Ukrainian society. Stalin's party had finally won the civil and national wars of 1918–1921.[22]

The Communist Party now highlighted a single Soviet identity, with Russian culture as its primary modern component. Stalin's insistence on Russian culture as the only key to modernization promoted stratification

---

*Literary Politics in the Soviet Ukraine, 1917–1934* (New York: Columbia University Press, 1956); Robert S. Sullivant, *Soviet Politics and the Ukraine, 1917–1957* (New York: Columbia University Press, 1962); James E. Mace, *Communism and the Dilemmas of National Liberation: National Communism in Soviet Ukraine, 1918–1933* (Cambridge, MA: Harvard Ukrainian Research Institute, 1983); Krawchenko, *Social Change*; George O. Liber, *Soviet Nationality Policy, Urban Growth, and Identity Change in the Ukrainian SSR, 1923–1934* (Cambridge, UK, and New York: Cambridge University Press, 1992), 121–42; Terry Martin, *The Affirmative Action Empire: Nations and Nationalism in the Soviet Union, 1923–1939* (Ithaca, NY: Cornell University Press, 2001), 211–72; and Matthew D. Pauly, *Breaking the Tongue: Language, Education, and Power in Soviet Ukraine, 1923–1934* (Toronto: University of Toronto Press, 2014).

21   See Liudmyla Hrynevych, *Khronika kolektyvizatsii ta Holodomoru v Ukraini 1927–1933 rr.* (Kyiv: Krytyka, 2008–2012), vol. 1, Books 1–3; and Liudmyla Hrynevych, *Holod 1928–1929 rr. u Radianskii Ukraini* (Kyiv: Natsionalna Akademiia Nauk Ukrainy, Instytut istorii Ukrainy, 2013).

22   See Luckyj, *Literary Politics in the Soviet Ukraine;* Myroslav Shkandrij and Olga Bertelsen, "The Soviet Regime's National Operations in Ukraine, 1929–1934," *Canadian Slavonic Papers* 55, nos. 3–4 (2013): 417–47; O. L. Kirianova, *Naukovo-pedahohichna i vchytelska intelihentsiia radianskoi Ukrainy v umovakh kulturno-osvitnykh peretvoren 20-30-kh rr. XX st.: istoriohrafiia* (Pereiaslav-Khmelnytskyi: Pereiaslav-Khmelnytskyi derzhavnyi pedahohichnyi universytet im. Hryhoriia Skovorody, 2013); T. H. Komarenko and M. A. Shypovych, *Vlada i literaturno-mystetska intelihentsiia Radianskoi Ukrainy, 20-ti roky XX st.* (Kyiv: Instytut istorii Ukrainy, 1999); H. Kasianov, *Ukrainska intelihentsiia 1920-kh—30-kh rokiv: sotsialnyi portret ta istorychna dolia* (Kyiv: "Globus" and "Vik," 1992); and H. Kasianov and V. M. Danylenko, *Stalinizm i ukrainska intelihentsiia: 20—30 roky* (Kyiv: Naukova dumka, 1991).

and ultimately Russification. In the 1920s non-Russians could perceive themselves as modern; by the 1930s the Soviet mass media identified modernization solely with Russia and with those who spoke Russian. In the early 1920s, the Soviet political leadership, grasping that "national" did not necessarily equal "nationalist," subsidized the blossoming of non-Russian national cultures. But in the harsh political climate of the 1930s, "national" increasingly corresponded with "nationalist."[23] The Soviet state then responded to all "national" and "nationalist" manifestations with unprecedented ruthlessness.

With collectivization and industrialization, Stalin did not completely nullify the formal arrangements established between the Russian center and the non-Russian periphery in 1918–1923. Instead, he left a contradictory legacy for his successors. Even though he purged the indigenous elites and intelligentsia in the non-Russian regions, the multi-national structure of the USSR remained, although more so in name only (it now operated on more hyper-centralized, not federal, lines). Although Stalin dissolved or re-arranged many Ukrainian institutions, he did not abandon the previous commitments to national homelands or the party's national-territorial divisions (both became more symbolic than real). Instead, he purged the elites (and their active and potential supporters) and replaced them with his own compliant ones. Stalin, in effect, forged a unitary state divided against itself.[24]

After 1933, the Soviet government and Communist Party limited the idea of a Ukrainian imagined community. By narrowing the social functions of "Ukrainian" in public life, blurring the differences between Ukrainians and Russians, and marginalizing Ukrainian culture, Soviet institutions (even those that survived Stalin's purges) reduced the options Ukrainians could use to define their own national identity and narrowed the already slender psychological distance between the Ukrainians and Russians. As millions of Ukrainians became urbanized after 1933, an increasing proportion of them became Russified.[25]

---

23 Hiroaki Kuromiya, *The Voices of the Dead: Stalin's Great Terror in the 1930s* (New Haven and London: Yale University Press, 2007), 124.

24 Seweryn Bialer, "Comment—The Impact of Common RSFSR/USSR Institutions," in *Ethnic Russia in the USSR: The Dilemma of Dominance*, ed. Edward Allworth (New York: Praeger, 1980), 198–99.

25 Ivan Dzyuba, *Internationalism or Russification?: A Study in the Soviet Nationalities Problem* (New York: Monad Press, 1974).

After 1938, the population of the Ukrainian SSR started to recover demographically from the famines, mass deportations, and purges of the 1930s, replenished to a large degree by the Soviet conquest and incorporation of majority Ukrainian-speaking territories in Poland and Romania in 1939 and 1940. But the German invasion of 1941 and the long German, Hungarian, and Romanian occupations skewed the demographic relationship between Russians and Ukrainians within the USSR and within Ukraine even further, to the disadvantage of the Ukrainians.

Ukraine also experienced extensive border changes. Soviet authorities had already incorporated eastern Galicia and Volhynia from Poland and Bukovyna and Bessarabia from Romania into the Ukrainian SSR before the end of the war and Transcarpathia from Czechoslovakia in 1945. (Only small numbers of Ukrainians remained in these countries after these boundary rectifications). With the conclusion of the Second World War, Stalin and his colleagues united the majority of Ukrainians living in East Central Europe into a single Soviet republic, a highly popular move among those Ukrainians living in territories under Soviet control since 1920, but not necessarily among those annexed after 1939.[26]

These border changes, however, did not transform the Ukrainian SSR into a nationally homogeneous entity.[27] After 1945 Ukraine remained nationally diverse, but regionally homogeneous. In the post-war period, it contained four different sets of territories. The western Ukrainian territories, those areas the Soviet Union acquired from Poland, Czechoslovakia, and Romania in 1939–1945, became more Ukrainian demographically.[28] In the central, agricultural regions under Soviet control since 1920,

---

26 Amir Weiner, *Making Sense of War: The Second World War and the Fate of the Bolshevik Revolution* (Princeton, NJ: Princeton University Press, 2001), 337–38.

27 According to the 1939 Soviet census (taken before the annexation of Ukrainian territories from Poland, Romania, and Czechoslovakia), 23,667,509 individuals (or seventy-six percent of the total population of the Ukrainian SSR) identified themselves as Ukrainians. According to the 1959 census, the first since the end of the war, 32,158,493 people (or seventy-seven percent of the total population) identified themselves as Ukrainians. Sources: (1939): Tsentralnyi gosudarstvennyi arkhiv narodnogo khoziaistva (TsGANKh), f. 1562, op. 529, d. 4535, l. 72; (1959): USSR, Tsentralnoe statisticheskoe upravlenie, *Itogi Vsesoiuznoi perepisi naseleniia 1959 goda: Ukrainskaia SSR* (Moscow: Gosstatizdat, 1963), 168.

28 In the 1930s, 63.4 percent of the population of the territories annexed to the Soviet Union from Poland, 61.6 percent of the population from Czechoslovakia, and 43.4 percent of the population from Rumania identified themselves as Ukrainians.

the percentage of those who identified themselves as Ukrainians also increased in the 1939–1959 period.[29] Yet, the industrial eastern and southern regions under Soviet control since 1920 became more Russian (with the exception of Zaporizhzhia and Mykolaiv and the city of Kyiv).[30] As the authorities reconstructed one of the major industrial heartlands of the USSR after the war, they transferred many Russian and Russified cadres to the eastern and southern regions.

Ukraine's western, central, eastern, and southern territories established different clusters of "tipping points," that critical mass needed to maintain the Ukrainian language and culture or to abandon it. These demographic changes and the introduction of new institutional arrangements provided a limited social and political menu of options. The masses could make choices after 1945, but only from the list the Soviet authorities provided them.

With Soviet Ukraine's extensive demographic losses and territorial gains in the course of the war, Stalin imagined that he had solved East Central Europe's festering "Ukrainian question." His successors sought to integrate the Ukrainians into the victorious Soviet system by providing a refurbished state-sponsored narrative. According to the evolving paradigm encompassing the celebrations of the three hundredth anniversary of the Treaty of Pereiaslav in January 1954, the history of Ukraine was intimately intertwined with that of Russia:

---

See Piotr Eberhardt, *Ethnic Groups and Population Changes in Twentieth-Century Central Eastern-Europe: History, Data, Analysis* (Armonk, NY: M. E. Sharpe, 2003), 212, 213, 214. According to the Soviet census of 1959, Ukrainians comprised 91 percent of the Lviv, Ivano-Frankivsk, and Ternopil oblasts (which constituted Poland's interwar Galicia) and 94 percent of the Volyn and Rivne oblasts (which comprised Poland's interwar Volhynia); 75 percent of the Zakarpatska Oblast (Czechoslovakia's former Transcarpathia), and 67 percent of the Chernivtsi Oblast, Rumania's interwar Bukovyna). See *Itogi Vsesoiuznoi perepisi naseleniia 1959 goda: Ukrainskaia SSR*, 176–78.

29  Source: (1939): TsGANKh, f. 1562, op. 329, d. 4535, ll. 72–74: (1959): USSR, Tsentralnoe statisticheskoe upravlenie, *Itogi Vsesoiuznoi perepisi naseleniia 1959 goda: Ukrainskaia SSR*, 174–79.

30  Ibid.

> Only thanks to the help of the great Russian people the workers of Ukraine overthrew the landlords and the capitalists, and established a Soviet government. Only with the great friendship of all Soviet peoples did Soviet Ukraine blossom and re-unite all Ukrainian lands in a single state.[31]

The treaty now became a teleological bridge not only for the progressive and mutually-enriching history of Russian and Ukrainian relations from Kyiv Rus to the period of acquisition and incorporation to the present, but also the model relationship for all of the non-Russians in the USSR. According to organizers of this celebration, Pereiaslav represented a permanent "reunion" of the Russian and Ukrainian peoples, not a "union" or a temporary military alliance.

The Communist Party of the Soviet Union presented the Treaty of Pereiaslav as a critical event in the long arc of the development of the Ukrainian and Russian peoples from their common origins within the framework of Kyiv Rus to the formation of the USSR and to the socioeconomic developments, spurred by rapid industrialization and mass collectivization within the USSR. This decree placed the Ukrainians at centerstage within the Soviet pantheon of nations, codifying a new hierarchy within the old paradigm of the "friendship of peoples." It presented the history of Ukraine, from Rus to the present, in broad, sweeping strokes. Each historical event conformed to the overarching theme, the ever-evolving friendship between the Russian and Ukrainian populations, "two great kindred Slavic peoples."[32]

These quotes highlight the idea that Ukraine possessed a long history with Russia and that these ties were, are, and will be permanent and inviolable. While it is easier to rewrite the past than to control the present or to predict the details of the future, these theses highlighted the importance of the Ukrainian SSR and Ukrainians. This campaign intended to enmesh the Ukrainians deeper into the Soviet project and keep them there.

---

31   O. Khablo, "Mohutnii zasib vykhovannia pobuttia druzhby narodiv: Do 15-richchia kyivskoho filialu Tsentralnoho muzeiu V. I. Lenina," *Radianska Ukraina*, Aug. 29, 1953, p. 3.

32   "Theses on the 300th Anniversary of the Reunification of Ukraine and Russia (1654–1954)," *Pravda* and *Izvestiia*, Jan. 12, 1954, p. 2. Also published in *Radianska Ukraina*, Jan. 12, 1953, p. 3–4, and cited in *The Current Digest of the Soviet Press (CDSP)* 6, no. 51 (1954): 3.

As an integral part of the Pereiaslav celebrations, the USSR Supreme Court transferred the Crimean Oblast, a part of the Russian Soviet Federal Socialist Republic, to the Ukrainian SSR. Due to the deportations of the Crimean Tatar, Armenian, Bulgarian, and Greek populations in early 1944, the peninsula's Russian population increased its size and majority in the post-war period.[33]

## Tectonic Plate C: Mixed Feelings about Ukraine in the First Decade after the Collapse of the USSR in the Ieltsin Era

Mikhail Gorbachev's reforms unleashed a cascade of nationalist mobilizations throughout the USSR, bringing to power individuals who sought to use Soviet institutions to further the interests of the fifteen union republics.[34] In 1990 and 1991, the Russian Federation's Boris Ieltsin and Ukraine's Leonid Kravchuk both challenged Gorbachev's leadership of the USSR. After the August 1991 coup, after the Ukraine's declaration of independence on August 24, 1991, and after the resounding pro-independence vote on December 1, Gorbachev spoke on television and "citing his own forebodings, he talked about the possibility that states that have decided to leave the Union may make territorial claims on one another. According to Gorbachev, Russia might, for example, demand some of the territory of present-day Kazakhstan or lay claim to Kharkov, the Crimea and the Donets Basin."[35]

Although Vladimir Zhirinovskii and other Russian ultra-nationalists raised territorial issues, Ieltsin did not make any demands on his new neighbors during his two terms as president. By concentrating on the Russian Federation, Ieltsin maintained—for the most part—good relations with Ukraine, culminating in the 1994–1996 denuclearization of Ukraine, the 1998 Russian-Ukrainian Treaty of Friendship, and the division of the Black Sea fleet between the Russian and Ukrainian navies. In this period,

---

33  See Gwendolyn Sasse, *The Crimea Question: Identity, Transition, and Conflict* (Cambridge, MA: Harvard Ukrainian Research Institute, 2007).
34  See Mark R. Beissinger, *Nationalist Mobilization and the Collapse of the Soviet State* (Cambridge, UK, and New York: Cambridge University Press, 2002); and Henry E. Hale, *The Foundations of Ethnic Politics: Separation of State and Nations in Eurasia and the World* (Cambridge, UK, and New York: Cambridge University Press, 2008).
35  Sergei Tsikora, "Presidents' Views Differ Fundamentally," *Izvestiia*, Dec. 9, 1991, p. 2; cited in *CDSP*, 43, no. 49 (1991): 4.

the Ieltsyn government did not support the growing separatist movement in the Crimea.[36]

Nevertheless, members of Ieltsin's elite and perhaps even Ieltsin himself possessed mixed feelings about Ukraine and Ukraine's borders. Despite the breakup of the USSR along national-republican lines, the post-Soviet elite in the Russian Federation did not de-colonize their minds. Many Russians referred to their closest neighbors as the "Near Abroad" and employed the term "the post-Soviet space." Both terms imply that these new nation-states do not constitute real political entities and that "what binds these countries is their common Soviet inheritance."[37] Both concepts imply the idea that Russia should enjoy a "special relationship" with the newly independent states of the former Soviet Union. Vladimir Lukin, the first post-communist Russian ambassador to the United States, best expressed these underlying assumptions by asserting that relations between Russia and the former Soviet states "should be treated as identical to those between New York and New Jersey," a sphere of influence, in other words.[38] According to Fiodor Lukianov, the Chair of the Council on Foreign and Defense Policy and the Editor-in-Chief of *Russia in Global Affairs*, "Russia still believes it is necessary to create a space around itself where it is recognized as the leader in every sense—political, economic, cultural, and ideological."[39] Just as Russians claim that the United States treats Russia "like a colony, not an equal," Russia treats its non-Russian neighbors in the post-Soviet space as "colonies, not equals."[40] Even more so.

In the 1990s the Russian media started to propagate myths which the West did not—or could not—challenge: that Russia had been "humiliated" by the West after the USSR's collapse in 1991; that the former USSR was "the lost territory" of historic Russia and that post-Soviet Russia had the right to play a "special role" in these areas (the post-Soviet space); and that Russia's historic fear of encirclement was replaying itself because of the expansion of the North Atlantic Treaty Organization

---

36 Sasse, *The Crimea Question*.
37 Angela Stent, *The Limits of Partnership: U.S.-Russian Relations in the Twenty-First Century* (Princeton, NJ: Princeton University Press, 2014), 98.
38 Stent, 19.
39 Fyodor Lukyanov, "Moment of Truth," *Rossiiskaia gazeta*, Oct. 16, 2013, p. 8; translated in *CDRP* 65, no. 42 (2013): 8.
40 Stent, 25.

(NATO) eastwards. (In truth, Russia's humiliations did not come from the West, but from other Russians, the oligarchs who dominated the Ieltsyn era and who now appear as Putin's "friends").[41] The mass acceptance of this interpretation has made it difficult for Russians to accept their reduced post-Cold War international status, to reconfigure their post-imperial national identity, or to come "to terms with the loss of empire."[42]

## Tectonic Plate D: Putin's Ascendency and View of the World

Vladimir Putin joined Moscow's post-Soviet political establishment in the mid-1990s, shortly after the collapse of the USSR and Russia's economy. He did not enter government service as a blank slate. He entered it as an adult, as someone who had formed his vision of the world based on his own experiences and those of Russia and the Soviet Union. In a series of interviews with journalists in preparation for his first presidential campaign in 2000, Putin admitted that he was "a pure and utterly successful product of Soviet patriotic education," someone who did not learn about Stalin's crimes or the blank spots of Soviet history. During his time in the KGB ranks, the organization's primary enemy was NATO.[43]

He spent sixteen years in the KGB, from 1975 to 1991, with nearly five years in Dresden, in East Germany. He went there in 1985 and left after the fall of the Berlin Wall in 1990, living in one of the most repressive countries in East Central Europe and in one of the few East German cities which could not receive West German television broadcasting.[44] His mission abroad coincided with Gorbachev's reforms, which sparked the anti-communist East European revolutions of 1989.

When the mass protests broke out that fall and when crowds attacked the East German Ministry of State Security near Putin's Dresden offices, he and his KGB team burned secret papers night and day until— by some accounts—the furnace broke. "We were afraid," Putin remembered, that "they would come for us too."[45]

---

41   Andrew Wilson, *Ukraine Crisis: What It Means for the West* (New Haven, CT and London: Yale University Press, 2014), 5.
42   Stent, 5.
43   Vladimir Putin et al, *First Person: An Astonishingly Frank Self-Portrait by Russia's President*, trans. Catherine Fitzpatrick (New York: Public Affairs, 2000), 42, 67.
44   Putin, *First Person*, 67, 69, 77.
45   Putin, *First Person*, 76.

This fear of personal danger and death was amplified when he could not get reinforcements from a nearby Soviet garrison because he did not have Moscow's permission and "Moscow was silent." With this crisis, "I got the feeling that the country [the USSR] no longer existed. That it disappeared. It was clear that the [Soviet] Union was ailing. And that it had a terminal disease without a cure—a paralysis of power."[46] Not surprisingly, Gorbachev and his reforms, which led to the loss of eastern Europe and to the disintegration of the USSR itself, were to blame.

Although Putin claimed that the 1989 revolutionary events in East Central Europe were inevitable, he asserted that "[he] only really regretted that the Soviet Union had lost its position in Europe, although intellectually [he] understood that a position built on walls and dividers cannot last. But [he] wanted something different to rise in its place. And, nothing different was proposed. That's what hurt. They just dropped everything and 'went away.'"[47]

In light of his Soviet upbringing, his experiences in the KGB, and the 1989 events in East Germany, Putin is vehemently opposed to regime change and chaos, which flows from it. The US-led NATO intervention against Serbia on behalf of Kosovo in 1999, the U.S.-led invasion of Iraq in 2003, the Tulip Revolution in Georgia in late 2003, the NATO expansion into Estonia, Latvia, and Lithuania in the spring of 2004, and the US-led intervention in Libya inspired Putin and the Russian political establishment to draw the line on Ukraine in 2004 and again in 2013–2014. Russia's invasion of Georgia and subsequent occupation of Abkhazia and South Ossetia in August 2008 represented a warning to Georgia—and to Ukraine as well. According to Angela Stent,

> [f]or the Kremlin, the stakes in Ukraine were higher than in Georgia—Ukraine's population was ten times larger than Georgia's, eighty percent of Russia's gas exports to Europe pass through Ukraine, the Black Sea Fleet is headquartered in the Crimea, which is on Ukrainian territory, and roughly one-sixth of the country's population is ethnically Russian.[48]

In the course of Ukraine's 2004 presidential election campaign, Putin and his colleagues openly supported Viktor Ianukovych over his opponent, Viktor Iushchenko. When the United States, the European Union, and the

---

46   Putin, *First Person*, 79.
47   Putin, *First Person*, 80.
48   Stent, 110.

Organization for Security and Cooperation in Europe (OSCE) denounced the fairness of the November 21 election, Iushchenko's supporters mobilized millions throughout Ukraine and attracted hundreds of thousands to Kyiv's Independence Square to protest the election outcome. They paralyzed the government's operations, and launched the successful, nonviolent Orange Revolution, which brought Viktor Iushchenko and Iuliia Tymoshenko to power in January 2005.[49]

During this balloting, Russia bet on the wrong horse and lost. But the Russian leadership learned a brutal lesson, as expressed by Valerii Khomiakov, General Director of the Council on National Strategy. The principle reason for any "orange revolution," he asserted, is to overturn the electoral process. The opposition no longer believes that the government can be changed through elections and "if it does not believe that, it thinks: 'Why do we need these elections? We will take to the streets and get rid of the lot of them.'"[50]

For Putin and his supporters, the Orange Revolution did not represent democracy in action (as most in the West interpreted this phenomenon), but as a direct challenge to the well-ordered authoritarian state Putin sought to build. Russia's president would not accept the Orange Revolution's victory. He understood that it solidified Ukraine's velvet divorce from Russia after the collapse of the USSR. In early 2005, shortly after Iushchenko's inauguration as president of Ukraine, Putin claimed that the collapse of the USSR was "a major geo-political catastrophe of the twentieth century. For the Russian people, it was a genuine

---

[49] See Stanislav Vladyslavovych Kulchytskyi, *Pomarancheva revoliutsiia* (Kyiv: Heneza, 2005); Andrew Wilson, *Ukraine's Orange Revolution* (New Haven, CT: Yale University Press, 2005); Anders Aslund and Michael McFaul, eds., *Revolution in Orange: The Origins of Ukraine's Democratic Breakthrough* (Washington, DC: Carnegie Endowment for International Peace, 2006); Taras Kuzio, ed., *Democratic Revolution in Ukraine: From Kuchmagate to the Orange Revolution* (London and New York: Routledge, 2009); Paul D'Anieri, ed., *Orange Revolution and Aftermath: Mobilization, Apathy and the State in Ukraine* (Washington, DC: Woodrow Wilson Center and Baltimore, MD: The Johns Hopkins University Press, 2010); and Lincoln A. Mitchell, *The Color Revolutions* (Philadelphia: University of Pennsylvania Press, 2012).

[50] Pyotr Tverdov and Alexandra Samarina, "The State Generates Demand for Political Radicalism," *Nezavisimaia gazeta*, Sep. 5, 2013, p. 1; translated in *CDRP* 65, no. 36 (2013): 13.

drama. Tens of millions of our co-citizens and compatriots found themselves outside Russian territory. What's more, the epidemic of disintegration infected Russia itself."[51] This epidemic divorced Ukraine from Russia.

Putin reviled the Iushchenko government and sought to manipulate Ukraine's parliamentary elections of 2006 with the gas cutoff of January-February 2006 and with another one in early 2009. In early 2008, he was infuriated over NATO's Membership Action Plan (MAP) program for Georgia and Ukraine, the next step for these two post-Soviet states to gain full membership. In the summer of 2008, provoked by Georgia's President Mikheil Saakashvili, he invaded Georgia in August and occupied Abkhazia and South Ossetia.

During the presidential elections of 2010 in Ukraine, Russia's favored candidate—Viktor Ianukovych—won a narrow victory over Iuliia Tymoshenko. The OSCE, the European Union, and the United States certified that this election was "free and fair," unlike the first two rounds of the 2004 elections. Ianukovych did not disappoint Putin. Shortly after being sworn in, the new Ukrainian president asserted that Ukraine would never become a member of NATO and signed the Kharkiv Accords, which extended the end of the lease on the Russian naval base in Sevastopol from 2017 to 2042. In enacting a set of highly-arbitrary laws, Ianukovych consolidated his control over Ukraine's parliament, restricted the scope of Ukraine's civil society, and jailed his primary and most charismatic opponent, Iuliia Tymoshenko. By the end of 2011, Putin may have imagined that Ianukovych's illegal and unconstitutional maneuvers would thwart the efforts of those Ukrainians who wanted their country to join the EU and NATO. Thanks to Ianukovych, Putin may have convinced himself, Ukraine would remain in Russia's orbit.

Or so it seemed, if one discounted the political tremors unleashed in the Middle East and spread across the digitally-connected world. But no authoritarian political leader could ignore the Arab Spring's inspiration to all who opposed dictatorships and "managed democracies." The Arab masses in the streets expressing their hopes, aspirations, and frustrations, the outbreak of civil war in Libya, the subsequent NATO-led

---

51   Vladimir Putin, "Annual Address to the Federal Assembly of the Russian Federation," *President of Russia* (official site), April 25, 2005, http://en.kremlin.ru/events/president/transcripts/22931; *Rossiiskaia gazeta*, Apr. 26, 2005; and translated in *CDRP* 57, no. 17 (2005): 1.

intervention there, and then the civil war in Syria, Russia's most important ally in the Middle East, reaffirmed that the post-Soviet world was very messy and chaotic. In a speech delivered one year after the start of the Arab Spring, Putin asserted that it

> was initially received with hope for positive change. People in Russia sympathized with those who were seeking democratic reform. However, it soon became clear that events in many countries were not following a civilized scenario. Instead of asserting democracy and protecting the rights of the minority, attempts were being made to depose an enemy and to stage a coup, which only resulted in the replacement of one dominant force with another even more aggressive dominant force . . .
> 
> Generally, the current developments in the Arab world are, in many ways, instructive. They show that a striving to introduce democracy by use of force can produce—and often does produce—contradictory results. They can produce forces that rise from the bottom, including religious extremists, who will strive to change the very direction of a country's development and the secular nature of a government.[52]

If the unfolding of the Arab Spring into an Arab Winter frustrated Putin and his colleagues, the demonstrations in Moscow against Putin and his candidacy for a third presidential term in the fall of 2011 and in the spring of 2012 shook him to the core and strengthened his resolve to chart a new, more insular course for Russia.

After his victory at the March 2012 presidential elections, Putin sought to discredit those who rallied against him as the vanguard of the decadent West, unrepresentative of the "real Russia."[53] He then launched a new Russian narrative based on the need to protect Russians and the Russian-speaking populations in the near abroad, to promote the imperial notion of Eurasia and the Eurasian Customs Union, and in wake of Pussy Riot's provocative public protests to defend the "conservative values" championed by the Orthodox Church.[54]

Increasingly, he also expressed his security service mentality. According to his thinking, the Russian Federation was still constantly surrounded by enemies, not just NATO, but the EU as well. In Putin's view of the world, America's disregard of Russian interests in Kosovo, Iraq, the

---

52  See Vladimir Putin on Foreign Policy "Russia and the Changing World," *RT*, February 27, 2012, https://www.rt.com/politics/official-word/putin-russia-changing-world-263/; *Moskovskie novosti*, March 1, 2012; excerpts in *CDRP* 64, no. 9 (2012): 3.
53  Wilson, *Ukraine* Crisis, 5.
54  Wilson, *Ukraine Crisis*, 3.

near abroad, and Syria "remains a key driver of Russian policy."[55] According to Dmitrii Rogozin, Russia's former ambassador to NATO (2008–2012) and deputy minister of defense, "Putin symbolizes policy that's independent from the 'Washington apparatchiks'—he is the only leader in Europe who has not been crushed by the steamroller of U.S. hegemony."[56] According to this logic, Ukraine's efforts to join the European Union represented a diminishment of Russia's hegemony over the post-Soviet space and a strengthening of the American one, a totally unacceptable proposition.

When the demonstrations broke out in Kyiv in late November 2013, Putin and his entourage took actions in Crimea and in southeastern Ukraine. After Ianukovych and his inner circle escalated the violence against the demonstrators and after the demonstrators responded in kind in January 2014, Putin began to intervene more openly in Ukraine, a country he does not recognize as a legitimate political actor independent of Russia.[57] Putin nearly lost Ukraine in 2004. With an Arab Spring-type scenario unfolding in Ukraine, he tried to take advantage of every opportunity to thwart the anti-Ianukovych forces from coming to power. But he failed.

On the night between Friday, February 21, 2014, and Saturday, February 22, President Ianukovych fled Kyiv. On Saturday morning, Ukraine's parliament met and deposed him from office. Three hundred seventy-two deputies (80 percent of the total number of members of parliament), including men and women from Ianukovych's Party of Regions, voted in favor of this legislation. Oleksandr Turchynov, a Tymoshenko ally, became the new speaker of parliament and acting president. On Thursday, February 27, parliament established a new unity government, with Turchynov as speaker and acting president and Arsenii Iatsenyuk as prime minister. Shortly afterwards, they set the election for a

---

55  Stent, 50.
56  Dmitry Rogozin, "The Russian Answer to Vladimir Putin," *Izvestiia*, Feb. 1, 2012, p. 1; translated in *CDRP* 64, no. 5 (2012): 8.
57  At the 2008 NATO Conference in Bucharest, Putin allegedly told President George W. Bush: "George," he said, "you have to understand that Ukraine is not even a country. Part of its territory is in Eastern Europe and the greater part was given to us." Cited in Stent, 168; originally in "NATO Was Sold to a Blocking Stake," *Kommersant*, April 7, 2008, http://www.kommersant.ru/doc/877224.

new president on Sunday, May 25, which Petro Poroshenko won on the first ballot.

Despite this legitimate transfer of power from Ianukovych to Turchynov to Poroshenko, many in Ukraine's majority Russian-speaking regions in the Crimea and eastern Ukraine, stoked by inflammatory newscasts they received from Russian television channels, expressed unease, if not hostility to the new Ukrainian government. Already on December 2, 2013, barely two weeks after the anti-Ianukovych demonstrations started in Kyiv, a city councilman in Crimea's Sevastopol organized a petition, asking President Putin to send troops from Russia to protect the Russian population of Crimea and other regions of Ukraine. Within hours after Ukraine's parliament created its post-revolutionary unity government on February 27, masked men in unmarked camouflage suits ("the little green men," as they were called) who carried highly sophisticated Russian military weapons took over the regional parliament building in Simferopol and installed a radical pro-Russian zealot as the leader of the Crimean parliament. The legislature then called a referendum concerning the peninsula's status on March 16, 2014.

On Saturday morning, March 1, Russia's parliament unanimously approved President Putin's request to employ Russian military forces in Ukraine to protect Russian citizens and the Russian-speaking population "until the social and political conditions in that country normalize."

On March 4, Putin in one of his first interviews after the Euromaidan Revolution claimed that the Ukrainian parliament was "partially legitimate," but that the acting president was not. Ianukovych, Putin asserted, was Ukraine's only legitimate president. Shortly after Russia's parliament passed a resolution making it easier to add territories to the Russian Federation, Putin expressed his support for the March 16, 2014 referendum in Crimea.

The Russian media claimed that ninety-eight percent of all eligible Crimeans voted to join the Russian Federation. Two days later, on March 18, Russia officially annexed Crimea from Ukraine. By mid-April, pro-Russian separatists stormed buildings in eastern Ukraine and raised the Russian tri-colored flag over Ukrainian administrative buildings. Supported and financed by "volunteers" from the Russian armed forces, the "separatists" took power over large swathes of territory in two of Ukraine's easternmost provinces, Donetsk oblast and Luhansk oblast.

Armed conflict between the Ukrainian government and the so-called pro-Russian separatists (who were not necessarily citizens of Ukraine) broke out over the summer of 2014. Troops loyal to the Ukrainian government experienced slow, but steady success on the battlefield until the Russian Army's intervention in mid-August 2014. Under intense international pressure, Presidents Poroshenko and Putin met in Minsk and signed a ceasefire protocol on September 5.

Despite small-scale violations of the ceasefire, the truce held until January 2015, when the pro-Russian forces successfully beat back the Ukrainian Army. Poroshenko and Putin signed a new ceasefire agreement on February 11–12. This agreement has been constantly violated, primarily by the Russians, who for the most part still deny the presence of the Russian Army on the territory of Ukraine.

## Conclusion

Each of the above-mentioned themes, these tectonic plates, build on and re-inforce each other, and provide the environment which inform official Russian pronouncements concerning Ukraine and its revolutionary upheavals. As Russia's integration with the West came to an end in the late 1990s, Putin formulated and sought to implement four major foreign policy goals:

1) For Russia to participate in all major international decisions.
2) To maintain the status quo in the Euro-Atlantic area and ensure that there is no more eastern enlargement of either NATO or the European Union in the former Soviet states.
3) To contain and push back Western democracy-promotion efforts in Russia and its neighbors and minimize the possibility of regime change or instability in Eurasia.
4) Russia offers itself as a defender of the autocratic rulers in the neighborhood.
5) To promote Russia's economic interests and, by implication, those of its political elite by enlisting Western investment and technology in Russia's modernization project.[58]

---

58  Stent, 263.

Ukraine is an important component of at least three of the above four goals. Putin seeks to prevent Ukraine from establishing closer ties with the EU and NATO, and to draw it closer to the Russian Federation, even if Ukraine never joins Putin's Eurasian Union. Moscow authorities seek to establish political control over Ukraine, at least indirect political control by creating a frozen conflict in eastern Ukraine, similar to those in Transnistria, Abkhazia, South Ossetia, and Nagorno-Karabakh. In doing so, they hope to maintain veto power over Ukraine's legitimately elected government.

Whether or not Vladimir Putin is an impulsive gambler or a grand strategist, he is certainly influenced by Russian imperial and Soviet views of Ukraine as a region in the Russian orbit. The post-Soviet humiliations of the 1990s and his own frustrations with Ukraine's democratic experiments in the twenty-first century, which have upended his vision of what the post-Soviet order should look like, have only strengthened his convictions. He seeks to restore the primacy of the Russian Federation in the post-Soviet space, following in the footsteps of the late Gorbachev period's "empire savers," who regarded the Soviet Union in its 1989 boundaries "as the proper and legitimate national 'space' of the Russian nation. Indeed, some of them extend it to the Soviet bloc."[59]

At the same time, President Putin and his state-controlled media are not just manipulating the Russian public's responses to the Euromaidan Revolution, he is also seeking to pro-actively respond to the Russian public. He hopes to divert attention from his own government's non-transparent "managed democracy" and from his own serious economic problems, exacerbated by the fall in the price of world oil and Western sanctions imposed after Russia's annexation of Crimea.

For President Putin, who constantly emphasizes the question of Russian national security, Ukrainians and their aspirations to join Western institutions are a serious threat. He may have combined this highly subjective threat with a perception of a personal affront. In his eyes, much like the Ukrainian Hetman Ivan Mazepa betrayed Tsar Peter the Great in the early eighteenth century, Ukrainian democracy betrayed him in the twenty-first. Inasmuch as this injury must be avenged, the prospects for a

---

59 Roman Szporluk, "Dilemmas of Russian Nationalism," *Problems of Communism* 38, no. 4 (1989): 18; also in Roman Szporluk, *Russia, Ukraine, and the Breakup of the Soviet Union* (Stanford, CA: Hoover Institution Press, 2000), 187.

mutually-agreeable compromise between the post-revolutionary Ukrainian government and Putin's government are dim in the near future. As the citizens of Ukraine demanded international respect, national sovereignty, the rule of law, and the right to choose their own future, Russia's president launched a low-intensity, hybrid war against them. For Putin, they must pay for their European choice. And the costs must outweigh the EU's benefits.

## Bibliography

Anderson, Benedict. *Imagined Communities: Reflections on the Origins and Spread of Nationalism.* London and New York: Verso, 1991.

Andriewsky, Olga. "The Making of the Generation of 1917: Towards a Collective Biography." In *Synopsis: A Collection of Essays in Honour of Zenon E. Kohut,* edited by Serhii Plokhy and Frank E. Sysyn, 19–37. Edmonton, Alberta: Canadian Institute of Ukrainian Studies Press, 2005.

Aslund, Anders, and Michael McFaul, eds. *Revolution in Orange: The Origins of Ukraine's Democratic Breakthrough.* Washington, DC: Carnegie Endowment for International Peace, 2006.

Beissinger, Mark R. *Nationalist Mobilization and the Collapse of the Soviet State.* Cambridge, UK and New York: Cambridge University Press, 2002.

Bialer, Seweryn. "Comment—The Impact of Common RSFSR/USSR Institutions." In *Ethnic Russia in the USSR: The Dilemma of Dominance,* edited by Edward Allworth, 197–99. New York: Praeger, 1980.

*Budivnytstvo Radianskoi Ukrainy: Zbirnyk, No. 1.* Kharkiv: Derzhavne vyd. Ukrainy, s.a..

Chernenko, Yelena. "Even Pork Fat Threat Will Not Stop Ukraine." *Kommersant.* Oct. 29, 2013; cited in *The Current Digest of the Russian Press (CDRP)* 65, no. 44–45 (2013): 3.

Cumming-Bruce, Nick. "Death Toll in Ukraine Conflict Hits 9,160, U.N. Says." *The New York Times.* March 3, 2016. http://www.nytimes.com/2016/03/04/world/europe/ukraine-death-toll-civilians.html?_r=0.

D'Anieri, Paul, ed. *Orange Revolution and Aftermath: Mobilization, Apathy and the State in Ukraine.* Washington, DC: Woodrow Wilson Center and Baltimore, MD: The Johns Hopkins University Press, 2010.

Dmytryshyn, Basil. *Moscow and the Ukraine, 1918–1953: A Study of Russian Bolshevik Nationality Policy.* New York: Bookman Associates, 1956.

Dzyuba, Ivan. *Internationalism or Russification? A Study in the Soviet Nationalities Problem.* New York: Monad Press, 1974.

Eberhardt, Piotr. *Ethnic Groups and Population Changes in Twentieth-Century Central Eastern-Europe: History, Data, Analysis.* Armonk, NY: M. E. Sharpe, 2003.

Edelman, Robert. *Proletarian Peasants: The Revolution of 1905 in Russia's Southwest.* Ithaca, NY: Cornell University Press, 1987.

Eley, Geoff. "Remapping the Nation: War, Revolutionary Upheaval and State Formation in Eastern Europe, 1914–1923." In *Ukrainian-Jewish Relations in Historical Perspective*, edited by Peter J. Potichnyj and Howard Aster, 205–46. Edmonton, AL: Canadian Institute of Ukrainian Studies, 1988.

Gigova, Radina. "Ukraine Crisis: Growing Sense of Despair." *CNN*. March 4, 2016. http://www.cnn.com/2016/03/03/world/ ukraine-un-report/index.html.

Hale, Henry E. *The Foundations of Ethnic Politics: Separation of State and Nations in Eurasia and the World*. Cambridge, UK, and New York: Cambridge University Press, 2008.

Holquist, Peter. *Making War, Forging Revolution: Russia's Continuum of Crisis, 1914–1921*. Cambridge, MA: Harvard University Press, 2002.

Hroch, Miroslav. *Social Preconditions of National Revival in Europe: A Comparative Analysis of the Social Composition of Patriotic Groups Among the Smaller European Nation*. Cambridge, UK, and New York: Cambridge University Press, 1985.

*Itogi Vsesoiuznoi perepisi naseleniia 1959 goda: Ukrainskaia SSR*. Moscow: Gosstatizdat, 1963.

Ivzhenko, Tatyana. "Kyiv Heads West." *Nezavisimaia gazeta*, Sep. 19, 2013; cited in *CDRP* 65, no. 38 (2013): 19.

Kasianov, H., and V. M. Danylenko. *Stalinizm i ukrainska intelihentsiia: 20—30 roky*. Kyiv: Naukova dumka, 1991.

Kasianov, H. *Ukrainska intelihentsiia 1920-kh—30-kh rokiv: sotsialnyi portret ta istorychna dolia*. Kyiv: "Globus" and "Vik," 1992.

Khablo, O. "Mohutnii zasib vykhovannia pobuttia druzhby narodiv: Do 15-richchia kyivskoho filialu Tsentralnoho muzeiu V.I. Lenina." *Radianska Ukraina*, Aug. 29, 1953, p. 3.

Kirianova, O. L. *Naukovo-pedahohichna i vchytelska intelihentsiia radianskoi Ukrainy v umovakh kulturno-osvitnykh peretvoren 20–30-kh rr. XX st.: istoriohrafiia*. Pereiaslav-Khmelnytskyi: Pereiaslav-Khmelnytskyi derzhavnyi pedahohichnyi universytet im. Hryhoriia Skovorody, 2013.

Komarenko, T. H., and M. A. Shypovych. *Vlada i literaturno-mystetska intelihentsiia Radianskoi Ukrainy, 20-ti roky XX st.* Kyiv: Instytut istorii Ukrainy, 1999.

Krawchenko, Bohdan. *Social Change and National Consciousness in Twentieth Century Ukraine*. New York: St. Martin's Press, 1985.

Kulchytskyi, Stanislav Vladyslavovych. *Pomarancheva revoliutsiia*. Kyiv: Heneza, 2005.

Kuromiya, Hiroaki. *The Voices of the Dead: Stalin's Great Terror in the 1930s*. New Haven and London: Yale University Press, 2007.

Kuzio, Taras, ed. *Democratic Revolution in Ukraine: From Kuchmagate to the Orange Revolution*. London and New York: Routledge, 2009.

Laqueur, Thomas W. "Toward a Cultural Ecology of Literacy in England, 1600–1850." In *Literacy in Historical Perspective*, edited by Daniel P. Resnick, 43–57. Washington, DC: The Library of Congress, 1983.

Liber, George O. *Soviet Nationality Policy, Urban Growth, and Identity Change in the Ukrainian SSR, 1923–1934*. Cambridge, UK, and New York: Cambridge University Press, 1992.

Lohr, Eric. *Nationalizing the Russian Empire: The Campaign Against Enemy Aliens During World War I.* Cambridge, MA: Harvard University Press, 2003.

Lorimer, Frank. *Population of the Soviet Union: History and Prospects.* Geneva: League of Nations, 1946.

Luckyj, George S. N. *Literary Politics in the Soviet Ukraine, 1917–1934.* New York: Columbia University Press, 1956.

Lukyanov, Fyodor. "Moment of Truth." *Rossiiskaia gazeta,* Oct. 16, 2013, p. 8; translated in *CDRP* 65, no. 42 (2013): 8.

Mace, James E. *Communism and the Dilemmas of National Liberation: National Communism in Soviet Ukraine, 1918–1933.* Cambridge, MA: Harvard Ukrainian Research Institute, 1983.

Martin, Terry. *The Affirmative Action Empire: Nations and Nationalism in the Soviet Union, 1923–1939.* Ithaca, NY: Cornell University Press, 2001.

Mitchell, Lincoln A. *The Color Revolutions.* Philadelphia: University of Pennsylvania Press, 2012.

"NATO Was Sold to a Blocking Stake." *Kommersant.* April 7, 2008. http://www.kommersant.ru/doc/877224.

Pauly, Matthew D. *Breaking the Tongue: Language, Education, and Power in Soviet Ukraine, 1923–1934.* Toronto: University of Toronto Press, 2014.

"Pro zakhody zabezpechennia rivnopravnosty mov i pro dopomohu rozvytkovi ukrainskoi movy." In *Kulturne budivnytstvo v Ukrainskii RSR: Naivazhlyvishi rishennia komunistychnoi partii i radianskoho uriadu: Zbirnyk dokumentiv,* vol. 1, 242–47. Kyiv: Derzhavne vyd. politychnoi literatury URSR, 1959.

Putin, Vladimir. "Address by the President of Russia at Crimea's Annexation." *President of Russia* (official site). March 18, 2014. http://en.kremlin.ru/events/president/news/20603.

———. "Annual Address to the Federal Assembly of the Russian Federation." *President of Russia* (official site). April 25, 2005. http://en.kremlin.ru/events/president/transcripts/22931.

———. "Russia and the Changing World." *RT.* February 27, 2012. https://www.rt.com/politics/official-word/putin-russia-changing-world-263/.

Putin, Vladimir et al. *First Person: An Astonishingly Frank Self-Portrait by Russia's President.* Translated by Catherine Fitzpatrick. New York: Public Affairs, 2000.

Rogozin, Dmitry. "The Russian Answer to Vladimir Putin." *Izvestiia,* Feb. 1, 2012, p. 1.

Rudnytsky, Ivan L. *Essays in Modern Ukrainian History.* Edmonton, AL: Canadian Institute of Ukrainian Studies, 1987.

Sasse, Gwendolyn. *The Crimea Question: Identity, Transition, and Conflict.* Cambridge, MA: Harvard Ukrainian Research Institute, 2007.

Saunders, David. "Russia's Nationality Policy: The Case of Ukraine (1847–1941)." In *Synopsis: A Collection of Essays in Honour of Zenon E. Kohut,* edited by Serhii Plokhy and Frank E. Sysyn, 399–419. Edmonton, Alberta: Canadian Institute of Ukrainian Studies Press, 2005.

Shevelov, George Y. *The Ukrainian Language in the First Half of the Twentieth Century (1900–1941): Its State and Status*. Cambridge, MA: Harvard Ukrainian Research Institute, 1989.

Shkandrij, Myroslav, and Olga Bertelsen. "The Soviet Regime's National Operations in Ukraine, 1929–1934." *Canadian Slavonic Papers* 55, nos. 3–4 (2013): 417–47.

Stent, Angela. *The Limits of Partnership: U.S.—Russian Relations in the Twenty-First Century*. Princeton, NJ: Princeton University Press, 2014.

Sullivant, Robert S. *Soviet Politics and the Ukraine, 1917–1957*. New York: Columbia University Press, 1962.

Szporluk, Roman. "Dilemmas of Russian Nationalism." *Problems of Communism* 38, no. 4 (1989): 15–35.

———. *Russia, Ukraine and the Breakup of the Soviet Union*. Stanford, CA: Hoover Institution Press, 2000.

———. *Ukraine: A Brief History*. Detroit: Ukrainian Festival Committee, 1979.

"Theses on the 300th Anniversary of the Reunification of Ukraine and Russia (1654–1954)." *Pravda* and *Izvestiia*. Jan. 12, 1954, p. 2.

Tolz, Vera. *Russia: Inventing the Nation*. London: Arnold, 2001.

Troinitskii, N. A., ed. *Pervaia vseobshchaia perepis naseleniia Rossiiskoi Imperii 1897 g*. Saint Petersburg: Izd. Tsentralnogo statisticheskogo komiteta Ministerstva vnutrennikh del, 1899–1905. Vols. 8, 13, 16, 32, 33, 41, 46, 47, and 48.

Tsikora, Sergei. "Presidents' Views Differ Fundamentally." *Izvestiia*, Dec. 9, 1991, p. 2.

Tverdov, Pyotr, and Alexandra Samarina. "The State Generates Demand for Political Radicalism." *Nezavisimaia gazeta*, Sep. 5, 2013, p. 1.

*Vsesoiuznaia perepis naseleniia 1926 goda*. Vols. 11, 12, and 13. Moscow: Tsentralnoe statisticheskoe upravlenie SSSR, otdel perepisi, 1928–29.

Weiner, Amir. *Making Sense of War: The Second World War and the Fate of the Bolshevik Revolution*. Princeton, NJ: Princeton University Press, 2001.

Weinstein, H. R. "Land Hunger and Nationalism in the Ukraine, 1905–1917." *Journal of Economic History* 2, no. 1 (1942): 24–35.

Wilson, Andrew. *Ukraine Crisis: What It Means for the West*. New Haven, CT and London: Yale University Press, 2014.

———. *Ukraine's Orange Revolution*. New Haven, CT: Yale University Press, 2005.

# 2
# Ukraine is the Epicenter of the "World Hurricane"

Yurii Scherbak

### A "Dark Rising Tide" Prior to the Hurricane

My book entitled *Ukraina v zoni turbulentnosti* (Ukraine in the Zone of Turbulence) was published in Kyiv in 2010, and included a collection of essays and public speeches dated from 2003 to 2010. The texts were permeated by my concerns for Ukraine's future. Having reread them recently, I was amazed at the premonitions I expressed in the past which today sound almost like prophecies. But apparently these premonitions did not emanate from my prophetic gift but rather from my ability to sense the social atmosphere of uncertainty and collective concerns associated with increasing neo-imperial revanchist tendencies in neighboring Russia. The distant thunder rumbled at our borders, and it has been heard.

In 2004 I wrote that the battle unravelling as a result of these tendencies was not a local affair but rather a development of geopolitical significance, and its consequences were crucial to Ukraine's status, whether Ukraine would become a NATO or EU member and leave the "gray security zone," or whether it would remain the southwestern borderland of a "revived Eurasian empire." I suggested that we should carefully listen to Putin, and pay attention to how successively he had been rejuvenating the "great indivisible Russia" which of course was inconceivable without Ukraine.[1] Already in 2004, having identified the existent regimes in Kyiv and Tbilisi as extremely dangerous, Russia began a massive attack on Ukraine. In other words, a "dark rising tide" (*temnyi pryplyv*) occurred then, the third or the fourth one over the thirteen years of independent Ukraine's history, an attack that was more sophisticated

---

1 Iurii Shcherbak, "Peizazh pered bytvoiu," in *Ukraina v zoni turbulentnosti* (Kyiv: Ukrainskyi pysmennyk, 2010), 87–96.

and systematic than the earlier ones from an economic and intelligence point of view.[2]

The vectors of Russia's 2004–2005 attacks were consistent with the latest one—in Crimea, the East, and the South of Ukraine. For instance, since 1991, semi-privately and semi-officially, the Russian political elites have claimed that Crimea belonged to Russia. They have also been quite vocal about their desire to force Ukraine into surrendering its plans to join NATO and the EU. The meaning of this rhetoric is transparent: Ukraine, if Russia's plan succeeded, would be transformed into Russia's satellite, a submerged province of a new empire.

The "dark rising tide" seems to be a long-term campaign and the most serious challenge to the very existence of Ukraine. It was designed to forcibly change Ukraine's political course and the legitimate Ukrainian government. Russia's aggression in Ukraine constitutes a clear violation of the 1994 agreements, in which Ukraine was guaranteed territorial integrity, peace, security, and protection in exchange for its nuclear arsenal.[3] Today the Kremlin attempts to compromise Ukraine in the eyes of the international community, claiming that a group of fascist came to power in Kyiv. In reality, Ukraine rejects the idea of hostile relations with Russia and advocates peace and cooperation with its neighboring states. It asserts, however, its place in these relations as an equal and sovereign state.

My concerns in 2010, the time when Viktor Ianukovych came to power, were also associated with the putinization of Ukraine and the authoritarian practices of the then Ukrainian government. There were grounds to believe that the regime would proceed in a direction where democratic changes in Ukraine would be rolled back, and people's civil rights and freedoms would be thwarted. What would the Ukrainian political leaders do if there were protests in the streets? Their methods appeared then to be crystal clear—to fight Ukrainian nationalism and Western influences mercilessly.[4]

These allusions from my earlier writings were included here not for self-aggrandizing purposes but in order to illuminate growing anxieties

---

2    Iurii Shcherbak, "Temnyi pryplyv," in *Ukraina v zoni turbulentnosti* (Kyiv: Ukrainskyi pysmennyk, 2010), 324.
3    Shcherbak, "Temnyi pryplyv," 327.
4    Iurii Shcherbak, "Vlada temriavy," in *Ukraina v zoni turbulentnosti* (Kyiv: Ukrainskyi pysmennyk, 2010), 362.

and understandings of Ukraine as a state that was approaching a cataclysmic world storm, although back then there were still hopes that Ukraine would avoid the worst.

It has not.

Today it is rather obvious that Russia's aggression in Ukraine in 2014–2015 was not spontaneous or "situationally conditioned," as Putin and the followers of his regime attempt to persuade us. Prepared in advance, this strategic operation was designed to destroy Ukraine's statehood, and has been continuously implemented through gas, milk, and other wars, anti-Ukrainian propaganda and intelligence operations, and systematic attempts at grabbing Ukrainian lands (i.e. the 2003 Tuzla Island conflict[5]). From a geopolitical perspective, this operation prepared by the Kremlin should be identified as a "world hurricane" that disrupts world politics, national security, and the international norms of political ethical behavior.

## A Tragic Historical Turn

In future textbooks on World History, the year 2014 might be identified as the beginning of the Third World War, yet initially very few people had seen the situation in these terms. Similarly, the events of the 1930s—the war between Japan and China, Italy's war in Abyssinia, the Spanish civil war with the participation of Stalin's USSR and Hitler's Germany—were not perceived by contemporaries as harbingers, or rather components, of the Second World War. Even the Anschluss in Austria and the Munich Agreement of 1938 were not treated as undeniable signs of the beginning of the Second World War. Many peoples and politicians prefer to live in the illusory world, disregarding the truth of the realities and facts that deny the inertia of peaceful co-existence.

In a somewhat mysterious way, the chimeric stream of small and large events that occurred in post-war Europe and the Middle East, including the disintegration of the "evil empire"—the Soviet Union, created a logistical space, where their continuity can be traced over a hundred years since the eruption of the First World War.

---

5  Tuzla Island is part of Kerch city in eastern Crimea and located in the middle of the Strait of Kerch between the Kerch Peninsula in the West and the Tasman Peninsula in the East.

As far as contemporary world history is concerned, in February 2014 in Kyiv, Europe's periphery, in its central square a local conflict developed: the government authorities executed a hundred rebels, an act that provoked the eruption of protests against Ianukovych's larcenous regime, protests that were carried out by millions of people. Later on, however, these events began to unravel rapidly, and they appeared to be of global significance, a totally unexpected development for prudent European politicians who were largely accustomed to play by the rules: on Putin's order, Russia invaded and annexed a part of sovereign Ukraine, the strategically important Crimean peninsula, which was followed by the invasion of the Donbas by Russia's intelligence forces. A civil conflict inspired by the fifth column that has been nurtured by Russia for quite some time camouflaged its aggression in eastern Ukraine, which resulted in the creation of Novorosiia, a fictitious pseudo-state formation that has never existed, for the purpose of slicing the largest and most developed eight (sic!) oblasts from Ukraine. Capturing and annexing these oblasts under the banner of "*Russkii mir*" (the Russian World) would cut Ukraine off from the Black and Azov Seas, transforming it into a marginal non-viable stump of a former developed country.

As a response to Russia's barely hidden aggression, the political leadership of Ukraine took legitimate steps to preserve its territorial integrity, launching an anti-terrorist operation (ATO). The chain reaction of spilling blood had begun: first minor casualties called for more on both sides; the hatred generated more hatred; the desire for revenge on one side echoed with the same acute desire on the other side.

From day one of the conflict, Russia employed the poisonous weapon of mass disinformation, announcing that "the Ukrainian Nazis and banderites" who took power in Kyiv with the aid of the US and NATO allegedly wanted to destroy the Russian-speaking population of the Donbas, to forcibly Ukrainize this region, transforming the "glorious Russian Donbas land" into a field of bloody crimes. Rhetorically and methodologically, this was typical Goebbels-like propaganda, extensively used during the Communist times, a popular appeal that employed the same old stereotypes which targeted the Ukrainian national liberation movements, OUN and UPA, during and after the Second World War in western Ukraine.

For the majority of Ukrainian citizens, everything that happened in the spring of 2014 appeared like a dream, eerie, tenacious, and dark, from which one cannot wake up. The pre-war existence (1991–2013), a borderline of poverty and unfair but nevertheless free and peaceful life, was left behind, with doubtful prospects for its return in the nearest future. Having accumulated over the years of Ukraine's independence, people's frustration with and hatred toward oligarchic and corrupt power exploded with unmatched force in all Ukraine's oblasts without exception. Yet the protests were aimed not at the destruction of the Ukrainian state but at Ukraine's reformation. Interestingly, Russia fully exploited the protest movement to its advantage only in Crimea and the Donbas when on February 20, 2014 it launched a hybrid war against Ukraine to grab a significant part of the Ukrainian territory.

This was the starting point of incessant funerals and cries of widows and their children who bewailed the deceased soldiers and volunteers, fallen victims of Russia's aggression. Every day, Ukrainian TV channels broadcast these funerals where the caskets were carried under the melody of the melancholic Lemko folklore song "*Plyve kacha*" (A Duck Is Swimming) and exclamations "*Heroi ne vmyraiut!*" (Heroes do not die!).

Ukraine fell into emotional depression. As if resuscitated from black-and-white documentary footage, the images of the forgotten Second World War have made a return to Ukrainian lands in the form of ruined cities, destroyed villages, blown-up bridges, hundreds of thousands of refugees, the corpses of soldiers burned by "Grads" (Hails) and distorted by mortar fire, the dead bodies of aged women ruptured at the markets and bus stops, and of children who were killed in the playgrounds.

The morgues in the war zone were overfilled, and the horrific images of naked, bloody, and mutilated bodies, piled up on tables and on the floor, were placed on the internet with the warning 18+, as if individuals who were older than 18 could tranquilly contemplate this orgy of death. The three generations of Ukrainians born after 1945 have not seen so many killed, wounded, and mutilated people, and almost no one has remembers what it is like to hide in moldy cellars during shelling, fearing for children's lives.

In 1941 I was seven years old, and I remember the scent of the soil in cellars where our kindergarten was hiding when the Germans bombarded Ukrainian cities and villages. Now new generations of Ukrainians were introduced to the menacing features of war, those who will live in the twenty-first century. Ukraine will never forget this new war, including its old enduring features intermingled with super-modern particularities.

Fighters on both sides were hiding their faces behind balaclavas. This was a time of masks, a time of an ominous masquerade. First and last names disappeared, having been replaced by callsigns: "Tur," "Koleso," "Kino," "Motorola," "Kokh," "Shark," "Kulia," "Tsyhan," "Veider," and "Doctor."

The hopes for a quick and victorious end of the war in the Donbas, assertively promised by political leaders and their military advisors[6] in the early summer of 2014, evaporated when Russia dispatched its fully armed troops who regularly defeated Ukrainian fighters. A feeling of hopelessness enveloped Ukraine after each lost battle.

Dropping the last pre-war illusions and awakening from a severe shock entitled the "Russian spring," the outdated myths about eternal peace in the territories of the former Soviet Union and the peacefulness of the Russians, the majority of free-thinking people in Ukraine began to see things more clearly, grasping the new and frightening truth: hundreds of thousands if not millions of Ukrainian citizens in the East and the South (Crimea, the Donbas, parts of Kharkiv, and Odesa) are not united by the same national or any other identity; they are not rooted in the Ukrainian soil, and were poisoned by Russian-Soviet propaganda ("we are the same Soviet people"); they *hate* and *disrespect* the Ukrainian state, the Ukrainian language, and Ukrainian culture. The ethnic roots of this war became quite clear. Traditionally, since the Soviet era, the Russians were proclaimed the titular nation of the empire which tried to absorb and dilute other nationalities. These attitudes have been cultivated and reinforced, and only in 2014 did this hidden abscess burst.

As if in the grasp of a somnambular or epileptic seizure, many of those who belonged, or who believed they belonged, to the Russians, laid down in front of the tracks of Ukrainian tanks, became fire control volunteers or joined the local militia, identifying themselves as *opolchentsy* (insurgents), running with Russian flags and Putin's portraits, and destroying everything that reminded them of the much hated, corrupt, and unfair Ukraine. Yet in reality, they were governed not by independent

---

6   In Ukraine they have been identified as "parquet generals" (*parketni heneraly*), a definition of military officials who have only seen the real war from their comfortable offices.

Ukraine but by the local mafia of Akhmetov, Ianukovych, Kolesnikov, Iefremov, and other bandits, a mafia that was overwhelmingly pro-Russian and anti-Ukrainian.

In their desire to break free from one prison (Ukrainian, according to Russian propagandists), the people of the Donbas paved the way toward another prison for themselves, a prison which is much more violent and ruthless, empowered by the spatial capacities of Siberia and the regime of dictatorship.

In the barbarous euphoria, anticipating the Manna and Safe Haven of increased pensions ("like in Russia"), these unfortunate and impoverished people were making a return to the past, back to the USSR, a discernible entity marked by Iosif Kobzon's supercilious Soviet songs, parades, and rockets in Red Square in Moscow, and monuments to Stalin—a return to the NKVD-KGB state and informants, to the interrogation cellars, torture, and illegal appropriation of businesses by the state, a return to corrupt judges, gangsters, and bandits, and to the state governed by the officers of the Russian secret services. That is precisely the state that they received quite quickly in the form of the fake republics such as the DNR (Donetsk People's Republic) and LNR (Luhansk People's Republic).

Intelligence and ideological subversion conducted in Ukraine by the FSB expedited the creation of these republics. Moreover, the key institutions of Ukraine's political power—the military, the police, and the security services—had been deliberately destroyed by the previous regimes through the efforts of the Russian intelligence: they were demoralized and incapable of defending Ukraine from an outside invasion and from internal aggression of anti-state forces. Tens of thousands of the Ukrainian military and law enforcement men and women betrayed their oath to Ukraine and deserted, running to the Russians in Crimea and the Donbas. This phenomenon of mass betrayal remains to be understood.

Moscow, "the older brother," who for centuries has been disseminating a poisonous narrative among the subjugated Ukrainians about the special relative link between the Russians and Ukrainians (in reality disrespecting "*khokhly*"[7] and "*malorosy*"[8] and considering them a subservient servile force), has revealed itself as an insolent enemy. Having abandoned Lenin's rhetoric of internationalism and "friendship of peoples," Russia functions as a treacherous murderer of its "brothers and sisters," as an invader of their territories, and as a plunderer of Ukrainian wealth. In its war against Ukraine, Russia acts as an arrogant imperial and racist force. Over the last two years, this has become abundantly clear for the majority of Ukrainian citizens. Regardless of the language they speak, they seem to have heard the call of their ancestors, "independentists," freedom-loving Cossacks, and rebels of Makhno: they have awakened and realized that there was more than a grain of truth in the beliefs of Ukrainian nationalists who identified Russia as the most vicious enemy of Ukraine.[9]

Indeed, the bloody split of two "brotherly peoples" in 2014 might have fundamental and permanent ramifications: Russia might lose Ukraine forever.

However, the hopes of Ukrainians for the effective and swift intervention of the West—Europe and the United States which have been idealized by the Ukrainians—have been disappointed. Weak and tranquilized by the long peace, welfare, and liberal values "without boundaries," European states have been watching the conflict in trepidation, the fiery flaming steppe which encompasses the East of Ukraine and which at any moment may spill over to the West—old Europe.

The American government, weakened by Barack Obama, a dreamer and a peace-maker, was reluctant to interfere and unleash a potential military conflict with Putin. Obama believed that the war in eastern Ukraine was a distant regional conflict, which was no danger to the national interests of the United States. Fortunately for Ukraine, many influential American politicians and generals disagreed with him.

---

7    *Khokhly* is a derogatory term for Ukrainians used in Russia.
8    According to the official state concept of the Russian empire, Ukrainians or Little Russians, *malorosy* (in Russian, *malorossy*), represented one of the three branches of the all-Russian people (the other two are Russians and Belorussians).
9    See Alexander J. Motyl's similar analysis in "A Grand Strategy for Ukraine: How to Navigate Between Russia and the West," *Foreign Affairs*, April 5, 2016, https://www.foreignaffairs.com/articles/ukraine/2016-04-05/grand-strategy-ukraine.

Nevertheless, the realities appear quite gloomy: instead of decisive intervention by the United States, Great Britain, and France, states which, like Russia, solemnly promised to guard Ukraine's sovereignty in exchange for its surrendering its nuclear weapons (the Budapest Memorandum of 1994), these Western states found Russia's actions with respect to Ukraine undermining "democratic processes and institutions in Ukraine," threatening "its peace, security, stability, sovereignty, and territorial integrity," and contributing to "the misappropriation of its assets," and, in response, authorized limited sanctions,[10] but denied essential help to Ukraine through military support, lethal weapons, modern radio-electronic equipment, space intelligence and the like. Certainly, the West has not repeated the Munich crime of 1938, yet it once again exhibited unpardonable weakness and indecisiveness in relations with the aggressor.

In 2014 Ukraine found itself in a situation of 1940, when through great efforts and sacrifice Great Britain beat back Hitler's attacks without sufficient support from the United States, due to President Franklin D. Roosevelt's obligations to follow the Neutrality Acts. Because of Russia's aggression, Ukraine became an extremely unstable state and found itself on the brink of extinction. The epicenter of world history once again moved to the Ukrainian lands, acquiring the most tragic features—the features of war with its hurricane of fire and blood. The destructive and violently rotating column of a world tornado moved from the Asian, Middle Eastern, and African peripheries to Europe, reminding humanity of 1914 and 1939. The ambivalent attitudes of the West toward the Russian-Ukrainian conflict emboldened Russia's adventurism and incursions into Ukraine and other foreign territories, reshaping international security strategies and procedures in this region.

## The International Aspects of Russia's Aggression against Ukraine

For the first time in the post-war history of Europe, the great nuclear Eurasian state and member of the United Nations Security Council, Russia, carried out large-scale unprovoked aggression against its

---

10   "Ukraine and Russia Sanctions," *U.S. Department of State*, 2014, http://www.state.gov/e/eb/tfs/spi/ukrainerussia/.

neighboring state, violating a series of fundamental international agreements, first and foremost the Charter of the United Nations of 1945.

Ruining the common European security system and destroying the Westphalian concept of sovereign states and the post-Yalta and post-Helsinki world order built on the principle of the integrity of state borders, Putin, like Hitler, has opened Pandora's box and created a sense of déjà vu, returning us to the first half of the twentieth century: he rejuvenated the "dictatorship of power," pursuing a course that leads to the liquidation of the global system of international relations. The consequences of Putin's efforts are far-reaching—the destabilization of the extant world order and the emergence of military conflicts in various parts of the world.

In 2014 the United Nations General Assembly condemned Russia's political behavior, when 100 members of the UN supported the anti-Putin resolution and only 11 members, Russia's allies, voted against it. Russia's actions unequivocally fall into the category of aggression according to the 1974 United Nations General Assembly Resolution (XXIX) (Definition of Aggression), which reads:

> Any of the following acts, regardless of a declaration of war, shall, subject to and in accordance with the provisions of article 2, qualify as an act of aggression:
> (a) The invasion or attack by the armed forces of a State of the territory of another State, or any military occupation, however temporary, resulting from such invasion or attack, or any annexation by the use of force of the territory of another State or part thereof,
> (b) Bombardment by the armed forces of a State against the territory of another State or the use of any weapons by a State against the territory of another State;
> (c) The blockade of the ports or coasts of a State by the armed forces of another State;
> (d) An attack by the armed forces of a State on the land, sea or air forces, or marine and air fleets of another State;
> (e) The use of armed forces of one State which are within the territory of another State with the agreement of the receiving State, in contravention of the conditions provided for in the agreement or any extension of their presence in such territory beyond the termination of the agreement;
> (f) The action of a State in allowing its temtory, which it has placed at the disposal of another State, to be used by that other State for perpetrating an act of aggression against a third State;
> (g) The sending by or on behalf of a State of armed bands, groups, irregulars or mercenaries, which carry out acts of armed force against another State of

such gravity as to amount to the acts listed above, or its substantial involvement therein.[11]

Point (e) accurately identifies the participation of the Russian military in the invasion of Crimea, personnel who were stationed in Sevastopol, a part of Ukraine's territory. Russia's further actions in the Donbas in the summer of 2014, a mass invasion of the territory of Ukraine by detachments of the Russian military, also qualify as an act of aggression. There is little doubt that, as the initiator and the leader of aggression, Putin will eventually be accused of crimes against peace (planning, preparing, inflaming, and conducting an aggressive war) and humanity (murders, imprisonment, persecution on political and ethnic bases, the theft of state and private property, the destruction of cities and villages) by a future Nuremberg-like tribunal.

Over a fairly brief period of time, Putin's regime transformed Russia into a dangerous transgressor of international law and order, into a state which today can be identified as a sponsor of international terrorism.[12] After the collapse of Putin's regime (according to my prognosis, this will happen in 2017), the international community may face serious and very complex dilemmas: how to revitalize the international security system? How to revive faith in international agreements? How to reform the Organization of United Nations, in general, and the Security Council in particular, limiting the abuse of its "veto power?" What will happen to the nuclear non-proliferation and missile technology control regimes (MTCR)?

In the realm of international relations during the post-Putin era, the key challenge will focus on whether the world community is able to stop the chaos and to discontinue the chain reaction which might lead to a Third World War.

## "*Russkii Mir*" (the Russian World)—the Ideology of Aggressors

To the great surprise of Western democrats, the fall of the totalitarian Communist regime in 1991 did not lead to Russia's moral and democratic

---

11   See Article 3 of the 1974 Declaration on the Definition of Aggression (GAR 3314), adopted in New York (U.S.A.) on December 14, 1974, *United Nations*, 1974, http://www.un-documents.net/a29r3314.htm.

12   See Alexander J. Motyl, "Putin's Russia as a State Sponsor of Terrorism," *World Affairs*, April 14, 2014, http://www.worldaffairsjournal.org/blog/alexander-j-motyl/putin%E2%80%99s-russia-state-sponsor-terrorism.

revival. Under Putin, Russia returned to the monarchical and chauvinist roots of tsarism, preserving and promoting the most pernicious traditions of the Communist era. Gradually, a fusion of the Stalin-Andropov state and the obscurant version of aggressive Orthodoxy occurred. As a result, with Putin's support, red and brown Russian Nazi-like radical individuals, such as Aleksandr Dugin, Aleksandr Prokhanov, and Sergei Glaziev, became the leading voices in contemporary Russia in formulating and promoting the doctrine of the "Russian World"—an association of people of various nationalities who speak Russian and actively support the ideology of Russian exclusivity and chauvinism. Concurrently, attempts at erasing the democratic traditions established by Andrei Sakharov, Galina Starovoitova, Anna Politkovskaia, Iurii Afanasiev, and Valeriia Novodvorskaia were undertaken and appear to be rather effective.

The principles of the "Russian World" include the code of the Russian "condottieri," wondering tumbleweed (*perekaty-pole*), rootless adventurers, mercenaries, and marauders—all those operetta-like Don Cossacks and otamans who fully revealed themselves in Crimea and the Donbas, establishing a "new order" by force of arms in the occupied lands. Essentially, the "Russian World" is a tool of the Kremlin's foreign policy and a concept that undermines stability in Russia's "near abroad," which was founded on the principles of chauvinism with the goal to revive the Eurasian empire and to create a new Russia that could overpower the West.

This policy seems to be grounded in principles once formulated by Hitler. In 1935 in countries neighboring the Third Reich, the "People's Union for Germandom Abroad" (Volksbund für das Deutschtum im Ausland) was created, which oversaw thousands of German organizations and 400 chapters of the Nazi party abroad. In other words, in the territories of sovereign states places of sabotage and treason emerged which were in essence the embryos of the fifth column: they incited ethnic hatred against their own citizens, eliminating national (Czech, Polish and other) schools and promoting the German language.

Unfortunately, despite being aware of the consequences of Hitler's politics, contemporary European, especially German, politicians do not pay sufficient attention to the *ethnic* aspect of conducting war in Ukraine: the scale of ethnic violence and crimes committed by Russian chauvinists is tremendous in the districts they have occupied: Ukrainian activists have been murdered, Ukrainian schools and churches have been closed, and Ukrainian newspapers, radio and television have been prohibited there.

Aleksandr Dugin, the "theoretician" of Eurasianism, gives voice and sustenance to ethnic violence: "We should kill, kill and kill Ukrainians! . . . I am telling you that as a professor."[13] Similarly and equally "eloquently," one of the representatives of the "Russian World" and the Vice-President of "Novorossiia's Parliament" Aleksandr Kofman has stated: "If this was in my power, the very name of Ukraine would disappear. This state formation should not exist. Its roots should be incinerated."[14] These calls echo those of the Nazi past. On August 14, 1939, shortly before Germany's invasion of Poland, the Nazi newspaper *National Zeitung* wrote: "The existence of the Polish state is a shame for the world culture and a danger for peace."

Moscow terrorist and the former Prime Minister of the self-proclaimed DNR Aleksandr Borodai offered a clear definition of goals of the "Russian World" in Ukraine: "The borders of the 'Russian World' are much broader than those of the Russian Federation. I am fulfilling a historic mission in the name of the Russian nation, a super-ethnos, sealed by the Orthodox state. As in the Caucasus, I am fighting the separatists in Ukraine . . . who are sitting in Kiev and fighting against the Russian empire."[15]

The "Russian World," the "Russian Black Hundreds," "polite little green men," bandits in Crimea and the Donbas, and millions of Russian citizens, zombified by television propaganda, follow their "leader and teacher"—the main inspiration of the war against Ukraine and the West. His name is Putin.

## Putin, the Main Firebrand of the War

Today Putin is a hybrid leader and a student of Russian chauvinism and Black Hundreds anti-Western forces in Russia. He is a contemporary product of the new information age who learned from the experiences of Stalin, Hitler, Goebbels, Brezhnev, Andropov, the white generals, and red

---

13  "Aleksandr Dugin: Ubivat, ubivat i ubivat," *YouTube*, June 15, 2014, https://www.youtube.com/watch?v=sX4r1eXpUSI.
14  "Budni telepropagandy. Octiabr-Noiabr 2014," *Grani.ru*, October 24, 2014, http://grani.ru/Society/Media/Television/m.234271.html.
15  Quoted in Aleksandr Skobov, "Rekonstruktsiia ada," *Grani.ru*, July 21, 2014, http://grani.ru/opinion/skobov/m.231294.html.

chekists who functioned during the Civil War in Russia in 1917–1920. Putin represents a new phenomenon of the twenty-first century who managed to merge the illusory features of false democracy (i.e. elections conducted in the absence of opposition that has been suffocated) and the traditions of the KGB's total control over society. Inspired by a hatred of Western liberal and democratic principles, his idée fixe is to build a special Russian model of "civilization" which would be based on anti-Western and anti-liberal principles. The overarching power of total Goebbels-like propaganda serves Putin's regime as a tool to maintain Putin's power and to sustain the large-scale information war. The cynicism of the main "troll" of contemporary Russia—Putin—seems to border on conscious sadism: in the presence of the frightened leaders of the Jewish community of the Russian Federation, Putin identified Goebbels as a "talented person."[16]

Instead of being a guarantor of peace, Putin launched a war against Ukraine, and recently against Syrian "rebels," becoming an extremely dangerous transgressor of international order and peace. Many observers have noted that in addition to Putin's delusion of grandeur boosted by the successful takeover of Crimea, he suffers from an inferiority complex: the West, and first and foremost the United States, so hated by Putin, rejected him as an equal partner—they are unwilling to negotiate with him the spheres of influence in the world.

Importantly, according to Putin's former advisor Andrei Illarionov, Russia's share in total world military expenditures has increased dramatically—from 0.95% in 1999 to 4.94% in 2013, which constituted a world record. At the same time, the indices of political rights and civil liberties in Russia dropped from 42 to 26 (the indices of countries where civil liberties are abused are lower than 34). Russia has the same indices (26) as Afghanistan, Myanmar, Oman, Yemen, and Rwanda. Countries, such as Zimbabwe, Qatar, and Angola, are among those states that have higher indices of civil liberties than Russia.

In their book *Russia After Putin* (Kyiv, 2015), Ukrainian authors Valentin Badrak and Dmitry Kozlov, among other things, consider Vladimir Putin's personality and potential scenarios of Russia's development after Putin. The titles for the book's sections appear symptomatic: "The Player With Marked Cards," "Conscience Split and Resulting Dominance of

---

16   "Putin: Gebbels byl talantlivyi chelovek," *YouTube*, July 10, 2014, https://www.youtube.com/watch?v=zLEOlA5O8aw.

Illusion Over Reality," "Bearing of the Lonely KGB Veteran," "Putin and Ukraine: Will Erostratus Be Given a Chance?"[17] Analyzing the personality of Russia's president, the authors have concluded that "Putin has long become a national tragedy of Russia."[18]

How can one be more accurate?

## The Bloody Parameters of War

Speaking at the September 2015 Session of the UN General Assembly, President of Ukraine Petro Posroshenko announced that eight thousand people had died as a result of the Russian aggression in the Donbas. This number included six-thousand civilians. Forty-four thousand square kilometers of Ukrainian territory have been occupied, and over 1.5 million people lost their homes and were displaced.[19] The industrial and transport infrastructure of the Donetsk and Luhansk oblasts has been destroyed, as well as a considerable part of residential buildings.

The April 2014 armed attacks by Russian terrorists against administration buildings and the headquarters of the Ministry of Internal Affairs and the Security Service in the Donbass provoked the bloody war: Kyiv launched an anti-terrorist operation (ATO) in the region. Several months after the beginning of the war in the Donbas, the casualties of the ATO comprise 2100 dead and 7000 wounded. The Russian terrorist armies lost 9000 people—7421 were Russian citizens. Both sides lost substantial quantities of heavy military equipment, artillery, and mortar systems.

The occupation of Crimea and the Donbas resulted in tremendous monetary loss for Ukraine which has been estimated in the billions of dollars. How can one, however, measure the depth of people's sorrow, those who lost their dearest family and friends, those who lost their homes and have no means for survival?

---

17  The book is "by-lingual"—in Russian and English. See the full text at *Slideshare.net, Center for Army, Conversion and Disarmament Studies,* March 3, 2015, http://www.slideshare.net/OleksandrMykhalik/center-for-army-conversion-and-disarmament-studies.
18  Badrak and Kozlov, 51.
19  "Poroshenko: Zhertvami voiny na Donbasse stali 8 tys. chelovek," *Gordonua.com,* September 29, 2015, http://gordonua.com/news/politics/poroshenko-zhertvami-voyny-na-donbasse-stali-8-tys-chelovek-100022.html.

## Conclusion

What is happening in the Donbas is not a civil war and not a local conflict. This is a war with Russia, an aggressor that invaded Ukraine's territory. This is a war of liberation for Europe's future. The Ukrainian soldiers fight not only for their land but also for the values of the Euro-Atlantic civilization, for people's right to choose the European democratic path of independent development. If Ukraine loses this war, Georgia and Moldova may become the next victims of Russia's aggression, as well as the Baltic states, and the states of Central and Southern Europe.

Russia's main goal in Ukraine is not only the destruction of Ukrainian statehood, subjugation of the Ukrainian people, and their transformation into "Russians." The war in Ukraine and in Syria is a war against the United States and the states of the European Union. This is an ideological and religious war which was designed to destroy the liberal and democratic values of the West. In this war, several methods have been used, including conventional warfare, terrorism, information and propaganda warfare, and psychological subversion.

Putin's regime has transformed Russia into a terrorist state which threatens world stability and blackmails the world by the threat of the potential use of nuclear weapons. This makes Russia an extremely dangerous state which pushes the world toward a Third World War. Thus, support of Ukraine by the world community, including military support, is crucial to strengthening world stability based on the principles of justice, democracy, and peace.

The war has become a new important phase in Ukraine's history. The liberation struggle against Russian occupants has amplified the best features of the Ukrainian people: patriotism and the ability to sacrifice and unite at the moment of truth. The soldiers of the Ukrainian military forces and volunteers have prevented the enemy from moving forward into the main lands of Ukraine sacrificing their lives for Ukraine's sovereignty. During the war an unprecedented volunteer movement emerged in all Ukrainian cities: the volunteers provided the Ukrainian troops with clothes, food, water, and other vital supplies for the front, replacing the ineffective state structures. Moreover, as a result of the Revolution of Dignity of 2013–2014 and the liberation war of 2014–2015, new political and civic organizations emerged in Ukraine that now work toward the purification of power and construction of a new Ukrainian state of the European type.

They are helping to build a democratic and economically strong Ukraine purged of corruption, which would become attractive for those who still reside in the occupied Ukrainian territories.

The destructive hurricane of chaos and war, a moment in history, will eventually come to an end and leave Ukrainian territory. A new Ukraine, consolidated and tempered in its struggle for independence, will be established. We, Ukrainians, believe in this, fight for this, and live for this.

Translated by Olga Bertelsen

## Bibliography

"Aleksandr Dugin: Ubivat, ubivat i ubivat." *YouTube*. June 15, 2014. https://www.youtube.com/watch?v=sX4r1eXpUSI.

Badrak, Valentin, and Dmitry Kozlov. *Russia After Putin*. Available at *Slideshare.net*, Center for Army, Conversion and Disarmament Studies. March 3, 2015. http://www.slideshare.net/OleksandrMykhalik/center-for-army-conversion-and-disarmament-studies.

"Budapest Memorandums on Security Assurances, 1994." *Council on Foreign Relations*. December 5, 1994. http://www.cfr.org/nonproliferation-arms-control-and-disarmament/budapest-memorandums-security-assurances-1994/p32484.

"Budni telepropagandy. Octiabr-Noiabr 2014." *Grani.ru*. October 24, 2014. http://grani.ru/Society/Media/Television/m.234271.html.

Kulyk, Volodymyr. "Ukrainian Nationalism Since the Outbreak of Euromaidan." *Ab Imperio*, no. 3 (2014): 94–122.

Motyl, Alexander J. "A Grand Strategy for Ukraine: How to Navigate Between Russia and the West." *Foreign Affairs*. April 5, 2016. https://www.foreignaffairs.com/articles/ukraine/2016-04-05/grand-strategy-ukraine.

_____. "Here's Why More Ukrainians Admire Nationalists, and Why the West Shouldn't Freak Out." *Atlantic Council*. July 8, 2015. http://www.atlanticcouncil.org/blogs/new-atlanticist/understanding-contemporary-ukraine.

_____. "Putin's Russia as a Fascist Political System." *Communist and Post-Communist Studies* 49, no. 1 (2016): 25–36.

_____. "Putin's Russia as a State Sponsor of Terrorism." *World Affairs*. April 14, 2014. http://www.worldaffairsjournal.org/blog/alexander-j-motyl/putin%E2%80%99s-russia-state-sponsor-terrorism.

"Poroshenko: Zhertvami voiny na Donbasse stali 8 tys. chelovek." *Gordonua.com*. September 29, 2015. http://gordonua.com/news/politics/poroshenko-zhertvami-voyny-na-donbasse-stali-8-tys-chelovek-100022.html.

"Putin: Gebbels byl talantlivyi chelovek." *YouTube*. July 10, 2014. https://www.youtube.com/watch?v=zLEOlA5O8aw.

Shcherbak, Iurii. "Peizazh pered bytvoiu." In *Ukraina v zoni turbulentnosti* by Iurii Shcherbak. Kyiv: Ukrainskyi pysmennyk, 2010.

——————. "Temnyi pryplyv." In *Ukraina v zoni turbulentnosti* by Iurii Shcherbak. Kyiv: Ukrainskyi pysmennyk, 2010.

——————. "Vlada temriavy." In *Ukraina v zoni turbulentnosti* by Iurii Shcherbak. Kyiv: Ukrainskyi pysmennyk, 2010.

Skobov, Aleksandr. "Rekonstruktsiia ada." *Grani.ru*. July 21, 2014. http://grani.ru/opinion/skobov/m.231294.html.

"The 1974 Declaration on the Definition of Aggression (GAR 3314)." *United Nations*. December 14, 1974. http://www.un-documents.net/a29r3314.htm.

"Ukraine and Russia Sanctions." *U.S. Department of State*. 2014. http://www.state.gov/e/eb/tfs/spi/ukrainerussia/.

# Part Two

## War of Narratives

Part Two

# 3

# Ukraine and Russia: Entangled Histories, Contested Identities, and a War of Narratives

Igor Torbakov

How much do words matter in power politics? A historian's answer to this question is: a great deal. After all, words form narratives, narratives shape identities and other forms of political imagination, and the latter act as drivers of policies that might lead to, or even purposefully provoke, hostilities. Furthermore, a "war of words" or information warfare usually accompanies any hot conflict and is meant to rally the allies, disorient the rivals, and undermine the enemy. Thus, the characterization of the smoldering conflict in the Donbas as a "war of narratives and arms"[1] is an apt one. Remarkably, as early as the fifth century B.C., Thucydides, a political thinker and a general, articulated a crucial link between *arms* and *narratives*.[2] In his celebrated *History of the Peloponnesian War*, Thucydides famously distinguished the real reasons (*prophasis*) and the stated reasons (*proschemata*) for waging war. There are three primary real reasons for waging war, he argued: fear, honor, and interest, while the stated reasons involve appeals to nationalism and fear mongering (which is not the same as "reasonable" causes for fear).[3]

Over the last two years, Moscow's explanations of its conduct vis-à-vis Ukraine resemble a page out of the ancient Greek philosopher's writings. Seeking to justify its direct aggression and the land grab in Crimea, as well as its open and covert support for the Donbas separatist insurgents, the Kremlin deploys historical myths, such as the myths of

---

[1] James Sherr, "A War of Narratives and Arms," in *The Russian Challenge: The Chatham House Report* by Keir Giles et al. (London: Royal Institute of International Affairs, 2015), 23–32.
[2] I am grateful to my Uppsala University colleague Dr. Martin Kragh for valuable insights which he shared with me during our discussion of Thucydides's political theory.
[3] For a comprehensive analysis of Thucydides's political thinking, see Geoffrey Hawthorn, *Thucydides on Politics: Back to the Present* (Cambridge: Cambridge University Press, 2014).

perennial "Russo-Ukrainian unity" and of the artificial nature of Ukrainian statehood, geopolitical imagination grounded in the notion of the *Russkii Mir* (Russian World), and scare tactics which are caricaturized by an image of "Ukrainian fascism" blown out of proportion. Simultaneously, the Kremlin has been boosting patriotic feelings, and has been crushing the opposition movement domestically. Yet, the real reasons behind Russia's "hybrid war" against Ukraine appear to be consistent with Thucydides's thesis: fear, honor, and interest. The Russian leadership is seriously concerned about the prospect of losing geopolitical competition with the West in what it regards as its key strategic neighborhood; it resents the fact that its Western "partners" do not accord it all due respect; and it holds that keeping post-revolutionary Ukraine off balance is crucial for consolidating the authoritarian political regime in Russia.

There looms, however, a larger and trickier question: why do Russia's governing elites see things as they do? The answer to this question should be analyzed through the prism of the Russian leadership's perspective on the Russo-Ukrainian conflict which has been shaped by its understandings of complex processes associated with histories and geopolitics of the two countries. These processes include: protracted and painful imperial disintegration and postimperial readjustment; immature national/political identity in post-Soviet Russia and Ukraine; and alternating expansion and contraction of the "spheres of identity" in what is usually designated as "historical borderlands" between "Russia" and "Europe." This essay thus investigates how Russia's and Ukraine's entangled histories gave rise to various historical interpretations, focusing in particular on two conflicting narratives: one highlights a distinct Ukrainian national identity as a basis for the independent and sovereign Ukrainian state; the other blurs national distinctions and emphasizes "pan-Russian" unity. The reasons behind the Russian ruling elites' perception of a distinct Ukrainian identity and of a sovereign Ukrainian state as inimical to what are designated as Russia's "national" interests will also be discussed.

Some insights offered by scholars of colonial and postcolonial studies might enhance understandings of Ukrainian-Russian multifaceted entanglements. In (re)directing attention toward cultural aspects of subordination, "postcolonial" scholars have highlighted the complexity of identity formation in imperial/colonial polities. By introducing the notions of "hybridity" and "subalternity," they have prompted other scholars to examine more closely the discontinuity and ambivalence in the relationship between the rulers and the ruled within empires.[4] This thought-provoking (but admittedly also controversial) approach was first adopted by literary scholars, anthropologists, and specialists in cultural studies, but later also emerged in the works of historians who explored the complexities of the postcolonial paradigm.[5] Analyses of Ukrainian-Russian relations that employed this paradigm appeared immediately after Ukraine attained independence in 1991.[6]

The 2014 revolution and war gave new impetus to this discourse. Some scholars have boldly proclaimed the Euromaidan as the first truly "postcolonial revolution" in post-Soviet space. They have argued that the Kyiv uprising allowed the subaltern—Ukraine—to regain its subjectivity and to begin speaking with its own voice.[7] However, other scholars have retorted, correctly, that "[i]f Ukraine is to be considered postcolonial, then so should Russia, and indeed the whole post-communist region would share in this condition."[8] An insightful concept of Russia as a "subaltern empire," "a space which is both imperial and postcolonial," has recently been advanced.[9] Not surprisingly, both Ukraine and Russia find themselves in a kind of postcolonial condition, because their histories had been closely entangled throughout the imperial and Soviet eras, and both have been struggling to adapt to the postimperial realities after 1991.[10]

But what is similar and what is different in the ways Ukraine and Russia are affected by the postcolonial condition? It would seem that both Ukraine and Russia exhibit extreme "hybridity" and ambivalence in several

---

4   For an analysis of postcolonial discourse, see Ania Loomba, *Colonialism/Postcolonialism* (London: Routledge, 1998).
5   See e.g. Mark von Hagen, "From Imperial Russia to Colonial Ukraine," in *The Shadow of Colonialism on Europe's Modern Past*, eds. Roisin Healy and Enrico Dal Lago (New York: Palgrave Macmillan, 2014), 173–93.
6   See a concise historiographical survey in von Hagen, "From Imperial Russia," 173–79. The limitations of applying the postcolonial paradigm to the study of Ukrainian history have been recently discussed by Yaroslav Hrytsak in "The Postcolonial Is Not Enough," *Slavic Review* 74, no. 4 (2015): 732–37.
7   Ilya Gerasimov, "Ukraine 2014: The First Postcolonial Revolution. Introduction to the Forum," *Ab Imperio*, no. 3 (2014): 22–44.
8   Richard Sakwa, "Ukraine and the Postcolonial Condition," *Open Democracy*, September 18, 2015, https://www.opendemocracy.net/od-russia/richard-sakwa/ukraine-and-postcolonial-condition.
9   Viatcheslav Morozov, *Russia's Postcolonial Identity: A Subaltern Empire in a Eurocentric World* (New York: Palgrave Macmillan, 2015).
10  Ilya Gerasimov and Marina Mogilner, "Deconstructing Integration: Ukraine's Postcolonial Subjectivity," *Slavic Review* 74, no. 4 (2015): 722.

spheres, including social, cultural and political. For instance, Ukraine is desperately striving to break out of Soviet legacies. Many Ukrainians bemoan the ruinous effect of "Soviet imperialism" on the nation as a whole. It was Soviet modernity, however, that shaped the Ukrainian nation which for the first time became fully literate and predominantly urban under Soviet rule. Moreover, its elites were mostly formed by ethnic Ukrainians rather than by representatives of other ethnicities. In foreign policy, Ukraine's hybridity and uncertain identities were on full display for the past twenty-five years as it was searching for a new format of relations with Russia, and maneuvering between its former "master" and its potential "hegemon," the European Union.

Remarkably, the postcolonial condition in Russia also assumes a double hybridity. First, following the collapse of the Soviet Union, post-Soviet Russia was formally reconstituted as a civic nation of *rossiiane*—an ethnically diverse community of the Russian Federation's citizens. Yet, in the Russian elites' political imagination, the Russian Federation is viewed as being co-equal to the entire "historic Russia," thus endowing its self-image with an imperial dimension. Second, for the last three centuries in its relations with Europe, Russia has been a subaltern simply because it did not generate its own vision of modernity but adopted a European one. An alternative communist modernity that had been constructed during the Soviet era was also European both in its philosophical roots and in aspirations but it failed miserably. However, while today *objectively* being a subaltern in the sense of economic, social, and political developments, Russia, driven by its *subjective* self-understanding, challenges these realities by claiming the status of a great power whose voice, unlike that of a subaltern, must be heard. The pattern of Ukraine's and Russia's hybridities and ambivalent behaviors during the postimperial period seem to be similar, but one might also observe a crucial difference: "Ukraine is only a subaltern, whereas Russia is both subaltern and an empire."[11]

It is also important to keep in mind that history is not a teleological process, and "[t]he past is not a single path leading to a predetermined future."[12] Soviet legacies, embedded in Ukraine's and Russia's realities,

---

11   Sakwa, "Ukraine;" Viatcheslav Morozov, "Subaltern Empire? Toward a Postcolonial Approach to Russian Foreign Policy," *Problems of Post-Communism* 60, no. 6 (2013): 16–28.

12   Jane Burbank and Frederick Cooper, *Empires in World History: Power and Politics of Difference* (Princeton: Princeton University Press, 2010), 22.

condition multiple alternatives for historical development. Significantly, politicians, ideologues, and intellectuals shaped the histories of these countries in the past and continue to fashion their present and future. Their imaginations and beliefs about the intertwined historical paths of Ukraine and Russia contribute to an uneasy relationship between the two countries, characterized by some historians as an unstable combination of "intimacy and antipathy."[13] But most importantly, the particular historical views held by people who wield power in both states, as well as their concrete political decisions, created a precondition for the current conflict that led to bloodshed.

I.

Ukraine's and Russia's histories have been symbiotically linked together since the dawn of the history of Eastern Slavdom. Both Ukraine and Russia claim the primacy of their origins from the Kyivan Rus, a loose confederation of early medieval East Slavic principalities. This alleged early beginning of Ukrainian and Russian historical trajectories has long been the subject of highly divergent interpretations.[14] One recent commemorative event illustrates the depth of this long-standing Ukrainian-Russian controversy which has arguably grown even more acrimonious under war conditions. On July 28, 2015, the thousandth anniversary since the death of Vladimir (Volodymyr) the Great, "a saint equal to the apostles" who is revered for having introduced Christianity to Kyivan Rus, was celebrated both in Russia and in Ukraine. Interestingly, while at the center of festivities in both countries was one and the same historical figure, Moscow and Kyiv advanced divergent narratives concerning what it was that the ancient Slavic prince ruled over. In his address at a posh reception in the Grand Kremlin Palace, Russian President Vladimir Putin defined Vladimir as the Prince who "laid the foundation for the formation of a united Russian (*russkaia*) nation," having "baptized the *people of Rus'* into Christianity." "In fact," Putin added, "he cleared the way for establishing a

---

13   Faith Hillis, "Intimacy and Antipathy: Ukrainian-Russian Relations in Historical Perspective," *Kritika: Explorations in Russian and Eurasian History* 16, no. 1 (2015): 121–28.
14   Jaroslaw Pelenski, *The Contest for the Legacy of Kievan Rus'* (Boulder, CO: East European Monographs, 1998); Aleksei Tolochko, *Kievskaia Rus i Malorossiia v XIX veke* (Kyiv: Laurus, 2012).

strong, centralized Russian state."[15] In contrast, the Ukrainian president's administration referred to Vladimir as the "Prince of Kyiv" who Christianized *"Kyivan Rus'—Ukraine."*[16] Furthermore, the Ukrainian lawmaker Oksana Korchynska has contended that the terms *Russia* and *Rus* are historical names of contemporary Ukraine, and proposed a draft law to ban the use of these terms in reference to the present-day Russia in official documents, media, school textbooks, and road maps.[17]

The rhetoric deployed by Moscow and Kyiv in this most recent altercation over their shared history neatly reflects the two countries' antithetical strategies. As noted elsewhere,

> [w]hile the Russian historical myth seeks to question Ukraine's distinctiveness (and thus to undermine its right to sovereignty), the Ukrainian nationalist narrative responds by reasserting Ukraine's distinctiveness and championing its efforts to forge a separate historical path. This is the crux of the matter: whereas Russia's grand story emphasizes togetherness, the Ukrainian one stresses separateness."[18]

But what exactly is distinctive about the Ukrainian story? How legitimate is Leonid Kuchma's claim that "Ukraine is not Russia" which became the title for his 2004 book?[19] Kyiv's celebrations of the aforementioned anniversary suggest that the Ukrainian leadership, following the venerable Hrushevskian historiographic tradition, struggles to uphold the narrative that would date the split between Ukrainians' and Russians' historical paths all the way to the early Middle Ages. Some commentators have noted that Ukrainian president Petro Poroshenko's speechwriters crafted

---

15   Vladimir Putin, "Vystuplenie na torzhestvennom prieme po sluchaiu tysiacheletiia prestavleniia sviatogo ravnoapostolnogo kniazia Vladimira," July 28, 2015, http://kremlin.ru/events/president/transcripts/speeches/50068.
16   Petro Poroshenko, "Zvernennia z nahody Dnia khreshchennia Kyivskoi Rusi," July 28, 2015, http://www.president.gov.ua/news/zvernennya-z-nagodi-dnya-hreshennya-kiyivskoyi-rusi-35736.
17   Verkhovna Rada Ukrainy, "Proekt zakonu pro zaboronu vykorystannia istorychnoi nazvy terytorii Ukrainy ta pokhidnykh vid nei sliv v iakosti nazvy abo synonimu Rosiiskoi Federatsii," July 3, 2015, http://w1.c1.rada.gov.ua/pls/zweb2/webproc4_1?pf3511=55883.
18   Igor Torbakov, "'This Is a Strife of Slavs among Themselves': Understanding Russian-Ukrainian Relations as the Conflict of Contested Identities," in *The Maidan Uprising, Separatism and Foreign Intervention: Ukraine's Complex Transition*, eds. Klaus Bachmann and Igor Lyubashenko (Frankfurt am Main: Peter Lang, 2014), 197.
19   Leonid Kuchma, *Ukraina—ne Rossiia* (Moscow: Vremia, 2004).

a storyline which mirrored Putin's narrative. The essential difference between Poroshenko's and Putin's narratives was in their protagonists: Poroshenko spoke of the "Ukrainian nation," while Putin discussed the history of the "unified Russian people."[20]

Most professional historians observe problems with both interpretations: Kyivan Rus was of course neither a Ukrainian nor a Russian state, and some scholars even doubt whether it was a full-fledged state at all.[21] More importantly, the Ukrainian leaders' desperate attempts at finding solid historical evidence for the Ukrainian nation's glorious antiquity and at identifying the ethno-cultural factors that distinguish Ukrainians from Russians appear to be a failing strategy. Focusing on ethnicity and culture, and comparing and contrasting a thousand year-long history of the "Ukrainian nation" with the supposedly shorter history of Russia plays straight into the hands of Kremlin-run propaganda that cast the ongoing conflict as the one resulting from the clash between two well defined and clearly bounded ethnic groups: the "Ukrainian ultra-nationalists" who seized power in Kyiv in the February 2014 "coup d'état" and the inhabitants of Ukraine's eastern provinces. The latter have been characterized by Putin as peaceful "coal miners" and "tractor drivers" who took up arms to protect their cultural affinity with Russia that allegedly was gravely endangered by the "Kyiv fascists."[22]

There is, however, a more promising way of looking at Ukraine's historical uniqueness based on a different kind of historiographic tradition. This tradition focuses on practices of governance and the relations between the state and society[23] in the territories that constitute contemporary Ukraine. These territories include those Ukrainian lands that either

---

20   Yaroslav Hrytsak, "Vrazhda narodov: Podeliat li Ukraina i Rossiia Kievskuiu Rus," *Novoe Vremia*, August 29, 2015, http://nv.ua/opinion/grytsak/vrazhda-narodov-podeljat-li-ukraina-i-rossija-kievskuju-rus-66201.html.
21   Ironically, the first scholar who bluntly stated that Kyivan Rus was neither Russia nor Ukraine, and that it was not a state but rather a loose federation of principalities, appeared to be the nineteenth-century Russian historian and journalist Nikolai Polevoi. See Volodymyr Kravchenko, *Ukraina, Imperiia, Rosiia* (Kyiv: Krytyka, 2011), 359.
22   Vladimir Putin, "Zaiavleniia dlia pressy i otvety na voprosy zhurnalistov po itogam rossiisko-vengerskikh peregovorov," February 17, 2015, http://kremlin.ru/events/president/transcripts/press_conferences/47706.
23   Arguably, the very possibility of this approach is rooted in the definition of "nation" that can be found in Samuel Johnson's *Dictionary* of 1755: nation is "a people distinguished from another people; generally by their language, origin, or

enjoyed a short-lived autonomy (e.g. the Cossack Hetmanate) or were at different times incorporated into polities, such as the Grand Duchy of Lithuania, the Polish-Lithuanian Commonwealth, and the Habsburg Empire. Back in the 1860s, the prominent historian Nikolai (Mykola) Kostomarov appeared to be the first among the students of Ukrainian and Russian history who argued that "the basic differences between Ukrainians and Russians rested more on socio-political factors than on ethnicity, language or religion."[24] In the 1920s, continuing this line of argument, the conservative political thinker Viacheslav Lypynskyi, who, in Ivan L. Rudnytsky's words, "was the antithesis of Hrushevsky,"[25] formulated his seminal concept of a socially and politically differentiated Ukraine. Lypynskyi contended that

> [t]he basic difference between Ukraine and Muscovy does not consist in language, race or religion . . . but in a different, age-old political structure, a different method of organization of the elite, in a different relationship between the upper and the lower social classes, between the state and society.[26]

When applied to the analyses of the current situation, such a perspective helps one observe more clearly that it is not the supposedly intractable ethnic contradictions that lie at the heart of the present-day conflict. Rather, it is grounded in the intrinsic societal differences that conditioned Ukraine's and Russia's diverging post-Soviet political trajectories. These differences mostly concern the degree of Ukraine's and Russia's sociocultural homogeneity, the role that regionalism plays in both countries, and Ukrainians' and Russians' attitudes towards the state and revolution.

## II.

What is striking about Russia is that for a country of such a gigantic size it enjoys a paradoxically high level of cultural homogeneity. With the exception of some non-Russian Muslim enclaves (in the Middle Volga and

---

government." See also Adrian Hastings, *The Construction of Nationhood: Ethnicity, Religion and Nationalism* (Cambridge: Cambridge University Press, 1997), 14.
24   Pelenski, *The Contest*, 222.
25   Ivan L. Rudnytsky, *Essays in Modern Ukrainian History* (Cambridge, MA: Harvard University Press, 1987), 444.
26   Viacheslav Lypynskyi, *Lysty do brativ-khliborobiv* (Vienna, 1926), xxv; quoted in Rudnytsky, *Essays*, 18.

in the North Caucasus), the Russian people—although not an "imperial race" by any means but definitely an ethnic backbone of the Romanov Empire and the Soviet Union—developed a relatively uniform culture in the process of the colonization of the vast Eurasian expanses. Across nine time zones stretching from Kaliningrad in the far west to Vladivostok in the Far East, one would not discern significant regional cultural differences or pronounced regional identities.[27] In part, this can be explained by the fact that, as in the other post-Soviet states, contemporary Russia remains institutionally underdeveloped and administratively centralized. The state's domination over individual, and societal atomization exacerbates Russia's cultural homogeneity. As the late Russian political thinker Dmitrii Furman has aptly noted, in Russia "there is an individual and there is the state, and there is nothing in between."[28]

Ukraine presents a starkly different picture. Despite all the cataclysms that the Ukrainians suffered in the twentieth century, the cataclysms that turned the ethno-cultural patchwork of most of Central European societies into neatly homogenized nation-states, Ukraine remains boisterously diverse, displaying regional, political, social, and religious pluralism. There are strong regional differences and highly developed regional identities; there are four Eastern Christian denominations (three Orthodox and one Uniate) and two widely spoken languages—Ukrainian and Russian. This remarkable diversity of Ukrainian society partially compensates for a lack of civil society institutions, serving at the same time as a basis for their formation.[29] Establishing autocratic rule in such a diverse society is extremely difficult, unless it is suppressed by force. This

---

27 Siberian regionalism (*oblastnichestvo*), which was very pronounced at the turn of the twentieth century, lost its significance after the Bolshevik victory in the civil war. See Mark von Hagen, "Federalisms and Pan-Movements: Re-imagining Empire," in *Russian Empire: Space, People, Power, 1700–1930*, eds. Jane Burbank, Mark von Hagen, and Anatolyi Remnev (Bloomington, IN: Indiana University Press, 2007), 494–510.
28 Dmitrii Furman, "Neizbezhnoe vzroslenie: interviu s Dmitriem Furmanom," *Polit.ru*, December 26, 2004, http://www.polit.ru/analytics/2004/12/26/furm.html.
29 Dmitrii Furman, "Diialektyka bratnioho viddaliannia," *Krytyka* 10, no. 6 (2006), http://krytyka.com/ua/journal/rik-x-chyslo-6-104. Likewise, the Ukrainian historian Andrii Portnov has suggested that in their analyses of Ukraine's complexity, scholars "should try to free themselves from the temptation to treat heterogeneity and hybridity as signs of weakness or underdevelopment." See Andrii Portnov, "Post-Maidan Europe and the New Ukrainian Studies," *Slavic Review* 74, no. 4 (2015): 726.

factor has always been a consideration for Ukraine's powers that be, and it continues to play a role in the state's decisions regarding domestic and foreign policies.

Furthermore, Russians and Ukrainians seem to differ in their attitudes toward state authority, in their acceptance of trade-offs between unchecked power and social stability, and in their attitudes toward revolutionary upheavals. Rooted in the past experiences of both peoples, these differences have arguably become more pronounced over the last twenty-five years of post-Soviet development.

Since its early years as the Tsardom of Muscovy, Russia has been building a strong autocratic imperial state that could also act as a great power in the international arena. Russian autocratic rule was closely associated with the state's imperial nature because no land empire, where the distinction between the "center" and the "colonial peripheries" is blurred, can embark on even the most moderate democratization in the central provinces (the empire's putative "national core") without running a risk of destabilizing the entire imperial polity across the board. There were only two periods in Russia's history when its autocratic rule completely collapsed: the Time of Troubles (*Smuta*) in the early seventeenth century and the 1917 Revolution followed by civil war. Both upheavals have been etched in Russian collective memory as sheer catastrophes replete with chaos, social dislocation, and massive human losses. The turbulent early 1990s ushered in by the Soviet Union's breakup were generally viewed in Russia as the advent of the third *smuta*: the times of lawlessness, mass poverty, and increasing secessionist movements in the outlying regions—all due to the extreme weakening of the central government. It should come as no great surprise that under Putin, Russia's memory politics sought to contrast the chaos brought about by the revolutionary upheaval (be it in 1917 or in 1991) with the "order" and "stability" secured and protected by the strong and centralized state.[30] Turning its back on the

---

30 In Putin's words, "For us, the state and its institutions and structures have always played an exceptionally important role in the life of the country and the people. For Russians, a strong state is not an anomaly to fight against. Quite the contrary, the state is the source and guarantor of order, the initiator and the main driving force of any change." Vladimir Putin, "Rossiia na rubezhe tysiacheletii," *Nezavisimaia gazeta*, December 30, 1999, http://www.ng.ru/politics/1999-12-30/4_millenium.html; see also Andrei Tsygankov, *The Strong State in Russia: Development and Crisis* (New York: Oxford University Press, 2014).

traditions of Soviet culture that romanticized and sanctified revolutions, the Kremlin propaganda machine portrayed them in negative connotations: to discredit revolutionary ideals, it would make use of long quotations from works written by the philosopher Nikolai Berdiaev and the writer Alexander Solzhenitsyn, Russian luminaries and intellectual and moral authorities who were no great champions of any revolution. It would appear that the Kremlin's efforts to mold public attitudes have proven to be successful. "This politics of memory resonates with today's Russians," the prominent Russian historian Boris Kolonitsky has noted. He has maintained that "'stability' has become a core political value" in Russia.[31]

The situation in Ukraine seems to be very different. The political system and state-like entities that the Ukrainians had been trying to build before 1991 differed markedly from the Russian Empire's autocratic structure and traditions, which have been mostly state-centered throughout Russia's history. This factor has been stressed in Lypynskyi's and Kostomarov's writings.[32] For significant numbers of the national-minded Ukrainians, the glory of the (national) state and the authoritarian system of government were not necessarily interdependent notions, as they were for most Russians. In other words, unlike the Russians, the Ukrainians did not develop what some political scientists call "nondemocratic hegemonic national identity."[33] Importantly, the Ukrainians also have a different attitude toward revolutions. This is of course not to say that they hold dear the myth of the Bolshevik revolution any more than the Russians do. Yet, the Ukrainian national narrative is all about the struggle for national liberation. Therefore, the heroics and romantic aura of a national revolution (a valiant popular revolt against foreign oppression), driven by a historically conditioned combination of social and national factors, clearly strikes a chord with millions of Ukrainians. Some commentators have even sug-

---

31   Boris Kolonitsky, "Why Russians Back Putin on Ukraine," *New York Times*, March 12, 2014, http://www.nytimes.com/2014/03/12/opinion/why-russians-back-putin-on-ukraine.html?hp&rref=opinion&_r=1.
32   Lypynsky, *Lysty*; Nikolai Kostomarov, "Two Russian Nationalities," in *Towards an Intellectual History of Ukraine: An Anthology of Ukrainian Thought from 1710 to 1995*, eds. Ralph Lindheim and George Luckyj (Toronto: University of Toronto Press, 1996), 122–34.
33   Yitzhak M. Brudny and Evgeny Finkel, "Why Ukraine Is Not Russia: Hegemonic National Identity and Democracy in Russia and Ukraine," *East European Politics and Societies* 25, no. 4 (2011): 813–33.

gested that it would not hurt if the Ukrainians' rebelliousness was counterbalanced by a healthy dose of conservatism. As Lypynskyi once sadly remarked in a letter to a friend, "The trouble is not that we have revolutionaries. The trouble is that we have *only* revolutionaries."[34]

Moreover, the Ukrainian political culture has recently been enriched by a new revolutionary impetus—the 2004 Orange Revolution—which in turn served as a powerful symbolic resource for the 2014 Euromaidan Revolution. Viktor Ianukovych's win in the 2010 presidential election that almost immediately prompted him to grab more power in an attempt at establishing a Putinesque authoritarian regime reignited the question of revolution and placed it on the list of people's priorities. Notably, some more astute analysts clearly saw it coming. For instance, Yitzhak Brudny and Evgeny Finkel presciently wrote in 2011

> that Yanukovych's attempts to turn Ukraine into a softer version of Putin's Russia . . . would encounter a much stiffer opposition than Putin ever faced. Moreover, we believe the fierce opposition from a significant section of the political and intellectual elite and especially from the majority of the population in Western Ukraine would ultimately either force Yanukovych to abandon his authoritarian agenda or bring another Orange style uprising."[35]

This rebellious spirit, the capacity for societal self-organization, and the readiness to rise up against oppressive power seem to substantiate the main contention of Kuchma's otherwise lackluster memoir *Ukraina—ne Rossiia*.

Ukraine's most fundamental distinction, however, lies in the character and ambitions of the latest Ukrainian revolutionary movement. As some observers have argued, "[t]rue revolutions do not just change the political regime or the composition of the government; they transform the people and their political culture."[36] In its attempt at establishing societal control over the state, the Euromaidan was striving to do just that. In his erudite book *The Construction of Nationhood*, Adrian Hastings has in-

---

34 See Lypynsky's February 18, 1925 letter to Osyp Nazaruk in *Lysty Osypa Nazaruka do Viacheslava Lypynskoho*, ed. Ivan L. Rudnytsky (Philadelphia: Skhidnoievropeiskyi doslidnyi instytut im. V. K. Lypynskoho, 1976), xlvi. Emphasis added.
35 Brudny and Finkel, 828.
36 Stefan Auer, "Carl Schmitt in the Kremlin: The Ukraine Crisis and the Return of Geopolitics," *International Affairs* 91, no. 5 (2015): 958.

sightfully noted that a nation "is not a [true] nation until it senses its primacy over and against the state."[37] Indeed, the implications of the Euromaidan have been tremendously important: the world observed dramatic changes in Ukraine in 2013–2014—the dismissal of the authoritarian political regime and the emergence of a new Ukrainian civic nation.

## III.

Although the ousting of the kleptocratic Ianukovych cabal was essentially Ukraine's domestic affair, Russia remained a key player throughout the conflict, attempting to manipulate the outcome of the revolution. The main thrust of the Euromaidan (which came to be known also as the Revolution of Values or the Revolution of Dignity) was the struggle, led by broad segments of the Ukrainian society, against corruption and lawlessness, and for transparent governance and the rule of law. Importantly, seeking to expand the repertoire of explanatory paradigms, the historian Ilya Gerasimov has suggested considering the notion of "postcolonial revolution."

"The Ukrainian revolution," Gerasimov argues, "is a postcolonial revolution because it is all about the people acquiring their own voice, and in the process of this self-assertive act they forge a new Ukrainian nation as a community of negotiated solidary action by self-conscious individuals."[38] Gerasimov is convinced that in 2013–2014 a new Ukrainian collective subjectivity was forged. For the Russian governing elite, this phenomenon seemed threatening, as throughout the entire post-1991 period Russia has been asserting, with varying degrees of aggressiveness, its entitlement to determine how Ukraine should be governed. The belief in such entitlement is grounded in Moscow ruling circles' (mis)understanding of what kind of Russia and what kind of Ukraine emerged after the Soviet Union's disintegration. The Kremlin's idiosyncratic views of "post-imperial" relations between Russia and Ukraine had been in gestation for quite some time, germinating in the process of the Euromaidan and presented in more clear contours in the official pronouncements of Russia's top leaders, above all of President Putin. These views have become Russia's official master narrative which was designed to promote

---

37  Hastings, *The Construction of Nationhood*, 25.
38  Gerasimov, "Ukraine 2014," 23; Gerasimov and Mogilner, "Deconstructing Integration," 721.

a new political imagination and to guide policy. The main problem with this narrative, of course, is that it is fundamentally flawed and, when used as a political blueprint, leads to disastrous results.

Let us take a closer look at how present-day Moscow elites imagine historical links and interconnections among contemporary Russia, the defunct Soviet Union, and the Romanov Empire. All three state entities seem to represent for them various incarnations of "historic Russia." According to Putin, "the Soviet Union has traditionally been called Russia, Soviet Russia, and it was indeed the greater Russia,"[39] while the post-Soviet Russian Federation is viewed as a "truncated Russia," a "rump empire" that lost fourteen of its borderland dependencies. It is worth noting that the 1993 Constitution rechristened the former Russian Soviet Federative Socialist Republic (RSFSR) into the *Russian Federation* commonly known as *Russia* (Rossiia), with both names being used interchangeably.

Again, words matter. This particular choice of the state's name is paramount to what can be considered as the forging of a false identity. In the Soviet Union, all union republics (with a notable exception of the largest one—the RSFSR) were constructed as quasi-states of particular *titular* nationalities/nations—the Georgians, the Uzbeks, the Ukrainians, and others. These nations had their *national* homelands and were encouraged (de-jure) to foster their individual *national* identities and cultures within the framework of the well-known Soviet formula: "national in form, socialist in content." Throughout the entire Soviet period, the RSFSR was the only republic where this formula was purposefully not adopted. The Soviet nationalities policy's main goal was to keep Russian and Soviet identities blurred so that the majority of Russians would view the entire Soviet Union as their own state, rather than the RSFSR. The Russians played the role of the "imperial glue" in the Soviet empire which was becoming increasingly Russocentric. As a result, the imperial character of Russian national identity and the imperial consciousness of the Russians were strengthened.[40]

This hegemonic national identity manifested itself in the immediate aftermath of the Soviet breakup. Although the political leadership of the RSFSR was instrumental in bringing down the USSR, it claimed for "new

---

39 Vladimir Putin, "Interview with American TV Channel CBS and PBS," September 29, 2015, http://kremlin.ru/events/president/news/50380.

40 Brudny and Finkel, 816–19.

Russia" the status of the successor of the Soviet Union, reincarnated "historic Russia" or the Russian Empire. Such a line of succession has been solidly embedded in the political imagination of several generations of Russians, sustaining a geopolitical fantasy to rejuvenate "historic Russia" at some point during the post-Soviet period. Already in the early 1990s some astute observers maintained that the new Russian governing elites were indulging in such pipe dreams. For instance, in 1992 Gasan Guseinov noted that those politicians who had chosen to identify the former RSFSR as Russia

> demonstrated a perfect example of wishful thinking because they believed that the old "all-Union" status of the Russian Federation would remain in force even after the Soviet Union's disappearance. This same mistake was repeated by the majority of international organizations where the Russian Federation almost automatically inherited positions of the USSR.[41]

The immediate political implications of this move for Ukraine were outlined by Daniel Beauvois, a leading French historian specializing in East European history. In the introduction to the Ukrainian-language edition of his magisterial work *La bataille de la terre en Ukraine* Beauvois has written:

> On February 7, 1992, France signed a Friendship Treaty with Russia, "proceeding from the fact that Russia is the successor state of the USSR . . . and also from [France's] recognition of the Commonwealth of Independent States." Our diplomats did not notice in this *contraditio in adjecto*. What kind of independence [and what type of sovereignty] then does Ukraine possess if France, while opening its embassy in Kyiv, recognizes Russia as the *exclusive inheritor of the entire imperial legacy*?[42]

The result of this notorious case of mistaken identity is twofold. In the political imagination of Moscow elites, post-Soviet Russia's status as the sole successor to both the Soviet Union and the Russian Empire, as well as its historic inheritance, have been artificially inflated. By contrast, in Ukraine's case, its post-Soviet status, as well as its share in imperial inheritance, was artificially diminished, not least because in a fit of strategic shortsightedness, the governing elites in Kyiv in the early 1990s themselves chose to pursue policies of nationalizing the state, viewing

---

41  Gasan Guseinov, "Istoricheskii smysl politicheskogo kosnoiazychiia," *Znamia* no. 10 (1992), http://gefter.ru/archive/12381.

42  Daniel Bovua [Beauvois], *Bytva za zemliu v Ukraini, 1863–1914: Poliaky v sotsioetnichnykh konfliktakh* (Kyiv: Krytyka, 1998). Emphasis added.

Russia's "closeness" as intrinsically harmful to Ukraine's state and nation building. In other words, Guseinov's suggestion is that the contemporary Russian Federation is "smaller" than its elites imagine it to be (the Russian Federation does not equal "Russia"), while Ukraine is "larger" than the Moscow (and Kyiv) leadership imagined in the early 1990s.[43]

This optical aberration prevents both the Russian *derzhavniki* (champions of imperial great power) and narrow-minded Ukrainian ethnic nationalists from seeing post-Soviet Ukraine as an equal inheritor of Russia's historical imperial legacies. Seen through a different kind of lens, the one that produces a much less distorted social picture, the multiethnic Crimea with its presently dominant Russian cultural component, as well as Kyiv, Kharkiv, and Odesa with their vibrant urban Russian-language culture and millions of Russian-speaking Ukrainians, would appear as parts of the social landscape produced by the imperial and Soviet periods of *Ukrainian* history. These phenomena that can be interpreted as clear manifestations of the country's postcolonial hybridity contribute to the richness and diversity of present-day Ukrainian social life and relate to today's Russian Federation only in a historical sense: both post-Soviet nations' histories indeed have been closely entwined for several centuries.

Crucially, the imperial epoch and the Soviet era differ markedly as far as the development of a distinct Ukrainian identity is concerned. Until the end of the Russian Empire, the struggle between the two national projects—the Ukrainian nationalist project and the project of a "larger Russian nation" pursued by imperial bureaucracy—remained an open ended process. The establishment of the Ukrainian socialist (quasi) state by the Bolsheviks has arguably made the process of Ukrainian-Russian disentanglement irreversible. The Romanov Empire did not distinguish between "Ukraine" and "Russia," or for that matter, among other *ethnically* marked territorial units.[44] In a broad political sense, the vast multiethnic imperial polity in its entirety was considered to be "Russia" autocratically ruled by the "Russian" Romanov dynasty. Besides being used as a politonym in this very broad sense, from the 1850s the word *Russian* was also used as a fuzzy politonym *cum* ethnonym in a narrower sense—specifically, in the

---

43  Guseinov, "Istoricheskii smysl."
44  For instance, the Kingdom of Poland was renamed to Privislinsky Krai following the 1863 Uprising, thus leaving the Grand Duchy of Finland the only exception to the rule.

notion of the "larger Russian nation" that was imagined as comprising three Eastern Slavic peoples—Russians (Great Russians), Ukrainians (Little Russians), and Belarusians.[45] In the beginning of the twentieth century, a number of top imperial bureaucrats argued that confusing "Russia" with the "Russian Empire" was a flawed intellectual premise for pursuing practical policies. Sergei Witte has noted that

> [i]f 35 per cent of the population are ethnic minorities, and if the Russians are divided into Great Russians, Little Russians, and Belarusians, then in the nineteenth and twentieth centuries it is impossible to conduct a policy that disregards this historical fact of capital importance, that disregards the national traits of the other nationalities composing the Russian Empire, their religion, language, and so on.[46]

The "historical fact of capital importance" that Witte stressed so forcefully had remained largely ignored until the First World War and the 1917 Revolution which brought the history of the Russian Empire to an end and simultaneously launched Ukraine onto the world stage.[47] According to the interwar Ukrainian historian Vasyl Kuchabsky, political upheavals in Eastern Europe in 1917–1920 resulted in three extremely important geopolitical developments—the victory of Bolshevism, the reestablishment of Poland, and the reemergence of Ukraine as the third key East European actor alongside *Velikorossiia* (Great Russia) and the reconstituted Polish state.[48] This critical geopolitical factor—the "reemergence of Ukraine"—ultimately led to the establishment of the Ukrainian Soviet Socialist Republic which, according to Ivan L. Rudnytsky, had become "the embodiment of a compromise between Ukrainian nationalism and Russian [Soviet] centralism."[49] This compromise, whose formal expression was the creation of the USSR and the whole system of Soviet federalism based on the principle of the territorialization of ethnicity, was an inherently shaky

---

45 Alexei Miller, "The Romanov Empire and the Russian Nation," in *Nationalizing Empires*, eds. Stefan Berger and Alexei Miller (Budapest: Central European University Press, 2015), 309–68.
46 Sergei Vitte [Witte], *Vospominaniia*, in 3 vols. (Moscow: Izdatelstvo sotsialno-ekonomicheskoi literatury, 1960), 3:274–75.
47 See Eric Lohr et al., eds., *The Empire and Nationalism at War* (Bloomington, IN.: Slavica Publishers, 2014).
48 Vasyl Kuchabsky, *Western Ukraine in Conflict with Poland and Bolshevism, 1918–1923* (Toronto: Canadian Institute of Ukrainian Studies Press, 2009).
49 Rudnytsky, *Essays*, 464.

affair. This formation's instability was perceptively analyzed by Arnold Toynbee back in the 1950s, at a time when the Soviet Union, one of the principal victors in the Second World War and the emerging world superpower, seemed to be at the peak of its geopolitical might. Toynbee wrote that

> [it would] be seen that Stalin's administrative map of the Soviet Union was not to be taken at its face value; but a moral commitment cannot be wiped out through being dishonored by its makers; and, in a world that had emerged from the Second World War, Stalin's map might live to be translated, after all, from the limbo of camouflage into the realm of reality . . . .[50]

The dissolution of the USSR in December 1991 appeared to be exactly what Toynbee outlined as a possible geopolitical result of a "politico-cartographic transformation": what once were administrative borders within the highly centralized Soviet "federation" were converted by national-minded republican elites into *real* state borders dividing sovereign nations, and the union state fell apart at the seams. The leaders of both republics, the Ukrainian SSR and the RSFSR, Leonid Kravchuk and Boris Ieltsin played leading roles in the Soviet Union's demise. More precisely, it was the nationalist stance taken by Ieltsin that delivered a *coup de grâce* to the ailing communist empire.[51] If the Russian Republic were to rush to the exit, George Kennan asked rhetorically, "what, beyond the name, would be left of the Soviet Union? It would have become an empty shell, without people, without territory, and with no more than a theoretical identity."[52]

## IV.

Both Ukraine and the Russian Federation have emerged from the imperial debris as independent states that had liberated themselves from what their political leadership characterized as a centralizing, oppressive, and supranational union metropole. Each state's sovereignty was rooted in a distinct identity of, respectively, the Ukrainian and the Russian peoples.

---

50 Arnold J. Toynbee, *A Study of History* (New York: Oxford University Press, 1954), 9:551; quoted in Rudnytsky, *Essays*, 473.
51 Serhii Plokhy, *The Last Empire: The Final Days of the Soviet Union* (New York: Basic Books, 2014).
52 George F. Kennan, "Witness to the Fall," *New York Review of Books*, November 16, 1995, http://www.nybooks.com/articles/archives/1995/nov/16/witness-to-the-fall/.

This distinction, however, was not a completely novel affair. As mentioned above, the recognition of separate Ukrainian and Russian identities lay at the heart of the formation of the Ukrainian SSR and the subsequent establishment of the Soviet Union. It was also one of the key arguments in Vladimir Lenin's seminal 1914 article "On the National Pride of the Great Russians."[53]

More remarkably, the narrative that President Putin is currently advancing seeks to undo the long-standing political principle underpinning the Ukrainian-Russian relations throughout the Soviet and post-Soviet periods, namely conceiving Russians and Ukrainians as culturally and linguistically close but still separate peoples. In early September 2013, soon before the Euromaidan protest erupted in the center of Kyiv, Putin informed the Russian and international audiences that whatever the Ukrainians might do or whichever direction they might travel, their path is destined to cross with that of the Russians. He then explained why:

> Because we are one people. Although nationalists on both sides (and there are nationalists among us and in Ukraine) may be offended by what I have just said, that is the actual fact of the matter. Because we have the same Kyivan baptismal font in the Dnieper; we certainly have common historical roots and common fates; we have a common religion, a common faith; we have a very similar culture, languages, traditions, and mentality . . ..[54]

Putin's embrace of the archaic notion of the "larger (or triune) Russian nation" which subsumes the Ukrainians and the Belarusians with the Great Russians into a single ethno-political entity is significant in more than one sense. Politically, the claim that the Russians and the Ukrainians are "one people" destabilizes a distinct Ukrainian identity and questions the legitimacy and the very raison d'être of the independent Ukrainian state. Similarly, such statements also destabilize and delegitimize a post-Soviet Russian identity that underpins the existence of the contemporary Russian Federation. Putin's rhetorical persistence, however, should be explained by the tenacity of a hegemonic imperial identity among Russia's ruling elites and the way they understand the reasons behind the Soviet Union's disintegration and its implications.

---

53 Roman Szporluk, "Lenin, 'Great Russia,' and Ukraine," *Harvard Ukrainian Studies* 28, no. 1–4 (2006): 611–26.
54 Vladimir Putin, "Interviu Pervomu kanalu i agentstvu Associated Press," September 4, 2013, http://kremlin.ru/transcripts/19143.

In the 2005 State of the nation address, Putin invited his audience to take a closer look at what he termed as the "genesis of contemporary Russian history." This was the speech in which Putin famously characterized the collapse of the Soviet Union as the "major geopolitical catastrophe of the [twentieth] century."[55] Most significantly, he deciphered the meaning of this catastrophe for the Russian people. According to Putin, the demise of the Soviet Union became "a true drama" for them: "Tens of millions of our fellow citizens *and* compatriots found themselves beyond the borders of Russia."[56] As previously mentioned, in the Moscow ruling elites' political imagination, the distinction between the images of the Russian Federation and of "historic Russia" are blurred, which prompts them to employ the notions of "citizens" and "compatriots" interchangeably. At the same time, these notions seemed to be subtly juxtaposed in their public speeches. According to the message inserted in them, the Russian Federation might well be a formal homeland for the body of Russian citizens but not a "genuine" Russia that is destined to embrace all "compatriots" stranded in various postimperial "formations" and to bring all other "people of Russian culture" into its fold.

This view is "premised on the incompleteness of the Russian Federation and its incongruence with the idea of a 'genuine Russia,' which supposedly should be extended beyond its current borders."[57] Such a political outlook is unmistakably imperial precisely because at its core lies the idea of the fluidity of Russia's borders. Most students of empire agree that empire as a polity is characterized by unstable, movable boundaries, a feature that derives from the imperial ideal of universalism. Alfred Rieber has argued that

---

55 There appears to be a meeting of the minds between the rulers and the ruled in contemporary Russia. See cogent analyses of the Russians' social and cultural longing for the Soviet past in Liudmila Mazur, "Golden Age Mythology and the Nostalgia of Catastrophes in Post-Soviet Russia," *Canadian Slavonic Papers* 57, no. 3–4 (2015): 213–38, and Laura Piccolo, "'Back in the USSR': Notes on Nostalgia for the USSR in Twenty-First Century Russian Society, Literature, and Cinema," *Canadian Slavonic Papers* 57, no. 3–4 (2015): 254–67.
56 Vladimir Putin, "Poslanie Federalnomu Sobraniiu Rossiiskoi Federatsii," April 25, 2005, http://archive.kremlin.ru/appears/2005/04/25/1223_type63372type63374type82634_87049.shtml. Emphasis added.
57 Andrey Makarychev, "Reassembling Lands or Reconnecting People? Geopolitics and Biopower in Russia's Neighborhood Policy," *PONARS Eurasia Policy Memo*, no. 367 (July 2015): 2.

> [e]mpires differ most strikingly from nation states in their way of imagining and fixing their boundaries. The contrast stems from diverse conceptions of universalism and power. Imperial ideologies are inspired by the ideal of universal domination but accept limitations imposed by their own cultural traditions and the constraints of power politics.[58]

Similarly, Toshiteru Matsuura has posited that empires are "another name for ceaseless struggles to expand their frontiers." Empires' territorial frontiers are

> constantly obscure and never fixed, because they are the fluid spheres of conflict between two momentums that expand and push back. When an empire gains demarcated, visible fringes, it is even possible to say that this 'empire' is already dead.[59]

In all its historical guises, Russia has been an empire for almost half a millennium. Quite naturally, the Russian Federation, "as the largest portion of the empire that collapsed less than a quarter century ago has inherited one of the most important features of imperial spatial arrangement: the uncertain and dynamic nature of borders."[60] Due to imperial inertia, Russia seems more inclined to "define its borders *from within, marking the limits of its sovereignty by its own action*," instead of relying on mutual recognition of boundaries based on international law.[61] Notably, all prominent ideologues championing the Russian empire (*russkie impertsy*) equate their imaginary *Russkaia imperiia* with expansion. Iegor Kholmogorov, a leading nationalist thinker who promotes an image of Russia as a "national empire," has recently written that "Russian psyche is immersed in geography," adding that "our Sacred History is the history of Russian spatial expansion."[62] For numerous champions of Russia's "imperial mission," the notion of Russianness has been forever blended

---

58  Alfred J. Rieber, "The Comparative Ecology of Complex Frontiers," in *Imperial Rule*, eds. Alexei Miller and Alfred J. Rieber (Budapest: Central European University Press, 2004), 198.
59  Kimitaka Matsuzato, "Cultural Geopolitics and the New Border Regions of Eurasia," *Journal of Eurasian Studies*, no. 1 (2010): 47.
60  Aleksandr Filippov, "Granitsy gosudarstva i resurs solidarnosti," *Russkii zhurnal*, December 30, 2014, http://russ.ru/Mirovaya-povestka/Granicy-gosudarstva-i-res urs-solidarnosti.
61  Ibid. Emphasis added. This trait is nicely captured in the old Soviet joke: "Which countries does the Soviet Union border on?—Whichever country it wishes."
62  Iegor Kholmogorov, "Russkaia geografiia," *Izvestia*, November 11, 2014, http://izvestia.ru/news/579239.

with the notion of empire: there can be no genuine Russia without the Russian-led Eurasian empire.[63]

To be sure, *impertsy* are not the only ones whose anger has been aroused by the violation in Russia of Gellner's main principle of nationalism. Russian ethnic nationalists are also concerned that the present-day Russian Federation's political and cultural unit, "ethnie and nation," do not coincide.[64] To repair this unfortunate situation, they suggest three ways in which Russian nationhood can be defined today. Depending on a particular ethnonationalist school of thought, Russia is conceived as a community of ethnic Russians, or as a community of Eastern Slavic peoples, or as a community of Russian speakers.[65] However, analyses of the Russian leadership's nation building practices, as well as its neighborhood policy over the past twenty-five years, demonstrate that the Kremlin's policies until very recently have been extremely ambiguous, vacillating at different times between statist/imperial and ethno-cultural options.[66] The conceptual toolkit that official Moscow has deployed with considerable skill included elastic notions such as *sootechestvenniki* (compatriots), *Russkii Mir*, and various permutations of *evraziistvo* (Eurasianism). Vaguely defined and broadly interpreted, these notions helped Russia's governing elites pursue policies of their choice, perpetuating the ambiguity of their approaches to nation building and extracting maximum benefit from this ambiguity. At their core, however, these operative notions have strong imperial connotations and are ultimately designed to redefine the

---

63  V. I. Terekhov, "Rossiia: neizbezhnost imperii," *Vestnik Moskovskogo universiteta*, Series 8 (History), no. 5 (1993): 52–57.
64  See Anthony D. Smith, *Nationalism: Theory, Ideology, History* (Cambridge: Polity Press, 2001).
65  Vera Tolz, "'Homeland Myths' and Nation-State Building in Postcommunist Russia," *Slavic Review* 57, no. 2 (1998): 267–94.
66  Marlene Laruelle, "Russia as a 'Divided Nation,' from Compatriots to Crimea," *Problems of Post-Communism* 62, no. 2 (2015): 88–97; Yuri Teper, "Official Russian Identity Discourse in Light of the Annexation of Crimea: National or Imperial?" *Post-Soviet Affairs* 32, no. 4 (2016): 378–96; Alexander Kozin, "'The Law of Compatriot': Toward a New Russian National Identity," *Russian Journal of Communication* 7, no. 3 (2015): 286–99; Oxana Shevel, "Russian Nation-building from Yel'tsin to Medvedev: Ethnic, Civic or Purposefully Ambiguous?" *Europe-Asia Studies* 63, no. 2 (2011): 179–202; Petr Panov, "Nation-building in Post-Soviet Russia: What Kind of Nationalism Is Produced by the Kremlin?" *Journal of Eurasian Studies* 1, no. 1 (2010): 85–94.

established state borders. Moreover, as Andrey Makarychev has persuasively argued, the war in Ukraine has also shown that these

> doctrines are prone to radicalization and militarization. Geopolitical reasoning [Eurasianism] easily evolves from calculating Russian resources and advantages in the "near abroad" to militarily conquering parts of neighboring states, while biopolitics [the Russian World] shifts from protecting the linguistic rights of Russian speakers to enforcing a family-type of union with post-Soviet nations.[67]

The "pan-Russian" idea advocated by Putin which cast the Russians and the Ukrainians as one people effectively extends the notion of the *Russkii Mir*, including the space of contemporary Ukraine, and thus reducing Ukraine's independence to an obsolete phenomenon. Ultimately, the concept of *Russkii Mir* and the "unity paradigm" cast serious doubts on Ukraine's political subjectivity and sovereignty.

The roots of this outlook go deep into seventeenth-century Kyiv where the learned bookmen from the community of monks of the Kyivan Cave Monastery produced the first major historical work, *Sinopsis* (1674), which explicitly advanced the "unity paradigm." It tells a story of the unified Orthodox Slavo-Russian people (*pravoslavny slaveno-rossiiskii narod*) and treats "Ukrainian" territories of the old Kyivan Rus (which later came to be known as Little Russia) within a larger pan-Russian context. These ideas were then developed by Russian imperial scholars in the course of the nineteenth century, particularly by the St. Petersburg historian Nikolai Ustrialov (1805–1870), into a Russian grand narrative that

> became an assertion of historical priority, a claim to privileged possession of territory and statehood, and a justification of a Great Russian ethnolinguistic definition of 'Russianness' and Russian identity.[68]

Piotr Struve deployed this grand narrative to prop up his arguments in the famous polemic with Ukrainian intellectuals on the pages of *Ukrainian Life* and *Russian Thought* journals in the early 1910s. Struve dreamed about Russia as a great power. A key precondition for attaining such status, he believed, was the existence and further development of the great pan-Russian culture within a unified Russian state which he held was in the

---

67 Makarychev, "Reassembling Lands," 6.
68 Zenon Kohut, "Origins of Unity Paradigm: Ukraine and Construction of Russian National History (1620–1860)," *Eighteenth-Century Studies* 35, no. 1 (2001): 75.

process of becoming a "national empire." Because Struve defined Russian unity in cultural rather than ethnic terms, the emergence of the Ukrainian movement upholding a distinct Ukrainian cultural *and* political identity was an intolerable notion for him. He rejected the Ukrainians' right to self-determination as well as their cultural distinctiveness.[69]

By 1917, the Russian grand narrative championing the "one and indivisible Russian state" and a "single, indissoluble Russian nation" became so pervasive that the upsurge of Ukrainian nationalism triggered by the First World War and revolutionary upheavals caught the Russian educated public off guard. Their lack of awareness is probably best epitomized by General Anton Denikin wondering, "Where did all those Ukrainians come from?" (*Otkuda zhe poiavilos stolko ukraintsev?*)[70] Truth be told though, the Russian public should blame itself for being so unprepared for the emergence of a strong Ukrainian movement, argued Bogdan Kistiakovskii, one of Struve's main intellectual opponents in the earlier Russo-Ukrainian debates. Having blind faith in the "pan-Russian idea" with its main contention that Little Russians (*malorosy*) are part of a larger "Russian tribe," "educated Russians had no interest in those petty Ukrainians," wrote Kistiakovskii in 1917. "They regarded their [Ukrainians] existence as a little matter pertaining to provincial life."[71]

Not all Russians, though, thought along those lines. As noted above, the Bolsheviks, seeking to reestablish control over the rebellious borderland, unequivocally discarded the concept of the larger Russian nation and recognized Ukrainian identity as the principal one on the territory of the Ukrainian republic that they established as part of the Soviet socialist "federation." The Soviets replaced the "pan-Russian" idea with the "friendship of peoples" concept.[72] Yet, the old "unity paradigm"

---

69   Richard Pipes, *Struve: Liberal on the Right, 1905–1944* (Cambridge, MA: Harvard University Press, 1980).
70   Denikin quoted in Olga Andriewsky, "The Russian-Ukrainian Discourse and the Failure of the 'Little Russian Solution,' 1782–1917," in *Culture, Nation, and Identity: The Ukrainian-Russian Encounter, 1600–1945*, eds. Andreas Kappeler et al. (Edmonton: Canadian Institute of Ukrainian Studies Press, 2003), 214.
71   Kistiakovskii quoted in Andrei Portnov, "Kak razgliadet Ukrainu: Izbrannye mesta iz russkoi literatury," *Uroki istorii: XX vek*, January 12, 2015, http://urokiistorii.ru/node/52376.
72   Lowell Tillett, *The Great Friendship: Soviet Historians on the Non-Russian Nationalities* (Chapel Hill: University of North Carolina Press, 1969); Pål Kolstø, "Faulted for the Wrong Reasons: Soviet Institutionalization of Ethnic Diversity and Western (Mis)interpretations," in *Institutional Legacies of Communism: Change*

and the Russian grand narrative that was built on it did not vanish into thin air. They shaped a number of deep-seated perceptions that survived throughout the Soviet period and into the post-Soviet era. These perceptions powerfully affect the political imagination of significant segments of Russia's population and political elites and can be summed up as follows:

*an almost mystical attachment to the territory "from where Rus had originated," which is seen as the cradle of "Russian" history, statehood, religion, and "national spirit."

**a strong sense of Ukraine's central role in Russia's historical destiny. It is broadly held that incorporating a substantial portion of Ukraine into Muscovy in the seventeenth century laid the foundation for the powerful Russian Empire, and the "loss" of Ukraine would likewise lead to the demise of "historic Russia." The upshot of such a development, many Russians believe, would be an "incomplete Russia."

***a belief that most of the Russians and Russian-speakers who reside in Ukraine have a strong desire to reunite with their "historic homeland."

****a sense that Ukraine's independence weakens Russia strategically as it allows other centers of power (such as the European Union and/or the United States) to broaden their sphere of influence in the region that Russia considers vitally important for its own security and for its status as a great (European) power.

## V.

To justify the Russian Empire's participation in the partitions of the Polish Commonwealth, Catherine the Great famously stated: "We took only what was rightfully ours." The empress's remark appears to have neatly encapsulated Russian strategic thinking in which the issues of geopolitics and of identity are tightly intertwined. The three successive eighteenth-century land grabs that greatly expanded Russia's borders westwards at the expense of "historic Poland" brought under St. Petersburg's rule largely "Ukrainian" lands which, it was claimed, were previously ruled by the Rurikid princes whose lawful successors were the tsars of the Romanov dynasty. Another important storyline interpreting Catherine's involvement

---

*and Continuities in Minority Protection*, eds. Karl Cordell, Timofey Agarin and Alexander Osipov (New York: Routledge, 2013): 31–44.

in "Polish affairs," however, was that the lands absorbed by the Russian Empire were populated mostly by eastern Slavs, all of whom were viewed, according to the mainstream perception of the age, as "ours," that is the "Russians." This territorial expansion, adding the Right Bank Ukraine to the Left Bank lands that were included in the Tsardom of Muscovy in the middle of the seventeenth century, was instrumental in shaping two crucial facets of Russian self-understanding. First, it was these new imperial possessions that firmly anchored Russia in "Europe" as one of the continent's great powers. Second, by turning millions of "our" eastern Slavs into new imperial subjects, Russia's governing elites came to view the "Ukrainian question" as a key aspect of forging a "pan-Russian" nation. From the Russian rulers' standpoint, in the "historical borderlands" between Europe and Russia, the latter's "sphere of identity" was a handy geopolitical instrument that would be repeatedly used to expand Russia's sphere of influence.

Roughly the same vision seems to be widespread both among politicians and broader publics in the present-day Russian Federation. As noted above, Moscow political elites see Russia's sphere of identity extending far beyond the Russian Federation's borders, with Ukraine playing a central role within it—by virtue of perceived historical, cultural, and affective ties. All the key aspects of Russian "neighborhood policy"—*Russkii Mir*, *sootechestvenniki*, and efforts to preserve a unified mnemonic community based on shared historical memories—were designed to portray Ukraine, albeit formally an independent state, as an inalienable part of the imagined "historic Russia," and thus to keep it within the Russian Federation's sphere of influence.

Unlike in the eighteenth century, however, today the East European "borderlands" constitute a neighborhood shared by Russia and the European Union. The latter also has a "sphere of identity" but its modus operandi is diametrically opposite to that of Russia. Being a norms- and values-based entity, the EU cultivates identity that essentially is not territory-bound. "To the extent that European identity is connected to the European space, identity is as flexible as the interpretation of what Europe means geographically in a given moment."⁷³ This incompatibility of principles makes the EU-Russia accommodation in the sense of the delimitation of their respective "spheres" extremely difficult if not altogether impossible. Whereas Russia's sphere of identity is limited to the "Russian World" (although broadly understood), for the EU, figuratively speaking, the sky is a limit as, technically, it can expand as far as where its norms and values are accepted and interiorized. Quite naturally, Ukraine became a battlefield where Russia's and the EU's principles clashed. So long as Moscow managed to keep Kyiv within its orbit and Brussels at bay by manipulating identity as a soft power tool, it largely remained a status quo power. When the Kremlin leadership sensed that Ukraine was about to "defect" to the West (as the "European values" upheld by Euromaidan protesters seemed to have triumphed over the Moscow-sponsored ideal of "Slavic unity"), Russia turned revisionist. Russia seized Crimea and claimed that it took what was rightfully hers, and in Ukraine's East the "pan-Russian" idea was deployed with a vengeance. But we would be well advised to follow Thucydides's insight and see this as *proschemata*—Russia's narrative aimed to justify its aggression. Lying deeper are the true reasons behind Russia's conduct—ones that reveal its nature as a "subaltern empire." Unable to advance a viable alternative to the Western social model, Russia's leaders resent Western hegemony, crave equal status within the "concert" of great powers, and seek to perpetuate their political regime. Meanwhile, Ukraine remains a "mere" subaltern, to which a crueler Thucydides maxim applies: "the strong do what they can and the weak suffer what they must."

## Bibliography

Andriewsky, Olga. "The Russian-Ukrainian Discourse and the Failure of the 'Little Russian Solution,' 1782–1917." In *Culture, Nation, and Identity: The Ukrainian-Russian Encounter, 1600–1945*, edited by Andreas Kappeler, Zenon Kohut, Frank Sysyn, and Mark von Hagen, 182–214. Edmonton: Canadian Institute of Ukrainian Studies Press, 2003.

Auer, Stefan. "Carl Schmitt in the Kremlin: The Ukraine Crisis and the Return of Geopolitics." *International Affairs* 91, no. 5 (2015): 953–68.

---

73   Philipp Casula, "Russia's and Europe's Borderlands: Between Sovereign Intervention and Security Management," *Problems of Post-Communism* 61, no. 6 (2014): 9.

Bovua [Beauvois], Daniel. *Bytva za zemliu v Ukraini, 1863–1914: Poliaky v sotsio-etnichnykh konfliktakh*. Kyiv: Krytyka, 1998.

Brudny, Yitzhak M., and Evgeny Finkel. "Why Ukraine Is Not Russia: Hegemonic National Identity and Democracy in Russia and Ukraine." *East European Politics and Societies* 25, no. 4 (2011): 813–33.

Burbank, Jane, and Frederick Cooper. *Empires in World History: Power and Politics of Difference*. Princeton: Princeton University Press, 2010.

Casula, Philipp. "Russia's and Europe's Borderlands: Between Sovereign Intervention and Security Management." *Problems of Post-Communism* 61, no. 6 (2014): 6–17.

Filippov, Aleksandr. "Granitsy gosudarstva i resurs solidarnosti." *Russkii zhurnal*. December 30, 2014. http://russ.ru/Mirovaya-povestka/Granicy-gosudarstva-i-resurs-solidarnosti.

Furman, Dmitrii. "Neizbezhnoe vzroslenie: interviu s Dmitriem Furmanom." *Polit.ru*. December 26, 2004. http://www.polit.ru/analytics/2004/12/26/furm.html.

──────. "Diialektyka bratnioho viddaliannia." *Krytyka* 10, no. 6 (2006). http://krytyka.com/ua/journal/rik-x-chyslo-6-104.

Gerasimov, Ilya. "Ukraine 2014: The First Postcolonial Revolution. Introduction to the Forum." *Ab Imperio*, no. 3 (2014): 22–44.

Gerasimov, Ilya, and Marina Mogilner. "Deconstructing Integration: Ukraine's Postcolonial Subjectivity." *Slavic Review* 74, no. 4 (2015): 715–22.

Guseinov, Gasan. "Istoricheskii smysl politicheskogo kosnoiazychiia." *Znamia* no. 10 (1992). http://gefter.ru/archive/12381.

Hagen, Mark von. "Federalisms and Pan-Movements: Re-imagining Empire." In *Russian Empire: Space, People, Power, 1700–1930*, edited by Jane Burbank, Mark von Hagen, and Anatolyi Remnev, 494–510. Bloomington, IN: Indiana University Press, 2007.

──────. "From Imperial Russia to Colonial Ukraine." In *The Shadow of Colonialism on Europe's Modern Past*, edited by Roisin Healy and Enrico Dal Lago, 173–93. New York: Palgrave Macmillan, 2014.

Hastings, Adrian. *The Construction of Nationhood: Ethnicity, Religion and Nationalism*. Cambridge: Cambridge University Press, 1997.

Hawthorn, Geoffrey. *Thucydides on Politics: Back to the Present*. Cambridge: Cambridge University Press, 2014.

Hillis, Faith. "Intimacy and Antipathy: Ukrainian-Russian Relations in Historical Perspective." *Kritika: Explorations in Russian and Eurasian History* 16, no. 1 (2015): 121–28.

Hrytsak, Yaroslav. "The Postcolonial Is Not Enough." *Slavic Review* 74, no. 4 (2015): 732–37.

──────. "Vrazhda narodov: Podeliat li Ukraina i Rossiia Kievskuiu Rus." *Novoe Vremia*. August 29, 2015. http://nv.ua/opinion/grytsak/vrazhda-narodov-podeljat-li-ukraina-i-rossija-kievskuju-rus-66201.html.

Kennan, George F. "Witness to the Fall." *New York Review of Books*. November 16, 1995. http://www.nybooks.com/articles/archives/1995/nov/16/witness-to-the-fall/.

Kholmogorov, Iegor. "Russkaia geografiia." *Izvestiia*. November 11, 2014. http://izvest ia.ru/news/579239.

Kohut, Zenon. "Origins of Unity Paradigm: Ukraine and Construction of Russian National History (1620–1860)." *Eighteenth-Century Studies* 35, no. 1 (2001): 70–76.

Kolonitsky, Boris. "Why Russians Back Putin on Ukraine." *New York Times*. March 12, 2014. http://www.nytimes.com/2014/03/12/opinion/why-russians-back-putin-on-ukr aine.html?hp&rref=opinion&_r=1.

Kolstø, Pål. "Faulted for the Wrong Reasons: Soviet Institutionalization of Ethnic Diversity and Western (Mis)interpretations." In *Institutional Legacies of Communism*, edited by Karl Cordell, Timofey Agarin, and Alexander Osipov, 31–44. New York: Routledge, 2013.

Kostomarov, Nikolai. "Two Russian Nationalities." In *Towards an Intellectual History of Ukraine: An Anthology of Ukrainian Thought from 1710 to 1995*, edited by Ralph Lindheim and George Luckyj, 122–34. Toronto: University of Toronto Press, 1996.

Kozin, Alexander. "'The Law of Compatriot': Toward a New Russian National Identity." *Russian Journal of Communication* 7, no. 3 (2015): 286–99.

Kravchenko, Volodymyr. *Ukraina, Imperiia, Rosiia*. Kyiv: Krytyka, 2011.

Kuchabsky, Vasyl. *Western Ukraine in Conflict with Poland and Bolshevism, 1918–1923*. Toronto: Canadian Institute of Ukrainian Studies Press, 2009.

Kuchma, Leonid. *Ukraina—ne Rossiia*. Moscow: Vremia, 2004.

Laruelle, Marlene. "Russia as a 'Divided Nation,' from Compatriots to Crimea." *Problems of Post-Communism* 62, no. 2 (2015): 88–97.

Lohr, Eric, Vera Tolz, Alexander Semyonov, and Mark von Hagen, eds. *The Empire and Nationalism at War*. Bloomington, IN.: Slavica Publishers, 2014.

Loomba, Ania. *Colonialism/Postcolonialism*. London: Routledge, 1998.

Lypynskyi, Viacheslav. *Lysty do brativ-khliborobiv*. Vienna, 1926.

Makarychev, Andrey. "Reassembling Lands or Reconnecting People? Geopolitics and Biopower in Russia's Neighborhood Policy." *PONARS Eurasia Policy Memo*, no. 367 (July 2015): 1–6.

Matsuzato, Kimitaka. "Cultural Geopolitics and the New Border Regions of Eurasia." *Journal of Eurasian Studies*, no. 1 (2010): 42–53.

Mazur, Liudmila. "Golden Age Mythology and the Nostalgia of Catastrophes in Post-Soviet Russia." *Canadian Slavonic Papers* 57, no. 3–4 (2015): 213–38.

Miller, Alexei. "The Romanov Empire and the Russian Nation." In *Nationalizing Empires*, edited by Stefan Berger and Alexei Miller, 309–68. Budapest: Central European University Press, 2015.

Morozov, Viatcheslav. *Russia's Postcolonial Identity: A Subaltern Empire in a Eurocentric World*. New York: Palgrave Macmillan, 2015.

―――. "Subaltern Empire? Toward a Postcolonial Approach to Russian Foreign Policy." *Problems of Post-Communism* 60, no. 6 (2013): 16–28.

Nazaruk, Osyp. *Lysty Osypa Nazaruka do Viacheslava Lypynskoho*, edited by Ivan L. Rudnytsky. Philadelphia: Skhidno-Ievropeiskyi doslidnyi instytut im. V. K. Lypynskoho, 1976.

Panov, Petr. "Nation-building in Post-Soviet Russia: What Kind of Nationalism Is Produced by the Kremlin?" *Journal of Eurasian Studies* 1, no. 1 (2010): 85–94.

Pelenski, Jaroslaw. *The Contest for the Legacy of Kievan Rus*. Boulder, CO: East European Monographs, 1998.

Piccolo, Laura. "'Back in the USSR': Notes on Nostalgia for the USSR in Twenty-First Century Russian Society, Literature, and Cinema." *Canadian Slavonic Papers* 57, no. 3–4 (2015): 254–67.

Pipes, Richard. *Struve: Liberal on the Right, 1905–1944*. Cambridge, MA: Harvard University Press, 1980.

Plokhy, Serhii. *The Last Empire: The Final Days of the Soviet Union*. New York: Basic Books, 2014.

Poroshenko, Petro. "Zvernennia z nahody Dnia khreshchennia Kyivskoi Rusi." *Prezydent Ukrainy* (official site). July 28, 2015. http://www.president.gov.ua/news/zvernennya-z-nagodi-dnya-hreshennya-kiyivskoyi-rusi-35736.

Portnov, Andrii. "Kak razgliadet Ukrainu: Izbrannye mesta iz russkoi literatury." *Uroki istorii: XX vek*. January 12, 2015. http://urokiistorii.ru/node/52376.

——— . "Post-Maidan Europe and the New Ukrainian Studies." *Slavic Review* 74, no. 4 (2015): 723–31.

Putin, Vladimir. "Interviu Pervomu kanalu i agentstvu Associated Press." *Prezident Rossii* (official site). September 4, 2013. http://kremlin.ru/transcripts/19143.

——— . "Interview to American TV Channel CBS and PBS." *Prezident Rossii* (official site). September 29, 2015. http://kremlin.ru/events/president/news/50380.

——— . "Poslanie Federalnomu Sobraniiu Rossiiskoi Federatsii." *Prezident Rossii* (official site). April 25, 2005. http://kremlin.ru/events/president/transcripts/22931.

——— . "Rossiia na rubezhe tysiacheletii." *Nezavisimaia gazeta*. December 30, 1999. http://www.ng.ru/politics/1999-12-30/4_millenium.html.

——— . "Vystuplenie na torzhestvennom prieme po sluchaiu tysiacheletiia prestavleniia sviatogo ravnoapostolnogo kniazia Vladimira." *Prezident Rossii* (official site). July 28, 2015. http://kremlin.ru/events/president/transcripts/speeches/50068.

——— . "Zaiavleniia dlia pressy i otvety na voprosy zhurnalistov po itogam rossiisko-vengerskikh peregovorov." *Prezident Rossii* (official site). February 17, 2015. http://kremlin.ru/events/president/transcripts/press_conferences/47706.

Rieber, Alfred J. "The Comparative Ecology of Complex Frontiers." In *Imperial Rule*, edited by Alexei Miller and Alfred J. Rieber, 177–207. Budapest: Central European University Press, 2004.

Rudnytsky, Ivan L. *Essays in Modern Ukrainian History*. Cambridge, MA: Harvard University Press, 1987.

Sakwa, Richard. "Ukraine and the Postcolonial Condition." *Open Democracy*. September 18, 2015. https://www.opendemocracy.net/od-russia/richard-sakwa/ukraine-and-postcolonial-condition.

Sherr, James. "A War of Narratives and Arms." In *The Russian Challenge: The Chatham House Report* by Keir Giles, Philip Hanson, Roderic Lyne, James Nixey, James Sherr and Andrew Wood, 23–32. London: Royal Institute of International Affairs, 2015.

Shevel, Oxana. "Russian Nation-building from Yel'tsin to Medvedev: Ethnic, Civic or Purposefully Ambiguous?" *Europe-Asia Studies* 63, no. 2 (2011): 179–202.

Smith, Anthony D. *Nationalism: Theory, Ideology, History*. Cambridge: Polity Press, 2001.

Szporluk, Roman. "Lenin, 'Great Russia,' and Ukraine." *Harvard Ukrainian Studies* 28, no. 1–4 (2006): 611–26.

Teper, Yuri. "Official Russian Identity Discourse in Light of the Annexation of Crimea: National or Imperial?" *Post-Soviet Affairs* 32, no. 4 (2016): 378–96.

Terekhov, V. I. "Rossiia: neizbezhnost imperii." *Vestnik Moskovskogo universiteta*, Series 8 (History), no. 5 (1993): 52–57.

Tillett, Lowell. *The Great Friendship: Soviet Historians on the Non-Russian Nationalities*. Chapel Hill: University of North Carolina Press, 1969.

Tolochko, Aleksei. *Kievskaia Rus i Malorossiia v XIX veke*. Kyiv: Laurus, 2012.

Tolz, Vera. "'Homeland Myths' and Nation-State Building in Postcommunist Russia." *Slavic Review* 57, no. 2 (1998): 267–94.

Torbakov, Igor. "'This Is a Strife of Slavs among Themselves': Understanding Russian-Ukrainian Relations as the Conflict of Contested Identities." In *The Maidan Uprising, Separatism and Foreign Intervention: Ukraine's Complex Transition*, edited by Klaus Bachmann and Igor Lyubashenko, 183–205. Frankfurt am Main: Peter Lang, 2014.

Toynbee, Arnold J. *A Study of History*. New York: Oxford University Press, 1954.

Tsygankov, Andrei. *The Strong State in Russia: Development and Crisis*. New York: Oxford University Press, 2014.

"Proekt zakonu pro zaboronu vykorystannia istorychnoi nazvy terytorii Ukrainy ta pokhidnykh vid nei sliv v iakosti nazvy abo synonimu Rosiiskoi Federatsii." *Verkhovna Rada Ukrainy*. July 3, 2015. http://w1.c1.rada.gov.ua/pls/zweb2/webproc4_1?pf3511=55883.

Vitte [Witte], Sergei. *Vospominaniia*. In 3 Vols. Moscow: Izdatelstvo sotsialno-ekonomicheskoi literatury, 1960.

# 4
# Living with Ambiguities: Meanings of Nationalism in the Russian-Ukrainian War

## Myroslav Shkandrij

Manipulation of language plays an important role in the way Vladimir Putin's regime presents the war in Ukraine. Concepts take on an Orwellian ability to mean the opposite of what we think they should. One could speak of the weaponization of language, in much the same way as Peter Pomerantsev and Michael Weiss, among others, have spoken of the weaponization of information.[1] In the current conflict with Ukraine perhaps no word has been more abused that "nationalism." This essay examines seven ways the word is manipulated within narratives. It takes account both of pro-Kremlin narratives and the way a shift has occurred in the minds of many Ukrainians concerning the issues of nation and self-identification.

Because of the Russian disinformation campaign the word nationalism is now contested both in Ukraine and in the world media. It is instructive to begin by casting our minds back a couple of decades. Twenty-five years ago one might have wondered whether there were any nationalists left in Ukraine. Soviet propaganda insisted on their complete marginalization in political life and described them as a pathological phenomenon. They only existed abroad and represented a kind of Western virus smuggled into the country by émigrés; a sickness that needed quarantining and removing. Today, however, Putin would have us believe that nationalists of the most nightmarish, "Banderite" variety rule the country, that a Nazi fascist "junta" is in power in Kyiv, and every Ukrainian citizen from border to border is forced by the junta to wave the yellow-and-blue flag.

---

[1] Peter Pomerantsev and Michael Weiss, "The Menace of Unreality: How the Kremlin Weaponizes Information, Culture and Memory," *The Interpreter* (New York: Institute of Modern Russia, Inc.), 2014, http://www.interpretermag.com/wp-content/uploads/2014/11/The_Menace_of_Unreality_Final.pdf. See also http://www.interpretermag.com/the-menace-of-unreality-how-the-kremlin-weaponizes-information-culture-and-money/.

Since 2014 the confusion surrounding the term "nationalist" (and its linking to the words "Banderite," "fascist," "junta" and "Kyiv") has been deliberate, a conscious policy of equating opposition to Russian military invasion and dominance with chauvinism, racism, and political violence. The Putin narrative presents any anti-Russian sentiment as a perversion of the natural order in which Russia is the irresistible great power that rightfully attracts and controls the geopolitical bloc to which Ukraine belongs.

An observer is left wondering how after seventy years of Soviet campaigns raging against nationalism (then the attached adjectives were "bourgeois," "zoological"), and after seventy years of extolling the friendship of Soviet peoples, all Ukraine has suddenly turned out to be one nationalist camp. The "virus" was first portrayed in Soviet propaganda as a nasty element restricted mainly to Western Ukraine's Carpathian mountains. If Putin's propaganda is to be believed, it now appears that these ghosts from the past have crawled out of their Second World War bunkers and imposed their anti-Russian ideology and Ukrainian language on the rest of the country. Is any of this true? Should Ukrainian nationalism be equated with the partisans of the 1940s? Have the ghosts from the OUN and UPA bunkers captured the country?

Some Ukrainians, like Serhii Kvit, the Minister of Education and Science and former Rector of the National University "Kyiv-Mohyla Academy" in Kyiv, would have us believe that, indeed, there is a continuity with the nationalism of the thirties, but this is of course untrue. Earlier in his career Kvit wrote a flattering portrait of Dmytro Dontsov, the journalist who supported the development of a Ukrainian fascist ideology in the thirties. Recently, the Minister of Education stated: "The struggle for genuine independence resumed on the Euromaidan, and quickly adopted the ideological legacy, organizational, and structural forms of 20th Century Ukrainian nationalism, which is today performing an integrative function for society as a whole."[2] However, it is telling that in this article Kvit does not identify which nationalism he is referring to. Is it Dontsov's, the OUN's, or the democratic nationalism that always represented the majority of Ukrainian society, whether in the 1930s, 1960s or the 1990s? Which particular

---

2  Serhiy Kvit, "The Ideology of the Euromaidan," *Social, Health, and Communication Studies Journal. Contemporary Ukraine: A Case of Euromaidan* 1, no. 1 (2014): 34.

nationalism referred to is left vague. It is not clear what time-frame and which party he is describing, or what constitutes the content of his nationalism. Time-frames and contents, however, are important; they represent different phenomena that should not be conflated.

In today's Ukraine, both Ukrainian- and Russian-speaking citizens, along with all other language-speakers, have united against a military intervention and an attempt to dismember their country. The ideological glue binding them together is belief in a civil society, in European norms and ideals (democratic elections, incorruptible judges, respect for the law, freedom of the press and assembly). Ironically, Putin's war has been the primary factor in transforming Ukrainian citizens into supporters of the nation-state. It has also created a generation of Russophobes, particularly among those citizens who are Russian speakers (including those of Russian background) who live in the country's eastern oblasts. The political scientist and journalist Volodymyr Kulyk argues that the previous ambivalence of this population toward national identity has changed dramatically in the last year. The slogans, symbols, and rituals that first manifested themselves in Kyiv have now spread throughout the country. The Euromaidan's original impetus came from the idea of defending democracy and expressing popular outrage with President Viktor Ianukovych. This shifted in early 2014 toward the idea of defending the nation. The shift was gradual. After the violent attacks against protestors on November 30, 2013 the older generation spoke of "protecting our children." The Euromaidan at that point became a struggle, conducted under the national flag, against tyranny. Then, after Ianukovych's trips to Moscow in late December 2013 came the realization that most Russians supported the policies of president Putin, which resulted in a hardening of attitudes toward the Russian regime and nation.[3] Nonetheless, the focus remained on becoming a "normal" European country, meaning a democratic society, in which the rights of all citizens were protected by the law and adhered to by the government.

During the Euromaidan protests Putin's narrative of terrifying nationalists bent on bloodthirsty repression was used to obscure this reality. Andreas Umland has argued that what the Russian president was fishing for was "a scary story of economic fiasco, ethnic division, bloody

---

3   Volodymyr Kulyk, "Ukrainskyi natsionalizm u chas Ievromaidanu," *Krytyka*, no. 7–8 (2015): 3.

conflict, and social chaos," so that he could present Ukraine's failure as the inevitable consequence of any democratic uprising and rapprochement with the West.[4] Many commentators agree that the lesson was and still is aimed primarily at the president's own population. Umland has posited that Putin is not concerned with a frank discussion of Russia's national interests, but is focused on "the mundane issue of personal power and domestic control."[5] This issue drives Russia's promotion of armed separatism and military intervention. In short, not the interests of the Russian state and nation, "but the continuing stability of Putin's increasingly autocratic rule and corrupt system" are Moscow's major concern.[6] Ukraine's successful Europeanization threatens the etatist, neo-authoritarian regime that has emerged in Russia. Therefore, Putin needs a spectacular failure of this Europeanization to protect himself and his regime.

The Putin narrative is contradictory, incoherent, and exploits terminological confusion. Here are a few examples.

## 1. Nationalism as National Solidarity

In the Putin narrative those who support the government in Kyiv are nationalists. Today this means that almost the country's entire population should be classified as nationalist. In the same breath, however, Putin argues that there is no Ukrainian nation, that Ukrainians, even though they deny this, are really Russians. The reality is that the enormous number of volunteers helping the army, those who are aiding the war effort, and those who have been politicized by the war, although they would probably call themselves patriots, not nationalists, have created a new sense of solidarity.

A people who express this sense of solidarity and desire to live as an independent nation, to control their own fate, belong to a type of movement we associate with the creation of nations in the nineteenth century. This is a democratic form of nationalism fueled by the recognition of a shared culture and common language. In the nineteenth century it

---

4   Andreas Umland, "Understanding Russia's Role and Aims in the 'Ukraine Crisis,'" *Harvard International Review*, August 11, 2014, http://hir.harvard.edu/understanding-russias-role-and-aims-in-the-ukraine-crisis/; or https://www.academia.edu/8672924/Understanding_Russia_s_Role_and_Aims_in_the_Ukraine_Crisis_.
5   Ibid.
6   Ibid.

challenged imperial rulers and led eventually to the creation of national states throughout Europe.

The Euromaidan was clearly like this. In the early months of protest, political parties were shunned, especially Svoboda, whose slogans were viewed as dissonantly anti-democratic and anti-European. Svoboda's decision to organize a pro-Bandera march in early January 2014 was denounced as divisive, as putting party interests before national. Significantly, at this moment the Euromaidan activists separated national liberation slogans from those suggesting ethnic exclusivity. Svoboda's "Ukraine above all" slogan, for example, was dropped.[7]

Russia too proposes its own sense of solidarity based on a shared cultural history and language. It describes this sense of identity as an allegiance to the Russkii Mir (Russian World), the Russian-language space that includes many neighboring states and sees the EU and USA as foreign imperialists who are preventing the Kremlin's desire to expand the "Russian" space. But the Kremlin refuses to use the words conquest or imperialism in describing its desire to impose its own rule on neighboring countries.

## 2. Nationalism as Belief in a Shared History

In Putin's narrative Ukraine does not have its own history but must view itself within the framework of Russian history, within a story describing the expansion of the Russian state, and development of the Russian language and culture. However, incongruously, this Putin narrative argues that Ukrainians have always (from Ivan Mazepa, Mykhailo Hrushevskyi, Symon Petliura, Mykola Skrypnyk, Stepan Bandera, and to Petro Poroshenko) been disloyal, treacherous anti-Russians. This schizophrenic attitude is typical of imperialist thinking and has been observed in postcolonial studies: natives are loved as long as they behave like grateful subordinates or loyal regionals, but when they refuse to conform to this imposed role and instead develop a resistant self-image, the imperial imagination suddenly transforms them into subversives.

Within the Putin narrative any identification with a completely different historical account is viewed as dangerous nationalism. Ukrainian history books teach that the late medieval states of Kyivan Rus and

---

7   Kulyk, "Ukrainskyi natsionalizm u chas Ievromaidanu," 5.

Galicia-Volhynia, the association with the Polish-Lithuanian Commonwealth, the period of the baroque and the Cossack state of early modernity are part of a tradition that has produced a distinct and unique identity. However, for Putin and many Russians such an opinion is considered an impermissible expression of nationalism because it refuses to identify with their imagined grand narrative of Russian history. For example, Putin has on several occasions affirmed the sacredness of Crimea to Russians. The framework of this sacred story allows no room to argue that there was no Russia when Kyivan Rus was a state, that Crimea is also sacred to Ukrainians and Tatars, or that the Tatars perhaps have the strongest historical claim to Crimea, having settled, ruled and dominated it the longest. Today, however, even to assert the multicultural nature of this peninsula's history is to be accused of anti-Russian feeling and, of course, nationalism. Ukrainian and Tatar schools are being closed in the peninsula and the Ukrainian language is banned from public life and meetings. Forgotten is the fact that a majority of Crimeans voted to be part of independent Ukraine after the fall of the Soviet Union, and that prior to the Russian invasion in 2014 polls consistently showed that most Crimeans wanted to remain part of Ukraine.

## 3. Nationalism as Support for a Common Language

In the Putin narrative Ukraine persecutes Russian speakers. However, in the same time breath this narrative argues that most people in central and eastern Ukraine speak only Russian. The implication behind this latter statement is that the population there does not want to share a linguistic space with Ukrainian, that it wants Russian to be treated as the exclusive language of high culture, commerce, scholarship and official life. This, as Timothy Snyder has pointed out, resembles the old Soviet class-based approach to language. From the 1970s "the USSR was perceived as needing one thinking class, and not multiple national ones. As a result the Ukrainian language was driven from schools, and especially from higher education."[8] In response Ukrainian patriots of almost all political persuasions embraced a civic understanding of Ukrainian identity. In fact, both Russian and Ukrainian speakers were equally accepted by Euromaidan

---

8   Timothy Snyder, "Europe and Ukraine: Putin's Project," *Frankfurter Allgemeine*, April 16, 2014, http://www.faz.net/suche/.

activists. Today, because the soldiers fighting on the eastern front are frequently, and sometimes predominantly, Russian-speaking, they have, in Kulyk's words, legitimized Russian-language citizens as full members of the Ukrainian nation. It has become clear to all Ukrainian citizens that the language issue is a red herring.

In fact, throughout today's Ukraine the Ukrainian language is mandated to be taught in schools but not necessarily to serve as the main language of instruction. Russian has official status in parts of the east. In any case, it has now become clear to unbiased commentators that all Ukrainians are to varying degrees bilingual in both Ukrainian and Russian, and in most cities of central and eastern Ukraine Russian predominates: there are more Russian than Ukrainian programs on TV, more Russian than Ukrainian films, more Russian than Ukrainian books in bookstores. In these parts of Ukraine it is the Ukrainian language space that needs support. The dual language space has been accepted, and the population has consolidated around this idea. Most Russian speakers now sympathize with the presence of Ukrainian, which distinguishes their country from Russia. Nonetheless, hysterical claims that Russian speakers are being persecuted continue to be a staple of Russian propaganda and are used in an attempt to divide the population. Ironically, it is in today's Russian-ruled Crimea and Donbas that linguistic persecution has become the norm. For example, Ukrainian schools in Crimea (those in which Ukrainian was the language of instruction) even though they were few and far between (about six out of 600), have been shut down, and Ukrainian broadcasts have been banned. Crimea has also witnessed the public burning of Ukrainian books.

## 4. Nationalism as Ethnic/Racial/National Exclusivity

Putin's narrative describes the Kyiv government as antisemitic and xenophobic. At the same time it argues that Ukrainian Jews (such as the Prime Minister Arsenii Iatseniuk, along with the speaker of the house, and figures like the Jewish oligarch Ihor Kolomoiskyi who in Dnipropetrovsk has supported the largest Ukrainian-Jewish community) are Ukrainian nationalists and fascists. The term Judeo-Banderite (*Zhydo-Banderivets*) is used in the Russian internet and media to denounce Kyiv's leaders.[9] However, there never was any persecution of minorities during Euromaidan or afterwards. There are some nationalist sects that propagate a racist ideology but they are marginal and elected no members to the parliament on October 26, 2014. Even one of the two elected members of parliament from the Right Sector is a practicing Jew. Observers only have to compare this situation to the one that exists in Russia to see the cynical hypocrisy of these charges.

The use of violence after January 19, 2014 radicalized the Maidan. At this time the Right Sector (*Pravyi Sektor*) garnered more sympathy, particularly after Dmytro Iarosh, its leader, spoke of his group's differences with Svoboda. He stated that he did not accept "some things of a racist character" in Svoboda's ideology.[10] Iarosh said that he adhered to "the idea of Ukrainian nationalism in the interpretation of Stepan Bandera." By this he meant that all ethnic groups who supported an independent Ukrainian state were part of the nation. Although the role in the 1940s of the OUN (Organization of Ukrainian Nationalists) and UPA (Ukrainian Insurgent Army) remained a controversial issue, at this juncture one began to hear comments on the Maidan (on January 20) like: "a new Konovalets and new UPA will appear if violence is used against the Maidan."[11] Ukrainian and Jewish activists fought side-by-side against the Berkut special police and hired goons (popularly known as *titushky*) that served President Ianukovych. Those who participated in defending the protestors against attacks even included a group of Ukrainians who were Israeli army veterans. Since that time the T-shirt "Judeo-Banderite" has been worn by many Ukrainian Jews in defiance of Putin's propaganda.

---

9   It should be pointed out that in Russian the word "zhid" is a slur, but in Ukrainian, as in most Slavic languages, the word has long been used as a neutral term. There are two standard words for "Jew" in Ukrainian. In western Ukraine the term "zhyd" is common, while in central and eastern Ukraine the term "ievrei" is most often used. The Russian term "Zhido-Banderovets" is therefore pejorative, while the Ukrainian term "Zhydo-Banderivets" is not.

10  *Ukrainska pravda*, February 9, 2014; quoted in Kulyk, "Ukrainskyi natsionalizm u chas Ievromaidanu," 8.

11  Quoted in Kulyk "Ukrainskyi natsionalizm u chas Ievromaidanu," 8.

## 5. Nationalism as Fascism

Putin's propaganda brands anyone who thinks Ukraine should be independent as a "Banderite" and argues that a self-appointed "junta" is now in power in Ukraine. The Russian media constantly tries to make a connection between independence, Banderites and fascism. According to this mythology, any drive for Ukrainian independence equals fascism, and Moscow, of course, represents the struggle against fascism.

Since the thirties the anti-fascist scenario has been standard cover for all Soviet failures. In Stalin's worldview (already evident in the 1920s) the fascists served as the omnipresent other, the enemy that infiltrated, undermined and subverted all Soviet projects. Putin has now revived this anti-fascist politics. By arguing that, under instructions from the US and the EU, the Ukrainian population voted overwhelmingly for a "fascist junta," he is also indicating that the West is responsible for installing fascism in Ukraine.

## 6. Nationalism as a Renewal of Second World War Mythmaking

By casting the present events as a replay of the Second World War Putin is attempting to impose Soviet wartime mythmaking on contemporary politics. This, of course, is the major reason why Ukrainian citizens are described in his propaganda as Banderites.

How do contemporary Ukrainians see the issue? It should be said that there is a gulf between popular perceptions of the OUN(B) or Banderites and the historical reality. For example, Svoboda and the groups that make up the Right Sector view the OUN, and Bandera's wing in particular, as heroic freedom fighters, and celebrate the history of the UPA, which until the 1950s was still fighting in the underground against the imposition of Soviet rule. The memory of this struggle for independence has been described with admiration in films and in books like Oksana Zabuzhko's *Muzei pokynutykh sekretiv* (Museum of Forgotten Secrets).[12] In recent years many individuals have embraced the term Banderite in much the same way as some Russian liberals in 1918 embraced the Western view of themselves as barbarians. In this year Aleksandr Blok famously and threateningly wrote "Yes, we are Scythians, we are

---

12   Oksana Zabuzhko, *Muzei pokynutykh sekretiv* (Kyiv: Fakt, 2009).

Asiatics." The important point is that the term "Banderite" has been adopted by many Ukrainians as an act of defiance, a way of throwing the challenge back at Putin. The Second World War slogan "Glory to Ukraine! Glory to the heroes!"—also associated with the OUN and UPA—was adopted after February 20, 2014 when on the streets of Kyiv over a hundred people were killed by government forces. The population appropriated this slogan as an expression of commitment to the current struggle. At this time some insignia of the wartime guerillas, such as the red-and-black flag, were also appropriated as symbols of the struggle for independent statehood and the resistance to the imposition of foreign, Kremlin-directed rule.

In this sense, the present-day context shares two things with the OUN's nationalism of the 1930s and 1940s: a belief in militant struggle as a necessity for independent statehood to be won and maintained, and a commitment to an anti-Kremlin orientation. However, identification with the partisan movement of the forties does not translate into admiration for the interwar OUN's ideology, which was contemptuous of democracy and parliamentary rule; nor does it signify an attraction to a totalitarian model in which civil society, the press, the judiciary are subordinated to the authoritarian state. Still less does it translate into sympathy for those who helped round up and murder Jews in the weeks following the outbreak of the German-Soviet war on June 22, 1941. Quite the opposite: the vast majority of contemporary citizens reject the views held by the OUN(B) in the 1930s and early 1940s, and are appalled by the actions of those who participated in the machinery of the Holocaust. Even Serhii Kvit and the Right Sector are not prepared to recall these views and actions. They prefer to reinterpret the OUN and UPA exclusively according to later, post-1943, pronouncements by these groups, which were anti-imperialist and pro-democratic.

This has not stopped Putin's propaganda machine from trying to replay the Second World War in a scenario that casts Russia as the victim of an aggressive and simultaneously degenerate West. The war and the politics of fascism/anti-fascism are used, as Snyder has pointed out, to portray Moscow as a defender of all that is good, and its critics as evil. As Snyder explains when commenting on 1939–41:

> This very effective rhetorical pose did not preclude an actual Soviet alliance with the actual Nazis. Given the return of Russian propaganda today to anti-fascism,

this is an important point to remember: the whole grand moral Manichaeism was meant to serve the state, and as such did not limit it in any way. The embrace of anti-fascism as a strategy is quite different from opposing actual fascists.[13]

In fact, it is Putin's Russia that today represents the aggressive, quasi-fascist state. As were Germans in the thirties, contemporary Russians are being taught to resent the loss of their superpower status and to view their post-Soviet condition as humiliating. They are encouraged to identify with a strong leader and a powerful state, to admire an aggressive masculinity that expresses itself in violence and war, and to despise the weakness that is associated with liberalism, femininity, homosexuality and a decaying Europe.[14] The aggressive Russian state is paradoxically portrayed as a victim whose majesty and power have been reduced or go unrecognized. A first step toward recovering self-respect, Russians are told, is to regain the satellites they once controlled. The Russian fascist, as Mikhail Iampolskii calls him, today feels simultaneously "omnipotent and persecuted," and is therefore prone to believe invented stories of martyrdom, such as that of the boy crucified by Ukrainian troops.[15]

Some collectives have been described by Iampolskii as "basic assumption" groups. Their unity, he argues, is based on illusions and a denial of individual differentiation:

> Their primary task is the rejection of the ego in order to merge with some narcissistic primordial unity and become part of a homogenous and undifferentiated mass. Such groups are homogenous on principle; their members are utterly intolerant of any deviation from their single style of thought and behavior.[16]

---

13   Snyder, "Europe and Ukraine."
14   See, for instance, "The Catechesis of a Member of the Eurasian Union of Youth," *Rossiia-3 (Ievraziiskii soiuz molodiozhi)*, April 26, 2016, http://www.rossia3.ru/kat ehizis.html.
15   Mikhail Iampolski, "Judging the Victors: Why Victimhood is a Bad Fit for Russia," *Jordan Russia Center*, March 5, 2015, http://jordanrussiacenter.org/news/judging -victors-victimhood-bad-fit-russia/. See Mikhail Iampolskii's original article in Russian "Kak sudiat pobeditelei," *Colta: Shkola grazhdanskoi zhurnalistiki*, January 26, 2015, http://www.colta.ru/articles/specials/6088.
16   Ibid.

This kind of consciousness is described by Iampolskii as paranoid and quasi-fascist. In his view, it dominated Hitler's Germany and is now prevalent in Putin's Russia.

The way history is told in today's Russia increasingly requires the framing of conquest and use of brute force in positive terms. The victory against Germany in 1945 is appropriated as a national—exclusively Russian—achievement, and today's events are cast as a repetition of the fight against Nazi Germany. However, the dominant message to be learned from this narrative is the need to recover lost greatness through reconquest. The question of what the fight is for appears to have only one answer: a strong Russia. No mention is made of a tolerant and strong civil society, and the pro-state rhetoric allows almost no investment in the vision of a democratic order, freedom of the press and association, an independent judiciary, and the application of the rule of law to government officials. If democracy, media freedoms and the accountability of rulers to judicial oversight are mentioned, the references are often made in order to illustrate the internal divisions in Western society, and to suggest that authoritarianism is preferable to chaos, weakness and decadence.

## 7. Russian Nationalism as Dismissal of the International Community

In Putin's bi-polar world, nationalism, authoritarianism and expansionism are viewed as acceptable, even admirable, if they strengthen the Russian state. According to this logic, to limit Russian authoritarianism and expansionism is to be anti-Russian and to open oneself to charges of serving foreign states and fascism. By the same token, oppositionists within Russia who call for civil rights are seen as behaving in an unpatriotic, un-Russian, culturally alien manner—as dupes of foreign powers.[17]

Hiding behind this propaganda is the vision of a strong, monolithic state supported enthusiastically by all Russians, before which neighboring states quake with fear. An example of strength and sovereignty, as the fascist theorist Carl Schmitt argued, can be found in the right to suspend the law and begin war. To follow international norms, keep agreements,

---

17   Will Stewart, "President Putin's Critics Are Denounced in a Soviet-style 'Wall of Shame,'" *Daily Mail*, April 17, 2014, http://www.dailymail.co.uk/news/article-2607099/President-Putins-critics-denounced-Soviet-style-wall-shame-erected-Crimea-slams-opposition-figures-like-Pussy-Riot-singers-tools-West.html.

negotiate in good faith, and defer to the larger community is, by contrast, seen as a mark of weakness. The strong, according to this view, can stand alone.

## 8. Russian Nationalism as Support of Western Far-Right Parties

This stance has won Putin admirers, particularly in Europe's far-right parties, many of which are today promoted and financed by Russia. Aleksandr Dugin, the influential theorist of Eurasianism, is in fact openly pro-fascist, as were many of the first separatist leaders and supporters of rebellion in the Donbas.[18]

After all, goes the thinking, what is wrong with fascism if it helps the Russian state? Eurofascists weaken the EU by pitting individual nations against Brussels and each other. Domestically neo-fascists work to expand the Russian state's boundaries, and overcome internal dissent and disorder. However, this line of argument is not used by the Russian government in public discourse. It is reserved for influential propagandists of Russian fascism, such as Aleksandr Dugin and Aleksandr Barkashov. In mainstream Russian propaganda the term "fascist" is only applied to Euromaidan protesters and opponents of the Russian invasion of Ukraine, never to Putin's fascist and far-right allies in the West or at home.

The support for far-right groups leads to a politics that is racialized and sexualized. The Western far-right parties receive money from Putin

---

18    For an introduction to Aleksandr Dugin, see Anton Shekhovtsov, "Russian Fascist Aleksandr Dugin's Dreams of Dictatorship in Russia," *Anton Shekhovtsov Blogspot*, February 27, 2014, http://anton-shekhovtsov.blogspot.ca/2014/02/russian-fascist-aleksandr-dugin-is.html. See also Umland, "Understanding Russia's Role." On Aleksandr Barkashov, who founded the Russian National Unity Party in 1990 and holds defiantly pro-Nazi views, see Walter Laqueur, *Fascism: Past, Present, Future* (New York: Oxford University Press, 1996), 189–90. On May 7, 2014 Barkashov phoned the Donbas with instructions from Moscow to proceed with the vote for a "Donetsk People's Republic" and forge the results. This conversation is available at *Euromaidan Press*, May 7, 2014, http://euromaidanpress.com/2014/05/07/russia-orchestrating-donetsk-referendum/. On the Novorossiia (New Russia) Party, which held its first congress in Donetsk in the presence of Aleksandr Dugin, Pavel Gubarev (a leader of Donetsk Republic and previously a member of Russian National Unity) and Aleksandr Prokhanov, a Stalinist, antisemite, and fascist who is fascinated by the idea that Russia is the true "mystical womb" of Aryan civilization, see Mat Babiak, "Welcome to New Russia," *Ukrainian Policy*, May 23, 2014, http://ukrainianpolicy.com/welcome-to-new-russia.

in order to promote an anti-immigrant, anti-multicultural, anti-gay, anti-EU policy that is seen as benefitting the Kremlin. Although these far-right parties claim to be for family values and tradition, theirs is a traditionalism that incorporates minority bashing, religious intolerance, homophobia, chauvinism, support of violent criminal gangs and corrupt regimes. Just beneath the surface lies a political agenda that is anti-parliamentary, intolerant of minorities, and opposed to press and media freedom.

All the above contradictions and incoherencies in the Putin narrative are solved by accepting a simple construct: those who resist the imposition of Russian rule, a Russocentric history and identity are to be classified as the regime's opponents, and the entire rhetorical arsenal can be used against them: they can be called imperialists, nationalists, aggressors, fascists or Nazis.

When we begin to unpack the term "nationalism," therefore, we encounter its use in a range of key narratives. As illustrated in the seven cases outlined above, the term is employed to discredit another nation state, while the same underlying concept is used to glorify or strengthen the Russian nation state. In all cases the Putin regime applies a single test: Do you agree with its version, its interpretation of solidarity, history, the meaning of shared language, the fascist/anti-fascist divide, the Second World War, the decline of the West, and with the need to support extremist parties in the EU? If you do not, you are viewed as a dupe of Western imperialism, a nationalist, or a fascist.

## Bibliography

Babiak, Mat. "Welcome to New Russia." *Ukrainian Policy*. May 23, 2014. http://ukrainianpolicy.com/welcome-to-new-russia.

Iampolski, Mikhail. "Judging the Victors: Why Victimhood is a bad fit for Russia." *NYU Jordan Center for the Advanced Study of Russia*. March 5, 2015. http://jordanrussiacenter.org/news/judging-victors-victimhood-bad-fit-russia.

Iampolskii, Mikhail. "Kak sudiat pobeditelei." *Colta: Shkola grazhdanskoi zhurnalistiki*. January 26, 2015. http://www.colta.ru/articles/specials/6088.

Kulyk, Volodymyr. "Ukrainskyi natsionalizm u chas Ievromaidanu." *Krytyka*, no. 7–8 (2015): 2–7.

⸺. "Ukrainskyi natsionalizm u chas viiny z Rosiieiu." *Krytyka*, no. 9–10 (2015): 15–18.

Kvit, Serhiy. "The Ideology of the Euromaidan." *Social, Health, and Communication Studies Journal. Contemporary Ukraine: A Case of Euromaidan* 1, no.1 (2014): 27–39.

Laqueur, Walter. *Fascism: Past, Present, Future.* New York: Oxford University Press, 1996.

Pomerantsev, Peter, and Michael Weiss. "The Menace of Unreality: How the Kremlin Weaponizes Information, Culture and Memory." *Interpreter.* 2014. http://www.interp retermag.com/the-menace-of-unreality-how-the-kremlin-weaponizes-information-c ulture-and-money/. Full pdf text: http://www.interpretermag.com/wp-content/upload s/2014/11/The_Menace_of_Unreality_Final.pdf.

Shekhovtsov, Anton. "Russian Fascist Aleksandr Dugin's Dreams of Dictatorship in Russia." *Anton Shekhovtsov Blogspot.* February 27, 2014. http://anton-shekhovtsov .blogspot.ca/2014/02/russian-fascist-aleksandr-dugin-is.html.

Snyder, Timothy. "Europe and Ukraine: Putin's Project." *Frankfurter Allgemeine.* April 16, 2014. http://www.faz.net/aktuell/politik/ausland/timothy-snyder-about-europe-a nd-ukraine.

Stewart, Will. "President Putin's Critics Are Denounced in a Soviet-style 'Wall of Shame.'" *Daily Mail.* April 17, 2014, http://www.dailymail.co.uk/news/article-260709 9/President-Putins-critics-denounced-Soviet-style-wall-shame-erected-Crimea-sla ms-opposition-figures-like-Pussy-Riot-singers-tools-West.html.

"The Catechesis of a Member of the Eurasian Union of Youth." *Rossiia-3 (Ievraziiskii soiuz molodiozhi).* April 26, 2016. http://www.rossia3.ru/katehizis.html.

Umland, Andreas. "Understanding Russia's Role and Aims in the 'Ukraine Crisis.'" *Harvard International Review.* August 11, 2014. http://eap-csf.eu/en/news-events/articles-anal ytics/understanding-russias-role-and-aims-in-the-ukraine-crisis/; or http://www.acade mia.edu/8672924/Understanding_Russia_s_Role_and_Aims_in_the_Ukraine_Crisis.

———. "Who is Alexander Dugin?" *Open Democracy.* September 26, 2008. https://www.opendemocracy.net/article/russia-theme/who-is-alexander-dugin.

Zabuzhko, Oksana. *Muzei pokynutykh sekretiv.* Kyiv: Fakt, 2009.

# Part Three

# The Euromaidan, War, and Cultural Change in Ukraine

## Part Three

# 5
# Ideologies of Language in Wartime

Laada Bilaniuk

The ongoing war in eastern Ukraine has fueled two opposed tendencies in language ideologies and practices, which may be summed up thus: "language does not matter" versus "language matters." These opposed trends have implications for the definition of what Ukraine is and should be. Those who believe that language does not matter embrace the existing widespread Ukrainian and Russian bilingualism in the country, whether simply because it is the status quo, or due to an ideology rejecting a unitary ethnolinguistic definition of a nation. In contrast, those who believe that language matters consider a titular language to be an important attribute of nationhood. This ideological tendency is divided, based on stance toward Ukraine's sovereignty: those who support it consider linguistic Ukrainization to be critical, while those who would deny it, particularly in Russian-occupied Crimea and the separatist regions in eastern Ukraine, push for Russification. The tugs of war between bilingualism and monolingualism, Ukrainian and Russian languages, ethnonational and civic definitions of the nation are played out everywhere—from parliament to private spaces. This study examines each tendency in turn, how it is manifested, and how it relates to the existing language legislation.[1]

## The First Trend: "It Does Not Matter Which Language You Speak"

This tendency is exemplified in the practice of non-accommodating bilingualism, where people speak whichever language they prefer, Ukrainian

---

[1] Field research for this paper was funded by a Fulbright-Hays Faculty Research Abroad grant and an International Research & Exchanges Board Individual Advanced Research Opportunities grant. The views expressed are my own and not those of the funding agencies. I am grateful to the many interviewees and colleagues, too many to name individually here, without whom this research would not be possible, who have shared their opinions, observations, and experiences with me.

or Russian, and do not accommodate to the language of their interlocutor.[2] This practice is widespread in Ukraine, both in everyday life and in the media, in public and in private. Non-accommodating bilingualism works best when language choice is transparent, or at least accepted as neutral. When language is transparent, code choice is not noticed, and so the use of a divergent code does not signal any social antagonism.[3] Such transparency is evident in cases where, immediately after a conversation, individuals could not tell for sure which language they were just speaking, or what was the language of a broadcast they just heard.[4] Even if language choice is noticed, it should be seen as politically neutral, and the language a person speaks should not be taken as a symbol of ethnic or political allegiance. According to this ideology, it is the content of words and actual deeds that matter, not which language is used. Transparency and neutrality of language, however, are not ubiquitous, as language choice is frequently noticed and politicized, leading to heated debates over the language issue.

The non-accommodating bilingual mode can be seen as liberal, as on the surface it gives people freedom in language choice. For this system to work, everyone must be at least passively bilingual, able to understand both languages, if not actually speak them. One could also say that non-

---

2   In the sociolinguistic literature this practice is also referred to as nonreciprocal bilingualism, receptive bilingualism, and intercomprehension. The term "non-accommodating bilingualism" is used here to highlight the fact that in Ukraine, the interlocutors are often both fully bilingual, and so would be able to switch to the same language, but they choose not to do so.

3   The connection between linguistic divergence and social antagonism is posited by communication accommodation theory (CAT). This theory assumes that positive attitudes between interlocutors will lead to convergence, with each speaking more similarly to the other, to the extent possible, as outlined by Howard Giles, Richard Y. Bourhis, and Donald M. Taylor, "Towards a Theory of Language in Ethnic Group Relations," in *Language, Ethnicity and Intergroup Relations*, ed. Howard Giles (New York: Academic Press, 1977), 307–48; and Carolyn A. Shepard, Howard Giles, and Beth A. Le Poire, "Communication Accommodation Theory," in *The New Handbook of Language and Social Psychology*, eds. W. Peter Robinson and Howard Giles (Toronto: John Wiley & Sons, 2001), 36–39. The widespread practice of non-accommodating bilingualism in Ukraine poses a challenge to the explanatory model of CAT.

4   For example, a blog about people who identify as "Russophone Ukrainian nationalists" states: "After watching a film, with difficulty we try to remember what language it was in, Russian or Ukrainian." Serge, "Russkogovoriashchie Ukrainskie Natsionalisty," *Ukrainska pravda—Narodni blohy*, January 12, 2008, http://narodna.pravda.com.ua/nation/4788131ac2ffe/. All translations into English by the author.

accommodating bilingualism keeps the door open for change in language tendencies, leaving it to individual choice which language will be more prevalent.

The bilingual Ukrainian Russian slogan "Iedyna kraina—Iedinaia strana" (a united/single country) portrays this desired unity in duality. This slogan was popularized by a series of videos produced by a consortium of Ukraine's major media groups. These videos aired on Ukraine's television channels beginning on March 2, 2014, while the unmarked Russian forces were invading Crimea, just weeks before Russia announced its annexation of the peninsula.[5] The video clips featured popular television hosts and newscasters, speaking in both Ukrainian and Russian, sometimes switching between the two, expressing their belief that Ukraine's unity transcends differences of language, ethnicity, or regional background. At the end of 2014, the slogan was highlighted in President Poroshenko's New Year's address to the country, with the addition of "Bir devlet," the same slogan in Crimean Tatar.[6] In this address the President used primarily Ukrainian, but he did include brief well-wishes in Russian and Crimean Tatar as well. As the Russian government was putting forward the argument that it needed to protect the rights of "its" Russian speakers in Ukraine, Ukrainians were countering it by asserting that language did not determine their political inclinations or citizenship.

Another symbol of the "language does not matter" trend is the figure of the "Russophone Ukrainian nationalist." I first encountered this identity online in a 2008 blog.[7] In 2012, Sergei Zamiliukhin formalized and popularized the identity by founding the organization RUN, "Rosiiskomovni ukrainski natsionalisty" (Russophone Ukrainian Nationalists), with

---

5   An example of one of the videos and an explanation of the initiative is provided on *YouTube* by Kanal Ukraina, "Iedyna kraina. Iedinaia strana," March 5, 2014, https://www.youtube.com/watch?v=8i0_TmiPBqE. Another video in this series is from Telekanal 1+1, "Iedyna kraina. Iedinaia strana," *YouTube*, March 4, 2014, https://www.youtube.com/watch?v=WPNoQQjRYNQ.
6   "'Iedyna kraina'—'Iedinaia strana'—'Bir devlet': Poroshenko pozdravil Ukrainu s Novym Godom," *Obozrevatel*, January 1, 2015, http://obozrevatel.com/politics/20 139-novogodnee-pozdravlenie-poroshenko.htm; see also a video of the 2015 New Year's greeting "Novorichne pryvitannia Prezydenta Ukrainy Petra Poroshenka," *YouTube*, December 31, 2014, https://www.youtube.com/watch?v=xAV N2h3rbwg.
7   Serge, "Russkogovoriashchie ukrainskie natsionalisty."

chapters in various cities, predominately in southeastern Ukraine.[8] This organization also has a robust online presence, with its own internet page and groups in various social media.[9] Zamiliukhin asserted that language does not matter in determining his own allegiances. However, he saw the wide use of Russian in Ukraine as a result of imperialist forced assimilation, and so he believed that eventually the Ukrainian language should return to use as the dominant language of the country. Thus his own position is that in the long run, language does matter. Online comments show that not everyone who identifies as a Russophone Ukrainian nationalist holds the same opinion regarding the desired future sociolinguistic situation.[10]

Russian speakers were a prominent part of the Euromaidan protests. An image that was widely circulated in reporting of the Euromaidan showed an older man with a bushy white mustache holding a sign proclaiming, in Russian, "I am a Russian-speaking Ukrainian nationalist." Another sign on a nearby tent proclaimed, "Ukrainian nationalist is a state of the soul, independent of language!" Now in the ongoing war in eastern Ukraine, Russian speakers of various ethnic backgrounds fight against the Russia-backed separatists and terrorists, and many have given their lives. Many people's deeds show that being Russophone often goes along with being a Ukrainian patriot. In principle, this fact could defuse the politicization of language choice. So what are the problems with this tendency?

The idea that speaking whichever language one wants allows one the most freedom erroneously assumes that language could be a purely individual choice. Indeed, one can choose, but communication depends on the connotations and habits of language that are cultivated in a social

---

8 Semion Semionych, "Russkoiazychnye ukrainskie natsionalisty," *Zrada.org*, February 8, 2011, http://zrada.org/hot/25-mova/248-russkojazychnye-ukrainskie-natsionalisty.html; Ievgenii Bulavka, "Nashi deti budut ukrainomovnymi—v strane razvivaetsia dvizhenie russkoiazychnykh ukrainskikh natsionalistov," *Tsenzor. Net*, June 26, 2013, http://censor.net.ua/n245680; Severin Nalyvaiko, "V Ukraine razrastaetsia dvizhenie russkoiazychnykh banderovtsev," *Gazeta.ua*, July 15, 2013, http://gazeta.ua/ru/articles/sogodennya/506906.

9 See the website of the organization "Rosiiskomovni ukrainski natsionalisty (RUN)," http://run-ua.org; their Vkontakte group with over 23,000 members, http://vk.com/o_run; their Facebook group with over 15,000 members, https://www.facebook.com/groups/run.groups/; and their Livejournal blog, http://run-ukr.livejournal.com.

10 Nalyvaiko, "V Ukraine razrastaetsia dvizhenie."

environment. Language ideology is not a conscious choice, but is part of one's habitus, the predispositions that are inculcated throughout one's lifetime and then deployed in practices and judgments, leading to the reproduction of existing regimes of language.[11] Non-accommodating bilingualism may sometimes work with neutrality and transparency, but it does not cancel the fact that language carries not just referential content, but social information about its speakers as well. Going against a dominant status quo or using a less prestigious language can have negative social repercussions. According to sociolinguist Larysa Masenko, the figure of the Russophone Ukrainian nationalist has become "like a mantra" to justify a bilingual regime and to undermine the revival of Ukrainian.[12] This brings us to the opposite trend in language ideology, that "language choice matters."

**The Second Trend: "Language Choice Matters"**

The importance of language choice was highlighted by the fact that all of the Soviet republics declared their titular language to be their official language even before declaring independence from the USSR. This was in line with a Romantic Herderian idea that "language is the soul of the nation," which was often invoked in the early years of independence.[13] Identification with a unique state language provided a powerful justification of aspirations for independent nationhood.

The declaration of Ukrainian as the sole state language of the Ukrainian SSR, and then of independent Ukraine, was symbolically powerful, but in practice, Ukrainian was at a disadvantage. Both historical and contemporary conditions had not been a level playing field for Ukrainian and Russian. The conflicted relationship between Ukrainian and

---

11  Pierre Bourdieu, *Language and Symbolic Power* (Cambridge: Harvard University Press, 1991).
12  Maia Orel, "Nam potriben movnyi kordon iz Rosiieiu. Suchasna movna polityka v Ukraini ochyma sotsiolinhvista," *Ukraina Moloda*, December 26, 2014, http://language-policy.info/2014/12/nam-potriben-movnyj-kordon-iz-rosijeyu-suchasna-movna-polityka-ukrajini-ochyma-sotsiolinhvista/.
13  See Johann Gottfried Herder's "Letters for the Advancement of Humanity," originally published in 1783–87, in *Herder: Philosophical Writings,* ed. Michael N. Forster (New York: Cambridge University Press, 2002), 380–424. For a more detailed explanation of Herder's ideas, see Paul Robert Magocsi, *A History of Ukraine* (Seattle: University of Washington Press, 1998), 353.

Russian languages rested on a long history in which Ukrainian was both openly persecuted and implicitly discriminated, in the Russian Empire and then in the Soviet Union. A long legacy of institutional suppression of the public use of Ukrainian and discrimination against Ukrainian speakers led to widespread disdain for Ukrainian as an unrefined language, associated with lack of education and with the rural sphere.[14]

This historical legacy continues to have repercussions on language choice, dissuading many people from using Ukrainian—sometimes simply due to the dominance of Russian language in their environment, and sometimes also because of negative views of Ukrainian.[15] Urban areas in particular have been sites of Russian language dominance, which, as Masenko argues, created "psychologically comfortable conditions for the Russian-speaking part of the population, and uncomfortable conditions for those who remained faithful to Ukrainian language."[16] Thus what seemed like freedom of choice resulted in Russification:

> Today we do not need liberalism in the linguistic self-affirmation of the state, but a language border with Russia. Liberalism in this issue today works towards the same goal that totalitarianism worked for in the past, and that is linguistic assimilation. A postcolonial country cannot allow itself to weaken the status of the state language as a main consolidating factor of the population within its borders, all the more so during a time of war with a neighbor-aggressor.[17]

The symbolic role of Ukrainian language as an emblem of independence has now become a security issue. This was incited by Putin's assertions that Russia's military incursions are driven by the imperative to defend Russian "compatriots"—defining compatriots as Russian speakers, not just ethnic Russians.[18] This policy undermined the bilingual regime in

---

14   For an overview of the recent history of the sociolinguistic situation in Ukraine, see Laada Bilaniuk, *Contested Tongues: Language Politics and Cultural Correction in Ukraine* (Ithaca: Cornell University Press, 2005); George Liber, *Total Wars and the Making of Modern Ukraine, 1914–1954* (Toronto: University of Toronto Press, Scholarly Publishing Division, 2016).

15   Volodymyr Kulyk explained many such situations of pressure to assimilate to Russian that continue to exist in Ukraine in a press conference on the topic of "Ukrainian Language. Society. Government," *Glavkom*, November 9, 2015, https://www.youtube.com/watch?v=hAK5n8nnOZM.

16   Masenko quoted in Orel, "Nam potriben movnyi kordon."

17   Ibid.

18   See Catherine Wanner, "'Fraternal' Nations and Challenges to Sovereignty in Ukraine: The Politics of Linguistic and Religious Ties," *American Ethnologist* 41,

Ukraine, and made Russian a language that threatened Ukraine's sovereignty. Some people asserted their right to have Russian as a native language and to speak it while rejecting Russia's so-called "protection."[19] However, many people were also compelled by Russia's actions to learn Ukrainian, or if bilingual, to use Ukrainian more often.[20]

Conversions from Russian speech to Ukrainian speech have become a growing trend since independence. Founded in 2005, the NGO "Ne bud' baiduzhym" (Don't Be Apathetic) organized various campaigns to encourage increased use of Ukrainian and improved attitudes towards the language. The campaigns have included Ukrainian-language rock concerts and dance club nights in cities and small towns all over Ukraine, visits to schools to promote edgy contemporary Ukrainian literature, a nation-wide historical essay competition, and the distribution of brightly illustrated booklets urging people to "Give a gift to Ukraine! Switch to Ukrainian!" The executive director of this organization, Oksana Levkova, is herself an ethnic Russian, born in Ukraine in a military family. She spent much of her childhood in Russia and returned to Ukraine at the age of seventeen, and she did not embrace Ukrainian until her university years. She now works tirelessly to promote the language and the country's democratic development. During my research in 2009, in recording life histories of activists, musicians, journalists, and other media workers, I found many people who were "converts" like Levkova—people of various ethnicities who grew up speaking Russian but had switched to speaking Ukrainian, either partially, or categorically. Indeed, it seemed that those who had grown up speaking Russian and taken up Ukrainian later in life

---

no. 3 (2014): 428, and Lara Ryazanova-Clarke, "Russian with an Accent: Globalisation and the Post-Soviet Imaginary," in *The Russian Language Outside the Nation*, ed. Lara Ryazanova-Clarke (Edinburgh: Edinburgh University Press, 2014), 249–50, http://www.jstor.org/stable/10.3366/j.ctt9qds27.

19   Volodymyr Kulyk, "Ukrainian Nationalism Since the Outbreak of Euromaidan," *Ab Imperio*, no. 3 (2014): 108. Also see the results of a 2014 opinion survey of residents of Kharkiv and Odesa oblasts, presented in Aleksei Navalnyi, "Russkii Mir Ukrainy protiv Zolotoi Ordy Putina. Kross-tablitsy nashego sotsoprosa," *Navalny*, September 24, 2014, https://navalny.com/p/3840/.

20   For instance, many ordinary Kharkivites joined the Ukrainian club "Apostrof," which is part of the Kharkiv Ukrainian cultural and linguistic club. The Orange revolution, the Euromaidan, and Russia's aggression in Ukraine served as powerful motivation for many to learn the Ukrainian language. See the official website of "Apostrof" at http://club.apostrof.in.ua/index.php?option=com_content&view=article&id=9&Itemid=104.

were often more ardent supporters of the Ukrainian language than those who had grown up speaking it.

In February 2016, the website of the southeastern city of Zaporizhzhia showcased the stories of five individuals who had made the switch to Ukrainian, as part of a feature about people who "have done something different than the rest," aligning linguistic conversion with actions such as "volunteering for the war, becoming vegetarian, quitting smoking, practicing extreme sports, taking in animals from shelters."[21] Indeed, linguistic conversion can be part of a broader self-transformation, as in the case of Andrii Khlibets, who proudly announced on Facebook on June 2, 2014, that he gave up smoking and alcohol, became vegetarian, began exercising, lost 23 kilograms of excess weight, and switched to Ukrainian in 85 percent of his communications (his native language is Russian). He wrote, "I can announce with pride that the language of my rebirth is Ukrainian."[22]

Following the Euromaidan protests, self-Ukrainization picked up momentum and urgency.[23] The scale of this trend remains to be investigated, although there is some evidence in online testimonials. A social media group called "Perekhod' na ukrainsku" (Switch to Ukrainian) was created on Facebook by Oleksandr Ivanov on November 9, 2015, to document and promote linguistic conversions to Ukrainian.[24] Every week the page features a new personal story, receiving between 40,000 and 80,000 views. This group produced a video titled "Ukrainian language is our security," urging people to switch to Ukrainian.[25] In this video, male and female volunteers and military personnel explain the reasons for their own conversion and explain the security dimensions of language choice:

---

21  Tamara Gonchenko, "5 istorii zaporozhtsev, kotoryie pereshli na ukrainskii iazyk," *Sait Zaporizhzhia*, February 11, 2016, http://www.061.ua/news/1118487.
22  Facebook post archived in Andrii Khlibets, "Iak Andrii Khlibets diishov do takoho zhyttia," *Sasha.tsyba.org*, June 2, 2014, http://sasha.tsyba.org/archive/tilo/yak-andrij-khlibets-dijshov-do-takogo-zhittya.html.
23  Ievgen Vorobiov, "Why Ukrainians Are Speaking More Ukrainian," *Foreign Policy*, June 26, 2015, https://foreignpolicy.com/2015/06/26/why-ukrainians-are-speaking-more-ukrainian/.
24  "Kyiv rusyfikuiut dytiachi sadky: Zasnovnyk initsiatyvy 'Perekhod na ukrainsku,'" *Gazeta.ua*, February 12, 2016, http://gazeta.ua/articles/sogodennya/678123. Ivanov has set up a corresponding page on VKontakte as well.
25  Iaryna Chornohuz and Oleksandr Ivanov, *"Ukrainska mova—nasha bezpeka"* (Ukrainian Language is Our Security), *YouTube*, November 9, 2015, https://www.youtube.com/watch?v=tF6fVQ-k_tM.

Our enemies do not hide that their weapon against Ukraine is Russification. They declare openly that where there is Russian language, there are Russia's interests. . . . If you don't want the Russian army to come rescue you and your relatives, use your most powerful weapon against them. Speak Ukrainian. Switch to Ukrainian. Demand from the government decisive policy in protection and support of the Ukrainian language. Remember, the Ukrainian language is the guarantor of our peace. Ukrainian language is our security.[26]

This video implies that continuing to speak Russian can undermine Ukraine's peace and security, and that language choice is not just a decision about expressing personal identity, but an activity with real political repercussions.

Other initiatives that support Ukrainization include education, campaigns to ensure consumer access to information in Ukrainian, and media campaigns to influence attitudes. Free Ukrainian language lessons aim to assist those who want to make the switch, or just to feel more comfortable conversing in Ukrainian. Two such programs include one for soldiers of the Dnipro-1 volunteer battalion in Dnipropetrovsk[27] and another for state employees in Donetsk oblast.[28] The organization "I tak poimut!" (They Will Understand Anyway!), founded in 2012, continues to press businesses to provide publications, labeling, and information in Ukrainian.[29] Billboards promoting Ukrainian language went up in Kyiv in November 2015,[30] stating "Ie mova, ie ukraintsi, ie derzhava—ie maibutnie" (If there is the language, there are Ukrainians, there is the state—there is a future). Another billboard stated that "Kyiv is Ukrainian-speaking" (Kyiv ukrainskomovnyi), with smaller text stating that "72.1% of Kyiv residents are Ukrainophone," "according to data from the 2001 census." Other billboards quoted Ukrainian writers, including Lina

---

26 Ibid.
27 "Biitsi 'Dnipra-1' sily za partu, shchob udoskonalyty svoiu ukrainsku movu," *Radio Svoboda*, October 22, 2015, http://www.radiosvoboda.org/content/news/27321242.html.
28 Announced on November 8, 2015 in a Facebook post by Pavlo Zhebrivskyi, head of the Donetsk civil-military administration, as reported in "Na Donechchyni derzhsluzhbovtsi vchytymut ukrainsku movu," *Portal movnoi polityky*, November 12, 2015, http://language-policy.info/2015/11/2097/.
29 Vasylyna Duman, "Spilnota 'I tak poimut!' efektyvno perekonuie biznes spilkuvatysia ukrainskoiu," *Teksty.org.ua*, February 26, 2013, http://texty.org.ua/pg/article/editorial/read/43757/.
30 As posted on the Facebook page of *hromadske.tv*, November 11, 2015.

Kostenko: "Nations don't die from heart attacks. They first lose their language."[31]

Linguistic conversion—that is, self-motivated change in one's predominant linguistic behavior—both challenges and upholds essentialism. On the one hand, it allows self-construction and freedom, in that anyone of any ethnic background is welcome to be Ukrainian by speaking Ukrainian. But conversion also reinforces an essentialization of ethnolinguistic identity—the idea that true or good Ukrainians should speak Ukrainian, and that Russian speakers are not true patriots. This is problematic in a country where Russian is the native language of many people, and where Russian has a deep presence in everyday life, and here it is important to make a distinction between attitudes and practices. It may be difficult for some people to switch their language habits, but if they care about Ukraine's independence, one would expect them to be supportive of those who do use Ukrainian and embrace the broader use of the language in their society. The possibility of balanced bilingualism and neutrality of language choice has been undermined by the importance of language in justifying Russia's aggression against Ukraine. A rejection of Ukrainian language can no longer be passed off as a nonpolitical personal choice.

## Language Matters in the Russian Separatist Areas

In Crimea, occupied by Russia since the spring of 2014, the situation of the Ukrainian language is dire. None of the seven Ukrainian-language schools that existed before the Russian invasion remain. Whereas there used to be 400 class-groups taught in Ukrainian in various Crimean schools, by the spring of 2015 there were no more than fifty. Schools that had been named after Ukrainian writers were renamed. Even though legally Ukrainian remains one of three official languages of Crimea, along with Russian and Crimean Tatar, pupils in ninth through eleventh grade are no longer permitted to study in Ukrainian. Almost all of the departments of Ukrainian language and literature in Crimean universities have

---

31 Olha Chernysh, "Khto i navishcho zavisyv Kyiv bilbordamy z tsytatamy Liny Kostenko," *Depo kraina ukropiv*, November 20, 2015, http://ukrop.depo.ua/ukr/molodoy_ukrop/hto-i-navishcho-zavisiv-kiyiv-bilbordami-z-tsitatami-lini-kostenko-19112015203600.

been eliminated. All of the Crimean Ukrainian-language printed periodicals have been closed down, and many Ukrainian and Crimean Tatar books were burned or otherwise destroyed. Activists and supporters of Ukrainian and Crimean Tatar languages have been intimidated, kidnapped, beaten, and tortured. Many opponents of Russification have left the peninsula for fear of reprisals.[32]

The situation of the Ukrainian language also deteriorated rapidly in the portions of Luhansk and Donetsk oblasts that are not currently under control of the Ukrainian government, as the war on the border of these areas continues. The regions controlled by Russian-backed separatist groups, the so-called "Donetsk People's Republic" (DNR), and the "Luhansk People's Republic" (LNR), passed legislation and implemented broad changes to remove Ukrainian and promote Russian language. "Constitutions" adopted by both regions designated both Russian and Ukrainian as state languages, with the additional specification in the LNR that Russian was the language of government administration. The inclusion of Ukrainian as a "state language" belied the actions that were implemented to exclude Ukrainian. During 2014 and 2015 in both regions Ukrainian language schools were converted to Russian language schools, and time devoted to studying Ukrainian language and literature was reduced to as little as one hour per week. In some cases the conversion of schools and class-groups to Russian language was carried out by militia members who threatened parents that they had to write letters requesting the change, for fear of negative repercussions for the children and teachers.[33] While reliable statistics are lacking, all evidence suggests that by the beginning of the 2015–16 school year, there were few if any remaining schools with Ukrainian as the language of instruction in these regions.[34]

In the DNR and LNR, all television programming in Ukrainian has been eliminated, there are no Ukrainian language periodicals available, and internet providers block access to various Ukrainian news sources.

---

32  "Stanovyshche ukrainskoi movy v Ukraini v 2014-2015 rokakh," *Rukh Dobrovoltsiv "Prostir Svobody,"* July 8, 2015 (11–14), http://dobrovol.org/files/2015/Stan_movy_2014_15.doc.
33  "V Donetske okkupanty pereveli shkoly na russkii iazyk obucheniia," *LIGA. Novosti,* May 29, 2015, http://news.liga.net/news/politics/5878299-v_donetske_okkupanty_pereveli_shkoly_na_russkiy_yazyk_obucheniya.htm.
34  "Stanovyshche ukrainskoi movy," 16-17.

Signage, advertising, and public announcements are exclusively in Russian. One sphere where Ukrainian language was still present, at least in the first half of 2015, was in movie screenings. Foreign films such as "The Hobbit" were shown with Ukrainian dubbing, although the separatist authorities stated that they were working to get access to Russian-produced and Russian-dubbed foreign films.[35] In sum, the aggressive policy of Russification and elimination of use of Ukrainian in the regions occupied by Russia and pro-Russian separatists underscore the central role that language plays in the current conflicts. According to the actions of the Russian occupiers and separatists, language definitely matters.

## The Current Legal Context: Laws Regulating Language Status and Use

By definition, regulation of language status and use follows the ideology that "language matters." The designation of Ukrainian as the sole state language of Ukraine has been consistent since the Law on Languages of 1989, passed before Ukraine's independence from the USSR, and then reaffirmed in independent Ukraine's Constitution in 1996. However, along with this clear assertion, the Constitution also includes contradictory and ambiguous statements. For example, Article 10 not only declares support for the state language, Ukrainian, but also guarantees the "free development, use and protection of Russian and other languages of national minorities of Ukraine."[36] Regarding education, Article 53 assures that the state will provide free education at all levels, but later also states that "citizens belonging to national minorities shall be guaranteed, in accordance with law, the right to education in their native language, or to study their native language at the state and communal educational establishments or through national cultural societies."[37] It was not clear to what extent or in which cases the state would take on the financing of minority language education, as the provision of education in every citizen's native language is logistically practically impossible. In 1999 the Ukrainian Parliament also ratified the European Charter for Regional or Minority Languages, which

---

35 "Stanovyshche ukrainskoi movy," 18.
36 See *The Constitution of Ukraine* (official English translation), *Uriadovyi portal*, accessed February 15, 2016, http://www.kmu.gov.ua/document/110977042/Constitution_eng.doc.
37 Ibid.

also supports minority language education, but again without any explanation of how minorities were to be identified and how the law was to be implemented.

In 2006, the regional councils of Donetsk and Luhansk, and the city councils of Kharkiv, Dnipropetrovsk, Mykolaiv, and Sevastopol, voted to give Russian language official status in their regions, alongside Ukrainian. A regional court ruled that this was unconstitutional. In Donetsk, an appeals court overturned that decision in 2007, supporting the status of Russian as a regional language in that oblast.[38]

The struggles over official language status continued. In 2012, during Ianukovych's presidency, a controversial law "On the Principles of the State Language Policy" was passed, amid street protests, fistfights in Parliament, and accusations of procedural violations. This law, informally known as the "Kivalov-Kolesnichenko" law after two of its authors, allowed regions with at least 10% minority populations to declare their language an official regional language. The law was portrayed by its proponents as fulfilling the European Charter on Minority Languages, but in reality it mainly served to support the existing dominance of Russian language, and provided no protection for Ukrainian. The Kivalov-Kolesnichenko law conflicted with the state status of Ukrainian, as it eroded efforts to increase the use of the previously subjugated Ukrainian language. Well before the events of 2014, lawmakers were concerned that the Kivalov-Kolesnichenko law would undermine Ukraine's unity and feed Russia's imperial ambitions of taking over Ukraine's territory.[39]

A move to repeal the Kivalov-Kolesnichenko law was one of the first actions of the post-Ianukovych government. However, this move was portrayed by pro-Russian media as "banning Russian," as supposed proof of discrimination against Russian speakers, and it was used to justify Russia's military incursions into Ukrainian territory. Even though removing the regional official status of Russian was very different from "banning Russian," in the tense and tenuous situation of post-Euromaidan Ukraine, the media rhetoric played an inflammatory role. Although the Parliament

---

[38] Laada Bilaniuk and Svitlana Melnyk, "A Tense and Shifting Balance: Bilingualism and Education in Ukraine," *International Journal of Bilingual Education and Bilingualism* 11, no. 3/4 (2008): 350–51.

[39] Miriam Elder, "Ukrainians Protest against Russian Language Law," *The Guardian*, July 4, 2012, http://www.theguardian.com/world/2012/jul/04/ukrainians-protest-russian-language-law.

voted to repeal the law in February 2014, then-acting president Oleksandr Turchynov did not sign the repeal into law. So the Kivalov-Kolesnichenko law continues to be in effect, even though it can be seen as contradicting the country's constitution. Ukrainian-language activists and politicians have joined efforts to continue to push for the repeal of the law, but in July 2016, the process remained in limbo.[40]

One could say that the repeal of the Kivalov-Kolesnichenko law would "ban" the exclusive dominant status of Russian, and that could be seen as threatening to Russophones. But is it an infringement on the rights of speakers to not grant a language official status? "Language rights" are a murky area, because language is so intertwined with power. First one must acknowledge that any official language (or languages), whether explicitly designated or implicit in dominant use, is an imposition on someone, and it is not possible to have a functioning country without it. This has not stopped people from using "rights discourse" as a basis for supporting a particular language policy. In Ukraine, a "language rights" discourse was most often invoked by supporters of Russian who rejected needing to learn Ukrainian for official public interactions. Such individuals argued that it is an infringement on their rights to need to know Ukrainian, and that they should have state services provided in Russian. But a Russian-dominant language regime is just as much of an infringement on the rights of speakers of other languages. Even in seemingly liberal regimes, there are implicit and explicit means of imposing a language, and power differences are always involved in bringing a language to prominence and wide use. Any language regime is a regime of power. We can agree that people should be free to speak whichever language they want in their private lives, but it is very costly and inefficient, if not impossible, to extend that freedom to officials in state-supported institutions.

## Language in Institutions and the Media

Institutions constrain individual language choice, but practices do not always conform to institutionalized regulations. People in government jobs

---

40   See a scan of the signed letter "Zvernennia do Holovy Konstytutsiinoho Sudu Ukrainy Baulina Iu. V.," in "Hromadski aktyvisty zvernulysia do Konstytutsiinoho Sudu z pryvodu movnoho zakonu," *Portal movnoi polityky*, June 5, 2015, http://language-policy.info/2015/06/hromadski-aktyvisty-zvernulysya-dokonstytut sijnoho-sudu-z-pryvodu-movnoho-zakonu/.

are required to speak Ukrainian, and in some regions, according to the Kivalov-Kolesnichenko law, to be bilingual, but the laws are often not carried out in practice. In some urban areas, Russian monolingualism prevails, sometimes along with open disdain for Ukrainian. It is here that the idea of "individual freedom of choice" faces a major obstacle. In these situations it is a risk to speak Ukrainian and potentially antagonize a Russian-speaking state official, if that person has power in providing needed certification or services.[41] And so a Russian-dominant (and non-bilingual) status quo continues in some regions, disrupting the idea that "language does not matter." Right now it is more common for people who are native Ukrainian speakers to be bilingual in Russian, than the other way around.[42] If areas where Russian now dominates embraced bilingualism and non-bilingual Russophones made the effort to learn Ukrainian, this could lead to a more balanced situation for both languages. But given the country's history of control by the Russian Empire, Russia's current aggressive policies, and the politicization of language in this time of war, balanced bilingualism in the long run seems less likely than it did three years ago.

There is one sphere that has been de-Russified significantly since Ukraine's independence, and that is the school system. When Ukraine became independent in 1991, only 45% of children studied in schools with Ukrainian as the language of instruction, and 54% studied in Russian-language schools.[43] In 2005, the percentage of children instructed in Ukrainian had grown to 78%, with 21% instructed in Russian, and the remaining 1% of students taught in other minority languages.[44] By 2013, the percentage of schoolchildren taught in Ukrainian as the primary language of instruction had increased to almost 82%. The statistics for the 2014–2015 school year showed yet another increase in the proportion of students learning in Ukrainian, to 89%, but this did not reflect a shift in the

---

41    See Volodymyr Kulyk (press conference on "Ukrainian Language. Society. Government"), *Glavkom TV, YouTube*, November 9, 2015, https://www.youtube.com/watch?v=hAK5n8nnOZM.
42    See Tetiana Burda's research, discussed in Orel, "Nam potriben movnyi kordon."
43    See statistical tables prepared by Vladimir Malinkovich based on information from the Ministry of Science and Education of Ukraine (2001–2004), "Stepen ukrainizatsii obrazovaniia na Ukraine," *Mezhdunarodnyi Institut Gumanitarno-Politicheskikh Issledovanii,* March 10, 2005, http://www.igpi.ru/info/people/malink/1111152776.html.
44    Bilaniuk and Melnyk, 352.

instructional language of schools, but rather was the result of Ukraine's loss of control of Crimea and parts of Luhansk and Donetsk oblasts, and thus the exclusion from the count of territories that had higher concentrations of Russian-language schools.[45] The increase in Ukrainian language instruction has facilitated increased use of the language in everyday life, but there continue to exist spheres that are dominated by Russian language as in Soviet times.

The situation of Ukrainian in the broadcast media remains especially weak. Monitoring of the eight most highly rated television channels of Ukraine in December 2014 showed that approximately 30% of programming time was in Ukrainian, 26% was partly Ukrainian (bilingual), and 44% was in Russian.[46] Another survey comparing television programming of the top ten commercial Ukrainian television channels in June and in November 2015 showed a 5% decrease in Ukrainian programming during the five-month span, from 28% to 23%. The remaining programming was either in Russian exclusively, Russian with Ukrainian subtitles, or bilingual. The portion of bilingual programming during the same period grew by 9%, from 24% to 33%.[47] Ukrainian language is often scantly represented in bilingual shows,[48] so this trend most likely reveals a net loss for the presence of Ukrainian language on television. While trends do not favor Ukrainian language, the percentage of Ukrainian-produced programming increased during the five-month period from 33% to 51%, and Russian produced programming decreased from 29% to 19%. This change is a result of legislation regarding national security, which banned films that constituted propaganda for the government of an "aggressor nation."[49] Overall these data show that the place of Ukrainian language in

---

45  "Stanovyshche ukrainskoi movy," 20–23. Based on data from the Ministry of Science and Education of Ukraine.
46  "Stanovyshche ukrainskoi movy," 28–31.
47  "Na Ukrainskykh telekanalakh zmenshuietsia kilkist Ukrainomovnoho kontentu," *Portal movnoi polityky*, November 17, 2015, http://language-policy.info/2015/11/na-ukrajinskyh-telekanalah-zmenshujetsya-kilkist-ukrajinomovnoho-kontentu/.
48  Laada Bilaniuk, "Language in the Balance: The Politics of Non-accommodation in Bilingual Ukrainian-Russian Television Shows," *International Journal of the Sociology of Language*, no. 201 (2010): 115.
49  See the database "Laws of Ukraine," "Zakon Ukrainy pro vnesennia zmin do deiakykh zakoniv Ukrainy shchodo zakhystu informatsiinoho teleradioprostoru Ukrainy," *Verkhovna Rada*, February 5, 2015, http://zakon5.rada.gov.ua/laws/show/159-19.
50  "Stanovyshche ukrainskoi movy," 28–31.

television programming is not secure, as this field continues to favor a Russophone environment.

In radio broadcasting the situation was even direr for Ukrainian language. Monitoring of the top five music radio stations of Ukraine in December 2014 revealed that an average of 5% of songs were in Ukrainian, 40% in Russian, and 55% in other languages, mostly English.[50] A law passed in June 2016 promises change, by establishing a quota of 35% of all broadcast music during prime hours to be in Ukrainian. This law also requires 60% of announcements, discussions, and other talk programming conducted by program hosts to be in Ukrainian.[51] The passage of this law marks a small but significant step in legal and institutional protection of Ukrainian.

## The Martial Art of Mixed Language

So what exists between the two ideological extremes—one where language doesn't matter, and one where it does? One where bilingualism and Russophone Ukrainians are embraced, and the other where Russian is seen as a danger, and Ukrainian language is seen as critical for Ukraine's security and survival? A phenomenon that blurs the logic of the two opposed tendencies is "*boiovyi surzhyk*" (martial or fighting *surzhyk*), a literary and social media movement that gained momentum during the Euromaidan protests, in which people write in mixed Ukrainian-Russian nonstandard language. One of the major gatherings of *boiovyi surzhyk* writers and performers is the website Repka.club, with postings on Facebook and other social media, on a wide range of topics, from politics to everyday life. It is this group that came up with the *boiovyi surzhyk* label (modeled after the "*boiovyi hopak*" martial art). Repka club includes Parliament deputy Vitalii Chepynoha, who has over 94,000 Facebook followers. People have long been using this language style on the internet to express irony and solidarity. What differentiates *boiovyi surzhyk* from generic *surzhyk* is that it is used by people who are fluent in standard Ukrainian and Russian, who choose to use mixed nonstandard language for its specific communicative impact. So just what is this impact?

---

51  "Rada pryiniala ukrainomovni kvoty na radio," *Ukrainska pravda*, June 16, 2016, http://life.pravda.com.ua/culture/2016/06/16/214032/.

*Boiovyi surzhyk* is carnivalesque—it thumbs its nose at accepted social authority by flouting linguistic conventions of correctness and propriety. *Boiovyi surzhyk* writers reject the very logic of those who deny the legitimacy of Ukrainian language and culture, by using a code that refuses to be defined by the usual standards of legitimacy and correctness. And yet, in rejecting Ukrainian language standards, they are claiming Ukrainianness and full creative freedom in how to express it. Given that much of the population either speaks a *surzhyk* as a native language, or is familiar with the *surzhyk* of friends and relatives, this nonstandard language evokes a sense of familiarity and solidarity. Practitioners of *boiovyi surzhyk* distance themselves from the sterile, bureaucratese connotations of Ukrainian as an official governmental language, and are especially effective in criticizing the corruption of officials.

*Boiovyi surzhyk* disrupts the barrier between the two languages, asserting that both are part of Ukraine and that they do not have to be segregated. However, it still supports the idea of Ukrainization—one not shackled by a narrow definition of correctness, but a Ukrainian language repertoire that is free to expand and embrace the vernacular. While some find this rebellious approach to language use liberating, others view it as dangerous, in that it accepts the historical Russification that has had a degrading impact on the Ukrainian language, and ultimately could lead to its demise.

So what role can *boiovyi surzhyk* play in mediating the opposed tendencies that either embrace Russian language and bilingualism, or insist on Ukrainization? There are various possibilities. A greater acceptance of *surzhyk* as a normal part of Ukraine's landscape would include many people who do not recognize their own language in the standard Ukrainian language. One could retain a privileged position for the standard in formal contexts, but still cultivate a more positive attitude towards nonstandard linguistic variations. Such an attitude would also remove one of the obstacles for Russian speakers who might want to learn Ukrainian or use it occasionally—the stigma associated with imperfectly learned Russian-influenced Ukrainian, which is an unavoidable part of the learning process.

As a carnivalesque mode of expression that flouts standards, *surzhyk* cannot provide a standard for nation building. The government will still have to set policies that either support a bilingual regime with Russian, or just Ukrainian. At this point, given Russia's proprietary stance regarding Russian speakers and the disadvantaged position of Ukrainian language, it would make more sense for the government to lend extra support to Ukrainian, especially in broadcast and print media. This would also make it easier for people to switch to Ukrainian, a tendency that is likely to grow as long as Ukraine's borders and sovereignty are threatened.

## Conclusions

I have illustrated two opposed tendencies in language ideologies and practices in Ukraine, one in which "language does not matter," and the other in which "language matters." On the surface, the ideology that "language does not matter" appears to be the most liberal, allowing individual freedom of choice. However, neutrality in language choice is elusive, all the more so in a society at war with a neighbor using language as partial justification for that war. As I have shown here, when push comes to shove, *language always matters*. For example, while the organization of Russophone Ukrainian Nationalists asserts that language does not determine their allegiance, they still envision a Ukrainophone future as the best path for their children. Those who say that the government's concern with promoting Ukrainian is misplaced in a time of economic woes are often Russophones for whom language does matter, because they do not want their habitual language environment to change. Ultimately, as long as there are social differences, language will reflect these differences. The war has politicized language choice, making the possibility of neutrality of language choice more elusive. Meanwhile, more people are engaging in determining just how language matters, both in their personal choices and in activism to shape the choices of the rest of society.

## Bibliography

"Biitsi 'Dnipra-1' sily za party, shchob udoskonalyty svoiu ukrainsku movu." *Radio Svoboda*. October 22, 2015. http://www.radiosvoboda.org/content/news/27321242.html.

Bilaniuk, Laada, and Svitlana Melnyk. "A Tense and Shifting Balance: Bilingualism and Education in Ukraine." *International Journal of Bilingual Education and Bilingualism* 11, no. 3/4 (2008): 340–72.

Bilaniuk, Laada. *Contested Tongues: Language Politics and Cultural Correction in Ukraine.* Ithaca: Cornell University Press, 2005.

_____. "Language in the Balance: The Politics of Non-accommodation in Bilingual Ukrainian-Russian Television Shows." *International Journal of the Sociology of Language*, no. 201 (2010): 105–33.

Bourdieu, Pierre. *Language and Symbolic Power*. Cambridge: Harvard University Press, 1991.

Bulavka, Ievgenii. "Nashi deti budut ukrainomovnymi—v strane razvivaetsia dvizhenie russkoiazychnykh ukrainskikh natsionalistov." *Tsenzor.net*. June 26, 2013. http://censor.net.ua/n245680.

Chernysh, Olha. "Khto i navishcho zavisyv Kyiv bilbordamy z tsytatamy Liny Kostenko." *Depo kraina ukropiv*. November 20, 2015. http://ukrop.depo.ua/ukr/molodoy_ukrop/hto-i-navishcho-zavisiv-kiyiv-bilbordami-z-tsitatami-lini-kostenko-19112015203600.

Chornohuz, Iaryna, and Oleksandr Ivanov. "Ukrainska mova—nasha bezpeka" (Ukrainian Language is Our Security). *YouTube*. November 9, 2015. https://www.youtube.com/watch?v=tF6fVQ-k_tM.

*Constitution of Ukraine* (official English translation). *Uriadovyi portal*. Accessed February 15, 2016. http://www.kmu.gov.ua/document/110977042/Constitution_eng.doc.

Duman, Vasylyna. "Spilnota 'I tak poimut!' efektyvno perekonuie biznes spilkuvatysia ukrainskoiu." *Teksty.org.ua*. February 26, 2013. http://texty.org.ua/pg/article/editorial/read/43757/.

Elder, Miriam. "Ukrainians Protest Against Russian Language Law." *The Guardian*. July 4, 2012. http://www.theguardian.com/world/2012/jul/04/ukrainians-protest-russian-language-law.

Giles, Howard, Richard Y. Bourhis, and Donald M. Taylor. "Towards a Theory of Language in Ethnic Group Relations." In *Language, Ethnicity and Intergroup Relations*, edited by Howard Giles, 307–348. New York: Academic Press, 1977.

Gonchenko, Tamara. "5 istorii zaporozhtsev, kotoryie pereshli na ukrainskii iazyk." *Sait Zaporizhzhia*. February 11, 2016. http://www.061.ua/news/1118487.

Herder, Johann Gottfried. "Letters for the advancement of humanity." In *Herder: Philosophical Writings*, edited by Michael N. Forster, 380–424. New York: Cambridge University Press, 2002.

"Hromadski aktyvisty zvernulysia do Konstytutsiinoho Sudu z pryvodu movnoho zakonu." *Portal movnoi polityky*. July 5, 2015. http://language-policy.info/2015/06/hromadski-aktyvisty-zvernulysya-do-konstytutsijnoho-sudu-z-pryvodu-movnoho-zakonu/.

"'Iedyna kraina'—'Iedinaia strana'—'Bir devlet': Poroshenko pozdravil Ukrainu s Novym Godom." *Obozrevatel*. January 1, 2015. http://obozrevatel.com/politics/20139-novogodnee-pozdravlenie-poroshenko.htm.

Khlibets, Andrii. "Iak Andrii Khlibets diishov do takoho zhyttia." *Sasha.tsyba.org*. June 2, 2014. http://sasha.tsyba.org/archive/tilo/yak-andrij-khlibets-dijshov-do-takogo-zhittya.html.

Kulyk, Volodymyr. Press conference on "Ukrainian Language. Society. Government." *Glavkom TV, YouTube*. November 9, 2015. https://www.youtube.com/watch?v=hAK5n8nnOZM.

_____. "Ukrainian Nationalism Since the Outbreak of Euromaidan." *Ab Imperio*, no. 3 (2014): 94–122.

"Kyiv rusyfikuiut dytiachi sadky: zasnovnyk initsiatyvy 'Perekhod na Ukrainsku.'" *Gazeta.ua.* February 12, 2016. http://gazeta.ua/articles/sogodennya/678123.

Liber, George. *Total Wars and the Making of Modern Ukraine, 1914–1954.* Toronto: University of Toronto Press, Scholarly Publishing Division, 2016.

Magocsi, Paul Robert. *A History of Ukraine.* Seattle: University of Washington Press, 1998.

Malinkovich, Vladimir. "Stepen ukrainizatsii obrazovaniia na Ukraine." *Mezhdunarodnyi institut gumanitarno-politicheskikh issledovanii.* March 10, 2005. http://www.igpi.ru/info/people/malink/1111152776.html.

"Na Donechchyni derzhsluzhbovtsi vchytymut ukrainsku movu." *Portal movnoi polityky.* November 12, 2015. http://language-policy.info/2015/11/2097/.

Nalyvaiko, Severin. "V Ukraine razrastaetsia dvizhenie russkoiazychnykh banderovtsev." *Gazeta.ua.* July 15, 2013. http://gazeta.ua/ru/articles/sogodennya/506906.

"Na ukrainskykh telekanalakh zmenshuietsia kilkist ukrainomovnoho kontentu." *Portal movnoi polityky.* November 17, 2015. http://language-policy.info/2015/11/na-ukrajinskyh-telekanalah-zmenshujetsya-kilkist-ukrajinomovnoho-kontentu/.

Navalnyi, Aleksei. "Russkii Mir Ukrainy protiv Zolotoi Ordy Putina. Kross-tablitsy nashego sotsoprosa." *Navalny.* September 24, 2014. https://navalny.com/p/3840/.

"Novorichne pryvitannia Prezydenta Ukrainy Petra Poroshenka." *YouTube.* December 31, 2014. https://www.youtube.com/watch?v=xAVN2h3rbwg.

Orel, Maia. "Nam potriben movnyi kordon iz Rosiieiu. Suchasna movna polityka v Ukraini ochyma sotsiolinhvista." *Ukraina Moloda.* December 26, 2014. http://language-policy.info/2014/12/nam-potriben-movnyj-kordon-iz-rosijeyu-suchasna-movna-polityka-ukrajini-ochyma-sotsiolinhvista/.

"Rada pryiniala ukrainomovni kvoty na radio." *Ukrainska pravda.* June 16, 2016. http://life.pravda.com.ua/culture/2016/06/16/214032/.

Ryazanova-Clarke, Lara. "Russian with an Accent: Globalisation and the Post-Soviet Imaginary." In *The Russian Language Outside the Nation*, edited by Lara Ryazanova-Clarke, 249–81. Edinburgh: Edinburgh University Press, 2014. http://www.jstor.org/stable/10.3366/j.ctt9qds27.

Semionych, Semion. "Russkoiazychnye ukrainskie natsionalisty." *Zrada.org.* February 8, 2011. http://zrada.org/hot/25-mova/248-russkojazychnye-ukrainskie-natsionalisty.html.

Serge. "Russkogovoriashchie ukrainskie natsionalisty." *Ukrainska pravda—Narodni blohy.* January 12, 2008. http://narodna.pravda.com.ua/nation/4788131ac2ffe/.

Shepard, Carolyn A., Howard Giles, and Beth A. Le Poire. "Communication Accommodation Theory." In *The New Handbook of Language and Social Psychology*, edited by W. Peter Robinson and Howard Giles, 33–56. Toronto: John Wiley & Sons, 2001.

"Stanovyshche ukrainskoi movy v Ukraini v 2014-2015 rokakh." *Rukh Dobrovoltsiv "Prostir Svobody."* July 8, 2015. http://dobrovol.org/files/2015/Stan_movy_2014_15.doc.

"V Donetske okkupanty pereveli shkoly na russkii iazyk obucheniia." *LIGA. Novosti.* May 29, 2015. http://news.liga.net/news/politics/5878299-v_donetske_okkupanty_pereveli_shkoly_na_russkiy_yazyk_obucheniya.htm.

Vorobiov, Ievgen. "Why Ukrainians Are Speaking More Ukrainian." *Foreign Policy*. June 26, 2015. https://foreignpolicy.com/2015/06/26/why-ukrainians-are-speaking-more-ukrainian/.

Wanner, Catherine. "'Fraternal' Nations and Challenges to Sovereignty in Ukraine: The Politics of Linguistic and Religious Ties." *American Ethnologist* 41, no. 3 (2014): 427–39.

"Zakon Ukrainy pro vnesennia zmin do deiakykh zakoniv Ukrainy shchodo zakhystu informatsiinoho teleradioprostoru Ukrainy." *Verkhovna Rada*. February 5, 2015. http://zakon5.rada.gov.ua/laws/show/159-19.

# 6
# Ukrainian Euromaidan as Social and Cultural Performance

Tamara Hundorova

The Ukrainian Euromaidan of 2013–2014 represents both political and aesthetic phenomena, a space of socio-cultural performance where new kinds of identities were constructed—national, social, political and gender. The perception and consideration of the Euromaidan through the prism of the performance theory does not suggest a reduction of the political and ideological substance of the Ukrainian revolution. But, through the means of pseudo-aesthetical discourses, its opponents attempt to obscure the perfomative aspect of the Euromaidan by diminishing the political aspects of this phenomenon of civic protest and emphasizing the purely theatrical and entertaining nature of the Euromaidan that occurred in the center of Kyiv.[1] One Russian blogger emphatically claimed that the Maidan was a performance because "'maidowns,'[2] to be more precise, their inspirers were concerned a great deal with the appearance of the Maidan and the behavioral code of its participants to impress their European sponsors and the liberal [*liberastvuiushchaiia*] public." According to this blogger, for this purpose all necessary elements of performance were at play at the Maidan: the spectators who were in fact the overseers—"sponsors" and "*liberasty*," the stage ("time, place, and the aesthetics of these ugly tents, tires, and garbage . . . all the conditions were preserved"), the actors

---

[1] Interdisciplinary readings on the theory of performance include among others: Henry Bial and Sara Brady, eds., *The Performance Studies Reader*, 3rd ed. (London and New York: Routledge, 2016); Caoimhe McAvinchey, ed., *Performance and Community: Commentary and Case Studies* (London: Bloomsbury Methuen Drama, 2014); Richard Schechner, *Performance Theory*, revised and expanded ed. (New York: Routledge, 2003); Andrew Parker and Eve Kosofsky Sedgwick, eds., *Performativity and Performance* (New York: Routledge, 1995); Susan Sontag, ed., *Antonin Artaud, Selected Writings*, trans. Helen Weaver (Berkeley: University of California Press, 1988); Victor W. Turner, *The Anthropology of Performance*, 1st ed. (New York: PAJ Publications, 1986).

[2] "Maidowns" is the blogger's concoction which cynically utilizes an interplay between two words—Maidan" and the Down syndrome.

(Ukrainian politicians who behaved "like People's Artists of Ukraine: dancers [*tantsiurysty*], bandura players [*bandurysty*], comedians or emcees [*mastera rasgovornogo zhanra*] . . . everything is in one bottle").³

Truly, the Euromaidan was rich in artistic performances, installation art and the like.⁴ For instance, on December 6, 2013 a performance entitled "Ianukovych! Let's go, good bye!" took place on the Maidan, which the organizers identified as an "art manifesto of free Ukrainians." On January 19, 2014, another artistic performance was presented, "Ukrainian women against the future of subjugation," which included a scene where the unresponsive and shield-protected row of "Berkut" special forces were "attacked" by a hail of flying children's toys. Many performances employed the image of the Ukrainian poet Taras Shevchenko whose 200th birth anniversary was celebrated during the Euromaidan. A new Ukrainian project "Babylon-13," a cinema innovation, became memorable: it presented the footage of artistic performances during the revolutionary events—"Re minor in Kyivrada," "Shame," and "We exist:" a girl was playing the piano in the Kyivrada headquarters; another was singing for the combatants; and several students were reciting poems written by poets of the Executed Renaissance of the 1920s.⁵ A Ukrainian named Bohdan who received the nickname "pianist-extremist" became famous during the revolution: even the cold January winter did not prevent him from playing piano at the Maidan.⁶ Indeed, the Euromaidan produced phenomena such

---

3    AK-47, Prosvetlennyi, "Maidan eto samyi bolshoi performans za vsiu istoriiu ili byli bolshe?," *Otvety.mail.ru*, accessed July 26, 2016, https://otvet.mail.ru/questio n/165153241. Interestingly, the word "liberal" was linguistically modified in Russian to resemble a slang term for a homosexual, a person who belongs to a group largely denigrated in Russia.

4    Installation art implies the use of techniques and three-dimensional works and objects that allow the audience to better understand, observe and "transcend" a space. Often this genre is site- and space-specific, and employs modern technologies. For a discussion on installation art, see Barbara Ferriani and Marina Pugliese, eds., *Ephemeral Monuments: History and Conservation of Installation Art* (Los Angeles: Getty Conservation Institute, 2013); Mark Rosenthal, *Understanding Installation Art: From Duchamp to Holzer* (Munich: Prestel Verlag, 2003); Michael Fried, "Art and Objecthood," in *Art and Objecthood: Essays and Reviews* (Chicago: University of Chicago Press, 1998), 148–72.

5    Dariia Badior, "Puteshestviie na krai bezdny," *Korydor*, December 23, 2013, http://old.korydor.in.ua/spectema/33-yevromaidan/1551-puteshestvie-na-kraj-be zdny.

6    "Ekstremist z Ievromaidanu dorvavsia do pianino," *YouTube*, January 26, 2014, https://www.youtube.com/watch?v=1JBjOe7B27k; and "Ekstremist dorvavsia do

as theatricality and performance, which have become inseparable parts of our lives, as well as politics, culture, and sport. Maidan was permeated by theatricality and performance, and in this respect this place and space was a product of the contemporary post-modern world, a world of new opportunities and social practices that helped improve it morally, politically and intellectually.

## Maidan as an Intellectual Challenge

The Ukrainian revolution of 2013–2014 has been referred to by various names. During the first days of the revolution, in December 2013, Anton Shekhovtsov called it the Euromaidan.[7] In 2014, Volodymyr Viatrovych defined the Euromaidan as an "anti-Soviet revolt,"[8] and Iaroslav Hrytsak held that this was a "Revolution of Values."[9] Others believe that the Ukrainian revolution of 2013–2014 produced "the Maidan of intelligent romantics"[10] and prefer the title "The Revolution of Dignity," which in their view accurately defines the essence of the events which occurred in the Kyiv Maidan. The proliferation of names in itself is an interesting phenomenon, which demonstrates that the Maidan became an extremely significant political event, and also generated an intellectual paradigm where new socio-cultural and geopolitical meanings emerged. Ideologically and symbolically, the Maidan encapsulated democratic ideas and a true European spirit, inspiring the emergence of civil society, which contextualizes this revolution in the post-Soviet and the postcolonial discourse. Simultaneously, the Maidan produced various cultural associations and new artistic forms. For Iurii Andrukhovych, for instance, the faces of Maidan embodied the images of classic literature, associatively

---

pianino," *YouTube*, January 25, 2014, https://www.youtube.com/watch?v=PiEJ b5oU-6s.

7  Anton Shekhovtsov, "The Ukrainian Revolution is European and National," *Eurozine*, December 13, 2013, http://www.eurozine.com/articles/2013-12-13-shekhovtsov-en.html.

8  See Volodymyr Viatrovych's interview with Iaroslava Muzychenko, "Maidan stav anty-ukrainskym povstanniam," *Ukraina moloda*, April 11, 2014, http://www.umoloda.kiev.ua/number/2445/222/86888/.

9  Iaroslav Hrytsak, "Revoliutsiia tsinnostei," *Ukrainska pravda*, November 7, 2014, http://life.pravda.com.ua/society/2014/11/7/183467/.

10 Svetlana Volnova, "Maidan sobral intelligentnykh romantikov," *Viva.ua*, December 20, 2013, http://viva.ua/lifestar/news/24730-svetlana-voljnova-maydan-sobral-intelligentnih-romantikov.html.

transforming Maidan into a Don-Quixote-like masquerade where hundreds of Ukrainians were wearing "colanders and pots" instead of helmets: this was a rebellious attempt to express their discontent and their mocking and contemptuous attitudes toward the government's abusive power.[11]

But what is more interesting is that the Maidan provided new models for social practices. In hindsight, actionism and the performative aspect of Maidan have become more transparent, gaining special meaning, because over the last several decades "political actionism has taken firm root as a form of social protest in Ukraine," as many contemporary scholars have aptly noted.[12] At the peak of human tragedy and mass killings at the Maidan, the Ukrainian philosopher Serhii Datsiuk posited that "the Maidan offered the world its own innovation," which can be identified as "web-confidentiality" or trust, and the "economics of donation" or giving.[13] He was certain that "Maidan became a social network that advanced in the topological space of confidential and trustworthy relations where geography played an insignificant role."[14] This implies that Maidan has become a new social net-reality, part of the world community that opposes hierarchical criminal corporative power, "a proto-image of a new world" and a quasi-political structure that is capable of fighting criminal regimes by transcending geography: Maidans as net-communities can emerge anywhere.[15] In a sense, Maidan restructured the existing social and geo-cultural imagination because Ukraine and Kyiv are no longer perceived as the marginal hinterlands at the edge of Europe. They were

---

11    Iurii Andrukhovych, "1984. 2014?," *Ievromaidan. Khronika vidchuttiv* by Taras Prokhasko, Ivan Tsyperdiuk, Iurii Andrukhovych, Serhii Zhadan, Iurii Vynnychuk (Brustiriv: Dyskurs, 2014), 71.
12    N. M. Khoma, "Sotsializuiuchyi vplyv aktsionizmu: mystetsko-politychnyi syntez v proektsii modeliuvannia politychnoi povedinky," *Aktualni problemy polityky* no. 53 (2014): 41. For a discussion about "actionism," the "art of action" that emerged in the 1960s–1970s, see, for instance, Mechtild Widrich, "The Informative Public of Performance. A Case Study in Viennese Actionism," *TDR. The Drama Review* 57:1, no. 217 (2013): 137–51; Philip Auslander, "The Performativity of Performance Documentation," *PAJ: A Journal of Performance and Art* 28, no. 3 (2006): 1–10; Peter Weibel, ed., *The Vienna Group, A Moment of Modernity 1954–1960: The Visual Works and Actions* (New York: Springer, 1997).
13    Sergei Datsiuk, "Chto takoie Maidan?," *Ukrainskaia pravda*, February 20, 2014, http://blogs.pravda.com.ua/authors/datsuk/5305cb8896062/.
14    Ibid.
15    Ibid.

transformed into the outposts of the struggle for European values. Volodymyr Iermolenko, a blogger and philosopher, has defined the framework for Maidan performance: "Today we must think in terms of all-encompassing history. Our stage today is not a small European province. Our stage is the whole continent, the whole world."[16]

## Semiosis of the Maidan

Undoubtedly, politically, socially, linguistically, and culturally, the representations of the Euromaidan are associated with the most dramatic societal changes of the twenty-first century: Maidan has become an "institution" and a form of consciousness. If the Maidan is considered a meaningful semiotic practice, there are at least four main symbolic codes of this event: Cossack, apocalyptic, carnivalesque, and performative. Precisely these codes or socio-cultural meanings associated with aesthetics and style place the Maidan in the historical and cultural context, providing us with an opportunity to perceive it as a meaningful text. The Cossack code was one of the most influential. An appeal to the Zaporizhian Cossacks' free spirit became extremely popular in the Maidan's discourse. The presence of the Cossack myth as a nation-building myth was quite distinguishable from a practical structural perspective (constructing the barricades, organizing battalions [*sotni*], styling men's haircuts that featured a Cossack forelock [*chupryna*] and the like), and was also detectible at the unconscious social level on the Maidan. Taras Liutyi has emphasized the vitality of this myth: ". . . relatively speaking, the Zaporizhian Sich is one such prototype, which was prominent in certain mythological attributes during the Maidan."[17]

The apocalyptic myth also plays a substantial role in the rhetoric of the Maidan: the Independence Square in Kyiv has been frequently perceived as a sacral place, a cathedral where the fate of Ukraine is determined. In these perceptions, a special place is allotted to people and their

---

16  Volodymyr Iermolenko, "Pro te, shcho nasha stsena—tsilyi svit," *Krytyka*, November 26, 2013, http://krytyka.com/ua/community/blogs/pro-te-shcho-nasha-stsena-tsilyy-svit.
17  See Taras Liutyi's interview with Maryna Dorosh, "Iakshcho my ne osmyslymo radiansku epokhu, istoriia dali ne rukhatymetsia," *Media Sapiens*, November 18, 2014, http://osvita.mediasapiens.ua/trends/1411978127/taras_lyutiy_yakscho_mi_ne_osmislimo_radyansku_epokhu_istoriya_dali_ne_rukhatimetsya/.

representations as a corporeal sacral body, and the tragic events evoke associations with a liturgy and resurrection. "Everything there is like the Divine Liturgy on Sunday," the Ukrainian writer Taras Prokhasko confessed. "The passion for a better Ukraine invigorated the awakening of lightness in the people," he stated,[18] the "unbearable lightness of being," as Milan Kundera would say, a cognitive realization of lightness that signifies freedom and conscious free choice.

Cordo-centrism, the philosophy that echoed from Hryhorii Skovoroda to Pamfil Iurkevych and, what the famous Ukrainian philosopher Dmytro Czyżewski viewed as a special characteristic of Ukrainian consciousness, puts an additional emphasis on Maidan's sacral meaning. The Ukrainian writer Ivan Tsyperdiuk has decoded it as "an invisible church" and a place where "the heart of Ukraine beats."[19] He also has deciphered the apocalyptic plot of the Maidan in the pages of Holy Scriptures. In Tsyperdiuk's view, the intrinsic components of an apocalyptic discourse are all there; they had traversed through space and time, having materialized during the Euromaidan:[20] the introduction (a promise of the European integration), the development of events (beating of students, multiple gatherings of hundreds of thousands of protesters), the continuation (the confrontations with the "Berkut," building barricades, taking hold of the Ukrainian House), and the culmination on February 19, 2014, when at the Maidan approximately one-hundred protesters were shot and killed.[21]

---

18   Taras Prokhasko, "Svitlo i tin," in *Ievromaidan. Khronika vidchuttiv*, 21.
19   Ivan Tsyperdiuk, "Vira," in *Ievromaidan. Khronika vidchuttiv*, 40.
20   For a discussion about apocalyptic discourse, see Gregory Carey, "Introduction: Apocalyptic Discourse, Apocalyptic Rhetoric," in *Vision and Persuasion: Rhetorical Dimensions of Apocalyptic Discourse*, ed. Gregory Carey and L. Gregory Bloomquist (St. Louis: Chalice, 1999), 10. Carey wrote: "Apocalyptic discourse refers to the constellation of apocalyptic topics as they function in larger early Jewish and Christian literary and social contexts. Thus, apocalyptic discourse should be treated as a flexible set of resources that early Jews and Christians could employ for a variety of persuasive tasks. Whenever early Jews and Christians appealed to such topics as visions and revelations, heavenly journeys, final catastrophes, and the like, they were using apocalyptic discourse." See also Vernon K. Robbins, "The Intertexture of Apocalyptic Discourse in the Gospel of Mark," *Emory.edu*, accessed July 26, 2016, http://religion.emory.edu/faculty/robbins/Pdfs/ApocIntertexture.pdf.
21   Tsyperdiuk, "Kulminatsiia," in *Ievromaidan. Khronika vidchuttiv*, 51.

The reception of the Maidan also includes an eschatological meaning associated not only with the demolition of Ianukovych's regime but also with the clash between Good and Evil, sacral death, the resurrection of the Heavenly Hundred heros [*nebesna sotnia*], and the future of Ukraine as a free European country. Analyzing the reception of Maidan in contemporary Ukrainian information space, Iaroslav Potapenko has argued that "[i]n this context, the perception of Maidan as a worldview and an existential place of victory over fear, and as *topoi* of liberation from a paralyzing power of fear, characteristic of a post-genocidal nation, . . . is quite popular."[22]

However, aside from the Cossack Sich and the Apocalypses, the most powerful cultural associations Maidan provoked were carnival and performance. There are primarily two reasons for this: first, in post-Soviet Ukraine a carnival became one of the most commanding forms of self-consciousness and socio-cultural critique;[23] second, Maidan has demonstrated that the use of the latest information technologies, such as the Internet, Facebook, blogs, stringer journalism, and street art, the means that take advantage of the remarkable influence of actionism, virtuality and performance, were extremely effective in promoting mass protest actions.[24] A carnival and performance overlapped on Maidan, yet there was an essential difference between them: the Carnival was an aesthetic form, while performance became a social practice of the revolution.

## Carnivalization and Revolution

Many observers have stressed the carnivalesque character of the Maidan. Hryhorii Nikonov, for instance, has noted that "up to the Epiphany [January 19, 2014] carnivalization was a socio-psychological and aesthetic

---

22  Iaroslav Potapenko, "Spryiniattia Ievromaidanu v suchasnomu ukrainskomu informatsiinomu prostori," *Visnyk Pereiaslavshchyny*, November 9, 2015, http://visnik-press.com.ua/?p=44064.
23  Tamara Hundorova, "Bu-Ba-Bu, karnaval i kich," *Journal of Ukrainian Studies* 27, no. 1–2 (2002): 233–56.
24  Precisely ". . . new media technologies made the Ukrainian protest movement possible in a real space." See Liliia Tulupenko, "Maidan iak kultura protestu," *Mediakrytyka*, February 26, 2014, http://www.mediakrytyka.info/ohlyady-analityka/maydan-yak-kultura-protestu.html.

*dominanta* of the protest in the center Kyiv."[25] In his December, 2013 interview to Radio Liberty, Iurii Andrukhovych warned against Maidan's transformation into a Carnival.[26] To be sure, Andrukhovych cautioned against people's beliefs that actors and musicians might save the revolution—they were not the main actors of the revolution; neither was acting the foundation of the revolutionary process. "They are, of course, needed there, and they are doing a big job but, apparently, [he suggested], this is not of primary importance."[27] Nevertheless, the performative character, carnivalization and theatricality of the Maidan had persisted until "the theater of war actions" dramatically changed it.[28] The Carnival of the 2014 Maidan echoed that of the 2004 Maidan but the blood spilled in January 2014 and subsequent deaths unequivocally erased the Carnival spirit of the former.

The carnivalization pattern of the Euromaidan allows us to trace the geography of the phenomenon, and to view Maidan as a closed space located in the center of Kyiv and a triangle created by the Independence Square, Hrushevskoho and Instytutska Streets. Importantly, as Mikhail Bakhtin has noted, a Carnival usually unfolds in a confined space within a short period of time. The events on Maidan followed the same pattern, only sometimes spilling over into the nearest streets: this reflected the topology of a carnival described in Andrukhovych's 1992 novel *Rekreatsii* (Recreations). Through the carnival, Andrukhovych symbolically identified a space of various transformations and the subjectivities of his characters, at the same time revealing that the carnival might be an imitation and may be ambivalent toward power. Similarly, Mikhail Bakhtin has illuminated a special and important role of social upheavals and cultural re-orientation which "carnivalize" to a certain degree people's entire lives, narrowing the boundaries of the world. In turn, the world itself "loses its structure and certainty," while "the boundaries of the square [the carnival] expand, and its atmosphere absorbs everything."[29]

---

25  Hryhorii Nikonov, "Teatr boiovykh dii," *Comentari: Cholovichi ihry*, no. 3 (387) (2014): 4.
26  "Andrukhovych predostereg Maidan ot prevrashcheniia v karnaval," *Dzerkalo tyzhnia (Zn.ua)*, December 28, 2013, http://zn.ua/UKRAINE/andruhovich-predostereg-maydan-ot-krovi-136004_.html.
27  Ibid.
28  Nikonov, "Teatr boiovykh dii," 4.
29  M. M. Bakhtin, "Dopolneniia i izmeneniia k 'Rable,'" *Voprosy filosofii*, no. 1 (1992): 154.

Let us take a closer look at the Maidan as a carnivalesque social performance by going beyond the traditional aesthetical perception of the Carnival. The carnivalesque performance on Maidan challenged the boundaries of political, social, national and gender relations during the crisis period, uniting politics and aesthetics. This phenomenon became one of the most important and meaningful markers in developing the Ukrainian revolution. From the first days of the protest, carnivalization served as a means of maturing the emotional and cultural "body" of the Maidan.[30] One of the protesters wrote in December 2013: "The contemporary Maidan is a true art space. Here the oldest traditions are disseminated through super-modern technologies," through wi-fi connection.[31] This witness and participant viewed the barricades as art objects, and the famous Maidan Christmas tree as street art. Elements, such as ornamented helmets and tires, anecdotes, poetry, slogans, people wearing different costumes, and hybrid-style colored flags and banners, constituted the masquerading and performative structure of the Maidan. This place represented a fusion of the virtual and the real, and even more—the fluidity of reality where the virtually imagined reality of the Middle Age Carnival unraveled in front of everyone's eyes. The contemporary world represented by computers, Internet, and videos collided with the Middle age world and its attributes— catapults, shields, improvised knight-like helmets, and the *viche*.[32] A small-scale simulacrum (replica) of the Cossack Sich appeared to be located in the center of contemporary Kyiv.

Importantly, the site acquired all the elements of performance, including the actors—heroes, victims, volunteers, and the audience. The tent camps and barricades in flames became not only a field of battles and defense but also a popular tourist attraction: people came to see the

---

30 In my book *Transit Culture* (Tranzytna kultura), I have analyzed the symptoms of post-colonial trauma. Among others, the phenomenon of the "sick body" seems one of the most prominent. Maidan became a factor that helped collective post-traumatic consciousness awaken and to a certain degree recover, although there is still a long and torturous pathway to full recovery. See Tamara Hundorova, *Tranzytna kultura. Symptomy postkolonialnoi travmy* (Kyiv: Hrani-T, 2013), 548; Tamara Hundorova, "Maidan iak symptom: travma, rana i krypta," *Krytyka*, April 16, 2014, http://krytyka.com/ua/community/blogs/maydan-yak-symptom-travma-rana-i-krypta.
31 "Maidan iak performans," *Livejournal* (*marisa_t*), December 17, 2013, http://marisa-t.livejournal.com/480580.html.
32 *Viche* is a term defining a collective gathering of citizens in Kyivan Rus.

Maidan even on the day of fierce fighting on Hrushevskoho Street. The touristization and commodification of the Maidan signified the sublimation of the protesters' and the tourists' aesthetic energy and Maidan's belonging to the contemporary society of the spectacle, where the "most important change lies in the very continuity of [this] spectacle."[33] The sublimation of the feeling of danger, while one was taking pictures of the burning tires and explosions, amplified excitement and satisfaction due to the self-perception of belonging to the Maidan's community. Consequently, the color of the revolution mattered, as it was important during the Orange revolution: it clarifies the strategy of the performance. As some contemporary observers have stressed, "a color, in many cases, has been a way to express dissent without speaking, has had a substantial visual impact, and has been a symbol that united the protesters, emotionally and politically."[34]

## Performance as Social Construction

Generally, all forms of theatrical presentation involving body, temporality, and space served as a means of political, national, social, and lingual transformations on the Maidan. As some scholars have argued, "performance is a complex communicative action where the roles of actors and the audience are equally important. The essence of performance is in its function to manifest and deliver their political ideas and to declare the role of their supporters."[35] Maidan's cultural symbols imputed a performative character to the revolution. Their main goal was to create a community of the Maidan, a microcosm of a new Ukrainian society. Interestingly, Bakhtin has argued that routinely the Carnival community resembles a grotesque body in its totality. But postmodern realities offered a new code, where the carnivalization and grotesque produced unity, which was not equal to totality and/or homogeneity; it was multi-dimensional and plural, a phenomenon that adds a new dimension to Bakhtin's ideas.

---

33  Guy Debord, *The Society of the Spectacle*, trans. Donald Nicholson-Smith (New York: Zone Brooks, 1995), cover page.
34  Abel Polese and Donnacha Ó. Beacháin, "The Color Revolution Virus and Authoritarian Antidotes: Political Protest and Regime Counterattacks in Post-Communist Spaces," *Demokratizatsiya* 19, no. 2 (2011): 112.
35  Khoma, "Sotsializuiuchyi vplyv aktsionizmu," 44.

The Maidan became a catalyst of social changes which facilitated the construction of new kinds of collective solidarity and community in Ukraine. This space and place embraced people of various social backgrounds and professions, the youth and elderly, and people of many nationalities who came to Kyiv from Ukrainian and foreign cities, towns and villages. The Maidan became for them a communicative space where individual strivings, practices and experiences, as well as subjectivities, enriched and to some extent created a new community—dynamic, colorful, and rhizomatic: everyone brought his or her own world, habits, and behavior to the Maidan, yet a common feeling of civic duty, as well as human and national pride and dignity, united these people who learned and developed new behavioral patterns of socialization, new subjectvities, and a taste for collective urban practices. In these experiences, demographic diversity defined by age, sex, social status, and place of origin remained important, yet not dominant. Rather shared democratic values, the language of protest, and common goals became the foundation for understanding, compassion, and unity among Maidan's participants.

People's collective awakening and their awareness of Ukraine's necessary transformation into civic society and a truly democratic state which is crucial to its survival became one of the most important legacies of the Maidan. United by the protest movement against Ianukovych's criminal regime and by their collective gravitation toward European civilization and values, Maidan's participants subscribed to equality and pluralism as the ideal form of a new democratic Ukraine. The space and place of dignity—Maidan—annihilated social hierarchies instantaneously, erasing the boundaries between the center and peripheries: Independence Square became a place where different Ukraines and generations co-existed, befriended one another, built and fought, for the first time experiencing the powerful feeling of togetherness. Their consciousness, individual and collective accountability for everyone and for all, and the "lightness of being" were channeled and sustained through multiple contacts, connections, and links, a phenomenon necessary for effective interactions among the protesters and the advancement of their social, national and gender subjectivities at the moment of a national calamity and revolution.

Taras Prokhasko, for instance, has identified this phenomenon as the one that transcended the space of Maidan, and even Ukraine. He has argued that during the Maidan people gained invaluable individual (and collective) experiences, something that had been taken from them during the Soviet era. In ironic fashion, paraphrasing the Ukrainian national poet Taras Shevchenko, he claimed: "Everyone has the right to exist: those who peacefully stand in Maidan; and those who non-peacefully storm the positions held by *sylovyky*.[36] And so do *sylovyky*, who do not like this situation at all. Someone is throwing stones, and someone defends himself or herself from them. Someone does something there, in Kyiv, and someone is sitting at home. To each his own... In fact, we are fighting for this."[37] In his blog, Prokhasko emphasized the diversity of faces which intellectually and aesthetically were in opposition to the faces that comprised Ianukovych's circle. Prokhasko identified the Maidan as a new Zone that gathered various people: "There are idiots [*lokhi*], imbeciles, botanists, homeless, homosexuals, paralytics, cops [*musory*], and four eyes [*ochkaryky*] who do not want to follow criminal patterns of behavior,"[38]—they became part of a new Zone where the code of honesty and dignity was supreme. In a similar fashion, Oleksandr Irvanets has suggested that despite the multi-facial character of the Maidan community, people's individual unique features and faces created a unique common portrait of the Carnival—the Ukrainian revolution in which they are the main actors: "there are many faces in this revolution . . . . They are our faces! We are the main actors of this performance!"[39]

As has been demonstrated earlier, the Maidan's performative strategy challenges the notions of totality and homogeneity of Ukrainian society and its official power institutions, and also invites us to consider it in binary terms ("center/periphery," "ours"/"foreign," "Maidan/Anti-Maidan," "good/bad," "young/old"). Yet, the Maidan certainly facilitated the emergence of diverse net-communities in the form of "*sotnias*": there were art *sotnia*, medical *sotnia*, volunteers *sotnia*, female *sotnia*, self-defense *sotnia*, and *Nebesna sotnia*. In a sense, in the Independence Square, we

---

36    *Sylovyky* (in Ukrainian) or *siloviki* (in Russian) is a term defining those who serve as police special forces. These term is equally applicable to Russian special forces and their Ukrainian counterparts.
37    Taras Prokhasko, "Kozhnomy svoie," in *Ievromaidan. Khronika vidchuttiv*, 20.
38    Taras Prokhasko, "Oznaky zrilosti," in *Ievromaidan. Khronika vidchuttiv*, 14.
39    Quoted in Oksana Zahakailo, "Poeziia i proza Ievromaidanu," *Dzerkalo tyzhnia* (*Zn.ua*), December 6, 2013, http://gazeta.dt.ua/CULTURE/poeziya-i-proza-yevromaydanu-_.html.

observed multiple and diverse Maidans that represented diverse Ukrainian society, Maidans that changed and reformatted people's feeling of belonging and unity through the multiplicity of subjectivities conditioned by generational, geographical, ideological, ethnic, and gender identities. Under pressure of coercion and potential death, from December 2013 to February 2014 the Maidan underwent not an incremental, but a dramatic change that was destined to be challenged again by the Russian invasion.

## Maidan as a Cornucopia of Opportunities

Carnivalization played an important role in the formation of the Maidan community. The Maidan, however, was not transformed into a Carnival, as happened with the Orange Maidan in 2004. The 2013–2014 Maidan became a social and political phenomenon where performance enacted forms of new socializing experiences for Ukrainian citizens and their political development. The socio-cultural performative nature of the Maidan modified its carnivalesque formula and transformed this space and place into a *cornucopia of opportunities*. Its pluralities and multiplicities were grounded not only in the theatrical potential of the Maidan that included a game, life, heroism, tragedy and death. Rather the performative nature of the revolution developed the abilities and enhanced opportunities for every participant, prompting him or her to be creative and politically and socially active. People wrote poetry, even if they were not poets; they were singing, even if they were not singers; and they were fighting, even if they were not professional soldiers. In other words, the Maidan became the stage for the realization of everyone's potential. Actors have to change their costumes, and the participants of the Maidan did. They performed social and cultural roles, other than those they engaged in during peaceful times. Poetry was ubiquitous in Maidan, inspiring students to cook, retired men and women to build the barricades, and professors to serve food.

      Performance is deeply embedded in all human experiences and actions. The Maidan encouraged the protesters to play multiple roles as fighters, cooks, nurses, and volunteers. Moreover, Maidan was a product of city culture, and even its participants who came from small villages with their patriarchal traditions learned how to survive in a new urban environment. They performed many tasks and gained new skills. In turn, residents of big cities learned the skill of collective survival. These cultural adjustments and exchanges accelerated the processes of forming a new modern Ukrainian nation, a community of people belonging to their own territory and imagining it as one marked by their own rich culture and history, as well as by their feeling of "common good," as Serhii Zhadan has suggested. "[This feeling] allows us to stay together, something that holds us in our cities, within our borders. Something that makes us part of this territory," Zhadan has insisted.[40]

Many scholars have argued that the era of postmodernism dictates new rules of communication and forms new types of identities. Theatricality, performance, and representation play an immense role in these processes because identities are fluid, and there are neither definitive restrictions nor firm rules for their construction. In the early twenty-first century sociology embraced the notion of performance, examining it as one of the most important social practices. The theory of performance and the theory of society are based on the premise that performance is an inseparable part of social practices, and people's desire for unity. For instance, American sociologist Jeffrey C. Alexander has proposed to study social events as a performance but he placed a great deal of emphasis on the theatrical concept of performance. He wrote: "Cultural performance is the social process by which actors, individually or in concert, display for others the meaning of their social situation."[41] Yet there is an attempt among sociologists to bring this discussion to another level, and analyze the social and cultural significance of performance. Peter Snow, for example, has criticized Alexander's theory of performance as "being grounded in a theatre of dramaturgy of actors, characters and scripts," and suggested that one should consider other important features in this process, such as "embodiment, creativity and imagination."[42] According to Snow, social events become performances when people activate their creative imagination and open up "the horizon of alternative

---

40 Serhii Zhadan, "Pro spilne mizh riznymy Zakhodom ta Skhodom," in *Ievromaidan. Khronika vidchuttiv*, 102.
41 Jeffrey C. Alexander, "Cultural Pragmatics: Social Performance Between Ritual and Strategy," in *Social Performance: Symbolic Action, Cultural Pragmatics and Ritual*, eds. Jeffrey C. Alexander, Bernhard Giesen, and Jason L. Mast (London and New York: Cambridge University Press, 2006), 32.
42 Peter Snow, "Performing Society," *Thesis Eleven* 103, no. 1 (2010): 78.

possibilities for changing this or that situation."[43] Creativity or, in other words, an ability to engender new forms of existence or alternative possibilities is one of the criteria for considering a social event as a performance. Alexander has posited that

> social performances, like theatrical ones, symbolize particular meanings only because they can assume more general, taken-for-granted meaning structures within which their performances are staged. Performances select among, reorganize, and make present themes that are implicit in the immediate surround of social life—though these are absent in a literal sense. Reconfiguring the signifiers of background signifiers, performances evoke a new set of more action-specific signifiers in turn.[44]

In regard to Maidan, precisely this aspect of performance—the emergence of alternative realities and possibilities, and "a new set of more action-specific signifiers" which helped re-organize the extant social, political, and cultural conditions—seems to be the most important feature of critical analyses. Considering the Maidan from this vantage point helps us better understand the construction of a new civic society: Maidan created the possibility for another reality of which Maidan's actors wanted to be a part. This reality would become a solid foundation for constructing a truly democratic society in Ukraine. The post-Maidan social and political developments have demonstrated that the new skills and the new intellectual horizons that Maidan awakened in people found their further applications in their post-revolutionary activities. Giving became the motto of their lives: many of Maidan's actors became active participants in the volunteer movement.

## Beyond the Maidan: Politics and Culture

In retrospect, Maidan appears to be a truly heroic era, but at the same time it provokes new painful questions. Mykhailo Minakov, for instance, has spoken of the society's inability to build a new reality. He has posited that Maidans seem to be a "temporal tool of renovation" and lamented that

---

[43] Nail Farkhatdinov, "Peter Snow. 'Performans obshestva,'" *Sotsiologicheskoie obozreniie* 10, no. 1–2 (2011): 77. In this article, Farkhatdinov analyzes Peter Snow's debates with Jeffrey C. Alexander.

[44] Jeffrey C. Alexander, "From the Depths of Despair: Performance, Counterperformance, and 'September 11," in Alexander, Giesen, and Mast, 94.

Ukrainians appear to be "satisfied with the minimum."[45] Certainly, Maidan requires new analyses and new critical reflections. It is, however, difficult to deny that this most recent Maidan created the foundations for new political institutions and facilitated the processes of modernization in Ukraine.

The Maidan's social and cultural performance produced new civil initiatives and new cultural and aesthetical forms, such as "Babylon-13," "The Library of the Maidan," "The Museum of the Maidan," and various art performances. Immediately after the Maidan, exhibitions, such as "Art of Freedom: (R)evolutionary Culture of the Maidan" located in the Honchar Museum, have become frequent and popular: by means of interactive space, exhibitions told the individual stories of the Maidan's participants and exposed authentic objects used during the revolution—flags and slogans that decorated the famous Christmas tree during the revolutionary events, Molotov lights, painted helmets and the like. The performative element took post-Maidan art to another technological level: the aforementioned exhibition, for example, invited the guests to participate in a virtual tour "Maidan 3D," to share their own memories about the Maidan on the stage called "The Stage of Histories," and to write their thoughts and perceptions on a special wall called "The Voices of Attendees."[46]

In all, the Euromaidan has become a significant political and revolutionary event that accentuated a close link between cultural and political practices. Crucially, the Euromaidan has demonstrated that in the post-postmodern era performance remains not only an actual art phenomenon but a form of social practice, carrying strong socio-cultural and political messages.

---

45  See Mykhailo Minakov's interview with Ievheniia Syzontova, "Maidan stav chastynoiu suchasnoi politychnoi kultury Ukrainy," *Dialog.ua*, February 28, 2014, http://dialogs.org.ua/ru/dialog/page160-2477.html.

46  "Interaktyvnyi vystavkovyi proekt 'Tvorchist svobody: (R)evoliutsiina kultura Maidanu," *Muzei Ivana Honchara* (*Honchar.org.ua*), accessed July 27, 2016, http://honchar.org.ua/events/interaktyvnyj-vystavkovyj-proekt-tvorchist-svobody-revolyutsijna-kultura-majdanu/.

## Bibliography

AK-47, Prosvetlennyi. "Maidan eto samyi bolshoi performans za vsiu istoriiu ili byli bolshe?" *Otvety.mail.ru.* Accessed July 26, 2016. https://otvet.mail.ru/question/165153241.

Alexander, Jeffrey C. "Cultural Pragmatics: Social Performance Between Ritual and Strategy." In *Social Performance: Symbolic Action, Cultural Pragmatics and Ritual*, edited by Jeffrey C. Alexander, Bernhard Giesen, and Jason L. Mast, 29–90. London and New York: Cambridge University Press, 2006.

──────. "From the Depths of Despair: Performance, Counterperformance, and 'September 11." In *Social Performance: Symbolic Action, Cultural Pragmatics and Ritual*, edited by Jeffrey C. Alexander, Bernhard Giesen, and Jason L. Mast, 91–114. London and New York: Cambridge University Press, 2006.

Andrukhovych, Iurii. "1984. 2014?" *Ievromaidan. Khronika vidchuttiv* by Taras Prokhasko, Ivan Tsyperdiuk, Iurii Andrukhovych, Serhii Zhadan, and Iurii Vynnychuk, 70–72. Brustiriv: Dyskurs, 2014.

"Andrukhovych predostereg Maidan ot prevrashcheniia v karnaval." *Dzerkalo tyzhnia (Zn.ua).* December 28, 2013. http://zn.ua/UKRAINE/andruhovich-predostereg-maydan-ot-krovi-136004_.html.

Auslander, Philip. "The Performativity of Performance Documentation." *PAJ: A Journal of Performance and Art* 28, no. 3 (2006): 1–10.

Badior, Dariia. "Puteshestviie na krai bezdny." *Korydor.* December 23, 2013. http://old.korydor.in.ua/specterna/33-yevromaidan/1551-puteshestvie-na-kraj-bezdny.

Bakhtin, M. M. "Dopolneniia i izmeneniia k 'Rable.'" *Voprosy filosofii*, no. 1 (1992): 134–64.

Bial, Henry, and Sara Brady, eds. *The Performance Studies Reader*, 3rd ed. London and New York: Routledge, 2016.

Carey, Gregory. "Introduction: Apocalyptic Discourse, Apocalyptic Rhetoric." In *Vision and Persuasion: Rhetorical Dimensions of Apocalyptic Discourse*, ed. Gregory Carey and L. Gregory Bloomquist, 8–10. St. Louis: Chalice, 1999.

Datsiuk, Sergei. "Chto takoie Maidan?" *Ukrainskaia Pravda.* February 20, 2014. http://blogs.pravda.com.ua/authors/datsuk/5305cb8896062/.

Debord, Guy. *The Society of the Spectacle.* Translated by Donald Nicholson-Smith. New York: Zone Brooks, 1995.

"Ekstremist dorvavsia do pianino." *YouTube.* January 25, 2014. https://www.youtube.com/watch?v=PiEJb5oU-6s.

"Ekstremist z Ievromaidanu dorvavsia do pianino." *YouTube.* January 26, 2014. https://www.youtube.com/watch?v=1JBjOe7B27k.

Farkhatdinov, Nail. "Peter Snow. 'Performans obshestva.'" *Sotsiologicheskoie obozreniie* 10, no. 1–2 (2011): 75–78.

Ferriani, Barbara, and Marina Pugliese, eds. *Ephemeral Monuments: History and Conservation of Installation Art.* Los Angeles: Getty Conservation Institute, 2013.

Fried, Michael. "Art and Objecthood." In *Art and Objecthood: Essays and Reviews* by Michael Fried, 148–72. Chicago: University of Chicago Press, 1998.

Hrytsak, Iaroslav. "Revoliutsiia tsinnostei." *Ukrainska pravda*. November 7, 2014. http://life.pr avda.com.ua/society/2014/11/7/183467/.

Hundorova, Tamara. "Bu-Ba-Bu, karnaval i kich." *Journal of Ukrainian Studies* 27, no. 1–2 (2002): 233–56.

──────────. "Maidan iak symptom: travma, rana i krypta." *Krytyka*. April 16, 2014. http://krytyka.com/ua/community/blogs/maydan-yak-symptom-travma-rana-i-krypta.

──────────. *Tranzytna kultura. Symptomy postkolonialnoi travmy*. Kyiv: Hrani-T, 2013.

Iermolenko, Volodymyr. "Pro te, shcho nasha stsena—tsilyi svit." *Krytyka*. November 26, 2013. http://krytyka.com/ua/community/blogs/pro-te-shcho-nasha-stsena-tsilyy-svit.

"Interaktyvnyi vystavkovyi proekt 'Tvorchist svobody: (R)evoliutsiina kultura Maidanu." *Muzei Ivana Honchara* (*Honchar.org.ua*). Accessed July 27, 2016. http://honchar.or g.ua/events/interaktyvnyj-vystavkovyj-proekt-tvorchist-svobody-revolyutsijna-kultur a-majdanu/.

Khoma, N. M. "Sotsializuiuchyi vplyv aktsionizmu: mystetsko-politychnyi syntez v proektsii modeliuvannia politychnoi povedinky." *Aktualni problemy polityky* no. 53 (2014): 40–47.

Liutyi, Taras (interview with Maryna Dorosh). "Iakshcho my ne osmyslymo radiansku epokhu, istoriia dali ne rukhatymetsia." *Media Sapiens*. November 18, 2014. http://osvita.m ediasapiens.ua/trends/1411978127/taras_lyutiy_yakscho_mi_ne_osmislimo_radyan sku_epokhu_istoriya_dali_ne_rukhatimetsya/.

"Maidan iak performans." *Livejournal* (*marisa_t*). December 17, 2013. http://marisat.livej ournal.com/480580.html.

McAvinchey, Caoimhe, ed. *Performance and Community: Commentary and Case Studies*. London: Bloomsbury Methuen Drama, 2014.

Minakov, Mykhailo (interview with Ievheniia Syzontova). "Maidan stav chastynoiu suchasnoi politychnoi kultury Ukrainy." *Dialog.ua*. February 28, 2014. http://dialog s.org.ua/ru/dialog/page160-2477.html.

Nikonov, Hryhorii. "Teatr boiovykh dii." *Comentari: Cholovichi ihry*, no. 3 (387) (2014): 4–5.

Parker, Andrew, and Eve Kosofsky Sedgwick, eds. *Performativity and Performance*. New York: Routledge, 1995.

Polese, Abel, and Donnacha Ó. Beacháin. "The Color Revolution Virus and Authoritarian Antidotes: Political Protest and Regime Counterattacks in Post-Communist Spaces." *Demokratizatsiya* 19, no. 2 (2011): 111–132.

Potapenko, Iaroslav. "Spryiniattia Ievromaidanu v suchasnomu ukrainskomu informatsiinomu prostori." *Visnyk Pereiaslavshchyny*. November 9, 2015. http://visnik-press.com.ua/?p=44064.

Prokhasko, Taras. "Kozhnomy svoie." In *Ievromaidan. Khronika vidchuttiv* by Taras Prokhasko, Ivan Tsyperdiuk, Iurii Andrukhovych, Serhii Zhadan, and Iurii Vynnychuk, 19–21. Brustiriv: Dyskurs, 2014.

──────────. "Oznaky zrilosti." In *Ievromaidan. Khronika vidchuttiv* by Taras Prokhasko, Ivan Tsyperdiuk, Iurii Andrukhovych, Serhii Zhadan, and Iurii Vynnychuk, 13–14. Brustiriv: Dyskurs, 2014.

———. "Svitlo i tin." In Ievromaidan. Khronika vidchuttiv by Taras Prokhasko, Ivan Tsyperdiuk, Iurii Andrukhovych, Serhii Zhadan, and Iurii Vynnychuk, 21–23. Brustiriv: Dyskurs, 2014.

Robbins, Vernon K. "The Intertexture of Apocalyptic Discourse in the Gospel of Mark." *Emory.edu*. Accessed July 26, 2016. http://religion.emory.edu/faculty/robbins/Pdfs/ApocIntertexture.pdf.

Rosenthal, Mark. *Understanding Installation Art: From Duchamp to Holzer*. Munich: Prestel Verlag, 2003.

Schechner, Richard. *Performance Theory*, revised and expanded ed. New York: Routledge, 2003.

Shekhovtsov, Anton. "The Ukrainian Revolution is European and National." *Eurozine*. December 13, 2013. http://www.eurozine.com/articles/2013-12-13-shekhovtsov-en.html.

Snow, Peter. "Performing Society." *Thesis Eleven* 103, no. 1 (2010): 78–87.

Sontag, Susan, ed. *Antonin Artaud, Selected Writings*. Translated by Helen Weaver. Berkeley: University of California Press, 1988.

Tsyperdiuk, Ivan. "Kulminatsiia." In *Ievromaidan. Khronika vidchuttiv* by Taras Prokhasko, Ivan Tsyperdiuk, Iurii Andrukhovych, Serhii Zhadan, and Iurii Vynnychuk, 51–52. Brustiriv: Dyskurs, 2014.

———. "Vira." In *Ievromaidan. Khronika vidchuttiv* by Taras Prokhasko, Ivan Tsyperdiuk, Iurii Andrukhovych, Serhii Zhadan, and Iurii Vynnychuk, 39–40. Brustiriv: Dyskurs, 2014.

Tulupenko, Liliia. "Maidan iak kultura protestu." *Mediakrytyka*. February 26, 2014. http://www.mediakrytyka.info/ohlyady-analityka/maydan-yak-kultura-protestu.html.

Turner, Victor W. *The Anthropology of Performance*, 1st ed. New York: PAJ Publications, 1986.

Viatrovych, Volodymyr (interview with Iaroslava Muzychenko). "Maidan stav antyukrainskym povstanniam." *Ukraina moloda*. April 11, 2014. http://www.umoloda.kiev.ua/number/2445/222/86888/.

Volnova, Svetlana. "Maidan sobral intelligentnykh romantikov." *Viva.ua*. December 20, 2013. http://viva.ua/lifestar/news/24730-svetlana-voljnova-maydan-sobral-intelligentnih-romantikov.html.

Weibel, Peter, ed. *The Vienna Group, A Moment of Modernity 1954–1960: The Visual Works and Actions*. New York: Springer, 1997.

Widrich, Mechtild. "The Informative Public of Performance. A Case Study in Viennese Actionism." *TDR. The Drama Review* 57:1, no. 217 (2013): 137–51.

Zahakailo, Oksana. "Poeziia i proza Ievromaidanu." *Dzerkalo tyzhnia (Zn.ua)*. December 6, 2013. http://gazeta.dt.ua/CULTURE/poezyia-i-proza-yevromaydanu-_.html.

Zhadan, Serhii. "Pro spilne mizh riznymy Zakhodom ta Skhodom." In *Ievromaidan. Khronika vidchuttiv* by Taras Prokhasko, Ivan Tsyperdiuk, Iurii Andrukhovych, Serhii Zhadan, and Iurii Vynnychuk, 100–102. Brustiriv: Dyskurs, 2014.

# Part Four

# Crimea, the Black Sea, and the Straits

Part Four

# 7

# The Annexation of Crimea: Russia's Response to Ukraine's Revolution

Nedim Useinov

In late 2013 and early 2014 Kyiv once again drew the attention of the entire world. In November 2013 Ukraine's Prime Minister Mykola Azarov announced that, despite earlier arrangements, his government would not sign the European Union (EU)-Ukraine (UA) Association Agreement during the upcoming Eastern Partnership summit in Vilnius. Apparently, this sudden turn took everyone by surprise except Russian president Vladimir Putin. Western European leaders and the majority of Ukrainians seemed to be caught off guard by President Viktor Ianukovych's decision. Since a miracle had not occurred in the Lithuanian capital, and since Ukrainian officials had not changed their minds, some European politicians and journalists hastily made a disappointing forecast about Ukraine drifting toward authoritarianism and a growing dependence on Russia. Moreover, they predicted that the West was about to lose Ukraine for years to come.

In 2013 Ianukovych found himself caught in a conundrum of personal ambitions, Ukraine's domestic problems, and Russian geopolitical subterfuge. After the 2012 parliamentary elections in Ukraine, which were accompanied by numerous violations[1] against the backdrop of a difficult economic situation, sociologists warned about the growing level of public

---

1     In its election observation mission final report, the OSCE concluded that (inter alia) "while voters had a choice between distinct parties and election day was calm and peaceful overall, certain aspects of the pre-election period constituted a step backwards compared with recent national elections," and that "widespread evidence of intimidation, abuse of administrative resources, pressure on public employees, and indirect vote-buying" were registered. See "Ukraine. Parliamentary Elections. 28 October 2012: OSCE/ODIHR Election Observation Mission Final Report," *OSCE: Office for Democratic Institutions and Human Rights* (Warsaw), January 3, 2013, http://www.osce.org/odihr/98578?download=true. 1.

discontent, which might easily turn into protests.[2] In this context, for Ianukovych the upcoming EU-UA Association Agreement could be a mitigating factor. However, on the eve of the summit in Vilnius, Russia dramatically increased pressure on Ukrainian officials.[3] Ianukovych's calculations of potential gains from rejecting the European integration seemed to be crucial to his decision, as his regime was largely dependent on financial and political support from Moscow. Subsequent events in Kyiv demonstrated that Ianukovych made a political mistake which became fatal for him and his corrupt accomplices: he underestimated the disappointment of Ukrainian society provoked by the reorientation of state policies towards the East, and, most importantly, the growing political activism of Ukrainian society galvanized by the Orange revolution.

On November 21, 2013, hundreds of protesters gathered on the Maidan Nezalezhnosti, the central square in Kyiv, to express their support for integration and closer cooperation with the European Union (EU). Within a brief period of time, peaceful demonstrations spread across the entire country. When the authorities used lethal force to disperse the protesters, peaceful popular discontent was quickly transformed into active confrontation with the police who were specially trained and well-armed. The police received an order to use lethal weapons and, as a result, over 100 protesters were killed on Hrushevskoho and Instytutska Streets. Bloody clashes between the police and demonstrators exacerbated the intensity of the conflict. Ianukovych lost control over the situation, and during the night of February 21, 2014 he fled Kyiv. Later on, on October 24, 2014 at the annual Valdai Club meeting in Sochi, Putin revealed that Russians had assisted the Ukrainian president's move to Crimea and then to Russia.[4]

---

2   "Ukraina-2013: mizh vyboramy i pered vyborom (analitychni otsinky)," *Tsentr Razumkova* (Kyiv), 2013, http://www.razumkov.org.ua/upload/Ukraine-2013_ukr.pdf. For a discussion about the determinants of protest moods in Ukraine, see also "Hradus protestnyh nastroiiv v Ukraini zrostaie—doslidzhennia," *News.ru.ua*, March 23, 2013, http://www.newsru.ua/arch/ukraine/23mar2013/boiling_cattle.html.
3   Christiane Hoffmann, Marc Hujer, Ralf Neukirch, Matthias Schepp, Gregor P. Schmitz, and Christoph Schult, "Summit of Failure: How the EU Lost Russia over Ukraine," *Spiegel Online International*, November 24, 2014, http://www.spiegel.de/international/europe/war-in-ukraine-a-result-of-misunderstandings-between-europe-and-russia-a-1004706-2.html.
4   Stepan Kravchenko, "Putin Says Russia Helped Yanukovych to Escape Ukraine," *Bloomberg*, October 24, 2014, http://www.bloomberg.com/news/articles/2014-10-24/putin-says-russia-helped-yanukovych-to-escape-ukraine.

While the protesters on the Maidan Nezalezhnosti were counting their losses, in Crimea, local separatists together with Russian security forces activated Putin's "little green men" and "Crimean spring" special operations. Despite the presence of Ukrainian military bases in Crimea, Russia's fully armed special troops (without visible insignia) faced no perceptible resistance when they appeared on Crimean streets. This might be partially explained by the temporary power vacuum in Kyiv and the general disorganization of the Ukrainian army leadership after Ianukovych's escape, which gave the Russian president a brief window of opportunity to annex the peninsula. But it would be problematic to deny the fact that the Kremlin's operation was a brilliantly prepared campaign, which surprised and paralyzed the Ukrainian military forces stationed on the peninsula. Similarly, this operation astonished the West and left the majority of Western politicians totally flabbergasted.[5]

Many questions arise in this context, but the most crucial relate to the political and economic future of the peninsula under Russian rule, including Russia's treatment of political opposition in Crimea. In a geographical sense, Crimea found itself isolated: it is connected by land only with Ukraine, and has always relied on Ukraine for water, energy, and food supplies, which presents a number of economic challenges for Crimean residents. Politically, the Russian authorities exhibited signs of hostility and intolerance to Crimean Tatars and those who support official Kyiv, prosecuting them for extremist activities. These post-annexation dynamics dramatically reconfigure the social, cultural and demographic landscape of the peninsula, making Crimea's return to Ukraine highly problematic.

This study offers an analysis of the anatomy of the Russian military operation in Crimea in February–March 2014, which constituted the initial stage of the ongoing Russian-Ukrainian military, economic, and political conflict, and assesses the influence of annexation on the prospects of Ukraine-Russia relations and on the economic and political future of the Crimean peninsula and its inhabitants. A brief overview of the financial and political situation in Ukraine on the eve of the Eastern Partnership

---

5    For a discussion about Russia's annexation of Crimea and the condition of the Ukrainian army at the moment, see Taras Berezovets, *Aneksiia: ostriv Krym. Khroniky "hibrydnoi viiny"* (Kyiv: Bright Star Publishing, 2015).

Summit in Vilnius in autumn 2013, and Russia's involvement in the Ukrainian revolution of 2013–2014 seem necessary to clarify the foundations for Russia's take over of Crimea.

## Prelude to the Annexation of Crimea: Russia's Involvement in Maidan

On October 28, 2012 Ukrainian citizens elected new members of parliament. In Ukraine, the election campaign is usually accompanied by an increased scale of protest activity and 2012 was no exception. Dissatisfaction escalated due to the worsening economic situation, the high unemployment rate, and the government's inability to effectively deal with omnipresent corruption.[6] Moreover, Ianukovych used parliamentary elections to strengthen his vertical power, which further deepened existing political divisions in society. To alleviate these tensions, the ruling elites actively exploited the Euro-integration theme. State television broadcast promotional video-spots praising European integration, a visa-free regime, educational opportunities, and access to Europe's high standards of living. To a certain extent, these tactics allowed the government to temporarily divert people's attention from unsolved economic problems and a lack of reforms vital for Ukraine. The government's abrupt refusal to sign the EU-UA Association Agreement frustrated many Ukrainians, who believed in previous declarations about maintaining the Western course. Dissatisfied by the unexpected change of the Euro-integration plans combined with rapidly declining living standards and shrinking political freedoms, Ukrainian citizens gathered at the Maidan Nezalezhnosti in Kyiv to protest.

Between February 18 and February 22, 2014, the Maidan and the adjacent Hrushevskoho and Instytutska Streets turned into a battlefield: on one side of the barricades there were protestors, sheltered by wooden

---

6    For a discussion of the public mood in Ukraine in 2012–2013, see Bohdana Kostiuk, "Protestni nastroi sered Ukraintsiv zrostaiut, ale brakuie lideriv—eksperty," *Radio Svoboda*, March 21, 2013, http://www.radiosvoboda.org/content/article/24934512.html; Bohdan Butkevych and Andrii Skumin, "Chy povstane Ukraina," *Tyzhden.ua*, July 18, 2013, http://tyzhden.ua/Politics/84289; see also "Protests, Concessions and Repressions in Ukraine: Monitoring Results of 2013," *Centre for Society Research*, 2014, http://www.cedos.org.ua/system/attachments/files/000/000/043/original/CSR_-_Protests_in_2013_-_29_Apr_2014_Eng.pdf?1400090323.

shields and plastic helmets, on the other—"Berkut" units armed with lethal weapons and backed by professional snipers. In the period between December 2013 and February 2014, in Kyiv alone, approximately one-hundred protesters (the "Heavenly Hundred") were shot and killed under the orders of Ianukovych and the minister of interior Vitalii Zaharchenko. In addition, unconfirmed numbers of Ukrainian citizens, activists of local Maidans, had gone missing all over the country.

On February 21, in order to support negotiations between the government and the opposition, a group of mediators consisting of three EU foreign ministers (Frank-Walter Steinmeier, Radoslaw Sikorski, and Laurent Fabios) arrived in Kyiv. Russia delegated its ombudsman Vladimir Lukin. During the meeting with Ianukovych, the leaders of the Ukrainian opposition signed an agreement, which, *inter alia*, included a reference to the 2004 Constitution and early presidential elections. But this did not satisfy the majority of protesters who demanded Ianukovych's immediate resignation from office and an investigation of the massacre of the "Heavenly Hundred."[7] The swift development of the conflict and failed negotiations with the opposition undermined Ianukovych's desperate attempts to preserve his power.

It appeared abundantly clear to Ianukovych that he would be arrested and accused of crimes against the Ukrainian people. Certainly, he would be questioned about the involvement of Russian security services in the killings of Maidan protesters. In February 2015, relying on information provided by Valentyn Nalyvaichenko, Ukraine's State Security Service chief at that time, President Petro Poroshenko claimed that Russian security services were involved in the bloody crackdown in Kyiv. He also stated that foreign snipers operating on the Maidan were supervised by Vladislav Surkov, Putin's advisor. According to Nalyvaichenko, the investigation of the crimes established that on February 21–22, 2014, during the clashes between militia and protesters, Surkov and FSB officers visited Kyiv:

---

7    For a discussion about the Maidan activists' demand that abolished agreements reached in Kyiv between the Ukrainian opposition and president and forced Ianukovych to flee the country, see Richard Balmforth, "In Ukraine Turbulence, a Lad from Lviv Becomes the Toast of Kiev," *Reuters*, February 25, 2014, http://www.reuters.com/article/us-ukraine-crisis-hero-insight-idUSBREA1O0JT20140225.

> ... we have the positions of those people, their surnames, copies of their passports, dates of arrival and departure how they communicated and where they were. We also know how and when Surkov, an assistant to President Putin, supervised them in Kyiv, [and] when they visited Yanukovych. [8]

Yet the Russian political leadership and Ukraine's fugitive president consistently denied their involvement in the shootings at the Maidan Nezalezhnosti.

Although the FSB operation in Kyiv failed, Russian special forces succeeded in Crimea. Let us take a closer look at Russia's "little green men" operation in Crimea.

## Evacuation of Ianukovych and Russia's "Little Green Men" Operation

Ianukovych left Kyiv on the night of February 21 and flew to Kharkiv, where he stayed overnight. The next day he headed to the Kharkiv airport and flew to Donetsk from where he planned to escape to Moscow. His plan failed to materialize as the staff at the Donetsk airport prevented Ianukovych from boarding a charter plane. The border patrol and the militia, however, did not dare to arrest the fleeing president, letting him continue his escape. Ianukovych directed his escort toward the southern Ukrainian city of Mariupol. A few hours later he freely passed the administrative border of the Autonomous Republic of Crimea (ARC) and headed to Yalta. Ukraine's newly appointed minister of the interior Arsen Avakov launched an operation to capture the fugitive. Logistically, because it takes approximately an hour to get from Yalta to Sevastopol by car, Avakov had a good chance of success. Nevertheless, on February 23 Ianukovych's escort reached Sevastopol, the base of the Russian Black Sea fleet, from where, with the assistance of the Russian marines brigade, he was transported to Novorossiisk. [9] In this context, it is important to keep in mind that by the time the "little green men" operation was launched in Crimea, Kyiv officials realized that they could not rely on the Crimean

---

8 "President Poroshenko Says Russia Was Involved in Shooting Euromaidan Protesters," *Ukraine Today*, February 24, 2015, http://uatoday.tv/politics/president-poroshenko-says-russia-was-involved-in-killing-euromaidan-protesters-410787.html.
9 "Marshrut vtechi Ianukovycha: ekskluzyvni podrobytsi," *TSN*, April 21, 2014, http://tsn.ua/politika/zhurnalisti-vidnovili-marshrut-vtechi-yanukovicha-v-rosiyu-346299.html.

administration, because many of them, sensing the changing wind of history, began to openly question the new government in Kyiv.

The Kremlin's intervention in the peninsula was preceded and supported by powerful anti-Ukrainian information warfare—both in the Russian and Crimean mass media. The latter, incidentally, had been generously subsidized by the Kremlin throughout the entire period of Ukraine's independence after the fall of the USSR.

After the bloody clashes on the Maidan Nezalezhnosti, events on the peninsula began to develop rapidly. On February 17, 2014 one of the most popular local newspapers *Krymskaia Pravda* (The Crimean Truth) published a brief announcement about the visit of the Crimean Supreme Council's chairman Vladimir Konstantinov to Moscow that had been planned for February 19–21, 2014, where he intended to meet the Chairman of the State Duma Sergei Naryshkin.[10] The purpose of this visit was to reach an agreement with Russian leaders on joint humanitarian projects in the ARC. Answering the State Duma deputies' questions about probable scenarios in Crimea, Konstantinov stated that if "extremists" in Kyiv used violence in order to come to power, the Russian Federation should not recognize their illegal government. He also suggested that at the moment there was no need for Russia to intervene to protect Crimean residents from "Ukrainian fascists." On February 20, the aforementioned newspaper appealed to Ukraine's minister of the interior: "Zaharchenko, wake up!" asking:

> Why are the militia units, who are attacked by armed militant groups, equipped only with batons, stun and gas grenades, and non-lethal weapons? How many more wounded officers and civilians do they need to finally pacify the radicals?[11]

To mobilize public opinion, Kremlin propaganda frightened Crimean Russians by spreading fictitious rumors that "Ukrainian radical nationalists" were heading to Crimea to take revenge on Russians for their political affinity, and that the Americans would place a NATO base in Sevastopol. These manipulations proved to be an extremely effective tool of the

---

10  "Predsedatel VS ARK vstretitsia so spikerom Gosdumy RF," *Krymskaia Pravda*, February 17, 2014, http://c-pravda.ru/news/2014/02/17/predsedatel-vs-arkvstretitsya-so-spikerom-gosdumy-rf.

11  Maksim Golovan, "Zaharchenko, prosnis! Banderovtsy ubivaiut militsionerov i mirnykh grazhdan," *Krymskaia Pravda*, February 20, 2014, http://c-pravda.ru/newspapers/2014/02/20/zakharchenko-prosnis.

escalation strategy aimed at justifying Russian military intervention in Crimea.[12] Many Russian inhabitants of the peninsula took this propaganda very seriously and indeed felt unsafe.

Shortly after Ianukovych's departure to Novorossiisk, on February 23 in Sevastopol, Russia-backed activists organized a demonstration "against the fascism in Ukraine," which gathered a few thousand participants. The protest officially aimed at supporting the so-called Anti-maidan, which was designed as a counterweight to the Maidan movement to demonstrate solidarity with Ianukovych's government. Interestingly, the protesters were carrying Russian flags and chanting "Russia!", "Putin—our president!" and the like. The crowd elected Aleksei Chalyi, a local businessman and pro-Russian activist, as the People's Mayor of Sevastopol, who promised to protect the city from illegitimate authorities in Kyiv.[13]

As there was no coherent reaction from Kyiv or local authorities, the separatists took the next step. On February 24 unidentified trucks blocked all the roads leading to the city, while pro-Russian residents formed a "Volunteer People's Squad" to "protect the city from the Banderites."[14] In response to these events, on February 25, in his speech to the parliament, the future Ukrainian Prime Minister Arsenii Iatseniuk emphasized that the government would not allow any separatism. Yet, beyond this warning, Ukrainian political leaders did little to prevent Russia's annexation of Crimea.

On February 25, two military trucks with Russian license plates carrying men without insignia arrived in Yalta. The Ukrainian social media were checkered with messages posted by Internet users about the increasing presence of unidentified soldiers in the city. While Internet users and local residents seemed to have no doubts about the soldiers' country of origin,[15] the Kremlin categorically denied the presence of any

---

12   For a discussion about the Russian information war strategy during Crimea's annexation, see Jolanta Darczewska, "The Anatomy of Russian Information Warfare. The Crimean Operation, a Case Study," *Centre for Eastern Studies* (OSW), Warsaw, no. 42, May 2014, http://www.osw.waw.pl/en/publikacje/point-view/2014-05-22/anatomy-russian-information-warfare-crimean-operation-a-case-study.

13   "Pobeda Sevastopolia 24 fevralia!" [incomplete title], *YouTube*, February 24, 2014, https://www.youtube.com/watch?v=Nqhdh-hRuDw.

14   Ibid.

15   "V Krymu rossiiskiie voiennyie s oruzhiiem zaniali Yaltu", *Neftegaz.ru*, February 25, 2014, http://neftegaz.ru/news/view/120391.

Russian troops in Crimea. On the same day, a group of deputies of the Russian State Duma came to the Crimean capital—Simferopol. Leonid Slutskii, head of the State Duma Committee on the "Commonwealth of Independent States, Eurasian Integration and Connections with Compatriots," delivered a speech which clearly formulated the Russian foreign policy doctrine: "If the life and health of Russian compatriots [*sootechestvenniki*] in Ukraine are threatened, we will not stand aside."[16]

By the next day, political tensions in Crimea had grown considerably. The Russian security services' activities in the peninsula became more brazen; the secessionists no longer concealed their intentions. Konstantinov convened an extraordinary session of the Supreme Council of Crimea. Its official agenda included the socio-political situation in the ARC and the government's annual report. Crimean Tatars, however, organized a rally outside the parliament building because their leaders had been alarmed about the plans of the regional authorities to vote for Crimea's secession from Ukraine. Refat Chubarov, head of the Mejlis, the single highest executive-representative body of the Crimean Tatars, called pro-Ukrainian activists to block the parliament building. Within a few hours, thousands of activists gathered outside the parliament. At the same time, another group of protesters, who represented pro-Russian organizations, opposed the Crimean Tatars' efforts by hanging Russian flags and chanting pro-Russian slogans. When the demonstrators from the two opposite camps clashed and the situation got out of control (two people died in the clashes), Refat Chubarov and the leader of the anti-Ukrainian group Sergei Aksionov persuaded people to go home, assuring them that a compromise was reached and the planned session of the parliament was cancelled.[17]

On the night of February 27, armed men in uniforms without insignia occupied local parliament and government buildings in Crimea. They did not voice any demands but warned that in case of assault they would

---

16   Berezovets, 55.
17   Two years after the annexation, February 26 became a day of commemoration in Ukraine, a day of Crimean peaceful civil resistance to Russian occupation. It has a symbolic meaning, as Kyiv's official narrative states that in February 2014 pro-Ukrainian activists abstaining from violence thwarted Putin's plans to incite local separatists to proclaim Crimea's separation from Ukraine, and then formally to ask the Russian president to send troops to protect its Crimean residents from the Banderites.

open fire. In response to these actions, the Crimean internal troops' commander Mykola Baran called the "Berkut" and "Alfa" special police forces for support, but they refused to cooperate. He also suggested closing the Kerch Straight, in case Russians tried to redeploy their troops to the peninsula, but the border guards ignored the request as well.[18] In the morning, deputies of the Supreme Council of the ARC arrived at their work place and the armed men wearing "balaclavas"[19] let them enter the occupied building. The deputies voted for the resolution to dismiss the Crimean government and for holding a referendum on the status of Crimea.[20] They also appointed the leader of the pro-Kremlin all-Crimean political movement "Russkoie iedinstvo" (Russian Unity) Sergei Aksionov as the new Prime Minister. The Kyiv authorities, however, considered the appointment illegal, arguing that this violated the constitution of ARC,[21] according to which the appointment of the head of the regional government should be approved by Ukraine's president. Yet the separatists explained that they had received Ianukovych's oral confirmation, whom they still considered as legitimate president, despite his escape to Russia. Ignoring Kyiv's denial to accept his new position, Aksionov took control of the local Ukrainian security forces and officially appealed to Putin to provide military assistance in "assuring peace" on the peninsula.[22]

On March 1 the Federation Council (the upper house of the Federal Assembly) gave the Russian president official permission to send troops to Ukraine.[23] Justifying the decision, the Russian authorities explained that they could not ignore the Crimean leader's request and promised to

---

18  Berezovets, 73–74.
19  "Balaclavas" are a type of headwear used by armed men to mask their faces during the occupation of the Crimean public buildings in February 2014.
20  Initially, the referendum was scheduled for May 25, but it was moved to an earlier date and held on March 16.
21  "Pro zatverdzhennia Konstytutsii Avtonomnoi Respubliky Krym," *Verkhovna rada Ukrainy, Zakon, Konstytutsiia № 350–XIV*, December 23, 1998, http://zakon4.rada.gov.ua/laws/show/350-14/page2.
22  "Ukraine Crisis: Crimea Leader Appeals to Putin for Help," *BBC News*, March 1, 2014, http://www.bbc.com/news/world-europe-26397323.
23  "Sovet Federatsii dal soglasie na ispolzovanie vooruzhennykh sil Rossii na territorii Ukrainy," *Sovet Federatsii Federalnogo Sobraniia Rossiiskoi Federatsii*, March 1, 2014, http://council.gov.ru/press-center/news/39851/.

help.[24] As mentioned earlier, several days before the decision, heavily armed men wearing uniforms without insignia and driving unidentified vehicles, surrounded airports and the most important communication centers. They appeared in major Crimean cities and towns. A year after Crimea's annexation Putin officially acknowledged that he had ordered the deployment of troops to the peninsula in February 2014 to "support Crimean self-defense forces."[25] The "little green men" attacked Ukrainian military bases and other strategic facilities in order to disable and commandeer them. They took charge of the state television and radio station buildings under the pretext that they had to "protect" these important objects from "provocateurs."

The decision about the annexation of the peninsula had been made before the referendum. Under the protection of the Russian army, the local separatists announced a referendum on the status of Crimea which was held on March 16, 2014. At gunpoint, 97% of voters in Crimea agreed to join Russia.[26] Ukrainian officials did not recognize the referendum as legitimate and called on the peninsula's inhabitants to boycott the voting. The ballot contained two questions:

> 1. "Do you support the reunification of Crimea with Russia with all the rights of the federal subject of the Russian Federation?"
> 2. "Do you support the restoration of the Constitution of the Republic of Crimea in 1992 and the status of the Crimea as part of Ukraine?"

There was no option to preserve the status quo. According to the data released by Russian authorities, over 96% of inhabitants eligible to vote supported Crimea's and Sevastopol's "reunification" with Russia. The Mejlis, however, stated that the majority of Crimean Tatars boycotted the "referendum." Importantly, the Crimean Parliament adopted an independence declaration, necessary for holding a March 16 referendum, which

---

24 "Moscow Says It Won't Ignore Crimean PM's Call for Help," *QHA*, March 1, 2014, http://qha.com.ua/en/search?q=Moscow+says+it+won%27t+ignore+Crimean+PM%27s+call+for+help.
25 At the beginning of the Kremlin's special operation in Crimea, pro-Russian separatists created what they were calling "self-defence units" that included, among others, veterans from the Afghan and Chechen wars, bikers, "Cossacks," and former "Berkut" officers from Crimea who participated in brutal dispersing of Maidan in January and February 2014.
26 "Putin Reveals Secrets of Russia's Crimea Takeover Plot," *BBC News*, March 9, 2015, http://www.bbc.com/news/world-europe-31796226.

paved the way for the March 16 referendum on Crimea and for the city of Sevastopol to join Russia.[27] On March 18 in his speech in the Kremlin, Putin stated that Russia was ready to accept Crimea as part of its territory, offering the following justification:

> In people's hearts and minds, Crimea has always been an inseparable part of Russia. This firm conviction is based on truth and justice and was passed from generation to generation, over time, under any circumstances, despite all the dramatic changes our country went through during the entire 20th century.[28]

## Why Crimea?

There are many versions of the reasons behind Putin's decision to annex Crimea in March 2014.[29] Some believe that the Kremlin had been preparing the ground for annexation for a long time. Others claim that Russia's final decision to annex Crimea was shaped immediately after the Orange Revolution in 2004/2005, when then Ukrainian president Viktor Iushchenko announced that his government would not prolong the Ukraine-Russia agreement on the stationing of the Russian Black Sea Fleet in Sevastopol (the agreement was to expire in 2017).[30] There is,

---

27 "Crimea Parliament Signs Independence Declaration ahead of Referendum," *Independent.mk*, March 11, 2014, http://www.independent.mk/articles/2502/Crimea+Parliament+Signs+Independence+Declaration+ahead+of+Referendum.

28 "Address by President of the Russian Federation," *President of Russia* (official website), March 18, 2014, http://en.kremlin.ru/events/president/news/20603.

29 For a discussion about the reasons for the annexation of Crimea, see Maria Gołda-Sobczak, *Krym jako przedmiot sporu ukraińsko-rosyjskiego* (Poznań: Wydawnictwo Naukowe Silva Rerum, 2016), 183–87.

30 For an analysis of the Orange Revolution's achievements and losses, see Maciej Wapiński, "The Orange Revolution and its Aftermath," in *The Maidan Uprising, Separatism and Foreign Intervention: Ukraine's Complex Transition*, eds. Klaus Bachmann and Igor Lyubashenko (Frankfurt am Main: Peter Lang, 2014), 43–61. According to well-known political analyst Vitalii Portnikov, one has to take into consideration intelligence operations and the pre-history of Crimea's occupation and parts of Lugansk and Donetsk regions in eastern Ukraine which began not in 1990s, as many believe, but earlier—in 1988–1989. The Soviet leaders realized that they could lose control over the national republics and initiated a range of projects in Abkhazia, North Ossetia, Transnistria and Gagauzia which were designed to deepen their internal contradictions and tensions. When the time was ripe, Russia thawed the frozen conflicts to reach its own political objectives by destabilizing these regions. See Berezovets, 44.

however, another opinion according to which the Russian leader's decision to annex Crimea was a direct response to the Maidan protests in Kyiv. The infamous official excuse expressed by Putin was the necessity to "protect Russian-speaking inhabitants of the peninsula from Ukrainian nationalists." A potential underlying reason for Putin's decisive actions might have been his need to preserve his image as a strong Russian leader in the eyes of Russian compatriots, Russian citizens who expected an "appropriate" reaction to Maidan from their president and, most importantly, in the eyes of the Western political elite. This explanation seems quite plausible in light of Putin's declining approval ratings domestically. The Crimean annexation was to boost them. Let us take a closer look at the periods of Putin's greatest popularity, which may, at least partially, confirm this argument.

The Russian leader's approval rating reached one of its peaks in November 1999, when the country was sunk into the second Chechen War (1999–2009). Putin's decisive and uncompromising position and Russia's military actions in Chechnia inspired Russian patriotism and convinced 80% of Putin's fellow citizens of the Russian leader's fitness for his post. Furthermore, in September 2008, during the military conflict with Georgia, Putin's popularity as Prime Minister jumped to 88%.[31] The latest explosion of citizens' approval ratings came after the annexation of Crimea, when Russians rewarded their president's "brilliant special operation" with an 82% endorsement in April 2014 and even 86% a few months later.[32]

Indeed, Putin managed to persuade the majority of Russian citizens that Ukraine's return to the European integration path and Kyiv's political orientation toward the West meant a step away from Moscow's political orbit, a negative development fraught with geopolitical ramifications for Russia. Moreover, in the case of Ukraine's successful reforms, this shift could become an attractive model for other post-Soviet countries, including the Russian Federation itself. In fact, a neighboring democratic

---

31  "Vsio ruhnulo, krome reitinga prezidenta (an interview with the expert of "Levada Center" Denis Volkov), *BBC Russkaia sluzhba*, January 6, 2015, http://www.bbc.com/russian/russia/2015/01/150105_levada_volkov_putin_15_years?ocid=wsrus_rus_psc_facebook_mkt_fe_news_na.
32  See more data about Putin's ratings in "Maiskiie reitingi odobreniia i doveriia," *Levada-Tsentr*, May 23–26, 2014, http://www.levada.ru/old/29-05-2014/maiskie-reitingi-odobreniya-i-doveriya.

state with too many freedoms would be lethal for Putin's regime, jeopardizing the survival of the well-established Russian regimented society.

Significantly, Crimea has always played a very special role in the Russian founding myth. It is associated with dramatic episodes of Russian history, such as the Crimean War (1853–1856) and the Great Patriotic War (1941–1944).[33] Although Russian dominance over the peninsula dates back only to 1783, when Catherine the Great took control over the territory disintegrating the Crimean Khanate, the Russian official narrative treats Crimea as a "native Russian land," ignoring the fact that Russian presence in the peninsula accounts for only 170 years of the region's almost three-thousand year history. Andrew Wilson's calculation is even more modest:

> The Russian Empire annexed Crimea in 1783, but it was only ever truly Russian from the Crimean War of 1853–56 until 1917, and then from 1945–54 (it was a separate Soviet Republic from 1921–1945) . . . By my calculation, Crimea was Russian for seventy-three years after 1853; then it was Ukrainian for for sixty years from 1954 to 2014, which isn't so different. Before that, it belonged to the Crimean Tatars for at least 400 years.[34]

Moreover, Russians outnumbered other ethnic groups in the peninsula only in 1917, when the population of Crimea's indigenous people, the Crimean Tatars, dramatically declined as a result of mass emigration to the Ottoman Empire.[35] Yet the takeover of Crimea in 2014 has been recognized by many Russians as the restoration of historical justice, and it comes as no surprise that the Kremlin ruling elites fully share this sentiment.

---

33 For instance, on the contemporary myth of Sevastopol as the city of Russian glory, see Serhii Plokhy, "The City of Glory: Sevastopol in Russian Historical Mythology," *Journal of Contemporary History* 35, no. 3 (2000): 369-83.
34 Andrew Wilson, *Ukraine Crisis: What it Means for the West* (New Haven and London: Yale University Press, 2014), 100.
35 Pavel Kazarin and Olga Dukhnich, eds., "Antologiia sovremennoi krymskoi mifologii. Rossiiskiie i ukrainskiie mify o Kryme, krymchanakh, krymskikh tatarakh i anneksii," *Krym. Realii*, February 26, 2016, http://ru.krymr.com/media/photogallery/27575254.html.

## The Kremlin's Policy toward Ukraine: Undermining Its Sovereignty

Ianukovych's presidency weakened Ukraine's independence and its ability to resist serious external threats. In 2010 under Kharkiv Accords, Kyiv extended the lease on the Russian Black Sea Fleet base in Sevastopol for another twenty-five years in exchange for a discount on Russian gas. As a result, Moscow increased its naval and military capabilities in Crimea, and used them during the Crimean occupation in February–March 2014.[36] The annexation of Crimea and the military aggression in the Donbas region forced the Ukrainian post-Maidan government to adopt a new version of the military doctrine in which for the first time since 1991, the Russian Federation was recognized as a threat to Ukraine's sovereignty.[37] The earlier 2004 version of Ukraine's military doctrine was identified as defensive, as no specifications regarding potential security threats were included in it.[38] Instead, the doctrine made a reference to the Budapest Memorandum on Security Assurances, a political agreement signed on December 5, 1994 in Hungary, which provided Ukraine with security assurances by its signatories in exchange for Ukraine's compliance with the Treaty on the Nonproliferation of Nuclear Weapons.[39] The Memorandum was originally signed by three nuclear powers—the Russian Federation, the United States of America, and the United Kingdom. China and France joined the initiative later, signing separate sets of documents.

---

36  Dmitrii Orlov, "Kharkovskiie soglasheniia v tsifrakh i faktakh," *Fokus*, April 29, 2013, http://focus.ua/country/268583; see also "Dohovir Ianukovycha i Medvedeva pro bazuvannia flotu do 2042 roku. Tekst dokumentu," *Ukrainska pravda*, April 22, 2010, http://www.pravda.com.ua/articles/2010/04/22/4956018.

37  "Ukaz Prezydenta Ukrainy pro rishennia Rady natsionalnoi bezpeky i oborony Ukrainy vid 2 veresnia 2015 roku 'Pro novu redaktsiiu Voiennoi doktryny Ukrainy,'" *Verkhovna Rada Ukrainy*, September 24, 2015, http://zakon5.rada.gov.ua/laws/show/555/2015.

38  "Ukaz Prezydenta Ukrainy pro voiennu doktrynu Ukrainy," *Verkhovna Rada Ukrainy*, June 15, 2004 (ed. June 8, 2012), http://zakon4.rada.gov.ua/laws/show/648/2004.

39  "Memorandum on Security Assurances in Connection with Ukraine's Accession to the Treaty on the NPT," *Permanent Mission of the Republic of Poland to the United Nations Office and International Organizations in Vienna*, December 19, 1994, https://www.msz.gov.pl/en/p/wiedenobwe_at_s_en/news/memorandum_on_security_assurances_in_connection_with_ukraine_s_accession_to_the_treaty_on_the_npt.

As Russia's puppet, Ianukovych facilated the Kremlin's efforts to keep Ukraine in its orbit by using a carrot and stick approach. When the EU delayed signing the association agreement with Kyiv (planned for March 30, 2012) in response to violations of the electoral law as well as the imprisonment of former Prime Minister and prominent opposition leader Iuliia Tymoshenko, the Russians exploited the opportunity, pressing Kyiv to join the Eurasian Customs Union. The Kremlin promised economic benefits if Kyiv agreed, and threatened Ukraine with sanctions if the answer was negative.[40] The Ukrainian government's vacillation further provoked Putin who did not seem to give up on Ukraine. Before the next EU-UA summit in Vilnius, Moscow strengthened its political and economic pressure on Ianukovych's regime, combining it with an attractive offer of a $15 billion loan for joining the Eurasian Customs Union. In Ianukovych's world, this offer was attractive from both economic and political perspectives: Russia's support would make his governing smoother and less vulnerable.[41] Yet, accepting Russia's offer cost Ianukovych his presidency: as in the past, he ignored popular attitudes toward the values he represented, and disregarded the resilience and increased political activism of a new generation of Ukrainians. None of Ukraine's previous political leaders dared to deceive their citizens as arrogantly as Ianukovych did by granting them hope for closer ties with Europe and then withdrawing his promise for his own personal gain.

During its history as an independent state, Ukraine should be considered a non-typical case: Ukrainian citizens had an opportunity to elect five presidents. In the post-Soviet period, Russia had three presidents, including Putin who has been governing the country for over 15 years. In Belarus, President Aleksandr Lukashenka has been in office since 1994. In Kazakhstan, Nursultan Nazarbaiev has been ruling since 1991. Indeed, Ukraine's presidential history differs from that of its neighboring states. Ukraine's second president Leonid Kuchma was the only one reelected for a second term. His predecessor Leonid Kravchuk and the third

---

40   Marcel H. Van Herpen, *Viiny Putina. Chechnia, Hruziia, Ukraina: nezasvoieni uroky mynuloho*, trans. from English (unknown translator), the original title: *Putin's Wars: The Rise of Russia's New Imperialism* (Kharkiv: Vivat, 2015), 296–302.

41   Timothy Heritage and Katya Golubkova, "Russia Eyes Loan, Gas Deal to Keep Ukraine in its Orbit," *Reuters,* December 16, 2013, http://www.reuters.com/article/us-ukraine-russia-idUSBRE9BF0GV20131216.

president Viktor Iushchenko each served only one term. After five years as president, Iushchenko failed to be re-elected in 2010 and voluntarily relinquished power to his opponent from the Orange Revolution, Ianukovych. Clearly, the Soviet gerontological tendencies empowering General Secretaries to govern until their complete senility or death, or post-Soviet authoritarian trends symptomatic of Russia, Belarus, and Kazakhstan, which allow politicians to stay in power for several consecutive terms do not seem to survive in the Ukrainian political and social climate. These dynamics demonstrate that Ianukovych made a serious mistake, underestimating the power of Ukrainian civil society. The scale of corruption of Ianukovych's administartion combined with the president's lack of modesty and sense of proportion sealed his fate. Had he been more humble in his pursuit of power and wealth, he might have occupied the president's office much longer, and Ukraine's latest history would have been very different.

After the 2010 elections, because of Ianukovych's pro-Russian stance, many experts forecast an improvement in relations between Russia and Ukraine. Under Iushchenko, they deteriorated, and Russia increasingly radicalized its rhetoric related to Ukraine, and also strengthened its economic pressure on Kyiv. The logic behind Russia's aggressive policies toward Ukraine rested in Iushchenko's political course that was aimed at solidifying independent Ukrainian institutions and transforming the Ukrainians' historical memory which was burdened by Soviet taboos and stereotypes. The Kremlin's strategy between 2005 and 2010 was designed to marginalize the pro-Western "orange" elites of Ukraine and to expose their inability to solve growing economic and political problems without Moscow's protection. Fortunately for the Kremlin, a political split in the "orange camp," which occurred soon after Iushchenko appointed his political ally Iuliia Tymoshenko as Prime Minister, facilitated Moscow's efforts to discredit the Ukrainian leaders and undermine their agenda to join the North Atlantic Treaty Organization. In April 2008, during the NATO-Russia Council meeting in Bucharest, Putin identified Ukraine as

> . . . a very complicated state. Ukraine, in the form it currently exists, was created in the Soviet times, it received its territories from Poland—after the Second World war, from Czechoslovakia, from Romania—and at present not all the problems have been solved as yet in the border region with Romania in the Black Sea. Then, it received huge territories from Russia in the east and south

of the country. It is a complicated state formation. If we introduce into it NATO problems, other problems, it may put the state on the verge of its existence. Complicated internal political problems are taking place there. We should act also very-very carefully. We do not have any right to veto, and, probably, we do not pretend to have. But I want that all of us, when deciding such issues, realize that we have there our interests as well. Well, seventeen million Russians currently live in Ukraine. Who may state that we do not have any interests there? South, the south of Ukraine, completely, there are only Russians.[42]

In contrast to Iushchenko, Ianukovych gravitated toward Russia, and Moscow embraced this opportunity to return Ukraine, a "complicated state formation," to its sphere of influence.

Traditionally, the Russian political elites' anti-Ukrainian rhetoric was disseminated and reinforced by the Kremlin-controlled media which shaped popular hostile attitudes in Russia toward Ukraine. Numerous high-ranking politicians, such as Moscow's former mayor Iurii Luzhkov, actively promoted Russia's historical claims to Crimea and Sevastopol, demanding the Russian parliament denounce Nikita Khrushchev's 1954 decree on transferring the Crimean oblast' to the Ukrainian SSR. They also appealed to the Kremlin's commitment to defend Russian-speaking residents in the peninsula and in the Donbas from the Ukrainian nationalists. Moreover, since 2008 Russia launched a mass campaign of distribution of Russian passports to the residents of Sevastopol and other cities of Crimea.[43] Routinely, Aleksandr Zaldostanov, Putin's friend and the leader of the "Night Wolves," Russia's largest motorcycle club which happened to be a recipient of considerable funding in the form of state grants, organized motocycle rallies with Russian flags in many Crimean cities and towns, advocating Crimea's cessation from Ukraine.[44] All these activities, involving intelligence operations, laid the foundation for the Russian annexation of the peninsula in 2014.

The most substantial barrier that somewhat disturbed Russian propaganda, which claimed that Crimea for years "dreamed about returning

---

42  "Text of Putin's Speech at NATO Summit (Bucharest, April 2, 2008)," *UNIAN*, April 18, 2008, http://www.unian.info/world/111033-text-of-putins-speech-at-nato-summit-bucharest-april-2-2008.html.
43  Adrian Blomfield, "Russia 'Distributing Passports in the Crimea,'" *The Telegraph*, August 17, 2008, http://www.telegraph.co.uk/news/worldnews/europe/ukraine/2575421/Russia-distributing-passports-in-the-Crimea.html.
44  "Putin's Patriotic Biker-Friend Says Crimea is Only Start, Kyiv is Next," *Independent.mk*, April 8, 2014, http://www.independent.mk/articles/3596/Putins+Patriotic+Biker-Friend+Says+Crimea+is+Only+Start,+Kyiv+is+Next.

to the bosom of its motherland,"[45] were the Crimean Tatars. Despite their relatively small size among Crimea's two million population, Crimean Tatars are a politically unified and well mobilized group of pro-Ukrainian residents in the penninsula. To neutralize the Crimean Tatars' national movement and its leadership, the Kremlin drove a wedge between them. After 2010 Moscow began to finance new organizations led by little-known activists, who identified themselves as the opposition to the Mejlis. They began to attack its leaders Mustafa Dzhemilev, famous Soviet dissident and member of the Ukrainian parliament, and Refat Chubarov, head of the Mejlis. After the annexation of Crimea in 2014, the Kremlin used these activists to create a group of loyal Crimean Tatar politicians and appointed them as high-ranking officials in the Crimean government. Importantly, some Crimean Tatar NGOs, which supported the annexation of the peninsula, demanded delegalization of the Mejlis as an extremist organization, accusing its leaders Dzhemilev and Chubarov, who were earlier banned from entering Crimea by the Crimean prosecutor general, of provoking ethno-political conflicts in the region.[46] On April 18, 2016, Crimea's Ministry of Justice suspended the Mejlis for what it called "extremist activities." According to the Ministry, the Mejlis is now prohibited "from using all state and municipal media, holding various public mass events, using bank accounts or conducting any type of work."[47] The Ministry claimed that the decision was grounded in the April 13 order of Crimea's Moscow-backed prosecutor Natalia Poklonskaia, who called for the suspension of the Mejlis. The international community reacted to this instantly. For instance, on April 21, 2016, John Kirby, Assistant Secretary and U.S. Department of State Spokesperson (Bureau of Public Affairs in Washington, DC) released a press statement on the Russian Federation's decision to suspend the Crimean Tatar Mejlis, which reads:

> We call on the Russian Federation to reverse the Ministry of Justice's recent decision to designate the Crimean Tatar Mejlis as an "extremist" organization and the decision by de facto authorities in Crimea to suspend this democratic

---

45 For a discussion about Kremlin-produced myths about "Native Russian Crimea," see Kazarin and Dukhnich, "Antologiia sovremennoi krymskoi mifologii."
46 "Zaboronyty Mejlis—mriia prokuratury aneksovanoho Krymu," *Deutsche Welle Ukraine*, February 19, 2016, http://dw.com/p/1HwvL.
47 "Russia Suspends Crimean Tatar Mejlis for 'Alleged Extremist Activities,'" *Daily Sabah*, April 19, 2016, http://www.dailysabah.com/europe/2016/04/19/russia-suspends-crimean-tatar-mejlis-for-alleged-extremist-activities.

institution. The Mejlis has long been a representative body for the traditionally under-represented and historically oppressed Crimean Tatar population. It has also served as an important independent voice in preserving their culture and protecting them from discrimination.

Russian authorities have no basis or jurisdiction to assert Russian law over Tatar conduct in Ukraine. A ban on the Mejlis would prohibit it from convening, publishing its views in mass media, or holding public events, which contravenes basic democratic principles. This action is the latest in a series of abuses perpetrated by de facto authorities against those in Crimea who oppose the occupation, including Crimean Tatars and members of other ethnic and religious minorities in Crimea. Such abuses include arbitrary detentions, beatings, and police raids on their homes and places of worship.

We again call on Russia to end its occupation of Crimea and return control over this piece of Ukrainian territory. Sanctions related to Crimea will remain in place as long as the occupation continues.[48]

Yet the Russian authorities remained deaf to this call, and a new wave of repressions was launched against the Mejlis's regional leaders and local journalists, those who have not yet left Crimea. Chubarov informed the international community that on April 19–21, 2016, the authorities conducted searches in the homes of seven Tatar journalists. He revealed only four names of Mykola Semena, Ruslan Liumanov, Zair Akadyrov, and Leniara Abibullaieva.[49] In all, it should be recognized that the Kremlin's intimidation tactics and the "divide and conquer" strategy against Crimean Tatar political leaders and organizations have thus far been successful.

## From a Peninsula to an Island: Crimea in Isolation

Ukraine, the United States, Canada, Australia and other countries as well as international organizations such as the United Nations, NATO, the European Union, and the Venice Commission have condemned the annexation of Crimea by the Russian Federation as illegal and dismissed the 2014 Crimean "referendum" results. The United Nations General Assembly's resolution on Crimea affirmed its

---

48  See Kirby's press statement at *U.S. Department of State* official site, April 21, 2016, http://www.state.gov/r/pa/prs/ps/2016/04/256480.htm.
49  "Pro novu khvyliu represii u Krymu zaiavliaie Mejlis," *Ekspres.ua*, April 21, 2016, http://expres.ua/news/2016/04/21/183608-novu-hvylyu-represiy-krymu-zayavlyaye-medzhlis. See also "Zair Akadyrov Told Details of Yesterday's Raid," *QHA*, April 20, 2016, http://qha.com.ua/en/politics/zair-akadyrov-told-details-of-yesterday-s-raid/136889/.

commitment to Ukraine's sovereignty, political independence, unity and territorial integrity within its internationally recognized borders, underscoring the invalidity of the March 16 referendum held in autonomous Crimea.[50]

Furthermore, the West responded to Russian military intervention in Ukraine by imposing painful sanctions on the country and high-ranking Russian officials as well as many Crimean companies, isolating them from Western markets and contracts. Tourism, which has always been an important source of income for the residents of the peninsula, collapsed in the summer of 2014 and since that time mainly relies on visitors from Russia and the occupied parts of Luhansk and Donetsk regions. Due to sanctions as well as a communication blockade, Ukrainians, who traditionally accounted for two-thirds of tourists in the region, are now snubbing it in favour of other destinations.[51]

The isolation continued to deepen when in December 2014 Ukraine's government cancelled train connections with the peninsula.[52] Later, on September 20, 2015, Crimean Tatars along with other Ukrainian activists, including the members of Right Sector, Automaidan, Maidan Self-Defense and territorial defense battalions, launched a "Crimean Blockade"—a civil initiative aimed at blocking the flow of goods from mainland Ukraine to Crimea.[53] The blockade activists demanded that the Kremlin release Ukrainian political prisoners held in Russia, enable the independent media to work in Crimea, and lift the ban on Crimean Tatar leaders Mustafa Dzhemilev and Refat Chubarov from entering the peninsula.[54] In addition, the "Crimean civic blockade" activists appealed

---

50   "General Assembly Adopts Resolution Calling upon States Not to Recognize Changes in Status of Crimea Region," *United Nations. Meeting Coverage and Press Releases*, March 27, 2014, http://www.un.org/press/en/2014/ga11493.doc.htm.
51   Stas Yurchenko, Usein Dzhabbarov, and Claire Bigg, "Tourist Season A Washout In Annexed Crimea," *Radio Free Europe. Radio Liberty*, July 5, 2014, http://www.rferl.org/content/tourist-season-washout-in-annexed-crimea/25446604.html.
52   "Ukrainian Railways Cuts Rail Links with Crimea Over Security Fears," *UNIAN*, December 26, 2014, http://www.unian.info/society/1026678-ukrainian-railways-cuts-rail-links-with-crimea-over-security-fears.html.
53   Rafał Sadowski, "The Blockade of Crimea," *The Centre for Eastern Studies* (OSW), September 30, 2015, http://www.osw.waw.pl/en/publikacje/analyses/2015-09-30/blockade-crimea.
54   For more information about the human rights violations in annexed Crimea, see "Human Rights in Crimea. Rollback Three Centuries," *Crimea SOS*, accessed April 23, 2016, http://crimeamap.krymsos.com/eng/map.html. See also Taras

to Kyiv's officials to invalidate the free economic zone in Crimea, established by the Ukrainian parliament, which allowed private companies to trade with the occupied territories on preferential terms. Initially, both Russian and Ukrainian officials did not pay much attention to the blockade, although it certainly had the unofficial support of Kyiv's authorities. The situation changed on November 21–22, 2015, when a series of powerful explosions at the administrative border with Crimea cut off power delivered from Ukraine, forcing the peninsula, as well as some parts of the Ukrainian Kherson oblast, to rely on generators.

In November, the Crimean prosecutor began a criminal investigation against one of the leaders of the blockade and former Russian businessman Lenur Isliamov. He is the owner of the Crimean Tatar TV channel ATR, which after the annexation had to move its headquarters from Crimea to Kyiv.[55] Isliamov was accused by the Crimean authorities of organizing the blockade and leading the extremists who blew up the high-voltage power transmission lines supplying Crimea with Ukrainian energy.[56] In December 2015, the government in Kyiv yielded to the pressure of the blockade activists and announced the suspension of power supplies to occupied Crimea, beginning in January 2016. Ukraine's officials, however, emphasized that the contract could be resumed if Russia would agree to identify Crimea as a "temporarily occupied territory of Ukraine." This condition, however, was unacceptable for Putin. Such a concession would tarnish his reputation as an indomitable politician. The Kremlin's indirect but clear answer came on January 1, 2016, when the Russian Public Opinion Research Center released an opinion poll, in which Crimean residents were asked via telephone whether they wanted to receive Ukrainian power under the aforementioned condition. According to the released data, the majority of the respondents answered that they were willing to endure rolling blackouts until the construction of the

---

Burnos, "V Ukraine nachalas aktsiia—'Grazhdanskaia blokada Kryma,'" *Golos Ameriki,* September 20, 2015, http://www.golos-ameriki.ru/content/medzhlis-starts-blocade-of-crimea/2971279.html.

55 For more details about the situation with the Ukrainian mass media under Russian rule, see Sergey Suhoboychenko, *Crimean Media after Annexation. Analytical Report* (Warsaw: The Eastern European Democratic Center Association, 2015).

56 "Lenur Islyamov's Property Is Seized—Poklonskaya," *QHA,* December 3, 2015, http://qha.com.ua/en/politics/lenur-islyamov-s-property-is-seized-poklonskaya/135153/.

planned second line of the energy bridge from the Kuban region is completed.[57] At the end of 2015, Russia finished the project—the energy bridge to the peninsula via the Kerch Straight (with a capacity of approximately 460 MW), which, together with a significant increase in the amount of energy produced in the peninsula (according to the official Russian statistics, approximately 450 MW), noticeably reduced the need for power from Ukraine.[58]

Meanwhile, due to the Russian-Ukrainian "trade war," which began with the formal accession of Ukraine to the free trade zone with the European Union on January 1, 2016, Kyiv has not restored the power flow to the peninsula. Undoubtedly, Crimea's complete freedom from Ukraine's energy supplies, which Russia scheduled for 2016, requires considerable financial investments, including the renovation of Crimea's entire infrastructure. Yet it seems likely that sooner rather than later the Kremlin will be able to solve the energy deficit problem. It is also likely that Crimea's dependence on Ukraine and Crimea's problems with food supplies and transport communications will persist at least until 2018, if a mega-project, the construction of the Kerch Strait Bridge, is completed. The Western sanctions, low oil prices, challenging climate conditions in the area, and Russia's growing economic difficulties may delay the project for an indefinite time. It is also possible that the project might be cancelled, and Russia's "historic mission" of building the bridge (Putin's definition)[59] within coming years would fail for both economic and political reasons.

## Conclusion

Russia's military intervention and annexation of Crimea in March 2014 has become the most serious challenge to Ukraine's sovereignty since 1991. The Revolution of Dignity erupted as people's reaction to the government's resignation from the European integration plans in November 2013. The protesters went into the streets of Kyiv and other Ukrainian

---

57   "Problema postavok elektroenergii v Krym: itogi vserossiiskogo oprosa," *WCIOM*, Press-Vypusk, no. 3026, January 27, 2016, http://wciom.ru/index.php?id=236&uid=115562.

58   Tadeusz Iwański and Jan Strzelecki, "Energia elektryczna znów płynie na Krym," *OSW*, December 16, 2016, http://www.osw.waw.pl/pl/publikacje/analizy/2015-12-16/energia-elektryczna-znow-plynie-na-krym.

59   Mikhail Metzel, "Putin Calls Construction of Bridge Across Kerch Strait Historic Mission," *TASS*, March 18, 2016, http://tass.ru/en/politics/863439.

cities to defend democracy and their civil rights. The brutality of the police and special forces transformed the peaceful protests into a bloodbath. Ukrainians paid a high price for changing the corrupt government and restoring the European vector of Ukraine's development—human lives and lost territories.

The international community of politicians and scholars advocate a return of the Crimean peninsula to Ukraine, but both Ukrainian and Western experts agree that there is no military solution to the Crimean problem. Russia's annexation created a dangerous precedent and set an example for other regions of frozen conflicts marked by separatist tendencies (i.e. Venetism [a regionalist movement], Catalan, Basque, and Scottish movements for independence). Regardless of the political and economic situation in Russia, which in 2016 continued to deteriorate due to, *inter alia*, falling global oil prices, the effects of Western sanctions, and the costs of maintaining the Crimean peninsula and the separatist republics in the occupied parts of the Donbas, the issue of resolving the Crimean occupation problem for Ukraine largely depends on its ability to carry out in-depth fundamental reforms and to create an effective economic model, which could be attractive for the residents of post-Soviet states, including occupied Crimea. Some analysts have argued that Russian incorporation of Crimea as one of the units of the Federation will complicate the legal procedure for potential restoration of Crimea as part of sovereign Ukraine.

According to the Ukrainian journalist and political analyst Vitalii Portnikov, Crimea's return to Ukraine is possible only after the disintegration of Russia.[60] In this context, two questions seem especially relevant: how long would it take to formally "transfer" the peninsula back to Ukraine, and what to do with hundreds of thousands of Russia-oriented inhabitants of Crimea who believe that the current Ukrainian state is governed by fascists? The social, cultural and demographic forcible reconfiguration of the peninsula, which is associated with de-Ukrainization and the elimination of Tatar opposition, significantly problematizes Crimea's potential return to Ukraine's orbit. Importantly, a large part of the

---

60  For an analysis of potential conditions for Crimea's return to Ukraine by the Russian Federation, see "Portnikov: Krym vernut mozhno lish putiom territorialnoi dezintegratsii Rossii," *15 Minut,* February 26, 2016, http://www.15minut.org/news158041-portnikov-krym-vernut-mozhno-lish-putem-territorialnoj-dezigracii-rossii.

pro-European political elites in Kyiv might contest the reintegration of Crimea into Ukraine's political system due to their concerns about the growing influence of the pro-Russian electorate on Ukraine's political life and its vector of development. What is clear is that conditions that might potentially force the Russian political elites to discuss the issue of Crimea's return appear unimaginable under Putin's rule.

Apart from these considerations, it seems obvious today that the annexation of Crimea was only part of Moscow's broader geopolitical strategy. It would be naïve to believe that Russia used aggression against Ukraine only to punish it for its "disloyalty." The recent dynamics in the Donbas region suggest that Putin's plan includes the long-term destabilization of Ukraine to hinder its government's efforts to implement democratic reforms which would bring Ukraine closer to the West, out of Russia's sphere of influence. For many reasons that have been discussed in this volume, Moscow considers Ukraine's close cooperation with the West as a threat to its strategic interests in the region.

Similarly, in the early 1990s Russia, less aggressively, opposed the integration of Poland and the Baltic states into the Euro-Atlantic structures. Twenty years later, the Russian Federation seems to be better positioned (financially and militarily) to embark on conventional warfare with its neighboring states to return them to Russian control. Ukraine proved to be important for Russia today, as it was in the past. And as in the past, in the face of aggression, the Ukrainians' perceptions are shaped by it: they feel that they are a "constantly besieged community," and the "orphans of the universe" who "had no external protectors or patrons."[61]

Indeed, serious geopolitical challenges, such as the economic and migration crisis, the fight against Islamic fundamentalism, and the rise of right-wing political movements in Europe, weakens the West, preventing it from strong financial and political support for Ukraine. Nevertheless, in becoming a modern European state, a great deal depends on Ukraine itself and on how wisely the Ukrainian government will use the trust of the Ukrainian people granted to them during the Euromaidan.

---

61 George Liber, *Total Wars and the Making of Modern Ukraine, 1914–1954* (Toronto: University of Toronto Press, 2016), 107.

## Bibliography

"Address by President of the Russian Federation." *President of Russia* (official website). March 18, 2014. http://en.kremlin.ru/events/president/news/20603.

Balmforth, Richard. "In Ukraine Turbulence, a Lad from Lviv Becomes the Toast of Kiev." *Reuters*. February 25, 2014. http://www.reuters.com/article/us-ukraine-crisis-hero-insight-idUSBREA1O0JT20140225.

Berezovets, Taras. *Aneksiia: ostriv Krym. Khroniky "hibrydnoi viiny."* Kyiv: Bright Star Publishing, 2015.

Blomfield, Adrian. "Russia 'Distributing Passports in the Crimea.'" *The Telegraph*. August 17, 2008. http://www.telegraph.co.uk/news/worldnews/europe/ukraine/2575421/Russia-distributing-passports-in-the-Crimea.html.

Burnos, Taras. "V Ukraine nachalas aktsiia—'Grazhdanskaia blokada Kryma.'" *Golos Ameriki*. September 20, 2015. http://www.golos-ameriki.ru/content/medzhlis-starts-blocade-of-crimea/2971279.html.

Butkevych, Bohdan, and Andrii Skumin. "Chy povstane Ukraina." *Tyzhden.ua*. July 18, 2013. http://tyzhden.ua/Politics/84289.

"Crimea Parliament Signs Independence Declaration ahead of Referendum." *Independent.mk*. March 11, 2014. http://www.independent.mk/articles/2502/Crimea+Parliament+Signs+Independence+Declaration+ahead+of+Referendum.

Darczewska, Jolanta. "The Anatomy of Russian Information Warfare. The Crimean Operation, a Case Study." *Centre for Eastern Studies* (OSW), Warsaw, no. 42 (2014). http://www.osw.waw.pl/en/publikacje/point-view/2014-05-22/anatomy-russian-information-warfare-crimean-operation-a-case-study.

"Dohovir Ianukovycha i Medvedeva pro bazuvannia flotu do 2042 roku. Tekst dokumentu." *Ukrainska pravda*. April 22, 2010. http://www.pravda.com.ua/articles/2010/04/22/4956018.

"General Assembly Adopts Resolution Calling upon States Not to Recognize Changes in Status of Crimea Region." *United Nations. Meeting Coverage and Press Releases*. March 27, 2014. http://www.un.org/press/en/2014/ga11493.doc.htm.

Gołda-Sobczak, Maria. *Krym jako przedmiot sporu ukraińsko-rosyjskiego.* Poznań: Wydawnictwo Naukowe Silva Rerum, 2016.

Golovan, Maksim. "Zaharchenko, prosnis! Banderovtsy ubivaiut militsionerov i mirnykh grazhdan." *Krymskaia Pravda*. February 20, 2014. http://c-pravda.ru/newspapers/2014/02/20/zakharchenko-prosnis.

Heritage, Timothy, and Katya Golubkova. "Russia Eyes Loan, Gas Deal to Keep Ukraine in its Orbit." *Reuters*. December 16, 2013. http://www.reuters.com/article/us-ukraine-russia-idUSBRE9BF0GV20131216.

Hoffmann, Christiane, Marc Hujer, Ralf Neukirch, Matthias Schepp, Gregor P. Schmitz, and Christoph Schult. "Summit of Failure: How the EU Lost Russia over Ukraine." *Spiegel Online International*. November 24, 2014. http://www.spiegel.de/international/europe/war-in-ukraine-a-result-of-misunderstandings-between-europe-and-russia-a-1004706-2.html.

"Hradus protestnyh nastroiiv v Ukraini zrostaie—doslidzhennia." *News.ru.ua*. March 23, 2013. http://www.newsru.ua/arch/ukraine/23mar2013/boiling_cattle.html.

"Human Rights in Crimea. Rollback Three Centuries." *Crimea SOS*. Accessed April 23, 2016. http://crimeamap.krymsos.com/eng/map.html.

Iwański, Tadeusz, and Jan Strzelecki. "Energia elektryczna znów płynie na Krym." *OSW*. December 16, 2016. http://www.osw.waw.pl/pl/publikacje/analizy/2015-12-1 6/energia-elektryczna-znow-plynie-na-krym.

Kazarin, Pavel, and Olga Dukhnich, eds. "Antologiia sovremennoi krymskoi mifologii. Rossiiskiie i ukrainskiie mify o Kryme, krymchanakh, krymskikh tatarakh i anneksii." *Krym. Realii*. February 26, 2016. http://ru.krymr.com/media/photogallery/27575254.html.

Kirby, John. "Russia's Decision To Suspend the Crimean Tatar Mejlis (Press statement)." *U.S. Department of State* (official website). April 21, 2016. http://www.state.gov/r/pa /prs/ps/2016/04/256480.htm.

Kostiuk, Bohdana. "Protestni nastroi sered Ukraintsiv zrostaiut, ale brakuie lideriv— eksperty." *Radio Svoboda*. March 21, 2013. http://www.radiosvoboda.org/content/a rticle/24934512.html.

Kravchenko, Stepan. "Putin Says Russia Helped Yanukovych to Escape Ukraine." *Bloomberg*. October 24, 2014. http://www.bloomberg.com/news/articles/2014-10- 24/putin-says-russia-helped-yanukovych-to-escape-ukraine.

"Lenur Islyamov's Property Is Seized—Poklonskaya." *QHA*. December 3, 2015. http://qha.com.ua/en/politics/lenur-islyamov-s-property-is-seized-poklonskaya/135 153.

Liber, George. *Total Wars and the Making of Modern Ukraine, 1914–1954*. Toronto: University of Toronto Press, 2016.

"Maiskiie reitingi odobreniia i doveriia."*Levada-Tsentr*. May 23–26, 2014. http://www.lev ada.ru/old/29-05-2014/maiskie-reitingi-odobreniya-i-doveriya.

"Marshrut vtechi Ianukovycha: ekskluzyvni podrobytsi." *TSN*. April 21, 2014. http://tsn.ua/politika/zhurnalisti-vidnovili-marshrut-vtechi-yanukovicha-v-rosiyu-346 299.html.

"Memorandum on Security Assurances in Connection with Ukraine's Accession to the Treaty on the NPT." *Permanent Mission of the Republic of Poland to the United Nations Office and International Organizations in Vienna*. December 19, 1994. https://www.msz.gov.pl/en/p/wiedenobwe_at_s_en/news/memorandum_on_security _assurances_in_connection_with_ukraine_s_accession_to_the_treaty_on_the_npt.

Metzel, Mikhail. "Putin Calls Construction of Bridge Across Kerch Strait Historic Mission." *TASS*. March 18, 2016. http://tass.ru/en/politics/863439.

"Moscow Says It Won't Ignore Crimean PM's Call for Help." *QHA*. March 1, 2014. http://qha.com.ua/en/search?q=Moscow+says+it+won%27t+ignore+Crimean+PM %27s+call+for+help.

Orlov, Dmitrii. "Kharkovskiie soglasheniia v tsifrakh i faktakh." *Fokus*. April 29, 2013. http://focus.ua/country/268583.

Plokhy, Serhii. "The City of Glory: Sevastopol in Russian Historical Mythology." *Journal of Contemporary History* 35, no. 3 (2000): 369–83.

"Pobeda Sevastopolia 24 fevralia!" [incomplete title]. *YouTube*. February 24, 2014. https://www.youtube.com/watch?v=Nqhdh-hRuDw.

"Portnikov: Krym vernut mozhno lish putiom territorialnoi dezintegratsii Rossii." *15 Minut*. February 26, 2016. http://15minut.org/news/158041-portnikov-krym-vernut-mozhno-lish-putem-territorialnoj-dezintegracii-rossii.

"Predsedatel VS ARK vstretitsia so spikerom Gosdumy RF." *Krymskaia Pravda*. February 17, 2014. http://c-pravda.ru/news/2014/02/17/predsedatel-vs-ark-vstretits ya-so-spikerom-gosdumy-rf.

"President Poroshenko Says Russia Was Involved in Shooting Euromaidan Protesters." *Ukraine Today*. February 24, 2015. http://uatoday.tv/politics/president-poroshenko-says-russia-was-involved-in-killing-euromaidan-protesters-410787.html.

"Problema postavok elektroenergii v Krym: itogi vserossiiskogo oprosa." *WCIOM*. Press-Vypusk, no. 3026. January 27, 2016. http://wciom.ru/index.php?id=236&uid=115562.

"Pro novu khvyliu represii u Krymu zaiavliaie Mejlis." *Ekspres.ua*. April 21, 2016. http://expres.ua/news/2016/04/21/183608-novu-hvylyu-represiy-krymu-zayavlyaye-medzhlis.

"Protests, Concessions and Repressions in Ukraine: Monitoring Results of 2013." *Centre for Society Research*. 2014. http://www.cedos.org.ua/system/attachments/files/000/0 00/043/original/CSR_-_Protests_in_2013_-_29_Apr_2014_-_Eng.pdf?1400090323.

"Pro zatverdzhennia Konstytutsii Avtonomnoi Respubliky Krym." *Verkhovna rada Ukrainy, Zakon, Konstytutsiia № 350–XIV*. December 23, 1998. http://zakon4.rada.gov.ua/laws/show/350-14/page2.

"Putin Reveals Secrets of Russia's Crimea Takeover Plot." *BBC News*. March 9, 2015. http://www.bbc.com/news/world-europe-31796226.

"Putin's Patriotic Biker-Friend Says Crimea is Only Start, Kyiv is Next." *Independent.mk*. April 8, 2014. http://www.independent.mk/articles/3596/Putins+Patriotic+Biker-Frie nd+Says+Crimea+is+Only+Start,+Kyiv+is+Next.

"Russia Suspends Crimean Tatar Mejlis for 'Alleged Extremist Activities.'" *Daily Sabah*. April 19, 2016. http://www.dailysabah.com/europe/2016/04/19/russia-suspends-cri mean-tatar-mejlis-for-alleged-extremist-activities.

Sadowski, Rafał. "The Blockade of Crimea." *The Centre for Eastern Studies* (OSW). September 30, 2015. http://www.osw.waw.pl/en/publikacje/analyses/2015-09-30/bl ockade-crimea.

"Sovet Federatsii dal soglasiie na ispolzovanie vooruzhennykh sil Rossii na territorii Ukrainy." *Sovet Federatsii Federalnogo Sobraniia Rossiiskoi Federatsii*. March 1, 2014. http://council.gov.ru/press-center/news/39851.

Suhoboychenko, Sergey. *Crimean Media after Annexation. Analytical Report*. Warsaw: The Eastern European Democratic Center Association, 2015.

"Text of Putin's Speech at NATO Summit (Bucharest, April 2, 2008)." *UNIAN*. April 18, 2008. http://www.unian.info/world/111033-text-of-putins-speech-at-nato-summit-bu charest-april-2-2008.html.

"Ukaz Prezydenta Ukrainy pro rishennia Rady natsionalnoi bezpeky i oborony Ukrainy vid 2 veresnia 2015 roku 'Pro novu redaktsiiu Voiennoi doktryny Ukrainy.'" *Verkhovna Rada Ukrainy*. September 24, 2015. http://zakon5.rada.gov.ua/laws/show/555/2015.

"Ukaz Prezydenta Ukrainy pro voiennu doktrynu Ukrainy." *Verkhovna Rada Ukrainy.* June 15, 2004 (ed. June 8, 2012). http://zakon4.rada.gov.ua/laws/show/648/2004.

"Ukraina-2013: mizh vyboramy i pered vyborom (analitychni otsinky)." *Tsentr Razumkova* (Kyiv). 2013. http://www.razumkov.org.ua/upload/Ukraine-2013_ukr.pdf.

"Ukraine Crisis: Crimea Leader Appeals to Putin for Help." *BBC News.* March 1, 2014. http://www.bbc.com/news/world-europe-26397323.

"Ukraine. Parliamentary Elections. 28 October 2012: OSCE/ODIHR Election Observation Mission Final Report." *OSCE: Office for Democratic Institutions and Human Rights* (Warsaw). January 3, 2013. http://www.osce.org/odihr/98578?download=true.

"Ukrainian Railways Cuts Rail Links with Crimea Over Security Fears." *UNIAN.* December 26, 2014. http://www.unian.info/society/1026678-ukrainian-railways-cuts-rail-lin ks-with-crimea-over-security-fears.html.

Van Herpen, Marcel H. *Viiny Putina. Chechnia, Hruziia, Ukraina: nezasvoieni uroky mynuloho.* Transated from English (unknown translator). The original title: *Putin's Wars: The Rise of Russia's New Imperialism.* Kharkiv: Vivat, 2015.

"V Krymu rossiiskiie voiennyie s oruzhiiem zaniali Yaltu." *Neftegaz.ru.* February 25, 2014. http://neftegaz.ru/news/view/120391.

"Vsio ruhnulo, krome reitinga prezidenta (an interview with the expert of "Levada Center" Denis Volkov). *BBC Russkaia sluzhba.* January 6, 2015. http://www.bbc.com/russia n/russia/2015/01/150105_levada_volkov_putin_15_years?ocid=wsrus_rus_psc_fa cebook_mkt_fe_news_na.

Wapiński, Maciej. "The Orange Revolution and its Aftermath." In *The Maidan Uprising, Separatism and Foreign Intervention: Ukraine's Complex Transition,* edited by Klaus Bachmann and Igor Lyubashenko, 43–60. Frankfurt am Main: Peter Lang, 2014.

Wilson, Andrew. *Ukraine Crisis: What it Means for the West.* New Haven and London: Yale University Press, 2014.

Yurchenko, Stas, Usein Dzhabbarov, and Claire Bigg. "Tourist Season A Washout In Annexed Crimea." *Radio Free Europe. Radio Liberty.* July 5, 2014. http://www.rf erl.org/content/tourist-season-washout-in-annexed-crimea/25446604.html.

"Zaboronyty Mejlis—mriia prokuratury aneksovanoho Krymu." *Deutsche Welle Ukraine.* February 19, 2016. http://dw.com/p/1HwvL.

"Zair Akadyrov Told Details of Yesterday's Raid." *QHA.* April 20, 2016. http://qha.com.u a/en/politics/zair-akadyrov-told-details-of-yesterday-s-raid/136889.

# 8
# Russian Hegemony in the Black Sea Basin: The "Third Rome" in Contemporary Geopolitics

Dale A. Bertelsen and Olga Bertelsen

Russia's annexation of the Crimean peninsula and invasion of eastern Ukraine have significantly altered the post-Cold War political landscape, and with it, the regional and global power and security dynamics. Indeed, Russia's actions, when seen in a broader spatial context, pose an alarming threat geographically, strategically, politically, and economically. Initially understood as an attempt to control Russia's "near abroad," the incursions into Ukraine's sovereign territory are emerging as harbingers of a much more extensive expansion of Russian power then first anticipated.

    Russia's rather spurious initial justification for annexing the Crimean peninsula and supporting "separatists" in eastern Ukraine was grounded in the desire to protect Russian citizens "no matter where they are." Observers have since offered a number of reasonable competing explanations for Russia's actions. Quite often the Ukrainian invasion is rationalized as a Russian response to perceptions of NATO expansion. Other, equally interesting, explanations for Russian adventurism in the region are attributed to Russia's desire to break up NATO and the European Union, or to limit European integration.[1] But when combined with past incursions into Georgia and Chechnya, more recent forays into Syria, increased arms sales to Armenia and Azerbaijan, and threats to the sovereignty of Turkey and Romania, the constriction of NATO expansion and European integration lack sufficient explanatory power to fully account for Russia's actions in the Black Sea region.

---

[1] For a very thoughtful discussion of Russian activity in the Black Sea littoral, see Stephen Blank, "Russia and the Black Sea's Frozen Conflicts in Strategic Perspective," *Mediterranean Quarterly* 19, no. 3 (2008): 23–54.

Instead, Russia appears to be engaged in the encirclement of the Black Sea basin which offers sufficient geopolitical and economic advantages to warrant the inherent risks of such a maneuver. For example, Russia's annexation of the Crimean peninsula was followed quickly by the "nationalization" of Ukraine's extensive on-and off-shore gas and oil interests, as well as control of distribution pipelines in the Crimea.[2] This economic coup also may reasonably explain the invasion of eastern Ukraine, the vital landline and lifeline of supplies for the newly acquired territory.

Although all of these gains have supporting rationales, the question remains, what is the ultimate goal? Surely the wealth and power generated through the control of vast natural resources could be the end goal, or the protection of Russians in the near abroad, or fighting terrorists in Syria and other areas of the Black Sea littoral so they do not have to be fought at home. Perhaps broader interests like limiting NATO expansion and halting European integration provide the impetus for Russian adventurism in the Black Sea basin. Yet the acquisition of this territory comes at a very high price, both in loss of human life and in the loss of international standing. Seen individually, Russia's actions in the Black Sea basin and its littoral region might even be explained away by using the euphemism of post-Soviet expansion or colonialism. But when seen collectively, Russian militarism in the Black Sea basin suggests a scenario at once more concerning and far-reaching.

The region of the Crimean peninsula, the Black Sea, and its coastline are important for Russia strategically. Their bold annexation of the Crimea peninsula confirms that the Russians consider their control over the Black Sea extremely important for their economy and geopolitics. In essence, when taken collectively, Russian military and political activity in and around the Black Sea suggests that Russia is currently waging war for the control of this strategically important area. The recent political behavior of the Russian Federation and its leaders signals that, beyond Ukraine's destruction as an independent and sovereign state, and the destruction of NATO and the European Union, Russia's plans include complete control of the Black Sea basin.

---

2   For a quick synopsis, see John C.K. Daly, "Russia Claims Ukraine's Black Sea Oil and Gas Bounty," *OilPrice.com*, May 7, 2014, http://oilprice.com/Energy/Energy-General/Russia-Claims-Ukraines-Black-Sea-Oil-And-Gas-Bounty.html.

Ultimately, Russian dominance in the Black Sea basin cannot be realized without taking control of the Turkish Straits (the Bosporus and Dardanelles, and the Sea of Marmara), the primary means of ingress and egress to the vast riches that lie under the sea itself, and the militarily strategic positions that control maritime traffic in the Black Sea. To accomplish this goal, the continued destabilization of the Black Sea region will be vital. Thusfar, ongoing military and political conflicts in Ukraine, Georgia, Moldova, Syria, and Nagorno-Karabakh will continue to destabilize large portions of the Black Sea basin.[3] In addition, and perhaps most importantly at the moment, destabilizing Turkey, Romania, and Bulgaria will become more prominent tasks. Romania and Bulgaria are increasingly important to Russia as they control huge offshore mineral rights.[4] But Turkey's control of the Turkish Straits has long been a point of contention for Russia. Gaining control of the Straits has been a historic goal for Russia and has become increasingly significant for the success of their plans in the Black Sea basin.

Russian desires to control the Turkish Straits are often attributed to the rhetoric of the myth of the "Third Rome," a manifest destiny rationale for Russian dominance in the Black sea region. In this narrative, Russia serves as the hereditary guardian of Orthodoxy, an international shield to ward off the heresy and sin of the decadent (typically cast as the West). Moreover, the Russian people are the chosen people, devoted to the messianic mission of saving the world, but especially acting as the

---

3   For a thorough discussion of the implications of Russian military action in Georgia on Russo-Turkish relations, and the regional balance of power, see Igor Torbakov's report, "The Georgia Crisis and Russia-Turkey Relations" (Washington, D.C.: Jamestown Foundation, 2006), *The Jamestown Foundation*, accessed 24 July, 2016, http://www.jamestown.org/uploads/media/GeorgiaCrisisTorbakov.pdf.

4   For a consideration of Bulgaria's and Romania's mineral resources, see Yadira Soto-Viruet, "The Mineral Industry of Bulgaria," *USGS* (U.S. Geological Survey; U.S. Department of Interior), March 2014, http://minerals.usgs.gov/minerals/pubs/country/2012/myb3-2012-bu.pdf; "Focus: East Central Europe: Better Times to Come," *Mining-journal.com*, July 18, 2014, http://www.euromines.org/files/publications/mining-journal-feature-july-2014-east-central-europe.pdf; Walter G. Steblez, "The Mineral Industries of Bulgaria and Romania," *USGS* (U.S. Geological Survey; U.S. Department of Interior), 2000, http://minerals.usgs.gov/minerals/pubs/country/2000/9408000.pdf.

protectors of Russian/Slavic peoples no matter where they may be. Ultimately, Russia will fulfill the "Third Rome" myth by unifying the Orthodox faith and recovering Constantinople, the historic seat of Orthodoxy.[5]

To understand how Russia conceptualizes its right to control the Straits, indeed, to control the Black Sea, a brief discussion of the "Third Rome" rationale is necessary. Although the Third Rome myth may not be a causative factor in Russian foreign or domestic policy, it seems likely that because it infiltrates Russian identity and is often referred to as a rationale for any number of ideological assumptions and foreign incursions, it may have predictive value, particularly as it relates to the Black Sea basin. After exploring the nature and power of the narrative force of the "Third Rome" myth as a discursive formation, Russia's efforts to destabilize Turkey and the balance of the Black Sea littoral states, and the ultimate implications of such acts, will be clearer.

## The Discursive Formation of Power and Knowledge in the "Third Rome" Myth

According to Michel Foucault, a discursive formation acts as an interpretative framework, a lens through which we construct and understand our world.[6] These structures govern cultural knowledge and emerge through cultural discourse. Importantly, humans are born into a "system of discourse" that largely defines and creates "the world of human experience."[7] Discursive formations follow a set of unwritten rules that identify what is and is not communicated, and, correspondingly, what is

---

[5] Multiple variations of the "Third Rome" myth are available, among them: Peter J.S. Duncan, *Russian Messianism: Third Rome, Revolution, Communism and After* (London and New York: Rutledge, 2000); Maria Engstrom, "Contemporary Russian Messianism and New Russian Foreign Policy," *Contemporary Security Policy*, no. 3 (2014): 356–79; Jardar Ostbo, *The New Third Rome: Readings of a Russian Nationalist Myth* (Stuttgart, Germany: ibidem-Verlag, 2016); Marshall T. Poe, "'Moscow, the Third Rome': The Origins and Transformations of a Pivotal Movement" (a report submitted to the National Council for Soviet and East European Research, Title VIII Program, Washington, DC, October 10, 1997, i–22), *University Center for International Studies* (Pittsburgh), accessed July 6, 2016, https://www.ucis.pitt.edu/nceeer/1997-811-25-Poe.pdf.

[6] Michel Foucault, *The Archeology of Knowledge and the Discourse on Language*, trans. A. M. Sheridan Smith (New York: Pantheon Books, 1972).

[7] See Ann Gill, *Rhetoric and Human Understanding* (Prospect Heights, Ill: Waveland Press, Inc., 1994), especially pp.178–86.

known. In other words, every culture, every society, embodies a cultural encyclopedia of sorts—a storehouse of information that shapes knowledge and behavior. The power of a discursive formation is sustained so long as the specific narrative of the discursive formation is reiterated in the culture's discourse, or remains a part of the cultural memory. For example, the power of the "Third Rome" myth does not rest solely in its nature to prescribe belief and action in specific fulfillment of its edicts. Nor is it imperative to determine the "true" source of the myth. The power resides in the myth's infiltration of Russian discourse in general. In that sense, its influence guides and shapes the national discourse. Because the "Third Rome" myth may commonly be found in "virtually every Russian history textbook," it likely plays a key role in the formation of Russian identity.[8]

To further clarify, myth may be understood as a cultural narrative insofar as a myth tells a story about a culture and its people. Walter Fisher has held that narratives are moral ideological constructs and are often taken as imperatives to believe or act in a certain way. Typically, the narrative ideological imperative acts as a constraining force in the conduct of the people who ascribe to that narrative. Moreover, the ascendance of a narrative, or in this case a myth, "forecloses discussion and debate."[9] In the case of the "Third Rome" narrative, its dominance in Russian discourse imbues it with such explanatory force that it infiltrates the Russian psyche and, therefore, Russian self-identity. This has occurred through a number of means, not the least of which is the political value the myth imparts for national identity building.

In all, the "Third Rome" myth maintains its dominance over the Russian psyche as a prominent discursive formation. An examination of the emergence of the "Third Rome" myth and the extensive role it plays in Russian national discourse should clarify its nature as a discursive formation and identify its prominent features. Once this framework becomes

---

8   Ostbo, *The New Third Rome*, 55.
9   Walter R. Fisher, "Narration as a Human Communication Paradigm: The Case of Public Moral Argument," *Communication Monographs* 51, no. 1 (1984): 13. See also Walter R. Fisher, *Human Communication as Narration: Toward a Philosophy of Reason, Value, and Action* (Columbia, SC: University of South Carolina Press, 1987). Foucault also makes a similar point in *History of Human Sexuality: Volume I: An Introduction* (New York: Vintage Books/A Division of Random House, 1978), especially p. 6.

evident, the narrative of the "Third Rome" should provide the ground for assessing and anticipating Russian actions in the Black Sea basin.

## The "Third Rome" Myth in Russian Intellectual History

The concept of the "Third Rome" has traditionally been traced to ancient Byzantium. Constantinople was founded as Byzantium in the seventh century BC by the Greeks, became the capital of the Roman Empire in AD 330, and became the capital of the Ottoman Empire in 1453. Historically, Constantinople—"Greek," "Roman," and "Turkish," controls the only passage that connects the Mediterranean and Black Seas.[10] As a result, its geopolitical and commercial significance is difficult to overlook.[11] Serhii Plokhy has argued that Ukraine has historically constituted the gates of Europe.[12] In similar fashion, Istanbul, the guardian of the Turkish Straits, may be reasonably identified as the southern gateway to Europe and beyond. Moreover, as the former State Minister for EU Affairs Egemen Bağış stated in 2010, "Istanbul is [not just] a European city; it is the city which shaped European Culture."[13] As far as the historic destiny of the Russians is concerned, Constantinople and Russia's "right" to transform it into Russian Tsargrad (the old Russian name for Constantinople), once again serves as an inner moral justification for encroaching into the Turkish geographical and political space.

Many contemporary scholars contend that the myth of the "Third Rome" stems from some plaintive letters written by Filofei, a monk in the monastery of Eleazar at Pskov (ca. 1465–1542).[14] In 1510, Grand Prince of Moscow Vasilii III annexed Pskov. For most of its citizens it was difficult

---

10  Constantinople was often simultaneously referred to as Istanbul, and officially became Istanbul in 1923 under Turkish rule. See, for example, Ira M. Lapidus, *A History of Islamic Societies*, 2nd ed. (New York: Cambridge University Press, 2002), 211, 253, 263, 272, 274–76; Jerry H. Bentley and Herbert F. Zeigler, *Traditions & Encounters: A Global Perspective on the Past*, vol. II, 4th ed. (New York: The McGraw-Hill Companies, Inc., 2008), 755; Serhii Plokhy, *The Gates of Europe: A History of Ukraine* (New York: Basic Books, 2015), 74.
11  Norman Davies, *Vanished Kingdoms: The Rise and Fall of States and Nations* (London: Penguin Books, 2011), 312.
12  Plokhy, *The Gates of Europe*.
13  Quoted in Davies, *Vanished Kingdoms*, 313.
14  For a discussion about the theory of the Third Rome, see works by Serhii Plokhy (2006), N. V. Sinitsyna (1998), Donald Ostrowski (1998), Paul Bushkovitch (1986), David M. Goldfrank (1981).

to surrender the idea of independence and accept the supremacy of Moscow. But not for Filofei. He actively promoted Moscow's dominance and argued that Moscow should take the lead in the Orthodox fight against heresy. In this way, he is largely credited as the original source of the idea of Moscow as the "Third Rome."[15] The messages he sent to the Grand Princes of Moscow beginning in 1530 until his death emphasized that Muscovy was the spiritual successor of the Roman and Byzantine Empires, and had to "defend true Orthodoxy against heresy."[16] Filofei argued that "[a]ll former Christian states disappeared due to their moral deterioration . . . the First Rome fell in the same fashion as the Second—Byzantium. The Third Rome—Muscovy, however, is unconquered. And there will not be the Fourth Rome."[17]

Marshall T. Poe, however, suggests that the "Third Rome" is largely a product of revisionist history, a desire to find a historical path that justifies a desired future.[18] In his view, the "'Third Rome,' then, is the result of the projection of a modern idea—notably, the 'Russian mission'—onto a superficially analogous early modern concept."[19] Poe further contends that the notion of the "Third Rome" largely disappeared from "mainstream Russian thought," only circulating among some clerics and reappearing sporadically through the sectarian Old Believers of the late seventeenth century, and among historians in the mid-1800s after Filofei's letters were published. It was at this time that the "Third Rome" was cast as an ideological foundation for Russian messianic expansion. From the late nineteenth century onward, the "Third Rome" gained currency as a Russian discursive formation with some degree of influence over the Russian psyche. Poe argued strongly that the "Third Rome" was an "abuse of historical information," and as a "creation of late nineteenth-century Russian scholars" should not be employed as an explanation for Russian "foreign policy or Russian national psychology."[20] Yet, there seems to be sufficient evidence to suggest that the "Third Rome" narrative

---

15    Francis Dvornik, *The Slavs in European History and Civilization* (New Brunswick, NJ: Rutgers University Press, 1962), 311.
16    Serhii Plokhy, *The Origins of the Slavic Nations: Premodern Identities in Russia, Ukraine, and Belarus* (New York: Cambridge University Press, 2006), 145.
17    Quoted in Ievhen Kaliuzhnyi, "Kyivska Rus—tse ne Rosiia," *Literaturna Ukraina*, July 16, 2015, p. 10.
18    Poe, i–22.
19    Ibid, 15.
20    Ibid, ii.

has been more deeply ingrained in the Russian psyche than Poe supposed.

Some have suggested, consistent with Poe's position, that the "Third Rome" myth, attributed to Filofei, had little to do with *translatio imperii* (succession of the transfer of ruling power to command the empire),[21] and was in fact not a "semi-official political manifesto."[22] Allegedly, this was a concept that helped establish the notion of the grand prince's duties and responsibilities toward the Church, an "inheritance of the Byzantine Empire in a religious sense," not in a political or territorial sense.[23] Whatever the case might be, it is interesting that the *Tale of the Taking of Tsargrad* by Nestor-Iskander reinforced the idea that one day Constantinople which fell in 1453 would be liberated by the Christians. The rise of Moscow became the hope of salvation for Orthodox Christians. Other narratives, such as the *Tales of the Babylonian Empire*, were invented and modified to establish the right of Russia to the Byzantine territory and heritage.[24] Although Filofei's idea did not become the official state ideology and little had been heard about it until the late sixteenth century, it certainly awakened Moscow's confidence as the legitimate heir of Constantinople, and probably stimulated the Russian messianism of the nineteenth century.[25] The idea that Russia was the leader of the Orthodoxy and that its moral right to Constantinople was legitimate was illuminated in various forms in the writings of Fiodor Dostoevsky (1821–1881), Nikolai Danilevskii (1922–1895), Dmitrii Merezhkovskii (1865–1941), Aleksandr Blok (1880–1921), Viacheslav Ivanov (1866–1949), Mikhail Bulgakov (1891–1940) and many other Russian writers and thinkers.[26] Pan-Slavist ideologist Danilevskii, for example, argued strenuously that Russia had an inevitable moral obligation and a historic

---

21 Maria Engstrom argues that *translatio imperii romani* grants the "Third Rome" rights to an empire with "no constant temporal or spatial characteristics [which] can manifest itself on the territory of different states." Engstrom, 363.
22 See, for example, Von Edgar Hösch, "Die Idee der Translatio Imperii im Moskauer Russland," *EGO*, March 12, 2010, http://ieg-ego.eu/de/threads/modelle-und-stereotypen/modell-antike/edgar-hoesch-die-idee-der-translatio-imperii-im-moskau er-russland/?searchterm=H%C3%B6sch,%20Von%20Edgar.%20%E2%80%9C Die%20Idee%20der%20Translatio%20Imperii%20im%20Moskauer%20Russlan d.%E2%80%9D&set_language=de.
23 Ibid.
24 Dvornik, 312–15.
25 Hösch, "Die Idee der Translatio Imperii im Moskauer Russland."
26 Ibid.

maternal right to "possess Constantinople" and that as the "real Tsargard" Constantinople would be "the capital not just of Russia, but of the entire Slavic union," a symbol of enlightenment, glory, luxury, and power, and the center of Orthodoxy.[27] Similarly, Dostoevsky believed that Constantinople should be "ours,"[28] and a century later, displaying the enduring intellectual power of the "Third Rome," Joseph Brodsky stated that Crimea should be Russian.[29]

Evidence of the "Third Rome" rationale also has been identified in the film *Fall of the Empire: Byzantium's Lesson* broadcast by RTR in January 2008. According to Irina Papkova, the film was "produced and directed by Father Tikhon Shevkunov, head of the Sretenskii monastery in Moscow" and rumored spiritual advisor to Vladimir Putin.[30] She interprets the film as a parable for Russia's "contemporary geopolitical position" that "perpetuates the '"Third Rome' paradigm," largely functions to "legitimize . . . Putin's policies," and reasserts the link between Russian Orthodoxy and contemporary Russian politics.[31]

But the "Third Rome" myth is not restricted to Russian history, literature, or the arts. Maria Engstrom has convincingly shown that the "Third Rome" myth has infiltrated Russian foreign policy in rather dramatic ways. She contends that "the Foreign Policy Concept of the Russian Federation, signed by Putin in February 2013"[32] clearly embodies significant ideological sustenance and rationale grounded in the "Third Rome"

---

27   Quoted in Ievhen Hutsalo, *Mentalnist ordy* (Kyiv: KMA, 2007), 192–93.
28   See an analysis of Dostoevsky's claim in Hutsalo, 111–12.
29   Olga Bertelsen, "Joseph Brodsky's Imperial Consciousness," *Scripta Historica*, no. 21 (2015): 272.
30   For those readers who might wish to ponder the degree to which Putin subscribes to the "Third Rome" myth, or how it may fulfill his public image, or the role it might play in his psyche and decision-making, or the enduring relationship between the Orthodox church and the members of the FSB, see "Putin Sat in the Chair of Byzantine Emporers," *RUSHINCRASH*, May 28, 2016, http://rushincrash.com/russia/putin-sat-in-the-chair-ofbyzantine/emporers/; "Putin Visits Russian Orthodox Monastic Community in Greece," *Yahoo News*, May 28, 2016, https://www.yahoo.com/news/putin-visits-orthodox-monastic-community-mount-athos-114538932.html; Paul Coyer, "Putin's Holy War and the Disintegration of the 'Russian World,'" *Forbes*, June 4, 2015, http://www.forbes.com/sites/paulcoyer/2015/06/04/putins-holy-war-and-the-disintegration-of-the-russian-world/#35c396601097.
31   Irina Papkova, "Saving the Third Rome: 'Fall of the Empire', Byzantium and Putin's Russia," in *Reconciling the Irreconcilable*, ed. I. Papkova, vol. 24 (Vienna: IWM Junior Visiting Fellows' Conferences, 2009).
32   Engstrom, 362.

narrative. Engstrom argues that the "Third Rome" myth serves as the ideological foundation for the turn toward conservatism in Russian politics and foreign policy, with Russia being cast as an independent sovereign nation, employing a re-actualization of the "messianic Katechon-ideologeme and the extensive use of collective cultural memory in contemporary political discourse" acting as a primary influence in "the popularity of Putin's politics" in foreign and domestic policy and among all levels of Russian citizens.[33] In all, she suggests that re-emergent Russian messianism (Katechon), where Russia is the guardian against the apocalyptic chaos of immorality and heresy (typically emanating from the West), acting without impunity in virtually any geographic theatre (*translatio imperii romani*), provides a shield and has the capacity to employ any means necessary to protect the people and the nation. Engstrom opines that while

> [t]he ideologization of domestic, foreign and security policy can be analysed as Putin's attempt to legitimize his own power, and his rising support can be critiqued as the result of propaganda... such explanations ignore the important factor of collective memory and identity, the deep roots of the Katechonic discourse in Russian culture, both pre-revolutionary and Soviet. In times of open confrontation the mobilization potential of this old new messianism can and will be used.[34]

There is also confirmation that the "Third Rome" myth has penetrated the depths of the Russian intellectual elites. Jardar Ostbo traces the fundamental characteristics of the "Third Rome" myth through the views of four prominent Russian nationalist intellectuals (Vadim Tsymburskii, Aleksandr Dugin, Nataliia Narochnitskaia, and Egor [Iegor] Kholmogorov) and examines how the myth infiltrates their contributions to debates about nationalism, national identity, and the relationship between church (Orthodox Christianity) and politics (Russian territorial ambitions). Ostbo observes that the "Third Rome" myth plays an important role in Russian culture and is fit into existing ideological perspectives to justify the Russian invasion of and war in Ukraine. Moreover, he finds that the rhetoric of the four Russian intellectuals largely accommodates and rationalizes Russia's annexation of the Crimean peninsula and invasion of eastern

---

33  Engstrom, 357.
34  Engstrom, 376. Both British and American spellings have been used by the author in the original: "analysed" and "legitimize."

Ukraine, and demonstrates how they view these events as a celebration of Russia's status as the "Third Rome," with a corresponding increase in Russian national pride and self-identity as a great nation. In all, he argues that the "Third Rome" myth primarily serves as a founding myth that has entered the mainstream of Russian society through a variety of discourse forms, and contributes to nation building in post-Soviet Russia.[35]

Certainly the "Third Rome" myth is a common feature and regular part of contemporary Russian discourse, and a discursive formation with deep roots in Russian cultural memory. But the question now becomes, how have the imperatives of the myth indulged Russia's enduring quest to control the Turkish Straits, a significant geographical lynchpin of the "Third Rome" narrative, one of the gateways to Europe?

## Russia's Quest in Historical Perspective: Constantinople and the Straits

As Norman Davies has noted, two unstoppable late seventeenth century processes ignited events of geopolitical significance: the Russian Empire's obsessive expansion from 1683 and the Ottoman Empire's perpetual retreat. Traceable in their causality and continuity, these events shook the world, creating new states, nations, and identities in the nineteenth and twentieth centuries: they provoked the rise of the Balkan nations' independence, the Crimean War (1854–56), and ultimately the First World War.[36]

The decline and the eventual demise of the Ottoman Empire was desirable for the Russians for several reasons. Among other justifications, they wanted to re-establish their power over the Turkish Straits, to take advantage of that unique geographical location, and to protect the population of the Christian faith. The history of these attempts goes back to the reign of the Russian Tsar Nikolai I, when he tried to negotiate with England

---

35 Ostbo, *The New Third Rome*. For an interesting discussion of the influence of the "Third Rome" myth throughout Russian history, see Sergei Margaril, "The Mythology of the 'Third Rome' in Russian Educated Society," *Russian Politics and Law* 50, no. 5 (2012): 7–34. For a detailed examination of Third Romism in post-Soviet ideologies, see Dmitrii Sidorov, "Post-Imperial Third Romes: Resurrection of a Russian Orthodox Geopolitical Metaphor," *Geopolitics* 11, no. 2 (2006): 317–47.
36 Norman Davies, *Europe: A History* (New York: HarperPerennial, 1998), 869.

a plan for taking over Constantinople. According to this plan, England would help Russia to annex Constantinople, in turn receiving control over Egypt that belonged then to Turkey. England rejected the offer. Nikolai also demanded a Russian protectorate over the Orthodox population from the Sultan. When his demands were rebuffed, in 1853 the Russians launched the Crimean war against the Turks. Russia lost the war to Turkey which had been supported by England, France, Austria, and Sardinia. The Western powers sent troops to the Crimean peninsula, and after fierce trench warfare Sevastopol fell. In 1877 Russia undertook another attempt to assert control over Constantinople. Russian troops invaded Ottoman territory on the Danube and in Armenia. By early 1878, the Russians were near Constantinople's walls. Through tedious diplomatic negotiations, Turkey's Western allies managed to once again restrain Russia's ambitions.[37]

The myth of the "Third Rome" became more perceptible in the eighteenth century when Russia expanded southward against the Ottomans, down to the Black Sea. These victories enriched Russia commercially and spatially. Control over the coastline of the Black Sea was acquired under Catherine the Great and the area was colonized by the 1780s. The next goal was to ensure control over the Bosporus in the east toward the Dardanelles in the west.[38] Not surprisingly, such rapid expansion toward Constantinople provoked opposition from the West. Russia realized that further territorial gains in Europe would be unjustifiably costly. Yet the prospects of being the champion of the Orthodox faith if Constantinople fell were seductive for many Russian Slavophiles and politicians, including the Tsar. The motivations for the expansion were more significant than mere geopolitics. Conquering Constantinople would serve as evidence for the uniqueness of the Slavic civilization, expediting the collapse of decadent Europe.[39]

However, there was no consensus in Russia about restoring Christian rule in Constantinople. Even some Slavophiles, such as Serge Sazonov, foreign minister from 1910 to 1916, questioned the idea of attempting to gain control of Constantinople which would meet hostility from other

---

37 Davies, *Europe*, 870.
38 Dominic Lieven, *The End of Tsarist Russia: The March to World War I and Revolution* (New York: Viking, 2015), 70.
39 Lieven, 71.

great powers and would complicate the issue of Russia's other strategic goal—the Straits.[40] The Russian dream had always been to dominate the Black Sea. Only then could Russia control the Straits. Due to international conventions, the waters of the Straits were controlled by the Ottomans, which made the Russians vulnerable to Turkish attacks or attacks by foreign powers: the Sultan's allies could be given permission to enter the Black Sea in wartime. Dominic Lieven has aptly noted that "whoever controlled the Black Sea would therefore have crucial advantages in any Russo-Turkish war," a reality that proved to be catastrophic for Russia during the Crimean war.[41]

Over the long history of Russia's struggle for the Bosporus, Russian rulers considered many scenarios. Among them were diplomatic negotiations about securing waterways for Russian ships, and a military takeover of the Bosporus at the eastern end. In 1896, St. Petersburg seriously pondered the latter solution but rejected it as "too risky."[42] Had Russia been hypothetically offered the option of choosing between control of Constantinople and the Straits, it would likely have chosen the Straits, as the Russian fleet could be relocated from the Baltic Sea, and the northern Pacific Ocean to the warmer Black Sea. At that time, this strategic relocation of the Russian fleet would have provided the Russians with an advantage to react quickly to a threat in Russia's three main maritime theatres.[43]

In addition, Russia's dynamic trade conducted through the Black Sea has always depended on the issue of the Straits, and their interdependence continues to occupy the minds of the Russians today as they try to solve the dilemma of energy export and intercontinental trade. The nature of Russian exports has changed over the centuries but the interconnectedness of politics, geography, and economic considerations appears to be crucial to the Russian political elites' policies.

Grigorii Trubetskoi, Russian diplomat and politician who exercised tremendous influence over Russia's foreign policy before 1914, understood the significance of Constantinople and the Straits. For him Slav interests were more important than the Straits: they could not be sacrificed

---

40 Lieven, 73.
41 Ibid.
42 Lieven, 74.
43 Ibid.

in negotiating control over the Bosporus. In order to gain this control, Russia "needed a firm base among the Balkan Slavs."[44] Thus, from 1906 to 1914 Russia delayed any solutions or activities in the Straits. The Balkan Wars of 1912–13 and the defeat of the Ottomans encouraged the Russians to return to this crucial question. For Trubetskoi the acquisition of both Constantinople and the Straits was the most desirable option:

> Such a solution would correspond to the national mission created by our history. Russia would possess one of the great centers of world trade and the key to the Mediterranean Sea. As regards strategy, the short land border with Bulgaria and the possibility to create invulnerable defenses on the Chataldja position were big advantages. Combined with the natural geographic strength of the Dardanelles, which could also easily be enhanced by formidable fortifications, this would provide a new and secure foundation for an unprecedented growth in Russian power. On the other hand, the transfer of Constantinople to Russia would necessarily confirm Russia's unequivocal leadership over all the Balkan states. In a word, this would create for Russia a position in the world that is the natural crowning of all the efforts and sacrifices of the last two centuries of our history. The majesty of such a project and all its innumerable consequences in the ecclesiastical, cultural, economic, and political spheres would bring healing in our domestic life and would give both government and society goals and an enthusiasm that would unite them in the service of so unquestionably important a national cause.[45]

In 1914, when the Turks declared war on Russia, the British and the French seriously considered giving Constantinople and the Straits to the Russians, but the revolution of 1917 upset those plans.[46] In all, although Sazonov and Nikolai II did not share Trubetskoi's ideas, the pre-revolutionary Russian regime's war goals and policies nevertheless maintained the desire to acquire control over Constantinople and the Straits.

As Russia's enduring quest demonstrates, the "Third Rome" myth dovetails conveniently with Russian geostrategic goals. Control of the Turkish Straits would, in large measure, move toward confirmation of the "Third Rome" compulsions, and, simultaneously, grant Russia a degree of

---

44 Lieven, 130.
45 Lieven, 254–55.
46 Lieven, 130. The British promised the Russians control of Istanbul and the Straits in return for British control over Iran's neutral zone rich with oil. A secret treaty was signed in March 1915. See Nikki R. Keddie, *Modern Iran: Roots and Results of Revolution*, updated ed. (New Haven & London: Yale University Press, 2006), 73.

hegemonic control of Back Sea resources, shipping, and military position. Not surprisingly, Turkey, part of the original threat to Orthodoxy, remains a principle obstruction in Russia's quest to control the Turkish Straits, and to Russia's fulfillment of the prophecies of the "Third Rome" myth. Russia's continued military excursions in the Black Sea littoral, particularly those that involve Turkey, reinforce the traditional scenario where all aggressive military actions can be excused through the permissions of the "Third Rome" narrative, with slight modifications to accommodate contemporary events.

## The Escalation of Tensions between Russia and Turkey: Continued Military Expansion

Russian interests in the Black Sea basin ebb and flow like the sea itself. At times, Russia has made strenuous attempts to gain control of the entire basin, especially the Turkish Straits. Indeed, the Russian drive to control the Black Sea basin is ancient, and, most importantly, largely continuous, irrespective of the form of government in Russia. For example, in late 1940 the talks between Ribbentrop and Molotov about how to partition Europe regularly returned to considerations of Soviet military control of the Straits. The Soviet Union also tried to convince Turkey to join them in a mutual assistance agreement that would include the joint defense of the Dardanelles. Much to the chagrin of the Soviet leaders, Turkey refused. Yet the Soviets persisted, again in 1940–41 pushing for a Turco-Soviet mutual assistance agreement which would include "the establishment of a Soviet military base on the Straits 'on the basis of a long-term lease.'"[47] Despite Soviet guarantees to assure Turkey's "territorial integrity," the Turkish government, based on their historical experiences with the Russians, would not accede to the Soviet's wishes, as the historian Wolfgang Wagner notes:

---

[47] For a more detailed discussion of the Soviet Union's attempts to gain control of the Straits, see Wolfgang Wagner, *The Partitioning of Europe: A History of the Soviet Expansion up to the Cleavage of Germany 1918–1945* (Stuttgart, Germany: Deutsche Verlags-Anstalt, 1959), especially pp. 51, 133–35. The Russian-Soviet tactic of establishing quasi-permanent military bases during and post-war in Abkhazia, Crimea, Nagorno-Karabakh, South Ossetia, Syria, and Transnistria has proven especially successful in facilitating Russia's post-Soviet expansion or nascent colonialism, and in aiding in the encirclement of Turkey.

> As a result of long historical experience, the Turkish leaders of State knew that Russia had always regarded the Straits as one of the goals most worth striving for, and in times when the Russians were strong they had been moved by an uncontrollable desire to expand up to the Bosphorus.[48]

In 1945, at the conclusion of the war, Turkey fell victim to an onslaught of Soviet propaganda designed to substantiate a new Turco-Soviet pact, arguing that that world had changed and that Turkey should adjust to the "new conditions." Again, the victorious Soviets, through Molotov, demanded "military bases in the Straits" and an "adjustment of the Turco-Soviet frontier" which included the cessation of large territories in eastern Anatolia. Once again, Turkey resisted, invoked the assistance of the Western Powers, and largely evaded the looming crisis by proclaiming that the Straits "would be accessible to the whole world."[49] In all, the Western Powers recognized "a new direction of Soviet expansion, from the Black Sea via the Bosphorus to the Near East" and combined to thwart "Soviet claims on Turkey."[50]

But tensions between Russia and Turkey are only one aspect of Russian military expansion. Prior to and since the Russian Federation's annexation of the Crimean peninsula and invasion of eastern Ukrainian territories, high-ranking Russian officials have accused NATO of provocations, enlargement, and the encirclement of Russia. These accusations go back at least to 1991, and their quintessence is that NATO continues to escalate tensions in the relations between Russia and the West, exhibits a Cold-War mentality, and is generally hostile to modern democratic Russia.[51] Moreover, Russia blames NATO for instigating the

---

48   Wagner, 133.
49   Wagner, 135.
50   Ibid.
51   For current examples of this sort of rationale, see Joshua R. Itkowitz Shifrinson, "Russia's Got a Point: The U.S. Broke a NATO promise," *Los Angeles Times*, May 30, 2016, http://www.latimes.com/opinion/op-ed/la-oe-shifrinson-russia-us-nato; Rick Rozoff, "Black Sea: Pentagon's Gateway to Three Continents and the Middle East," *Antiwar Literary and Philosophical Selections* (Rick Rozoff), August 27, 2009, https://rickrozoff.wordpress.com/2009/08/27/79/; Damion Sharkov, "Russia Fears NATO 'Global Strike' from Eastern Europe," *Newsweek*, June 6, 2016, www.newsweek.com/russia-fears-nato-global-strike-eastern-europe-senator-466853; Patrick Goodenough, "As NATO Plans More Troops for Poland, Russia Decries 'Cold War-Era Security Schemes,'" *CNS News*, May 31, 2016, http://www.cnsnews.com/news/article/patrick-goodenogh/nato-plans-send-more-troops-poland-russia-decries-cold-war-era.

Maidan revolutions in Kyiv, and claims NATO was planning to establish a military base in Crimea.[52] Russian propaganda that attempts to discredit the alliance, however, is not the only method employed over the last few years. Intimidation tactics have become part of Russia's broader attack on the West and Western values, consistent with the edicts of the "Third Rome" narrative. In 2012, for example, a Russian submarine travelled undetected in the Gulf of Mexico for more than a month, at the same time that Russian bombers encroached on U.S. airspace over Alaska and California. Similar Russian naval probes were apparently carried out against Sweden and the United Kingdom in 2014.[53]

Since the last Ukrainian revolution and Russia's subsequent military success in the Crimean peninsula, Russia has routinely tested NATO defense systems, trying to intimidate Europe by increasing military flights close to NATO air space.[54] In November 2014, Jens Stoltenberg, secretary-general of NATO, noted:

> We (NATO) are intercepting the Russian planes whether it is in the Atlantic Sea or in the Baltic Sea or in the Black Sea. The numbers of intercepts have so far this year been over 100, which is about three times as much as the total number of intercepts the whole of last year.[55]

---

52 For dethroning these myths, fruit of Russian propaganda, see "NATO-Russia Relations: The Facts," *North Atlantic Treaty Organization*, last updated December 17, 2015, http://www.nato.int/cps/en/natohq/topics_111767.htm.

53 Bill Gertz, "Russian Attack Submarine Sailed in Gulf of Mexico Undetected for Weeks, U.S. Officials Say," *The Washington Free Beacon*, August 14, 2012, http://freebeacon.com/national-security/silent-running/; Tom Parfitt, "Sweden Widens Search for 'Russian Submarine,'" *The Telegraph*, October 20, 2014, http://telegraph.co.uk/news/worldnews/europe/sweden/11175832/Sweden-widens-search-for-Russian-submarine.html; Chris Hughes, "Royal Navy Chases Four Russian Ships from the North Sea out into English Channel," *Mirror*, November 28, 2014, http://www.mirror.co.uk/news/uk-news/royal-navy-chases-four-russian-4715149.

54 Christopher Harress, "Russia's Cold War Tactics: A Map of Where Russian Planes are Probing Air Defenses," *IB Times*, November 13, 2014, http://www.ibtimes.com/russias-cold-war-tactics-map-where-russian-planes-are-probing-air-defenses-1723480.

55 Adrian Croft, "NATO: Russia Moves Troops Closer To Ukraine Border," *The World Post*, November 4, 2014, http://www.huffingtonpost.com/2014/11/04/russia-nato-ukraine_n_6101662.html.

Russian fighter planes have repeatedly entered the airspace of the Baltic states and Finland, performing maneuvers in an "unsafe and unprofessional" way, which could be identified as attempts to provoke a conflict.[56] Although two Russian bombers did not enter UK airspace, they were escorted out of an "area of UK interest" in February 2016.[57] Canadian fighter jets intercepted two Russian bombers flying about 75 kilometers off Canada's Arctic coast in September 2014.[58] Similarly, Russian bombers circled around NATO airspace, coming close to infringing above the territory of a French Delta-class ballistic missile submarine near the Bay of Biscay. Such actions were designed to send a "political message" to the West and to heighten anxieties.[59]

In mid-October 2015, the Turkish defense system shot down an unmarked Russian-made drone. Then, on November 24, 2015, after multiple overflights of its territory by Russian fighter jets, Turkey shot down a Russian military jet which had violated its airspace along the Syrian border.[60] Turkey claimed that ten warnings had been issued within five

---

56 Lidia Kelly (ed. Gareth Jones), "Russia: Here's Why We Sent a Fighter Plane to Intercept a US Aircraft," *Business Insider*, April 30, 2016, http://www.businessinsider.com/r-russia-defends-intercept-of-us-reconnaissance-plane-over-baltic-2016-4; "An 'Unsafe and Unprofessional' Intercept Over the Baltic Sea," *The Aviationist*, 2016, https://theaviationist.com/tag/baltic-air-policing/; Kati Pohjanpalo and Kasper Viita, "Finland's Fighter Jets on Alert as Russia Violates Airspace," *Bloomberg*, August 29, 2014, http://www.bloomberg.com/news/articles/2014-08-28/finland-puts-fighter-planes-on-alert-as-russia-violates-airspace.

57 "RAF Jets Intercept Russian Bombers Heading to UK," *BBC*, February 17, 2016, http://www.bbc.com/news/uk-35598892.

58 "Canadian Fighter Jets Intercept Russian Bombers in Arctic," *CBS News*, September 19, 2014, http://www.cbc.ca/news/canada/canadian-fighter-jets-intercept-russian-bombers-in-arctic-1.2772440. In an eight month span during 2014, NATO recorded nearly 40 specific instances of Russian violations of NATO airspace. See Lizzie Deardon, "Full List of Incidents Involving Russian Military and NATO since March 2014," *Independent*, November 10, 2014, http://www.independent.co.uk/news/world/europe/full-list-of-incidents-involving-russian-military-and-nato-since-march-2014-9851309.html.

59 Stephen Pifer, "Putin's Reckless Nuclear Saber-Rattling Is Just Show, *Newsweek*, March 18, 2016, http://www.newsweek.com/putin-reckless-nuclear-saber-rattling-just-show-biscay-437200; Helene Cooper, "Close Encounters with Jets Show Russia's Anger at NATO Buildup, U.S. Says," *NY Times*, May 8, 2016, http://www.nytimes.com/2016/05/09/world/europe/russia-us-jets-anger-nato-buildup.html?_r=0.

60 Dion Nissenbaum, Emre Peker, and James Marson, "Turkey Shoots Down Russian Military Jet," *The Wall Street Journal*, November 24, 2015, http://www.wsj.com/articles/turkey-shoots-down-jet-near-syria-border-1448356509.

minutes but the Russian pilot remained unresponsive, a declaration that was confirmed by U.S. intelligence. This particular encroachment of Turkish airspace was not an isolated event. The Turkish leadership had repeatedly warned Russia about breaching Turkish airspace from Syria.[61] Vladimir Putin claimed that the Russian jet was over Syria, and characterized Turkey's actions as a "stab in the back" and providing aid to terrorists, and emphasized that this event would have "serious consequences for Russian-Turkish relations"[62]—and it did. Russia launched a powerful propaganda campaign against Turkey; the Ministry of Defense suspended all military contracts with Turkey; Russia ceased all diplomatic contacts with Ankara, and Russian tourists were advised not to travel to Turkey.[63]

Importantly, since Russia was invited by the regime of Bashar al-Assad to intervene in the Syrian civil war in the beginning of October 2015, on the pretext of fighting terrorism, the Russian military completed its mission (as they claimed), and in mid-March 2016 withdrew troops from Syria.[64] In the process, Russia killed hundreds of civilians and destroyed Syrian hospitals with massive airstrikes, "using unguided or dumb bombs, far less precise than the satellite-guided weapons used by the U.S. military."[65] However, according to recent evidence, Russia's narrative about the alleged withdrawal of their military is untrue. The Russians built a new military base in Palmyra in Syria, although they continue to deny it.[66] A recently released video by Andrey Borodulin confirms that the Syrian desert city of Palmyra has been turned into a Russian military base

---

61 Nick Penzenstadler, "Turkey, NATO Call on Russia to Stop Airspace Violations," *USA Today*, January 30, 2016, http://www.usatoday.com/story/news/world/2016/01/30/turkey-says-another-russian-jet-violated-turkey's-airspace/79563500/.
62 Ibid.
63 Ibid.
64 According to Putin, Russia spent 33 billion rubles from the funds of the Ministry of Defense for the operation in Syria. See "Rossiia ukhodit iz Sirii: chto dalshe?," *News.mail.ru*, accessed July 6, 2016, https://news.mail.ru/card/70/.
65 Lucas Tomlinson, "Video of Military Convoy New Evidence Russia Not Pulling Out of Syria," *Military.com*, April 4, 2016, http://www.military.com/daily-news/2016/04/04/video-military-convoy-evidence-russia-not-pulling-out-of-syria.html.
66 Roman Kretsul, "Are Russia and the U.S. Building Military Bases in Syria?," *Russia Beyond the Headlines*, January 26, 2016, http://rbth.com/international/2016/01/26/are-russia-and-the-us-building-military-bases-in-syria_562379; "Russia Denies Report on New Military Base in Northern Syria," *Defense News*, January 25, 2016, http://www.defensenews.com/story/defense/2016/01/25/russia-denies-report-new-military-base-north-syria/79317974/. Taking a page from the tactics

where "a combined short to medium range surface-to-air missile and anti-aircraft artillery weapon system" called Pantsir-S1was installed.[67]

Videos of a Russian military convoy that was sent to Syria under the guise of a humanitarian mission in early April 2016 (a grim reminder of a tactic that largely shifted the tide of battle in the Ukrainian war) suggest that the Russians are increasing their military presence in Syria: according to a US defense official, "the Russians installed underground fuel tanks in their air base in Latakia," which suggests the Russians are pursuing long-term goals in Syria.[68] Interestingly, Russia's goals in Syria are not just about fighting terrorists, but include a major effort to be identified as a serious international power-broker, what some have called the "great power" image, an identity consistent with the "Third Rome" mythical avenging savior, able to project their power beyond the spatial constraints of their own borders.[69]

Russian military actions in Syria are quite similar to those employed in Ukraine. After the invasion and annexation of the Crimean peninsula, Russia transformed it into a huge military base that hosts sophisticated military equipment, including tactical nuclear weapons. TU-22M3 bombers constitute the core of a Russian special aviation group that is located at one of the Crimean airports. According to an official of the Russian Ministry of Defense, this was a response to the United States which had established a PRO global missile system in Romania.[70] In February 2016,

---

of ISIS fighters, Russia's base in Palmyra is sheltered by an important archeological site. See Bassem Mroue, "Russia Builds Military Camp Near Ancient Site in Palmyra," *Yahoo News*, May 17, 2016, http://finance.yahoo.com/news/report-russians-building-army-syrias-palmyra-103558096.html.

67 Zen Adra, "In Video: Russia Sets Up New Military Base in Palmyra," *Al Masdar News*, May 7, 2016, https://www.almasdarnews.com/article/video-russia-sets-new-military-base-palmyra/.

68 Tomlinson, "Video of Military Convoy New Evidence."

69 Margaret Klein, "Russia's Military Capabilities: 'Great Power' Ambitions and Reality," *German Institute for International and Security Affairs* (SWP Research Paper), October 12, 2009, https://www.swp-berlin.org/fileadmin/contents/products/research_papers/2009_RP12_kle_ks.pdf; Ali Hashem, "Goals of Russia's Recent Military Action Go Beyond Syria," *U.S. News*, October 8, 2015, http://www.usnews.com/news/articles/2015/10/08/goals-of-russias-recent-military-action-go-beyond-syria.

70 "Rosiia rozmistyt v aneksovanomy Krymu raketonostsi-bombarduvalnyky TU-22M3," *Ekspres.ua*, July 22, 2015, http://expres.ua/world/2015/07/22/144592-rosiya-rozmistyt-aneksovanomu-krymu-raketonosci-bombarduvalnyky-tu-22m3; "Russia Turned Crimea Into a Military Base: Tatar Leader," *Yahoo News*, March

Sergei Shoigu, Russian Minister of Defense, reported to Putin about a large-scale Russian military training exercise that took place in Opuk (Crimea) and was designed to advance the participants' skills in neutralizing foreign marines and protecting the coastline of the Black Sea.[71] Official conservative estimates put Russian troop strength in Russian-occupied Crimea at somewhere near 20, 000 soldiers and seamen, with other estimates ranging as high as 28, 000.[72]

Russia's military campaigns in Ukraine and Syria have sandwiched Turkey between at least two naval/military bases, in Tartus and Sevastopol.[73] Both have extensive naval facilities which increases Russia's wartime potential and capacities. As the earlier historical discussion has demonstrated, for Russia, warm-water Black Sea ports have long played a crucial role in Russian foreign policy, and in the Russian imagination to gain permanent control of the Straits. Edward Delman has observed that

> Russia isn't landlocked, of course, but Europe-facing ports such as Arkhangelsk and St. Petersburg were historically ice-locked for part of the year before the advent of the icebreaker in the 20th century (Russia's post of Murmansk is ice-free, but it was built in 1915, and the Russian port of Vladivistok is on the Pacific). Moreover, none of these ports, even when open for business, allow for easy access to the bustling Mediterranean Sea. This has left Russia with an economic and military incentive to expand toward warmer waters.[74]

Control of the Black Sea, and of the Black Sea basin, particularly the Turkish Straits, will make Russia's access to the Mediterranean possible, and this is a powerful consideration that guides the Russian Federation's

---

19, 2015, https://www.yahoo.com/news/russia-turned-crimea-military-tatar-leader-221751657.html?ref=gs.

71   "Chernomorskii flot i VDV zashchishchaiut bereg Kryma ot 'vrazheskogo' dissanta," *News.mail.ru*, February 11, 2016, https://news.mail.ru/politics/24814067/?frommail=1. The Russian fortifications in Latakia suggest further encroachment toward Turkish territory.

72   Phil Stewart, "Pentagon Says 20,000 Russian Troops May Be in Crimea," *Reuters*, March 7, 2014, http://www.reuters.com/article/us-ukraine-crisis-pentagon-id USBREA261RC20140307; "Russian Invasion of Ukraine," *Ukrainian Policy*, March 1, 2014, http://ukrainianpolicy.com/russian-invasion-of-ukraine/.

73   Edward Delman, "The Link Between Putin's Military Campaigns in Syria and Ukraine," *The Atlantic*, October 2, 2015, http://www.theatlantic.com/international/archive/2015/10/navy-base-syria-crimea-putin/408694/.

74   Ibid.

foreign policy today. U.S. Navy Captain Sean R. Liedman has contended that the annexation of the Crimean peninsula in March of 2014 and the release of the "Maritime Doctrine of Russian Federation 2020" in July of 2015, as well as deployment of Russian military forces to Syria, confirmed that maintaining naval access "has become a centerpiece of President Putin's foreign policy and may shed light on future Russian foreign policy goals."[75] Indeed, restoring Russian naval power seems to be a priority for Putin in his endeavor to achieve Russian geopolitical dominance in several regions: the Atlantic, Arctic, Antarctic, Caspian, Indian Ocean, and Pacific. Putin's "Maritime Doctrine" emphasizes that "[h]istorically, Russia [is] the leading maritime power," and, according to the majority of Russian politicians, its power is meant to be restored because of NATO expansion. For instance, Deputy Prime Minister Dmitrii Rogozin believes that because of this threat, there is a pressing need "to integrate Crimea and the Sevastopol naval base into the Russian economy, and to re-establish a permanent Russian Navy presence in the Mediterranean."[76] The scope of the "restoration" initiative appears to be quite broad, and might in the nearest future reach levels similar to those of the Soviet Union's capacities during the Cold War, when "the Soviet Navy enjoyed access to bases in Algeria, Libya, Egypt, and Yugoslavia to sustain continuous naval influence in the Mediterranean Sea."[77]

The Russian military base in Tartus that is located on Syria's western coast was established in 1971. By using economic and political pressure, as was the case with Ukraine when throughout its independence Russia negotiated the presence of the Russian fleet in Sevastopol, Russian political leaders managed to preserve the Tartus base after 1991, manipulating Syria into an agreement of mutual interest: The Russians would forgive the Syrian multi-billion dollar debt to the Soviet Union, and in return the Syrians would allow the Russian navy to expand there to maintain its presence in the Mediterranean. Today, together with the

---

75 Sean R. Liedman, "Vladimir Putin's Naval Ambitions Have Only Begun," *Defense in Depth* (Janine Davidson's blog), September 30, 2015, http://blogs.cfr.org/davidson/2015/09/30/vladimir-putins-naval-ambitions-have-only-begun/; see "Morskaia doktrina Rosiiskoi Federatsii" (*Maritime Doctrine of Russian Federation*), *Static.Kremlin.ru*, 2015, http://static.kremlin.ru/media/events/files/ru/uAFi5nvux2twaqjftS5yrIZUVTJan77L.pdf.
76 Quoted in Liedman "Vladimir Putin's Naval Ambitions Have Only Begun."
77 Liedman "Vladimir Putin's Naval Ambitions Have Only Begun."

Latakia base, Russia has establish a strong foothold in Syria. Clearly, fighting ISIS and terrorism allowed the Russians to camouflage their long-standing goal to eventually gain control over the Straits.[78] Turkey still remains the main obstacle but the process of its destabilization, or shaking (*rasshatyvaniie*), seems to have begun.

Recep Tayyip Erdoğan, President of Turkey, has expressed legitimate concerns about Russia's actions in Syria. According to him, Russia's actions in Syria are nothing less than its occupation, and the creation of a quasi-state for Assad that would be fully controlled by Russia. He has emphasized that Russia bears the ultimate responsibility for the deaths of 400,000 people in Syria, and Turkey is naturally nervous: "Our border with Syria constitutes 911 kilometers. Do Russia and Iran have borders with Syria? What are they doing there?" Erdoğan has also opined that the Russians' justification for being in Syria is that Assad invited them: "One should not accept every invitation," especially when the president of Syria is a "tyrant and murderer," and those who support him are his "accomplices."[79]

The hostile rhetoric employed by Turkey and Russia escalated when the Russian Deputy Minister of Foreign Affairs Aleksei Meshkov demanded that Turkey pay compensation for the Russian military jet shot down by the Turkish missile defense.[80] Tanju Bilgiç, Turkish Foreign Ministry spokesperson, rejected the demand, advising the Russians to stop violating international laws. In response, Russia introduced sanctions in the political and economic spheres, including trade, the closing of Russian ports to Turkish ships, and restrictions on the use of Russian airspace for Turkish aircraft. Moreover, the sanctions would affect the functioning of the gas pipeline "The Turkish Stream."[81]

---

78    Russia's dominance in Syria has of course other goals. But the Straits play a key role in Russia's foreign policies and strategies.

79    "Erdogan obvinil Rossiiu i Asada v gibeli 400,000 tys. Siriitsev," *Infox.ru*, February 5, 2016, http://www.infox.ru/authority/foreign/2016/02/05/Erdogan_obvinil_Ross.phtml?ntvk1_source=sem_recommend.

80    Denis Rakhuba, "Turtsiia ne budet vozmeshchat ushcherb RF za cbityi SU-24—Tanju Bilgiç," *Top.novostimira.com*, December 16, 2015, http://top.novostimira.biz/fulltext_164422.html.

81    "Sanktsii protiv Turtsii zatronut gazoprovod 'Turetskii potok'—Aleksei Uliukaev," *Top.novostimira.com*, November 26, 2015, http://www.novostimira.com.ua/news_163607.html.

Russia's economic sanctions and Russia's general attitude toward Turkey prompted Erdoğan to look at Ukraine in a new light—as a partner and a potential ally in search of economic and military cooperation. Turkey's early response to Russia's invasion of Ukraine was largely muted, essentially for economic reasons, not the least of which is Turkey's strong dependence on Russia for natural gas and oil.[82] But in February 2016, Turkey approached Arsenii Iatseniuk's government with a proposition to create a zone of free trade that would facilitate economic cooperation between their two countries.[83] On April 4, 2016, two military ships of the Turkish Navy, TCG "Salihreis" and TCG "Bartin," entered the Odesa port, where they were met by Oleh Doskato, commander of the Western Naval Base, and Denys Ivanin, commander of the warship "Hetman Sahaidachnyi." The meeting was organized at the highest level to design an effective program of exchange and military cooperation between Turkey and Ukraine.[84]

As a central discursive formation in Russian national consciousness, the "Third Rome" myth can be identified as a conceptual element in Russian intellectual history, as a pragmatic instrument in the implementation of Russian domestic and foreign policy, and as a rationale for Russian military adventurism and expansion in Georgia, Ukraine, Turkey, and other littoral states of the Black Sea basin. In this context, it seems appropriate to turn the reader's attention to the appeal of the "Third Rome" narrative to account for prospective Russian actions designed to restore Russian greatness.

## Implications

The "Third Rome" myth greatly influences Russian self-identity and Russian nationalism, and often infiltrates Russian foreign and military policies. Domestically, the myth serves as a significant point of unification for a

---

[82] Soner Cagaptay and James F. Jeffrey, "Turkey's Muted Reaction to the Crimean Crises," *Washington Institute*, March 4, 2014, http://www.washingtoninstitute.org/policy-analysis/view/turkeys-muted-reaction-to-the-crimean-crisis.

[83] "Turechchyna proponuie Ukraini nehaino pidpysaty uhodu pro ZVT," *Ekspres.ua*, February 15, 2016, http://expres.ua/news/2016/02/15/173468-turechchyna-proponuye-ukrayini-negayno-pidpysaty-ugodu-zvt.

[84] "Turetski viiskovi korabli zaishly v Odeskyi port," *Ekspres.ua*, April 4, 2016, http://expres.ua/news/2016/04/04/180794-turecki-viyskovi-korabli-zayshly-odeskyy-port.

nation newly emerged from nearly a century of Soviet control. Indeed, the post-Ukrainian invasion imposition of sanctions by the European Union, United States, and others serves to reinforce the "Third Rome" narrative, and unite the Russian people by once again adopting their messianic mantle and struggling through difficult times. Among the Russian ruling elite, military, political and economic leaders, the "Third Rome" myth provides a convenient subterfuge for neo-colonialism, expansionism, and the pursuit of military advantage. Although the implications of recent Russian gains acquired through the tacit substantiation of the "Third Rome" myth are extensive, the geographic, political and economic gains seem most significant. Additionally, the myth of the "Third Rome" may provide a framework for anticipating future Russian actions in the Black Sea basin and beyond.

The implications of Russia's activities in the Black Sea basin begin with the geopolitical repercussions that are just now being realized. Initially, a policy of benign appeasement seemed to be the international response to Russia's invasion of Georgia's and Ukraine's sovereign territories. In other words, the limited sanctions against Russia for its military adventurism signaled an international willingness to grant Russia some degree of control in its "near abroad," or its "sphere of influence." But Russian expansion into Turkey, or gaining control of the Straits, would immeasurably upset the geostrategic balance in the region. Russian military and naval bases in Georgia, Russian-occupied Crimea, and Syria would prove very formidable, flanking Turkey and the Straits with bases which very likely have become permanent fixtures in the littoral regions of the Mediterranean and Black Seas, around what is currently open international waters.

The present manifestation of Russia's interest in the Black Sea region should not be viewed as a new occurrence, nor should it be understood as a series of disconnected military events. As noted earlier, Russia's desire to control the Black Sea basin has its roots in ancient and modern history. The prohibitive factor in Russia attaining its goals in this region has been and continues to be Turkey. The lack of a contiguous land mass makes it decidedly difficult for Russia to invade the sovereign territory of Turkey to gain control of the Straits. Yet recent provocations may provide just such an excuse. Although the Russian military tactic of encirclement has been underway with great sincerity for at least the past 20 years, their closest approach right now emanates from enclaves in

Syria on the south, Georgia and Nagorno-Karabakh on the east, and Russian-occupied Crimea and eastern Ukraine on the north. But given the historical geostrategic significance of the Straits for the Russians, it should be expected that they will continue to pursue control in this region, and may have already achieved it. Recent reports of Russian warships and fighter jets harassing U.S. naval vessels in the eastern Mediterranean and Black Seas offer a sobering glimpse of Russia's degree of control over a strategic space they have pursued for centuries.[85] Indeed, Turkish President Erdoğan, recognizing the impending danger, signaled a shift in his country's Black Sea policies by noting NATO's absence had essentially turned the Black Sea "into a Russian lake." Turkey has since provided naval reinforcement to Romania and Bulgaria, and "political and military support to Ukraine."[86]

In essence, Russia has established de facto control over the Turkish Straits through the use of frozen conflicts, essentially controlling a geographic position which they had heretofore been unable to control through other means. These stalemates serve Russian purposes in controlling the Black Sea basin by providing wedges, or opportunities for Russia to quasi-legally inject their forces and ultimately their control in many countries of the Black Sea littoral.[87] Georgia and Ukraine are already deeply entangled in this process. Important ports and coastal regions of both countries have

---

[85] See, for example Luis Martinez, Patrick Reevell, and Elizabeth Mclaughlin, "US Officials Say Russian Warship Intentionally Interfered With Navy Operations," *ABC News*, June 2, 29, 2016, https://gma.yahoo.com/us-officials-russian-warship-intentionally-interfered-navy-operations-160004019--abc-news-topstories.html; Idrees Ali, "Russian Warship Made 'Unprofessional' Maneuver: U.S. Official," *Reuters*, July 1, 2016, https://www.yahoo.com/news/russian-warship-made-unprofessional-maneuver-u-official-235446945.html; Doug Stanglin, "Russia Vows Response to U.S. Naval Ship's Entry into Black Sea," *USA Today*, June 10, 2016, http://www.usatoday.com/story/news/2016/06/10/russia-vows-response-us-naval-ships-entry-into-black-sea/85686822; Steve Scherer, "U.S. Says It Will Stay in Black Sea Despite Russian Warning," *Reuters*, June 6, 2016, http://www.reuters.com/article/us-usa-defense-navy-blacksea-idUSKCN0Z30WG; Richard Weitz, "After Ukraine, Black Sea Becomes Contested Zone for Russia, NATO," *World Politics Review*, December 2, 2014, http://www.worldpoliticsreview.com/articles/14556/after-ukraine-black-sea-becomes-contested-zone-for-russia-nato.

[86] "Erdogan to Lead NATO Challenge against Russia on Black Sea?," *Guardian*, May 18, 2016, https://off-guardian.org/2016/05/20/erdogan-to-lead-nato-challenge-against-russia-on-black-sea/.

[87] For a discussion of the value of frozen conflicts in Russian military strategy, see Blank, "Russia and the Black Sea's Frozen Conflicts in Strategic Perspective."

been annexed and Russian forces have moved in to fortify those strategic positions. There is sufficient evidence to suggest that Turkey is currently threatened with encirclement, and the slightest provocation may force Turkey to yield control over strategic areas such as the Straits. Moving forward, it seems quite plausible that Russia may attempt to destabilize the Turkish countryside further, and there are events that suggest the sort of provocation that may tip the balance toward more overt destabilization in Turkey. For example, in the explanatory context of the "Third Rome" myth, Russia stands as the guardian shield against the chaos of the world that threatens the Orthodox conservative values that undergird the Russian Foreign Policy concept. In Turkey, the increasing dangers of regular terrorist bombings in Istanbul, in the area nearest the "golden gates" of the Straits, or attempted coups by the Turkish military, may indeed represent the sort of chaos that proves too unsettling for the Russians. International waterways, such as the Turkish Straits, cannot be safely traversed if there are regular terrorist attacks or military uprisings in the immediate area.[88] Any imminent terrorist threat to shipping would have to be curtailed. To fight terrorism and to control chaos, Russia may be forced to establish military bases on the Straits, or increase the pressure of encirclement, to force the Turks to concede such strategic ground—for the good of international interests. One recent example seems especially noteworthy. Because NATO nations have not been outwardly supportive of Turkey's more hard-line stance in the Black Sea basin, Turkey has adopted a more conciliatory tone toward Russia. In a recent statement, Turkish Foreign Minister Mevlut Cavusoglu hinted at a major strategic

---

88  Krishnadev Calamur, Matt Vasilogambros, J. Weston Phippen, David A. Graham, Yasmeen Serhan, and Matt Ford, "What's Going On in Turkey?" *The Atlantic*, July 21, 2016, http://www.theatlantic.com/news/archive/2016/07/turkey-government/491579/?utm_source=yahoo&yptr=yahoo; Erin Cunningham and Hugh Naylor, "Turkish Authorities Granted Emergency Powers Amid 'Cleansing' after Failed Coup," *The Washington Post*, July 21, 2016, https://www.washingtonpost.com/world/state-of-emergency-begins-in-turkey-with-new-arrests-of-judges-generals/2016/07/21/604afada-4eb2-11e6-bf27-405106836f96_story.html; Katy Lee, "Istanbul Nearly a Ghost Town as Tourists Stay Away," *AFP*, July 3, 2016, https://www.yahoo.com/news/istanbul-nearly-ghost-town-tourists-stay-away-032207062.html; "Deadly Car Bomb Attack in Istanbul, Turkey," *Yahoo news*, June 7, 2016, https://www.yahoo.com/news/deadly-car-bomb-attack-istanbul-171728272.html.

concession to the Russians, allowing them access to the Incirlik airbase, an airbase traditionally reserved for use by NATO member nations.[89]

Logistically, taking and holding the sovereign territory of other countries is costly; economically, as supply lines would be difficult to maintain, and as scarce resources are diverted to a full war economy; geopolitically, as Russia would become more and more isolated as the West finally recognizes the need to respond in a manner other than appeasement; and domestically, when dead soldiers are returned to their families, and people are forced to endure shortages. But the nature of "frozen conflicts" offers several decided advantages: militarily, proxy forces often take on a good deal of the burden of the actual fighting; economically, stalemates restrict the inflow of investment capital and resources contributing to further destabilization, and the actual costs of maintaining an occupational force are greatly reduced; thus, a strategic initiative is therefore gained with a minimum of long-term investment or risk. Frozen conflicts do not necessarily result in the acquisition of territory, but they do keep opponents off balance and unable to muster an appropriate defense.

As the noose of frozen conflicts slowly strangles Turkey, it may be reasonable to explore possible future conflicts or potential military campaigns. Since Russia does seem to have established some degree of control over the Black Sea, any offshore oil or gas exploration will likely require some form of appeasement or exaction, perhaps a share in the offshore leases that already have been established by Romania and Bulgaria.[90] The "Third Rome" narrative also provides a convenient rationale for Russian attempts to control energy exploration, development, and distribution in the Black Sea basin and beyond. Insofar as the development of these Black Sea resources might make Europe and the

---

[89] Ece Toksabay and Dmitry Solovyov, "Turkey Proposes Cooperation with Russia in Fighting Islamic State," *Reuters/Yahoo News*, July 4, 2016, https://www.yahoo.com/news/turkey-proposes-cooperation-russia-fighting-foreign-minister-091805123.html.

[90] For a broad discussion of the Russian energy industry and its control, see, for example, John Biersack and Shannon O'Lear, "The Geopolitics of Russia's Annexation of Crimea: Narratives, Identity, Silences, and Energy," *Eurasian Geography and Economics* 55, no. 3 (2014): 247–69; Karen Dawisha, *Putin's Kleptocracy: Who Owns Russia?* (New York: Simon and Schuster, 2014); Marshall I. Goldman, *Petrostate: Putin, Power, and the New Russia* (New York: Oxford University Press, 2010).

littoral states of the Black and Mediterranean Seas less dependent on Russian energy supplies, the Russians may feel justified to pursue control of these resources to maintain their messianic position, to protect these resources so the decadent, and by implication, untrustworthy West, does not misuse or destroy them, or worse, employ them against Russia. There is some evidence to indicate that Russian attempts to influence international decisions about the means of energy distribution in and around the Black Sea are being addressed politically, and, if political avenues are unproductive, Russia seems well-positioned to facilitate their energy goals in other ways as well.[91] Of course, the myth of the "Third Rome" continues to function as cover for such coercion, at home, where the threat from the West (i.e., NATO) must be combatted by the guardian forces. Additional threats and expansion can be expected in many directions—westward toward an increasingly fragmented European Union, particularly Romania and Bulgaria; southward where the disruption of everyday life in Turkey may be expected to continue until chaos reigns—increasing terror attacks near the Straits, airport attacks in Istanbul, growing Syrian advances toward Aleppo and the Turkish border.

Whether the "Third Rome" myth truly influences Russian foreign and military policy may be open to conjecture. But there certainly seem to be some pragmatic opportunities where some elements of the myth are invoked to justify foreign incursions, and to contribute to the ideology that sustains the development of Russia's national identity that everyday takes deeper hold of the Russian people.[92] Like any narrative, the power of the "Third Rome" myth rests in its flexibility, its capacity to accommodate incremental alterations without surrendering the essential character of the myth, or the moral of the story. When the social reality of a powerful

---

91   Nick Cunningham, "Greek Pipeline Breakthrough to Challenge Russian Gas Dominance," *Oilprice*, May 18, 2016, http://finance.yahoo.com/news/greek-pipeline-breakthrough-challenge-russian-214200101.html; Kalyeena Makortoff, "Putin Courts Athens Ahead of Vote on Sanctions Extension," *CNBC*, May 27, 2016, http://www.cnbc.com/2016/05/27/putin-courts-athens-ahead-of-vote-on-sanctions-extension.html; Tugce Vargol, "Russia Remains Determined to Stop Israel-Turkey Pipeline Deal," *Oilprice*, June 17, 2016, http://finance.yahoo.com/news/russia-remains-determined-stop-isreal-205026182.html.

92   Richard Arnold, "Surveys Show Russian Nationalism is on the Rise. This Explains a Lot about the Country's Foreign and Domestic Politics," *The Washington Post*, May 30, 2016, https://www.washingtonpost.com/news/monkey-cage/wp/2016/05/30/surveys-show-russian-nationalism-is-on-the-rise-this-explains-a-lot-about-the-countrys-foreign-and-domestic-politics/.

discursive formation is confronted with a profound threat to its epistemological and ontological foundations, events that might ultimately result in the negation of the self-concept and national identity constructed by the myth, strong responses should be anticipated.[93] For example, NATO's placement of missile defense systems in Romania tests the ideological devotion of the Russian people as well as Russian military pretensions,[94] and equally importantly, the avaricious hunger of the Russian energy sector. No matter how the missile sites are characterized, as defensive or not, their mere presence challenges fundamental Russian ideological positions. The placement of these missile sites serves as symbolic tears in the rhetorical power of the narrative of the "Third Rome" myth, rends in the fabric of the myth that may be of sufficient magnitude to shake the foundations of the myth itself. In this context, Putin's threats that Romania is now "in the crosshairs" should be taken not just as a reaction to the placement of the missiles, but as the recognition of a more dangerous threat to the "Third Rome" narrative.[95] Were the narrative of the myth to unravel, so too might Putin's power. Accordingly, when challenges to the social reality constructed in and through the "Third Rome" myth occur, threatening the narrative that unifies the Russian people and which thereby supports the power base for Russian leadership, some transformative action should be expected in an attempt to transcend the divergent event.

---

93  For an elaboration of the manner in which myth and narrative coopt and assimilate divergent views, see James E. Ettema and Theodore L. Glasser, "Narrative Form and Moral Force: The Realization of Innocence and Guilt Through Investigative Journalism," *Journal of Communication* 38, no. 3 (1988): 8–26; Leroy G. Dorsey and Rachel M. Harlow, "'We Want Americans Pure and Simple': Theodore Roosevelt and the Myth of Americanism," *Rhetoric & Public Affairs* 6, no. 1 (2003): 55–78; William F. Lewis, "Telling America's Story: Narrative Form and the Reagan Presidency," *Quarterly Journal of Speech* 73 no. 3 (1987): 280–302.

94  Vladimir Isachenkov, "Putin Warns Russia Will Respond to NATO Missile Shield," *AP The Big Story*, May 13, 2016, http://bigstory.ap.org/article/ea2043f4d9154d03b857ed49e5ac6b9d/putin-warns-russia-will-respond-nato-missile-shield.

95  For a brief analysis of Putin's threat against Romania, see, for example, Patrick Goodenough, "As NATO Plans More Troops for Poland, Russia Decries 'Cold War-Era Security Schemes,'" *CNS News*, May 31, 2016, http://www.cnsnews.com/news/article/patrick-goodenogh/nato-plans-send-more-troops-poland-russia-decries-cold-war-era.

There may be disagreement over the origins of the "Third Rome" myth, but the employment of the myth to unify the Russian nation and to sustain its post-Soviet identity provides a dynamic empowering force behind belief, decision, and ultimately action. Insofar as changes external to the controlling narrative can be subsumed or accommodated within the dominant narrative, if there is sufficient space to incorporate such alterations, then the narrative will maintain its centrality. But if the narrative is inflexible, there are at least two potential courses that may ensue: first, the dominant narrative may be dropped—an unlikely alternative as it requires a drastic, almost sacrilegious transformation of identity; second, the eradication of the objectionable interjections, correcting the narrative by eliminating or coopting the new events that challenge it.

In the context of the narrative of the "Third Rome" myth, the fundamental identity so constructed should not be expected to change dramatically, because to do so would require a denial of that narrative. Without a unifying narrative, chaos would ensue. In this context, the "Third Rome" myth sanctions Russian hegemony in the Black Sea basin. More importantly, without an alternative belief system or a competing narrative, events such as the invasion of Ukraine, the annexation of the Crimean peninsula, and gains in Georgia and elsewhere will not likely be easily undone. Insofar as they can be justified at home under the narrative of the "Third Rome," the popularity of such invasions is sacrosanct and consistent with the Russian national identity and individual self-identify, and should be expected to endure.

## Bibliography

Adra, Zen. "In Video: Russia Sets Up New Military Base in Palmyra." *Al Masdar News.* May 7, 2016. https://www.almasdarnews.com/article/video-russia-sets-new-military-base-palmyra/.

Ali, Idrees. "Russian Warship Made 'Unprofessional' Maneuver: U.S. Official." *Reuters.* July 1, 2016. https://www.yahoo.com/news/russian-warship-made-unprofessional-maneuver-u-official-235446945.html.

"An 'Unsafe and Unprofessional' Intercept Over the Baltic Sea." *The Aviationist.* 2016. https://theaviationist.com/tag/baltic-air-policing/.

Arnold, Richard. "Surveys Show Russian Nationalism is on the Rise. This Explains a Lot about the Country's Foreign and Domestic Politics." *The Washington Post.* May 30, 2016. https://www.washingtonpost.com/news/monkey-cage/wp/2016/05/30/surveys-show-russian-nationalism-is-on-the-rise-this-explains-a-lot-about-the-countrys-foreign-and-domestic-politics/.

Bentley, Jerry H., and Herbert F. Zeigler. *Traditions & Encounters: A Global Perspective on the Past*, vol. II, 4th ed. New York: The McGraw-Hill Companies, Inc., 2008.

Bertelsen, Olga. "Joseph Brodsky's Imperial Consciousness." *Scripta Historica*, no. 21 (2015): 263–89.

Biersack, John, and Shannon O'Lear. "The Geopolitics of Russia's Annexation of Crimea: Narratives, Identity, Silences, and Energy." *Eurasian Geography and Economics* 55, no. 3 (2014): 247–69.

Blank, Stephen. "Russia and the Black Sea's Frozen Conflicts in Strategic Perspective." *Mediterranean Quarterly* 19, no. 3 (2008): 23–54.

Cagaptay, Soner, and James F. Jeffrey. "Turkey's Muted Reaction to the Crimean Crises." *Washington Institute*. March 4, 2014. http://www.washingtoninstitute.org/policy-analysis/view/turkeys-muted-reaction-to-the-crimean-crisis.

Calamur, Krishnadev, Matt Vasilogambros, J. Weston Phippen, David A. Graham, Yasmeen Serhan, and Matt Ford. "What's Going On in Turkey?" *The Atlantic*. July 21, 2016. http://www.theatlantic.com/news/archive/2016/07/turkey-government/491579/?utm_source=yahoo&yptr=yahoo.

"Canadian Fighter Jets Intercept Russian Bombers in Arctic." *CBS News*. September 19, 2014. http://www.cbc.ca/news/canada/canadian-fighter-jets-intercept-russian-bombers-in-arctic-1.2772440.

"Chernomorskii flot i VDV zashchishchaiut bereg Kryma ot 'vrazheskogo' dissanta." *News.mail.ru*. February 11, 2016. https://news.mail.ru/politics/24814067/?frommail=1.

Cooper, Helene. "Close Encounters with Jets Show Russia's Anger at NATO Buildup, U.S. Says." *NY Times*. May 8, 2016. http://www.nytimes.com/2016/05/09/world/europe/russia-us-jets-anger-nato-buildup.html?_r=0.

Coyer, Paul. "Putin's Holy War and the Disintegration of the 'Russian World.'" *Forbes*. June 4, 2015. http://www.forbes.com/sites/paulcoyer/2015/06/04/putins-holy-war-and-the-disintegration-of-the-russian-world/#35c396601097.

Croft, Adrian. "NATO: Russia Moves Troops Closer To Ukraine Border." *The World Post*. November 4, 2014. http://www.huffingtonpost.com/2014/11/04/russia-nato-ukraine_n_6101662.html.

Cunningham, Erin, and Hugh Naylor. "Turkish Authorities Granted Emergency Powers Amid 'Cleansing' after Failed Coup." *The Washington Post*. July 21, 2016. https://www.washingtonpost.com/world/state-of-emergency-begins-in-turkey-with-new-arrests-of-judges-generals/2016/07/21/604afada-4eb2-11e6-bf27-405106836f96_story.html.

Cunningham, Nick. "Greek Pipeline Breakthrough to Challenge Russian Gas Dominance." *Oilprice*. May 18, 2016. http://finance.yahoo.com/news/greek-pipeline-breakthrough-challenge-russian-214200101.html.

Daly, John C.K. "Russia Claims Ukraine's Black Sea Oil and Gas Bounty." *OilPrice.com*. May 7, 2014. http://oilprice.com/Energy/Energy-General/Russia-Claims-Ukraines-Black-Sea-Oil-And-Gas-Bounty.html.

Davies, Norman. *Europe: A History*. New York: HarperPerennial, 1998.

———. *Vanished Kingdoms: The Rise and Fall of States and Nations*. London: Penguin Books, 2011.

Dawisha, Karen. *Putin's Kleptocracy: Who Owns Russia?* New York: Simon and Schuster, 2014.

"Deadly Car Bomb Attack in Istanbul, Turkey." *Yahoo news.* June 7, 2016. https://www.yahoo.com/news/deadly-car-bomb-attack-istanbul-171728272.html.

Deardon, Lizzie. "Full List of Incidents Involving Russian Military and NATO since March 2014." *Independent.* November 10, 2014. http://www.independent.co.uk/news/world/europe/full-list-of-incidents-involving-russian-military-and-nato-since-march-2014-9851309.html.

Delman, Edward. "The Link Between Putin's Military Campaigns in Syria and Ukraine." *The Atlantic.* October 2, 2015. http://www.theatlantic.com/international/archive/2015/10/navy-base-syria-crimea-putin/408694/.

Dorsey, Leroy G., and Rachel M. Harlow. "'We Want Americans Pure and Simple': Theodore Roosevelt and the Myth of Americanism." *Rhetoric & Public Affairs* 6, no. 1 (2003): 55–78.

Duncan, Peter J. S. *Russian Messianism: Third Rome, Revolution, Communism and After.* London and New York: Routledge, 2000.

Dvornik, Francis. *The Slavs in European History and Civilization.* New Brunswick, NJ: Rutgers University Press, 1962.

Engstrom, Maria. "Contemporary Russian Messianism and New Russian Foreign Policy." *Contemporary Security Policy*, no. 3 (2014): 356–79.

Ettema, James E., and Theodore L. Glasser. "Narrative Form and Moral Force: The Realization of Innocence and Guilt Through Investigative Journalism." *Journal of Communication* 38, no. 3 (1988): 8–26.

"Erdogan obvinil Rossiiu i Asada v gibeli 400,000 tys. Siriitsev." *Infox.ru.* February 5, 2016. http://www.infox.ru/authority/foreign/2016/02/05/Erdogan_obvinil_Ross.phtml?ntvk1_source=sem_recommend.

"Erdogan to Lead NATO Challenge against Russia on Black Sea?" *Guardian.* May 18, 2016. https://off-guardian.org/2016/05/20/erdogan-to-lead-nato-challenge-against-russia-on-black-sea/.

Fisher, Walter R. *Human Communication as Narration: Toward a Philosophy of Reason, Value, and Action.* Columbia, SC: University of South Carolina Press, 1987.

―――. "Narration as a Human Communication Paradigm: The Case of Public Moral Argument." *Communication Monographs* 51, no. 1 (1984): 1–22.

"Focus: East Central Europe: Better Times to Come." *Mining-journal.com.* July 18, 2014. http://www.euromines.org/files/publications/mining-journal-feature-july-2014-east-central-europe.pdf.

Foucault, Michel. *History of Human Sexuality: Volume I: An Introduction.* New York: Vintage Books/A Division of Random House, 1978.

―――. *The Archeology of Knowledge and the Discourse on Language.* Translated by A. M. Sheridan Smith. New York: Pantheon Books, 1972.

Gertz, Bill. "Russian Attack Submarine Sailed in Gulf of Mexico Undetected for Weeks, U.S. Officials Say." *The Washington Free Beacon.* August 14, 2012. http://freebeacon.com/national-security/silent-running/.

Gill, Ann. *Rhetoric and Human Understanding.* Prospect Heights, Ill: Waveland Press, Inc., 1994.

Goldman, Marshall I. *Petrostate: Putin, Power, and the New Russia.* New York: Oxford University Press, 2010.

Goodenough, Patrick. "As NATO Plans More Troops for Poland, Russia Decries 'Cold War-Era Security Schemes.'" *CNS News.* May 31, 2016. http://www.cnsnews.com/news/article/patrick-goodenogh/nato-plans-send-more-troops-poland-russia-decries-cold-war-era.

Harress, Christopher. "Russia's Cold War Tactics: A Map of Where Russian Planes are Probing Air Defenses." *IB Times.* November 13, 2014. http://www.ibtimes.com/russias-cold-war-tactics-map-where-russian-planes-are-probing-air-defenses-1723480.

Hashem, Ali. "Goals of Russia's Recent Military Action Go Beyond Syria." *U.S. News.* October 8, 2015. http://www.usnews.com/news/articles/2015/10/08/goals-of-russias-recent-military-action-go-beyond-syria.

Hösch, Von Edgar. "Die Idee der Translatio Imperii im Moskauer Russland." *EGO.* March 12, 2010. http://ieg-ego.eu/de/threads/modelle-und-stereotypen/modell-anti ke/edgar-hoesch-die-idee-der-translatio-imperii-im-moskauer-russland/?searchterm=H%C3%B6sch,%20Von%20Edgar.%20%E2%80%9CDie%20Idee%20der%20 Translatio%20Imperii%20im%20Moskauer%20Russland.%E2%80%9D&set_lang uage=de.

Hughes, Chris. "Royal Navy Chases Four Russian Ships from the North Sea out into English Channel." *Mirror.* November 28, 2014. http://www.mirror.co.uk/news/uk-news/royal-navy-chases-four-russian-4715149.

Hutsalo, Ievhen. *Mentalnist ordy.* Kyiv: KMA, 2007.

Isachenkov, Vladimir. "Putin Warns Russia Will Respond to NATO Missile Shield." *AP The Big Story.* May 13, 2016. http://bigstory.ap.org/article/ea2043f4d9154d03b857ed49e5ac6b9d/putin-warns-russia-will-respond-nato-missile-shield.

Itkowitz Shifrinson, Joshua R. "Russia's Got a Point: The U.S. Broke a NATO promise." *Los Angeles Times.* May 30, 2016. http://www.latimes.com/opinion/op-ed/la-oeshifrinson-russia-us-nato.

Kaliuzhnyi, Ievhen. "Kyivska Rus—tse ne Rosiia." *Literaturna Ukraina,* July 16, 2015, p. 10.

Keddie, Nikki R. *Modern Iran: Roots and Results of Revolution,* updated ed. New Haven & London: Yale University Press, 2006.

Kelly, Lidia (ed. Gareth Jones). "Russia: Here's Why We Sent a Fighter Plane to Intercept a US Aircraft." *Business Insider.* April 30, 2016. http://www.businessinsider.com/r-russia-defends-intercept-of-us-reconnaissance-plane-over-baltic-2016-4.

Klein, Margarete. "Russia's Military Capabilities: 'Great Power' Ambitions and Reality." *German Institute for International and Security Affairs* (SWP Research Paper). October 12, 2009. https://www.swp-berlin.org/fileadmin/contents/products/research_papers/2009_RP12_kle_ks.pdf.

Kretsul, Roman. "Are Russia and the U.S. Building Military Bases in Syria?" *Russia Beyond the Headlines.* January 26, 2016. http://rbth.com/international/2016/01/26/are-russia-and-the-us-building-military-bases-in-syria_562379.

Lapidus, Ira M. *A History of Islamic Societies*, 2nd ed. New York: Cambridge University Press, 2002.

Lee, Katy. "Istanbul Nearly a Ghost Town as Tourists Stay Away." *AFP*. July 3, 2016. https://www.yahoo.com/news/istanbul-nearly-ghost-town-tourists-stay-away-03220 7062.html.

Lewis, William F. "Telling America's Story: Narrative Form and the Reagan Presidency." *Quarterly Journal of Speech* 73 no. 3 (1987): 280–302.

Liedman, Sean R. "Vladimir Putin's Naval Ambitions Have Only Begun." *Defense in Depth* (Janine Davidson's blog). September 30, 2015. http://blogs.cfr.org/davidson/ 2015/09/30/vladimir-putins-naval-ambitions-have-only-begun/.

Lieven, Dominic. *The End of Tsarist Russia: The March to World War I and Revolution*. New York: Viking, 2015.

Makortoff, Kalyeena. "Putin Courts Athens Ahead of Vote on Sanctions Extension." *CNBC*. May 27, 2016. http://www.cnbc.com/2016/05/27/putin-courts-athens-ahead -of-vote-on-sanctions-extension.html.

Margaril, Sergei. "The Mythology of the 'Third Rome' in Russian Educated Society." *Russian Politics and Law* 50, no. 5 (2012): 7–34.

Martinez, Luis, Patrick Reevell, and Elizabeth Mclaughlin. "US Officials Say Russian Warship Intentionally Interfered With Navy Operations." *ABC News*. June 2, 29, 2016. https://gma.yahoo.com/us-officials-russian-warship-intentionally-interfered-n avy-operations-160004019--abc-news-topstories.html.

"Morskaiia doktrina Rosiiskoi Federatsii" (Maritime Doctrine of Russian Federation). *Static.Kremlin.ru*. 2015. http://static.kremlin.ru/media/events/files/ru/uAFi5nvux2tw aqjftS5yrIZUVTJan77L.pdf.

Mroue, Bassem. "Russia Builds Military Camp Near Ancient Site in Palmyra." *Yahoo News*. May 17, 2016. http://finance.yahoo.com/news/report-russians-building-army -syrias-palmyra-103558096.html.

"NATO-Russia Relations: The Facts." *North Atlantic Treaty Organization*. Last updated December 17, 2015. http://www.nato.int/cps/en/natohq/topics_111767.htm.

Nissenbaum, Dion, Emre Peker, and James Marson. "Turkey Shoots Down Russian Military Jet." *The Wall Street Journal*. November 24, 2015. http://www.wsj.com/articl es/turkey-shoots-down-jet-near-syria-border-1448356509.

Ostbo, Jardar. *The New Third Rome: Readings of a Russian Nationalist Myth*. Stuttgart, Germany: ibidem-Verlag, 2016.

Papkova, Irina. "Saving the Third Rome: 'Fall of the Empire', Byzantium and Putin's Russia." In *Reconciling the Irreconcilable*, edited by I. Papkova, vol. 24. Vienna: IWM Junior Visiting Fellows' Conferences, 2009.

Parfitt, Tom. "Sweden Widens Search for 'Russian Submarine.'" *The Telegraph*. October 20, 2014. http://telegraph.co.uk/news/worldnews/europe/sweden/11175832/Sw eden-widens-search-for-Russian-submarine.html.

Penzenstadler, Nick. "Turkey, NATO Call on Russia to Stop Airspace Violations." *USA Today*. January 30, 2016. http://www.usatoday.com/story/news/world/2016/01/30/t urkey-says-another-russian-jet-violated-turkey's-airspace/79563500/.

Pifer, Stephen. "Putin's Reckless Nuclear Saber-Rattling Is Just Show. *Newsweek*. March 18, 2016. http://www.newsweek.com/putin-reckless-nuclear-saber-rattling-just-show-biscay-437200.

Plokhy, Serhii. *The Gates of Europe: A History of Ukraine*. New York: Basic Books, 2015.

_____. *The Origins of the Slavic Nations: Premodern Identities in Russia, Ukraine, and Belarus*. New York: Cambridge University Press, 2006.

Poe, Marshall T. "'Moscow, the Third Rome:' The Origins and Transformations of a Pivotal Movement" (a report submitted to the National Council for Soviet and East European Research, Title VIII Program, Washington, DC, October 10, 1997, i-22). *University Center for International Studies* (Pittsburgh). Accessed July 6, 2016. https://www.ucis.pitt.edu/nceeer/1997-811-25-Poe.pdf.

Pohjanpalo, Kati, and Kasper Viita. "Finland's Fighter Jets on Alert as Russia Violates Airspace." *Bloomberg*. August 29, 2014. http://www.bloomberg.com/news/articles/2014-08-28/finland-puts-fighter-planes-on-alert-as-russia-violates-airspace.

"Putin Sat in the Chair of Byzantine Emporers." *RUSHINCRASH*. May 28, 2016. http://rushincrash.com/russia/putin-sat-in-the-chair-of byzantine/emporers/.

"Putin Visits Russian Orthodox Monastic Community in Greece." *Yahoo News*. May 28, 2016. https://www.yahoo.com/news/putin-visits-orthodox-monastic-community-mount-athos-114538932.html.

"RAF Jets Intercept Russian Bombers Heading to UK." *BBC*. February 17, 2016. http://www.bbc.com/news/uk-35598892.

Rakhuba, Denis. "Turtsiia ne budet vozmeshchat ushcherb RF za cbityi SU-24—Tanju Bilgiç." *Top.novostimira.com*. December 16, 2015. http://top.novostimira.biz/fulltext_164422.html.

"Rosiia rozmistyt v aneksovanomy Krymu raketonostsi-bombarduvalnyky TU-22M3." *Ekspres.ua*. July 22, 2015. http://expres.ua/world/2015/07/22/144592-rosiya-rozmistyt-aneksovanomu-krymu-raketonosci-bombarduvalnyky-tu-22m3.

"Rossiia ukhodit iz Sirii: chto dalshe?" *News.mail.ru*. Accessed July 6, 2016. https://news.mail.ru/card/70/.

Rozoff, Rick. "Black Sea: Pentagon's Gateway to Three Continents and the Middle East." *Antiwar Literary and Philosophical Selections* (Rick Rozoff). August 27, 2009. https://rickrozoff.wordpress.com/2009/08/27/79/.

"Russia Denies Report on New Military Base in Northern Syria." *Defense News*. January 25, 2016. http://www.defensenews.com/story/defense/2016/01/25/russia-denies-report-new-military-base-north-syria/79317974/.

"Russia Turned Crimea Into a Military Base: Tatar Leader." *Yahoo News*. March 19, 2015. https://www.yahoo.com/news/russia-turned-crimea-military-tatar-leader-221751657.html?ref=gs.

"Russian Invasion of Ukraine." *Ukrainian Policy*. March 1, 2014. http://ukrainianpolicy.com/russian-invasion-of-ukraine/.

"Sanktsii protiv Turtsii zatronut gazoprovod 'Turetskii potok'—Aleksei Uliukaev." *Top.novostimira.com*. November 26, 2015. http://www.novostimira.com.ua/news_163607.html.

Scherer, Steve. "U.S. Says It Will Stay in Black Sea Despite Russian Warning." *Reuters.* June 6, 2016. http://www.reuters.com/article/us-usa-defense-navy-blacksea-idUSKCN0Z30WG.

Sharkov, Damion. "Russia Fears NATO 'Global Strike' from Eastern Europe." *Newsweek.* June 6, 2016. http://www.newsweek.com/russia-fears-nato-global-strike-eastern-europe-senator-466853.

Sidorov, Dmitrii. "Post-Imperial Third Romes: Resurrection of a Russian Orthodox Geopolitical Metaphor." *Geopolitics* 11, no. 2 (2006): 317–47.

Soto-Viruet, Yadira. "The Mineral Industry of Bulgaria." *USGS* (U.S. Geological Survey; U.S. Department of Interior). March 2014. http://minerals.usgs.gov/minerals/pubs/country/2012/myb3-2012-bu.pdf.

Stanglin, Doug. "Russia Vows Response to U.S. Naval Ship's Entry into Black Sea." *USA Today.* June 10, 2016. http://www.usatoday.com/story/news/2016/06/10/russia-vows-response-us-naval-ships-entry-into-black-sea/85686822.

Steblez, Walter G. "The Mineral Industries of Bulgaria and Romania." *USGS* (U.S. Geological Survey; U.S. Department of Interior). 2000. http://minerals.usgs.gov/minerals/pubs/country/2000/9408000.pdf.

Stewart, Phil. "Pentagon Says 20,000 Russian Troops May Be in Crimea." *Reuters.* March 7, 2014. http://www.reuters.com/article/us-ukraine-crisis-pentagon-idUSBREA261RC20140307.

Toksabay, Ece, and Dmitry Solovyov. "Turkey Proposes Cooperation with Russia in Fighting Islamic State." *Reuters/Yahoo News.* July 4, 2016. https://www.yahoo.com/news/turkey-proposes-cooperation-russia-fighting-foreign-minister-091805123.html.

Tomlinson, Lucas. "Video of Military Convoy New Evidence Russia Not Pulling Out of Syria." *Military.com.* April 4, 2016. http://www.military.com/daily-news/2016/04/04/video-military-convoy-evidence-russia-not-pulling-out-of-syria.html.

Torbakov, Igor. "The Georgia Crisis and Russia-Turkey Relations" (Washington, D.C.: Jamestown Foundation, 2006). *The Jamestown Foundation.* Accessed July 24, 2016. http://www.jamestown.org/uploads/media/GeorgiaCrisisTorbakov.pdf

"Turechchyna proponuie Ukraini nehaino pidpysaty uhodu pro ZVT." *Ekspres.ua.* February 15, 2016. http://expres.ua/news/2016/02/15/173468-turechchyna-proponuye-ukrayini-negayno-pidpysaty-ugodu-zvt.

"Turetski viiskovi korabli zaishly v Odeskyi port." *Ekspres.ua.* April 4, 2016. http://expres.ua/news/2016/04/04/180794-turecki-viyskovi-korabli-zayshly-odeskyy-port.

Vargol, Tugce. "Russia Remains Determined to Stop Israel-Turkey Pipeline Deal." *Oilprice.* June 17, 2016. http://finance.yahoo.com/news/russia-remains-determined-stop-isreal-205026182.html.

Wagner, Wolfgang. *The Partitioning of Europe: A History of the Soviet Expansion up to the Cleavage of Germany 1918–1945.* Stuttgart, Germany: Deutsche Verlags-Anstalt, 1959.

Weitz, Richard. "After Ukraine, Black Sea Becomes Contested Zone for Russia, NATO." *World Politics Review.* December 2, 2014. http://www.worldpoliticsreview.com/articles/14556/after-ukraine-black-sea-becomes-contested-zone-for-russia-nato.

# Part Five
Information and Religious Wars

Part Five

# 9

# The Invisible Front: Russia, Trolls, and the Information War against Ukraine

Peter N. Tanchak

The Euromaidan and the Russian-Ukrainian war received great attention from Internet users around the world, and have become the focus of extensive discussions in social media and online forums. Individuals familiar with these forums have likely come across postings that are clearly false or contain insulting content. These postings appear to be written in hopes of generating arguments or emotional responses from other contributors, and the authors of such postings have been termed as "trolls." A growing body of evidence suggests that nation-states have witnessed, and been smitten by, the utility of trolls as tools for manipulating online discussions. In fact, states now hire individuals to perform such tasks on their behalf. This chapter will examine the origins of contemporary Russian state-affiliated trolls and their evolution from earlier ideological warfare techniques, focussing on their roots in KGB subversion tactics. An analysis of potential effects of troll propaganda on other states as well as recommendations for countering the use and negative repercussions of online trolls resulting from the risks they pose to national security will be offered.

Although the phenomenon of trolling is not new, its militarization and use as a tool for promoting foreign policy aims present a fascinating case of technological innovation with widespread implications. Although ongoing events in Ukraine and the Russian-Ukrainian war provide ample examples of trolls' tactics and techniques, this analysis will demonstrate the overarching applicability of trolls beyond the current conflict to any field in which a state has interest in securing a particular result. Russia has been using these techniques for quite some time, yet state-sponsored trolling as a phenomenon has matured during the Euromaidan and advanced dramatically in its aftermath, playing a special role in the international discourse about the military conflict in Ukraine. Trolls have become an important weapon in the Russian foreign policy toolkit,[1] which helps undermine the Ukrainian government's reform agenda and shapes public opinion. Moreover, trolling as a propaganda method was designed with an eye to affecting state policy and agenda-setting capacities well beyond eastern Europe.

This study is not designed as a technical manual for identifying, tracking, or "mapping" trolls, yet a limited discussion of techniques and tools used for these purposes, including the methods for counterbalancing Russian trolls' influence, will be provided. Importantly, this research explores their origins and role within Russian ideological warfare, and illuminates the policy implications of permitting a relatively small group of malicious online users, operating on behalf of Russia, to populate and exert influence within the public online space.

## The Origins of Trolls

Although certainly aided by the advent of the Information Age, Russian involvement in information warfare has a lengthy history. One might in fact consider modern day trolls a natural progression in state learning, as techniques that were developed during Soviet times and have been updated to keep pace with Information and Communications Technology (ICT) advances and changing social realities.[2] The term troll, as defined by Claire Hardaker, professor of Linguistics and English Language at Lancaster University, describes

> a CMC [Computer-Mediated Communications] user who constructs the identity of sincerely wishing to be part of the group in question, including professing, or conveying pseudo-sincere intentions, but whose real intention(s) is/are to cause

---

1  Miriam Elder, "Emails Give Insight into Kremlin Youth Group's Priorities, Means and Concerns," *The Guardian*, February 7, 2012, http://www.theguardian.com/world/2012/feb/07/nashi-emails-insight-kremlin-groups-priorities.
2  Volodymyr V. Lysenko and Kevin C. Desouza, "Charting the Coevolution of Cyberprotest and Counteraction: The Case of Former Soviet Union States from 1997 to 2011," *Convergence: The International Journal of Research into New Media Technologies* 20, no. 2 (2014): 176–200.

disruption and/or to trigger or exacerbate conflict for the purposes of their own amusement.³

The expansion of state-related actors, in the form of Russia's troll armies, to an online space formerly dominated by independent users requires that Hardaker's definition be somewhat modified. Although the trolls she describes work for their personal amusement, those discussed in this chapter act at the behest of a third party, disseminating a predetermined narrative for personal financial gain, in the form of a salary. Importantly, while the goals of state-sponsored trolling remain similar to those of private trolls—to disrupt positive debate while triggering or exacerbating conflicts—there exists a critical difference. In addition to disrupting debate and sowing confusion among readers, state-sponsored trolls project a state's official narrative of events regarding any given sphere of human activity—political, economic, social, and cultural. In order to better understand the evolution of trolls as a component of modern Russian information warfare, a brief historical overview seems appropriate here.

Throughout the Cold War, Western states were viewed as the primary targets for Soviet Bloc intelligence services, with the United States in particular being labelled the "Main Adversary."[4] The clandestine means through which these enemies were engaged were carefully designed by Moscow to prevent the Cold War from going "hot." On the front lines was Section A of the KGB's First Chief Directorate, which in conjunction with Line PR (political intelligence) officers worked to undermine public opinion through the use of disinformation measures.[5] Such techniques were a part of the KGB active measures (*aktivnyie meropriiatiia*) handbook, also known as measures of ideological subversion, and made use of mass media to run what were termed "influence operations," with the ultimate goal of affecting the course of global events.[6] As an example, it was for this purpose that the KGB spent tens of thousands of dollars financing

---

3   Claire Hardaker, "Trolling in Asynchronous Computer-Mediated Communication: From User Discussions to Academic Definitions," *Journal of Politeness Research*, no. 6 (2010): 237.
4   Christopher Andrew and Vasili Mitrokhin, *The Sword and the Shield: The Mitrokhin Archive and the Secret History of the KGB* (New York: Basic Books, 1999), 224.
5   Nigel West, *Historical Dictionary of Cold War Counterintelligence* (Plymouth: Scarecrow Press Inc., 2007), 88–89, 198.
6   Andrew and Mitrokhin, 224.

Carl Aldo Marzani, a small-time publisher who helped promote alternative theories on John F. Kennedy's assassination, and Mark Lane, an author writing on the same topic. The KGB also made use of forgeries, such as the Hunt-Oswald letter prepared by the Third Department of the KGB's Technical Directorate.[7] The purpose of these actions was to discredit the explanations provided by the United States regarding the Kennedy assassination, and ultimately to erode the credibility of the US Government in the eyes of its own citizens.

For the same purpose, the KGB employed "agents of influence," individuals in prominent positions or with a broader following who were able to leverage their public image and/or positions of trust to promote the Kremlin's ideological line abroad. Christopher Andrew and Vasili Mitrokhin have provided ample documentary evidence of these sorts of subversion operations drawn from the KGB archives. For instance, the popular journalist and author Pierre-Charles Pathé became a KGB agent of influence who published anti-American articles in the 1970s aimed at souring relations between France and the United States.[8]

In addition to evidence of the Soviet secret police's involvement in media manipulation provided by investigative journalists such as Gareth Jones,[9] first-hand accounts of the KGB's involvement were offered by the Soviet defector Yuri Bezmenov (alias Tomas Schuman). As a reporter for the Novosti press agency (today divided into the *Rossiia Segodnia* and *Sputnik* networks), Bezmenov worked to promote the Soviet government's interests at home and abroad. By hospitably hosting Western journalists, academics, and activists in the Soviet Union, he indoctrinated them with positive images of Soviet communism. They were later expected to promote and publicize their favorable views of the USSR in their home states.[10] According to Bezmenov, the KGB did not have to play a continuous role in the process of ideological subversion. Rather, the

---

7   Andrew and Mitrokhin, 228.
8   Andrew and Mitrokhin, 470–71.
9   Gareth Jones, "Mr. Jones Replies: Former Secretary of Lloyd George Tells of Observations in Russia," *New York Times,* May 13, 1933. See also Margaret Siriol Colley, *More Than A Grain of Truth: The Biography of Gareth Richard Vaughan Jones* (Newark, Nottinghamshire: Nigel Linsan Colley and Margaret Colley, 2005).
10  Yuri Bezmenov, "Psychological Warfare Subversion & Control of Western Society (Complete)," *YouTube,* 1983, posted by "GBPPR2" February 22, 2011 (duration 1:03:15), https://youtu.be/5gnpCqsXE8g.

agency attempted to sow the seeds of doubt among foreign populations and to undermine their trust in their own governments in a manner stealthy enough to limit direct lines of responsibility leading to the USSR. The hope was that a situation would be achieved whereby a given population would be *unable* to come to a clear conclusion on how they should react to a threat emanating from the Soviet Union, despite possessing credible information about the reality of such a threat.[11]

The collapse of the USSR in 1991 brought considerable uncertainty and instability to an environment that had grown accustomed to a tightly controlled and enforced form of internal order. The KGB itself was plunged into chaos. The social, political and cultural renaissance that followed was accompanied by an economic disaster. At the same time as historical archives were partially opened and individual and press freedoms were exercised, "shock therapy" reforms provoked financial anarchy and disorder.[12] Among the changes pursued by President Boris Ieltsin at this time was the reorganization of the security services, including partial decentralization of the KGB. In the early post-Soviet years, this decentralization process led to a competition in the sphere of intelligence activities. As a result, several sub-agencies emerged: the FSK[13] (soon to become the FSB[14]), responsible for domestic counter-intelligence work; the foreign intelligence service (SVR [15]); the GRU [16] (military intelligence); and FAPSI[17] (signals intelligence).[18]

Since Vladimir Putin's rise to power, the FSB has emerged from within the myriad of acronyms as the true successor agency to the KGB,

---

11   Bezmenov, "Psychological Warfare."
12   Alena V. Ledeneva, *How Russia Really Works: The Informal Practices that Shaped Post-Soviet Politics and Business* (Ithaca, New York: Cornell University Press, 2006).
13   FSK is an acronym for the Federal Counterintelligence Service (Federalnaia Sluzhba Kontrrazvedki).
14   FSB is an acronym for the Federal Security Service (Federalnaia Sluzhba Bezopasnosti).
15   SVR is an acronym for the Foreign Intelligence Service (Sluzhba Vneshnei Razvedki).
16   GRU is an acronym for the Main Intelligence Directorate (Glavnoe Razvedyvatelnoe Upravlenie).
17   FAPSI is an acronym for the Federal Agency of Government Communications and Information (Federalnoe Agentstvo Pravitelstvennoi Sviazi i Informatsii).
18   Andrei Soldatov and Irina Borogan, *The New Nobility: The Rebirth of the Russian Security State* (New York: PublicAffairs, 2010), 13.

gradually re-absorbing the various departments that had been detached during the preceding period of reorganization, as well as resuming operations abroad.[19] In addition, many KGB staff members from Soviet times were promoted to leading positions within the FSB, or appointed to head various state (and state-related) institutions, including government ministries, energy companies, and media outlets.[20] As state control over television and media tightened, the widening availability of, and connection to, the Internet allowed Russian citizens to access alternative news sources worldwide.[21] Because of this, censoring national media alone was no longer a sufficient means of manipulating public opinion; those engaged in this task required the ability to influence debates globally through new means. A shift of attention to the newly developed social media and online discussion forums was needed to maintain informational control across time and space.[22]

Russia's gradual return to highly centralized, authoritarian rule supported by the security services has also affected the field of international relations, where the apparent continuity and evolution of the Soviet-era policy of ideological subversion can be traced. Once again, Europe (now the European Union) and the United States find themselves in the crosshairs of Russian propagandists whose ultimate objectives are to prevent Western actors from producing effective responses to ongoing global events, while at the same time legitimizing any actions taken by Moscow. These objectives have been pursued, in part, through the use of mass media sources and online trolls in an effort to discredit Western discourse and overwhelm media consumers (the general public) with distorted narratives. Instead of offering objective facts, trolls confuse existing debates by presenting a multitude of alternative and often mutually exclusive messages, effectively leaving notions of "truth" open to interpretation. This tactic is designed to decelerate, and ideally to prevent, policy responses to credible threats as confusion surrounds the topics

---

19    Soldatov and Borogan, *The New Nobility*, 201–26.
20    Alena V. Ledeneva, *Can Russia Modernize* (Cambridge: Cambridge University Press, 2013), 81.
21    Peter Pomerantsev, *Nothing is True and Everything is Possible: The Surreal Heart of the New Russia* (New York: Public Affairs, 2014), 6.
22    Seva Gunitsky, "Corrupting the Cyber-Commons: Social Media as a Tool of Autocratic Stability," *Perspectives on Politics* 13, no. 1 (March 2015): 42–54.

under consideration.²³ The ideologically subversive actions of trolls create an environment in which "nothing is true and everything is possible," as Peter Pomerantsev has famously stated.²⁴

Having established the revisions necessary to Hardaker's definition of trolls (2010) in order to account for those currently used by Russia, as well as a historical background of some Russian ideological subversion measures, it would be prudent to examine now the process of Russian trolls' transformation—from tools for internal control to instruments of external influence.

## Examining Trolls: Goals and Tactics

Christopher Walker and Robert W. Orttung have discussed at length the importance of state-controlled national media sources for authoritarian regimes in their quest to maintain power.²⁵ Trolls play an important role in this process as one of several possible reactions to the freedom of information provided by Internet access. Subtler than China's Great Firewall, trolls allow the state to *influence* online debate rather than censoring it outright.²⁶ Trolls should also be differentiated from "bots," a different sort of malicious social and online media commentators, by virtue of the fact that trolls are real individuals, authoring unique online content and engaging in conversations with other users, while bots exist solely as lines of computer code.²⁷

The Russian project of using online trolls began as an internal effort and was designed to promote Putin as Russia's leader by limiting the influence of NGOs and opposition groups operating within Russia.²⁸

---

23  Maria Snegovaya, "Russia Report I: Putin's Information Warfare in Ukraine," *Institute for the Study of War*, September 2015, http://understandingwar.org/sites/defaul t/files/Russian%20Report%201%20Putin's%20Information%20Warfare%20in%20 Ukraine-%20Soviet%20Origins%20of%20Russias%20Hybrid%20Warfare.pdf.
24  Pomerantsev, *Nothing is True*, 233.
25  Christopher Walker and Robert W. Orttung, "Breaking the News: The Role of State-Run Media," *Journal of Democracy* 25, no. 1 (January 2014): 71–85.
26  The Great Firewall of China, also known as the Golden Shield Project, is a notoriously famous Chinese government project that was initiated in 1998 and designed to screen and block potentially harmful and unfavorable Internet content.
27  Snegovaya, "Russia Report I."
28  Note the emphasis on the individual; bloggers were paid to promote Vladimir Putin specifically rather than any particular political party.

These trolls were individuals affiliated with "Nashi" (Ours), a Kremlin-backed youth movement. They were paid modest sums to post propagandistic comments on web portals, such as LiveJournal and Twitter.[29] At that time, trolls' involvement in online and social media was limited to a Russian audience and focused on domestic topics, particularly the elections and subsequent protests of 2012.[30] Having proved their effectiveness, trolling operations were institutionalized and expanded, with troll "operators" hired on as regular employees by firms such as the Internet Research Agency to work in language and media-specific departments, depending on the intended audiences.[31] Given the threat allegedly posed by Western states,[32] the use of trolls against these international targets became a logical extension of Russian foreign policy following the Walker and Orttung model (2014).

Although respectable news sources typically hold contributing authors to strict sets of rules (i.e. BBC Editorial Guidelines), comment sections found below online articles, blogging websites, and social media have few, if any, such standards.[33] Russian trolls work to populate this space with pre-determined narratives, crowding out legitimate debate. One of the only remaining liberal news sources in Russia, *The Moscow Times*, cited a flood of malicious users (trolls) as the reason for closing down *all* online comment sections. *The Moscow Times*' statement read:

> Due to the increasing number of users engaging in personal attacks, spam, trolling and abusive comments, we are no longer able to host our forum as a site for constructive and intelligent debate. It is with regret, therefore, that we have found ourselves forced to suspend the commenting function on our articles.[34]

---

[29] Elder, "Emails Give Insight into Kremlin."

[30] Max Seddon, "Documents Show How Russia's Troll Army Hit America," *Buzzfeed*, June 2, 2014, http://www.buzzfeed.com/maxseddon/documents-show-how-russias-troll-army-hit-america#.py0k2RO9Xy.

[31] Dmitry Volchek and Daisy Sindelar, "One Professional Russian Troll Tells All," *RFE/RL*, March 25, 2015, http://www.rferl.org/content/how-to-guide-russian-trolling-trolls/26919999.html.

[32] "Address by President of the Russian Federation," *President of Russia* (official site), March 18, 2014, http://eng.kremlin.ru/news/6889.

[33] "BBC Editorial Guideline," *BBC*, last modified 2015, http://www.bbc.co.uk/editorialguidelines/guidelines/accuracy/.

[34] Quoted in Paul Roderick Gregory, "Putin's New Weapon in the Ukraine Propaganda War: Internet Trolls," *Forbes*, December 9, 2014, http://www.forbes.com/

Across a variety of publications, journalists have put efforts into documenting the inner workings of what have been called "Troll Factories" or "Troll Farms," where employees spend their shifts writing blogs and social media posts, as well as commenting on news articles published in various countries.[35] As a part of the (un)official disinformation campaign, these facilities work to promote the Kremlin's line on particular topics of interest. Since late 2013–early 2014, among other topics, the events in Ukraine have been featured prominently. Trolls have also played a critical role in experiments with social media manipulation, as documented by *The New York Times Magazine*.[36] Ben Nimmo of the Central European Policy Institute has described the use of "networks of officials, journalists, sympathetic commentators, and Internet trolls to create an alternative reality in which all truth is relative, and no information can be trusted."[37] Collecting and leveraging sizeable networks of followers to lend themselves credibility, trolls disseminate propaganda among audiences in a manner similar to that of the KGB's "agents of influence."

Following intensive investigation, *The New York Times*' journalist Adrian Chen has documented several instances where networks of hundreds of social media accounts were active in spreading disinformation: among their efforts was a Twitter story about an apparent chemical plant explosion in Louisiana.[38] Repeated postings, combined with re-tweets, placed the story among those trending rapidly; some posts included doctored photos and videos designed to give the story greater credibility. A question emerged whether these actions seemed to be a test: was an online campaign able to induce substantial social media and real-life confusion? The answer to this question appears to be resoundingly affirmative, and an FBI investigation remains open to this day.[39] Social media tools have provided trolls with the ability to elicit panic and confusion on a

---

sites/paulroderickgregory/2014/12/09/putins-new-weapon-in-the-ukraine-propaganda-war-internet-trolls/.
35   Volchek and Sindelar, "One Professional Russian Troll Tells All."
36   Adrian Chen, "The Agency," *The New York Times Magazine,* June 2, 2015, http://www.nytimes.com/2015/06/07/magazine/the-agency.html?_r=4.
37   Ben Nimmo, "Anatomy of an Info-War: How Russia's Propaganda Machine Works, and How To Counter It," *Central European Policy Institute,* May 15, 2015, http://www.cepolicy.org/publications/anatomy-info-war-how-russias-propaganda-machine-works-and-how-counter-it.
38   Chen, "The Agency."
39   Ibid.

broader scale. Far from speculation, there appear to have been attempts at such a scenario when, in late 2014, a number of Twitter accounts began posting comments about a (non-existent) racially-motivated killing in Atlanta.[40] An analysis of these activities suggests that they repeated a pattern similar to that of the Louisiana incident and involved many the same users.[41] One could easily imagine a scenario in which a similar situation, albeit played out with a larger number of actors and utilizing more sophisticated means, affects financial markets or results in civil unrest. Focussed on fostering fear and exacerbating cleavages within a foreign society, these events provide an excellent example of ideological subversion as described by Bezmenov.[42]

Curiously, the troll tactics documented by Chen evolved, to some degree, from the world of marketing and public relations, involving a process identified by media expert Ryan Holiday as "Trading up the chain."[43] Through this process, a contrived story is promoted at the grass-roots level through blogs and social media in hopes that this story will eventually be picked up and republished by larger, more credible news sources, thereby granting legitimacy. Formerly employed for the promotion and sale of goods, these tactics now are utilised by trolls to facilitate the spread of disinformation.

Connecting the vast network of trolls to Russia, and more specifically, the current political leadership, is an arduous task. Although trolls utilize VPNs (Virtual Private Networks) to mask their whereabouts, Internet researchers and investigative journalists have managed to uncover several "troll farms," as well as the individuals behind them. The best-documented of these is the Internet Research Agency, located at 55 Savushkina Street in St. Petersburg and connected by financial records to Ievgenii Prigozhin, nicknamed "the Kremlin's chef."[44] Following leads from analytical tools, a Russian blogger identified other potential locations for troll factories based on the geolocation of Internet searches. By using Google Trends, sparsely populated locales, such as the village of Perekatny in the Adegei Republic, were identified as querying the key

---

40 Ibid.
41 Ibid.
42 Bezmenov, "Psychological Warfare."
43 Ryan Holiday, *Trust Me, I'm Lying: The Tactics and Confessions of a Media Manipulator* (New York: Portfolio/Penguin Group USA, 2012), 18.
44 Chen, "The Agency."

word "Obama" more often than the entire city of Moscow, suggesting the presence of a troll factory nearby.[45] Additionally, individuals who have worked as trolls have themselves claimed the existence of multiple sites across Russia operating for the same purpose.[46]

Open-source research by Lawrence Alexander has also helped link troll media accounts to the Internet Research Agency. Through the use of Paterva's Maltego tool and Google Analytics identifiers, Alexander has been able to link a variety of supposedly independent media sites, including the website for "Material Evidence," the travelling propaganda exhibition, to an individual named Nikita Podgorny, an employee of the Internet Research Agency.[47] The media sites found by Alexander operate in a manner similar to blogs or Twitter trolls, albeit on a larger scale, publishing propaganda with a veneer of legitimacy. Their design and stylization as legitimate media outlets, posting multiple original articles per day, provide seeming credibility to the information they present. The illusion of credibility forestalls many Internet users from investigating the origins of such websites or their content to the extent performed by Alexander. The malicious manipulation of social media and online discourse for Russia's benefit comes at a considerable financial cost to target states as they attempt to counter these activities, and also at a social cost as people are unknowingly affected by a campaign designed to induce emotional responses and influence their behaviors.

## Trolling in the Context of the Russian-Ukrainian War

The conflict along Ukraine's border has provided an excellent opportunity for the study of Russian disinformation campaigns, and particularly the use of trolls in this context. The Euromaidan was followed by Russia's first major international military engagement since its 2008 war with Georgia. Russia's experiences in Georgia, as well as domestically dealing with protests surrounding the 2012 presidential elections, facilitated the

---

45 Catherine A. Fitzpatrick, "Russian Blogger Finds Pro-Kremlin 'Troll Factories,'" *The Daily Beast,* August 20, 2015, http://www.thedailybeast.com/articles/2015/08/20/russian-blogger-finds-pro-kremlin-troll-factories.html.
46 Chen, "The Agency."
47 Lawrence Alexander, "Open-Source Information Reveals Pro-Kremlin Web Campaign," *Global Voices,* July 13, 2015, https://globalvoices.org/2015/07/13/open-source-information-reveals-pro-kremlin-web-campaign/.

development of new techniques designed to counter positive interpretations of events in Ukraine, narratives that have been promoted by Ukraine and other states. These techniques have not necessarily been of a military nature; writing for the *Small Wars Journal*, Bret Perry has noted that two different sets of tactics have been employed during this conflict: one against Ukrainians and another against the broader Western community.[48]

Inside Ukraine, Russia has pursued a strategy of promoting Russian media, language, and culture, including the issuance of passports, in contravention of Ukrainian citizenship laws.[49] The purpose of these actions has been to make Ukrainians, particularly those living in eastern portions of the country, more susceptible to Russian propaganda and narratives, and therefore more likely to support Russia's intervention in case of conflict. Russian-language trolls and fake media websites played an active role in promoting Russian narratives to this group of the population, delegitimizing Ukrainian authorities while reinforcing messages trumpeted through major Russian print and television media already popular in parts of Ukraine.[50] One such website, *whoswho.com.ua*, purports to reveal secrets about Ukrainian public figures, and includes claims that the Ukrainian government supports ISIL (Islamic State of Iraq and the Levant).[51] Although appearing to be Ukrainian (by virtue of the ".ua" top-level domain), this website is in fact connected to the Internet Research Agency.[52]

Among other instances, trolls attempted to confuse narratives surrounding events that took place in Odesa in May of 2014. In the Odesa scenario, a man identifying himself as Dr. Rozovsky posted an impassioned plea to Facebook, subsequently republished by John Pilger in *The Guardian*, asking Vladimir Putin to intervene in the conflict.[53] The doctor's Facebook account was soon exposed as a fake, with the profile photo

---

[48] Bret Perry, "Non-Linear Warfare in Ukraine: The Critical Role of Information Operations and Special Operations," *Small Wars Journal*, August 14, 2015, http://smallwarsjournal.com/printpdf/27014.
[49] Ibid.
[50] Alexander, "Open-Source Information."
[51] Ostap Samoed, "Ukraina dlia IGIL kak sanatorii," *Who is Who*, November 4, 2015, http://whoswho.com.ua/120148-ukraina-dlya-igil-kak-sanatoriy/.
[52] Alexander, "Open-Source Information."
[53] John Pilger, "In Ukraine, the US Is Dragging Us towards War with Russia," *The Guardian*, May 13, 2014, http://www.theguardian.com/commentisfree/2014/may/13/ukraine-us-war-russia-john-pilger.

belonging to an unrelated dentist from Stavropol, although this was never made clear in *The Guardian* article.[54] The vector of trolls' messages clarifies their role in the hybrid warfare campaign against Ukraine—they have been used as tools to provide justification for Russian military intervention in Ukraine, as Roland Freudenstein (Martens Centre for European Studies) has defined it.[55]

Although not a new concept, the term "hybrid warfare" has become a virtual buzzword in the context of events in Ukraine.[56] Trolls have played an invaluable role as part of Russian psychological operations (PSYOP) throughout the period of revolution and subsequent war. The evolution in thinking that brought PSYOP, and as a result trolls, to the forefront of Russian military operations has been discussed by a number of prominent figures, including presidential advisor Vladislav Surkov, Chief of the General Staff Valery Gerasimov, and former-KGB officer Igor Panarin.[57] The concept was further expanded on by two Russian military officers, writing that, "[i]n the ongoing revolution in information technologies, information and psychological warfare will largely lay the groundwork for victory."[58] The application of this thinking is visible in Russian responses in the sphere of information warfare, employing a new generation of tools built and reliant upon modern information and communications technologies in order to maximize influence and power projection surrounding the issue of Ukraine.

The trolls' task was relatively easy in the first months of the war. Referring to the MH17 tragedy, Peter Pomerantsev has written that

---

54   Michael Weiss and Peter Pomerantsev, "The Menace of Unreality: How the Kremlin Weaponizes Information, Culture and Money (Special Report)," *The Interpreter,* 2014, http://www.interpretermag.com/wp-content/uploads/2014/11/The_Menace_of_Unreality_Final.pdf.
55   Roland Freudenstein, "Facing Up to the Bear: Confronting Putin's Russia," *European View* 13, no. 2 (2014): 226.
56   Kacper Rękawek and Peter Tanchak, "Nie tylko dla orłów. Czy terroryści sięgają po hybrydowość?" *Sprawy Międzynarodowe* no. 2 (2015): 57–72.
57   Perry, "Non-Linear Warfare."
58   S. G. Chekinov and S. A. Bogdanov, "The Nature and Content of a New-Generation War," *Military Thought* no. 4 (October 2013): 16.

> [t]he stories were glaringly sloppy, as if their creators did not care about being caught and just wanted to distract from the evidence that Russian-backed militias had shot down the plane.[59]

However, as time went on, these narratives became more compelling, precisely due to their strong emotional appeals (such as the tale of an apparent crucifixion in the town of Sloviansk, a story which was subsequently debunked).[60] Far from a lone occurrence, multiple instances have been noted where brutal images from other conflicts, including Chechnia and Syria, as well as commercial film footage, were repurposed by trolls in their efforts to discredit Ukrainian military operations aimed at preserving sovereignty.[61] The incorporation of emotional manipulation in propaganda has been a disturbing development. This method takes advantage of the ability of emotions to shut down logical thought processing and rational decision-making abilities, a well-documented physiological response discussed in multiple fields, from psychology to, more recently, social engineering.[62] This manipulation can be particularly easy given that trolls are not interested in documenting facts or the events' logic. Instead, their goal is to confuse readers rather than to assist them.[63]

In an effort to counter the massive influx of Russian propaganda and large-scale media manipulation, a group of Ukrainian journalists and scholars created the StopFake website, designed to provide a platform for debunking Russia's disinformation being promoted in the media and through trolls. Although vitally important to counterbalancing the PSYOP campaign, this effort has its limitations due to a lack of experience, training, and sophistication in propaganda analysis and counterpropaganda.

---

59 Peter Pomerantsev, "Inside the Kremlin's Hall of Mirrors," *The Guardian*, April 9, 2015, http://www.theguardian.com/news/2015/apr/09/kremlin-hall-of-mirrors-military-information-psychology?CMP=share_btn_tw.
60 Unattributed, "Lies: Crucifixion on 'Channel One,'" *StopFake.org*, July 15, 2014, http://www.stopfake.org/en/lies-crucifixion-on-channel-one/.
61 Andrei Soldatov and Irina Borogan, *The Red Web: The Struggle Between Russia's Digital Dictators and the New Online Revolutionaries* (New York, NY: PublicAffairs, 2015), 284.
62 Christopher Hadnagy, *Unmasking the Social Engineer: The Human Element of Security* (Indianapolis, Indiana: John Wiley & Sons, Inc., 2014), iBooks edition, 257–58.
63 Nimmo, "Anatomy of an Info-War;" Weiss and Pomerantsev, "Menace of Unreality."

The use of trolls in this conflict has resulted in the PSYOP campaign waged not only against Russian and Ukrainian citizens, but also against audiences abroad. In concert with other media and diplomatic measures, the PSYOP campaign allowed Putin to operate militarily unchecked on the territory of Ukraine, which resulted in thousands of casualties on both sides and nearly 1.5 million displaced individuals.[64] Russia's invasion and hybrid warfare dramatically increased hurdles for the Ukrainian government, already struggling to meet international financial obligations, to conduct meaningful reforms, and to prevent further encroachment on Ukraine's sovereign territory. It is important to keep in mind that the term PSYOP refers to a *military* measure used against enemy combatants and civilian targets.[65] The following section will demonstrate that trolls, as tools in the PSYOP arsenal, are being utilized to attack targets well beyond the boundaries and purview of the traditional battlefield in the Russian-Ukrainian war.

## The Effects of Trolling: Beyond Ukraine, Beyond the Conflict

As previously mentioned, trolls were initially conceived as a measure to assist with the maintenance of control and stability domestically, obscuring voices of dissent and opposition within Russia. Learning experiences encouraged the Russian authorities to adopt these same techniques to meet foreign policy goals, including the annexation of a portion of another state. These routine techniques included polluting online information streams, casting doubt on genuine facts, and generally confusing rational discourse. Amazingly, Russian propaganda has been extremely effective among Russian citizens: while the conflict in Ukraine continues at a low simmer, Putin's approval ratings remain well above 80 percent.[66] Moreover, to a certain extent, trolls' activities have affected public opinion abroad. Although economic sanctions have been imposed on Russia, it has not been declared a party to the conflict in Ukraine. Lethal military aid

---

64    Lolita Brayman, "How Ukraine is Forgetting Its Most Desperate Citizens," *Foreign Policy,* October 23, 2015, http://foreignpolicy.com/2015/10/23/how-ukraine-is-forgetting-its-most-desperate-citizens-refugees-idps/.
65    Perry, "Non-Linear Warfare."
66    Alexey Eremenko, "Vladimir Putin's Approval Ratings Hit All-Time High, Boosted by Syria Airstrikes," *NBC News,* October 22, 2015, http://www.nbcnews.com/news/world/vladimir-putins-approval-rating-hits-all-time-high-boosted-syria-n449071.

has also been slow in coming, with the US President Barack Obama only committing to the first $50 million of such funding in late-2015.[67] It is critical to understand that these developments are not the *sole result* of trolls' activities. Rather, employed as part of the foreign policy toolkit, trolls have played a role in affecting public perceptions worldwide, facilitating Russian operations throughout the course of the war.[68]

The use of trolls against foreign targets is likely to continue well beyond the period of the current conflict. Russian involvement in the Syrian civil war has expanded considerably over the past year, from the provision of materiel and diplomatic cover for the Assad regime, to including air and ground units in combat support operations.[69] Given the major foreign and domestic implications of such activities, online trolling will likely continue to play a role in defending and lauding Russian actions over social media and other online forums. Indeed, trolls and their handlers have already put considerable effort into perfecting content and posting tactics for various fora, including *The Huffington Post* and *Fox News*, among others. These efforts have included careful analyses of users and editorial rules to determine the best means of targeting media users or media consumers of the respective publications.[70] Where Russian ownership of multiple news sources in a foreign state would be both costly and potentially prohibited by law, trolls' comments in mass media discussion forums on selected topics are cost-efficient and accessible for broader audiences in nearly all online publications. Trolls constitute a fascinating addition to the massive Russian propaganda machine, and help disseminate Russian regime viewpoints virtually free of charge to media consumers all over the world.

---

67  Kristina Peterson and Carol E. Lee, "Obama to Sign Defense Bill Despite Provisions to Keep Guantanamo Open," *The Wall Street Journal,* November 10, 2015, http://www.wsj.com/articles/barack-obama-faces-dilemma-over-defense-bill-1447175692.
68  Perry, "Non-Linear Warfare."
69  Andrew Roth, Brian Murphy, and Missy Ryan, "Russia Begins Airstrikes in Syria; U.S. Warns of New Concerns in Conflict," *The Washington Post,* September 30, 2015, https://www.washingtonpost.com/world/russias-legislature-authorizes-putin-to-use-military-force-in-syria/2015/09/30/f069f752-6749-11e5-9ef3-fde182507eac_story.html.
70  Ilya Klishin, "The Kremlin's Trolls Go West," *The Moscow Times,* May 21, 2014, http://www.themoscowtimes.com/opinion/article/the-kremlins-trolls-go-west/500641.html.

Given their malicious and highly visible nature as in the "Louisiana" and "racially motivated shooting" Twitter storms documented above,[71] trolls' potential to shape domestic policies in foreign states means that they pose critical threats to the agenda-setting ability of governments. In Western states, where politicians and political agendas are sensitive to public opinion, the manipulation of public sentiments by a foreign state may limit the policy options considered "acceptable" to governments. Thus, trolls provide a means of power projection through agenda setting, allowing Russia to adjust or confuse public preferences, thereby placing restrictions on political actors.

Further risks are posed by the potential for other states to adopt trolls as a means of influence projection abroad. Saudi Arabia has been known to employ both trolls and bots as means of controlling online dissent over internal policies.[72] States such as China and Bahrain have also utilized trolls domestically in recent years.[73] Given that China has already displayed few qualms with engaging in international cyberattacks, we are likely to see additional players engaging in the use of trolls to influence foreign public opinion, as long as the consequences of such activities remain minimal to non-existent.

In his discussion of information operations, Bret Perry has suggested that "actors employ *reflexive control* in order to secretly hijack the adversary's decision making cycle."[74] The concept of "reflexive control" very closely mirrors the concept of social engineering, which has been defined as "any act that influences someone to take an action that may or may not be in his or her best interest."[75] However, rather than influencing one individual at a time, state-run reflexive control operations are designed to target society as a whole, and the narratives and/or decisions these operations encourage ultimately run counter to the target's national interests, potentially compromising its national security.

---

71 Chen, "The Agency."
72 "Freedom on the Net 2013: Saudi Arabia," *Freedom House*, 2013, https://freedomhouse.org/report/freedom-net/2013/saudi-arabia#.U6Oo3hZ0VFQ.
73 Sheena Chestnut Greitens, "Authoritarianism Online: What Can We Learn from Internet Data in Nondemocracies?" *Political Science & Politics* 46, no. 2 (2013): 262-70.
74 Perry, "Non-Linear Warfare." Emphasis added.
75 Hadnagy, 63

Among trolls' foreign targets, states in Russia's "near abroad" have been favorites for exercising preference adjustment through reflexive control. The Finnish journalist Jessikka Aro, who works for the national broadcaster YLE, has documented the information warfare campaign waged against Finns, which included the hijacking of Twitter accounts and hashtags, bullying tactics against users, and attempts at emotional manipulation through the use of fake photos and inflammatory language.[76] Aro has consulted with McAfee cybersecurity expert Jarno Limnell who described the campaign as one that "aimed at changing the national public sentiment and create [sic] a feeling of uncertainty in the society."[77] Although troll campaigns neither reach all citizens nor affect all whom they do reach, altering the preferences of a minority is often sufficient for fostering indecision and achieving the desired goal of state inaction.

Another prominent publication, *The Guardian*, has faced numerous complaints from its users who noted the presence of large numbers of trolls in comment sections as early as May 2014. The discussion moderators themselves described "an orchestrated campaign" that took place, with the transparent goal of corrupting open debate.[78]

Ultimately, state-affiliated trolls implement a targeted attack against the freedoms of opinion and expression enjoyed in Western states, and provided by social media and online forums, an attack that furthers Russian foreign policy objectives. Former CIA director Michael Hayden has characterized these activities as part of an overall Russian strategy, stating:

> Here our Secretary of State is saying this is not the Cold War, it's win-win and it's not zero sum. But for Vladimir Putin it is zero sum. That's what we need to understand.[79]

---

[76] Jessikka Aro, "This is What Pro-Russia Internet Propaganda Feels Like—Finns Have Been Tricked into Believing in Lies," *Yle Kioski,* June 24, 2015, http://kioski.yle.fi/omat/this-is-what-pro-russia-internet-propaganda-feels-like.

[77] Quoted in Jessikka Aro, "Yle Kioski Investigated: This Is How Pro-Russia Trolls Manipulate Finns Online—Check the List of Forums Favored by Propagandists," *Yle Kioski,* June 24, 2015, http://kioski.yle.fi/omat/troll-piece-2-english.

[78] Chris Elliott, "The Readers' Editor on ... Pro-Russia Trolling Below the Line on Ukraine Stories," *The Guardian,* May 4, 2014, http://www.theguardian.com/commentisfree/2014/may/04/pro-russia-trolls-ukraine-guardian-online.

[79] Quoted in Eli Lake, Noah Shachtman, and Christopher Dickey, "Ex-CIA Chief: Why We Keep Getting Putin Wrong," *The Daily Beast,* March 2, 2014,

Unchecked, actors with the ability to act as spoilers against the foreign and domestic policies of another state, and operating under a realist zero-sum mindset, will use their abilities in the interests of gaining any relative advantage. This is precisely what has been observed in the context of the Russian propaganda campaign vis-à-vis Ukraine and other Western states.

In running its information warfare operations, Russia has also managed to violate the codified rules of international law inscribed in the United Nations Declaration of Human Rights, particularly Article 19, which states:

> Everyone has the right to freedom of opinion and expression; this right includes freedom to hold opinions without interference and to seek, receive and impart information and ideas through any media and regardless of frontiers.[80]

By intruding into social media and other online communities, state-affiliated trolls interfere with the freedom of individuals to hold and express opinions. Trolls subvert legitimate debate, populate the information space with false data, and attack individuals personally.[81]

## Countering Trolls: Engaging Strategies by Disengaging Ideology

Although new developments in the cyberwarfare field are continually emerging, one must be cognizant of their pace. While Russia has denied the allegations that it was behind the 2007 and 2008 cyberattacks in Estonia and Georgia respectively, these actions, generally attributed to Russia, proved that Moscow was willing to engage other states in the cyber realm.[82] Yet trolling constitutes a different form of information warfare; over the course of 2011–2012, trolls were employed internally on an ad-hoc basis to quell unrest and promote Putin's return to power. With the 2013–2014 revolution in Ukraine, trolls were once again active, though this time in non-Russian social and mass media forums, discussing events

---

http://www.thedailybeast.com/articles/2014/03/02/ex-cia-chief-why-we-get-putin-wrong.html.
80  "The Universal Declaration of Human Rights," *United Nations*, accessed May 2, 2016, http://www.un.org/en/universal-declaration-human-rights/.
81  Aro, "This is What Pro-Russia Internet Propaganda Feels Like."
82  Freudenstein, "Facing Up to the Bear."

occurring beyond Russia's borders. Finally, Russia's 2014 war in Ukraine saw a major global troll campaign kick-off, which included the targeting of multiple states. In well under a decade, state-affiliated online trolls have gone from virtual non-existence to playing a highly visible role as tools facilitating the spread of disinformation in the context of a major international conflict. Successes thus far suggest that the use of trolls *will* continue, and is likely be enhanced further by future developments in the ICT field.[83] One of Putin's former advisors has publicly admitted the seductive power of information as a weapon for Russian leaders: ". . . in modern information societies, information is a very affordable weapon. It's cheap, effective and capable of spreading over the borders of countries."[84] Trolls present an ideal and cost-effective means of disseminating disinformation.

To Western states, social media and the Internet exist as largely an "ungoverned space,"[85] and penalties for this sort of hybrid war have not been considered. Inter-state cooperation on this matter is in their best interests, as it promotes liberal democratic values, yet such cooperation has proven to be extremely limited. As Michael Weiss and Peter Pomerantsev have pertinently noted,

> [t]he conflict in Ukraine saw non-linear war in action. Other rising authoritarian states will look to copy Moscow's model of hybrid war—and the West has no institutional or analytical tools to deal with it.[86]

Indeed, the task of limiting the pernicious effects of trolls on target populations, and of dissuading other actors from engaging in this sort of warfare, appears to be highly complex and difficult. Nevertheless, cyber space should not be surrendered to trolls, and their talking points should not be left unchallenged. Contesting this space and acknowledging the

---

83 Ronald Deibert and Rafal Rohozinski, "Liberation vs. Control: The Future of Cyberspace," *Journal of Democracy* 21, no. 4 (2010): 43–57.
84 Andrei Illarionov is quoted in Aro, "This is What Pro-Russia Internet Propaganda Feels Like."
85 The term has been offered by Alberto Fernandez, coordinator of the U.S. State Department's Center for Strategic Counterterrorism Communications (CSCC); quoted in Tim Hume, "Why the U.S. Government Is 'Trolling' Jihadists On Social Media," *CNN*, June 3, 2014, http://www.cnn.com/2014/04/18/world/jihadist-twitter-state-department-trolls-terrorists/.
86 Weiss and Pomerantsev, "Menace of Unreality."

magnitude and the scope of Russia's information operations is the first critical step in conceiving countermeasures.

As seen in the work of Lawrence Alexander and Aric Toler, exposing the tactics of trolls is instrumental to understanding and combatting disinformation.[87] Educating citizens to help them recognize the presence of manipulative media/social media techniques provides a further barrier between individuals and malicious disinformation campaigns, when such campaigns do occur.[88] Governments and policymakers must also recognize the potential for their own actions, when conducted in a non-transparent or accountable manner, to serve as fodder for trolls. Maria Snegovaya of Columbia University has noted that

> Russia's disinformation works only where it finds prolific ground; not as much due to its own efficiency, but due to the failures and internal problems of Ukraine and Western countries, such as cooptation of policy-makers, anti-U.S. sentiment, corruption, frustration with capitalism, failure to implement reforms and achieve transparency.[89]

Eliminating domestic informational "grey areas" and promoting honesty among public figures and institutions through measures such as those recommended by Weiss and Pomerantsev will limit the space in which the seeds of disinformation are able to take root.[90] Ben Nimmo has further suggested that states work towards predicting when and where trolls are likely to strike next, and invest the time and effort necessary to pre-empt their attacks.[91] Although valuable, such ability should not be considered as critical as citizens' education in empowering individuals to spot and avoid active disinformation measures.

At the same time, ensuring that domestic media operate under a strict code of conduct and exercise rigorous journalistic ethics and standards further equips Western states to counterbalance the trolls' disinformation and rebuilds the trust of citizens. Weiss and Pomerantsev have argued that it would be prudent of media outlets to employ counter-

---

87  Alexander, "Open-Source Information;" Aric Toler, "Inside the Kremlin's Troll Army Machine: Templates, Guidelines, and Paid Posts," *Global Voices,* March 14, 2015, https://globalvoices.org/2015/03/14/russia-kremlin-troll-army-examples/.
88  Nimmo, "Anatomy of an Info-War."
89  Snegovaya, "Russia Report I."
90  Weiss and Pomerantsev, "Menace of Unreality."
91  Ibid.

disinformation editors to play a role similar to that of op-ed ombudsmen, ensuring that their own outlets' news stories are based on concretely verifiable information or fact.[92] Furthermore, homegrown anti-disinformation groups, such as the aforementioned StopFake, may become a model for adoption in other states, as disinformation campaigns progress to targets beyond Ukraine. These measures are likely to be effective among Western media organizations and foreign broadcasters hoping to rebroadcast in Western states. Finally, utilizing legislation and regulatory bodies to sanction broadcasters guilty of misinformation, as witnessed when the UK communications regulator Ofcom sanctioned Russia's RT news network for "misleading and biased articles" on topics including Ukraine and Syria, serves to discourage news networks from engaging in disinformation.[93]

Social media, blogs, and comment sections as a public space present a different set of challenges. These spaces were originally designed to promote conversation, although trolls' activities have stifled and confused productive debate. Thankfully, technology offers potential solutions to this problem. As has been mentioned, trolls utilize VPN technology to mask users' true identities and prevent the possibility of tracing online activity to its source (whether an organization or an individual). What might decelerate the trolls' activities and their postings through VPNs is a system of online verification, whereby VPN-protected users would retain the ability to browse websites, but contributors would be required to provide proof of genuine identity. For instance, for registration purposes, websites could require Internet Service Provider (ISP) email addresses (i.e. Comcast, Sympatico, etc.), which may prevent an individual from operating dozens of accounts, whether as a bot or a troll.

This suggestion is likely to face criticism from individuals concerned with digital privacy issues. Although it is important to acknowledge these concerns as legitimate, the seriousness of the problem, whereby trolls are able to influence public opinion in foreign states, should not be understated or underestimated. To be sure, the proposition here is not to limit *access* to online media, but to restrict *contribution* to only genuine users—

---

92   Ibid.
93   Jasper Jackson, "RT Sanctioned by Ofcom Over Series of Misleading and Biased Articles," *The Guardian,* September 21, 2015, http://www.theguardian.com/media/2015/sep/21/rt-sanctioned-over-series-of-misleading-articles-by-media-watchdog.

a possible middle-of-the-road solution. In this context, it is essential to recognize that the concepts of "reflexive control" and PSYOPs associated with trolls have emerged from the military intelligence realm, and that Russian state-sponsored trolls have been employed, alongside conventional warfare in the case of Ukraine, to influence the "hearts and minds" of targeted populations through surreptitious means. The suggestions provided here aim to address this military threat on an equivalent scale, rather than downplaying its potential to cause serious damage around the world.

With regards to disinformation websites, "unmasking" such websites presents another challenge: there are few means of oversight or regulation for these sites, and these websites effectively mimic genuine news providers. In addition, the pace with which false information is created and disseminated through such websites far outperforms the initiatives of groups such as StopFake; they lag behind due to the sheer volume of data being published by trolls. Thus, expanding on Nimmo's suggestions, disinformation websites should be included in a formal listing of propaganda "agents," those noted for disseminating false information for the benefit of a foreign state.[94]

Importantly, technological advances affect both sides equally, which means that any corrective steps suggested and/or implemented today must be subject to continual review, refinement, and innovation in order to maintain pace. Trolls have already managed to adapt from highly overt propaganda comments placed in blogs to more subtle means, i.e. hiding a couple of stories on Ukraine or Putin among a broader set of generally mundane writing.[95] Indeed, some of the conspiracy theories and other fabrications, such as narratives on MH17 promoted by trolls, continue to be published well over a year after Russia-backed separatists downed the aircraft using Russian military hardware.[96] For the purposes of addressing the damage caused by trolls, Weiss and Pomerantsev have suggested adopting best practices from work already done on countering violent extremism, "including the equivalent of person-to-person online

---

94 Nimmo, "Anatomy of an Info-War."
95 Shaun Walker, "Salutin' Putin: Inside a Russian Troll House," *The Guardian*, April 2, 2015, http://www.theguardian.com/world/2015/apr/02/putin-kremlin-inside-russian-troll-house.
96 Olga Ivshina, "Flight MH17: Russia and Its Changing Story," *BBC News*, October 16, 2015, http://www.bbc.com/news/world-europe-34538142.

social work."[97] Such work would be attempted on the assumption that an informed and insulated public decreases the ability of *any* other party to exert undue influence over it. Although such techniques may prove fruitful, overall success is maximized when trolls' activities are also curtailed through technical means. So long as large quantities of malicious users operating on behalf of a third party are able to maintain access to publics, these solutions will remain little more than a game of whack-a-mole in the broader information war.

## Conclusion: Understanding Changing Realities

As has been demonstrated, regimes have extraordinary capacities to learn and adapt to changing environments. In Western states, where due process, open debate, and freedom of speech are valued, the process of introducing changes seems to take longer than in rigid top-down systems, such as contemporary Russia. Moreover, through the assistance of trolls, Russian strategists use the fundamental strengths and freedoms of the West against it. Trolls as a tool of psychological warfare will likely outlast the current leadership of the Russian Federation. One might argue that they will remain in use as long as they remain useful. Russia will be able to shed practices such as trolling only through internal democratic changes, resulting in dramatic societal changes and an altered collective mentality in which qualities such as honesty, rectitude, and dignity prevail. Viewed as certainly positive, such changes in Russia, or in other states that employ trolls, cannot be expected instantaneously, providing additional impetus for the preparatory and preventative tactics recommended above.

The global nature of troll warfare, targeting publications and social media in many states and languages, suggests that, acting alone, Ukraine is no match for its unconventional enemy. It must also be recognized that while the war in Ukraine is ongoing, Ukraine serves as a "lightening rod," attracting online trolls' attention away from other states and topics. One, however, might guarantee with certainty that this situation will *not* last long. If the poisoning of social media and, what University of Toronto political scientist Seva Gunitsky has more broadly identified as the "cyber-

---

97  Weiss and Pomerantsev, "Menace of Unreality."

commons," is not something the modern world is willing to tolerate, innovative thinking must be applied to develop better ICT tools and other measures to alleviate the problem of trolls.[98] To postpone changes is the worst possible course of action, which would ultimately legitimize and perpetuate trolls' existence.

Drawing on the statements of President Putin himself, trolls in their present form serve as foot soldiers in an attempt to influence Ukraine's "civilisational [sic] choice."[99] The Yale scholar Timothy Snyder has defined the stakes of Russia's war in Ukraine as a much broader battle of civilizational values:

> I really think we are at a point of "to be or not to be" for the West . . . This policy of strategic relativism,[100] of bringing down the various kinds of connections that exist, the transatlantic one, the European one, the integrity of states themselves, civil society, it is ultimately about us as well.[101]

Viewed in this context, trolling is no minor problem. Russia's psychological warfare ultimately aims to corrupt Western publics and Western values, and has thus far faced *no* coordinated response from the targeted states. Serious actions are necessary as the stakes encompass far more than Internet freedoms. Trolls constitute a significant part of a concerted attack on a way of life—dignified, moral, and meaningful.

## Bibliography

"Address by President of the Russian Federation." *President of Russia* (official site). March 18, 2014. http://eng.kremlin.ru/news/6889.

Alexander, Lawrence. "Open-Source Information Reveals Pro-Kremlin Web Campaign." *Global Voices.* July 13, 2015. https://globalvoices.org/2015/07/13/open-source-information-reveals-pro-kremlin-web-campaign/.

---

98  Gunitsky, "Corrupting the Cyber-Commons."
99  "Orthodox-Slavic Values: The Foundation of Ukraine's Civilisational Choice Conference," *President of Russia* (official site), July 27, 2013, http://en.kremlin.ru/events/president/news/18961.
100 Defined by Snyder as Russia's intentional weakening of other states in order to appear (relatively) stronger in comparison.
101 See Timothy Snyder's speech at the Chicago Humanities Festival "Ukraine: From Propaganda to Reality," *YouTube*, November 9, 2014, posted by "Chicago Humanities Festival" November 14, 2014 (timestamp 53:00; duration 57:35), https://www.youtube.com/watch?v=eKFObB6_naw.

Andrew, Christopher, and Vasili Mitrokhin. *The Sword and the Shield: The Mitrokhin Archive and the Secret History of the KGB.* New York: Basic Books, 1999.

Aro, Jessikka. "This Is What Pro-Russia Internet Propaganda Feels Like—Finns Have Been Tricked into Believing in Lies." *Yle Kioski.* June 24, 2015. http://kioski.yle.fi/om at/this-is-what-pro-russia-internet-propaganda-feels-like.

_____. "Yle Kioski Investigated: This is How Pro-Russia Trolls Manipulate Finns Online—Check the List of Forums Favored by Propagandists." *Yle Kioski.* June 24, 2015. http://kioski.yle.fi/omat/troll-piece-2-english.

"BBC Editorial Guideline." *BBC.* Last modified 2015. http://www.bbc.co.uk/editorialguide lines/guidelines/accuracy/.

Bezmenov, Yuri. "Psychological Warfare Subversion & Control of Western Society (Complete)." 1983. *YouTube.* https://youtu.be/5gnpCqsXE8g.

Brayman, Lolita. "How Ukraine is Forgetting its Most Desperate Citizens." *Foreign Policy.* October 23, 2015. http://foreignpolicy.com/2015/10/23/how-ukraine-is-forgettin g-its-most-desperate-citizens-refugees-idps/.

Checkinov, S. G., and S. A. Bogdanov. "The Nature and Content of a New-Generation War." *Military Thought*, no. 4 (October 2013): 12–23.

Chen, Adrian. "The Agency." *The New York Times Magazine.* June 02, 2015. http://www .nytimes.com/2015/06/07/magazine/the-agency.html?_r=4.

Colley, Margaret Siriol. *More Than A Grain of Truth: The Biography of Gareth Richard Vaughan Jones.* Newark, Nottinghamshire: Nigel Linsan Colley and Margaret Colley, 2005.

Deibert, Ronald, and Rafal Rohozinski. "Liberation vs. Control: The Future of Cyberspace." *Journal of Democracy* 21, no. 4 (October 2010): 43–57.

Elder, Miriam. "Emails Give Insight into Kremlin Youth Group's Priorities, Means and Concerns." *The Guardian.* February 7, 2012. http://www.theguardian.com/world/2 012/feb/07/nashi-emails-insight-kremlin-groups-priorities.

Elliott, Chris. "The Readers' Editor on … Pro-Russia Trolling Below the Line on Ukraine Stories." *The Guardian.* May 4, 2014. http://www.theguardian.com/commentisfree/ 2014/may/04/pro-russia-trolls-ukraine-guardian-online.

Eremenko, Alexey. "Vladimir Putin's Approval Ratings Hit All-Time High, Boosted by Syria Airstrikes." *NBC News.* October 22, 2015. http://www.nbcnews.com/news/ world/vladimir-putins-approval-rating-hits-all-time-high-boosted-syria-n449071.

Fitzpatrick, Catherine A. "Russian Blogger Finds Pro-Kremlin 'Troll Factories.'" *The Daily Beast.* August 20, 2015. http://www.thedailybeast.com/articles/2015/08/20/ru ssian-blogger-finds-pro-kremlin-troll-factories.html.

"Freedom on the Net 2013: Saudi Arabia." *Freedom House.* 2013. https://freedomhouse .org/report/freedom-net/2013/saudi-arabia#.U6Oo3hZ0VFQ.

Freudenstein, Roland. "Facing Up to the Bear: Confronting Putin's Russia." *European View* 13, no. 2 (2014): 225–32.

Gregory, Paul Roderick. "Putin's New Weapon In the Ukraine Propaganda War: Internet Trolls." *Forbes.* December 9, 2014. http://www.forbes.com/sites/paulroderickgrego ry/2014/12/09/putins-new-weapon-in-the-ukraine-propaganda-war-internet-trolls/.

Greitens, Sheena Chestnut. "Authoritarianism Online: What Can We Learn from Internet Data in Nondemocracies?" *Political Science & Politics* 46, no. 2 (2013): 262–70.

Gunitsky, Seva. "Corrupting the Cyber-Commons: Social Media as a Tool of Autocratic Stability." *Pespectives on Politics* 13, no. 1 (March 2015): 42–54.

Hadnagy, Christopher. *Unmasking the Social Engineer: The Human Element of Security*. Indianapolis, Indiana: John Wiley & Sons, Inc., 2014, iBooks edition.

Hardaker, Claire. "Trolling in Asynchronous Computer-Mediated Communication: From User Discussions to Academic Definitions." *Journal of Politeness Research*, no. 6 (2010): 215–42.

Holiday, Ryan. *Trust Me, I'm Lying: The Tactics and Confessions of a Media Manipulator*. New York: Portfolio/Penguin Group USA, 2012.

Hume, Tim. "Why the U.S. Government Is 'Trolling' Jihadists On Social Media." *CNN*. June 3, 2014. http://www.cnn.com/2014/04/18/world/jihadist-twitter-state-department-trolls-terrorists/.

Ivshina, Olga. "Flight MH17: Russia and Its Changing Story." *BBC News*. October 16, 2015. http://www.bbc.com/news/world-europe-34538142.

Jackson, Jasper. "RT Sanctioned by Ofcom Over Series of Misleading and Biased Articles." *The Guardian*. September 21, 2015. http://www.theguardian.com/media/2015/sep/21/rt-sanctioned-over-series-of-misleading-articles-by-media-watchdog.

Jones, Gareth. "Mr. Jones Replies: Former Secretary of Lloyd George Tells of Observations in Russia." *New York Times,* May 13, 1933.

Klishin, Ilya. "The Kremlin's Trolls Go West." *The Moscow Times*. May 21, 2014. http://www.themoscowtimes.com/opinion/article/the-kremlins-trolls-go-west/500641.html.

Lake, Eli, Noah Shachtman, and Christopher Dickey. "Ex-CIA Chief: Why We Keep Getting Putin Wrong." *The Daily Beast*. March 02, 2014. http://www.thedailybeast.com/articles/2014/03/02/ex-cia-chief-why-we-get-putin-wrong.html.

Ledeneva, Alena V. *Can Russia Modernize*. Cambridge: Cambridge University Press, 2013.

_____. *How Russia Really Works: The Informal Practices That Shaped Post-Soviet Politics and Business*. Ithaca, New York: Cornell University Press, 2006.

"Lies: Crucifixion on 'Channel One.'" *StopFake.org*. July 15, 2014. http://www.stopfake.org/en/lies-crucifixion-on-channel-one/.

Lysenko, Volodymyr V., and Kevin C. Desouza. "Charting the Coevolution of Cyberprotest and Counteraction: The Case of Former Soviet Union States from 1997 to 2011." *Convergence: The International Journal of Research into New Media Technologies* 20, no. 2 (2014): 176–200.

Nimmo, Ben. "Anatomy of an Info-War: How Russia's Propaganda Machine Works, and How to Counter It." *Central European Policy Institute*. May 15, 2015. http://www.cepolicy.org/publications/anatomy-info-war-how-russias-propaganda-machine-works-and-how-counter-it.

"Orthodox-Slavic Values: The Foundation of Ukraine's Civilisational Choice Conference." *President of Russia* (official site). July 27, 2013. http://en.kremlin.ru/events/president/news/18961.

Perry, Bret. "Non-Linear Warfare in Ukraine: The Critical Role of Information Operations and Special Operations." *Small Wars Journal.* August 2015. http://smallwarsjournal.com/printpdf/27014.

Peterson, Kristina, and Carol E. Lee. "Obama to Sign Defense Bill Despite Provisions to Keep Guantanamo Open." *The Wall Street Journal.* November 10, 2015. http://www.wsj.com/articles/barack-obama-faces-dilemma-over-defense-bill-1447175692.

Pilger, John. "In Ukraine, the US Is Dragging Us towards War with Russia." *The Guardian.* May 13, 2014. http://www.theguardian.com/commentisfree/2014/may/13/ukraine-us-war-russia-john-pilger.

Pomerantsev, Peter. "Inside the Kremlin's Hall of Mirrors." *The Guardian.* April 9, 2015. http://www.theguardian.com/news/2015/apr/09/kremlin-hall-of-mirrors-military-information-psychology?CMP=share_btn_tw.

——————. *Nothing is True and Everything is Possible: The Surreal Heart of the New Russia.* New York: PublicAffairs, 2014.

Rękawek, Kacper, and Peter Tanchak. "Nie tylko dla orłów. Czy terroryści sięgają po hybrydowość?" *Sprawy Międzynarodowe*, no. 2 (2015): 57–72.

Roth, Andrew, Brian Murphy, and Missy Ryan. "Russia Begins Airstrikes in Syria; U.S. Warns of New Concerns in Conflict." *The Washington Post.* September 30, 2015. https://www.washingtonpost.com/world/russias-legislature-authorizes-putin-to-use-military-force-in-syria/2015/09/30/f069f752-6749-11e5-9ef3-fde182507eac_story.html.

Samoed, Ostap. "Ukraina dlia IGIL kak sanatorii." *Who is Who.* November 4, 2015. http://whoswho.com.ua/120148-ukraina-dlya-igil-kak-sanatoriy/.

Seddon, Max. "Documents Show How Russia's Troll Army Hit America." *Buzzfeed.* June 2, 2014. http://www.buzzfeed.com/maxseddon/documents-show-how-russias-troll-army-hit-america#.py0k2RO9Xy.

Snegovaya, Maria. "Russia Report I: Putin's Information Warfare in Ukraine." *Institute for the Study of War.* September 2015. http://understandingwar.org/sites/default/files/Russian%20Report%201%20Putin's%20Information%20Warfare%20in%20Ukraine-%20Soviet%20Origins%20of%20Russias%20Hybrid%20Warfare.pdf.

Snyder, Timothy. "Ukraine: From Propaganda to Reality." *YouTube.* November 9, 2014. https://www.youtube.com/watch?v=eKFObB6_naw.

Soldatov, Andrei, and Irina Borogan. *The New Nobility: The Rebirth of the Russian Security State.* New York: PublicAffairs, 2010.

——————. *The Red Web: The Struggle Between Russia's Digital Dictators and the New Online Revolutionaries.* New York, NY: PublicAffairs, 2015.

"The Universal Declaration of Human Rights." *United Nations.* Accessed October 12, 2015. http://www.un.org/en/universal-declaration-human-rights/.

Toler, Aric. "Inside the Kremlin's Troll Army Machine: Templates, Guidelines, and Paid Posts." *Global Voices.* March 14, 2015. https://globalvoices.org/2015/03/14/russia-kremlin-troll-army-examples/.

Volchek, Dmitry, and Daisy Sindelar. "One Professional Russian Troll Tells All." *RFE/RL.* March 25, 2015. http://www.rferl.org/content/how-to-guide-russian-trolling-trolls/26919999.html.

Walker, Christopher, and Robert W. Orttung. "Breaking the News: The Role of State-Run Media." *Journal of Democracy* 25, no. 1 (January 2014): 71–85.

Walker, Shaun. "Salutin' Putin: Inside a Russian Troll House." *The Guardian.* April 2, 2015. http://www.theguardian.com/world/2015/apr/02/putin-kremlin-inside-russian-troll-house.

Weiss, Michael, and Peter Pomerantsev. "The Menace of Unreality: How the Kremlin Weaponizes Information, Culture and Money (Special Report)." *The Interpreter.* 2014. http://www.interpretermag.com/wp-content/uploads/2014/11/The_Menace_of_Unreality_Final.pdf.

West, Nigel. *Historical Dictionary of Cold War Counterintelligence.* Plymouth: Scarecrow Press Inc., 2007.

# 10
# The Impact of Russia's Intervention in Ukraine on Muslim, Jewish and Baptist Communities

Andrii Krawchuk

Early discussions of the war in Ukraine focused mostly on its political, economic, military and propaganda dimensions. On the domestic front, pre-existing concerns were with ensuring the transition from oligarchic to democratic governance and from corrupt to transparent economic practices. On the international scene, the principal issue was the one that ultimately precipitated the conflict—the transition from a primary economic reliance on Russia to closer ties with the EU. The war quickly shifted the focus of attention to Russia's annexation of Crimea and the military confrontation in the eastern Donbas region. While political, economic and military considerations remained at the forefront of much discussion, another topic that drew interest was the war of words—the reciprocal exchange of accusations and denials around the "green men" of Crimea, antisemitic leaflets in Donetsk, the downing of MH-17, and a bewildering array of other disputed matters. Such were the main topics of much media coverage and information bytes for those who sought to make some sense of the conflict, and to understand its origins, meaning, and potential outcomes.

The religious dimension of Ukraine's war is significant but largely neglected. It includes the divisive effects of the war itself and of new policies introduced by occupation authorities: the splitting up of faith communities through divided political loyalties, refugee displacement, and the coercive restructuring of religious organizations. Yet religious communities were not only passive observers and recipients of the war's impact. They also demonstrated a capacity for pro-active agency, and a full account of the religious dimension of Ukraine's war must include their critical and reflective responses to polarizing forces in society, and their creative mobilization of operational skills to adapt, survive and remain socially engaged, especially in the area of humanitarian aid.

The present study attempts a preliminary reconstruction of that religious dimension by studying the war's impact on three religious minorities and their responses to it. As Crimea and Donbas changed hands, Muslims, Jews, and Baptists had to decide whether to remain under Russian rule or to escape as refugees. Those who stayed found themselves within a new legal and political framework, which imposed a different *modus operandi* on religious communities. Those who left made haste to find a stable foothold, to organize assistance for families at home, and to adapt as religious communities to a new identity and mode of existence as refugees. The study of three communities enables a comparative appreciation of common patterns and particularities of religious response, adaptation, and self-reflection. It sheds light on the deeper quest for religious meaning in the context of violent conflict. Hopefully, that will set the stage for a more thorough assessment of the religious and theological perceptions and interpretations of the war in Ukraine, and of constructive religious contributions to the restoration of peace.

## Organizational Divisions among Crimea's Muslims

For Crimea's 260,000 Muslims, the transitional year 2014 began with the Russian military takeover in February and the March 16 "referendum" in favor of union with Russia. Even before the "referendum," which many Crimean Tatars boycotted, their political sympathies were readily apparent to Russophile observers.[1] Together with other members of the Inter-

---

1   Crimean Mejlis leader Mustafa Dzhemilev estimated that 10,000 Crimean Tatars left the peninsula after the Russian annexation. Oleg Yegorov, "Crimean Tatars Split As World Congress Calls for Return to Ukrainian Rule," *Russia Beyond the Headlines*, August 10, 2015, http://rbth.com/international/2015/08/10/crimean_ta tars_split_as_world_congress_calls_for_return_to_ukra_48405.html. See also Cristina Silva, "To Defeat Russia, Ukraine Creates Muslim Military Unit Made Up of Crimean Tatars," *International Business Times*, August 3, 2015, ibtimes.com/ defeat-russia-ukraine-creates-muslim-military-unit-made-crimean-tatars-203661 8; and Mykhaylo Yakubovych, "A Muslim Voice from Ukraine: Praying for Peace, Struggling for Freedom," *European Muslim Union*, August 4, 2014, www.emunio n.eu/jupgrade/index.php/home/52-front-news/290-a-muslim-voice-from-ukraine. For a useful survey of Muslims in Ukraine from 1989 to 2009 and of emerging tensions between traditional, independent communities and more recent, centralized institutions, see Mykhaylo Yakubovych, "Islam and Muslims in Contemporary Ukraine: Common Backgrounds, Different Images," *Religion, State & Society* 38, no. 3 (2010): 291–304.

confessional Council of Crimea, Muslim leaders had overwhelmingly supported the territorial integrity of Ukraine, while mass rallies of Crimean Muslims included alternating chants of "Allahu Akbar" in Arabic and "Glory to Ukraine" in Ukrainian.[2] Despite objections from the international community, the transfer of power became a fait accompli and the Muslims of Crimea found themselves in a new political, legal, and social environment. The third pivotal moment that year came on August 21: in Symferopil, a new religious organization was created, the so-called Tauride Muftiate. More than any other event, it represented the religious dimension of the political transformation for the traditional community structures and religious identity of Crimean Tatars. To understand the situation of the Muslims of Crimea, this organizational innovation must be reckoned with first of all. It provides an insight into the mindset, motivations, and mechanisms behind the Russian takeover of Crimea. Contrary to the view that Crimea was basically Russian all along, the Crimean Tatar experience sheds light on a story of propaganda, brutal coercion, and human rights abuses ranging from harassment and intimidation to murder.

What is the Tauride Muftiate? On August 21, 2014 in Symferopil, under the ancient name of Crimea—"Tauridia," a Central Spiritual Board of Muslims of Crimea was established as an Islamic jurisdiction that claimed continuity with a similarly titled institution in imperial Russia: the Tauride Directorate. The new muftiate was intended as an alternative to, and ultimately a substitute for, the existing organization—the Spiritual Board of Muslims of Crimea (Dukhovne Upravlinnia Musulman Krymu: hereafter DUMK).[3] For the secessionist authority under Sergei Aksionov,

---

2    In their statement, the Crimean leaders exhorted: "In the circumstances of this difficult ordeal we must prevent all possible attempts at dividing our society and we must preserve the territorial integrity of our state. We are sure that the events of the beginning of 2014 will remain forever as the sad history of Ukraine." In "Religioznyie lidery Kryma prizvali k sokhraneniiu tselostnosti Ukrainy," *Relihiia v Ukraini*, March 5, 2014, http://www.religion.in.ua/news/ukrainian_news/25093-religioznye-lidery-kryma-prizvali-k-soxraneniyu-celostnosti-ukrainy.html. See also Andrew Wilson, "Tatar Sunni Muslims Pose a Threat to Russia's Occupation of Crimea," *The Guardian*, March 5, 2014, theguardian.com/world/2014/mar/05/tartar-ukraine-sunni-muslims-threat-russian-rule-crimea; and Mykhailo Yakubovych, "Ukrainian Muslims and Maidan," *Ukraine Business*, March 8, 2014, ukrainebusiness.com.ua/news/11444.html.

3    Roman Silantiev, "Vserossiiskiie ambitsii muftiiatov: Islamskiie organizatsii nachali peredel Kryma i Sibiri," *Nezavisimaia Gazeta*, September 17, 2014, http://www.ng.ru/facts/2014-09-17/6_muftiat.html.

the idea of historical continuity supported the legitimacy of the Russian annexation and of subsequent reforms. In addition, theological and security considerations were cited. According to the Tauride Muftiate's leader, Mufti Ruslan Saitvaliev, the organization would "combat the development of radical movements such as Wahhabis, Hizb-ut-Tahrir [the Islamic Party of Liberation], and the Muslim Brotherhood."[4] In his opinion, this was something that DUMK had failed to do. Saitvaliev alleged that it had supported the development of those sectarians and that "to this day the imams of most mosques in Crimea are representatives of Hizb-ut-Tahrir or Wahhabis."[5] On the other hand, the Tauride Muftiate proposed to guard against Islamic radicalism by promoting Sufism as the desirable form of traditional Islam and by training their own imams rather than sending young people to study abroad.[6]

This was the stated rationale for the Tauride Muftiate. However, its deeper meaning emerges in connection with the Russian occupation and

---

4   Igor Gashkov and Vladislav Maltsev, "Rossiiskii islam oblekaiut v novye formy: Umme strany predlozheny 'zhestkaia vertical vlasti' i sufizm kak sredstvo ot radikalizma," *Nezavisimaia Gazeta*, September 3, 2014, http://www.ng.ru/facts/2 014-09-03/1_islam.html.
    The seeds of the alarmist reading of the situation had been sown by Sergei Aksionov. In a report compiled prior to the occupation of Crimea, he singled out the Mejlis and DUMK as sects engaged in "Russophobic and anti-Orthodox" politics. See "Ekspert predosteregaiet krymskiie vlasti ot bezogovorochnoi podderzhki DUM Kryma," *NEWSru.com*, September 10, 2014, newsru.com/re ligy/10sep2014/silantiev.html.
    Hizb-ut-Tahrir is prohibited as extremist in the EU and Russia because of its ties with the Muslim Brotherhood. However, it is legal in Ukraine. According to a different perspective on the situation in Crimea published in *Die Welt*, Crimean Tatars are for the most part moderate Muslims and distance themselves from the radical movement. But the very existence of an Islamist organization in Crimea serves as a pretext for harassment by Russian *siloviki*. See "Siloviki vryvaiutsia v doma krymskikh tatar, prikryvaias poiskom "Islamistov,'" *Ukrainskaia Pravda*, October 2, 2014, http://www.pravda.com.ua/rus/news/2014/10/2/7039645/.
    The Tauride muftiate's rejection of extremism, radicalization, and the politicization of religion was also part of an agreement with the chief mufti of Russia, Talgat Tadjuddin, reached in Ufa in mid-August. Vladislav Maltsev, "Tavricheskii muftiiat vzial v soiuzniki Povolzhiie," *Nezavisimaia Gazeta*, September 3, 2014, http://www.ng.ru/ng_religii/2014-09-03/1_muftiat.html.
5   Maltsev, "Tavricheskii muftiiat."
6   A related objection came from Russia's Roman Silantiev: DUMK had imams who were Turkish or Arab citizens. By implication, DUMK was therefore not a worthy successor to the historical Tauride Muftiate, which was "created by Nicholas I *for the defense of traditional Islam.*" (Emphasis mine). See "Ekspert predosteregaet krymskie vlasti."

the larger context of events leading up to and following August 21, 2014. Those events and religious policies fill out the picture of a coordinated campaign of repression and control of Muslims in Crimea.

It was not long after the disputed Crimean referendum that the new authorities were implementing measures against Crimean Tatars because of their pro-Ukrainian sympathies. In fact, the referendum itself had taken place in the shadow of a brutal murder. Reshat Amet, an activist who had undertaken a solitary protest against the Russian occupation of Crimea on Symferopil's Lenin Square on March 3, was abducted and beaten to death. His body was found on March 15, the eve of the referendum. When three other Muslims disappeared at the end of May, DUMK urged Crimean authorities to investigate the crimes, which for many confirmed an alarming increase in human rights abuses in Crimea.[7] Also in May, the occupation authorities banned the annual commemoration of the Sürgün, the 1944 deportation of Crimean Tatars by Stalin's regime—the first such obstruction since the observance began twenty years before.[8]

In June, the harassment of Muslims extended to the storming and search of a *madrasa* (religious school) and of a family home by armed, masked and unidentified troops in Kolchugino, outside Symferopil.[9] The *madrasa*'s deputy director Aider Osmanov was taken in for questioning by the MVD.[10] In late June, some Crimeans accompanied by "guests from Russia" launched a propaganda campaign, accusing Crimea's Mejlis and

---

[7] The three—Leonid Korzh, Timur Shaimardanov, and Seiran Zinedin—were members of the Ukrainian Home association. "Muftiiat trebuiet ot Aksionova razobratsia s faktami ischeznoveniia i zverskikh ubiistv krymchan," *RISU*, June 12, 2014, risu.org.ua/ru/index/all_news/community/scandals/56717/.

[8] "Aksionov zapretil Krymskim tataram aktsii ko Dniu Pamiati Zhertv Deportatsii," *RISU*, May 16, 2014, risu.org.ua/ru/index/all_news/community/scandals/56438/; see also www2.stetson.edu/~psteeves/relnews/1405d.html. Most of Crimea's Tatars were deported to Central Asia in May 1944, after they were accused of Nazi collaboration. Repatriation began in 1989.

[9] V Krymu 'zelionyie chelovechki' zakhvatili islamskuiu shkolu s uchenikami," *Relihiia v Ukraini* June 24, 2014, http://www.religion.in.ua/news/ukrainian_news/26167-v-krymu-zelenye-chelovechki-zaxvatili-islamskuyu-shkolu-s-uchenikami.html.

[10] "Zaderzhannogo zamdirektora medrese pod Simferopolem otpustili posle doprosa v glavnom upravlenii MVD v Krymu," *Portal-credo.ru*, June 25, 2014, http://www.portal-credo.ru/site/?act=news&id=108282.

DUMK of Islamist extremism, supported and financed by Ukraine.[11] Responding on behalf of DUMK to those allegations, Mufti Said Ismailov appealed to the participants of this campaign to stop trying to split the Muslim community of Crimea.[12] The All-Ukrainian Muslim charitable association Al-raid also cited anti-Islamic provocations that accused DUMK, the Mejlis, and other Crimean Tatar organizations of having ties with radical Islamist organizations. It confirmed the pro-Ukrainian positions of many Muslim societies in Ukraine, but attributed the allegations of extremism to "the odious Russian Islamophobe Roman Silantiev, notorious for his scandalous anti-Islamic statements."[13]

In July, the chairman of the Mejlis (or Council of Representatives) of the Crimean Tatar People Refat Chubarov and his predecessor Mustafa Dzhemilev (1991–2013) met with Turkey's foreign minister Ahmet Davutoğlu to discuss concerns over an increase in repressions by the Russian federation in Crimea.[14] In May, Dzhemilev had been banned from entry into Crimea for five years, and Chubarov was denied entry in July. Those moves against the Muslim leadership effectively hamstrung the Mejlis. "They took away our best people," said the chairman of the Bakhchisarai district administration Ilmi Umerov, a critic of the annexation who later himself was threatened with expulsion from Crimea if he did not keep his mouth shut.[15]

In the months following the referendum, there were other covert actions, which only came to light after the establishment of the Tauride Muftiate. Mosques, *madrasas*, and private homes were subjected to summary searches and seizures of literature, along with intimidation and

---

11   "Information War Launched against Crimean Muslims Switched to Practice—Mufti of Ukraine," *Russia Religion News* (Stetson University), June 25, 2014, http://www2.stetson.edu/~psteeves/relnews/1406f.html.
12   "Muftii: V Krymu nachalas informatsionnaia voina protiv krymskotatarskogo naseleniia," *Krym.org*, June 24, 2014, http://ru.krymr.com/content/article/25433905.html.
13   "Information War against Muslim Organizations in Crimea," *Russia Religion News* (Stetson University), June 21, 2014, http://www2.stetson.edu/~psteeves/relnews/1406f.html.
14   "Organizatsiia islamskogo sotrudnichestva budet monitorit sobliudeniie prav musulman v Krymu," *Krym.org*, July 11, 2014, ru.krymr.com/content/article/25453327.html.
15   "Siloviki vryvaiutsia v doma krymskikh tatar."

warnings about extremism.[16] According to Refat Chubarov, the sole purpose of this campaign was to crush the Crimean Mejlis.[17]

The Crimean Field Mission for Human Rights, having analyzed the situation in Crimea from March to September 2014 in collaboration with the Council of Europe, the OSCE, and the UN High Commissioner for Human Rights, concluded that it was no longer a matter of isolated incidents, but that "persecutions on the basis of religious identity have acquired a systemic character." The report further attributed the repressions to the actions of local authorities as well as the Russian FSB, explicitly connected them with the creation of the Tauride Muftiate, and warned that the intensification of human rights abuses in Russian-occupied Crimea could exacerbate the situation and accelerate the radicalization of Crimean Tatars.[18]

The situation only worsened in late August, after the creation of the Tauride Muftiate. The assault on the Mejlis and DUMK became more pronounced and public, with acting head of Crimea Sergei Aksionov announcing that despite more than twenty years in operation, the Mejlis did not really exist because it had not been "registered in the necessary way."[19]

The Tauride Muftiate began recruiting member communities through questionable means that involved procedural irregularities or outright manipulation. In the port city of Ievpatoria, local Muslims reported the illegal takeover of their place of worship, the 450-year old Juma-Jami mosque. In mid-September, the imam Elmar Abdulganiev called a summary election of a new board, after which the money in the mosque's safe was seized and the community switched jurisdiction from DUMK to the Tauride Muftiate. Ousted board members, some of whom did not know of

---

16    Tatiana Kalenichenko-Mukhomorova, "Islam v Krymu: Zolotoie proshloe i neopredelionnoie segodnia," *RISU*, November 14, 2014, risu.org.ua/ru/index/excl usive/events_people/58210/.

17    "V Krymu proshli obyski desiatkov musulman,—Chubarov," *RISU*, September 9, 2014, risu.org.ua/ru/index/all_news/other_confessions/islam/57596/.

18    "Pravozashchitniki: v okkupirovannom Krymu presleduiut musulman i veruiushchikh YPTs KP," *RISU*, September 17, 2014, risu.org.ua/ru/index/all_news/comm unity/vandalism/57688/. See also "ES obespokoien zapugivaniiami krymskikh tatar v anneksirovannom Rossiiei Krymu," *RISU*, September 19, 2014, risu.org.u a/ru/index/all_news/ukraine_and_world/international_relations/57712/.

19    "Siloviki vryvaiutsia v doma krymskikh tatar."

the meeting, accused the new board of an illegal election and misappropriation of funds.[20]

In October, the Tauride Muftiate was itself co-opted into the repression campaign after authorities ordered the surrender of Islamic literature that was prohibited under Russian law. A list of banned literature was published with the instruction that any such material was to be turned over to the Muftiate by the end of the year. After December 31, such literature would be confiscated.[21]

In Russia, there was keen interest in the events surrounding Crimea's Tauride Muftiate, especially among the proponents of a reunified Great Russia. Saber-rattling propagandist Roman Silantiev was part of the campaign to discredit Crimean Tatars as Russophobic extremists. He now accused Mejlis Chair Refat Chubarov of calling for armed aggression against Russia, and revealed the essentialist priorities of like-minded Orthodox Russians:

> the World Russian People's Sobor, of which I am a board member, intends to cooperate both with the Tauride Muftiate and with all organizations of *pro-Russian minded Crimean Tatars*. And any Crimean Tatar who *respects the church and the Russian people* may count on our protection.[22]

---

20 "B Ievpatorii proizoshel reiderskii zakhvat znamenitoi mecheti 'Dzhuma-Dzhami,'" *RISU*, September 10, 2014, risu.org.ua/ru/index/all_news/community/land_and_property_problems/57606/.
21 "Aksionov prizyvaiet krymskikh tatar sdavat zapreshchennuiu literaturu," *Interfax-Religiia*, October 14, 2014, interfax-religion.ru/?act=news&div=56756.
22 "Ekspert predosteregaiet krymskiie vlasti." Emphasis mine.
As director of the World Russian People's Sobor's rights advocacy center and an "expert on Islam," Silantiev had formed his views on the basis of those of Sergei Aksionov, before the latter headed occupied Crimea: "Several years ago I had occasion to read his analytical notes on Muslim sects in Crimea, who conducted their russophobic and anti-Orthodox politics in accordance with the line of the Mejlis of the Crimean Tatar People and the DUMK that it controlled." Ibid.
The World Russian People's Sobor was founded in May 1993 and is headed by Russian Orthodox Patriarch Kirill. Its stated goal is the unification of all Russian people, who "became a divided people after 1991." See "O Sobore," *Vsemirnyi Russkii Narodnyi Sobor* n.d., accessed May 18, 2016, http://vrns.ru/o_sobore/.

Silantiev advised the occupation authorities in Crimea not to trust DUMK or its mufti, Emiral Ablaev.[23] The matter was urgent, since the fundamental division of Crimeans had already been carried over to the eastern front: members of the Tauride Muftiate were now "fighting for Novorossiia," while Kolomoiskyi and Dzhemilev were filling the ranks of their National Guard battalions with activists from DUMK mosques who had deserted to the west ("*iz uiekhavshykh na Zapadenshchynu*").[24] All the more reason for the occupation authorities to be strategic in their financial support of religious institutions. Accordingly, Silantiev advised, "[i]t is the Tauride Muftiate that should now become the chief recipient of state aid; after all, it is dangerous to give money to DUMK."[25]

Russia's Chief Mufti Talgat Tadjuddin likewise became involved. He met with the leaders of the traditional organizations, the Mejlis and DUMK, in an effort to persuade them to get in step with the times. Echoing Silantiev, Tadjuddin's message came in the form of a plea for pragmatic realism—their brand of traditionalism was no longer desirable or, as he put it: "*Now they are already a part of Russia* and the best thing, according to the will of the Almighty, would be for them to unite with one another on the basis of traditional Islam of the Hanafi school. Then we will be prepared to cooperate with them."[26]

But not everyone in Russia was singing from the same songbook. Ravil Gainutdin, head of the Council of Muftis of Russia and aligned with Crimea's DUMK, opposed the establishment of the Tauride Muftiate, arguing that it would only divide the Muslim community. He called Tadjuddin to task, and demanded an explanation of his role in that

---

23   "Ekspert predosteregaiet krymskiie vlasti." Silantiev also advised against supporting the activities of the Council of Muftis of Russia, which apparently were not entirely in line with Kremlin policy.
24   Ibid. If there had been any doubts about Silantiev's sympathies, his choice of Ukrainian crisis neologisms—"Novorossiia," "Zapadenshchyna"—removed them. "Novorossiia," despite its imperial Russian roots, is in the current context a deliberate provocation against independent Ukraine's sovereignty, while "Zapadenshchyna" is an ideologically-driven distortion of "Zapad" (the West).
     Among the Tauride Muftiate's pro-Russian fighters in Luhansk was imam Tanai Cholkanov. Silantiev, "Vserossiiskiie ambitsii muftiiatov."
25   Silantiev, "Vserossiiskiie ambitsii muftiiatov."
26   "Muftii Talgat Tadzhuddin oproverg svoio uchastiie v sozdanii Tavricheskogo muftiiata," *Newsru.com*, September 11, 2014, http://www.newsru.com/religy/11sep2014/tajuddin.html. Emphasis mine.

organizational innovation (Tadjuddin denied any direct involvement).[27] Gainutdin also supported the right of Mejlis leaders Mustafa Dzhemilev and Refat Chubarov to enter Crimea, suggesting that they appeal through to the Human Rights Court in Strasbourg.[28]

In fact, when the shoe was on the other foot, even Tadjuddin could see through the untenable logic of seeking unity by way of division. In Russia, when under Gainutdin's influence the Spiritual Board of Muslims suddenly changed its name from the DUM "of the European Part of Russia" to the DUM "of the Russian Federation," Tadjuddin warned that this would undermine the stability of the umma and that the new muftiate would not represent all Muslims of Russia. With evident exasperation he asked: "What can change with the change of a name? Changes occur in our hearts. But instead of that . . . [Gainutdin] declares the creation of parallel structures. *How many ecclesiastical boards of Muslims can there be?*"[29]

By the end of 2014, the aims of Crimea's religious policy were clear: the Tauride Muftiate would serve as a key instrument of the repression campaign, whose aim was to break down and ultimately liquidate traditional community organizations. Under a slogan of unification, its emergence sowed organizational confusion, polarization, and discord in the Muslim community. And while the final outcome of the policy was not yet known, the mobilization of Russian and Crimean authorities, as well as religious leaders and agitators in Russia, enabled a focused campaign of brutal repression, intimidation, and submission to Russian religious policy. On the pretext of combatting Islamic extremism, pro-Ukrainian activists were systematically removed and a pro-Russian line was put in place. The Tauride Muftiate, created specifically to assist in that transformation, was dedicated to imposing a new principle of unity in a Russian mold—even at the cost of dismembering the Crimean Tatar *umma*.[30] Inside Russia,

---

27  "Muftii Talgat Tadzhuddin oproverg svoio uchastiie." Silantiev alleged that, during his visit to Crimea on September 8, Gainutdin had asked the local authorities to crack down on the Tauride Muftiate. "Ekspert predosteregaiet krymskiie vlasti."
28  Silantiev, "Vserossiiskiie ambitsii muftiiatov."
29  "Dukhovnoie upravleniie musulman ievropeiskoi chasti Rossii pereimenovano v DUM RF," *Interfax-Religiia*, September 22, 2014, http://www.interfax-religion.ru/?act=news&div=56515. Emphasis mine.
30  On the growing rift among Tatars in Crimea, see Oleg Yegorov, "Crimean Tatars Split as World Congress Calls for Return to Ukrainian Rule," *Russia Beyond the*

ideologues drew a direct connection with the eastern front, urging the Crimean occupation authorities to buy into the Russian war effort and to eliminate any pro-Ukrainian opposition that remained on the peninsula.

Ultimately, the problem has deeper, historic roots. The Tauride Muftiate is just another variation of the "Spiritual Directorate" governance model, which originated in eighteenth-century Russia and which was continued in the Soviet period. According to Islamic scholar Mykhailo Iakubovych, in by-passing the traditional model of autonomous Islamic communities that were open to integration with mainstream society, the Russian system imposed centralized governance, bureaucracy, and state controls.[31] This, in turn, ghettoized and ethnicized the Muslim *umma*. The issue of Islamic governance was thus tied to the controversy over Ukraine's integration with Europe, and two very different policy orientations toward Muslims were in play: bureaucratic isolation and decentralized integration.

## The Jews of Eastern Ukraine: Displacement and Competing Loyalties[32]

The Euromaidan protests, which began in Kyiv in November 2013, may well be considered a turning point in Jewish-Ukrainian relations. On February 20, 2014, when three Ukrainian Jews lost their lives in Kyiv along

---

*Headlines*, August 10, 2015, rbth.com/international/2015/08/10/crimean_tatars_split_as_world_congress_calls_for_return_to_ukra_48405.html.

31 "Expert: Ukraine Must Evolve from Russian to Western Approach to Islamic Communities," *Euromaidan Press*, May 21, 2015, euromaidanpress.com/2015/05/21/expert-ukraine-must-evolve-from-russian-to-western-approach-to-islamic-communities/. For a perceptive analysis of Muslims in Ukraine up to the end of 2014, assessing the evolving situation on the mainland and in Crimea after the Russian annexation, repressions and the creation of the Tauride Muftiate, see Oleg Yarosh, "Islam and Muslims in Ukraine after the 'Revolution of Dignity': Current Challenges and Perspectives," *Euxeinos. Governance and Culture in the Black Sea Region* 17: "Religion and Political Crisis in Ukraine," ed. Catherine Wanner (University of St. Gallen, 2015), 35–41. In view of the diminished influence of the Mejlis, the author concludes that in order to avoid a split of the Muslim umma in Crimea the role of DUMK will be critical.

32 For a brief historical sketch on Jews in Ukraine, especially since independence, see the recent study by the Director of the Institute of Jewish Studies in Kyiv Yuliana Smilianskaya, "The Jews of Ukraine: Past and Present," *Euxeinos. Governance and Culture in the Black Sea Region* 17: "Religion and Political Crisis in Ukraine," ed. Catherine Wanner (University of St. Gallen, 2015), 20-34.

with other innocent victims of sniper fire, citizens of Ukraine took note of that supreme sacrifice and of the fact that many more Ukrainian Jews had participated in the demonstrations demanding political accountability, trade relations with the EU, and a less Soviet Ukraine.[33]

On April 15, as the Jewish community of Donetsk began to celebrate Passover, unidentified masked men approached the synagogue and distributed leaflets addressed to "respected citizens of Jewish Nationality" from the "Independent Donetsk Republic." The leaflet accused Jews of supporting the "Banderite junta in Kyiv" and of hostility toward the "*Orthodox* Donetsk Republic," and ordered all Jewish citizens aged 16 or older to register with the "commissar for nationality affairs" and provide notarized documents for all immovable property. The leaflet concluded with a threat: "In the event of refusal to register, guilty parties will be deprived of citizenship and forcibly deported outside of the republic and their property will be confiscated."[34] The document included a stamp of the Donetsk "People's Republic" (DNR). Despite subsequent denials by the "authorities" who were cited in the document, the Donetsk Council of Churches and Religious Organizations issued an immediate appeal to the police and government authorities to stop the "rabid xenophobia and blatant antisemitism" by the separatists of the so-called DNR.[35] Other analyses concluded that, while it was difficult to determine the source of the leaflets with any certainty, the incident was more likely either a

---

[33] The three were: Oleksandr Shcherbaniuk, 46, of Chernivsti; Iosif Shiling, 61, of Drohobych; and Ievhen Kotliar, 33, of Kharkiv. See Viacheslav Likhachev, "Ievreiiskii kuren Nebesnoi sotni," *Ievroaziatskii Ievreiskii Kongress*, March 9, 2014, eajc.org/page279/news43756.html; and Paul Berger, "Three Jews Among Those Killed in Ukraine Uprising," *Forward*, March 18, 2014, forward.com/news /world/194722/three-jews-among-those-killed-in-ukraine-uprising/. The presence of members of the right-wing Right Sector at Shcherbaniuk's funeral was no provocation, but a demonstration of respect for a fallen Jewish brother.
Writing with trepidation mere weeks before the massacre, historian Viacheslav Likhachev suggested that Jewish participation at the Maidan may have been partly motivated by Reform Judaism's ideal of "correcting the world" (*Tikkun Olam*). See Viacheslav Likhachev, "Ievrei na Maidane: Pochemu i dlia chego?" *Booknik*, January 23, 2014, booknik.ru/today/all/evrei-na-mayidane-pochemu-i-dlya-chego/.

[34] "Council of Churches of Donetsk Asks Authorities to Stop Manifestations of Xenophobia and Antisemitism on Part of Separatists," *Russia Religion News* (Stetson University), April 17, 2014, www2.stetson.edu/~psteeves/relnews/1404d.html.

[35] Ibid.

provocation to discredit the DNR, or the initiative of antisemitic agitators from Russia.[36]

While the local interreligious Council's response was a significant indication of religious cooperation in Ukraine's regions, a very different reading was not long in coming from the Jewish community in Russia. On May 2, after clashes in Odesa between supporters and opponents of the Maidan, Molotov cocktails were thrown into the House of Labor Unions, and forty-six people died. Rabbi Zinovii Kogan, vice-president of the Congress of Jewish Religious Communities and Organizations in Russia, attributed the tragedy to the emergence of fascism and Russophobia.[37] Kogan looked at the preceding upheavals in Ukraine and concluded that the Odesa tragedy was "a horrible murder committed by people who were nurtured by the Maidan and poisoned by nationalism, Russophobia, hatred, and cruelty." He compared the tragedy to the time "when during the Second World War Jews and non-Jews were herded into barns and

---

36  David Fishman, history professor at the Jewish Theological Seminary in New York, considered the flyers an act of political theatre, whose "intent was to frighten and intimidate Jews . . . and perhaps to spark antisemitic sentiments among other local inhabitants." He also suggested a possible connection to the sudden appearance in eastern Ukraine of a motley assortment of visitors from Russia— special forces, intelligence agents, political agitators, and provocateurs. Of particular relevance were a group called the Black Hundreds, unprecedented in Ukraine, whose ideology was marked by an aggressive Russian ethno-religious nationalism that rejected the existence of Ukraine and which propagated antisemitism. David E. Fishman, "The Real Truth About Those Anti-Semitic Flyers in Donetsk," *Forward*, April 22, 2014, forward.com/opinion/world/196864/the-real-truth-about-those-anti-semitic-flyers-in/.

Josef Zissels also dismissed the flyers as a provocation to discredit the separatist Donetsk People's Republic. David Mikics, "The Head of the Jewish Community of Ukraine Speaks Out against Putin," *Tablet*, April 29, 2014, tabletmag.com/jewish-news-and-politics/170735/josef-zissels-yivo.

Another incident involving antisemitic flyers occurred in Crimea at the end of 2015. On December 26 in the city of Kerch, Igor Dukhanin was convicted for distributing antisemitic flyers in late 2014. He was sentenced to two-and-a-half years in prison, then immediately his sentence was reduced to a ban on media work, teaching and organizing events for the same period. Sam Sokol, "Analysis: Propaganda Battle over Ukrainian Jews is Not Over," *The Jerusalem Post*, January 1, 2016, jpost.com/Diaspora/Analysis-Propaganda-battle-over-Ukrainian-Jews-is-not-over-439057.

37  "Ravvin Kogan sravnil tragediiu v Odesse s Kholokostom i obvinil ukrainskikh ievreiev v potvorstve neofashistam," *Interfax-Religiia*, May 5, 2014, http://www.interfax-religion.ru/?act=news&div=55193. Kogan did not specify which of Patriarch Kirill's pronouncements had addressed this issue.

buildings and burned alive." In Russia, he praised Patriarch Kirill's "firm and moving" pronouncement on the subject, but bemoaned the silence of the rabbis in Ukraine, who seemed to be acting as if nothing had happened.[38]

The issue of antisemitism was revisited in early July, when Alexander Boroda, president of the Federation of Jewish Communities of Russia, stated that the continued glorification of "the xenophobe Stepan Bandera" by the Svoboda Party in Ukraine was but one manifestation of a "rehabilitation of Nazism" in Ukraine.[39] At that same time, Russia's Chief Rabbi Berl Lazar thanked Putin for Russia's "genuine concern" about threats of neo-Nazism, even as leaders in other countries "prefer to remain silent about this."[40] In the context of the Russian-Ukrainian conflict, there was nothing oblique about the reference.

On the other side of the front, the Jewish community of Dnipropetrovsk undertook a line of action in support of Ukraine, mobilizing humanitarian aid for over 200 civilian refugees who had arrived in the city from the embattled eastern regions, and for Ukraine's armed forces on the front lines. Looking back at the developments of the previous months, Oleh Rostovtsev, press service Director of the Jewish Religious Community, explained his community's position and its rationale:

> The Jewish community of Dnipropetrovsk, like other national and public organizations, cannot remain aloof from the processes occurring in our country, and we fully support Ukraine in its struggle for independence and its attempt to defend its territorial integrity, to resist external aggression and to fight to complete victory with terrorists and armed bandit formations.[41]

---

38    "Ravvin Kogan sravnil tragediiu v Odesse s Kholokostom."
39  " V Federatsii ievreiskikh obshchin Rossii obespokoieny reabilitatsiiei fashizma na Ukraine," *Interfax-Religiia*, July 10, 2014, http://www.interfax-religion.ru/?act =news&div=55878. For the record, Boroda also offered a much more restrained, diplomatic interpretation of developments in Ukraine, specifically distancing himself from the direct charge of fascism: "If we are talking about brutality, then obviously it exists there. I cannot say whether it can be called fascism. Rather, it is a foreshadowing of civil war, which began because one part of the state did not want to respect the interests of another." Ibid.
40    "Ravvin Lazar blagodarit prezidenta Putina za podderzhku ievreiskoi obshchiny," *Interfax-Religiia*, July 10, 2014, http://www.interfax-religion.ru/judaism/?act=new s&div=55879.
41    "Iudei Dnepropetrovska aktivno pomogaiut bezhentsam i ukrainskoi armii," *Relihiia v Ukraini*, July 31, 2014, http://www.religion.in.ua/news/ukrainian_news/26503- iudei-dnepropetrovska-aktivno-pomogayut-bezhencam-i-ukrainskoj-armii.html.

The Jewish community of Luhansk organized the evacuation of its members to "secure provinces" in Ukraine and to Israel.[42] Organized and funded by the charitable foundation "Keren Yedidud", the repatriation and relief program involved an intricate web of activities—from restoring communication and letting people know about relief services, to resettling Jews to Israel or to displaced persons camps, and providing accommodation and material aid.[43] By mid-September, the synagogue in Donetsk had been closed for over a month, and the World Forum of Russian Jewry reported that, after the displacement of thousands of Jews from eastern Ukraine to Kyiv, Kharkiv, Dnipropetrovsk, and Israel, the Jewish religious communities of Donetsk and Luhansk had practically ceased to exist.[44]

It should be noted that, unlike the diverse forms of Judaism in other parts of Ukraine, including the Modern Orthodox community, the Karlin Hasidic community of Chief Rabbi Yaakov Dov Bleich, the Chabad-Lubavitch Hasidic community, and the Reform (Progressive/Liberal) community under Chief Rabbi Alexander Dukhovny, in eastern Ukraine the only established Jewish presence is Chabad-Lubavitch, a branch of Hasidic Judaism.[45] Before the war, many of the twenty-six Chabad institutions in the region (synagogues, schools, and community centers) were in Donetsk. Within a year after the outbreak of the war, the Jewish population in that city had plummeted by almost 90%, from a pre-war total of 15,000 to 2,000.[46]

---

42  "Ievreiskaia obshchina Luganska obiavila ob evakuatsii ievreiev v Izrail," *UNIAN*, August 7, 2014, http://religions.unian.net/judaism/948680-evreyskaya-obschina-luganska-obyyavila-ob-evakuatsii-evreev-v-izrail.html.

43  "Iudeiev Luganska gotoviat k evakuatsii v Izrail," *Interfax-Religiia*, August 7, 2014, http://www.interfax-religion.ru/?act=news&div=56119.

44  "Konflikt na Donbasse usilivaiet tendentsii repatriatsii ievreiev v Izrail—Vsemirnyi forum russkoiazychnogo ievreistva," *Interfax-Ukraina*, September 17, 2014, http://interfax.com.ua/news/interview/224217.html.

45  Dovid Margolin, "Telling the Story of Ukraine's Jews: An Interview with *The Jerusalem Post*'s Sam Sokol," *Chabad.org News*, November 11, 2015, chabad.org/news/article_cdo/aid/3125973/jewish/Telling-the-Story-of-Ukraines-Jews-An-Interview-With-The-Jerusalem-Posts-Sam-Sokol.htm.

46  Various sources confirmed these estimates, including the Federation of Jewish Communities of the CIS (2,000), cited in Dovid Margolin, "'There's No Road Home to Donetsk' as Jewish Community Prepares for Yom Kippur in Kiev," *Chabad.org News*, September 21, 2015, chabad.org/news/article_cdo/aid/3071552/jewish/Theres-No-Road-Home-to-Donetsk-as-Jewish-Community-Prepares-for-Yom-Kippur-in-Kiev.htm; and Rabbi Ari Schwartz (2,100–2,500), quoted in Joshua Tartakovsky, "Rabbi of Donetsk Says Separatists Are Not Anti-Semitic,

Donetsk Rabbi Ari Schwartz, responding to a journalist's questions about Ukrainian army bombs hitting civilian residences and about the Ukrainian government "praising Nazi war criminals," insisted that he did not involve himself in political questions. "Everyone has his own opinion and can express it," he said.[47] But what might first have appeared as the cautious neutrality of a Ukrainian patriot took a different turn further on in the interview. Schwartz described his relations with the separatist authorities as "tight," and declared he was certain that the antisemitic leaflets (which had appeared in mid-April under Donetsk People's Republic insignia) had not come from the rebel government. He denied that there had been an *aliyah* (migration of Jews to Israel), saying instead that "people just left the area."[48] Significantly, he made no mention of Chief Rabbi of Donetsk Pinchas Vishedski or of thirteen Chabad-Lubavitch *shluchim* (emissaries) who had left Donetsk after serving there for many years.[49] In his version, all was quiet:

> *Jewish communal life did not stop for a moment* since the beginning of events. Daily prayers in the synagogue continue as usual. Perhaps there was one time when there were no meetings for a period of a week. But *the synagogue was never closed down* . . . everything functions, the school functions, the kindergarten functions. We are working as usual.[50]

This was quite a different perspective on the situation from that given by Jewish refugees who had fled to other parts of Ukraine or to Israel. After serving as Chief Rabbi of Donetsk for some twenty years, Rabbi Pinchas Vishedski had fled to Kyiv in August 2014.[51] From a makeshift office in the capital, he was continuing to direct the Jewish center in Donetsk and to

---

Several Jews Killed in Bombing by Ukrainian Army," *OffGuardian*, October 24, 2015, http://off-guardian.org/2015/10/24/rabbi-of-donetsk-says-separatists-are-n ot-anti-semitic-several-jews-killed-in-bombing-by-ukrainian-army/.

47 Tartakovsky, "Rabbi of Donetsk."
48 Ibid.
49 They included Rabbi Vishedski's wife, Nechama Dina Vishedski, and ten other rabbis: Arye Leib Kaminshtein, Avraam Ribalchenko, Yehuda Gorban, Yakov Dovid Shamrayevsky, Chaim Luria, Yuriy Kelerman, Mendy Lison, Arye Spektor, Arie Konverskiy, and David Usimov. "Chabad Lubavitch of Donetsk," accessed May 19, 2016, chabad.org/centers/default_cdo/aid/118266/jewish/Chabad-Luba vitch-of-Donetsk.htm.
50 Tartakovsky, "Rabbi of Donetsk." Emphasis mine.
51 Amie Ferris-Rotman, "The Scattering of Ukraine's Jews," *The Atlantic*, September 21, 2014, theatlantic.com/international/archive/2014/09/ukraine-jewish-com munity-israel/380515/.

coordinate relief work for refugees.⁵² According to Chabad sources, thirteen emissary families had been serving in the Donetsk Jewish community before the war. By the end of the year, only three families were still working alongside the Vishedskis in Kyiv, while the rest had temporarily relocated to Israel.⁵³ As for the Donetsk synagogue, *Portal-Credo.ru* reported on September 18 that it had been closed since mid-August.⁵⁴ So it remained unclear whether any external, Russian interference or pressure was involved in the Donetsk Jewish community's change of leadership, from Rabbi Vishedski to Rabbi Schwartz.

As for *aliyah*, numerous Jewish sources had no trouble applying the religious term to the displacement of eastern Ukrainian Jews. In April 2014 Soviet dissident Josef Zissels anticipated the real possibility of an *aliyah* from Ukraine.⁵⁵ In September the International Fellowship of Christians and Jews estimated that more Ukrainian Jews would make *aliyah* in 2014 than in the previous three years combined, and Luhansk refugee Lida Rabbieva said that making *aliyah* was the only option for her family.⁵⁶ Similar stories of Chabad *shluchim* displacements included those of Rabbi Shalom Gopin of Luhansk,⁵⁷ Rabbi Eliyahu Kramer of Makiivka (Donetsk oblast),⁵⁸ and Rabbi Mendel Cohen of Mariupol.⁵⁹ Like Reform

---

52   Dovid Margolin, "Scattered Among States, Donetsk Jewish Community Inches Into 2015," *Chabad.org News*, January 8, 2015, chabad.org/news/article_cdo/aid/2821604/jewish/Scattered-Among-States-Donetsk-Jewish-Community-Inches-Into-2015.htm.
53   Ibid.
54   "Konflikt na Donbasse usilivaiet tendentsii repatriatsii ievreiev v Izrail."
55   "Any instability gives birth to thinking about *aliyah*. People are very rooted there, in Ukraine, so they think, 'Maybe it will pass quickly.' But a few weeks, a few months, pass and it hasn't gone away and they say, 'OK, time to leave.'" See Mikics, "The Head of the Jewish Community."
56   Ferris-Rotman, "The Scattering of Ukraine's Jews."
57   Chana Gopin, "'My City Is Being Shelled': Chabad Emissary to Lugansk, Ukraine, Relates Her Story," *Chabad.org News*, September 3, 2014, www.chabad.org/news/article_cdo/aid/2689252/jewish/My-City-Is-Being-Shelled-Chabad-Emissary-to-Lugansk-Ukraine-Relates-Her-Story.htm.
58   Dovid Margolin, "Refugees Themselves, East Ukraine Chabad Emissaries Strive On," *Chabad.org*, January 12, 2015, chabad.org/news/article_cdo/aid/2824584/jewish/Refugees-Themselves-East-Ukraine-Chabad-Emissaries-Strive-On.htm.
59   Margolin, "Refugees Themselves."

Rabbi Misha Kapustin from Crimea, many left with their families specifically because they refused to live under Russian rule.[60] Each of them typically represented a substantial part of their communities, also displaced by the war.

Outside of the war zone, Jewish communities also tried to negotiate their way between patriotic loyalty and political neutrality. Chabad Rabbi Moishe Moskovitz of Kharkiv did not object to individual Jews taking personal stands on the war, but felt that "the Jewish community should wait and see how things turn out, rather than taking political sides."[61] But for other members of the Kharkiv Jewish community, there was a substantive difference between patriotism and partisan politics. Elena Dankina, a supporter of the new government in Kyiv, had joined the Euromaidan protests calling for Ianukovych's ouster in Kharkiv and found herself alongside members of the right-wing Svoboda Party. "If someone had told me a year ago that I would stand calmly next to people from Svoboda, I would never have believed it. I categorically thought that Svoboda Party was not a party that I could stand next to."[62] But she noted that after the party was elected to parliament in 2012, it dropped its antisemitic rhetoric and went more mainstream.

---

60   Sam Sokol, "Analysis: Propaganda Battle over Ukrainian Jews Is Not Over," *The Jerusalem Post*, January 1, 2016, jpost.com/Diaspora/Analysis-Propaganda-battle-over-Ukrainian-Jews-is-not-over-439057. Kapustin was astonished when *Russia Today*, the Kremlin-run station, completely twisted his words to make it appear that he was fleeing because of antisemitism: "I did not expect anything like that, they just misused, . . . mislead, . . . perverted my words."

61   Katherine Jacobsen, "Kharkhiv Jews Stay Calm Amid Separatist Storm Elsewhere in Ukraine," *Forward*, May 8, 2014, http://forward.com/author/katherine-jacobsen/. Moskovitz would later explain the unique distribution of patriotism in Kharkiv: "It's split 50-50. Some people here want to look towards Europe, others towards Russia." At a mere 40 km from the Russian border, citizens of Kharkiv are well aware that "[w]hatever the Russians want to do, they'll do. If they'd like, they can be here within the day." Dovid Margolin, "As Lenin Statue Comes Tumbling Down, Kharkov Jews Watch and Wait," *Chabad.org*, September 29, 2014, http://www.chabad.org/news/article_cdo/aid/2716037/jewish/As-Lenin-Statue-Comes-Tumbling-Down-Kharkov-Jews-Watch-and-Wait.htm. Luhansk refugee Irina expressed a similar view of her home town: "A lot of people want our region to be Russia. Probably half want to live in Ukraine . . . I personally may not like certain things about Ukraine, but I don't want Russia. But after a month of living in a basement under shelling, I'm ready to live anywhere." See Margolin, "As Lenin Statue Comes Tumbling Down."

62   Jacobsen, "Kharkhiv Jews Stay Calm Amid Separatist Storm."

Even sharper differences of perspective among Jews were evident inside the conflict zone and on both sides of the front line. Kofman, the Jewish "foreign minister" of the Donetsk separatists, who had announced that "it is a sacred duty of Israel to recognize us diplomatically," later reported that several dozen former Israel Defense Forces soldiers were serving with the rebels in Donetsk.[63] Among them was communist Ina Levitan, who declared: "As an Israeli, I personally, viscerally hate fascists."[64] On the Ukrainian side, Asher Joseph Cherkassky was a local Hasidic Jew and soldier who had fought in Donetsk. He considered it "a 'civic obligation' to defend Ukraine."[65] Cherkassky's unit, the Dnipro Battalion, was funded by Dnipropetrovsk's Jewish former regional governor, billionaire oligarch Ihor Kolomoiskyi.

By 2015, with some hindsight a broader perspective on the war became possible, and the outline of a deeper reflection on the spiritual and moral dimensions of the war began to surface. In the midst of the armed conflict, traditional prayers acquired a special relevance. Displaced Rabbi Pinchas Vishedski explained: "The Rosh Hashanah prayers that discuss the exile and scattering of the Jewish people have a special meaning for us. It's no longer abstract."[66] And, reflecting on the painful separation from his *shlichus* (posting), and the partition of his community between those who left Donetsk and those who could not, he found resonance in a phrase borrowed from a great philosopher: "We are one soul in two bodies."[67] In Kharkiv, refugee Irina recalled her harrowing bus trip from Luhansk: "We heard shooting all around, and I didn't see anything to

---

63 Sam Sokol, "Israeli Communist Joins Ukrainian Rebels to Fight 'fascists and neo-Nazis," *The Jerusalem Post*, August 20, 2015, jpost.com/Diaspora/Israeli-communist-joins-Ukrainian-rebels-to-fight-fascists-and-neo-Nazis-412785.
Kofman described himself as agnostic and added that he is "probably not Jewish according to strict Orthodox law." But displaced Donetsk Chief Rabbi Pinchas Vishedski was quoted as saying that Kofman is fully "Jewish according to Halacha." See Sam Sokol, "Dozens of Israelis Fighting in Ukraine, Rebel Leader Claims," *The Jerusalem Post*, December 19, 2014, www.jpost.com/Diaspora/Dozens-of-Israelis-fighting-in-Ukraine-rebel-leader-claims-385170.
64 Sokol, "Israeli Communist Joins Ukrainian Rebels."
65 Ibid. According to Rabbi Boruch Gorin, a senior community official from Russia, at the beginning of the war both sides took the Jewish factor very seriously, from a public relations standpoint: ". . . it was very important to show to both sides that they have Jews [and] Israelis fighting for them, and that the Jewish community abroad are their supporters."
66 Margolin, "'There's No Road Home to Donetsk.'"
67 Ibid.

the right or left, only the car in front of me. We just prayed." She could never have foreseen the value of the *Tefilat HaDerech* (prayer for travel) card, which she carried in her wallet.[68] There were many similar accounts of a heightened religiosity among Jews in the war zone. Facing imminent threats to life on a daily basis, the Hasidic Jews of eastern Ukraine found solace and meaning in the spiritual practices of their tradition.

In addition to the inwardly oriented quest for meaning, Jewish community responses to the war involved an awakened sense of the moral imperative of social justice—to reach out to those in need. The mobilization of humanitarian work by Jewish communities throughout Ukraine is well documented. The sense of humanitarian obligation also became a top priority for outsiders, who had some first-hand experience of the war. In November 2015, *Chabad.org News* interviewed journalist Sam Sokol of *The Jerusalem Post*, who had covered the war in Ukraine extensively. When asked about a message for the Jewish community and its leaders, he addressed head-on a matter of conscience and moral responsibility:

> We need to make a *cheshbon hanefesh* [an "accounting of the soul"]. What are the long-term problems the Jews of Ukraine will be facing now? We're past the main events; we're now at: how do they survive? How do they maintain a viable semblance of a community? It behooves us to take responsibility for our brothers, and there are numerous things people can do.[69]

To be sure, not all Jews shared his sense of the duty to assist. As Sokol explained, "there's a pretty vocal minority opposed to what I do. Some people say the Jews of Ukraine deserve what they're getting because they didn't come to Israel after the Soviet Union fell."[70] In this, the Jewish community was no different from any other that was gripped by the war. As the human toll of the war reverberated through the entire country, its divisive impact was also felt far beyond the battle-lines in eastern Ukraine.

The Jewish communities of eastern Ukraine experienced a polarization similar to that of Crimean Muslims in at least one important

---

68    Margolin, "As Lenin Statue Comes Tumbling Down."
69    Sokol listed constructive actions that could make a difference: helping Chabad and the Joint [Distribution Committee], helping him tell the story, sharing a Facebook post, applying to a Jewish organization for a grant to a Jewish school in Ukraine or an orphanage in Odesa, spending a winter volunteering. Margolin, "Telling the Story of Ukraine's Jews."
70    Margolin, "Telling the Story of Ukraine's Jews."

respect—loyalty to the state was the crucial factor determining where one stood, and so the competing alignments with either Ukraine or Russia produced opposite perspectives on the war and its desired outcome. But unlike Crimea, which Russia claimed for itself after the disputed referendum, Ukraine's occupied eastern regions retained their hybrid republican status much longer. Except for some uncertainty about the personnel change in the position of Chief Rabbi of Donetsk, there was no coercive imposition of a new organizational structure for the Jewish communities that remained in Donetsk and Luhansk, and as long as the conflict remained unresolved, prudence for them seemed to favor a politically neutral posture. But those who managed to flee had the opportunity to express their Ukrainian patriotism openly.

**The Baptists of Eastern Ukraine: Different Readings of Scripture**

The Baptist internal debate was perhaps the most complex of the three groups considered here. Initially, it centered on two documents of the 34th Congress of the Russian Union of Evangelical Christians-Baptists (RUECB—St. Petersburg, May 30, 2014) and the controversy that erupted between Baptists in Russia and their brethren in Ukraine. On the surface, the polarization was similar to those noted in other religious communities—essentially, perspectives were divided along either pro-Russian or pro-Ukrainian lines. But unlike the other controversies, the Baptist one produced official documents and a wide-ranging, public debate, with each side putting forward well-developed arguments on the interpretation of scripture, the discernment of divine truth and the proper application of both to real human contexts. We will briefly outline that exchange.

The Baptist Congress in St. Petersburg produced two documents: a resolution on the situation in Ukraine and an open letter to Putin. Some days before they were made public, an early draft was leaked by way of an audiotape, and the tempest was unleashed. Mikhail Cherenkov, a professor at the Drahomaniv National Pedagogical University in Kyiv and Vice-President of the Association for Spiritual Renewal (the Ukraine branch of Peter Deineka Mission Eurasia), objected vehemently to the draft resolution's reference to the situation in Ukraine as a "domestic confrontation."[71] Frustrated that his Baptist brothers in Russia were blind to the facts of the "men in green" (Kadyrov-Chechen and Kuban Cossack mercenaries), as well as to the annexation of Crimea and other threats, Cherenkov noted with frustration: "What the whole world sees, Russians do not see at close range. They believe their own television more than their Ukrainian brethren. They believe government propaganda more than the UN Security Council."[72] Apparently his message found its mark, because when the document was published the phrase "domestic confrontation" was replaced by the more open-ended "armed conflict."

Another passage in the draft stirred controversy when it cited biblical principle in questioning the Ukrainian revolution. The passage affirmed the Baptist Union's "adherence to biblical teaching, which does not embrace the violent overthrow of the legal government, nationalism, and the resolution of social and political contradictions by means of arms. 'Do not associate with rebels' (Pr. 24.21)." To this, Cherenkov responded:

> They accuse Ukrainians, including Ukrainian Baptists, of the "violent overthrow of a legal government," and of "nationalism." Which legal government—the murderers and thieves of Ianukovich, who fled to Russia? Of what kind of nationalism do they accuse us? . . . Hitherto no kind of nationalism has been observed. Although now Russian Baptists, without thinking, are repeating the words of government propaganda.[73]

On this point, there had been no substantial change from the original draft to the final text. Pressed on the matter in an interview, Pastor Iurii Sipko, past president of the RUECB, indicated a very different reading of the same text:

> . . . read the document with a cool head. You will discover that all the words about the unacceptability of the overthrow of a legal government pertain to the current actions of militants in the Donetsk and Luhansk regions. After all, the government in Kyiv is legitimate. There are no armed actions there. There are no insurrections there. All insurrections are taking place in the east. And the condemnation of revolutionaries expresses very precisely the attitude of the

---

71 "Otrecheniie." *RISU*, June 1, 2014, http://risu.org.ua/article_print.php?id=56615&name=blog&_lang=ua&. See also Mikhail Cherenkov, "Otrecheniie ot ukrainskikh bratiev," *Mir vam*, June 11, 2014, https://www.facebook.com/permalink.php?story_fbid=685608508141690&id=153134584722421.

72 Ibid.

73 Ibid.

RUECB to the so-called militias from Russia and to everybody who supports them.[74]

Sipko's reading between the lines (if not words) suggests that he may have served on the resolution committee that composed the text in the first place. But any calculation on his part that an ambiguous text would kill two birds with one stone—by pleasing both Russians in Russia and Ukrainians in Ukraine—appeared to have backfired.

On June 4, pastor Iurii Symonenko in Alchevsk, Luhansk province, addressed an open letter to his Baptist brethren in Russia who had participated in the May Congress. He had felt a deep pain ever since the congress had completed its work. As compared with the blows that Christians may expect at any time for their faith, he concluded that nowadays "those blows are coming ever more often from . . . our own brothers in the faith . . . And those blows are all the more painful because they are delivered [with reference to] scripture."[75] A case in point was the often cited biblical idea that there is no authority but from God (Rom. 13:1). For Symonenko, there was considerably more to it than simply passive compliance to civil authorities:

> The Lord bestows authority on man, but He also takes it away when man proves unworthy of it. And God has plenty of ways to remove authority. As I watched the events of the Maidan, I clearly saw the hand of divine judgment taking power away from a man who was caught stealing and who had dared to make a mockery of his solemn promise to the electorate.[76]

Ihor Bandura, vice-president of the Baptist Council of Ukraine (Ukrainian Council of Churches of Evangelical Christians-Baptists—UCCECB) and pastor in Odesa, attended the May Congress and was alarmed and disturbed by the emerging difference of opinion among Baptists about the situation in Ukraine. To describe it as a domestic, civil conflict and a

---

74  See Iurii Sipko's interview by Vladimir Oivin "Mneniie," *Portal-credo.ru*, accessed May 19, 2016, http://www.portal-credo.ru/site/?act=authority&id=2088.

75  Iurii Simonenko and Galina Korolevskaia, "Razmyshleniia pastora: Ukraina-Rossiia," *VSTs IeKhB*, June 10, 2014, ecbua.info/index.php?option=com_content&view=article&id=3110%3Arazmyshleniya-pastora-ukraina-rossiya&catid=13%3As-&Itemid=53&lang=ua.

76  Ibid.

fratricidal war was inaccurate. "This," he said, "is external aggression."[77] The challenge lay in establishing that truth in a situation where propaganda had taken over the public discourse and consolidated a conflict of interpretations. It also made a huge difference whether one lived in a country where the will of the people was to move toward democracy, or in a society that was falling back into totalitarianism.[78] As for Christians, they were morally bound to pursue an "internal search for the truth" regardless where they lived. Whether they had access to accurate information or only to disinformation and propaganda, Bandura was convinced that, as long as they made an honest effort to discern the real truth, "the Lord will certainly reveal it."[79] Nor were these theological abstractions—the very unity of Baptists in Ukraine and Russia was at stake. Bandura was deeply troubled to note such an incapacity of religious discernment among his brethren in Russia:

> It seemed to me that some brothers had begun to recall the Soviet Union with nostalgia, when there was a single empire and when everybody spoke a single language and when everyone walked in step. And [now,] commenting on events in Ukraine, people are lamenting with the words: "It was different." I am appalled that some Baptist ministers are nostalgic for the Soviet Union. I think this is an unhealthy trend, and part of the reason for it is that people are swallowing propaganda uncritically.[80]

---

77   See Igor Bandura's interview "Tserkov podderzhivaiet narod v iego poiske pravdy, svobody, samovyrazheniia," *Baznica.info*, June 13, 2014, baznica.info/article/igor-bandura-cerkov-podderzhivaet-narod-v-ego-pois/.
78   "In a free country, a person has the choice of news media. He can choose and for the most part probably find the truth. In a country where there is no such freedom, and where a single commentary on all events dominates, it is more difficult for people to get oriented." See Bandura's interview.
79   Ibid.
80   Ibid. Bandura may have been referring to Iurii Sipko's response to a question whether the letter to Putin, in effect a kind of "pledge of allegiance," was really a necessary step for the Baptist Congress. Sipko replied: "In my opinion, there was no such urgent need. On the one hand, it is a need of the current moment. On the other hand, it is an ancient tradition. *We are all children of the USSR (rodom iz SSSR).*" See Sipko's interview by Oivin. Emphasis mine.
Bandura would return again later to the troubling difference between Baptists in Ukraine and their co-religionists in Russia: "Ukrainian churches feel more sharply the importance of personal freedom and the values of the individual, freedom of speech and confession, and the independence of the church from the state. [They] are more conscious of their responsibility to raise the prophetic voice in defense of these values. For us, the authorities are not 'a holy cow,' and the

On the one hand, Baptists were called to stand together across political borders and not to allow the armed conflict to undermine their spiritual unity. But once the truth was discerned the church in Ukraine was duty-bound to take a stand together with the people. For Bandura, his church had a duty to serve as "salt and light" for those who suffered—delivering consolation and support where needed, and bringing meaning to the deepest questions of human existence.[81]

A similar sense of Christian moral responsibility was affirmed by the president of the Baptist Council of Ukraine, Valerii Antoniuk. In his view, the difference between Ukrainian and Russian Baptists was not about language, ethnicity, or political ideology, but about the Christian thirst for truth and justice: "Ukraine is not Russia . . . The difference is that here in Ukraine the changes that occurred in recent months are directly connected with the fact that the people's thirst for truth and justice is manifest."[82]

As for the Ukrainian Baptist position on the Ukrainian "uprising against the government," Antoniuk explained that the Christian discernment of truth did not center on human vicissitudes, but on the constant values of truth and justice. The church was committed to constructive social change that began with a change in the human heart:

> The strength of the church is not demonstrated by standing on the side of the people or the government. The strength of the church is always to be on the side of truth, regardless of state structures, political confrontations, or public moods. When a nation speaks the truth and seeks justice, when it wants to eliminate corruption and live honestly, Christians are always called to support this.
>
> The church is separated from the state, but not from society. And when in times of crisis and upheaval the people experience a unique sense of justice, the church must serve them by pointing out the paths that lead to real transformations, both in the hearts of citizens and in the life of the country.
>
> . . . When Martin Luther King delivered his famous speech "I have a dream" not all American Christians applauded him. Many were convinced that this

---

source of power—according to the Constitution—is not the president and government but the people. We have thus a different situation regarding religious freedom and other prospects for the development of the church." See Paul Goble, "Moscow's Intervention in Ukraine Dividing Ukrainian Baptists from Russian Co-Religionists," *The Interpreter*, June 17, 2015, interpretermag.com/moscows-intervention-in-ukraine-dividing-ukrainian-baptists-from-russian-co-religionists/.

81  See Bandura's interview "Tserkov podderzhivaiet narod."
82  See Valerii Antoniuk's interview by Konstantin Teteriatnikov, *RISU*, July 15, 2014, risu.org.ua/ua/index/expert_thought/interview/57031.

Baptist pastor was acting incorrectly and provocatively. It took time to understand why all that happened.[83]

The Baptist church could not afford to align itself with any particular state, in Antoniuk's view. If it did, it ran the risk of becoming politicized and disconnected from the truth, and potentially of collaborating with evil structures of power:

> When the church is too partisan it cannot speak God's truth. When Christians make purely political statements, pleasing the powers that be, that is improper and undignified . . . I recall the balanced and proper position taken by church ministers during the rise of the Third Reich: "Obedience to tyrants is equal to disobedience towards God," according to Dietrich Bonhoeffer and a group of pastors. Unfortunately, they were few.[84]

Antoniuk's reflection brought the discussion back to the issue of self-serving or non-committal interpretations of Romans 13:1 ("there is no authority except from God"). Rather than justifying all political authority, including dictatorship, and encouraging Christian submissiveness, the Pauline principle was a reminder that human authority remained accountable to its divine source. In a Christian perspective, justice could only be achieved when human authority was aligned with its divine source, and no amount of political manipulation of the truth could ever produce authentic justice. Social favor had its own distinct dynamics and, in their time, not even the penetrating discernment of Dietrich Bonhoeffer or of Martin Luther King had always enjoyed the consensus of the entire Christian community. Yet all were called to the one truth.

In their extended controversy over the war, the Baptists of Ukraine considered the root cause of the difference between them and their brothers in Russia as neither ideological nor political. Rather, it had to do with the discernment of truth in light of scripture. So Ukrainian Baptists elaborated a fraternal correction of their brothers in Russia, whose reading and interpretation of scripture had gone off the rails and led them to capitulate to the state in matters of Christian conscience.[85]

---

83   Ibid.
84   Ibid.
85   A case in point was an article by an American-born journalist affiliated with the Russian Union of Evangelical Christians-Baptists and the Russian Evangelical Alliance in Moscow. See William Yoder, "Conclusions from the Crisis in Ukraine," *Russia Religion News* (Stetson University), July 24, 2014, www2.stetson.edu/

## Concluding Remarks

Our study of the religious dimension of Ukraine's war has explored the impact of the conflict on three communities of faith and their responses.

For Crimean Tatars, who supported the integrity of Ukraine and opposed Russia's annexation of Crimea, the imposition of new leaders, structures, and ideas from Russia threatened the stability of their social and religious traditions. The new order represented a sharp dissonance with the immediate past and, connected as it was with a brutal campaign of repression, harassment, and murder, it was a shocking reminder of their massive deportation, the Sürgün, in 1944. As Russia took control of the peninsula in 2014, many Tatars fled to other regions in Ukraine and retained their citizenship. Those who remained in their traditional lands under a different flag recognized that they could no longer commemorate the Sürgün or support Ukraine. Their religious adherence and practice would also be under constant surveillance and suspicion of extremism.

Many Hasidim of Donbas, like Jews throughout Ukraine, were strong supporters of Ukrainian sovereignty and the democratic, European values of the Maidan. The horror of seeing their cities and towns bombed was compounded by antisemitic incidents, which harked back to patterns not seen since the Holocaust. Uprooted and displaced from Donetsk and Luhansk, they left behind the bare traces of once vibrant communities. Torn between neutrality and engagement on the home front, they found themselves painfully at odds with their co-religionists in Russia, who subscribed to the official discourse of Ukraine as a hotbed of fascism, neo-

---

~psteeves/relnews/1407g.html. Like Iurii Sipko, Yoder proposed unusual interpretations of the St. Petersburg Baptist Congress and of the situation in Ukraine. He claimed that the letter to Putin commended only the president's "internal peacemaking role," but not his foreign policy; that the Maidan "robbed the eastern half [of Ukraine] of its political parity;" that "Russia's annexation of Crimea was one response to the destruction of that delicate balance;" and that "Russians fortunately have media choices" as demonstrated by the fact that "more than a few" choose not to watch TV propagandist Dmitrii Kiseliov.

On the transition of Ukrainian Protestants from a spiritual subculture that was disengaged from social issues to one that identifies with Ukrainian society, its history, and pursuit of social justice, see Mykhailo Cherenkov, "Ukrainian Protestants after Maidan," in Wanner, 42–48. This seminal reflection provides a more detailed, differentiated picture of Protestants in Donbas than was possible in this brief sketch. In particular, the opposing views treated here as primarily differences of perspective between Ukraine and Russia are shown to have been fully at play in Donbas.

Nazism, and Russophobia and who extended that critique to their Jewish brothers in Ukraine. In confronting the challenges of the war, many found that their traditional spiritual practices had immense power to nourish hope that their communities would, yet again, survive a war, displacement, and separation.

The Baptist story provided the gripping image of a community in the throes of an agonizing, critical self-reflection. For a religious community that had virtually no ethno-national baggage and which prided itself on its cosmopolitan distance from such concerns, it was remarkable how a deep, theological reflection about the real situation could generate such heated internal debate about divine truth and social justice as illuminated by the Gospel. As evangelical Christians, their first port of call in the crisis was scripture: exegesis and prayerful reflection were the way to discern the divine will and to define human moral responsibility. The prophetic witness of Baptist pastors and leaders of Ukraine manifested their discernment of the signs of the times, their sense of emergent ethical obligations, and their memory of the courageous stands of the few, who challenged their religious communities in times of social turmoil.

Despite the differences, there were also common threads among the religious minorities of Ukraine. The first and the most obvious was the replacement of Ukrainian political authority with a Russian or pro-Russian one. Whether they liked it or not, Crimean Tatars and Donbas Jews and Baptists were told, virtually overnight, that they were no longer citizens of Ukraine. While some welcomed the change as a sort of long-awaited "liberation," others remained skeptical, neutral, or opposed.

The primary effects of the war and of occupation on the three religious communities were an exacerbation of old divisions, the introduction of new ones, and the imposition of mechanisms of control, and cooptation by the authorities. While the ranks of combat troops on both sides of the front were quickly dotted with Muslims and Jews as "token representatives," their home communities were left with the daunting task of maintaining some semblance of unity and of grappling with a hellish question: how was mortal combat possible between people of the same faith tradition?[86] Religious communities found themselves fragmented

---

86 On Crimean Tatars fighting for Ukraine, see Christina Silva, "To Defeat Russia, Ukraine Creates Muslim Military Unit made up of Crimean Tatars," *International Business Times*, August 3, 2015, http://www.ibtimes.com/defeat-russia-ukraine-

and divided in various ways. What used to be a rich diversity of ethnic backgrounds, linguistic preferences, and even political loyalties now became a matter of categorical, mutually exclusive options. Any one religious community could have members who were pro-Russian or pro-Ukrainian, and time and again ethnicity had very little to do with where one stood. As families split over the conflict, religious communities also came to know the challenge of trying to hold things together. The departure and displacement of refugees divided communities physically, geographically, and politically. Even worse, each of these Ukrainian religious communities also felt the separation from its counterparts in Russia, who read the situation in a very different light. The widespread social fragmentation and polarization caused by the war thus spilled over into individual religious communities, aggravating pre-existing, internal differences and instigating new hostilities.

The secessionist authorities likewise used a variety of measures to assert control over and to co-opt the religious communities. Repression and intimidation were the preferred tools for removing undesirable community leaders and books, and for prohibiting traditional observances that were deemed subversive. The purported suspicion of extremism or pro-Ukrainianism became a carte-blanche for the authorities to "be the law." The co-optation of religious communities occurred in a variety of ways, including the imposition of new organizational structures, and flying in VIPs from Moscow to spell out how the life of minority religious communities would look after harmonization with Russian law.

---

creates-muslim-military-unit-made-crimean-tatars-2036618. For Silantiev's statement on members of the Tauride Muftiate fighting for Novorossiia in Donbas, see "Ekspert predosteregaiet krymskiie vlasti."

For Jewish "DNR foreign minister" Aleksandr Kofman's information on former Israel Defense Forces soldiers serving with the rebels in Donetsk; on Israeli communist Ina Levitan; and on Asher Joseph Cherkassky, local Hasidic Jew and soldier for the Ukrainian side in Donetsk, see Sokol, "Israeli Communist joins Ukrainian Rebels."

While no information was available to us about Baptist soldiers serving on the front lines, the gap between Russian Baptist champions of Putin and Ukrainian Baptist supporters of the Maidan was very significant, since members of the same denomination were citing biblical principle in support of opposing views of the Ukrainian revolution. For those who had been at the Maidan, that difference was neither partisan nor ideological, but proceeded from a divergence in the kind of fundamental values of governance and political culture that are usually found in constitutions.

But the impact of Russia's intervention was only part of the religious story. Ukraine's minority faith communities also mounted a wide range of responses in their home territories and in the diaspora: adjusting their activities in order to survive; providing assistance to the casualties of war and their families; organizing relief for refugees; lending support to the war effort; taking principled stands on matters of conscience; maintaining lines of communication among members of their divided communities; and upholding the fundamental human values over which the transformation had begun at the Euromaidan. Through social engagement in the time of national catastrophe they forged new internal bonds and created opportunities for crossing religious borders with assistance to others in need. In diverse situations, people of faith discovered anew how their traditional beliefs and practices were enduring sources of strength, resilience, and hope.

## Bibliography

Cherenkov, Mykhailo. "Ukrainian Protestants after Maidan." In *Religion and Political Crisis in Ukraine*. Special Issue of *Euxeinos. Governance and Culture in the Black Sea Region* 17, edited by Catherine Wanner, 42–48. St. Gallen, CH: University of St. Gallen, 2015.

Elliott, Mark R., ed. *The Impact of the Ukrainian Crisis on the Church and Christian Ministry*. Special Issue of *East-West Church and Ministry Report* 22, no. 3. Wilmore, KY: Asbury University, 2014.

Elliott, Mark R. "The Impact of the Ukrainian Crisis on Religious Life in Ukraine and Russia." In *The Impact of the Ukrainian Crisis on the Church and Christian Ministry*. Special Issue of *East-West Church and Ministry Report* 22, no. 3, edited by Mark R. Elliott, 6–16. Wilmore, KY: Asbury University, 2014.

Krawchuk, Andrii, and Thomas Bremer, eds. *Eastern Orthodox Encounters of Identity and Otherness. Values, Self-Reflection, Dialogue*. New York: Palgrave Macmillan, 2014.

_____. *Churches in the Ukrainian Crisis*. New York: Palgrave Macmillan, 2016 (in press).

Leustean, Lucian, ed. *Eastern Christianity and Politics in the Twenty-First Century*. New York: Routledge, 2014.

Lunkin, Roman. "The Ukrainian Revolution and Christian Churches." In *The Impact of the Ukrainian Crisis on the Church and Christian Ministry*. Special Issue of *East-West Church and Ministry Report* 22, no. 3, edited by Mark R. Elliott, 1–6. Wilmore, KY: Asbury University, 2014.

Panych, Olena. "Memory and Identity among Post-Soviet Evangelical Christians-Baptists in Contemporary Ukraine." *Religion, State & Society* 42, no. 4 (2014): 354–73.

Plokhy, Serhii. *The Gates of Europe: A History of Ukraine*. New York: Basic Books, 2015.

Smilianskaya, Yuliana. "The Jews of Ukraine: Past and Present." In *Religion and Political Crisis in Ukraine*. Special Issue of *Euxeinos. Governance and Culture in the Black Sea Region* 17, edited by Catherine Wanner, 20–34. St. Gallen, CH: University of St. Gallen, 2015.

Wanner, Catherine, ed. *Religion and Political Crisis in Ukraine*. Special Issue of *Euxeinos. Governance and Culture in the Black Sea Region* 17. St. Gallen, CH: University of St. Gallen, 2015.

Wood, Elizabeth et al. *Roots of Russia's War in Ukraine*. New York: Columbia University Press, 2016.

Yakubovych, Mykhailo. "Islam and Muslims in Contemporary Ukraine: Common Backgrounds, Different Images." *Religion, State & Society* 38, no. 3 (2010): 291–304.

Yarosh, Oleg. "Islam and Muslims in Ukraine after the 'Revolution of Dignity': Current Challenges and Perspectives." In *Religion and Political Crisis in Ukraine*. Special Issue of *Euxeinos. Governance and Culture in the Black Sea Region* 17, edited by Catherine Wanner, 35–41. St. Gallen, CH: University of St. Gallen, 2015.

# Part Six

# Reforming Ukraine

# Part 3

# 11
# The Perpetual Cycle of Political Corruption in Ukraine and Post-Revolutionary Attempts to Break Through It

Oksana Huss

The most important demands of the participants in the 2013–2014 Ukrainian revolution included the removal of the corrupt Ianukovych regime and punishment of those involved in political corruption.[1] According to the Global Corruption Barometer survey conducted in Ukraine in 2013, more than 80% believed that the state institutions and the government were run through personal connections—"by a few big entities looking out for their own interests."[2] This survey also revealed that every third Ukrainian was ready to protest actively against corruption in 2013. Ultimately, more than one hundred civilians gave their lives for a new Ukraine, democratic and non-corrupt. However, two years after the revolution, corruption still remains a rampant and urgent problem in Ukraine impeding its democratic development.[3] The objective of this study is to analyze the persistence of

---

1  According to the December *7–8, 2013* survey conducted by the Ilko Kucheriv Democratic Initiatives Foundation and the Kyiv International Institute of Sociology, 75.1% of Maidan participants claimed that the dismissal of the government was necessary, and 49.6% considered it crucial to punish the corrupt political elite. 1037 respondents were questioned. See "Maidan-2013," *Fond "Demokratychni initsiatyvy imeni Ilka Kucheriva,"* accessed May 21, 2016, http://www.dif.org.ua/en/events/gvkrlgkaeths.htm.
2  Mike Runey, "The Latest Transparency International Global Corruption Barometer, Released Today, Shows that Ukrainians Strongly Believe That Their State Has Become More Corrupt Over the Last Two Years," *Transparency International Ukraine*, September 7, 2013, *http://ti-ukraine.org/en/news/2815.html.*
3  According to Transparency International, the Global Coalition against Corruption, Ukraine's Corruption Perceptions Index (CPI) for 2015, a perceived level of public sector corruption on a scale of 0 (highly corrupt) to 100 (non-corrupt), identifies Ukraine as one of the most corrupt countries in the world, occupying the 130th position in the list of 168 countries and territories with a score of 27. See "Corruption Perceptions Index 2015," *Transparency International*, accessed February 18, 2016, http://www.transparency.org/cpi2015#results-table.

political corruption in Ukraine and to assess related post-revolutionary changes.

Methodologically, this discussion is based on interviews conducted in Kyiv in 2014 and 2015, and on prosecution cases available for scrutiny at the time. Works by prominent investigative journalists, and important scholarship on the subject by Anders Åslund, Henry E. Hale, Taras Kuzio, and Oliver Bullough, as well as findings of the Razumkov Centre study on political corruption, serve as the foundation for this discussion.[4] In order to better understand Ukraine's specificity, a closer examination of the state's system that perpetuates corruption among the Ukrainian political and business elites seems in order.

Political corruption usually occurs at the highest levels of the government and state institutions, targeting the mechanisms and procedures of their functioning and shaping the state's political system. In the Ukrainian case, corruption should be conceptualized as an informal institution which facilitates corrupt exchanges by producing stable expectations for the parties involved.[5] Consequently, all participating actors are familiar with underlying informal rules and do not question the norms of corrupt action. These rules and norms determine the behavior of the majority of decision makers. Thus, political corruption is more than a deviation from formal and written legal norms. According to Jens Christopher Andvig and Odd-Helge Fjeldstad, "political corruption is when

---

4   Anders Åslund, "Oligarchs, Corruption, and European Integration," *Journal of Democracy* 25, no. 3 (2014): 64–73; Anders Åslund, *Ukraine: What Went Wrong and How to Fix It* (Washington, DC: Peterson Institute for International Economics, 2015); Henry E. Hale, *Patronal Politics: Eurasian Regime Dynamics in Comparative Perspective*, Problems of International Politics (New York, NY: Cambridge University Press, 2015); Taras Kuzio, *Ukraine: Democratization, Corruption, and the New Russian Imperialism* (Santa Barbara, California: Praeger Security International, 2015); Oliver Bullough, "Looting Ukraine: How East and West Teamed up to Steal a Country," *Legatum Institute*, July 1, 2014, http://www.li.com/docs/default-source/publications/ukraine_imr_a4_web.pdf;
"Political Corruption in Ukraine: Actors, Manifestations, Problems of Countering," *National Security & Defence* no. 7 (2009), *Razumkov Centre*, accessed June 13, 2016, http://www.razumkov.org.ua/eng/files/category_journal/NSD111_eng_1.pdf.
5   Jean Cartier-Bresson, "Corruption Networks, Transaction Security and Illegal Social Exchange," *Political Studies* 45, no. 3 (1997): 463–76.

rulers abuse laws and regulations, or sidestep, ignore, and tailor laws and regulations to benefit their private interests."[6]

In order to explain the persistence of corruption in Ukraine, the *corruption system* approach seems useful. The term *system* has been used in post-Soviet countries to define a specific type of governance structure, including formal and informal institutions, as well as structures and processes that influence participants' behavior. [7] This system operates in the environment built by a state's society and international actors. It is important to highlight three essential points about this approach.

First, the *corruption system* approach implies that widespread corruption is not a cultural problem, but primarily a structural one. An alternative approach suggests that the problem with corruption is historically ingrained within culture.[8] Although history and unwritten societal norms deeply anchored in it cannot be neglected, this cultural approach is insufficient for an analysis of widespread corruption. It is impossible to change history, yet it is possible to analyze and change historical practices and their current structure.

Second, in cases when formal institutions are developed and state laws are adopted under corrupt conditions,[9] corruption should be analyzed not only at the output side (policy implementation),[10] but also at the

---

[6] Jens Christopher Andvig and Odd-Helge Fjeldstad, *Corruption: A Review of Contemporary Research* (Bergen: Chr. Michelsen Institute, Development Studies and Human Rights. 2001), 11.

[7] Lilia Shevtsova, *Putin's Russia,* rev. and exp. ed. (Washington, D.C: Carnegie Endowment for International Peace, 2005), 16; Rasma Karklins, *The System Made Me Do It: Corruption in Post-Communist Societies* (New York: M.E. Sharpe, 2005), 13.

[8] Åse Berit Grødeland, "Elite Perceptions of Anti-Corruption Efforts in Ukraine," *Global Crime* 11, no. 2 (2010): 237–60; William L. Miller, Åse Berit Grødeland, and Tatyana Y. Koshechkina, *A Culture of Corruption? Coping with Government in Post-Communist Europe* (Budapest: Central European University Press, 2001).

[9] Tobias Debiel and Birgit Pech, "Mit Korruptionsbekämpfung Zum Take off Bei Den MDGs? ZuMöglichkeiten Und Grenzen Einer Entwicklungspolitischen Strategie," in *"Simplizistische Lösungen verbeiten sich"—Zur Internationalen Zusammenarbeit Im 21. Jahrhundert,* edited by Eckhard Deutschner and Hartmut Ihne (Baden-Baden: Nomos, 2010), 53–67.

[10] Bo Rothstein, "What Is the Opposite of Corruption?" *Third World Quarterly* 35, no. 5 (2014): 737–52, 745 ff.

input side (aggregation of interests and decision-making) of the political process.[11]

Third, arguably, corruption is not a problem of the country's formal institutional framework but rather of the informal structure of governance which corruption instantiates. Therefore, it would be prudent to take a closer look at the informal structures of the political system in order to identify the role and persistence of corruption within it. Such an analysis has been underrepresented in literature on corruption and, importantly, has not been a part of anti-corruption policies.[12]

Both scholarship on corruption and anti-corruption policies are dominated by the neo-classical economic approach which suggests that the problem with corruption is primarily associated with formal institutional incentives enabling corrupt action. As a result of this assumption, since the mid-nineties the core elements of the anti-corruption agenda consisted of new laws and formal institutions. For instance, under each President of Ukraine a new National Anti-Corruption Strategy was introduced and an Anti-Corruption Agency was established.[13] However, these laws and institutions had no perceptible impact and were used as a "good governance façade."[14] In some extreme cases, the regime resorted to the

---

11   Tanja A. Börzel, Yasemin Pamuk, and Andreas Stahn, "The European Union and the Promotion of Good Governance in Its Near Abroad: One Size Fits All?," *SFB-Governance Working Paper Series*, no. 18 (2008): 1–44; also available at *Freie Universität—Berlin*, accessed June 13, 2016, http://edocs.fu-berlin.de/docs/servl lets/MCRFileNodeServlet/FUDOCS_derivate_000000000224/SFB-Governance _Working_Paper_Nr18.pdf.
12   For a literature review on corruption and democratization, see Brigit Pech, "Korruption und Demokratisierung: Rekonstruktion des Forschungsstandes an den Schnittstellen zu Institutionenökonomik und politischer Transformationsforschung," *INEF Report*, no. 99 (Duisburg: Institut für Entwicklung und Frieden, 2009), *edoc.vifapol*, October 17, 2011, http://edoc.vifapol.de/opus/volltexte/2011/3468/ (in German).
13   Under Kuchma, the Law on Prevention of Corruption and the Concept on Fight against Corruption for 1998–2005 were introduced. Iushchenko developed the Concept of Overcoming Corruption "On the Way Toward Integrity" and formed the National Bureau of Investigation subordinated to the Prosecutor General. Ianukovych advanced the National Anti-Corruption Strategy for 2011–2015 and set the National Anti-Corruption Committee.
14   The term "good governance façade" describes reforms which are "introduced deliberately to mislead observers and stakeholders to cover political theft." Kalle Moene and Tina Søreide "Good Governance Facades," in *Greed, Corruption and the Modern State*, eds. Susan Rose-Ackerman and Paul Lagunes (Cheltenham, UK, Northampton, MA, USA: Edward Elgar Publishing, 2015), 46.

elimination of the opposition (e.g. Iuliia Tymoshenko's and Iurii Lutsenko's imprisonment under Ianukovych).

Political elites knowingly introduced formal anti-corruption measures to please western partners and to respond to the emerging global anti-corruption agenda,[15] but all these attempts did not target the core of informal rules and corrupt practices of the country's political system. The corruption system approach addresses this informal structure of Ukrainian politics that was ignored by previous attempts to tackle corruption.

In a nutshell, this study considers the *system of corruption* an integral part of a stable hybrid political regime with distinct characteristics, where formally democratic and non-democratic elements coexist and are interdependent.[16] In this hybrid political regime, corrupt exchanges are both the fuel and a stabilizing factor that ensure the system's functionality.[17] By misuse of public power for private gain—which is the common definition of corruption—the ruling elite has an advantage before their opponents, creating an "uneven playing field."[18] In Ukraine, even though the new political leadership came into power after the revolution, operating

---

15  Under Iushchenko's Presidency, Ukraine became a Member of GRECO (Group of States Against Corruption), ratified the UN Convention against Corruption as well as the Criminal Law Convention on Corruption and Council of Europe Civil Law Convention on Corruption.
16  Timm Beichelt, "Forms of Rule in the Post-Soviet Space: Hybrid Regimes," in *Presidents, Oligarchs and Bureaucrats: Forms of Rule in the Post-Soviet Space*, eds. Susan Stewart, Margarete Klein, Andrea Schmitz, and Hans-Henning Schröder (Burlington, VT: Ashgate, 2012), 18; Hale, *Patronal Politics*.
17  Tobias Debiel and Andrea Gawrich, eds., "Dys-Functionalities of Corruption: Comparative Perspectives and Methodological Pluralism," *Zeitschrift für vergleichende Politikwissenschaft (ZfVP) / Comparative Governance and Politics* (Wiesbaden: Springer VS) 7, no. 1 Suppl. (2013): 1–264.
18  This term has been employed by Steven Levitsky and Lucan Way to describe conditions, when incumbents manipulate state institutions and resources to the extent which seriously limits political competition despite possibly free and fair elections. See Steven Levitsky and Lucan Way, *Competitive Authoritarianism: Hybrid Regimes after the Cold War*, Problems of International Politics (New York: Cambridge University Press, 2010). A related term has been used by Kenneth Greene—"hyper-incumbency advantage." Greene has argued that dominant political forces win elections before election day, despite meaningful electoral competition, because of the resource advantages they have, misusing their political power. See Kenneth F. Greene, "Creating Competition: Patronage Politics and the PRI's Demise" (Working Paper No. 345, 2007, 2), *Helen Kellogg Institute for International Studies*, accessed June 13, 2016, https://kellogg.nd.edu/publications/workingpapers/WPS/345.pdf.

principles of the old hybrid regime and a core set of informal institutions remained. Under this circumstance, the political will to combat corruption appears to be very low. However, several post-revolutionary attempts to tackle political corruption, emanating from the civil society, are worth examining. Although the Euromaidan did not eradicate the system of corruption, it offered considerable opportunities for the civil society to alter the *system* from outside.

### The System of Corruption in Ukraine

The *system* has certain particularities in each state.[19] The main feature of Ukraine's *system* is a close interdependency of politics and oligarchic business. Recently, Mikheil Saakashvili, head of the Odesa regional administration, has described Ukraine as a "joint-stock company" which is owned by oligarchs.[20] For them, politics is business: they invest considerable amounts of their private funds into politics for personal gain. The business logic defines their political behavior, which illuminates the structural preconditions for large-scale corruption in Ukraine. Thus, its model should be identified as *the system of corruption*, since corruption is the central element in the regime's hybridity. This model includes four core elements of the formal democratic political process, incorporating informal incentives and corrupt practices behind them (*Figure 1*).

---

19  See an example for Russia's "system" in Shevtsova, *Putin's Russia*; Alena Ledeneva, "From Russia with 'Blat': Can Informal Networks Help Modernize Russia?" *Social Research* 76, no. 1 (2009): 257–88.
20  "Ie 'tiniovyi uriad,' iakyi ie vlasnykom AT 'Ukraina'," *Ukrainska pravda*, September 12, 2015, http://www.pravda.com.ua/news/2015/09/12/7081086/.

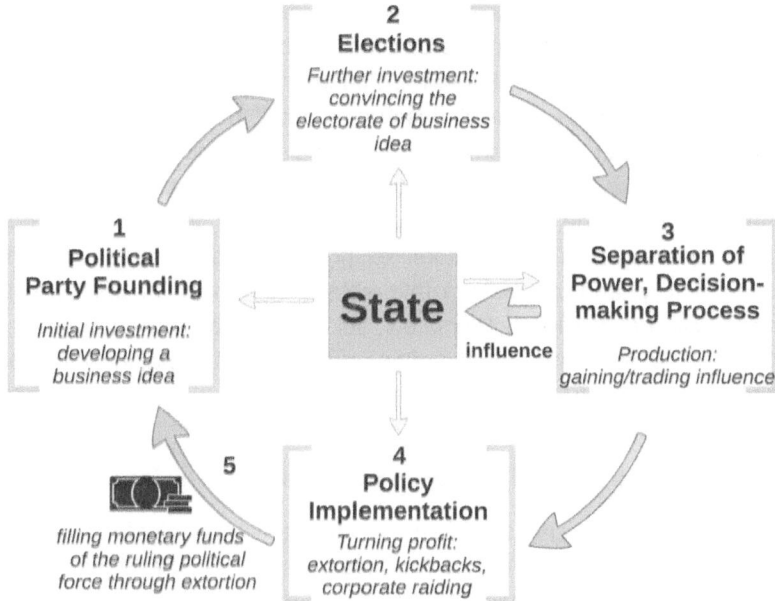

Figure 1: Perpetual cycle of corruption in Ukraine's political process.[21]

Corruption is the only "game in town,"[22] and serves as a tool for material gain of single actors and for securing their dominant positions in formal and informal "networks of power."[23] Traditionally, the ruling elite has an advantage playing the game, as they are able to modify its rules in their favor. This uneven playing field is a contested space but ultimately the competitors are forced to follow the rules of the game if they want to be successful. Although democracies fight their opponents through the rule

---

21  Created by the author. In the figure, the "state" represents formal institutions, such as the constitution and laws.

22  Anna Persson, Bo Rothstein, and Jan Teorell, "Why Anticorruption Reforms Fail-Systemic Corruption as a Collective Action Problem," *Governance* 26, no. 3 (2013): 465.

23  The term "networks of power" has been used by Ledeneva. It refers to informal structures of power, where decisions are made not on the basis of formal rules, but personal relationships. See Ledeneva, 267. Hale employed a related term, "patronalistic networks," where "networks" are the "sinews of power" used for informal distribution of resources and applied for coercion. See Hale, *Patronal Politics*, 10.

of law, authoritarian regimes employ repression tactics against the opposition. In hybrid regimes, such as Ukraine, the opponents simply "lose the game" when violating the rules of the system.[24]

The following section will describe in detail the particular elements of Ukraine's model offered in *Figure 1*. Special attention will be paid to political parties which serve as a vehicle for the oligarchs' influence, and to the elections as the actors' important investment in the scheme of corruption. An analysis of these actors' ability to influence the rules after the election victory, and to create a favorable environment for their private interests will be provided. Ultimately, this discussion will facilitate the understanding about the creation of an uneven playing field, in which corruption plays a significant role.

**Initial Investment: Political Parties as Business Projects**

Political parties in Ukraine are often viewed as an entry point for oligarchic influence in politics (*Fig. 1, No. 1*). Experts, such as Alla Voloshyna, a senior analyst of the civic organization "Transparency International Ukraine," consider them to be a "birth place" for political corruption in Ukraine.[25] The September 2015 corruption scandal involving the former Member of Parliament from the Radical Party Ihor Mosiichuk, who was taped while taking bribes, confirms this view.[26] In this tape, Mosiichuk revealed a simple "formula" of corruption and of how political parties are financed in Ukraine: "The party goes for elections, it needs money. Help the party, and the party will help you."[27] According to Voloshyna, this formula works for all political parties represented in the Parliament, even those that entered it after the Euromaidan.

---

24 For example, see Steven Levitsky and Lucan A. Way, "Democracy and a Level Playing Field," in *Presidents, Oligarchs and Bureaucrats: Forms of Rule in the Post-Soviet Space*, eds. Susan Stewart, Margarete Klein, Andrea Schmitz, and Hans-Henning Schröder (Burlington, VT: Ashgate Publishing Limited, 2012), 35.
25 Alla Voloshyna, "Politychna koruptsiia po-ukrainsky," *Transparency International*, October 6, 2015, http://ti-ukraine.org/news/media-about-us/5523.html.
26 "Verkhovna Rada proholosuvala za aresht nardepa vid Radykalnoi partii Ihora Mosiichuka," *Hromadske Radio*, September 17, 2015, http://hromadskeradio.org/2015/09/17/verhovna-rada-progolosuvala-za-aresht-nardepa-vid-radykalnoyi-partiyi-igora-mosiychuka.
27 "Shokin pokazal v Rade video, na kotorom Mosiichuk beret vziatki," *YouTube*, September 17, 2015, 04:25–04:39, https://www.youtube.com/watch?v=R462HKNEIR8.

According to the basic principles of democracy, political parties and elections are essential elements of the democratic representation process. As a rule, parties reflect the socio-economic cleavages in society. Elections allow different social groups to represent their interest on a fair competitive basis. However, political parties in Ukraine serve "as business platforms for certain groups or persons rather than as channels for citizen interests."[28] In other words, the majority of Ukraine's political parties are pre-conditioned and pre-positioned for political corruption.

The study conducted by the Razumkov Centre reveals that many political parties were established for possible sale to politicians who had no party affiliation but needed it before the elections.[29] For instance, in 2009, the ex-Prime Minister of Ukraine Arsenii Iatseniuk took over the already existing political party "Democratic front" (*Demokratychnyi front*) and renamed it using the same title of his own civil organisation "Front for Change" (*Front zmin*).[30] These realities might explain the parties' considerable fragmentation: by late 2015, there were 297 registered parties in the country.[31] Many existed only on paper and did not actively participate in Ukraine's political life. Parties' political ideologies have only a minor impact on their politics. In fact, many parties and blocs, such as the Petro Poroshenko's Bloc, or the Bloc of Iuliia Tymoshenko, were designed to feature their leaders.

Unsurprisingly, when political parties are created to protect private interests of individuals, be they politicians or oligarchs, popular trust in such parties is usually extremely low. The November 2015 survey conducted by the Ilko Kucheriv Democratic Initiatives Foundation and the Razumkov Centre demonstrated that 79.2% of survey respondents did not trust political parties and only 3.5% of survey respondents were

---

28  See a report on Ukraine by the Swedish Agency for Development Evaluation (SADEV) in Eva-Marie Kjellström, Sabiti Makara, and Peter Sjöberg, "Party Co-operation in a Results Perspective" (Karlstad: Swedish Agency for Development Evaluation [SADEV], 2010), 2.
29  "Political Corruption in Ukraine," *Razumkov Centre*, 9; Oleksandr Lavrynovych, Vice Chairman of the Parliament, has stated that some political parties in Ukraine have been created to protect business interests. See "Soratnyk Ianukovycha kazhe, shcho ne mozhna zaboronyty prodazh partii," *Ukrainska pravda*, April 29, 2009, http://www.pravda.com.ua/news/2009/04/29/3913586/.
30  "Iatseniuk otrymav partiiu," *Ukrainska pravda*, October 27, 2009, http://www.pravda.com.ua/news/2009/10/27/4269101/.
31  "Politychni partii," *Departament derzhavnoi reiestratsii*, accessed June 11, 2016, http://ddr.minjust.gov.ua/uk/ca9c78cf6b6ee6db5c05f0604acdbdec/politychni_partiyi/.

members of political parties.[32] This situation distances voters from politicians, significantly reducing political parties' accountability to citizens.

There are several factors that influence political parties' susceptibility to corruption. For instance, constitutional design of a political party's system, the division of power between Parliament and President and the form of the electoral system play an important role. The funding of Ukraine's political parties, however, currently constitutes the weakest point. Until recently, Ukraine's laws created a legal foundation for exclusive financial dependence of political parties on funding from oligarchs and financial-industrial groups (FIGs). Control over political parties represented in the Parliament allows oligarchs and FIGs to shape the state's legislation, the executive and indirectly, via the parliamentary majority, the judicial branches.[33]

Stable funding for political parties and its candidates is essential in democracies to provide free and fair political competition. Ukraine represents an exception in the Central and Eastern European region by declining state funding for political parties.[34] The membership fees are irrelevant for parties due to extremely low membership.[35] Consequently, the major source of party funding has been private corporate donations with minimal restrictions. Most importantly, there is no actual limit to how much money an individual or a corporate contributor can donate. As a result, one or two oligarchs are able to support a party "with hidden cash,"

---

32  The survey was conducted between the 14th and 22nd of November 2015 in all regions of Ukraine, except Crimea and the occupied territories of Donetsk and Luhansk regions. 2009 respondents were questioned. "Iakoiu miroiu vy doviriaiete politychnym partiiam?" *Tsentr Razumkova*, accessed March 2, 2016, http://razumkov.org.ua/ukr/poll.php?poll_id=1086; "Chy ie vy chlenom iakois politychnoi partii?" *Tsentr Razumkova*, accessed March 2, 2016, http://razumkov.org.ua/ukr/poll.php?poll_id=1085.
33  "Political Corruption in Ukraine," *Razumkov Centre*, 9.
34  For a comparative perspective of funding models for political parties in CEE, see Daniel M. Smilov and Jurij Toplak, eds., *Political Finance and Corruption in Eastern Europe: The Transition Period* (Aldershot, Hants, England; Burlington, VT: Ashgate, 2007).
35  Oleksii Khmara and Denys Kovryzhenko, "Karty, hroshi, dva stoly. Chomu tse dosi pratsiuie na vyborakh do parlamentu?" *Ukrainska pravda*, September 19, 2014, http://www.pravda.com.ua/articles/2014/09/19/7038105/.

and the voters are usually oblivious to who the party's donors are and what political course would be taken by the party.[36]

Another serious problem is associated with overseeing the funds of political parties. Political parties in Ukraine are accountable only to the state tax administration which makes sure that all taxes are paid, but it does not question the sources of funding. The lack of an independent body within the state that would effectively control private funding exacerbates the problem with political parties in Ukraine. Political parties are obliged to publicly report their yearly income, expenses, and assets. However, in their reports, they are not obliged to mention the names of their donors and the amounts of their contributions, as there are no precise content requirements for such reports. Furthermore, in Ukraine, there is no administrative or criminal responsibility for deception or fraud in financial reports. Some experts have suggested that most political parties have secret funds and the incomes they report are only the tip of the iceberg.[37]

After the Euromaidan, substantial changes regulating political parties' funding were introduced.[38] On October 8, 2015, under the considerable pressure of civil society, Parliament passed an important law designed to introduce public funding of political parties as well as to improve control over other sources of funding.[39] This law, which will be active from July 1, 2016, stipulates that all parties that pass the 2% threshold[40] in next parliamentary elections are entitled to receive state

---

36   Oleksii Khmara, "How and Why Party Financing Is Hidden," *Transparency International Ukraine*, October 7, 2014, http://ti-ukraine.org/en/news/media-about-us/4949.html.
37   Oleh Protsyk and Marcin Walecki, "Party Funding in Ukraine," in *Political Finance and Corruption in Eastern Europe: The Transition Period*, eds. Daniel M. Smilov and Jurij Toplak (Aldershot, Hants, England; Burlington, VT: Ashgate, 2007), 192.
38   For an analysis of post-revolutionary changes related to political parties' funding in Ukraine, see Oksana Huss, "Staatliche Parteienfinanzierung: Gelingt ein Meilenstein in der Bekämpfung der politischen Korruption?" *Ukraine-Analyse* (Bremen: Forschungsstelle Osteuropa / Deutsche Gesellschaft für Osteuropakunde e.V.), no. 164 (2016): 2–8.
39   "Zakon Ukrainy pro vnesennia zmin do deiakykh zakonodavchykh aktiv Ukrainy shchodo zapobihannia i protydii politychnii koruptsii," *Verkhovna Rada Ukrainy*, October 8, 2015, http://zakon3.rada.gov.ua/laws/show/731-viii.
40   Interestingly, there is an additional regulation for public funding for political parties elected between 2014 and 2016: in the original version of the law, public funding from July 1, 2016 was foreseen for parties that reached the barrier of 3% in the last parliamentary elections (2014). Yet the last-minute changes raised the

funding for their statutory activity, depending on the number of votes they received. Public funding of political parties aims at providing a platform for de-oligarchisation and fair competition among parties for their voters.

As a precondition for public financing, all political parties participating in elections should pass internal and independent external auditing. The law sets restrictions concerning the sources and amounts of donations. Also, it offers a clear definition of the term "contribution," including in-kind contributions, and prescribes criminal responsibility (2 years imprisonment) for non-disclosure of funding and liability for a wide range of deception in disclosing funding. Financial control of political parties' funds becomes the responsibility of the National Agency for the Prevention of Corruption. The Central Election Commission remains the key agency that controls election funds and is responsible for making public the information about political parties' and single candidates' incomes and expenses during the elections.

The main challenge to the effective application of this law is extremely high overall expenditures of political parties, especially for political advertising during elections.

**Further Investment: Elections**

Elections represent a substantial investment in the business of politics for both political parties and single candidates (*Fig. 1, No. 2*). As the long-standing economic advisor to different governments in Ukraine Anders Åslund has demonstrated,

> Ukrainian election campaigns are among the most expensive in the world. The 2010 presidential campaign and the 2012 parliamentary campaign each cost about $1 billion or 0.5 percent of GDP. In relation to GDP, that is 1,000 times more than a US election campaign.[41]

---

threshold to 5%. This means that until the next parliamentary elections, from July 1, 2016, only political parties which entered the Parliament will be eligible for public funding. This will give these parties additional advantage over their challengers. Perhaps, this was a necessary compromise, which allowed passage of this law, against the low political will to combat corruption.

41   Åslund, *Ukraine*, 121.

Even though the 2014 parliamentary elections were considerably cheaper (between $250 and $300 million),[42] these amounts appear to be too high to be affordable for political parties without oligarchic support. Moreover, according to Taras Kuzio, efficient control of electoral funds seems problematic, as the candidates spend for elections approximately three times more than they officially declare in financial reports.[43]

The mass media forms the main battlefield for political forces, where political advertising constitutes the lion's share of their expenses during elections. According to the NGO *Chesno* that monitored the 2014 presidential elections, candidates spent on average 70% of their electoral campaign funds for mass media advertising.[44] Petro Poroshenko's and Serhii Tyhypko's mass media expenditures were even higher than that of other candidates—85% and 95% respectively. Apart from presidential elections, in 2014 parliamentary elections political parties officially spent 90% of their expenses for mass media advertising.[45]

It comes as no surprise that Ukrainian oligarchs divided television space, the most important sphere of influence during election campaigns, among themselves. By late 2013, four oligarchs owned 85% of television broadcasting in Ukraine.[46] Kuzio has noted that

> Gas tycoon Dmytro Firtash owns the Inter channel, Ukraine's most popular channel. . . . Donetsk oligarch Rinat Akhmetov owns the Ukrayina channel. . . . Oligarchs Igor Kolomoyskyy owns 1 + 1 channel [as well as JN1—the Jewish news channel] while Viktor Pinchuk owns ICTV, New Channel and STB.[47]

---

42 Opora report from 2015 Hryhorii Sorochan, "Over 674 Million Spent on the Election Campaign by Parties," *Civil Network OPORA—Election in Ukraine*, accessed November 21, 2015, http://www.oporaua.org/en/news/38464-6192-1446982614-partiji-vytratyly-na-vyborchu-kampaniju-bilshe-674-miljoniv-gryven.

43 Taras Kuzio, "Impediments to the Emergence of Political Parties in Ukraine," *Politics* 34, no. 4 (2014): 316.

44 Taras Shevchenko and Tetyana Semiletko, "Zhyttia bez politychnoi reklamy: oliharkhy bez mikrofoniv," *Ukrainska pravda*, August 14, 2014, http://www.pravda.com.ua/articles/2014/08/14/7034794/.

45 Non-official expenses reached up to $1 billion, as some experts have estimated. Vadym Miskyi, "Chomu politychnu reklamu varto zaboronyty?" *Media Sapiens*, July 15, 2015, http://osvita.mediasapiens.ua/tv_radio/1411981046/chomu_politichnu_reklamu_varto_zaboroniti/.

46 "Ukrainskyi teleprostir: Akhmetov, Pinchuk, Kolomoiskyi ta Firtash," *Realna Ekonomika*, August 20, 2013, http://real-economy.com.ua/infographics/42686.html.

47 Kuzio, "Impediments," 316–17.

Traditionally, since Ukraine's independence, each President controlled the First National Channel (State Channel One), using it as part of the President's state-administrative resources. However, after the Euromaidan, in April 2015, Poroshenko signed law No. 1357, transforming State Channel One into a public broadcaster.[48] This was not as altruistic as it sounds, since he is the owner of the Fifth Channel.

Ukraine's broadcasting is overloaded with superficial, often camouflaged, political commercials and doubtful marketing tricks because legal restrictions that would enhance its quality are minimal.[49] To be sure, the imperfections and gaps in legislation and a serious contradiction between the laws on political parties and elections allow political parties to easily bypass those restrictions for electoral campaigns and political advertisement.[50] What makes the matter worse is that very little space is allotted to serious political debates and to interviews of the candidates which would familiarize the Ukrainian public with their political views and the ideological programs of their parties.

Transparency International Ukraine (TI Ukraine) executive director Oleksii Khmara and the legal advisor to the International Foundation for Electoral Systems (IFES) in Ukraine Denys Kovryzhenko have explained how legal gaps in regulating election funding have been used in practice: technically, the legislation on elections expressly forbids contributions to the electoral funds from private companies and enterprises. Also, Ukraine's law strictly regulates individual contributions. However, donations to political parties' funds are not subject to these regulations. The law allows private companies to support political parties. Thus ironically, no rules will be broken, if a political party receives funds from businesses. The party transfers these funds to its own electoral fund and uses them for political advertising.[51] As there was no clear definition of the term "contribution" in Ukraine until October 2015, the value of in-kind donations, such as services, transfers of property rights, non-monetary assets, and certain discounts were not specified in financial reports.

---

48   "V Ukraini prezentuvaly suspilne movlennia," *BBC Ukraina*, April 7, 2015, http://www.bbc.com/ukrainian/politics/2015/04/150407_ukraine_public_broadcaster_sx.
49   Khmara and Kovryzhenko, "Karty, Hroshi, Dva Stoly."
50   "Proekt zakonu pro vnesennia zmin do deiakykh zakonodavchykh aktiv Ukrainy shchodo zapobihannia i protydii politychnii koruptsii," *Verkhovna Rada Ukrainy*, June 19, 2015, http://w1.c1.rada.gov.ua/pls/zweb2/webproc4_1?pf3511=55653.
51   Khmara and Kovryzhenko, "Karty, hroshi, dva stoly."

On July 14, 2015, Ukraine's Parliament adopted a law on local elections. One of its drafts (2831-2)[52] was intended to prohibit paid political commercials on TV and radio. This restriction would essentially reduce political parties' and their candidates' campaign expenses, which would increase opportunities for new political forces without oligarchic support to emerge in elections. This idea was approved by the majority of civil society experts, as well as by the OSCE (Organization for Security and Co-operation in Europe) and the ODIHR (Office for Democratic Institutions and Human Rights).[53] Yet a subsequent draft (2831-3) did not include this provision. Political advertising remains a black hole that consumes substantial electoral funds. Most importantly, the problem of the legitimacy of these funds has not been solved which perpetuates political corruption.

The legal gaps described above refer directly to the problem of a long-term dependence of political parties on oligarchic finances. It is equally important to be aware of immediate corruption risks during elections, resulting from the problems described above.

According to the Razumkov Centre, there are three main types of corruption during elections: corruption during election list drawing, subornation of voters, and the use of administrative resources. First, considerable amounts of money circulate during the election list drawing—the seats in election lists are bought and sold. Corrupt actions seem to range from loyalty commitments ("parochial corruption") to monetary rewards ("political bribery"). The effective legislation on elections defining "closed" lists of political parties or blocs implies a strict order of candidates on the lists that cannot be changed or influenced by voters. The purchase and sale of ranks in election lists is common knowledge in Ukraine.[54] Politicians themselves raise this issue in the media. In 2014, Ihor Skosara, a Member of Parliament, reported paying $6 million for a "safe" seat in Parliament during the 2012 elections—to be placed on the list from the

---

52 "Proekt zakonu pro mistsevi vybory [2831-2]," *Verkhovna Rada Ukrainy*, May 28, 2015, http://w1.c1.rada.gov.ua/pls/zweb2/webproc4_1?pf3511=55376.
53 Halyna Petrenko, "Politychna reklama: zaboronyty ne mozhna rehuliuvaty," *Media Sapiens*, July 16, 2015, http://osvita.mediasapiens.ua/media_law/law/politich na_reklama_zaboroniti_ne_mozhna_regulyuvati/; Shevchenko and Semiletko, "Zhyttia bez politychnoi reklamy."
54 "Political Corruption in Ukraine," *Razumkov Centre*, 11. According to the Centre's public opinion poll, 73% of Ukrainian citizens are aware of such cases.

bloc "Batkivshchyna."[55] Although this form of corruption has been communicated publicly, it is not easy to prove payment for a list rank, especially when these transactions are disguised as legitimate funding for an election campaign. Meanwhile, this practice remains widespread in the majority of parties and blocs, and has been identified as "business as usual" during elections.[56]

Voter subornation technologies are another typical malpractice: subornation of voters "involves the influence on the citizens' will, encouraging its exercise in a way conducive to gaining (keeping) power by a certain political force or its candidate."[57] The most recent case of voter subornation practice occurred in Chernivtsi.[58] A local candidate engaged three students to organise vote buying at the university: the students offered $15–$20 per vote. They were brought to justice, but not their financier.

Finally, the use of state administrative resources, another form of corruption used during elections, implies the

> influence of officials using their powers on political developments, in particular the course, results and other elements of the election process with the purpose of staying in power.[59]

Ultimately, parties or candidates use their political power or state resources to their own advantage over the opposition. The civil network *Opora* provides an extensive list of different forms of administrative resources, such as institutional administrative resources (use of civil servants and state infrastructure for electoral campaigning), budgetary administrative resources (use of state budget funds or means for the benefit of parties or their candidate), enforcement administrative resources (use of law enforcement offices, such as militia, security services, the

---

55 "Za mistse u spysku 'Batkivshchyny'—$6 mln Iatseniuku, Turchynovu i Martynenku,—ziznannia nardepa," *ZIK*, October 9, 2014, http://zik.ua/news/2014/10/09/za_prohidne_mistse_u_spysku_batkivshchyny_zaplatyv_6_mln_dolariv_yatsenyuku_turchynovu_i_martynenku__skandalne_ziznannya_narodnogo_deputata_530365.
56 "Political Corruption in Ukraine," *Razumkov Centre*, 11.
57 Ibid.
58 Nadiia Virna, "V Chernivtsiakh za pidkup vybortsiv studentiv zasudyly do triokh rokiv," *Horamadske Radio*, November 11, 2015, http://hromadskeradio.org/2015/11/11/v-chernivcyah-za-pidkup-vyborciv-studentiv-zasudyly-do-troh-rokiv.
59 "Political Corruption in Ukraine," *Razumkov Centre*, 11.

Prosecutor's office in the interests of parties or their candidates to intimidate or repress their opponents), and others.[60] It might be instructive to observe local elections in regions and municipalities in order to understand how this type of corruption functions. Regional (oblast) governors are appointed by President of Ukraine and have the status of civil servants. In most cases, governors lead or are active members of political parties loyal to the President. Under Ianukovych the absolute majority of governors were representatives of the pro-presidential Party of Regions.[61] After the Euromaidan, through constitutional amendments, the President's political power was limited. Governors who represent the presidential party are no longer the majority. However, despite increased political competition, most of Ukraine's governors (10), or their deputies (7), were leading members of electoral lists of the Petro Poroshenko Bloc.[62] The new Law on Civil Service would prohibit gubernatorial participation in elections and political party membership. The law entered into force on May 1, 2016, so the progress of its implementation remains to be seen.

## Political Influence: Formal and Informal Separation of Power

The initial investments into a party and a single candidate during electoral campaigns serve the final goal—to extract profit by gaining personal power (*Fig. 1, No. 3*). For the "corrupt" mind, power means the ability to influence the decision-making processes at state institutions and to manage state resources through legislation in favor of personal wellbeing. In other words, the actors in power should be able to alter or modify the "rules of the game" at any moment, depending on their everyday goals and general interests.[63]

Beyond the formal division of power and the prescribed operating procedures of key political institutions, informal structures are of great importance for governing in hybrid regimes like Ukraine. In fact, informal arrangements among members of the ruling elite determine, who is in

---

60  Olha Aivazovska and Oleksandr Neberykut, "Adminresurs: Shcho tse take i iak ioho vyiavyty?" *OPORA*, accessed June 13, 2016, http://www.oporaua.org/news/1565-adminresurs-shcho-ce-take-i-jak-jogo-vyjavyty.
61  Vitalii Chervonenko, "Hubernatory na vyborakh: Adminresurs partii Poroshenka?" *BBC Ukraina*, October 1, 2015, http://www.bbc.com/ukrainian/politics/2015/10/151001_governers_local_election_vc.
62  Ibid.
63  "Political Corruption in Ukraine," *Razumkov Centre*, 15.

charge of formal institutions. After elections, the extensive trade of "formal" political positions begins. According to Åslund, the ruling party (or coalition) offers high bidders "profitable jobs" (*khlibni mistsia*), including posts chairing state committees and running state enterprises.[64] Additionally, there exists a beneficial trade in judgeships and provincial governorships, since governors are essentially presidential appointees in Ukraine.

In a hybrid regime, the constitution shapes informal expectation as to who embodies ultimate power in a country.[65] In Ukraine, for instance, constitutional changes in 2004 and 2014 formally redistributed the powers between President and Parliament, which empowered the parliamentary coalition to form the Government and greatly increased the importance and "political price" of the Prime Minister's post.[66] The informal power-sharing arrangement between President Poroshenko and Prime Minister Iatseniuk reflected this tendency: Iatseniuk received control over the Ministry of Interior, as well as the tax and customs services, both major political and economic resources.[67]

As in 2004, the 2014 constitutional changes resulted in the significant expansion of Ukraine's parliament's (Verkhovna Rada's) authority, which increased its influence on legislation and the formation of the executive branch. As a result, the parliament also became

> the main scene of conflict and tool of attainment of the interests of political actors and financial-industrial groups, which, in combination with the character of the election process, using closed party lists, makes the supreme state representative body susceptible to political corruption.[68]

Although during election campaigns political corruption can be characterized as "indirect," the legislation process illuminates corruption in its pure form as misuse of entrusted power for personal gain. Verkhovna Rada plays a key role in this process.

---

64  Åslund, "Oligarchs, Corruption, and European Integration," 67.
65  Hale, "*Patronal Politics*," 10.
66  In 2014 after Euromaidan, Ukraine returned to the 2004 Constitution, introducing a parliamentary-presidential form of rule. On dynamics of power sharing in 2004, see "Political Corruption in Ukraine," *Razumkov Centre*, 15.
67  For more details on the informal division of power between Poroshenko and Iatseniuk, see Oleksandr Fisun, "The Future of Ukraine's Neopatrimonial Democracy," *PONARS Eurasia*—Policy Memo, no. 394, October 2015, 1–7.
68  "Political Corruption in Ukraine," *Razumkov Centre*, 13.

Three groups of actors engaged in political corruption can be identified. The first group includes mainly oligarchs and financial-industrial groups, investors on a large scale who accumulated tremendous political power to increase and to preserve their assets. Oligarchs do not necessarily hold political positions, but they own political parties and influence the character of political forces in both legislative and executive branches. Typically, they use technologies of "encouragement" in the form of cash, posts, or pressure to create either a "situational majority" for voting on special issues (e.g. appointments and dismissals), or to build coalitions for major decisions.[69]

The second group consists of "businessmen"-politicians, profiting from their lobbying work in shaping the politics and economics in the country. They buy their seats in the party list or finance their own election campaigns from private resources, and trade their seats or votes at a profit.

In-between there is the third group, known as "grey cardinals," who are the informal leaders and who play a key role in the decision-making process. This small group of actors is of particular importance. They are not in the limelight of politics, but they initiate issues crucial to their interests and lead to their fruition.[70] Each political force in Parliament has its "grey cardinal." This group of actors consists of prominent businessmen, who also manage to become parliamentarians.[71] As a rule, "grey cardinals" are in charge of their political party's hidden funds (*obshchak*). In addition, these individuals are entrusted with trading the key positions.[72] Currently, investigative journalism and an interview with a Member of Parliament Serhii Leshchenko identified several "grey cardinals" in the new government. Among them are the first vice chairman of Petro Poroshenko's Bloc faction Ihor Kononenko and the Head of the Presidential Administration Borys Lozhkin. The "grey cardinals" of "The People's Front"

---

69 "Political Corruption in Ukraine," *Razumkov Centre*, 14.
70 Serhii Leshchenko and Mustafa Naiem, "Off-the-record: Siri kardynaly novoi vlady," *YouTube* (*Hromadske telebachennia*), April 20, 2014, https://www.youtube.com/watch?v=Fdc0VhrLso0&list=PLPnX89fQLdsk7sqSwLWGI1vmaxGxHzxS2&index=3.
71 Åslund, "Oligarchs, Corruption, and European Integration," 67.
72 Ibid.

(*Narodnyi front*), Iatseniuk's party, are Mykola Martynenko,[73] a businessman in the energy sector, and Andrii Ivanchuk, Chair of the Parliamentary Committee for Economics. Some sources identify the Minister of Internal Affairs Arsen Avakov and the co-chair of the parliamentary group "Vidrodzhennia" Vitalii Khomutynnik as influential individuals among state officials.[74]

The Ukrainian political elites seem to be extremely inventive: their corrupt "income" comes from several sources. First, many enrich themselves during different stages of legislative procedures,[75] beginning with the registration of a bill to its final reviews. "Outsiders" establish contacts with members of Ukraine's Parliament, and through them are able to influence the law-making process.[76] The second prominent source of corruption is vote selling. Finally, members of Parliament can profit from changing the faction. This is a quite typical phenomenon in Ukraine, when politicians blatantly changed factions in Parliament. This practice received a special term in Ukrainian—*tushkuvannia* (party-switching). Roman Zabzaliuk's case seems symptomatic: in 2012 the Member of Parliament Zabzaliuk published audio tapes of his conversation with the leader of the pro-government group Ihor Rybakov who offered him an initial payment of $500,000 and a monthly payment of approximately $25,000 for changing from the opposition faction to the pro-governmental one.[77] Clearly, once parliamentarians change parties, there are mechanisms in place to control their voting patterns. Along with the formal parliamentary division in factions, the informal groups are built around "grey cardinals" and other individual leaders, who succeed in gathering parliamentarians around them, independently of factional membership. As a result, the majority of

---

[73] In December 2015, after serious allegations of corruption, Mykola Martynenko resigned as a Member of Parliament.

[74] Khrystyna Berdynskykh, "Siri kardynaly vlady. Khto v otochenni premiera ta prezydenta vyrishuie, kudy rukhatys kraini," *Novoie vremia*, September 18, 2015, http://nv.ua/ukr/publications/siri-kardinali-vladi-hto-v-otochenni-prem-jera-ta-pre zidenta-virishujut-kudi-ruhatis-krajini-69919.html; "Leshchenko pro 'sirykh kardynaliv' vlady i pro te, khto naspravdi pravyt kraiinoiu," *Newsradio: Holos Stolytsi*, September 23, 2015, http://newsradio.com.ua/2015_09_23/Leshhenko-pro-s-rih-kardinal-v-vladi-pro-te-hto-naspravd-pravit-kra-noju-5137/.

[75] See the table of corruption risks and examples of misuse of power at every stage of the legislative process in "Political Corruption in Ukraine," *Razumkov Centre*, 18.

[76] "Political Corruption in Ukraine," *Razumkov Centre*, 17.

[77] "Rybakov—Zabzaliuku: 'Nachalo razgovora—500 tysiach...,'" *Ukrainska pravda*, February 8, 2012, http://www.pravda.com.ua/articles/2012/02/8/6958353/.

parliamentarians turn into "button-pushers" (this phenomenon is known in Ukraine as *knopkodavstvo*): instead of representing the will of their electorate or constituency, they follow instructions from "grey cardinals." Thus, actual decisions in the parliament are made by a few informal leaders, who arrange voting outcomes.

Corrupt activities are difficult to prove, and thus investigations have not been successful. The principle of checks and balances plays a limited role, and informal structures of governance and rules efficiently play into the hands of corrupt individuals. Introduced after the Euromaidan, the constitutional changes essentially limited presidential powers by increasing the Prime Minister's influence. However, this restriction is insufficient for a healthy balance among the branches of power. The pending judiciary reform[78] is the supreme obstacle to the success of other reforms. Judiciary and law enforcement institutions remain politically dependent on the ruling elites. Judges and prosecutors embody the concept of "legalized extortion"[79] and represent an integral part of corrupt networks. Thus, the informal rules still dominate the country's governing mechanisms and power sharing.

## Making Profit: Large-Scale Corruption on the Output Side

During the stage of policy implementation (*Fig. 1, No. 4*), the system of corruption is fully established with its actors securing key positions in executive power. Not surprisingly, the procedural rules of policy implementation are set in favor of the ruling political forces. This is the stage when oligarchs and various financial-industrial groups who invested throughout the process have an opportunity to make a handsome profit.

There are several ways of turning a profit from state resources.[80] The state budget is the largest source for embezzlement, therefore, main

---

78  On the progress of judicial reform, see "Judicial Reform," *National Reforms Council*, accessed June 12, 2016, http://reforms.in.ua/en/reforms/judicial-reform.

79  Anders Aslund used this term in his June 1, 2016 presentation at the European Centre for International Political Economy (ECIPE) in Brussels. See "How to understand Ukraine today?" *Ukrainian Think Tanks Liaison Office in Brussels*, accessed June 12, 2016, https://ukraine-office.eu/en/how-to-understand-ukraine-today/.

80  For various examples of corrupt schemes at the highest political level, see Åslund, "Oligarchs, Corruption, and European Integration;" Bullough, "Looting Ukraine."

corruption schemes target either the money on its way to the budget (e.g. taxation) or public spending from the state budget (e.g. public procurement). For instance, the corruption scheme withholding value-added tax (VAT) refunds from exporting companies is a very popular one. VAT forms around one third of the state budget, and it is the main source of state budget income.[81] Prime Minister Iatseniuk described VAT as "the most corrupt tax in the country."[82] State officials who are in charge of the State Tax Administration extort approximately 20% of the corresponding VAT refunds.[83] Under conditions of states' extreme indebtedness toward exporting companies, private business has no other choice but paying bribes and receiving at least a part of their refund. There are also numerous cases of illegitimate VAT refunds taken through the "taxation gap" (*podatkova iama*), which is an integral part in the shadow economy scheme for money laundering. Typically, the taxation gap implies the creation of a firm registered under a fake owner for a short period of time (no longer than two months), a measure designed to save tax payments or to receive an illegitimate VAT refund. In technical terms, the fake firm issues an invoice for delivering goods or services, which reduces the income of the real customer-company.[84] According to the Head of the State Tax Administration Ihor Bilous, between 2010 and 2014 the VAT fraud cost the country a quarter of its national budget.[85]

Another way of turning a profit is the scheme of embezzling funds directly from the state budget. For instance, a privileged circle of people in the energy sector enjoys state subsidies, amounting to approximately

---

81   For the overview on VAT in Ukraine, see Dmytro Boiarchuk, "Tsikavi fakty pro PDV," *Populiarna ekonomika: tsina derzhavy*, no. 26 (2014): 1–13; also available at *Open Society Foundation*, accessed June 13, 2016, http://cost.ua/files/vat-report.pdf.
82   "Iatseniuk: siohodni postavleno krapku u 'vidmyvanni' PDV," *Forbes Ukraina*, July 31, 2014, http://forbes.net.ua/ua/news/1376086-yacenyuk-sogodni-postavleno-krapku-u-vidmivanni-pdv.
83   The investigation by the US Department of Justice in the case of a subsidiary of Archer Daniels Midland Company (ADM) in Ukraine in 2013 demonstrated that in Ukraine firms were paying bribes around 20% of the corresponding VAT refunds between 2002 and 2008. For more details, see "ADM Subsidiary Pleads Guilty to Conspiracy to Violate the Foreign Corrupt Practices Act," *The US Department of Justice*, December 20, 2013, https://www.justice.gov/opa/pr/adm-subsidiary-pleads-guilty-conspiracy-violate-foreign-corrupt-practices-act.
84   Oleh Ivanov, "'Podatkovi iamy': Likviduvaty chy ocholiuvaty," *VOX Ukraine*, June 11, 2015, http://voxukraine.org/2015/06/11/podatkovi-yamy/.
85   Bullough, "Looting Ukraine," 8.

7.5% of the GDP, according to IMF.[86] To target the US$50 billion annual state procurement budget is another profitable corruption scheme.[87] At least 30% of the budget was systematically embezzled in the form of kickbacks between 2010 and 2014.[88] The amount of US$15 billion annually embezzled in Ukraine is nearly equal to the value of IMF loans approved in April 2014 in order to support Ukraine's economic reform program.

After the Euromaidan, considerable attempts at reducing corruption on the output side were made through legislation. To increase transparency and to advance accountability mechanisms, great expectations were placed in developing e-Governance—new technological mechanisms that would support the workflow in state bureaucracy and communication between public and private entities. Thus, in February 2015 the Government introduced an electronic system for monitoring VAT, an attempt to eliminate "taxation gaps" and to regulate VAT refunds. First assessments, however, identified this governmental initiative as imperfect—it disadvantaged private businesses.[89]

The new technological system was more successful in the public procurement sector. Unlike the VAT electronic system, which was a governmental initiative, the public procurement online platform ProZorro was the result of the civil society's initiative which received wide international recognition.[90] Thusfar, ProZorro is an example of the best practices of bottom-up anti-corruption initiatives. In spring 2014 legislation aimed at reaching transparency in public procurement was introduced.

---

86  Åslund, "Oligarchs, Corruption, and European Integration," 65.
87  Bullough, "Looting Ukraine," 8.
88  This is an average amount in cases under scrutiny during the Ianukovych regime. The calculations were made by "Nashi Hroshi," an online initiative of journalists and activists for uncovering corruption in public procurement. Additional information on public procurement frauds was collected during the interview of Oleksii Shalaiskyi, editor in chief of "Nashi Hroshi," conducted by the author in Kyiv on April 29, 2014.
89  Andrii Probytiuk, "Vidshkoduvannia PDV: prykryvaiuchy 'koruptsiinu lavku,' uriad stvoryv novi problemy," *Duetsche Welle,* February 10, 2015, http://www.dw.com/uk/відшкодування-пдв-прикриваючи-корупційну-лавку-уряд-створив-нові-пр облеми/a-18232879.
90  In May 2016, ProZorro received the international Procurement Leader Award for creating and implementing an electronic system with a unique architecture. See "ProZorro—the Best System in the World in the Sphere of Public Procurement," *Transparency International Ukraine,* May 19, 2016, http://ti-ukraine.org/en/news/monitoryng-deklaraciy/media/6039.html.

Simultaneously, a small group of young activists began to work as volunteers on implementing these reforms.[91] At the early stage they received support from Georgian experts[92] as well as from the EU project aimed at bringing Ukraine's public procurement system in line with European standards. As a result, the volunteers created an e-auction system ProZorro that helps design the mechanisms for transparent and effective public spending and for preventing corruption through monitoring and competition among suppliers. Today, this is the most dynamic and popular initiative for public procurement.[93]

Currently, every Ministry and state agency must use the new online system ProZorro, if they want to purchase any goods or services. Its mandatory use makes procurement more transparent and the competition among suppliers fiercer. This translates into lower prices and higher quality of goods and services that the state purchases. The issue of ownership of the ProZorro platform is an interesting one: typically, in countries other than Ukraine, the public procurement system is developed and administrated by the state only. In Ukraine, the activists from the civil society developed ProZorro independently from the state. Because of a lack of public trust of the Government, during the test phase, the activists transferred the ownership license for ProZorro not to the state, but to the NGO TI Ukraine on a free-of-charge basis. After the system was successfully tested, the state, under pressure of Western donors and civil

---

91 Interview with the ProZorro developer Andrii Kucherenko in Aliona Stadnik, "Po-tikhomu demontirovat nicheho uzhe ne poluchitsia," *Zmiya: Novoe vremia*, July 20, 2015, http://nv.ua/publications/po-tihomu-demontirovat-nichego-uzhe-ne-pol uchitsya-kak-psihi-volontery-iz-prozorro-pochti-poboroli-korrupciyu-v-goszakupk ah-60036.html.
92 Galina Tytysh (interview), "Prozrachno vse. Gruzinskie reformatory o smene sistemy goszakupok v Ukraine," *Ukrainska pravda*, May 14, 2015, http://life.pra vda.com.ua/society/2015/05/14/193908/.
93 Oleksandr Shatkovskyi and Grem Faivesh, "Elektroni derzhavni zakupli: Poshuk ukrainskoho shliakhu," *Project EU "Grown Agents,"* accessed June 1, 2016, http://eupublicprocurement.org.ua/e-procurement-finding-a-way-for-ukraine.html.
94 In November 2015, Ukraine joined the WTO Government Procurement Agreement. Moldova follows Ukraine's steps: in July 2016, it will join the WTO Government Procurement Agreement, and will use the system ProZorro. Russia and Kazakhstan have also expressed their interest in employing ProZorro. See "Government Procurement: Ukraine to Join WTO's Government Procurement Agreement," *World Trade Organization*, November 11, 2015, https://www.wto.org/engli sh/news_e/news15_e/gpro_11nov15_e.htm; "Susidnia derzhava vyrishyla zap-rovadyty ukrainsku systemu 'Prozorro,'" *Ekspres online*, June 18, 2016,

society, was authorized to employ ProZorro.[94] TI Ukraine remains responsible for ensuring the system's transparency, analyzing and controlling procurements and involving as many clients as possible.

Unfortunately, such examples as ProZorro are rare. Grand corruption in state services persists, especially in Tax and Customs Services, the natural resources sector, and state companies.

## Corruption as Fertile Soil for the Regime's Hybridity

The last element (*Fig. 1, No. 5*) in the system of corruption illuminates the ability of the ruling elite to refill the funds of their political party and to strengthen their own position through corruption. The extent to which the incumbents manipulate state institutions and resources through corruption is so large, that it seriously limits political competition. Other political actors replenish their electoral funds selling goods and services, while the ruling elites simply use state resources for their political and personal interests.[95] Consequently, corruption is not only the goal for politicians and oligarchs to enrich themselves but also a means to sustain the hybrid regime. Ultimately, corruption is an integral part of the system, which enables its smooth functioning.

This system in turn triggers the emergence of an uneven playing field which provides the ruling elites with a clear advantage over their opponents. In this situation, it is extremely unlikely that serious political opposition would appear on the stage and challenge the regime and its system of corruption. At best, political competitors might challenge some individuals in power, such as President or Prime Minister. The only challenge which is possible under these circumstances might emanate from outside of the *system,* in particular from Ukraine's civil society.

Under Ianukovych, political corruption in Ukraine reached its apogee.[96] The *family* (the term defines active members of the system of corruption perfected under Ianukovych) played a leading role in all

---

http://expres.ua/news/2016/06/18/190419-susidnya-derzhava-vyrishyla-zaprovadyty-ukrayinsku-systemu-prozorro.
95   Åslund, "Oligarchs, Corruption, and European Integration," 67.
96   For a detailed analysis of political corruption under Ianukovych's Presidency, see Oksana Huss's unpublished paper "Family Business Ukraine: Centralization of Political Corruption under the Presidency of Viktor Ianukovych," presented at the European Consortium for Political Research General Conference in Montreal, Canada (August 26–29, 2015).

schemes of state embezzlement. Ianukovych managed to monopolize the system of corruption and make it beneficial to a very few actors, efficiently eliminating political opposition and excluding potential competitors among oligarchs or other groups of influence from the system. As a result, only his political party, the Party of Regions, was able to consistently replenish its funds through extortion,[97] creating an uneven playing field. Political competition became impossible, and the authoritarian practices of the Ianukovych regime helped suppress civil society and free media in Ukraine.

Although the political opposition was extremely weak and fragmented, the Euromaidan succeeded in overthrowing the Ianukovych regime. This was the major victory of the Ukrainian society since the Orange revolution, which led to the decentralization of political power, establishing the limits to presidential authority through constitutional change. The *system of corruption* and informal structures continue to dominate the Ukrainian political landscape, yet post-Maidan changes produced a contested space associated with tensions between the *system* and its environment. This space made political competition possible, a favorable circumstance for Ukraine's civil society which helps strengthen its watchdog role in the reform process.

## Post-Revolutionary Attempts to Break Through the Perpetual Cycle of Corruption

As far as anti-corruption policy is concerned, corruption cannot be tackled from inside the system, as self-destruction seems an unlikely scenario. The system of corruption might be counteracted only by the environment it operates in. The Euromaidan and at least three novelties spelled out in new anti-corruption initiatives that were overlooked in previous anti-corruption campaigns arguably provide reasons for optimism.[98]

---

97  As Åslund has noted, "Before Yanukovych fled, he was rumored to have gathered a war chest of $3 billion in preparation for the scheduled March 2015 presidential election." See Åslund, "Oligarchs, Corruption, and European Integration," 67.

98  For more details about the 2014 anti-corruption reform package, see independent reports, conducted by TI Ukraine: Denys Kovryzhenko and Olena Chebanenko, "National Integrity System Assessment: Ukraine 2015," *Transparency International Ukraine*, June 2015, http://ti-ukraine.org/en/system/files/docs/news/nis_assessment_eng.pdf; the International Renaissance Foundation: Alla Voloshyna,

First, civil society organizations (CSO) became crucial to advancing anti-corruption reforms and monitoring how adopted legislation works in practice.[99] The relations between the government and the civil society changed dramatically after the Euromaidan. The Organization for Economic Co-Operation and Development's (OECD) 3rd monitoring report lists several factors which increase the role of civil society in post-revolutionary reforms. Among them are

> high public expectations from the new leaders of the country, including the pressure on the decision-makers that was created by the presidential and parliamentary election campaigns and anti-corruption conditions attached to the funding by international organisations and donors.[100]

Beyond the substantial pressure on politicians, the NGOs themselves improved considerably their proficiency level and set effective umbrella organizations, coordinating their work. All major anti-corruption CSOs participate in the "Reanimation Package of Reforms" (RPR) initiative that advocates reforms in various sectors of governance. This civic coalition developed its own agenda of priority reform measures, where the anti-corruption reform is listed second among the twenty-four most important fields that have been identified by the RPR in the Roadmap of Reforms[101] and which was provided to the Verkhovna Rada of the 8th convocation for consideration.

---

"Alternative Report on Evaluation of State Anticorruption Policy Efficiency: Research Resume," *Transparency International Ukraine; International Renaissance Foundation*, June 10, 2015, http://ti-ukraine.org/en/system/files/research/summary_alternative_report_en.pdf; and the Organization for Economic Co-Operation and Development—Anti-Corruption Network for Eastern Europe and Central Asia (ACN OECD), "Anti-Corruption Reforms in Ukraine: Round 3 Monitoring of the Istanbul Anti-Corruption Action Plan," *OECD*, March 24, 2015, http://www.oecd.org/daf/anti-bribery/Ukraine-Round-3-Monitoring-Report-ENG.pdf.

99  According to the recent assessment of the *National Integrity System* (NIS), civil society and anti-corruption agencies became the strongest pillars of the NIS in 2015, while the law enforcement and public sector are the weakest ones. The NIS assessment offers an evaluation of the legal basis and the actual performance of institutions ("pillars") relevant to the overall anti-corruption system. See Kovryzhenko and Chebanenko, "NIS Assessment Ukraine 2015."

100  "Anti-Corruption Reforms in Ukraine," 32.

101  "Roadmap of Reforms: For the Verkhovna Rada of Ukraine of the 8th Convocation," *Reanimation Package of Reforms*, 2015, https://drive.google.com/file/d/0B7G3FtLRKwh2Q21mbE4wcFhFRzQtNUNNR19qaUdMWTRHOFg0/view.

As an example of the effectiveness of such coordinated action, the critical National Anti-Corruption Strategy for 2014–2017 was developed in close cooperation between state institutions and experts from civil society. Hence, for the first time, professionals and experts—representatives of civil society, either took the lead or directly participated in shaping anti-corruption policy documents.[102] Moreover, several activists and investigative journalists became members of Parliament in October 2014. They have created an inter-factional union "Eurooptimists" and have written important laws, such as the law on public funding of political parties.

Second, such popular participation positively influenced the content of anti-corruption reforms. According to the legal expert Mykola Khavroniuk's analysis, for the first time new anti-corruption laws provide a working definition of corruption and imply the existence of political corruption, differentiating it from *petite* corruption in medicine or education.[103] Unlike earlier "facade" reforms that targeted individuals and *petite* corrupt activities, the National Anti-Corruption Strategy for 2014–2017[104] targets major corruption schemes and the political *system of corruption*. Both the Law on public funding of political parties issued on October 8, 2015 and the Amendments to the Law on Public Procurement issued on April 15, 2014 that were adopted as an essential part of the Anti-Corruption Strategy should be considered extremely healthy developments in Ukraine. The public procurement e-platform ProZorro, mentioned earlier, is an additional example of positive dynamics in regards to tackling massive corruption schemes rather than individual cases. Although there might be a limited political will to implement these anti-corruption measures, it appears that Ukraine's civil society recognizes the *system of corruption* as an urgent problem, which reinforces counteraction to corruption at all

---

102  "Anti-Corruption Reforms in Ukraine," 5.
103  The first extensive anti-corruption law package was adopted after the Euromaidan, on October 7, 2014. See Mykola Khavroniuk, "Zvykaimo: ani ia tobi, ani ty meni!," *Dzerkalo tyzhnia,* October 10, 2014, http://gazeta.dt.ua/internal/zvikaymo-ani-ya-tobi-ani-ti-meni-_.html.
104  For an overview of anti-corruption laws and institutions, see Halyna Kokhan, "Aufbau einer neuen Anti-Korruptions-Struktur in der Ukraine: ein Überblick über Fortschritt und Schwierigkeiten," *Ukraine-Analysen* (Bremen: Forschungsstelle Osteuropa / Deutsche Gesellschaft für Osteuropakunde e.V.), no. 165 (2016): 11–18.

levels. Importantly, the Euromaidan set in motion people's political activism, previously dormant, a factor that contributed to the civil society's anti-corruption initiatives.

Third, the new infrastructure of anti-corruption policies has been created which includes the National Anti-Corruption Bureau, an independent organization that investigates political corruption in Ukraine and prepares cases for prosecution, and the National Agency for the Prevention of Corruption, a special body that prevents corruption and regulates conflicts of interest.[105] A number of state anti-corruption institutions existed in Ukraine under the Ministry of the Interior, the Security Service, and the Prosecutor General. They, however, were ineffective, as they represented a part of the corrupt *system* and often were used to persecute the opposition. Against this background, only a politically independent body can deliver effective control and investigation. The main impediment to the effectiveness of the new anti-corruption infrastructure appears to be the absence of an independent judiciary in Ukraine. Although the Special Attorney Office for Anti-Corruption was created in December 2015, the appointment process was overshadowed by a sensational scandal: the Attorney General was trying to influence the appointment process.[106]

## Conclusion

As this discussion has demonstrated, the *system of corruption* dominates Ukrainian politics and sustains the regime's hybridity. At four stages of the political process that include building political parties, elections, separation of powers according to the checks and balances system and policy implementation, considerable legal inconsistencies and gaps are available, which not only allow corrupt activities that remain unpunished, but

---

[105] The National Anti-Corruption Bureau (NABU) began its work in June 2015. However, the investigations of its first cases were not initiated until December 2015, when the Special Attorney Office for Anti-Corruption was set. In December 2015 two regional NABU offices assumed their work. The National Agency for the Prevention of Corruption can begin its work after one third of its staff (approximately one hundred employees) is formed. As of June 2016, the Agency remains incomplete and will assume its duties with some delay.

[106] Serhii Sydorenko, "Viktor Shokin rozpochav velyku viinu. Proty MZS ta bezvizovoho rezhymu," *Ievropeiska pravda,* October 27, 2015, http://www.eurointegratio n.com.ua/articles/2015/10/27/7039965/.

also encourage corruption as the only way to operate in politics. An analysis of political corruption as a closed system reveals that those legal inconsistencies and gaps are introduced deliberately in hybrid regimes. Corruption is a tool to sustain their power and stability, to create new institutions, and to shape the system in a fashion that would make corrupt activities possible indefinitely.

As we have seen, members of Ukraine's Parliament receive bribes, sell their votes, change factions for monetary rewards, and participate in all kinds of corrupt schemes. Ukrainian oligarchs perceive the state as a business: large-scale political corruption helps them accumulate and protect their assets. The persistent loop of corruption is a key to understanding Ukrainian politics. As shown earlier, it is virtually impossible to enter Ukrainian politics without being engaged in corrupt activities because considerable investments are needed to build a political party or to win elections. Once those investments are made, they have to be returned with profit. Although in many democratic countries corruption is considered a violation of the rules of the game in politics, corruption in Ukrainian politics became a game in itself.[107]

In Ukraine, the political will to combat corruption is very low. This is not surprising, since the effective and real fight against corruption means self-destruction of the *system*. The governmental anti-corruption reforms tend to be illusory. Although the *system of corruption* remains in place after the Euromaidan, there have been considerable post-revolutionary attempts to break through the perpetual cycle of corruption. The most effective attempts are coming from civil society, from *outside the system*. Additionally, Western partners deliver strong support to these attempts, setting the Ukrainian government increasingly under pressure. The Euromaidan, as a genuine movement "from below," created circumstances that empowered people and NGOs to take the lead and to cooperate with the government in developing anti-corruption reforms. The signs of a strong popular will to tackle the *system* from the outside are pronounced and persistent, and inspire hope and confidence, so necessary for Ukrainians.

---

[107] Robert S. Leiken, "Controlling the Global Corruption Epidemic," *Foreign Policy*, no. 105 (1996): 61.

## Bibliography

"ADM Subsidiary Pleads Guilty to Conspiracy to Violate the Foreign Corrupt Practices Act." *US Department of Justice*. Last modified December 20, 2013. http://www.justice.gov/opa/pr/adm-subsidiary-pleads-guilty-conspiracy-violate-foreign-corrupt-practices-act.

Aivazovska, Olha, and Oleksandr Neberykut. "Adminresurs: Sho tse take i iak ioho vyiavyty?" *Civil Network OPORA—Election in Ukraine*. Accessed June 13, 2016. http://www.oporaua.org/news/1565-adminresurs-shcho-ce-take-i-jak-jogo-vyjavyty.

Andvig, Jens Christopher, and Odd-Helge Fjeldstad. "Corruption: A Review of Contemporary Research." Bergen: Chr. Michelsen Institute, Development Studies and Human Rights, 2001.

"Anti-Corruption Reforms in Ukraine: Round 3 Monitoring of the Istanbul Anti-Corruption Action Plan." *ACN OECD* (Anti-Corruption Network for Eastern Europe and Central Asia). March 24, 2015. https://www.oecd.org/daf/anti-bribery/Ukraine-Round-3-Monitoring-Report-ENG.pdf.

Åslund, Anders. "Oligarchs, Corruption, and European Integration." *Journal of Democracy* 25, no. 3 (2014): 64–73.

———. *Ukraine: What Went Wrong and How to Fix It*. Washington, DC: Peterson Institute for International Economics, 2015.

Beichelt, Timm. "Forms of Rule in the Post-Soviet Space: Hybrid Regimes." In *Presidents, Oligarchs and Bureaucrats: Forms of Rule in the Post-Soviet Space*, edited by Susan Stewart, Margarete Klein, Andrea Schmitz, and Hans-Henning Schröder, 15–28. Burlington, VT: Ashgate, 2012.

Berdynskykh, Khrystyna. "Siri kardynaly vlady. Khto v otochenni premiera ta prezydenta vyrishuie, kudy rukhatys kraini." *Novoie vremia*. September 23, 2015. http://nv.ua/ukr/publications/siri-kardinali-vladi-hto-v-otochenni-prem-jera-ta-prezidenta-virishujut-kudi-ruhatis-krajini-69919.html.

Boiarchuk, Dmytro. "Tsikavi fakty pro PDV." *Populiarna ekonomika: tsina derzhavy*, no. 26 (2014): 1–13; also available at *Open Society Foundation*. Accessed June 13, 2016. http://cost.ua/files/vat-report.pdf.

Börzel, Tanja A., Yasemin Pamuk, and Andreas Stahn. "The European Union and the Promotion of Good Governance in Its Near Abroad: One Size Fits All?" *SFB-Governance Working Paper Series*, no. 18 (2008): 1–44.

Bullough, Oliver. "Looting Ukraine: How East and West Teamed up to Steal a Country." *Legatum Institute*. July 1, 2014, http://www.li.com/docs/default-source/publications/ukraine_imr_a4_web.pdf.

Cartier-Bresson, Jean. "Corruption Networks, Transaction Security and Illegal Social Exchange." *Political Studies* 45, no. 3 (1997): 463–76.

Chervonenko, Vitalii. "Hubernatory na vyborakh: Adminresurs partii Poroshenka?" *BBC Ukraina*. October 1, 2015. http://www.bbc.com/ukrainian/politics/2015/10/151001_governers_local_election_vc .

"Chy ie vy chlenom iakois politychnoi partii?" *Tsentr Razumkova*. Accessed March 2, 2016. http://razumkov.org.ua/ukr/poll.php?poll_id=1085.

"Corruption Perceptions Index 2015." *Transparency International.* Accessed February 18, 2016. http://www.transparency.org/cpi2015#results-table.

Debiel, Tobias, and Andrea Gawrich, eds. *(Dys-)Functionalities of Corruption: Comparative Perspectives and Methodological Pluralism. Zeitschrift für vergleichende Politikwissenschaft (ZfVP) / Comparative Governance and Politics* (Wiesbaden: Springer VS) 7, no. 1 Supplement (2013): 1–264.

Debiel, Tobias, and Birgit Pech. "Mit Korruptionsbekämpfung zum Take off bei den MDGs? Zu Möglichkeiten und Grenzen einer entwicklungspolitischen Strategie." In *"Simplizistische Lösungen verbeiten sich"—Zur Internationalen Zusammenarbeit im 21. Jahrhundert*, edited by Eckhard Deutschner and Hartmut Ihne, 53–67. Baden-Baden: Nomos, 2010.

Fisun, Oleksandr. "The Future of Ukraine's Neopatrimonial Democracy." *PONARS Eurasia*—Policy Memo, no. 394, October 2015, 1–7.

"Government Procurement: Ukraine to Join WTO's Government Procurement Agreement." *World Trade Organization.* November 11, 2015. https://www.wto.org/english/news_e/news15_e/gpro_11nov15_e.htm;

Greene, Kenneth F. "Creating Competition: Patronage Politics and the PRI's Demise" [working paper, no. 345]. *Helen Kellogg Institute for International Studies.* December 2007. https://kellogg.nd.edu/publications/workingpapers/WPS/345.pdf.

Grødeland, Åse Berit. "Elite Perceptions of Anti-Corruption Efforts in Ukraine." *Global Crime* 11, no. 2 (2010): 237–60.

Hale, Henry E. *Patronal Politics: Eurasian Regime Dynamics in Comparative Perspective.* Problems of International Politics. New York, NY: Cambridge University Press, 2015.

"How to understand Ukraine today?" *Ukrainian Think Tanks Liaison Office in Brussels.* Accessed June 12, 2016. https://ukraine-office.eu/en/how-to-understand-ukraine-today/.

Huss, Oksana. "Family Business Ukraine: Centralization of Political Corruption under the Presidency of Viktor Ianukovych." Unpublished paper presented at the European Consortium for Political Research General Conference, Montreal, Quebec, August 26–29, 2015.

⎯⎯⎯⎯⎯⎯⎯⎯. "Staatliche Parteienfinanzierung: Gelingt ein Meilenstein in der Bekämpfung der politischen Korruption?" *Ukraine-Analyse* [Bremen: Forschungsstelle Osteuropa / Deutsche Gesellschaft für Osteuropakunde e.V.], no. 164 (2016): 2–8.

"Iakoiu miroiu vy doviriaiete politychnym partiiam?" *Tsentr Razumkova.* Accessed March 2, 2016. http://razumkov.org.ua/ukr/poll.php?poll_id=1086.

"Iatseniuk otrymav partiiu." *Ukrainska pravda.* October 27, 2009. http://www.pravda.com.ua/news/2009/10/27/4269101/.

"Iatseniuk: siohodni postavleno krapku u 'vidmyvanni' PDV." *Forbes Ukraine.* July 31, 2014. http://forbes.net.ua/ua/news/1376086-yacenyuk-sogodni-postavleno-krapku-u-vidmivanni-pdv.

"Ie 'tiniovyi uriad,' iakyi ie vlasnykom AT 'Ukraina.'" *Ukrainska pravda.* September 12, 2015. http://www.pravda.com.ua/news/2015/09/12/7081086/.

Ivanov, Oleh. "'Podatkovi iamy': Likviduvaty chy ocholiuvaty." *VOX Ukraine*. June 11, 2015. http://voxukraine.org/2015/06/11/podatkovi-yamy/.

"Judicial Reform." *National Reforms Council*. Accessed June 12, 2016. http://reforms.in.ua/en/reforms/judicial-reform.

Karklins, Rasma. *The System Made Me Do It: Corruption in Post-Communist Societies*. New York: M.E. Sharpe, 2005.

Khavroniuk, Mykola. "Zvykaimo: ani ia tobi, ani ty meni!" *Dzerkalo tyzhnia*. October 10, 2014. http://gazeta.dt.ua/internal/zvikaymo-ani-ya-tobi-ani-ti-meni-_.html.

Khmara, Oleksii, and Denys Kovryzhenko. "Karty, hroshi, dva stoly. Chomu tse dosi pratsiuie na vyborakh do parlamentu?" *Ukrainska pravda*. September 19, 2014. http://www.pravda.com.ua/articles/2014/09/19/7038105/.

Khmara, Oleksiy. "How and Why Party Financing Is Hidden | Transparency International." *TI-Ukraine*. October 7, 2014. http://ti-ukraine.org/en/news/media-about-us/4949.html.

Kjellström, Eva-Marie, Sabiti Makara, and Peter Sjöberg. "Party Cooperation in a Results Perspective: Evaluation of the Support to Democracy through Party Affiliated Organizations (PAOs)" [Report 2009:3; Karlstad: Swedish Agency for Development Evaluation, (SADEV), 2010]. *OECD*. Accessed June 18, 2016. https://www.oecd.org/derec/sweden/pao.pdf.

Kokhan, Halyna. "Aufbau einer neuen Anti-Korruptions-Struktur in der Ukraine: ein Überblick über Fortschritt und Schwierigkeiten." *Ukraine-Analysen* [Bremen: Forschungsstelle Osteuropa / Deutsche Gesellschaft für Osteuropakunde e.V.], no. 165 (2016): 11–18.

Kovryzhenko, Denys, and Olena Chebanenko. "National Integrity System Assessment Ukraine 2015." *Transparency International Ukraine*. 2015. Accessed June 18, 2016. http://ti-ukraine.org/en/system/files/research/nis_assessment_eng.pdf.

Kuzio, Taras. "Impediments to the Emergence of Political Parties in Ukraine: Political Parties in Ukraine." *Politics* 34, no. 4 (December 2014): 309–23.

_____. *Ukraine: Democratization, Corruption, and the New Russian Imperialism*. Santa Barbara, California: Praeger Security International, 2015.

Ledeneva, Alena. "From Russia with 'Blat': Can Informal Networks Help Modernize Russia?" *Social Research* 76, no. 1 (2009): 257–88.

Leiken, Robert S. "Controlling the Global Corruption Epidemic." *Foreign Policy*, no. 105 (1996): 55–73.

"Leshchenko pro 'sirykh kardynaliv' vlady i pro te, khto naspravdi pravyt kraiinoiu." *Newsradio*: *Holos Stolytsi*. September 23, 2015. http://newsradio.com.ua/2015_09_23/Leshhenko-pro-s-rih-kardinal-v-vladi-pro-te-hto-naspravd-pravit-kra-noju-5137/.

Leshchenko, Serhii, and Mustafa Naiem. "Off-the-record: Siri kardynaly novoi vlady." *YouTube*. April 20, 2014. https://www.youtube.com/watch?v=Fdc0VhrLso0&list=PLPnX89fQLdsk7sqSwLWGl1vmaxGxHzxS2&index=3.

Levitsky, Steven, and Lucan Way. *Competitive Authoritarianism: Hybrid Regimes after the Cold War*. Problems of International Politics. New York: Cambridge University Press, 2010.

_____. "Democracy and a Level Playing Field." In *Presidents, Oligarchs and Bureaucrats: Forms of Rule in the Post-Soviet Space*, edited by Susan Stewart, Margarete Klein, Andrea Schmitz, and Hans-Henning Schröder, 29–42. Burlington, VT: Ashgate Publishing Limited, 2012.

"Maidan-2013." *Ilko Kucheriv Democratic Initiatives Foundation.* Accessed May 21, 2016. http://www.dif.org.ua/en/events/gvkrlgkaeths.htm.

Miller, William L., Åse Berit Grødeland, and Tatyana Y. Koshechkina. *A Culture of Corruption? Coping with Government in Post-Communist Europe.* Budapest: Central European University Press, 2001.

Miskyi, Vadym. "Chomu politychnu reklamu varto zaboronyty?" *Media Sapiens.* July 15, 2015. http://osvita.mediasapiens.ua/tv_radio/1411981046/chomu_politichnu_reklamu_varto_zaboroniti/.

Moene, Kalle, and Tina Søreide. "Good Governance Facades." In *Greed, Corruption and the Modern State,* edited by Susan Rose-Ackerman and Paul Lagunes, 46–70. Cheltenham, UK, Northampton, MA, USA: Edward Elgar Publishing, 2015.

Pech, Brigit. "Korruption und Demokratisierung: Rekonstruktion des Forschungsstandes an den Schnittstellen zu Institutionenökonomik und politischer Transformationsforschung" [INEF Report, no. 99; Duisburg: Institut für Entwicklung und Frieden, 2009]. *Edoc.vifapol.* October 17, 2011. http://edoc.vifapol.de/opus/volltexte/2011/3468/.

Persson, Anna, Bo Rothstein, and Jan Teorell. "Why Anticorruption Reforms Fail-Systemic Corruption as a Collective Action Problem." *Governance* 26, no. 3 (2013): 449–71.

Petrenko, Halyna. "Politychna reklama: zaboronyty ne mozhna rehuliuvaty." *Media Sapiens.* July 16, 2015. http://osvita.mediasapiens.ua/media_law/law/politichna_reklama_zaboroniti_ne_mozhna_regulyuvati/.

"Political Corruption in Ukraine: Actors, Manifestations, Problems of Countering" [National Security and Defence Report; Kyiv: Ukrainian Centre for Economic and Political Studies named after Olexander Razumkov, 2009]. *Uceps.org.* Accessed June 18, 2016. http://www.uceps.org/eng/files/category_journal/NSD111_eng_1.pdf

"Politychni partii" [*Departament derzhavnoi reiestratsii*]. *Ministerstvo iustytsii* (official website). Accessed June 11, 2016. http://ddr.minjust.gov.ua/uk/ca9c78cf6b6ee6db5c05f0604acdbdec/politychni_partiyi/.

Probytiuk, Andrii. "Vidshkoduvannia PDV: prykryvaiuchy 'koruptsiinu lavku', uriad stvoryv novi problemy." *Deutsche Welle.* February 10, 2015. http://www.dw.com/uk/від шкодування-пдв-прикриваючи-корупційну-лавку-уряд-створив-нові-проблеми/a-18232879.

"Proekt zakonu pro mistsevi vybory Nr 2831-2." *Verkhovna Rada Ukrainy.* Last modified May 28, 2015. http://w1.c1.rada.gov.ua/pls/zweb2/webproc4_1?pf3511=55376.

"Proekt zakonu pro vnesennia zmin do deiakykh zakonodavchykh aktiv Ukrainy shchodo zapobihannia i protydii politychnii koruptsii Nr 2123a." *Verkhovna Rada Ukrainy.* Last modified June 19, 2015. http://w1.c1.rada.gov.ua/pls/zweb2/webproc4_1?pf3511=55653.

Protsyk, Oleh, and Marcin Walecki. "Party Funding in Ukraine." In *Political Finance and Corruption in Eastern Europe: The Transition Period*, edited by Daniel M. Smilov and Jurij Toplak, 189–208. Burlington, VT: Ashgate, 2007.

"ProZorro—the Best System in the World in the Sphere of Public Procurement." *Transparency International Ukraine*. May 19, 2016. http://ti-ukraine.org/en/news/monitoryng-deklaraciy/media/6039.html.

"Roadmap of Reforms for the Verkhovna Rada of Ukraine of the 8th convocation." *Reanimation Package of Reforms*. 2015. Accessed June 15, 2016. https://drive.google.com/file/d/0B7G3FtLRKwh2Q21mbE4wcFhFRzQtNUNNR19qaUdMWTRHOFg0/view.

Rothstein, Bo. "What Is the Opposite of Corruption?" *Third World Quarterly* 35, no. 5 (2014): 737–52.

Runey, Mike. "The Latest Transparency International Global Corruption Barometer, Released Today, Shows that Ukrainians Strongly Believe That Their State Has Become More Corrupt Over the Last Two Years." *Transparency International Ukraine*. September 7, 2013. http://ti-ukraine.org/en/news/2815.html.

"Rybakov—Zabzaliuku: 'Nachalo razgovora—500 tysiach...'" *Ukrainska pravda*. February 8, 2012. http://www.pravda.com.ua/articles/2012/02/8/6958353/.

Shatkovskyi, Oleksandr, and Graham Fiveash. "E-procurement: Finding a Way for Ukraine." *Harmonisation of Public Procurement System in Ukraine with EU Standards*. Accessed June 15, 2016. http://eupublicprocurement.org.ua/e-procurement-finding-a-way-for-ukraine.html?lang=en.

Shevchenko, Taras, and Tetyana Semiletko. "Zhyttia bez politychnoi reklamy: oliharkhy bez mikrofoniv." *Ukrainska pravda*. August 14, 2014. http://www.pravda.com.ua/articles/2014/08/14/7034794/.

Shevtsova, Lilia. *Putin's Russia*. Washington, D.C: Carnegie Endowment for International Peace, 2005.

"Shokin pokazal v Rade video, na kotorom Mosiichuk beret vziatki." *YouTube*. September 17, 2015. https://www.youtube.com/watch?v=R462HKNEIR8.

Smilov, Daniel M. "Political Finance and Corruption in Eastern Europe the Transition Period." In *Political Finance and Corruption in Eastern Europe: The Transition Period*, edited by Daniel M. Smilov and Jurij Toplak, 1–32. Burlington, VT: Ashgate, 2007.

"Soratnyk Ianukovycha kazhe, shcho ne mozhna zaboronyty prodazh partii." *Ukrainska pravda*. April 29, 2009. http://www.pravda.com.ua/news/2009/04/29/3913586/.

Sorochan, Hryhorii. "Over 674 Million Spent on the Election Campaign by Parties." *Civil Network OPORA—Election in Ukraine*. November 26, 2014. http://www.oporaua.org/en/news/38464-6192-1446982614-partiji-vytratyly-na-vyborchu-kampaniju-bilshe-674-miljoniv-gryven.

Stadnyk, Aliona. "Po-tikhomu demontirovat nicheho uzhe ne poluchitsia." *Zmiya: Novoe vremia*. July 20, 2015. http://nv.ua/publications/po-tihomu-demontirovat-nichego-uzhe-ne-poluchitsya-kak-psihi-volontery-iz-prozorro-pochti-poboroli-korrupciyu-v-gosakupkah-60036.html.

"Susidnia derzhava vyrishyla zaprovadyty ukrainsku systemu 'Prozorro.'" *Ekspres online*. June 18, 2016. http://expres.ua/news/2016/06/18/190419-susidnya-derzhava-vyrishyla-zaprovadyty-ukrayinsku-systemu-prozorro.

Sydorenko, Serhii. "Viktor Shokin rozpochav velyku viinu. Proty MZS na bezvizovoho rezhymu." *Ievropeiska pravda*. October 27, 2015. http://www.eurointegration.com.ua/articles/2015/10/27/7039965/.

Tytysh, Galina. "Prozrachno vse. Gruzinskiie reformatory o smene sistemy goszakupok v Ukraine." *Ukrainska pravda*. May 14, 2015. http://life.pravda.com.ua/society/2015/05/14/193908/.

"Ukraine's Party System: Specifics of Establishment, Problems of Functioning, Trends of Evolution" [National Security and Defence no. 5 (2010)]. *Razumkov Centre*. Accessed 18, 2016. http://www.razumkov.org.ua/eng/files/category_journal/NSD116_eng_1.pdf.

"Ukrainskyi teleprostir: Akhmetov, Pinchuk, Kolomoiskyi ta Firtash." *Realna Ekonomika*. August 20, 2013. http://real-economy.com.ua/infographics/42686.html.

"Verkhovna Rada proholosuvala za aresht nardepa vid Radykalnoi partii Ihora Mosiichuka." *Hromadske Radio*. September 17, 2015. http://hromadskeradio.org/2015/09/17/verhovna-rada-progolosuvala-za-aresht-nardepa-vid-radykalnoyi-partiyi-i gora-mosiychuka.

Virna, Nadiia. "V Chernivtsiakh za pidkup vybortsiv studentiv zasudyly do triokh rokiv." *Hromadske Radio*. November 11, 2015. http://hromadskeradio.org/2015/11/11/v-chernivcyah-za-pidkup-vyborciv-studentiv-zasudyly-do-troh-rokiv.

Voloshyna, Alla. "Alternative Report on Evaluation of State Anticorruption Policy Efficiency: Research Resume." *Transparency International Ukraine*. June 10, 2015. http://ti-ukraine.org/en/system/files/research/summary_alternative_report_en.pdf.

──────────. "Politychna koruptsiia po-ukrainsky." *Transparency International Ukraine*. October 6, 2015. http://ti-ukraine.org/news/media-about-us/5523.html.

"V Ukraini prezentuvaly suspilne movlennia." *BBC Ukraina*. April 7, 2015. http://www.bbc.com/ukrainian/politics/2015/04/150407_ukraine_public_broadcaster_sx.

"Zakon Ukrainy pro vnesennia zmin do deiakykh zakonodavchykh aktiv Ukrainy shchodo zapobihannia i protydii politychnii koruptsii." *Verkhovna Rada Ukrainy*. October 8, 2015. http://zakon5.rada.gov.ua/laws/show/731-viii.

"Za mistse u spysku 'Batkivshchyny'—$6 mln Iatseniuku, Turchynovu i Martynenku,— ziznannia nardepa." *ZIK.ua*. October 9, 2014. http://zik.ua/news/2014/10/09/za_prohi dne_mistse_u_spysku_batkivshchyny_zaplatyv_6_mln_dolariv_yatsenyuku_turchyn ovu_i_martynenku__skandalne_ziznannya_narodnogo_deputata_530365.

# 12
# Police Reform: Challenges and Prospects

Bohdan Harasymiw

On August 4, 2015, President Petro Poroshenko signed a new law creating the National Police of Ukraine (NPU).[1] The law went into effect in Kyiv on the date of its publication, August 6 but was delayed until the 20$^{th}$ in Odesa and Lviv. The NPU was expected to replace the Soviet-era *militsiia* in three months' time and also to have shed 30,000 personnel for a total force of 140,000. Structurally, it will consist of criminal, patrol, pretrial investigation, and special sections, with the notoriously corrupt highway inspection service having been absorbed into and replaced by the patrol police.[2] Since this is not the first such reform attempt—with the aim of reorienting the police from the principal task of shielding the state and its rulers from their subjects (repression) to serving and protecting the public, as well as curbing police corruption—in postcommunist Ukraine, what is the likelihood that this latest modernization effort will succeed in effecting fundamental change?

What is different this time? For one, it is no longer a stand-alone project but part of a comprehensively thorough program of reform of governance generally in Ukraine introduced by the post-Euromaidan administration.[3] According to the government's own monitoring website,

---

[1] "Petro Poroshenko pidpysav zakon pro Natsionalnu politsiiu," *Uriadovyi kurier*, August 4, 2015, http://ukurier.gov.ua/uk/news/petro-poroshenko-pidpisav-zakon-pro-nacionalnu-pol/. For the full text of the law, see "Pro natsionalnu politsiiu," *Verkhovna Rada*, 2015, ed. January 1, 2016, http://zakon3.rada.gov.ua/laws/show/58019.

[2] "Natsionalna politsiia povnistiu zaminyt militsiiu za 3 misiatsi,—MVS," *Den*, August 5, 2015, http://www.day.kiev.ua/uk/print/491250; "Zhuladze: reforma DAI vzhe rozpochalasia," *BBC Ukraina*, January 15, 2015, http://www.bbc.co.uk/ukrainian/politics/2015/01/150119_police_reform_started_zguladze_vc.

[3] See Prime Minister Arsenii Iatseniuk, "Recovery for Ukraine: Action Plan," n.p., n.d.; and "Agenda of the Cabinet of Ministers of Ukraine," *Ukraine Crisis Media Center*, December 12, 2014, http://uacrisis.org/agenda-cabinet-ministers-ukraine/. The head of the EU mission to Ukraine, which helped draft the law on police, has emphasized the necessity of police reform being undertaken within the context of thoroughly comprehensive and effective reform of governance. Serhii Sydorenko,

reform of law enforcement was 40 per cent accomplished within six months.[4] For another, it is for the first time being directed by outsiders (notably Iekateryna Zguladze-Gluksmann, First Deputy Minister of Internal Affairs, and Mikheil Saakashvili, Governor of Odesa oblast)[5] who have some record of accomplishment in the reform of police and policing away from the Soviet model toward the democratic in their native Georgia. But is this going to be adequate in overcoming inertia and effecting a wholesale transformation to democratic and European Union (EU) standards (or at least a reasonable facsimile), unachievable before? And will it be enough to overcome the hitherto intractable web of predatory criminal-business relations in which the police has been so willing a participant?[6] By looking carefully at past and present police reform efforts in Ukraine, as well as comparing experiences in other postcommunist states, this chapter hopes to make a fairly sound assessment as to the prospects of significant change.

For the tandem of Poroshenko and his prime minister, Arsenii Iatseniuk, since they began work on this project in 2014, it has been a tough slog. The new government was well aware that it faced widespread public dissatisfaction with the *militsiia* as currently constituted and a general expectation of radical reform.[7] Surveys conducted in Kharkiv, for example, in 2000 found that only 43 per cent of respondents reported any degree of trust in the *militsiia*, the major problem being corruption and bribery.[8] There was no shortage of prescriptions in the mass media, most of which agreed that restoration of public trust in the country's law enforcement bodies required, among other things: demilitarization of the

---

"Hlava misii IeS: 'U MVS maiut buty skorochennia. Bezrobitnykh stane bilshe, ta bez tsioho niiak,'" *Ievropeiska pravda*, September 1, 2015, http://www.eurointegrati on.com.ua/interview/2015/09/1/7037650/.

4 "Reforma pravookhoronnoi systemy," *Natsionalna rada reform*, accessed May 5, 2016, http://reforms.in.ua/ua/reforms/reforma-pravoohoronnoyi-systemy.
5 "Odesa Governor Saakashvili Trains with Ukrainian Police," *Ukraine Today TV*, August 19, 2015, http://uatoday.tv/society/new-odesa-police-officerrs-receive-trai ning-from-us-counterparts-478104.html.
6 Stanislav Markus, *Property, Predation, and Protection: Piranha Capitalism in Russia and Ukraine* (New York: Cambridge University Press, 2015), passim.
7 Serhii Hrabovskyi, "Khto doviriatyme MVS?," *Den*, February 18, 2014, http://day.kyiv.ua/uk/blog/politika/hto-doviryatime-mvs.
8 Adrian Beck and Yulia Chistyakova, "Crime and Policing in Post-Soviet Societies: Bridging the Police/Public Divide," *Policing and Society* 12, no. 2 (2002): 127, 129.

Ministry of Internal Affairs (MVS), within which law enforcement is housed; detachment of inappropriate functions from the *militsiia* to other government departments and agencies (e.g., issuance of motor vehicle licenses, customs control, passports, narcotics regulation, and security services), or to private operators; administrative decentralization and accountability to civilian authorities; fewer staff with better pay; curtailing involvement in business ventures; and reorienting personnel to the idea of serving and protecting the public. The economic crimes unit, they were saying, in reality a tool for shaking down businesses large and small, should be abolished; the interior troops should be transferred to the army.[9] When the government did issue its plans to reform the *militsiia*, these were criticized for superficiality and for not having taken into account expert opinion.[10] Such was expected, given that the reform process was in the hands of the Minister of Interior, Arsen Avakov. Summing up at year's end their assessment of the entire packet of government documents supposedly guiding the reform, two such experts offered a chapter-and-verse enumeration of its shortcomings: these "conceptual" or "strategic" papers were no substitute for a totally new law on the *militsiia*; no provision was made for actual mechanisms of accountability; citizens' concerns regarding local policing remained unaddressed; no concrete steps towards demilitarization of the MVS were evident, other than platitudes; functions inappropriate for policing had not been eliminated; rates of remuneration and staffing levels were unspecified; and no concrete provisions for political neutrality, or for an open public process of selecting the head of the national police force, were made.[11]

---

9     Hlib Kanevskyi, "Iak reformuvaty militsiiu," *Ekonomichna pravda*, March 5, 2014, http://www.epravda.com.ua/publications/2014/03/5/421628/; "Reforma militsii—neobkhodimo 'perelivanie krovi,'" *UNIAN*, April 4, 2014, http://www.unian.net/politics/904261-reforma-militsii-neobhodimo-perelivanie-krovi.html.

10    Inna Lykhovyd, "Reforma militsii . . . vidkladaietssia," *Den*, June 17, 2014, http://www.day.kiev.ua/uk/print/423533; Valentyn Torba, "Shcho robyty z 'mentom:' Reforma MVS—zmina suti chy kosmetyka?" *Den*, September 25, 2014, http://day.kyiv.ua/uk/article/podrobici/shcho-robiti-z-mentom.

11    Oleksandr Banchuk and Vadym Pyvovarov, "10 nedolikiv 'napivreformy' militsii," *Ukrainska pravda*, December 11, 2014, http://www.pravda.com.ua/articles/2014/12/11/7045767/. For a defense of the government's strategic orientation as revealed in the documents in question, on the other hand, see Ievhen Zakharov, "MVS ievropeiskoho gatunku: stratehiia reformatorskykh zmin," *Ukrainska pravda*, December 15, 2014, http://www.pravda.com.ua/columns/2014/12/15/7052035/.

A fresh start in the current effort at police reform came with the appointment of Eka Zguladze as Avakov's first deputy in the MVS in December 2014.[12] From 2004 to 2012, she had held the analogous post in Georgia and was largely responsible for the turnaround in that country. Directly on assuming office in Kyiv, Ms. Zguladze put into motion reform of the *militsiia*, beginning with: folding the State Highway Inspectorate (DAI) into the new patrol service, recruiting personnel (women as well as men) for the latter by open competition and testing, and raising salaries.[13] The patrol service, meant to assure safe streets and roads, or what in other countries is known as public order policing, began accepting applications in January 2015; this was to be followed by screening tests and training. Candidates were to be between the ages of 21 and 35, have at least secondary education, be free of criminal convictions, in good health, and fluent in Ukrainian. Initial pay was set at between 6,000 and 8,000 hryvni.[14] At the time, a police officer in Kyiv was earning, with bonuses, a salary of 2,100 to 2,200 hryvni, which, according to former Deputy Interior Minister Mykola Velychkovych, constituted "a direct path to corruption."[15] With US$15 million help from the U.S. Department of State, including uniforms, and C$5 million from Canada, the patrol service came into being; 2,000 personnel, schooled by American trainers and equipped with Japanese Toyota Prius hybrid cars, comprised the initial cohort.[16] Of the approximately 1,500 assigned to Kyiv, only 38 had previously worked in the DAI. The police were to expand into seven other

---

12  Ivan Farion, "Iakshcho ne rozzhene, to reformuie...," *Vysokyi zamok*, December 15, 2014, http://www.wz.lviv.ua/ukraine/129642.
13  "Eka Zhuladze anonsuvala reformu militsii," *BBC Ukraina*, December 25, 2014, http://www.bbc.com/ukrainian/politics/2014/12/141225_zguladze_reform_police_vc.
14  "Zhuladze: reforma DAI vzhe rozpochalas," and Mariia Prokopenko, "Tysiachi ukraintsiv khochut do ... politsii," *Den*, January 21, 2015, http://www.day.kiev.ua/uk/print/459650.
15  Roman Malko [Interview with Mykola Velychkovych], *Ukrainian Week*, February 19, 2015.
16  Kateryna Serhatskova, "'Politseiskyi—vzhe insha liudyna.' Iakoiu bude ukrainska patrulna sluzhba?," *Ukrainska pravda*, June 30, 2015, http://www.pravda.com.ua/articles/2015/06/30/7072910; Margarita Chornokondratenko and Elizabeth Piper, "Ukraine Launches Western-Style Police Force to Set a Marker for Reform," *Reuters*, July 6, 2015, http://www.trust.org/item20150706115230-xz7r9?view=print; and Ukraine Reform Monitor Team, "Ukraine Reform Monitor: August 2015," *Carnegie Endowment for International Peace*, accessed August 20, 2015, http://carnegieendowment.org/2015/08/19/ukraine-reform-monitor-august-2015/.

major cities; by the end of 2015, 6,000 patrolmen and women would be prepared. Ms. Zguladze pronounced herself satisfied with the new patrol police, who had comported themselves better than she expected.[17]

Meanwhile, starting in January 2015, the Verkhovna Rada began work on new legislation reforming the agencies of law enforcement. This was based on consultation with domestic experts as well as the experience of established (Canada, the United Kingdom, Germany, Austria, the Netherlands, Belgium, Spain, and Portugal) and newer (Poland, the Czech Republic, Slovakia, Slovenia, Croatia, and Moldova) democracies.[18] The draft bill: changed the name of the *militsiia* to "police;" took appointive power away from the Interior Minister placing it in the hands of an impartial commission; established open competition as the principle of recruitment; called for the creation of police commissions including civilians to be responsible for disciplinary matters; eliminated functions not proper for police; set rates of decent remuneration; gave police personnel the right to avoid unlawful commands; and strictly defined the conditions governing the use of force.[19] In February, the Verkhovna Rada passed a law eliminating the Main Administration for the Struggle against Organized Crime (HUBOZ).[20] While advocates argued its abolition on grounds that it duplicated the criminal investigation department, had failed to apprehend high-level crimes, and was itself a hive of crime and corruption, skeptics were unconvinced, believing the parliamentarians, together with the political elite in general, to be altogether uninterested in fighting organized crime rather than the unit having outlived its usefulness.[21]

---

17 "Zhuladze zadovolena robotoiu novykh patrulnykh," *Den*, July 6, 2015, http://www.day.kiev.ua/uk/print/486117; "Nova patrulna politsiia do kintsia roku zapratsiuie shche v 7 mistakh," *Den*, August 28, 2015, http://www.day.kiev.ua/uk/print/494542; and "Avakov rozpoviv, koly iakym mistam chekaty novu politsiiu," *Ukrainska pravda*, August 28, 2015, http://www.pravda.com.ua/2015/08/28/7079345/.
18 Oleksandr Banchuk and Borys Malyshev, "Shans na reformu: Chy zminyt pravookhoronnu systemu zakonoproekt pro politsiiu," *Ukrainska pravda*, February 2, 2015, http://www.pravda.com.ua/articles/2015/02/2/7057226/.
19 Ibid.
20 Dmytro Kryvtsun, "Reformuvannia MVS rozpochato," *Den*, February 13, 2015, http://day.kyiv.ua/uk/article/den-ukrayiny/reformuvannya-mvs-rozpochato.
21 Dmytro Kryvtsun, "Pro reformu militsii," *Den*, February 19, 2015, http://day.kyiv.ua/uk/article/podrobyci/pro-reformu-miliciyi.

Finally, on July 2, 2015, the Verkhovna Rada was presented with a packet of laws for scrutiny and approval respecting reform of law enforcement. According to the relevant parliamentary committee's secretary, these were bills on: the National Police; Internal Affairs organs; amendments to highway safety rules; and service centers.[22] The first, a replacement for the 1991 law on the *militsiia*, would mark a new departure for Ukraine in public order policing with competitive recruitment, respect for the rights of citizens, and strict rules on the use of force. The second was aimed at demilitarizing the Interior Ministry, making it into a civil service responsible for public order, fighting crime, administering migration policy, dealing with emergency situations, and safeguarding the security of all citizens. While the minister would have overall political responsibility for the portfolio, this would preclude interference in specific cases as had been allowed to happen up to now. Amendments to the highway and road traffic legislation were intended to bring this area into line with European practices, such as the use of photo-radar and video cameras to catch infractions, as well as a rationalization of the system of fines. Presumably, this would obviate loss of revenues otherwise going into the pockets of individual traffic officers. Finally, following the Georgian example, issuing licenses of various sorts, which formerly entailed considerable corruption, is to be cleaned up using the latest electronic technology and reducing the number of issuing centers from 300 to 80. Altogether, over 1,500 amendments had been introduced into this packet of legislation,[23] and provision was made for approximately two months' transition in respect of its implementation.[24]

---

22 Anton Gerashchenko, "Skazhem 'Da!' reforme MVD," *Ukrainska pravda: Blohy*, July 2, 2015, http://blogs.pravda.com.ua/authors/gerashchenko/55953ffb1567c/view_print/.

23 Which gave a measure of reassurance that the project may not have been fully captured by bureaucratic/institutional interests, as it was in a parallel reform in Russia in 2009–2011 under President Dmitrii Medvedev. See Brian D. Taylor, "Police Reform in Russia: The Policy Process in a Hybrid Regime," *Post-Soviet Affairs* 30, nos. 2–3 (2014): 226–55, especially 247.

24 "Novi patrulni vyidut na vulytsi shesty ukrainskykh mist," *Dzerkalo tyzhnia*, July 1, 2015, http://dt.ua/UKRAINE/novi-patrulni-viydut-na-vulici-shesti-ukrayinskih-mist-177548_.html.

Ultimately, therefore, following its adoption by the Rada on July 2, President Poroshenko did sign into law the new national police statute.[25] Published on August 6, most of its provisions were to go into effect in three months' time.[26] On November 4, Khatia Dekanoidze, adviser to minister Avakov and previously part of Georgian President Saakashvili's national security team as well as briefly minister of education in Georgia, was appointed head of the National Police.[27] Meanwhile, the transport *militsiia*—with, according to deputy minister Zguladze, an average caseload of three per month per investigator—was dissolved, its functions being taken over by the new criminal police.[28]

Among other noteworthy structural changes,[29] was replacement of the anti-narcotics operation with a new Counter Narcotic Crime Office (Biuro protydii narkozlochynnosti—BPN) with 80 percent new staff in two categories: agents and analysts. All special forces (Sokil, Omega, and Berkut) were to be liquidated and replaced by a single rapid-reaction force (Korpus operatyvno-raptovoi dii—KORD) consisting of 5,000 mostly fresh personnel untainted by association with the previous regime. A cybercrime unit is being established, and the analytical (expert) service is also being reorganized. A new department for safeguarding the economy replaces the economic crimes unit, with plans to hire civilian auditors, accountants, and property rights lawyers. On paper at least, these were laudatory moves.

---

25 "Prezydent Ukrainy Petro Poroshenko pidpysav zakon pro politsiiu," *UNIAN*, August 4, 2015, http://www.unian.ua/politics/1107966-poroshenko-pidpisav-zakon-pro-politsiyu.html#ad-image-0.

26 "Zakon pro politsiiu—Opublikovanyi zakon pro natsionalnu politsiiu," *Dzerkalo tyzhnia*, August 6, 2015, http://dt.ua/POLITICS/opublikovano-zakon-pro-nacionalnu-policiyu-180883_.html. For the full text, see "Pro Natsionalnu politsiiu," in the official government newspaper, *Holos Ukrainy*, August 6, 2015, http://www.golos.com.ua/article/257729.

27 "Avakov povidomyv, khto ocholyv Natsionalnu politsiiu," *Ukrainska pravda*, November 4, 2015, http://www.pravda.com.ua/news/2015/11/4/7087544/.

28 "MVS likviduvalo transportnu militsiiu," *Tyzhden*, July 22, 2015, http://tyzhden.ua/News/141610.

29 "Reforma MVS: planuiutssia kadrovi chystky 'zverkhu,' a biitsiv dobrobativ postavliat pered vyborom," *Dzerkalo tyzhnia*, October 24, 2015, http://dt.ua/POLITICS/reforma-mvd-planuyutsya-kadrovi-chistki-zverhu-a-biyciv-dobrobativ-postavlyat-pered-viborom-188762_.html; and Omar Uzarashvili, "Ukrainska militsiia nakazala dovho zhyty...," *Vysokyi zamok*, November 6, 2015, http://wz.lviv.ua/ukraine/147557-ukrainska-militsiia-nakazala-dovho-zhyty.

Instead of embarking on the tedious task of comparing clause-by-clause the old law on the *militsiia*[30] with the new police law, however, it will be more fruitful to assess the latter's conformity with the best-known principles of democratic policing. As formulated in the literature, these consist of: demilitarization, de-politicization, decentralization, professional competence, accountability and civilian oversight, transparency, and legitimacy.[31] According to David Bayley, acknowledged as the dean of police studies, the four essential elements of institutional reform of policing to align it with democratic government norms are: police accountability to the law rather than to the government of the day; protection of human rights; police accountability to external bodies; and citizens' needs being given top priority by the police service.[32] In pursuit of such reforms, Bayley adds, "six substantive programs ... are critically important.

1) Provide a legal basis for the new police.
2) Create specialized, independent oversight of the police.
3) Staff the police with the right sort of people.
4) Develop the capacity of police executives to manage reform.
5) Make the prevention of crime as it affects individuals the primary focus of policing.
6) Require legality and fairness in all actions."[33]

How does the 2015 law on the National Police of Ukraine as a basis for reform measure up to these criteria?

---

30  "Pro militsiiu: Zakon Ukrainy," *Verkhovna Rada*, 1991, http://zakon5.rada.gov.ua/laws/show/565-12.

31  Michael D. Wiatrowski and Jack A. Goldstone, "The Ballot and the Badge: Democratic Policing," *Journal of Democracy* 21, no. 2 (2010): 79–92; and Marina Caparini and Otwin Marenin, "Police Transformation in Central and Eastern Europe: The Challenge of Change," in *Transforming Police in Central and Eastern Europe: Process and Progress*, eds. Caparini and Marenin (Münster: LIT Verlag, 2004), 5–10. See also David H. Bayley, *Changing the Guard: Developing Democratic Police Abroad* (New York: Oxford University Press, 2006), chap. 1, and Otwin Marenin, "Democracy, Democratization, Democratic Policing," in *Challenges of Policing Democracies: A World Perspective*, eds. Diliip K. Das and Otwin Marenin (Amsterdam: Gordon and Breach Publishers, 2000), 311–31. For a skeptical view of democratic policing, however, see Graham Ellison and Nathan W. Pino, *Globalization, Police Reform and Development: Doing it the Western Way?* (New York: Palgrave Macmillan, 2012), 57–59.

32  Bayley, 18–20.

33  Ibid., 49, and elaborated 50–61.

*Demilitarization.* There is evidently no provision in the new legislation for even partial demilitarization of the police. The table of ranks, though keyed to the public service ("state service" in official Ukrainian parlance), parallels exactly that of the military, as it did before. Personnel are classed into three levels—junior (constable to sergeant), intermediate (junior lieutenant to colonel), and senior (several grades of general)—no detectives, inspectors, or superintendents here. Nor is there any mention of civilian employees as distinct from front-line officers: supposedly even analysts, IT personnel, forensics specialists, and police college instructors will carry ranks. It is remarkable in that where the new law specifies the table of ranks and the criteria for promotion (e.g., officers must have postsecondary education), the previous law made no mention of such it being merely taken for granted in the Soviet context. A step backward, it would seem, from the point of view of civilianizing the police force, and apparently criticized as such by the Council of Europe.[34]

Within the leadership of the Ministry of Internal Affairs as a whole, on the other hand, the presence of civilians was already significant at the time of the new law's passage. As of August 2015, civilians comprised a majority at the very apex, including Minister Avakov and three of his six deputy ministers; within the Ministry's Collegium 21 of 28 were civilians, including 11 parliamentarians.[35] Avakov himself, an ethnic Armenian born in 1964, is a notably successful businessman and politician. An engineer by training, he was one of the first to set up a shareholding company, "Investor," as early as 1990. In 2002, he was elected to the Kharkiv city council and campaigned for Viktor Iushchenko in the 2004 presidential election. The following year he became governor of Kharkiv. After a falling-out with Iushchenko, he quit the governorship and joined Iuliia Tymoshenko's Fatherland Party (Batkivshchyna). He spent 15 months in self-exile in Italy in 2011–12, evading political persecution by the Ianukovych regime. On returning, he won a seat in the Verkhovna Rada following the October 28, 2012 elections. Shortly after President Ianukovych's departure, on February 27, 2014, Avakov was appointed Minister of Internal Affairs, only the second civilian ever, reconfirmed on

---

34  Uzarashvili, "Ukrainska militsiia."
35  *Ministerstvo Vnutrishnikh Sprav Ukrainy* (official site), accessed August 18, 2015, http://www.mvs.gov.ua/.

December 2, 2014.[36] Like many other post-Euromaidan appointments, his was fraught with ambiguity.[37] Avakov's first deputy, Eka Zguladze, born in 1978, graduated in international journalism from Tbilisi University and then worked as a translator. As a teenager, she took a year of high school in Oklahoma on a U.S. Freedom Support Act program; in 2004–2005, she was employed at the Georgian branch office of the U.S. Millennium Challenge Corporation. She was then deputy interior minister in Georgia from 2005 to 2012, overseeing reform of the police.[38] The deputy minister for European integration within MVS, Tihran Avakian, born in 1975, was appointed on August 20, 2014. A specialist in international law and Eurointegration with a graduate degree in political science, he served briefly as a diplomat at Ukraine's embassy in Armenia and within the ministry of external affairs (MVS) before going into a succession of posts in business management. In 2013–2014, he was an advisor and consultant to a media magnate-turned-Rada parliamentarian, Mykola Kniazhytskyi. For the six months prior to his current appointment, Avakian was director of analysis and forecasting in the MVS.[39] Between them, these three have an impressive array of experience suitable for directing a genuine reform of police and policing in Ukraine, hopefully sufficient to break out of the Soviet mindset and to get off the treadmill. The new law says that appointment and dismissal of the chief of the National Police is

---

36  "Ministr vnutrishnikh sprav Ukrainy Avakov Arsen Borysovych," *Ministerstvo Vnutrishnikh Sprav Ukrainy*, accessed August 18, 2015, http://www.mvs.gov.ua/mvs/ control/main/uk/publish/article/986921. Iurii Lutsenko was the first, serving two terms between 2005 and 2010. For his troubles, he was promptly jailed in 2010 and only amnestied three years later on grounds of ill health.

37  Bohdan Butkevych, "Arsen Avakov: U vladi zibralysia vkrai tsynichni liudy, u iakykh nemaie zapobizhnykiv," *Tyzhden*, February 18, 2014, http://tyzhden.ua/ Politics/102227.

38  "Pershyi zastupnyk Ministra vnutrishnikh sprav Ukrainy Iekateryna Zhuladze-Gluksmann," *Ministerstvo Vnutrishnikh Sprav Ukrainy*, accessed August 22, 2015, http://www.mvs.gov.ua/mvs/control/main/uk/publish/article/1278363. For Zguladze's own account of her approach to police reform and her record in Georgia, see the extensive interview with her in Anastasia Ringis, "Eks-ministr MVD Gruzii Eka Zguladze: Novye idei nelzia rodit v tom zhe samom rabochem kabinete, gde ty provel vsiu zhizn," *Ukrainska pravda*, August 12, 2014, http://life.pravda.com.ua/per son/2014/08/12/177440/.

39  "Zastupnyk Ministra vnutrishnikh sprav Ukrainy z pytan ievropeiskoi intehratsii, Avakian Tihran Ashotovych," *Ministerstvo Vnutrishnikh Sprav Ukrainy*, accessed August 18, 2015, http://www.mvs.gov.ua/mvs/control/main/uk/publish/article/113 8325.

made by the Cabinet of Ministers on a proposal by the Prime minister, based on advice from the Interior Minister, all of which should ensure a continuing degree of civilian control of the police at the very top rather than their being a tool in the hands of the executive branch, ultimately the president. As mentioned, rounding out the top management team, the 38-year-old native of Georgia, Khatia Dekanoidze, was named head of the National Police in November 2015, on the eve of the new act's coming into force.

*De-politicization.* The newest version of the police law removes the provision giving full authority to the minister for managing the police, a component of the ministry, directly. This presumably would avoid grossly political use of the police, including at election-time, as happened when Iurii Kravchenko was minister and doing the bidding of President Leonid Kuchma.[40] The law now forbids any individual in the police establishment from belonging to a political party, taking orders from anyone outside the police structure, and accepting unlawful tasks; nor can anyone oblige such personnel to carry out improper acts or assignments (Section 62, arts. 3, 5, and 6). Political neutrality of the police is assured by art. 10. At the same time, the president will be allowed to bestow general's rank on whomever he pleases, leaving an opening for political interference, yet another shortcoming in the law as identified by the Council of Europe.[41]

*Decentralization.* As envisaged in the Law on the National Police (2015), there are to be two levels of administration: central and territorial. Structure of the central administration is set by the chief of the national police by consent of the Minister of Internal Affairs. Territorial offices are created in oblasts, cities, towns, and districts; territorial police chiefs are appointed by the national chief in consultation with the Interior Minister.

---

40 Bohdan Harasymiw, "Policing, Democratization and Political Leadership in Postcommunist Ukraine," *Canadian Journal of Political Science* 36, no. 2 (2003): 319–40. On the day he was to testify in regard to the killing of journalist Georgii Gongadze, in which Kuchma was implicated, Kravchenko was said to have conveniently avoided justice by committing suicide with two bullets to the head. Investigation into who exactly ordered the newspaperman's death was still ongoing thirteen years later. "Sprava Kravchenka mozhe vyvesty na slid zamovnyka vbyvstva Honhadze—advokat," *Dzerkalo tyzhnia*, January 6, 2016, http://dt.ua/UKRAINE/sprava-kravchenka-mozhe-vivesti-na-slid-zamovnika-vbiv stva-gongadze-advokat-195987_.html; and Valentyn Torba, "Sud nad vykonav-tsem—zamovnyky na voli," *Den*, January 6, 2016, http://www.day.kiev.ua/uk/ar ticle/polityka/sud-nad-vykonavcem-zamovnyky-na-voli.

41 Uzarashvili, "Ukrainska militsiia."

While the local police offices will now no longer be simply branch operations of a single administrative structure acting completely autonomously of local authorities, the degree of decentralization envisaged by the new law, it must be said, is modest. With financing still apparently allocated from the central budget, appointment of chiefs by the man at the top, and no discernible functions (apart from the patrol police) divided between the two levels, this measure hardly qualifies as effective decentralization.

By comparison, the draft prepared in January 2015 by the three-party ruling parliamentary coalition had included provision for a third, local community, level of administration. This would be funded from local government budgets and tasked with specific, if basic, functions. It may have been shelved pending implementation of a broader reform of territorial administrative decentralization.[42]

*Professional competence.* In the new police act considerable attention is devoted to the training of personnel, qualifications for various ranks, and requirements for promotion and time in rank. Initial recruitment is by open competition; for other vacancies and further advancement open competition is optional at the discretion of local commanders. This, as has been noted, leaves the door open beyond the entry level to favoritism, nepotism, and arbitrariness, although the new national police chief, Ms. Dekanoidze, has given assurances that aspirants for managerial and investigator positions will have to take polygraph tests in addition interviews.[43] There are also extensive rules on police officers' handling of encounters with the public so as to safeguard human rights of individuals as well as on the use of force, all of this being strictly regulated. Overall, the primacy of the rule of law is emphasized in the new act.

In pursuit of a higher degree professional competence, all personnel in the old *militsiia* have had to undergo a process of "re-certification" (*pereatestatsiia*) consisting of a standard general skills test (GST), a test of professional abilities, and an interview including members of the public. As of the end of 2015, some 47,000 policemen had failed their tests

---

42   Banchuk and Malyshev, "Shans na reformu."
43   "Spravzhnia reforma chy zvychaina pereatestatsiia?" *Vysokyi zamok*, September 17, 2015, http://wz.lviv.ua/ukraine/141537-spravzhnia-reforma-chy-zvychaina-pere atestatsiia; and "Kandydaty na kerivni posady v natspolitsiiu prokhodymut polihraf—Dekanoidze," *Den*, December 4, 2015, http://www.day.kiev.ua/uk/news/041215-ka ndydaty-na-kerivni-posady-v-nacpoliciyi-prohodymut-poligraf-dekanoidze.

nation-wide; in Kyiv and its oblast, the number was 3,386, or nearly 38 percent.[44] When some of these unsuccessful candidates picketed the Ministry of Internal Affairs building in the capital, National Police Chief Dekanoidze interpreted it as a sign she was on the right track, and prevailed on her Minister, Avakov, to replace the chief of police in Kyiv.[45] The road to reform was never smooth.

*Accountability and civilian oversight.* In a notable departure from Soviet practice, territorial police chiefs as well as the national chief are obliged to make and to publish on their web-sites an annual report (Chapter VIII). The local council (*rada*)—but not the Verkhovna Rada—may pass a vote of non-confidence in the chief or any subordinate, as a consequence of which the officer in question may be suspended, dismissed, reassigned, or reinstated, as appropriate. Highly detailed procedures regarding this are given in the act; a determined council can have an officer fired, contrary to the internal police investigation's recommendations.

The other innovation in this regard consists in creating permanent police commissions (art. 51). These are to adjudicate the competitive selection and promotion processes. At the central level it will consist of: two civilians designated by the minister; one, by the national chief of police; and two representatives of the public recommended by the Human Rights Commission of the Verkhovna Rada. In the territories there will be: one representative each nominated by the minister, the national chief of

---

44 "Z pochatku roku zvilneno 47 tysiach pravookhorontsiv—Avakov," *UNIAN*, December 8, 2015, http://www.unian.ua/society/1206278-z-pochatku-roku-zvilneno-47-tisyach-pravoohorontsiv-avakov.html; and "Bilshe tretyny kyivskykh militsioneriv ne proishly pereatestatsiiu dlia roboty v politsii," *Dzerkalo tyzhnia*, November 27, 2015, http://dt.ua/UKRAINE/bilshe-tretini-kiyivskih-milicioneriv-ne-proyshli-pereatestaciyu-dlya-roboti-v-policiyi-192415_.html.

45 "Dekanoidze o 'militseiskom maidane': znachit, my na pravilnom puti," *Obozrevatel*, December 13, 2015, http://obozrevatel.com/crime/90637-dekanoidze-o-militsejskom-majdane-znachit-myi-na-pravilnom-puti.htm; "Dekanoidze initsiiuvala vidstavku nachalnyka kyivskoi politsii Tereshchuka," *Dzerkalo tyzhnia*, December 14, 2015, http://dt.ua/UKRAINE/dekanoyidze-iniciyuvala-vidstavku-nachalnika-kiyivskoyi-policiyi-tereschuka-194056_.html; "Avakov pryznachyv Kryshchenka novym hlavoiu politsii Kyieva," *Den*, December 15, 2015, http://day.kyiv.ua/uk/news/151215-avakov-pryznachyv-kryshchenka-novym-glavoyu-policiyi-kyyeva;
and "Kyivsku politsiiu ocholyv Andrii Kryshchenko, iakyi zakhyshchav ukrainskyi prapor u Horlivtsi," *Dzerkalo tyzhnia*, December 15, 2015, http://dt.ua/UKRAINE/kiyivsku-policiyu-ocholiv-andriy-krischenko-yakiy-zahischav-ukrayinskiy-prapor-u-gorlivci-194129_.html.

police, and the local police chief; and two selected by the local council. Commissioners serve for a maximum of one three-year term. Each commission elects its own chair and secretary. Commission proceedings are open; their decisions are made public in written form. This is indeed a significant step, in principle, towards democratic policing.

In this regard, the parliamentary draft of January 2015 was much bolder.[46] It provided for the aforesaid adjudication commissions to be comprised of seven (rather than five) members, including four civilian human rights activists plus an outstanding lawyer, ensuring it not be dominated by bureaucrats. In addition, it foresaw the creation of regular five-member police commissions, three of whom would not be from police or government service, with disciplinary powers as per standard Western practice. Absence of those provisions in the actual NPU law implies the predominance of bureaucratic caution and interests over principles of genuine accountability.

*Transparency.* "Democratic policing," according to but one of many available definitions, entails or requires in part that "the police must be . . . transparent in their practices and not given to operating as a state within a state."[47] As a general doctrine of governance, transparency entails openness and accountability. Its advocates ascribe to it certain key characteristics:

> decisions governed by clearly established and published rules and procedures rather than by *ad hoc* judgements or processes; methods of accounting or public reporting that clarify who gains from and who pays for any public measure; and governance that is intelligible and accessible to the 'general public.'[48]

Closely related to notions of democratization, such doctrines are said to have several component elements,

> including the idea of government according to predictable rules, the idea of openness of government information to citizens and the idea of government

---

46  Ibid.
47  Wiatrowski and Goldstone, 81.
48  Christopher Hood, "Transparency in Historical Perspective," in *Transparency: The Key to Better Governance?*, eds. Christopher Hood and David Heald (Oxford: Oxford University Press, 2006), 5.

accounting and institutional arrangements that prevent covert cross-subsidization or opaque relationships between governments and their satellites, particularly state-owned enterprises.[49]

But a study of how transparency operates in practice in various spheres of political and economic life in the United Kingdom concludes on a cautious note. In the end, "prudence seems to justify a strong element of 'practical scepticism' about the way transparency measures work out on the ground."[50]

With this in mind, it is possible to discern a few rudimentary elements of transparency embedded for the first time in the new police law. One of these is a requirement for police officers to carry name tags with registration numbers which allows for identification in case of public complaints concerning their conduct. There is also in the law a detailed catalog of what an officer is and is not allowed to do in dealing with members of the public. In general, art. 9 covers openness and transparency; the police are: to act in accordance with such principles; to inform the public about their activity in respect of protecting rights, fighting crime, and maintaining public order; to afford access to public information as well as displaying on the central website the statutory basis which regulates police activity. Apart from the annual reports required of police chiefs, and police commissioners' participation in the hiring process, there is practically no possibility for the public to examine decision-making within the police force, according to the latest law. Police personnel are subject (art. 61) to the limitations sanctioned by the Law on Preventing Corruption; this explicit reference facilitates exposure of corrupt activity within the police. If the experience of other jurisdictions can serve as a guide, however, transparency is liable to remain more a hope than reality for the Ukrainian National Police.[51]

---

49  Ibid., 14.
50  Hood, "Beyond Exchanging First Principles? Some Closing Comments," in Hood and Heald, 224.
51  "One of the rather troublesome characteristics of all the systems we studied is their lack of transparency, as one of the more visible characteristics of democratic policing systems." Nils Uildriks and Piet van Reenen, *Policing Post-Communist Societies: Police-Public Violence, Democratic Policing and Human Rights* (Antwerp: Intersentia, 2003), 212. These authors' findings were based on interviews conducted in Lithuania, Perm (Russia), and Mongolia in 2001–2002, and compared with data on Bulgaria, Poland, and Romania.

*Legitimacy.* Considerable emphasis in the new law is placed at the outset on the defense of rights and freedoms of individuals as the primary duty of police (arts. 1 and 7). Chapter V very carefully spells out the means to be used, and under which conditions, by the police in dealing with the public in circumstances that may entail infringement of such rights and freedoms. In this regard, Chapter VIII, "Public Oversight of the Police," sounds more impressive than it is in substance. It provides, as mentioned above, for votes of non-confidence in police chiefs by local councils. The most positive provisions come at chapter's end, in arts. 89 and 90, which mandate joint police-public projects and programs "to satisfy public needs" as well as the inclusion of citizen representatives in the investigation of acts, or failures to act, on the part of police officers. At least on paper, this is a fundamental reorientation of the philosophy of policing in Ukraine, and constitutes a promising start for reform—even if not a watertight insurance policy.

Effective reforms will depend on implementation, but the track record in Ukraine itself is not good. At the end of 2006, for example, the first deputy minister of the MVS was advancing a third plan since independence for police reform, the previous two having been unrealized.[52] In 2011, Vasyl Hrytsak, parliamentarian with the Party of Regions, began work on legislation mirroring the reforms of the *militsiia* introduced by Russia. The following year, together with a colleague, he added a new proposal for a kind of praetorian guard for President Viktor Ianukovych. Critics pointed out that the Russian reform was, unfortunately, merely cosmetic.[53] This is the same Mr. Hrytsak who in July 2015 succeeded his boss, Valentyn Nalyvaichenko, as head of the Security Service of Ukraine (SBU), itself a notorious den of corruption.[54] But that is another story. More recently,

---

52   Mykhailo Korniienko, "Reforma militsii. Sproba nomer try," *Dzerkalo tyzhnia*, March 25–31, 2006, http://www.zn.kiev.ua/ie/print/52964/. For more detail on these earlier reform efforts, see Adrian Beck, Alexei Povolotskiy, and Alexander Yarmysh, "Reform of the Militia in Ukraine," in *Transforming Police in Central and Eastern Europe*, eds. Caparini and Marenin, 305–17.

53   "Hrytsak proponuie kardynalno reformuvaty MVS, stvoryvshy v Ukraini politsiiu i zhandarmeriiu," *Dzerkalo tyzhnia*, September 26, 2011, http://news.dt.ua/articles/88492; and "Nove vidomstvo na literu 'P,'" *Den*, July 11, 2012, http://day.kyiv.ua/uk/article/podrobici/nove-vidomstvo-na-literu-p.

54   Denys Kazanskyi, "Who are You, Mr. Hrytsak? Whose Interests will Guide the New SBU Chief," *Ukrainian Week*, July 14, 2015, http://ukrainianweek.com/Politics/140870.

President Ianukovych, in April 2013, pulled the plug on yet another police reform, undertaken as an obligation to the Council of Europe, which was to have been introduced that year and completed in 2015, following the European model.[55]

What can be anticipated in Ukraine, therefore, is neither sudden success nor abject failure, but a continuing struggle. Experience in other jurisdictions provides some guidelines. In Central and Eastern Europe, even 15 years after the fall of the Berlin Wall democratic policing had not been fully achieved—there had been institutional reforms, yes, but only modest successes in democratic control and accountability. Reforms had been slow, lacking in coherence, unsystematic.[56] The countries in this region had

> "not yet . . . effected fundamental change towards a service mentality among police officers, acceptance of the notions of policing by consent, public accountability and external supervision."[57]

Among the lessons to be learned from Central and Eastern European cases are that: (1) constitutional and legislative reforms are necessary, but not sufficient; (2) the essential contents of reforms are "three little d's and one big D"—decentralization, demilitarization, de-politicization, and Democratization; and (3) more legitimacy accruing to the police comes with more crime.[58] An increase in crime, in turn, slows down the process of reform as government devotes less attention to supervision and control, also becoming more cautious in the face of social change.[59] Ukraine is thus even farther behind in the process of police reform than its postcommunist cousins, and prospects of achieving their level (imperfect though it may be) is that much more remote.

---

55 Media speculation at that time explained the postponement as political: cutting down the size of the MVS would have entailed a loss to the presidential support base; the need for creating a finance police was still unclear; and infighting among law enforcement agencies over the illegal drug trade was ongoing. "Ianukovych vyrishyv vidklasty reformu militsii—ZMI," *Den*, April 17, 2013, http://day.kyiv.ua/uk/news/170413-yanukovich-virishiv-vidklasti-reformu-miliciyi-zmi.
56 Caparini and Marenin, "Process and Progress in the Reform of Policing Systems," in their *Transforming Police*, 321–39.
57 Ibid., 321.
58 Ibid., 327–34.
59 Ibid., 335.

In any case, it is the application of principles, not of models or a model that matters, because researchers now agree that there is no single model of police reform.[60] That point is forcefully made in a separate study of security sector reform examining seven cases from Europe, the Middle East, Africa, and Latin America. "Ultimately," its authors caution

> there is no one model of police reform that can be transposed from the West to the Rest. There is no guarantee that what works in Northern Ireland will work in South Africa, Brazil or Afghanistan—in spite of what some practitioners may like to think. Police reform is a highly contingent process; it depends ultimately on having a robust constitutional and political framework in place that is respectful and tolerant of rights, not the whims of regimes, and an economic system that is capable of meeting basic social needs.[61]

Empirical investigation of these varied cases leads them to conclude that "there is huge variation in terms of the success of police and security sector reform initiatives," with structural factors intervening.

> Second, . . . it appears highly unlikely that we will see . . . democratic policing, modeled on Western lines in a number of our case studies. . . . Perhaps the best we can hope for is to protect citizens from the more coercive machinations of the state.[62]

Clearly, they are not overly optimistic, as we, with respect to Ukraine, should not be, either. In general, according to Ellison and Peno, the conditions for successful police reform, with corresponding implications for the present study, are: coordination among outside aid providers; honoring of commitments; involvement of local actors in planning and implementation; state security and human rights being given equal emphasis; accountability and transparency are necessary; and long-term goals always must be emphasized.[63] Pre-conditions for these, however, and equally important, are: stable government; a political and economic system supportive of independent development; mutual and full commitment to reform from both donor and recipient countries; ethical leadership of donor country; simultaneous democratic reform of the political system;

---

60   Caparini and Marenin, "Police Transformation," in ibid., 10. Hence, also the emphasis in the present chapter on the law as a set of principles rather than on models of policing.
61   Ellison and Pino, 82.
62   Ibid., 206–07.
63   Ibid., 208–10.

and receptiveness of the police to change.[64] Insofar as their study falls under the larger umbrella of overseas development assistance, which is not the perspective adopted here, we may set aside the enumerated international factors, not that they are unimportant, to concentrate on the domestic political preconditions. In terms of such variables, as anyone familiar with that country's problems will easily surmise, the prognosis for Ukraine is indeterminate at best: while the Poroshenko-Iatseniuk/Hroisman government is indeed attempting to pursue democratic reform simultaneously on all fronts, its stability is undermined by chronic weakness and its very viability is threatened by the separatist war on its territory.[65] Models aside, the prospect of democratic policing in the best of conditions in a post-communist state would be ambiguous; in the Ukrainian government's present circumstances, which are verging on the catastrophic, it is even more so.

## Bibliography

"Agenda of the Cabinet of Ministers of Ukraine." *Ukraine Crisis Media Center.* Accessed February 17, 2016. http://uacrisis.org/agenda-cabinet-ministers-ukraine/.

"Avakov povidomyv, khto ocholyv Natsionalnu politsiiu." *Ukrainska pravda.* November 4, 2015. http://www.pravda.com.ua/news/2015/11/4/7087544/.

"Avakov pryznachyv Kryshchenka novym hlavoiu politsii Kyieva." *Den.* December 15, 2015. http://day.kyiv.ua/uk/news/151215-avakov-pryznachyv-kryshchenka-novym-glavoyu-policiyi-kyyeva

"Avakov rozpoviv, koly iakym mistam chekaty novu politsiiu." *Ukrainska pravda.* August 28, 2015. http://www.pravda.com.ua/news/2015/08/28/7079345.

Banchuk, Oleksandr, and Borys Malyshev. "Shans na reformu: Chy zminyt pravookhoronnu systemu zakonoproekt pro politsiiu." *Ukrainska pravda.* February 2, 2015. http://www.pravda.com.ua/articles/2015/02/2/7057226/.

Banchuk, Oleksandr, and Vadym Pyvovarov. "10 nedolikiv 'napivreformy' militsii." *Ukrainska pravda.* December 11, 2014. http://www.pravda.com.ua/articles/2014/12/11/7045767/.

Bayley, David H. *Changing the Guard: Developing Democratic Police Abroad.* New York: Oxford University Press, 2006.

Beck, Adrian, and Yulia Chistyakova. "Crime and Policing in Post-Soviet Societies: Bridging the Police/Public Divide." *Policing and Society* 12, no. 2 (2002): 123–37.

---

64  Ibid., 210–11.
65  Volodymyr Hroisman replaced Arsenii Iatseniuk as the Prime Minister of Ukraine on April 14, 2016.

"Bilshe tretyny kyivskykh militsioneriv ne proishly pereatestatsiiu dlia roboty v politsii." *Dzerkalo tyzhnia.* November 27, 2015. http://dt.ua/UKRAINE/bilshe-tretini-kiyivskih-milicioneriv-ne-proyshli-pereatestaciyu-dlya-roboti-v-policiyi-192415_.html.

Butkevych, Bohdan. "Arsen Avakov: U vladi zibralysia vkrai tsynichni liudy, u iakykh nemaie zapobizhnykiv." *Tyzhden.* February 18, 2014. http://tyzhden.ua/Politics/102227.

Caparini, Marina, and Otwin Marenin, eds. *Transforming Police in Central and Eastern Europe: Process and Progress.* Münster: LIT Verlag, 2004.

Chornokondratenko, Margarita, and Elizabeth Piper. "Ukraine Launches Western-Style Police Force to Set a Marker for Reform." *Reuters.* July 6, 2015. http://www.trust.org/item/20150706115230-xz7r9?view=print.

Das, Dilip K., and Otwin Marenin, eds. *Challenges of Policing Democracies: A World Perspective.* Amsterdam: Gordon and Breach Publishers, 2000.

"Dekanoidze initsiiuvala vidstavku nachalnyka kyivskoi politsii Tereshchuka." *Dzerkalo tyzhnia.* December 14, 2015. http://dt.ua/UKRAINE/dekanoyidze-iniciyuvala-vidstavku-nachalnika-kiyivskoyi-policiyi-tereschuka-194056_.html.

"Dekanoidze o 'militseiskom maidane': znachit, my na pravilnom puti." *Obozrevatel.* December 13, 2015. http://obozrevatel.com/crime/90637-dekanoidze-o-militsejskom-majdane-znachit-myi-na-pravilnom-puti.htm

Ellison, Graham, and Nathan W. Pino. *Globalization, Police Reform and Development: Doing it the Western Way?* New York: Palgrave Macmillan, 2012.

Farion, Ivan. "Iakshcho ne rozzhene, to reformuie . . ." *Vysokyi zamok.* December 15, 2014. http://www.wz.lviv.ua/ukraine/129642.

Gerashchenko, Anton. "Skazhem 'Da!' reforme MVD." *Ukrainska pravda: Blohy.* July 2, 2015. http://blogs.pravda.com.ua/authors/gerashchenko/55953ffb1567c/view_print/.

Harasymiw, Bohdan. "Policing, Democratization and Political Leadership in Postcommunist Ukraine." *Canadian Journal of Political Science* 36, no. 2 (2003): 319–40.

Hood, Christopher, and David Heald, eds. *Transparency: The Key to Better Governance?* Oxford: Oxford University Press, 2006.

Hrabovskyi, Serhii. "Khto doviriatyme MVS?" *Den.* February 18, 2014. http://day.kyiv.ua/uk/blog/politika/hto-doviryatime-mvs.

"Hrytsak proponuie kardynalno reformuvaty MVS, stvoryvshy v Ukraini politsiiu i zhandarmeriiu." *Dzerkalo tyzhnia.* September 26, 2011. http://news.dt.ua/articles/88492.

"Ianukovych vyrishyv vidklasty reform militsii—ZMI." *Den,* April 17, 2013. http://day.kyiv.ua/uk/news/170413-yanukovich-virishiv-vidklasti-reformu-miliciyi-zmi.

Iatseniuk, Arsenii. "Recovery for Ukraine: Action Plan." N.p., n.d.

"Kandydaty na kerivni posady v natspolitsiiu prokhodytymut polihraf—Dekanoidze." *Den.* December 4, 2015. http://www.day.kiev.ua/uk/news/041215-kandydaty-na-kerivni-posady-v-nacpoliciyi-prohodytymut-poligraf-dekanoidze.

Kanevskyi, Hlib. "Iak reformuvaty militsiiu." *Ekonomichna pravda.* March 5, 2014. http://www.epravda.com.ua/publications/2014/03/5/421628/.

Kazanskyi, Denys. "Who Are You, Mr. Hrytsak? Whose Interests will Guide the New SBU Chief." *Ukrainian Week.* July 14, 2015. http://ukrainianweek.com/Politics/140870.

Korniienko, Mykhailo. "Refoma militisii. Sproba nomer try." *Dzerkalo tyzhnia*. December 25-31, 2006. http://www.zn.kiev.ua/ie/print/52964/.

Kryvtsun, Dmytro. "Pro reformu militsii," *Den*. February 19, 2015. http://day.kyiv.ua/uk/article/podrobyci/pro-reformu-miliciyi.

──────────. "Reformuvannia MVS rozpochato." *Den*. February 16, 2015. http://day.kyiv.ua/uk/article/den-ukrayiny/reformuvannya-mvs-rozpochato.

"Kyivsku politsiiu ocholyv Andrii Kryshchenko, iakyi zakhyshchav ukrainskyi prapor u Horlivtsi." *Dzerkalo tyzhnia*. December 15, 2015. http://dt.ua/UKRAINE/kiyivsku-policiyu-ocholiv-andriy-krischenko-yakiy-zahischav-ukrayinskiy-prapor-u-gorlivci-194129_.html.

Lykhovyd, Inna. "Reforma militsii . . . vidkladaietsia." *Den*. June 17, 2014. http://www.day.kiev.ua/uk/print/423533.

Malko, Roman [Interview with Mykola Velychkovych]. *Ukrainian Week*, February 19, 2015.

Markus, Stanislav. *Property, Predation, and Protection: Piranha Capitalism in Russia and Ukraine*. New York: Cambridge University Press, 2015.

*Ministerstvo Vnutrishnikh Sprav Ukrainy* (official site). Accessed August 18 2015. http://www.mvs.gov.ua/.

"MVS likviduvalo transportnu militsiiu." *Tyzhden*. July 22, 2015. http://tyzhden.ua/News/141610.

"Natsionalna politsiia povnistiu zaminyt militsiiu za 3 misiatsi—MVS." *Den*. August 5, 2015. http://www.day.kiev.ua/uk/print/491250.

"Nova patrulna politsiia do kintsia roku zapratsiuie shche v 7 mistakh." *Den*. August 28, 2015. http://www.day.kiev.ua/uk/print/494542.

"Nove vidomstvo na literu 'P.'" *Den*. July 11, 2012. http://day.kyiv.ua/uk/article/podrobici/nove-vidomstvo-na-literu-p.

"Novi patrulni vyyidut na vulytsi shesty ukrainskykh mist." *Dzerkalo tyzhnia*. July 1, 2015. http://dt.ua/UKRAINE/novi-patrulni-viydut-na-vulici-shesti-ukrayinskih-mist-177548_.html.

"Odesa governor Saakashvili trains with Ukrainian police." *Ukraine Today TV*. August 19, 2015. http://uatoday.tv/society/new-odesa-police-officerrs-receive-training-from-us-counterparts-478104.html.

"Petro Poroshenko pidpysav zakon pro Natsionalnu politsiiu." *Uriadovyi kurier*. August 4, 2015. http://ukurier.gov.ua/uk/news/petro-poroshenko-pidpisav-zakon-pro-nacionalnu-pol/.

"Pro militsiiu: Zakon Ukrainy." *Verkhovna Rada*. 1991. http://zakon5.rada.gov.ua/laws/show/565-12.

"Pro natsionalnu politsiiu." *Verkhovna Rada*. 2015, edited January 1, 2016. http://zakon3.rada.gov.ua/laws/show/58019.

"Prezydent Ukrainy Petro Poroshenko pidpysav zakon pro politsiiu." *UNIAN*. August 4, 2015. http://www.unian.ua/politics/1107966-poroshenko-pidpisav-zakon-pro-politsiyu.html#ad-image-0.

Prokopenko, Mariia. "Tysiachi ukraintsiv khochut do . . . politsii." *Den*. January 21, 2015. http://www.day.kiev.ua/uk/print/459650.

"Reforma militsii—neobkhodimo 'perelivanie krovi.'" *UNIAN.* April 4, 2014. http://www.unian.net/politics/904261-reforma-militsii-neobhodimo-perelivanie-krovi.html.

"Reforma MVS: planuiutsia kadrovi chystky 'zverkhu,' a biitsiv dobrobativ postavliat pered vyborom." *Dzerkalo tyzhnia.* October 24, 2015. http://dt.ua/POLITICS/reforma-mvd-planuyutsya-kadrovi-chistki-zverhu-a-biyciv-dobrobativ-postavlyat-pered-viborom-188762_.html.

"Reforma pravookhoronnoi systemy." *Natsional'na rada reform.* Accessed February 16, 2016. http://reforms.in.ua/reforms/reforma-pravoohoronnoyi-systemi.

Ringis, Anastasia. "Eks-ministr MVD Gruzii Eka Zguladze: Novye idei nelzia rodyt v tom zhe samom rabochem kabinete, gde ty provel vsiu zhizn." *Ukrainska pravda.* August 12, 2014. http://life.pravda.com.ua/person/2014/08/12/177440/.

Serhatskova, Kateryna. "'Politseiskyi—vzhe insha liudyna.' Iakoiu bude ukrainska patrulna sluzhba?" *Ukrainska pravda.* June 30, 2015. http://www.pravda.com.ua/articles/2015/06/30/7072910.

"Sprava Kravchenka mozhe vyvesty na slid zamovnyka vbyvstva Honhadze—advokat." *Dzerkalo tyzhnia.* January 6, 2016. http://dt.ua/UKRAINE/sprava-kravchenka-mozhe-vivesti-na-slid-zamovnika-vbivstva-gongadze-advokat-195987_.html.

"Spravzhnia reforma chy zvychaina pereatestatsiia?" *Vysokyi zamok.* September 17, 2015. http://wz.lviv.ua/ukraine/141537-spravzhnia-reforma-chy-zvychaina-pereatestatsiia.

Sydorenko, Serhii. "Hlava misii IeS: 'U MVS maiut buty skorochennia. Bezrobitnykh stane bilshe, ta bez toho niiak.'" *Ievropeiska pravda.* September 1, 2015. http://www.eurointegration.com.ua/interview/2015/09/01/7037650/.

Taylor, Brian D. "Police Reform in Russia: The Policy Process in a Hybrid Regime." *Post-Soviet Affairs* 30, nos. 2–3 (2014): 226–55.

Torba, Valentyn. "Shcho robyty z 'mentom': Reforma MVS—zmina suti chy kosmetyka?" *Den.* September 25, 2014. http://day.kyiv.ua/uk/article/podrobici/shcho-robiti-z-mentom.

―――. "Sud nad vykonavtsem—zamovnyky na voli." *Den.* January 6, 2016. http://www.day.kiev.ua/uk/article/polityka/sud-nad-vykonavcem-zamovnyky-na-voli.

Uildriks, Niels, and Piet van Reenen. *Policing Post-Communist Societies: Police-Public Violence, Democratic Policing and Human Rights.* Antwerp: Intersentia, 2003.

Ukraine Reform Monitor Team. "Ukraine Reform Monitor: August 2015." *Carnegie Endowment for International Peace.* August 19, 2015. http://cargnegieendowment.org/2015/08/19/ukraine-reform-monitor-august-2015/.

Uzarashvili, Omar. "Ukrainska militsiia nakazala dovho zhyty. . . ." *Vysokyi zamok.* November 6, 2015. http://wz.lviv.ua/ukraine/147557-ukrainska-militsiia-nakazala-dovho-zhyty.

Wiatrowski, Michael D., and Jack A. Goldstone. "The Ballot and the Badge: Democratic Policing." *Journal of Democracy* 21, no. 2 (2010): 79–92.

Zakharov, Ievhen. "MVS ievropeiskoho gatunku: stratehiia reformatorskykh zmin." *Ukrainska pravda.* December 18, 2014. http://www.pravda.com.ua/columns/2014/12/15/7052035/.

"Zakon pro politsiiu—Opublikovanyi zakon pro natsionalnu politsiiu." *Dzerkalo tyzhnia.* August 6, 2015. http://dt.ua/POLITICS/opublikovano-zakon-pro-nacionalnu-policiyu-180883_.html.

"Zhuladze: reforma DAI vzhe rozpochalas." *BBC Ukraina.* January 15, 2015. http://www.bbc.co.uk/ukrainian/politics/2015/01/150119.

"Zhuladze zadovolena robotoiu novykh patrulnykh." *Den.* July 6, 2015. http://www.day.kiev.ua/uk/print/486117.

"Z pochatku roku zvilneno 47 tysiach pravookhorontsiv—Avakov." *UNIAN.* December 8, 2015. http://www.unian.ua/society/1206278-z-pochatku-roku-zvilneno-47-tisyach-pravoohorontsiv-avakov.html.

# Epilogue

Olga Bertelsen

There have been numerous attempts to decipher the conflict between Russia and Ukraine, as well as to understand the goals of Russia's foreign policies and Russian politicians' efforts at making their state great again.[1] The authors of this anthology view the conflict between Russia and Ukraine as a conflict of different collective identities and cultural realignment in both countries under internal and external pressures. Various interpretations of cultural, linguistic, political and social differences between Russians and Ukrainians confuse many, which often obscures people's deep understanding of today's on-going war between Russia and Ukraine. Russian historiography has traditionally placed an emphasis on

---

[1] Jeffrey Mankoff, *Russian Foreign Policy: The Return of Great Power Politics*, 2nd ed. (New York: Rowman & Littlefield Publishers, 2011); Andrew C. Kuchins and Igor A. Zevelev, "Russian Foreign Policy: Continuity in Change," *The Washington Quarterly* 35, no.1 (2012): 147–61; Timothy Snyder, "Fascism, Russia, and Ukraine," *The New York Review of Books*, March 20, 2014, http://www.nybooks.com/articles/archives/2014/mar/20/fascism-russia-and-ukraine/; Lubomyr Y. Luciuk, ed., *Jews, Ukrainians, and the Euromaidan* (Kashtan Press, 2014); Klaus Bachmann and Igor Lyubashenko, eds., *The Maidan Uprising, Separatism and Foreign Intervention: Ukraine's Complex Transition* (New York: Peter Lang, 2014); Peter Pomerantsev and Michael Weiss, *The Menace of Unreality: How the Kremlin Weaponizes Information, Culture and Money* (New York: The Interpreter; the Institute of Modern Russia, Inc., 2014); Andrew Wilson, *Ukrainian Crisis: What it Means to the West* (New Haven and London: Yale University Press, 2014); Alexander J. Motyl, "The Surrealism of Realism: Misreading the War in Ukraine," *World Affairs*, January/February 2015, http://www.worldaffairsjournal.org/article/surrealism-realism-misreading-war-ukraine; Serhy Yekelchyk, *The Conflict in Ukraine: What Everyone Needs to Know* (Oxford: Oxford Press, 2015); Rajan Menon and Eugene Rumer, *Conflict in Ukraine: The Unwinding of the Post-Cold War Order* (London, England, and Cambridge, Massachusetts: The MIT Press, 2015); Mikhail A. Molchanov, *Eurasian Regionalisms and Russian Foreign Policy*, in the International Political Economy of New Regionalisms series (London and New York: Routledge, 2015); Kimberly Marten, "Putin's Choices: Explaining Russian Foreign Policy and Intervention in Ukraine," *The Washington Quarterly* 38, no. 2 (2015): 189–204; Alexander Sergunin, *Explaining Russian Foreign Policy Behavior: Theory and Practice*, in the Soviet and Post-Soviet Politics and Society Series (Stuttgart: ibidem-Verlag, 2016).

the Russian nation: non-Russians' cultures and histories have been examined as "part of Russian regional history," and the histories of the nations, such as Ukrainians and Belarussians, have commonly been explained by a "desire for reunion" with the Russians.[2] The official Soviet interpretation deliberately minimized the differences between Russians and non-Russians and suppressed knowledge about the conflicts between them, simultaneously pretending to promote national histories and cultures.[3] Gorbachev's perestroika allowed Russians and "national minorities" to rediscover their pre-Bolshevik histories and cultures in their search for self-identification and to inform the world community about their national historical narratives. Yet the Soviet identity stereotypes mesmerized the consciousness of people around the world. Those stereotypes remain strong, continuing to shape understandings of new conflicts emerging in post-Soviet space. The task of this volume has been challenging—to analyze and explain changing identities on the collective level, transformations that occur during revolutions and wars at the most dramatic pace.[4] They can be frightening and encouraging, as well as the words and terms describing them. The conflict between Russia and Ukraine is largely an issue of different identities, and words had to be found to explain these differences and the war to which they led.

Identity and cultural realignment seem to be the underlying themes of each essay included in this collection. These issues are paramount to Ukraine's and Russia's politics and their social and cultural life. One scholar has identified the recent events in these two post-Soviet states as "the same old love-hate story": having stopped courting a woman and ultimately being rejected, her lover became violent and attempted to kill her. Regardless of such metaphors, this anthology certainly illuminates the violence in eastern Europe, unravelling before everyone's eyes, which opens a new era of uncertainties "in a continuous historic process of conflict between backwardness and development, between hopes for

---

2 Stephen Velychenko, *Shaping Identity in Eastern Europe and Russia: Soviet-Russian and Polish Accounts of Ukrainian History, 1914–1991* (New York: St. Martin's Press, 1993), 213.
3 Ibid.
4 For an assessment of wars, revolutions, and social engineering projects and their impact on Ukraine in the first half of the twentieth century, see George O. Liber, *Total Wars and the Making of Modern Ukraine, 1914–1954* (Toronto: University of Toronto Press, 2016).

change and given limitations, between autarky and opening to the outside world, between Europeanist claims and feelings of exclusion, between modern and post-modern."⁵ In a very general way, this epilogue attempts to trace identity changes in both Russia and Ukraine, rather than to summarize the findings of each essay. An analysis of these changes allows us to observe the emergence of new ideologies which define current foreign policies in Russia and Ukraine and shape the foundations for their future developments. This analysis reveals that these two states are developing in opposite directions, a phenomenon that hinders the processes of nation and state building in both countries. Moreover, the aesthetics of politics in modern Ukraine and Russia make the chasm between them unbridgeable, which inevitably distresses the global community and its security. Brief reflections on the nature and recent profound changes in Russian and Ukrainian identities will clarify this point.

## Russian Identity and Russia's Cultural Realignment under Putin

Intellectual efforts at understanding and explaining differences between various cultures and nations, including Russian and Ukrainian, are legion. For instance, in the early twentieth century, the famous Russian thinker, proletarian writer, and the founder of socialist realism Maksim Gorky (Peshkov) suggested that the dramatic differences between Russian and Ukrainian cultures, ethnopsychology, and mentality were largely environmental. He described the specificity of the landscapes and environments which, in Gorky's view, cultivated violence in "Moscovites," and harmony and freedom in Ukrainians. Gorky also extrapolated this idea to politics, claiming that a "Moscovite and a Ukrainian, having entirely different (even opposite) psyches and entirely different worldviews, naturally cannot have similar social systems."⁶ He argued that the worst feature of the Moscovite national character—violence—is diabolically and aesthetically sophisticated. "Here [he wrote], I mean mass psychology, people's soul, and collective violence."⁷ A century later, the Russian writer Viktor Ierofeev

---

5   Stefano Bianchini, *Eastern Europe and the Challenges of Modernity, 1800–2000*, trans. Carolyn Kadas (London and New York: Routledge, 2015), 204.
6   On the Russian people's violence, see Maksim Gorky, *O russkom krestianstve* (Berlin: Izd-vo I. P. Ladyzhnikova, 1922); quoted in Serhii Zhyzhko, *Natsiia iak spilnota* (Kyiv: Dnipro, 2008), 272.
7   Gorky, *O russkom krestianstve*; quoted in Zhyzhko, 270.

emphatically confirmed Gorky's thesis, deconstructing the notion of the "Russian soul."[8] The most critical readers might disagree with both Gorky's and Ierofeev's revelations but one element of Gorky's thinking seems to be profoundly prescient—the difference and irreconcilability of social systems in Ukraine and Russia. The roots of this difference rest in history, language, and culture, as the authors of this anthology argue, and these foundations account for a certain type of individual and collective identity which ultimately defines the type of social system.

Historically, relations between Russia and Ukraine shaped their people's identities: Russians continued to view Ukrainians in "traditionally narrow terms" as little brothers,[9] and Ukrainians' perceptions were shaped by Russia's oppressive imperial policies, cultivating an inferiority complex in them. Russia's imperial discriminatory language and institutional policies impeded the formation of the Ukrainian nation and identity. In her essay, Laada Bilaniuk has exposed the legacies of these policies—language wars between bilingualism and monolingualism, Ukrainian and Russian languages, which became a crucial element of Ukraine's and Russia's contemporary politics. Clearly, Ukraine suffers from colonial and imperial baggage. However, there are also, "domestic" problems that exacerbate the language problem in Ukraine and, as a result, inhibit the formation of a national identity. The inferiority complex, together with its opposite, intellectual arrogance, often contribute to popular resistance to monolingualism and complicate the process of consolidation of the Ukrainian nation. The Ukrainian scholar and writer Ivan Dziuba, for instance, believes that the linguistic "dictatorship" and personal ambitions of Ukrainian intellectuals obscure and to some degree prevent the natural development of the Ukrainian language and its maturity. He writes:

> I have a feeling that throughout their entire history Ukrainians fight with their own language—some fight with dialects (*dialektyzmy*), archaisms, neologisms; others—with russisms, polonisms, germanisms, old Slavonic-isms, in other words, with the very essence of the Ukrainian language, with its ability to assimilate all this, digest it and make it its own wealth, as the Russian language did, and more so English which is a great mixture, and has become the greatest world language, with the richest vocabulary . . . [e]ven the most prominent writer

---

8   Viktor Ierofeev, *Entsiklopediia russkoi dushi* (Sankt-Peterburg: Azbuka, 2010).
9   Roman Szporluk, *Russia, Ukraine, and the Breakup of the Soviet Union* (Stanford, CA: Hoover Institution Press, 2000), 356–57.

should not treat the language according to his or her own linguistic or aesthetical perception."[10]

Yet post-Soviet Russia's manipulation of the language issue seems to play a central role in Ukraine's indecisiveness and linguistic confusion. Interestingly enough, Russia's language wars also strengthen Ukrainian national identity, as they did in the late nineteenth and early twentieth centuries. Indeed, the policies of russification expanded the geography and the ethnographic borders of the Ukrainian language, in turn sharpening a sense of Ukrainian national identity within two empires, Russian and Austrian. Imperial practices of forbiddance and subversion led to the opposite effect of what was expected—more and more educated Ukrainians gravitated to the space of Ukrainian and "European" culture, a tendency that became especially pronounced in the early twentieth century.[11]

In contrast, the Russian language has never been threatened by extinction. Russian language, identity, and culture developed on the template of conquest and expansion. Construction of a collective historical memory through the narrative of a constant threat from outside and the necessity to fight external enemies accompanied the expansion. This narrative was shaped and reinforced by Russian history itself, "which still directs people to search for enemies and to make war against 'hostile forces.'"[12] Ideology, politics, and the personal ambitions of Russian rulers have always been pivotal to both expansion and its rationale.

The construct of "enemy" has been revived by the Putin regime, and anti-Western, anti-American, anti-European, and ultimately anti-Ukrainian sentiments became a quite typical filter for any discussions among the Russian intellectual and political elites. The intelligentsia appear to be especially susceptible to this appeal. It would be difficult to identify a great Russian writer who would not suffer from imperial consciousness and xenophobia, from Aleksandr Pushkin to Iosif Brodsky,

---

10  Quoted in Taras Salyha, "O natsie moia, rozderta i rozbyta (Nablyzhennia do portreta Ivana Dziuby)," *Literaturna Ukraina*, May 5, 2016, p. 11.
11  Valentyna Shandra, "Mova iak zasib formuvannia natsionalnoi identychnosti," in *Ukrainska identychnist i movne pytannia v Rosiiskii imperii: sproba derzhavnoho reguliuvannia*, ed. Hennadii Boriak (Kyiv: Klio, 2015), xxxvii.
12  R. R. Garagozov, "Collective Memory and the Russian 'Schematic Narrative Template,'" *Journal of Russian and East European Psychology* 40, no. 5 (2002): 86–87.

with the exception of Ivan Turgenev and a few others.[13] It also seems symptomatic that the prominent Russian intellectual and film director Andrei Konchalovskii, who was chastised for being a "Westerner" during Soviet times, today opposes "the civilizational pressures" of the West. He holds that the values of democracy, freedom, and equal rights, everything that the United States, the leader of world democracy, stands for, should not be applied universally. According to Konchalovskii, the period of absolute and unshakeable values of Western civilization "is coming to an end." He agrees with Gorky that the Russian culture was shaped by geography, climate, and history, but he is convinced that Russia developed on the periphery of Europe and the divide between Russia and Poland is philosophical, rather than ideological: there is a watershed between "Eastern philosophy—emotional; and Western philosophy—infatuation with order."[14] This cultural realignment among the Russian intellectual elites is in tune with the thesis formulated by Putin who managed to co-opt even the most vocal critics of Russia's cultural and political course. Igor Torbakov's essay has illustrated that the "Europeanization" of Russia under Putin seems to have ended, and the conflict in Ukraine serves as a reflection of this cultural realignment. Importantly, this realignment and Russia's persistent claims that Ukraine is a "non-existent" nation legitimize military solutions in Ukraine, and ultimately preclude "the development of a modern Russian national identity" by repressing Ukrainian national identity.[15]

As the studies in this anthology have demonstrated, Russia has returned to the rhetoric of "excessive patriotism" it exhibited during WWII, and gravitates toward isolationism characteristic of the post-war period. Isaiah Berlin has accurately grasped the essence of the same trends in

---

13 Isaiah Berlin, *The Soviet Mind: Russian Culture under Communism*, ed. Henry Hardy (Washington, D.C.: Brookings Institution Press, 2004), 90; Ewa M. Thompson, *Trubadury imperii: Rosiiska literatura i colonialism*, 2nd ed., trans. Mariia Korchynska (Kyiv: Vydavnytstvo Solomii Pavlychko "Osnovy," 2008); Myroslav Shkandrij, *Russia and Ukraine: Literature and the Discourse of Empire from Napoleonic to Postcolonial Times* (Montreal & Kingston: McGill-Queen's University Press, 2001); Olga Bertelsen, "Joseph Brodsky's Imperial Consciousness," *Scripta Historica*, no. 21 (2015): 263–89.
14 Bridget Kendall, "Cultural Struggle to Define Russia's Identity," *BBC News*, March 18, 2015, http://www.bbc.com/news/world-europe-31584221.
15 See the interview of Mykola Riabchuk by Alexander J. Motyl in "Ukrainian Identity After the Euromaidan," *World Affairs*, March 29, 2016, http://www.worldaffairsjournal.org/blog/alexander-j-motyl/ukrainian-identity-after-euromaiden.

Russia in the 1940s and 1950s, although he preferred the term "insulation" instead of "isolation." This meant Russia's strategy of insulation from the international community "without remaining isolated from it:" Russian nationalism encroached into the spaces of other nationalisms, disturbing them intellectually and militarily.[16] Russia's intrinsic mistrust of the West, which is so profound today, exacerbates the problem of Russia's effective integration into the community of equal states, further complicating Russian identity: by not being a part of Europe for long and by not blending into European nationhood, the inferiority complex seems to be severe and to be entering an acute stage in Russia under Putin. Western sanctions dramatically worsened the economic situation in the Russian Federation, which amplified the Russians' feeling of belonging to a "lesser" nation and perpetuated their mistrust toward the West and their traditional xenophobia. Moreover, these perceptions have been recently institutionalized through a variety of laws in Russia. The Extremism Law stands out among other laws issued under Putin: it is being applied arbitrarily, criminalizing the works of "other" cultures on the basis of a vague definition of extremism.[17] In the virtual absence of public debates, the authoritarian monopolization of the "mistrust" discourse by Putin and the Russian political elites further escalates the mistrust hysteria and promotes excessive nationalism, which essentially shapes the attitudes of the Russian intelligentsia and finds mass support.[18]

This collection of essays accentuates a clear link between Russian foreign policy, Russia's cultural realignment, and Russian national identity. The pragmatism of Putin's regime and Russia's current political behavior suggest that this link is not only a theoretical concept but also a blueprint for future expansion and talking points that would support and

---

16   Berlin, *The Soviet Mind*, 12–13, 90.
17   Olga Bertelsen, "A Trial *in Absentia*: Purifying National Historical Narratives in Russia," *Kyiv-Mohyla Humanities Journal,* no. 3 (2016): 57–87.
18   These trends are characteristic of fascist political systems, and a number of recent studies have drawn persuasive parallels between a fascist political system and that of the Russian Federation. See, for instance, Alexander J. Motyl, "Putin's Russia as a Fascist Political System," *Communist and Post-Communist Studies* 49, no. 1 (2016): 25–36. Motyl argues that four features are the key components of the fascist system of governing: full authoritarianism, mass support, a personality cult, and an active, personalistic leadership style, features that can be applied to Putin's Russia (p. 25).

justify it.[19] Recent studies have demonstrated that, although the idea of Russia as expansionist is not fully embraced on a popular level, the new Russian generation tends to welcome "Eurasianist foreign policy" and gravitates toward "more active cooperation or even deeper integration within the post-Soviet space."[20] It is of course difficult to assess to what degree the myth of the "Third Rome" that has recently been vocalized and popularized by Russian officials penetrated the Russians' consciousness. This volume invites readers to consider the Russian political elites' world in which the possession of the Turkish Straits and Constantinople, for instance, would serve multiple purposes—military, strategic, ideological, geopolitical, and "private." Russian national security is "not a question of frontier security," although it is important.[21] It seems to be a question of Putin's vision of respect to him personally as a strong Russian leader and the acceptance of the basic principles of the Russian military and political system, a respect that, in Russia's view, should be granted to Russia by the West. The military "drills" in Abkhazia, Georgia, Ukraine and other states in Russia's "near abroad," among other things, are reminders and signals to the West about Russia's expectations: the Russian system and general rules of the game have to be appreciated and accepted. Russia's ego is as enormous as its mistrust of the West, which returns the Russian state to the idea of a competition in an "imaginary race against time and in a ring of jealous enemies."[22] In this situation, the conflict between Russia and Ukraine is not only about territories, values, civil liberties, and

---

19   For a discussion about the concept of great power, a key element in Russian identity construction, see Iver Neumann, "Russia as a Great Power," in *Russia as a Great Power. Dimensions of Security under Putin*, eds. Jakob Hedenskog, Vilhelm Konnander, Bertil Nygren, Ingmar Oldberg, and Christer Pursiainen (Abington: Routledge, 2005), 24–41; Anne L. Clunan, *Social Construction of Russia's Resurgence: Aspirations, Identity, and Security Interests* (Baltimore, MD: Johns Hopkins University Press, 2009); Iver B. Neumann, "Russia in International Society Over the Longue Durée. Lessons from Early Rus' and Early post-Soviet State Formation," in *Russia's Identity in International Relations. Images, Perceptions, Misperceptions*, ed. Ray Taras (Abington: Routledge, 2013), 24–41.
20   Sirke Mäkinen, "Russia—a Leading or Fading Power? Students' Geopolitical Metanarratives on Russia's Role in the Post-Soviet Space," *Nationalities Papers* 44, no. 1 (2016): 92–113.
21   Berlin, *The Soviet Mind*, 92.
22   Berlin, *The Soviet Mind*, 93.

differences of social systems. For Russia, Ukraine has become a negotiating point with the West.

In these negotiations, Russian cultural realignment and identity is presented as intrinsically historical and thus legitimate, while Ukrainian identity allegedly lacks a historical foundation, mutating and degrading to a fascist one, and therefore it is not only illegitimate but also dangerous. It appears to be strategically easy to label Ukrainian nationalist movements as fascist and to blur the distinctions among patriotism, nationalism, and fascism. Russian propaganda plays a crucial role in denigrating Ukraine's efforts at nation and state building, as the essays by Peter Tanchak, Myroslav Shkandrij, and Igor Torbakov have shown. Words matter, but the matter is that words themselves mean next to nothing unless a person makes use of them, and even then they might be confusing. Interestingly, in 2008, at the peak of Russia's "anti-Orange" campaign when the Russian political elites claimed that nationalist and fascist tendencies had been rejuvenated in Ukraine, Serhii Zhyzhko, whose publications were criminalized in the Russian Federation as extremist materials, emphasized that, Ukraine in fact lacked nationalism, which resulted in its vacillation and indecisiveness: "Ukraine needs national identity, national consciousness, and national behavior so that the history of the twentieth century would not be repeated." [23] The Euromaidan and the Russian-Ukrainian war awakened Ukraine, producing a cultural change and creating a new civic identity which seems to be more stable and overarching than at the dawning of independent Ukraine in 1991.

Russian propaganda, however, continues to play a significant role in shaping public opinion and affecting Western scholarship marked by Russo-centric and pro-Putin biases. Words and notions often migrate unchanged from the Russian mass media to scholarly works, and the difference between Russian and Ukrainian interpretations of the war in Ukraine is routinely left out of the narrative, or simply ignored.[24] Under these circumstances, the meanings of the same words differ, depending on the interlocutor's interpretation and goals. Almost a century ago, the

---

23 Zhyzhko, 15.
24 Those who consider themselves Russia's experts and whose knowledge of Ukraine's history and culture is limited seem to be especially susceptible to Russian propaganda. See, for instance, Richard Sakwa, *Frontline Ukraine. Crisis in the Borderlands* (London: I. B. Tauris, 2015).

English linguist and philosopher Charles Koy Ogden and the literary critic and rhetorician Ivor Armstrong Richards noted that "the disputants are using the same words for different things, sometimes different words for the same things."[25] As a result, the truth and reality become obscured and non-transparent.

Indeed, our language shapes our way of thinking and the way we think generates a certain vocabulary. Words help enlighten people or confuse them. Identity and language are two inseparable elements, where ideology shapes both, inciting some to advance intellectually and to avoid ideological trappings, and provoking others to succumb to a certain ideology for various reasons. One scholar once stated that ideology became a "war of words. Through it, citizens had a stark choice: they could either find their 'true' political voice or be silenced."[26] Observing propaganda wars and a war of narratives in Russia and Ukraine, one might notice that this is truer now than ever before. This war accentuated the natural symbolism of words and people's deliberate use of words to misdirect those who listen. A word game intensified, and words became a "normal part of the mechanism of deceit."[27] Effective and powerful, the deceit of propaganda, however, has its cost like any other weapon employed in a war.[28] Meanings and symbols escape from people's control. The political lexicon becomes extremely selective, and the intention to offend becomes habitual, a phenomenon that tends to escalate the conflict. As many scholars, including Tanchak, have noticed, Russian propagandists outperformed their Ukrainian counterparts. The deputy of the Crimean Parliament Valerii Aksionov has recently suggested that along the Ukrainian border Crimea should install TV towers to broadcast Russian programs to Ukrainians who are subject to Ukrainian propaganda and "are oblivious" to the achievements of the peninsula.[29]

---

25 C. K. Ogden and I. A. Richards, *The Meaning of Meaning: A Study of The Influence of Language upon Thought and of The Science of Symbolism*, 3rd ed. (New York: Harcourt, Brace and Company, 1930), viii.
26 Michael Freeden, *Ideology: A Very Short Introduction* (New York: Oxford University Press, 2003), 92.
27 Ogden and Richards, 17.
28 Montaigue (*Disenchantment*, p. 101), quoted in Ogden and Richards, 18.
29 "Krymskyi separatyst proponuie zbuduvaty televyshku dlia transliatsii v Ukrainu brekhlyvoho rosiiskoho TB," *Ekspres Online*, June 6, 2016, http://expres.ua/news/2016/06/10/189420-krymskyy-separatyst-proponuye-zbuduvaty-televyshku-tran slyaciyi-ukrayinu.

Russian propaganda seems to be more aggressive than Ukrainian by far, and its techniques are more sophisticated as a result of the intense Soviet training that the KGB called ideological subversion. These techniques were designed at the dawn of the Cold War and meant to change individual and collective identity to subvert a nation.

Yet practices of ideological subversion in Ukraine, combined with state violence, began much earlier, immediately after the 1917 revolution. They led to a lack of Ukrainian national identity, which became one of the most salient factors contributing greatly to political instability and sluggish democratic changes in post-Soviet Ukraine.

## Ideological Subversion, Ukrainian Identity, and Its Reconceptualization

Ukraine is an ethnically diverse country due to complex historical and geographic reasons. Among the "titular" group of Ukrainians and other ethnic groups, Russians and Jews have been prominent in their numbers and influence in the political and cultural makeup of the country. In addition, for centuries various regions of Ukraine were part of imperial and colonial projects: under Poles, Russians, and the Soviets, Ukrainian culture in general and the Ukrainian language in particular were systematically suppressed by the authorities to prevent the formation of a Ukrainian ethnic and national identity. These two interdependent factors, ethnic diversity and the "under-development" of people's national consciousness in Ukraine, continued to play a significant role in Ukraine's post-Soviet development.

The processes of imperial expansion and domination, which help explain people's protracted search for identity in Ukraine, were far from peaceful: various ethnic groups in Ukraine were persecuted and prosecuted for their ethnic/cultural/national consciousness, and a large portion of them were physically exterminated by the Soviets from 1917 to 1991. In a cluster of Soviet autogenocides against national minorities in the Soviet Union, Moscow allotted a special place for defiant Ukrainians who resided in one of the largest and most significant Soviet republics.

As a result, cultural disruption of colossal proportions occurred in Ukraine after millions of Ukrainian peasants and thousands of the intelligentsia were eliminated by Stalin in the late 1920s and 1930s.³⁰ During the subsequent decades until the very end of the USSR, the Soviet government waged a war on Ukrainian national consciousness and culture. The period of late socialism claimed the lives of Ukrainians whose "ferment" of resistance had to be eradicated. They were intimidated, imprisoned, exiled, tortured by psychiatric terror, and murdered.³¹ Even shortly before 1991, the Soviet regime continued to isolate Ukrainian intellectuals from the rest of the society, and those who exhibited the signs of "morbid" Ukrainian nationalism and disobedience. In this context, the formation of an ethnic or national identity became increasingly problematic which precipitated the labyrinthine path of nation and state building in independent Ukraine.

Paradoxically, the brutality of Stalin's Soviet regime and political, ideological, and cultural subversion amplified the Ukrainians' aspirations to create an independent state. In some dormant form, the "ferment" of resistance was preserved: a new generation of intellectuals in the 1960s formed a cultural movement called the sixtiers' movement (*shistdesiatnytstvo*).³² Some scholars have argued that there was no continuity between the sixtiers and those who struggled for Ukraine's independence in 1918 and thereafter. Stalin effectively managed to excoriate national identity and Ukrainian nationalism in Ukraine, and raised an obedient generation of Soviet citizens. In their view, the sixtiers emerged as a non-political group, and were essentially a product of the Soviet system.³³ In many ways, they were. However, many sixtiers were children of those who were members of the nationalist organizations OUN and UPA, and some

---

30  Olga Bertelsen and Myroslav Shkandrij, "The Secret Police and the Campaign against Galicians in Soviet Ukraine, 1929–34," *Nationalities Papers: The Journal of Nationalism and Ethnicity* 42, no. 1 (2014): 37–62; Myroslav Shkandrij and Olga Bertelsen, "The Soviet Regime's National Operations in Ukraine, 1929–1934," *Canadian Slavonic Papers* LV, nos. 3–4 (2013).
31  Olga Bertelsen, "Rethinking Psychiatric Terror against Nationalists in Ukraine," *Kyiv-Mohyla Arts and Humanities*, no. 1 (2014): 27–76.
32  *Shistdesiatnytstvo* was a cultural movement of Soviet Ukrainian dissidents in the 1960s, which manifested itself in their creative art. Despite its cultural objectives, this movement also had a political vector. Ukrainian intellectuals fought against the Soviet system for human rights, freedom of self-expression, and the development of Ukrainian culture.
33  See, for instance, Yekelchyk, *The Conflict in Ukraine*, 58.

were themselves members of the UPA.³⁴ Leaving aside a controversy about the OUN and UPA, these men and women kept the Ukrainian national and cultural traditions alive, as well as the belief in Ukraine's independence. They inspired the creation of several dissident groups in Ukraine but in the 1960s and the 1970s, the organized dissident movement in Ukraine was crushed by the KGB.³⁵ The Ukrainian society was effectively pacified and submerged until 1986.

The nuclear disaster in Chernobyl near Kyiv that struck the world a few years before the USSR disintegrated united the Ukrainians to some degree. Tragically, this unification was provoked by human deaths caused by omnipresent radiation and the ecological catastrophe in Ukraine. Mikhail Gorbachev's perestroika and glasnost and its premise and promise to create a more open society, free of censorship and subversion, failed badly. The state's attempts to erase the tragedy at the expense of people's health and lives quickly elevated Chernobyl to a political issue. The emergence of the ecological movement and political activism in Ukraine began to exhibit the signs of a national awakening. In 1988 Ukrainian activists founded the first Ukrainian mass civic organization Green World (*Zelenyi svit*), which played a leading role in investigating the events at the Chernobyl Nuclear Power Plant. This organization became a symbol of a nascent civil society in Ukraine. For the first time in recent memory, the Ukrainians united, openly blaming the center and the Communist system for its exploitative and colonizing patterns of governing.³⁶ Catherine Wanner has suggested that "Chernobyl generated more anti-Soviet, pro-independence sentiment among the Ukrainian population than could ever have been dreamed of by the small group of Ukrainian nationalist intelligentsia struggling to create a ground swell of

---

34   The most prominent nationalist organizations that were active after WWII were the OUN (the Organization of Ukrainian Nationalists) and the UPA (the Ukrainian Insurgent Army). The Ukrainian poet-*shistdesiatnyk* Dmytro Pavlychko serves as an example, as in his youth he was a member of the UPA.

35   In the 1960s and the 1970s, the KGB designed a special secret operation entitled "Blok" and by the early 1980s the secret police crushed the organized dissident movement in Ukraine. For more details about operation "Blok," see Volodymyr Viatrovych, "Operatsiia 'Blok.' Diia persha," in *Istoriia z hryfom "Sekretno": Taiemnytsi ukrainskoho mynuloho z arkhiviv KGB* by Volodymyr Viatrovych (Lviv, Kyiv: Nash Format, 2011), 204–12.

36   Yekelchyk, *The Conflict in Ukraine*, 60–61.

support for independence."[37] One might argue that Chernobyl galvanized the Ukrainians' latent frustration with the Soviet state for the two other major crises in Soviet Ukrainian history—at least four million deaths during the Holodomor of 1932–1933 and nearly six million deaths during WWII in Ukraine, casualties that put the Ukrainian nation and culture on the brink of anthropological collapse. Undoubtedly, Chernobyl became a building block in the uneasy construction of a nation and a state that began in 1991.

The identity problem, however, persisted in Ukraine, becoming evident in Ukraine's domestic and foreign policies. As some scholars have pointed out, state building and nation building are two complex processes that go hand in hand, and influence the broader political and social situation in a country.[38] In the case of Ukraine, from the moment it gained independence in 1991, it has been in a "perennial political crisis" that might be partially explained by Ukraine's geography and ethnic and cultural diversity. Ukraine was sandwiched between Russia and Europe and seemed to be undecided about where it belonged culturally—in the West or in Russia.[39] This identity problem significantly impeded Ukraine's nation and state building, which found its reflection in often chaotic Ukrainian politics.[40]

Nation building suffered the most. From the habits developed during imperial and Soviet dominance, the Ukrainians continued to rely on the state which itself was in an embryonic form and in total disarray. Cultural construction, self-destruction, and reconstruction in Ukraine were

---

37   Catherine Wanner, *Burden of Dreams: History and Identity in Post-Soviet Ukraine* (University Park, PA: The Pennsylvania University Press, 1998), 31.
38   Juan J. Linz, "State Building and Nation-Building," *European Review* 1, no. 4 (1993): 356; Paul D'Anieri, Robert Kravchuk, and Taras Kuzio, "Nation Building and National Identity," in *Politics and Society in Ukraine* (Boulder, Colorado: Westview Press, 1999), 49.
39   Giulia Lami, "Ukraine's Road to Europe: Still a Controversial Issue," in *Contemporary Ukraine on the Cultural Map of Europe*, eds. Larissa M. L. Zaleska Onyshkevych and Maria G. Rewakowicz (London, England: M. E. Sharpe, 2009), 29–39.
40   Taras Kuzio has emphasized a close connection among national identity, political culture, and foreign policies. See Taras Kuzio, "European, Eastern Slavic, and Eurasian: National Identity, Transformation, and Ukrainian Foreign Policy," in *Ukrainian Foreign and Security Policy: Theoretical and Comparative Perspectives*, eds. Jennifer D. P. Moroney, Taras Kuzio and Mikhail Molchanov (Westport, Connecticut: Praeger, 2002), 197–225.

deeply Soviet, marked by Stalinism, territorial annexations, displacements, mass killings, and an enormous loss of cultural artifacts. These legacies cultivated chronic political passivity and indifference. The first Ukrainian president Leonid Kravchuk understood that the swift mobilization of Ukrainian society to build a new nation was going to be a gradual process, by far slower than state and institution building.[41] As a former Soviet propagandist, he also understood that the absence of a single history in Ukraine exacerbated the identity problem. Western Ukraine was annexed only in 1939–1940 by the Soviets, unlike other parts of Ukraine that became Soviet in 1919. Thus, a more developed sense of Ukrainian national identity in western Ukraine, which has been documented by many scholars, was in sharp contrast with that of Ukrainians in the East and in the South of Ukraine. Although the ethnic and linguistic lines between various regions in Ukraine have always been vague and fluid,[42] the differences in their histories and cultural traditions (language, art, literature and religion) were significant and shaped very distinct types of cultural identities and political affinities. The distorted national historical narrative and disrupted identity haunted the Ukrainians in their struggle to rejuvenate their traditions, the core of social cohesiveness and civilized political culture. Kravchuk tried to reconcile the histories of the less Sovietized West, the more Sovietized East, and the extremely Sovietized Donbas by limiting Russian influences on Ukraine. The situation was to some extent illogical: instead of the nation that was supposed to build a state, the state attempted to build the nation.[43] Not surprisingly, Kravchuk's presidency did not generate a consensus among Ukrainian nationalists and those Ukrainians who gravitated toward Russia.

Interestingly enough, the first and the second presidents of independent Ukraine, Leonid Kravchuk and Leonid Kuchma, were themselves the embodiments of polar identities. To simplify the matter, the former was pro-Ukrainian, and the latter was pro-Russian. Kravchuk

---

41  For a discussion about nation and state building in Ukraine, see D'Anieri, Kravchuk, and Kuzio, 50.
42  Graham Smith, Vivien Law, Andrew Wilson, Annette Bohr, and Edward Allworth, "Redefining Ethnic and Linguistic Boundaries in Ukraine: Indigenes, Settlers and Russophone Ukrainians," in *Nation-Building in the Post-Soviet Borderlands: The Politics of National Identities* (Cambridge, UK: Cambridge University Press, 1998), 119–38.
43  D'Anieri, Kravchuk, and Kuzio, 57–64.

attempted to isolate Ukraine from Russia which was portrayed as a security threat to Ukraine. Ukraine was depicted as a "buffer" and "'the front' line of Western civilization," while Russia was characterized as an "Asian" state.[44] No wonder that Kravchuk's stance alienated the East and the South. Kuchma, on the contrary, encouraged cooperation with Russia in all spheres—economic, cultural and social. He attracted the constituency of the East and of the South by placing a special emphasis on tackling the economic crisis through economic cooperation with Russia.[45] Russia was no longer portrayed as a threat, and Kuchma's rhetoric transformed Ukraine from a "buffer" to a "bridge" between Russia and Europe, which, of course, alienated western Ukraine and Kyiv.

Although Kravchuk's and Kuchma's approaches differed, they both proclaimed Ukraine's desire to return to Europe, and they both believed in a unitary state, despite the tensions between central and local governments. In their view, federalism would endanger Ukraine's territorial integrity. In addition, both realized that the identity problem in Ukraine seriously jeopardized the processes of nation and state building.

Indeed, the attributes that characterize a nation-state were nonexistent in Ukraine: the Ukrainian borders were contested; state institutions were yet to be created; and the Ukrainian language's role in the education system was minimal. Under pressure of russification policies Ukrainian culture was a culture of a small group of intellectuals who miraculously survived the purges of Soviet times. Ukrainian history that rejected the ideology of Pan-Slavism and Russo-centric narratives had to be rewritten. Due to a socioeconomic crisis, Ukraine's economy had to be built from scratch. Finally, the rule of law had to be restored. Neither Kravchuk nor Kuchma managed to mobilize the nation and to make progress in post-communist transition. A decade after the USSR's

---

44   Kuzio, "European, Eastern Slavic, and Eurasian," 211.
45   Ilya Prizel has noted that initially Kuchma's positions polarized the Ukrainian society but nevertheless in 1994 he was elected in peaceful democratic elections. "Traditionally, Ukrainian political activism had centered on Kiev and western Ukraine, while left-bank Ukrainians remained politically dormant," Prizel wrote. Kuchma managed to consolidate the Left Bank of Ukraine by his multi-vectoral program, and the East and the South played a decisive role in his victory. See Ilya Prizel, "Foreign Policy as a Means of Nation Building," in *National Identity and Foreign Policy: Nationalism and Leadership in Poland, Russia and Ukraine* (Cambridge, UK: Cambridge University Press, 1998), 388–89.

disintegration, Ukraine was still struggling to become a strong state, and suffered from a severe identity crisis and institutional deficit.

After a decade of Ukrainian independence, it became clear that nation building constituted the greatest challenge in Ukraine. The majority in the South and in the East have never been exposed to the abuse of the Poles or the Russians, and their language (Russian) has never been threatened with extinction. They were indifferent to any nationalist message emanating from Kyiv. The Crimea in particular and especially the Donbas were the regions where Soviet identity was the strongest.[46] In fact, the Soviet regime left its profound imprint in these regions: people's identity seemed to be a "fusion of Soviet nostalgia with Russian cultural identity."[47]

As recent events have demonstrated, regionalism (or separatism) continued to play a significant role in Ukrainian politics, and especially in the process of nation building. During the Orange revolution of 2004 and the Euromaidan, the strong opposition to the democratic movement that was initiated in Kyiv grew in the regions, such as the Crimea, the Donbass, and Kharkiv. The local authorities demanded the status of the Russian population be upgraded from a minority to the second titular nationality, their role and representation in the central government be expanded, and that they even be granted autonomy. There is evidence to suggest that the role of the Kremlin and the Russian secret service in supporting the anti-Orange and anti-Maidan forces was quite prominent, a factor that contributed to the fragmentation of Ukrainian society.[48] Nevertheless,

---

46 Taras Kuzio, "Soviet Conspiracy Theories and Political Culture in Ukraine: Understanding Viktor Yanukovych and the Party of Regions," *Communist and Post-Communist Studies* 44, no. 3 (2011): 221–232.
47 Yekelchyk, *The Conflict in Ukraine*, 20.
48 Taras Kuzio, *Ukraine: Democratization, Corruption, and the New Russian Imperialism* (Santa Barbara, CA, and Denver, CO: Praeger, 2015), 471–75; Andrew Wilson, *Ukraine's Orange Revolution* (New Haven and London: Yale University Press, 2005), 100; Taras Kuzio, "Russia Takes Control of Ukraine's Security Forces," *Eurasia Daily Monitor*, March 19, 2012 (*9:55*), p. 7–9; Andrei Soldatov, "The True Role of the FSB in the Ukrainian Crisis," *The Moscow Times*, April 15, 2014, http://www.themoscowtimes.com/opinion/article/the-true-role-of-the-fsb-in-the-ukrainian-crisis/498072.html; "20 Russian FSB Agents Suspected of Euromaidan Revolution Crimes Identified," *Ukraine Today*, February 24, 2014, http://uatoday.tv/politics/20-russian-fsb-agents-suspected-of-euromaidan-revolution-crimes-identified-411552.html; "SBU: Putin's Adviser and FSB Officers Involved in Maidan Killings," *UNIAN*, April 15, 2015, http://www.unian.info/politics/1067376-sbu-putin

Russia's efforts would fail if its political technologists miscalculated the situation on the ground in these regions.

The third president of independent Ukraine Viktor Iushchenko was also unable to solve the problem of regionalism, turning a blind eye on the Russian secret services' activities in Crimea and eastern Ukraine. In 2007, on an archival research trip in Crimea, my husband and I who are both American citizens were offered Russian passports in the streets of Sudak. The procedure was simple and quick: a person sitting on a chair at a little table in the street, a place similar to an ice-cream stand, invited people to be included in the list of those who were willing to become Russian citizens. It was sufficient to place your signature on a certain page of the passport, and provide necessary information for the list. The collectors of signatures completed other blanks in the passport for you. Our written reports about pro-Russian forces' criminal activities in the peninsula, reports that we submitted in person in the representative offices of Iuliia Tymoshenko in Crimea and of Iushchenko in Kharkiv remained unaddressed. It became obvious to us that popular political passivity was encouraged from above. Those who inspired political activism in Ukrainian society four years earlier were largely indifferent and deaf to civil democratic initiatives and impulses.

This discovery was shocking not only for us but for the majority of Ukraine's citizens. Iushchenko who seemed to be extremely sensitive to the issue of Ukrainian national identity and whose efforts in making the Ukrainian nation rested in the sphere of history and culture became unreachable. Moreover, the unattractive conflict between Iushchenko and Tymoshenko, and the impossibility of reuniting the Orange coalition during his tenure diminished and discredited Iushchenko's efforts in consolidating the nation. More tragically, the conflict provided Kremlin of-

---

s-adviser-and-fsb-officers-involved-in-maidan-killings.html; Jammie Dettmer, "New Evidence: Russian Spies Backed Kiev's Killers," *The Daily Beast*, March 4, 2014, http://www.thedailybeast.com/articles/2014/04/03/ukraine-fingers-russian-advisors-and-ex-president-yanukovych-in-february-massacre.html; "Dmitry Tymchuk: FSB Presence in Ukraine on February 20–21," *Voices of Ukraine*, April 5, 2014, http://maidantranslations.com/2014/04/05/dmitry-tymchuk-fsb-presence-in-ukraine-on-february-20-21/; Dmitry Chekalkin, "How Russia Invaded Ukraine as Told by FSB Colonel Girkin," *Euromaidan Press*, December 7, 2014, http://euromaidanpress.com/2014/12/07/fsb-colonel-girkin-tells-details-of-how-russia-invaded-ukraine-in-twice-censored-interview/.

ficials with an opportunity to regroup after their failure to install Ianukovych's puppet regime in Kyiv and to more effectively interfere in Ukrainian politics.[49] Iushchenko was pressed to create an alliance with Ianukovych, which resulted in Iushchenko's complete surrender of democratic principles and the demands of the Orange revolution. A compromise was reached on three key issues that satisfied the pro-Russian constituency in Ukraine and the leadership in the Russian Federation: NATO membership, federalism, and the status of the Russian language. In 2006, Ukraine lost its opportunity to join NATO: instead of a NATO Membership Plan for Ukraine, the parties signed an agreement about Ukraine-NATO cooperation. Federalism became a possibility along with Russia's hope to establish pro-Russian protectorates in the localities. Finally, Russian language status gained a new opportunity for expansion in Ukraine.[50]

As mentioned earlier, the language issue has always been a tool of manipulation employed by pro-Russian leaning citizens and separatists in Ukraine, as well as by Russian officials who support them. The East and the South remain the most russified regions in Ukraine. Moreover, the majority in the Ukrainian government spoke and continue to speak Russian, including the current president Petro Poroshenko. The history of russification policies goes back to imperial Russia and Catherine the Great. Then in the early 1920s, the Soviets embarked on Ukrainizing Ukraine, a campaign designed to be on the same ideological page and to "speak Bolshevik" (Kotkin's term) with the local population by using the local language, but by the early thirties Ukrainization was curtailed and its supporters were imprisoned and executed. For seventy years Moscow methodically russified Ukraine, eliminating Ukrainian schools and constraining the development of Ukrainian culture. As a result, a wholesale Ukrainization policy in contemporary Ukraine became problematic. Indeed, the 1996 Constitution contains the all-inclusive formula that reflects the Ukrainians' linguistic and ethnic diversity: "we, the Ukrainian people—citizens of Ukraine of all nationalities."[51] The inclusiveness of language policies are also evident today, although the government's position is somewhat ambiguous about whether to limit or to expand the

---

49    Lami, 30.
50    Lami, 32
51    Smith, Law, Wilson, Bohr, and Allworth, 124.

status of the Russian language, especially in light of separatist tendencies in the East and the Russian-Ukrainian war.

The Soviet and later Ukraine's language policies contributed greatly to the formation of people's multiple identities in Ukraine but this issue has been routinely overemphasized and manipulated by the Russian Federation. Russian officials claim that the rights of the Russian-speaking population in Ukraine have been violated on a regular basis, while in reality Russophone Ukrainians used and continue to use the Russian language freely with no constraints in all regions of Ukraine. Moreover, because of lethargic educational reforms in Ukraine, the Russian language gained prominence in government and business settings, and continues to remain the everyday language for many Ukrainians in central and eastern Ukraine, a factor that does not justify Russia's claims.

Returning to Iushchenko's presidency, his alliance with Viktor Ianukovych seriously undermined people's trust in the state and democratic changes in Ukraine. Mentally, people returned to the same state of mind and indifference that were shaped by the Soviet era: for decades ethnic and national identity had been driven from people's consciousness which paralyzed their capacity for self-governing and political activism. The ambiguous character of reforms and the corruption in independent Ukraine encumbered the formation of a civil society. People's social passivity and the acceptance of the status quo provided the grounds for many to identify the Ukrainian society as immature.[52] In other words, a civil society which presumes a coherent identity of its people, their clear understanding of their goals and objectives as a community, and their ability to interact with each other as private citizens to create organizations independent of the state in order to protect their freedom and human rights failed to materialize after the Orange revolution.[53] Although the main ultra-nationalist and far-right groups, such as Svoboda, were active in Ukraine for quite some time, they were unable to mobilize the Ukrainian society to fight corruption and defend Ukraine's national interests.

---

52    Mykola Riabchouk, "Civil Society and Nation Building in Ukraine," in *Contemporary Ukraine: Dynamics of Post-Soviet Transition*, ed. Taras Kuzio (New York: M.E. Sharpe, 1998), 81–98.

53    Ibid. See also a seminal work on democracy and civil society by Alexis de Tocqueville, a French political thinker and historian, best known for his book *Democracy in America*.

The pro-Russian president Ianukovych came to power in 2010, when the Ukrainian society as a whole was disillusioned, totally disgusted with Ukrainian politics, extremely fragmented and polarized. Ianukovych accelerated the russification process through his Minister of Education Dmytro Tabachnyk, and completely surrendered the principles of Ukraine's national security, which heightened the divide between pro-Russian and pro-Ukrainian identities in Ukraine. The emergence of oligarchic clans in the government that began during Kuchma's presidency dramatically decelerated democratic changes in Ukraine. As in the past, the agency of power played a leading role in the lack of a collective identity.

## Identity Change, Ideology, and Power

Theorizing about the construction of collective and individual identity, Eric R. Wolf has suggested that it is a complex societal process, which is closely connected with power, claims to power, and the issue of who has power over whom.[54] The aggressive methods of state governance in dealing with challenges, such as "ethnic rebellions" and calls for secession, are of great significance to the formation of a "defensive" national identity in those who are governed. A threat from above invites them to unite against the state. In the same vein, a constructed threat from within promulgated by the state consolidates a society against the enemy and aligns people with the state. Most importantly, Wolf has argued that the state might emerge as an ultimate beneficiary of "ethnic rebellions" and friction: they become a tool of manipulation, and make it easier for the state to divide and rule.

As far as Ukrainian-Russian relations were concerned, Russia and the pro-Russian Ukrainian government were direct beneficiaries of ethnic tensions in Ukraine, manipulating the existing realities—a bifurcated identity of Ukraine's citizens. According to Mykola Riabchuk, "the bifurcation concerns the degree of mental emancipation from the supra-ethnic, quasi-spiritual entity constructed 300 years ago by Peter the Great, who fused political loyalty to his new-born empire with the traditional religiosity of Orthodox Slavdom."[55] The degree and tempo of this mental liberation

---

54 Eric R. Wolf, "Comments on State, Identity and Violence," in *The State, Identity and Violence: Political Disintegration in the Post-Cold War World*, ed. R. Brian Ferguson (London and New York: Routledge, 2003), 61–67.
55 Mykola Riabchuk, "Ukrainian Identity After the Euromaidan."

were extremely uneven in different regions of Ukraine. Beyond the spatial factor (those territories under direct Russian and Soviet control were less successful in liberating themselves from the Russian/Soviet past and dogmas), generational and social factors were of great significance. The Russian and Ukrainian political elites manipulated and amplified ethnic/linguistic/social tensions to camouflage massive corruptive schemes that transcended the national borders.

By 2013, the reserves of popular tolerance were exhausted: people were ripe for a rebellion. Ianukovych's aggressive methods of governance, his sense of impunity, and kleptocratic tendencies inspired Ukrainians to protest. The Euromaidan fully awakened and united the majority of Ukrainian citizens, interestingly, not on the basis of nationalist or ethnic values. The revolution bonded the citizens of Ukraine on the basis of civic unity and democratic values, which accelerated the nation building process in Ukraine.[56] Riabchuk is correct, arguing that there is less ambiguity in Ukrainian society today regarding people's individual and collective identity: it is "becoming increasingly civic rather than ethnic, and increasingly incompatible with a supra-ethnic, non-civic, quasi-religious, East Slavonic identity."[57] The Russian invasion made it possible. It also revealed that Russia and Ukraine differ in popular responses to mobilization calls: in the Russian Federation nationalism and a nationalist appeal can easily promote political and social mobilization, while in Ukraine it would be a daunting task to seek support for nationalist slogans from the majority of the Ukrainian society.[58] Civic nationalism instead served that purpose.

---

56 Steffen Halling and Susan Stewart, "Identity and Violence in Ukraine: Societal Developments since the Maidan Protests," *Stiftung Wissenschaft und Politik; German Institute for International and Security Affairs* (March 2015): 1–7, available at http://www.swp-berlin.org/fileadmin/contents/products/comments/2015C 19_hln_stw.pdf.
57 Riabchuk, "Ukrainian Identity."
58 Riabchouk, "Civil Society," 84, 91. Indeed, nationalist parties (Svoboda and Right Sector) received minimal popular support during the parliamentary elections after the revolution. See Yekelchyk, *The Conflict in Ukraine*, 106; Ilya Gerasimov, "Ukraine 2014: The First Postcolonial Revolution. Introduction to the Forum," *Ab Imperio*, no. 3 (2014): 27. For a more detailed discussion about Svoboda and Right Sector, see Adrian Mandzy, "Nationalism and the Ideological Identities of Svoboda and Right Sector," in *The Maidan Uprising, Separatism and Foreign Intervention: Ukraine's Complex Transition*, eds. Klaus Bachmann and Igor Lyubashenko (Frankfurt am Main: Peter Lang GmbH, 2014), 157–82.

Importantly, the Euromaidan fundamentally restructured Ukrainian political life,[59] promoted patriotic feelings and sharpened civic consciousness among the majority of Ukraine's citizens. A deep re-evaluation of identities occurred on individual and collective levels, a dramatic change that propelled the state's nearly quiescent transition toward a more unified nation and civil society. The deaths of protesters in the Maidan and the desire to become a free and democratic nation, rather than a submerged nation, became powerful stimuli that encouraged the Ukrainians to reconsider the political status quo and their status as a people. A "new type of solidarity emerged, and a new Ukrainian nation came into being;" more precisely, a new "hybrid Ukrainness" emerged in Ukraine, as Ilya Gerasimov has posited.[60]

Already at the initial stages, immediately after the revolution, there was a clear indication of a newly emerging trend in Ukraine—people's cultural unity based on common values: politically active people were building their state.[61] Financial, banking, education and police reforms would not be possible without the contribution of ordinary Ukrainian citizens. Oksana Huss's and Bohdan Harasymiw's essays have persuasively demonstrated that ordinary Ukrainians contributed greatly to reforming Ukraine. They finally realized that an independent Ukraine had never been formed, and for nearly a quarter of a century they had been passively living in the Ukrainian Soviet Socialist Republic with all Soviet paraphernalia in the streets, preserved and untouched.[62] Now the time was right and ripe to change it. Individual contributions matter, and as Taras Prokhasko has proposed, "the era of collective responsibility has ended. Everyone is responsible for whatever he or she is capable of contributing [...] the societal organism has many functions. Someone is to

---

59 Serhiy Kvit, "The Euromaidan Revolution and the Struggle for Ukraine's Place in Europe," in *Jews, Ukrainians, and the Euromaidan*, ed. Lubomyr Y. Luciuk (Toronto: Kashtan Press, 2014), i.
60 Gerasimov, 27, 35, 41.
61 Gerasimov, 41.
62 Andrii Liubka, "Sizifova revoliutsiia," in *Maidan. (R)evoliutsiia dukhu*, ed. Antin Mukharskyi (Kyiv: Nash format, 2015), 213. As Iurii Lutsenko has stated in his book, "one gradually begins to understand that this can be observed everywhere—in [Ukrainian] laws, institutions, people—generally speaking, there is no independent Ukraine; it is simply a repainted UkrSSR." See Iurii Lutsenko, *Po obydva boky koliuchoho drotu*, 2nd ed., ed. Mustapha Nayem (Kyiv: "A-BA-BA-HA-LA-MA-HA, 2014), 101. See also *Literaturna Ukraina*, April 23, 2015, p. 12.

think, someone is to be quiet, someone is to fight, someone is to provide others with food, someone is to become a hero [...] that's how we will gain experience, the one we had not had."[63]

Indeed, ordinary people, such as Nadiia Savchenko, became heroes, creating new aesthetics in politics based on intuitive feelings of justice and morality, the foundations of democracy, which dismiss and destroy the old archetypes of political behavior. Many current Ukrainian politicians, especially those who were associated with the Party of Regions, cling to pro-Soviet beliefs. They continue to defend the old aesthetics and norms in politics which ensure the safety of their principles and welfare. Ordinary Ukrainians challenge the stability of the corrupt system in Ukraine and even the institution of the presidency, advocating a principle that is new for Ukraine—governing by the people.[64]

Cultural change that occurred in Ukraine over the last two years is fundamental: it is associated with values, memory, traditions, morality, and justice, notions that solidify the core and ensure the continuity of the Ukrainian nation. As many commentators have noted, cultural unity is a much more lasting and stable phenomenon than unity based on class or spatial factors.[65] The reconstruction of collective identity occurs systematically, in each generation, a process which is reshaped and re-codified through the influence of internal and external environments. The spirit of heroism, liberation, and sacrifice is axiomatic for new independent states.[66] In 2013–2014 in Ukraine these notions acquired special meanings in the imagination of the Ukrainians: these notions transcended the space of theory and romanticism, gaining the contours of practical applications. They became the modes of new social practices and everyday human behavior, a cultural foundation of unity and ethnopsychology, which were necessitated by revolution and war. Maidan represented a "space of socio-cultural performance where new kinds of identities were constructed—national, social, political and gender," as Tamara Hundorova has argued. In her essay, she has demonstrated that these new identities facilitated the emergence of a new creative Ukraine, "a

---

63   Taras Prokhasko, "Kozhnomu svoe," in Mukharskyi, 221.
64   Vania Herman, "Savchenko zaiavyla, shcho Ukraini ne potriben prezydent," *Presa Ukrainy*, June 28, 2016, http://uapress.info/uk/news/show/136043.
65   Zhyzhko, 240.
66   Zhyzhko, 241.

world of new opportunities, and social practices that helped improve it morally, politically and intellectually."

The issue of territory and space is as important as the issue of identity, and has been one of the central themes in several essays of this anthology. Both rest at the core of the Russian-Ukrainian conflict, and emerge in discourses on both sides. Indeed, Ukraine's territory is strategically and geopolitically important, and this importance has been stressed by many authors.[67] For the same reasons, the Ukrainian historian Viacheslav Lypynskyi identified the geographical location of Ukraine as "unfortunate,"[68] a contested space desired and invaded by many and marked by conflicts and wars. It appears that the routine loss and recovery of its territories empowers the Ukrainians' intellectual, spiritual and political will for independence. Invading eastern Ukraine and expecting the Crimean scenario with no resistance there, Russia was confronted by fierce fighting organized by the new Ukrainian government and the volunteer movement. Tragically, Ukraine found itself in the same boat with other post-Soviet states whose existence is jeopardized by contested borders and occupied (or secessionist) territories, a problem unsolvable in the nearest future. Approximately 10% of Ukraine's citizens reside in these territories, and thousands of people learned what war and displacement are all about in the twenty first century. Religious communities fragmented and "ethnic minorities" once again fell into the category of nationalists and extremists, as Andrii Krawchuk's and Nedim Useinov's essays have shown. Stripped of their possessions, jobs, and religious affiliations, they moved to other parts of Ukraine. Some emigrated abroad.

Spatial change produces new identity: for some this is extremely painful; others perceive it as an adventure. Revolutions, wars, displacement, and imprisonment are associated with coercion: they not only change people's geography but also traumatize, disfigure, and torment them. Displacement, however, may also temper and advance people morally and intellectually. Revolutions and wars transform environments and places, often beyond recognition. After Savchenko returned from the Russian prison, she was asked about whether Ukraine had changed. She

---

67  See, for instance, Timothy Snyder's *Bloodlands: Europe between Hitler and Stalin* (New York: Basic Books, 2010).
68  Quoted in Zhyzhko, 247.

claimed that after two years she discovered a new Ukraine: people had developed hyper-sensitivity to lies and injustice, and began to think and act independently.[69] Russia's imperial ambitions became more transparent to those who gravitated toward Russia in the past, culturally and politically. It also became abundantly clear for the majority of Ukraine's people that Russian de-colonization has never begun. Russia's war in Ukraine accelerated the processes of intellectual maturity and nation building in Ukraine.

Perhaps more important than the Ukrainians' perceptions about Russia, the majority of Ukrainians acquired the ability to assess Ukraine's internal problems. The revolution, the war, and a free Ukrainian media that eagerly support popular democratic initiatives made those problems more visible. The people's post-revolutionary expectations were high. Today many Ukrainians believe that Ukraine is moving in the wrong direction. They blame President Poroshenko and his close circle for massive corruption and the lack of political will to resist it. The Ukrainian scholar and poet Bohdan Zalizniak has utilized a famous saying, lamenting that in Ukraine, thusfar the fish is being cleaned from its tail, and it is still a long way to its head.[70] Any metaphor or analogy, however, is not powerful enough to capture the level of corruption in Ukraine, where a group of people positioned themselves outside the community, creating an environment in which notions such as rule of law, social contract, and civil rights are meaningless. As Oksana Huss has illustrated, the system of corruption can be changed only from the outside.

Some observers detect a close resemblance between Iushchenko and Poroshenko who tried to protect both their own oligarchic interests and the interests of Ukraine.[71] The former failed to create a new Ukraine; the latter will likely fail too and will be dismissed by Ukraine's people. Over

---

69 See Savchenko's interview with Savik Shuster in his talk show "Shuster LIVE," *YouTube*, June 3, 2016, http://3s.tv/content/video_player.php?show_id=1178&lang=ua&video=0joP5Rbev9U.

70 Bohdan Zalizniak (interview with Ihor Pavliuk), "Ihor Pavliuk: 'Chy mozhe nazyvatysia ukrainskym uriad, iakyi ne vvazhaie akademichnu nauku stratehichnym priorytetom?'" *Literaturna Ukraina*, March 17, 2016, p. 7. The saying goes in Ukrainian: *ryba hnyie z holovy*; in English: a fish rots from its head down.

71 Taras Kuzio, "Ukraine's Revolution Fatigue: Poroshenko Repeats Mistakes of Yushchenko," *Business Ukraine*, accessed June 4, 2016, http://bunews.com.ua/politics/item/ukraines-revolution-fatigue-oligarchs-still-in-control-as-poroshenko-repeats-mistakes-of-yushchenko?category_id=9.

the last two post-revolutionary years, a struggle has emerged between the young "Maidan" participants who became Members of the Ukrainian Parliament, and representatives of state institutions and oligarchical structures who keep Ukraine's "colonial-oligarchic economy" alive and active.[72] The oligarchs seem to be winning: corrupt schemes were uncovered but not demolished; the massive theft of Ukraine's resources continues; and no perpetrators have been put in prison. Popular frustration grows daily, and as some representatives of the voluntary movement claim, "there is not another Maidan now only because there is a war in the Ukrainian territories. The Russians will take the rest of the country if we exacerbate Ukraine's instability by mass protests and violence."[73] In the past Ukraine's citizens viewed Ukrainian politics through the lens of Soviet bureaucratic legacies. Today, after Russia's annexation of Crimea and invasion of eastern Ukraine, the majority of people in Ukraine discuss political developments in the colonial context, revealing their desire for Ukraine to break free from subjugation and to stop the foreign invasion. Yet many have realized that there is another, equally serious threat to Ukraine's sovereignty—Ukrainian oligarchs whose patterns of behavior have changed little. Taras Kusio, for instance, has argued that there are political forces in Ukraine that can be successful in challenging the oligarchs. These forces include

> Yulia Tymoshenko's Batkivshchina, Lviv Mayor Andriy Sadoviy's Samopomych, and the embryonic political party taking shape around former Georgian President Mikhail Saakashvili. If these political parties win election to the next parliament, they could conceivably create a coalition on a platform of de-oligarchisation. This reality could emerge sooner than many might imagine—there is widespread speculation of preterm parliamentary elections in autumn 2016.[74]

Popular ambivalent attitudes toward Tymoshenko might certainly prevent her political party from leading another revolution, even if its essence is democratic with the noble goals of liberating the Ukrainian society from oligarchical control. Whatever the case might be, revolutions are fraught

---

72    Kuzio, "Ukraine's Revolution Fatigue."
73    Private conversation with Liudmyla Shalaieva, a member of the voluntary association "Obolonski berehyni" (Kyiv), March 16, 2016.
74    Kuzio, "Ukraine's Revolution Fatigue."

with dangers, and the Ukrainians currently seem to exhibit revolution fatigue.

Indeed, in cultural, philosophical and practical terms, revolutions are threatened with dangers which might be lethal to the regimes established through revolutionary means. The most common danger is popular high expectations, radicalism, and the ultimate destruction of the ends for which people struggled. Isaiah Berlin has described a collective disillusionment, which is quite typical among the victors after the revolution:

> After the first intoxication of triumph is over, a mood of disillusionment, frustration and presently indignation sets in among the victors: some among the most sacred objectives have not been accomplished; evil still stalks the earth; someone must be to blame; someone is guilty of lack of zeal, of indifference, perhaps of sabotage, even of treachery. And so individuals are accused and condemned and punished for failing to accomplish something which, in all probability, could not in the actual circumstances have been brought about by anyone...[75]

Another danger is associated with popular passion, enthusiasm, and growing pragmatism. People experience a fatigue of heroism and personal and collective sacrifice, and return to their normal lives, rejecting the further destruction of their "souls," lives, and private property. They crave stability and comfort, creating spaces for indifference and corruption. As history has demonstrated, few, if any, revolutions live up to their objectives. What is undeniable is that they bring a cultural change in society which often determines its path for generations to come. The Ukrainian case confirms Berlin's thesis: Ukraine's prospects are unclear but its cultural change inspires optimism.

The most salient elements of success are remembering the goals and reasons for sacrifice and avoiding routine practices and modes of political behavior. The Serbian filmmaker, actor, and musician Emir Kusturica has argued that forgetting plays a significant role in the process of adjustment.[76] He ruminates: "How do people survive historical crises? Before and after them, forgetting reigns."[77] Political indifference, passivity, and disillusionment move them toward the abyss of forgetting. Soviet

---

75    Berlin, *The Soviet Mind*, 105.
76    Emir Kusturitsa, *Smert—neperevirena chutka* (Kyiv: Tempora, 2014), 8.
77    Kusturitsa, 6.

legacies are still strong, preventing people from searching for a new political aesthetics and civic innovations. Yet the social and cultural change that occurred after the Euromaidan might encourage the people of Ukraine to realize the overarching power behind the pronoun "we:" the Maidan and change occurred because of the individual sacrifice and contribution of thousands and millions of people in Ukraine. In sharp contrast to Russia, where dissolving similar "Maidans" (one of them, for instance, in Bolotnaia Street in Moscow) is possible through the decision of one man, in Ukraine the collective Maidan survived and changed the power in the country. The challenge now is to remember the purpose of the individual and collective sacrifice. David Sakvarelidze, ex-Deputy Prosecutor General of Ukraine and ex-Prosecutor of the Odesa oblast, has posited that the revolution and people's persistence and unity changed the power but did not change the bureaucracy associated with this power,[78] and forgetting this important element of revolutionary change will obscure the motivations that drove the revolution in the first place.

On a global level, the revolutionary events in Kyiv in 2013–2014, Russia's annexation of Crimea, and the invasion of Ukraine's eastern territories have significantly altered the post-Cold War political situation, and with it, the distribution of regional and global power. Indeed, Russia's actions provoked anxiety about world security among leaders of Western democracies, actions which went far beyond Russia's attempts to control its "near abroad." A much more extensive expansion of Russian power seems to be an extension of Russia's cultural and ideological realignment. George O. Liber's essay has analyzed the sources of Russia's response to revolutionary changes in Ukraine. More broadly, this anthology draws readers' attention to the authoritarian patterns of governing in Russia, and clarifies the historical and geopolitical significance of the "Third Rome" myth and its relevance to Russian policies in the Black Sea basin and beyond.

Importantly, the Russians have erected a new cult—the cult of Putin. Many dream to re-create Russia within its Soviet borders and worship Lenin's corpse which is still exposed in the Mausoleum in the Red Square. The most celebrated Russian theater director and filmmaker Mark Zakharov who advocates the idea of Lenin being removed from the Red

---

78  See Savik Shuster's talk show "Shuster LIVE," *YouTube*, June 3, 2016, http://3s.tv/content/video_player.php?show_id=1178&lang=ua&video=0joP5Rbev9U.

Square and buried appropriately, once stated with bitter irony: "A brave thought visited me one day: what if we begin to bury the deceased?"[79] This makes perfect sense, especially in light of the "corpse ideology," a notion formulated by the Ukrainian writer Ievhen Hutsalo. Almost two decades ago Hutsalo drew parallels between the Russians' desire to perpetuate Lenin's principles by mummifying Lenin's body, and mummifying/eternalizing themselves by erecting and maintaining the Mausoleum of their own illusions.[80] Hutsalo made a reference to the Russian philosopher Ivan Ilin who has been recently rejuvenated by Putin. Ilin has referred to Lenin and his associates as "Lenin and his gang," and has identified the Russian revolution as a "slide into a moral abyss."[81] Yet for the Russians, the Soviet slogan "Lenin lived, Lenin is alive, and Lenin will live forever" seems a powerful signifier, which perpetuates Soviet legacies, memories, and dreams which one day might come true. Having examined in detail these ambitions, Hutsalo wrote: "Can you imagine a giant Mausoleum on the scale of the SNG [*Sodruzhestvo Nezavisimykh Gosudarstv*—Commonwealth of Independent States], a Mausoleum of enormous proportions where all 'people of Russia' reside, walking alive and at the same time being 'mummified,' as it has been until recently?"[82] No wonder that Hutsalo's notion of "corpse ideology" and his analysis of the Russian empire as Asian despotism and of the Russian people as a nation that is deprived of aspirations for building a Western-like democratic state constituted the fundamental reasons behind Russia's criminalization of his book *The Mentality of the Horde* (*Mentalnist ordy*): under Putin, it was included in the Federal List of Extremist Materials.[83]

By now, more than two years after the Euromaidan, many aspects of Russia's politics and intentions in Ukraine and Europe have become

---

79 "'Vzgliadu'—25 let," *Segodnia vecherom* (Andrei Malakhov), *Pervyi Kanal*, October 6, 2012, (0:12:08), http://www.1tv.ru/shows/segodnya-vecherom/vypuski/-vzglyadu-25-let-segodnya-vecherom-vypusk-ot-06-10-2012.
80 Ievhen Hutsalo, *Mentalnist ordy* (Kyiv: KMA, 2007), 164.
81 Quoted in Hutsalo, 160, 164. See also Timothy Snyder's talk on Ilin's influence on Putin's worldview "The Ancient is the Modern" (IWMVienna), *YouTube*, June 2, 2016, https://www.youtube.com/watch?v=AkX6eBk4w-w.
82 Hutsalo, 164.
83 "Federalnyi spisok ekstremistskikh materialov," *Ministerstvo iustitsii Rossiiskoi Federatsii* (official website), accessed June 6, 2016, http://minjust.ru/extremist-materials?field_extremist_content_value=.

more transparent. Russian President Vladimir Putin's "Ukrainian complex," as well as his persistent desire to solve "the Ukrainian question" once and for all, may be similar to Stalin's "Polish complex," and Hitler's antisemitic paranoia.[84] Indeed, as the Ukrainian scholar and writer Yurii Scherbak has demonstrated, Ukraine might be a mortal illness for Putin.[85] Unfortunately, Putin's views are shared by millions of Russians, and his Eurasianist slogans are popular among the majority of Russian citizens. They overwhelmingly supported the annexation of Crimea, and individuals, such as Aleksandr Dugin, have called for the killing of Ukrainians. This ideological lexicon has been embraced by the Russian public at large, and the "corpse ideology" seems to be perpetuated by the Russian political elites, appealing to the darkest facets of people's consciousness. Russian society can choose from a variety of options offered by this ideology. Hopefully, Mausoleums erected at all levels will eventually evoke claustrophobia in Russian society, and their aesthetic appeal will decline substantially. Until then, revolutions and wars at all levels will continue, and the twenty-first century will be remembered as another century of violence and subversion.

## Bibliography

Bachmann, Klaus, and Igor Lyubashenko, eds. *The Maidan Uprising, Separatism and Foreign Intervention: Ukraine's Complex Transition*. New York: Peter Lang, 2014.

Berlin, Isaiah. *The Soviet Mind: Russian Culture under Communism*, edited by Henry Hardy. Washington, D.C.: Brookings Institution Press, 2004.

Bertelsen, Olga, and Myroslav Shkandrij. "The Secret Police and the Campaign against Galicians in Soviet Ukraine, 1929–34." *Nationalities Papers: The Journal of Nationalism and Ethnicity* 42, no. 1 (2014): 37–62.

Bertelsen, Olga. "A Trial *in Absentia*: Purifying National Historical Narratives in Russia." *Kyiv-Mohyla Humanities Journal*, no. 3 (2016): 57–87.

———. "Joseph Brodsky's Imperial Consciousness." *Scripta Historica*, no. 21 (2015): 263–89.

———. "Rethinking Psychiatric Terror against Nationalists in Ukraine." *Kyiv-Mohyla Humanities Journal*, no. 1 (2014): 27–76.

---

84 Yuri Felshtinsky and Mykhailo Stanchev, *Tretia svitova: Bytva za Ukrainu* (Kyiv: Tov "NF," 2014).
85 Iurii Shcherbak, "Putin smertelno bolen Ukrainoi," *Argument*, January 1, 2015, http://argumentua.com/stati/yurii-shcherbak-putin-smertelno-bolen-ukrainoi.

Bianchini, Stefano. *Eastern Europe and the Challenges of Modernity, 1800–2000.* Translated by Carolyn Kadas. London and New York: Routledge, 2015.

Chekalkin, Dmitry. "How Russia Invaded Ukraine as Told by FSB Colonel Girkin." *Euromaidan Press.* December 7, 2014. http://euromaidanpress.com/2014/12/07/fsb-colonel-girkin-tells-details-of-how-russia-invaded-ukraine-in-twice-censored-interview/.

Clunan, Anne L. *Social Construction of Russia's Resurgence: Aspirations, Identity, and Security Interests.* Baltimore, MD: Johns Hopkins University Press, 2009.

D'Anieri, Paul, Robert Kravchuk, and Taras Kuzio. "Nation Building and National Identity." In *Politics and Society in Ukraine,* 45–70. Boulder, Colorado: Westview Press, 1999.

Dettmer, Jammie. "New Evidence: Russian Spies Backed Kiev's Killers." *The Daily Beast.* March 4, 2014. http://www.thedailybeast.com/articles/2014/04/03/ukraine-fingers-russian-advisors-and-ex-president-yanukovych-in-february-massacre.html.

"Dmitry Tymchuk: FSB Presence in Ukraine on February 20–21." *Voices of Ukraine.* April 5, 2014. http://maidantranslations.com/2014/04/05/dmitry-tymchuk-fsb-presence-in-ukraine-on-february-20-21/.

"Federalnyi spisok ekstremistskikh materialov." *Ministerstvo iustitsii Rossiiskoi Federatsii* (official website). Accessed June 6, 2016. http://minjust.ru/extremist-materials?field_extremist_content_value=.

Felshtinsky, Yuri, and Mykhailo Stanchev. *Tretia svitova: Bytva za Ukrainu.* Kyiv: Tov "NF," 2014.

Freeden, Michael. *Ideology: A Very Short Introduction.* New York: Oxford University Press, 2003.

Garagozov, R. R. "Collective Memory and the Russian 'Schematic Narrative Template.'" *Journal of Russian and East European Psychology* 40, no. 5 (2002): 55–89.

Gerasimov, Ilya. "Ukraine 2014: The First Postcolonial Revolution. Introduction to the Forum." *Ab Imperio,* no. 3 (2014): 22–44.

Gorky, Maksim. *O russkom krestianstve.* Berlin: Izd-vo I. P. Ladyzhnikova, 1922.

Halling, Steffen, and Susan Stewart. "Identity and Violence in Ukraine: Societal Developments since the Maidan Protests." *Stiftung Wissenschaft und Politik; German Institute for International and Security Affairs* (March 2015): 1–7. Accessed July 4, 2016. http://www.swp-berlin.org/fileadmin/contents/products/comments/2015C19_hln_stw.pdf.

Herman, Vania. "Savchenko zaiavyla, shcho Ukraini ne potriben prezydent." *Presa Ukrainy.* June 28, 2016. http://uapress.info/uk/news/show/136043.

Hutsalo, Ievhen. *Mentalnist ordy.* Kyiv: KMA, 2007.

Ierofeev, Viktor. *Entsiklopediia russkoi dushi.* Sankt-Peterburg: Azbuka, 2010.

Kendall, Bridget. "Cultural Struggle to Define Russia's Identity." *BBC News.* March 18, 2015. http://www.bbc.com/news/world-europe-31584221.

"Krymskyi separatyst proponuie zbuduvaty televyshku dlia transliatsii v Ukrainu brekhlyvoho rosiiskoho TB." *Ekspres Online.* June 6, 2016. http://expres.ua/news/2016/06/10/189420-krymskyy-separatyst-proponuye-zbuduvaty-televyshku-translyaciyi-ukrayinu.

Kuchins, Andrew C., and Igor A. Zevelev. "Russian Foreign Policy: Continuity in Change." *The Washington Quarterly* 35, no.1 (2012): 147–61.

Kusturitsa, Emir. *Smert—neperevirena chutka*. Kyiv: Tempora, 2014.

Kuzio, Taras. "European, Eastern Slavic, and Eurasian: National Identity, Transformation, and Ukrainian Foreign Policy." In *Ukrainian Foreign and Security Policy: Theoretical and Comparative Perspectives*, edited by Jennifer D. P. Moroney, Taras Kuzio and Mikhail Molchanov, 197–225. Westport, Connecticut: Praeger, 2002.

——————. "Russia Takes Control of Ukraine's Security Forces." *Eurasia Daily Monitor*, March 19, 2012, p. 7–9.

——————. "Soviet Conspiracy Theories and Political Culture in Ukraine: Understanding Viktor Yanukovych and the Party of Regions." *Communist and Post-Communist Studies* 44, no. 3 (2011): 221–232.

——————. *Ukraine: Democratization, Corruption, and the New Russian Imperialism*. Santa Barbara, CA, and Denver, CO: Praeger, 2015.

——————. "Ukraine's Revolution Fatigue: Poroshenko Repeats Mistakes of Yushchenko." *Business Ukraine*. Accessed June 4, 2016. http://bunews.com.ua/politics/item/ukraines-revolution-fatigue-oligarchs-still-in-control-as-poroshenko-repeats-mistakes-of-yushchenko?category_id=9.

Kvit, Serhiy. "The Euromaidan Revolution and the Struggle for Ukraine's Place in Europe." In *Jews, Ukrainians, and the Euromaidan*, edited by Lubomyr Y. Luciuk, i-xvi. Toronto: Kashtan Press, 2014.

Lami, Giulia. "Ukraine's Road to Europe: Still a Controversial Issue." In *Contemporary Ukraine on the Cultural Map of Europe*, edited by Larissa M. L. Zaleska Onyshkevych and Maria G. Rewakowicz, 29–39. London, England: M. E. Sharpe, 2009.

Linz, Juan J. "State Building and Nation-Building." *European Review* 1, no. 4 (1993): 355–69.

Liubka, Andrii. "Sizifova revoliutsii." In *Maidan. (R)evoliutsiia dukhu*, edited by Antin Mukharskyi, 212–17. Kyiv: Nash format, 2015.

Luciuk, Lubomyr Y., ed. *Jews, Ukrainians, and the Euromaidan*. Kashtan Press, 2014.

Lutsenko, Iurii. *Po obydva boky koliuchoho drotu*, 2$^{nd}$ ed., edited by Mustapha Nayem. Kyiv: "A-BA-BA-HA-LA-MA-HA, 2014.

Mäkinen, Sirke. "Russia—a Leading or Fading Power? Students' Geopolitical Metanarratives on Russia's Role in the Post-Soviet Space." *Nationalities Papers* 44, no. 1 (2016): 92–113.

Mandzy, Adrian. "Nationalism and the Ideological Identities of Svoboda and Right Sector." In *The Maidan Uprising, Separatism and Foreign Intervention: Ukraine's Complex Transition*, edited by Klaus Bachmann and Igor Lyubashenko, 157–82. Frankfurt am Main: Peter Lang GmbH, 2014.

Mankoff, Jeffrey. *Russian Foreign Policy: The Return of Great Power Politics*, 2$^{nd}$ ed. New York: Rowman & Littlefield Publishers, 2011.

Marten, Kimberly. "Putin's Choices: Explaining Russian Foreign Policy and Intervention in Ukraine." *The Washington Quarterly* 38, no. 2 (2015): 189–204.

Menon, Rajan, and Eugene Rumer. *Conflict in Ukraine: The Unwinding of the Post-Cold War Order*. London, England, and Cambridge, Massachusetts: The MIT Press, 2015.

Molchanov, Mikhail A. *Eurasian Regionalisms and Russian Foreign Policy*. In the International Political Economy of New Regionalisms series. London and New York: Routledge, 2015.

Motyl, Alexander J. "Putin's Russia as a Fascist Political System." *Communist and Post-Communist Studies* 49, no. 1 (2016): 25–36.

──────────. "The Surrealism of Realism: Misreading the War in Ukraine." *World Affairs*. January/February 2015. http://www.worldaffairsjournal.org/article/surrealism-realism-misreading-war-ukraine.

Mukharskyi, Antin, ed. *Maidan. (R)evoliutsiia dukhu*. Kyiv: Nash format, 2015.

Neumann, Iver. "Russia as a Great Power." In *Russia as a Great Power. Dimensions of Security under Putin*, edited by Jakob Hedenskog, Vilhelm Konnander, Bertil Nygren, Ingmar Oldberg, and Christer Pursiainen, 24–41. Abington: Routledge, 2005.

Neumann, Iver B. "Russia in International Society Over the Longue Durée. Lessons from Early Rus' and Early post-Soviet State Formation." In *Russia's Identity in International Relations. Images, Perceptions, Misperceptions*, edited by Ray Taras, 24–41. Abington: Routledge, 2013.

Ogden, C. K., and I. A. Richards. *The Meaning of Meaning: A Study of The Influence of Language upon Thought and of The Science of Symbolism*, 3$^{rd}$ ed. New York: Harcourt, Brace and Company, 1930.

Pomerantsev, Peter, and Michael Weiss. *The Menace of Unreality: How the Kremlin Weaponizes Information, Culture and Money*. New York: The Interpreter; the Institute of Modern Russia, Inc., 2014.

Prizel, Ilya. "Foreign Policy as a Means of Nation Building." In *National Identity and Foreign Policy: Nationalism and Leadership in Poland, Russia and Ukraine*, 372–403. Cambridge, UK: Cambridge University Press, 1998.

Prokhasko, Taras. "Kozhnomu svoe." In *Maidan. (R)evoliutsiia dukhu*, edited by Antin Mukharskyi, 220–21. Kyiv: Nash format, 2015.

Riabchuk, Mykola. "Civil Society and Nation Building in Ukraine." In *Contemporary Ukraine: Dynamics of Post-Soviet Transition*, edited by Taras Kuzio, 81–98. New York: M.E. Sharpe, 1998.

Riabchuk, Mykola. "Ukrainian Identity After the Euromaidan" (interview by Alexander J. Motyl). *World Affairs*. March 29, 2016. http://www.worldaffairsjournal.org/blog/alexander-j-motyl/ukrainian-identity-after-euromaiden.

Sakwa, Richard. *Frontline Ukraine. Crisis in the Borderlands*. London: I. B. Tauris, 2015.

Salyha, Taras. "O natsie moia, rozderta i rozbyta (Nablyzhennia do portreta Ivana Dziuby). *Literaturna Ukraina*, May 5, 2016, p. 11.

Savchenko, Nadiia (interview with Savik Shuster). "Shuster LIVE." *YouTube*. June 3, 2016. http://3s.tv/content/video_player.php?show_id=1178&lang=ua&video=0joP5Rbev9U.

"SBU: Putin's Adviser and FSB Officers Involved in Maidan Killings." *UNIAN.* April 15, 2015. http://www.unian.info/politics/1067376-sbu-putins-adviser-and-fsb-officers-involved-in-maidan-killings.html.

Sergunin, Alexander. *Explaining Russian Foreign Policy Behavior: Theory and Practice.* In the Soviet and Post-Soviet Politics and Society Series. Stuttgart: ibidem-Verlag, 2016.

Shandra, Valentyna. "Mova iak zasib formuvannia natsionalnoi identychnosti." In *Ukrainska identychnist i movne pytannia v Rosiiskii imperii: sproba derzhavnoho reguliuvannia*, edited by Hennadii Boriak, vii–xxxvii. Kyiv: Klio, 2015.

Shcherbak, Iurii. "Putin smertelno bolen Ukrainoi." *Argument.* January 1, 2015. http://argumentua.com/stati/yurii-shcherbak-putin-smertelno-bolen-ukrainoi.

Shkandrij, Myroslav, and Olga Bertelsen. "The Soviet Regime's National Operations in Ukraine, 1929–1934." *Canadian Slavonic Papers* LV, nos. 3–4 (2013): 417–47.

Shkandrij, Myroslav. *Russia and Ukraine: Literature and the Discourse of Empire from Napoleonic to Postcolonial Times.* Montreal & Kingston: McGill-Queen's University Press, 2001.

Shuster, Savik. Talk show "Shuster LIVE." *YouTube.* June 3, 2016. http://3s.tv/content/video_player.php?show_id=1178&lang=ua&video=0joP5Rbev9U.

Smith, Graham, Vivien Law, Andrew Wilson, Annette Bohr, and Edward Allworth. "Redefining Ethnic and Linguistic Boundaries in Ukraine: Indigenes, Settlers and Russophone Ukrainians." In *Nation-Building in the Post-Soviet Borderlands: The Politics of National Identities*, 119–38. Cambridge, UK: Cambridge University Press, 1998.

Snyder, Timothy. *Bloodlands: Europe between Hitler and Stalin.* New York: Basic Books, 2010.

———. "Fascism, Russia, and Ukraine." *The New York Review of Books.* March 20, 2014. http://www.nybooks.com/articles/archives/2014/mar/20/fascism-russia-and-ukraine/.

———. "The Ancient is the Modern" (IWMVienna). *YouTube.* June 2, 2016. https://www.youtube.com/watch?v=AkX6eBk4w-w.

Soldatov, Andrei. "The True Role of the FSB in the Ukrainian Crisis." *The Moscow Times.* April 15, 2014. http://www.themoscowtimes.com/opinion/article/the-true-role-of-the-fsb-in-the-ukrainian-crisis/498072.html.

Szporluk, Roman. *Russia, Ukraine, and the Breakup of the Soviet Union.* Stanford, CA: Hoover Institution Press, 2000.

Thompson, Ewa M. *Trubadury imperii: Rosiiska literatura i colonialism*, 2nd ed. Translated by Mariia Korchynska. Kyiv: Vydavnytstvo Solomii Pavlychko "Osnovy," 2008.

"20 Russian FSB Agents Suspected of Euromaidan Revolution Crimes Identified." *Ukraine Today.* February 24, 2014. http://uatoday.tv/politics/20-russian-fsb-agents-suspected-of-euromaidan-revolution-crimes-identified-411552.html.

Velychenko, Stephen. *Shaping Identity in Eastern Europe and Russia: Soviet-Russian and Polish Accounts of Ukrainian History, 1914–1991.* New York: St. Martin's Press, 1993.

Viatrovych, Volodymyr. "Operatsiia 'Blok.' Diia persha." In *Istoriia z hryfom "Sekretno": Taiemnytsi ukrainskoho mynuloho z arkhiviv KGB* by Volodymyr Viatrovych, 204–12. Lviv, Kyiv: Nash Format, 2011.

"'Vzgliadu'—25 let" (talk show "Segodnia vecherom" with Andrei Malakhov). *Pervyi Kanal*. October 6, 2012 (0:12:08). http://www.1tv.ru/shows/segodnya-vecherom/vypuski/-vzglyadu-25-let-segodnya-vecherom-vypusk-ot-06-10-2012.

Wanner, Catherine. *Burden of Dreams: History and Identity in Post-Soviet Ukraine*. University Park, PA: The Pennsylvania University Press, 1998.

Wilson, Andrew. *Ukraine's Orange Revolution*. New Haven and London: Yale University Press, 2005.

_____. *Ukrainian Crisis: What it Means to the West*. New Haven and London: Yale University Press, 2014.

Wolf, Eric R. "Comments on State, Identity and Violence." In *The State, Identity and Violence: Political Disintegration in the Post-Cold War World*, edited by R. Brian Ferguson, 61–67. London and New York: Routledge, 2003.

Yekelchyk, Serhy. *The Conflict in Ukraine: What Everyone Needs to Know*. Oxford: Oxford University Press, 2015.

Zalizniak, Bohdan (interview by Ihor Pavliuk). "Ihor Pavliuk: 'Chy mozhe nazyvatysia ukrainskym uriad, iakyi ne vvazhaie akademichnu nauku stratehichnym priorytetom?'" *Literaturna Ukraina*, March 17, 2016, p. 7.

Zhyzhko, Serhii. *Natsiia iak spilnota*. Kyiv: Dnipro, 2008.

# Dictionary of Abbreviations

| | |
|---|---|
| ACN OECD | Anti-Corruption Network for Eastern Europe and Central Asia; the Organization for Economic Co-Operation and Development |
| ADM | Archer Daniels Midland Company (Ukraine) |
| ARC | Autonomous Republic of Crimea |
| ATO | anti-terrorist operation |
| BPN | Counter Narcotic Crime Office (Ukraine) |
| CAT | communication accommodation theory |
| CEE | Central and Eastern European region |
| CIA | Central Intelligence Agency |
| CMC | Computer-Mediated Communications |
| CSCC | U.S. State Department's Center for Strategic Counterterrorism Communications |
| CSO | civil society organizations |
| DAI | State Highway Inspectorate |
| DNR | Donetsk People's Republic |
| DUMK | Spiritual Board of Muslims of Crimea |
| ECIPE | European Centre for International Political Economy (Brussels) |
| EU | European Union |

| | |
|---|---|
| FAPSI | Federal Agency of Government Communications and Information |
| FIGs | financial-industrial groups |
| FSB | Federal Security Agency |
| FSK | Federal Counterintelligence Service |
| GDP | Gross Domestic Product |
| GRECO | Group of States Against Corruption |
| GRU | Main Intelligence Directorate |
| GST | standard general skills test |
| HUBOZ | Main Administration for the Struggle against Organized Crime |
| ICT | Information and Communications Technology |
| IFES | International Foundation for Electoral Systems |
| IMF | International Monetary Fund |
| ISIL | Islamic State of Iraq and the Levant |
| ISIS | Islamic State of Iraq and Syria |
| ISP | Internet Service Provider |
| KGB | Soviet secret police |
| KORD | rapid-reaction police force (Ukraine) |
| LNR | Luhansk People's Republic |
| MAP | NATO's Membership Action Plan |

| | |
|---|---|
| MTCR | missile technology control regimes |
| MVS | Ministry of Internal Affairs (Ukraine) |
| MZS | Ministry of Foreign Affairs (Ukraine) |
| NABU | National Anti-Corruption Bureau |
| NATO | North Atlantic Treaty Organization |
| NGO | a non-governmental organization |
| NIS | National Integrity System |
| NKVD | another acronym for the Soviet secret police |
| NPU | National Police of Ukraine |
| ODIHR | Office for Democratic Institutions and Human Rights |
| OECD | Organization for Economic Co-Operation and Development |
| OSCE | Organization for Security and Cooperation in Europe |
| OUN | Organization of Ukrainian Nationalists |
| OUN(B) | Organization of Ukrainian Nationalists—Bandera faction |
| PSYOP | psychological operations |
| PR | political intelligence |
| RPR | Reanimation Package of Reforms |
| RSFSR | Russian Soviet Federative Socialist Republic |
| RT | "Russia Today," Russian TV channel |

| | |
|---|---|
| RUECB | Russian Union of Evangelical Christians-Baptists |
| RUN | Russophone Ukrainian Nationalists |
| SADEV | Swedish Agency for Development Evaluation |
| SBU | Security Service of Ukraine |
| SNG | Commonwealth of Independent States |
| SVR | Foreign Intelligence Service |
| TI Ukraine | Transparency International Ukraine |
| UCCECB | Ukrainian Council of Churches of Evangelical Christians-Baptists |
| UN | United Nations |
| UPA | Ukrainian Insurgent Army |
| US | United States of America |
| USSR | Union of Soviet Socialist Republics |
| VAT | value-added tax |
| VPNs | Virtual Private Networks |
| WTO | World Trade Organization |
| WWII | Second World War |

# Index

## A

Abdulganiev, Elmar 289
Abibullaieva, Leniara 202
Abkhazia 59, 64, 384
Ablaev, Emiral 291
Abyssinia 71
'actionism' 164, 167
active measures 255
Afanasiev, Iurii 80
Afghanistan 82, 370
Africa 370
   African 77
aggression 19, 23, 27, 28, 70–73, 75, 77–79, 83, 84, 89, 115, 148, 197, 207, 290, 296, 306
Akhmetov, Rinat 75, 329
Aksionov, Sergei 191, 192, 285
Aksionov, Valerii 386
Alaska 229
Aleppo 241
Algeria 234
Amet, Reshat 287
Anatolia 228
Andropov, Iurii 80, 81
Angola 82
Ankara 231
annexation 16, 23, 26, 30, 64, 78, 141, 185, 190, 193–195, 197, 200–202, 204–207, 213, 214, 222, 228, 232, 234, 243, 267, 283, 286, 288, 304, 309, 403, 405, 407
   of Crimea 16, 23, 26, 64, 190, 195, 197, 201, 202, 205, 207, 283, 304, 309, 403, 405, 407
Anschluss (Austria) 71
Antarctic 234
Anti-maidan 190
antisemitism 294, 296
   antisemitic 127, 283, 295, 298, 300, 309, 407
Antoniuk, Valerii 307, 308
Arab 59, 60, 61
Arctic coast (Canada) 230
Arkhangelsk 233
Armenia 213, 224, 362
   Armenian 54, 361
arms trade 24
Association Agreement (EU agreement) 41, 183, 184, 186
Association for Spiritual Renewal 303
Atlantic 55, 63, 84, 199, 207, 229, 234
ATO 24, 72, 83
Austria 71, 224, 357
authoritarianism 132, 183
   authoritarian regime 100, 124, 259, 324
Avakian, Tihran 362
Avakov, Arsen 188, 336, 355, 356, 359, 361, 365
Azarov, Mykola 183
Azov Sea 72

## B

Bahrain 269
Bakhchisarai 288
Bakhtin, Mikhail 168, 170
Balkan nations 223
   Balkan Slavs 226
Baltic Sea 225, 229
Baltic states 84, 207, 230
Bandera, Stepan
   banderites 129, 190
Bandura, Ihor 305, 307
Baptists 31, 284, 303–305, 307, 308, 310
   Baptist Council of Ukraine 305, 307
Baran, Mykola 192
Barkashov, Aleksandr 133
Bashar al-Assad 231
Bay of Biscay 230
Belarus 41, 198
   Soviet Belarus 17
Belgium 357
Belorussians 17
Berdiaev, Nikolai 99

Berlin, Isaiah 22, 382, 404
Bessarabia 51
Bezmenov, Yuri (Tomas Schuman) 256
Bilgiç, Tanju, 235
bilingualism 139, 141, 143, 148, 153, 155, 156, 380
Black Sea 25, 30, 54, 57, 181, 188, 194, 197, 199, 213–216, 218, 224, 225, 227–229, 233, 236–238, 240, 243, 405
   basin 30, 214–216, 218, 227, 233, 236–238, 240, 243, 405
   fleet 54, 188
   region 25, 213, 215, 237
Bleich, Yaakov Dov 297
Blok, Aleksandr 129, 220
Bolsheviks 47, 48, 104, 112
Boroda, Alexander 296
Borodai, Aleksandr 81
Bosporus 215, 224–226
Brazil 370
Brezhnev, Leonid 81
Brussels 115, 133
Budapest Memorandum (1994) 77, 197
Budapest Memorandum on Security Assurances (1994) 197
Bukovyna 51
Bulgakov, Mikhail 220
Bulgaria 30, 215, 226, 238, 240
   Bulgarian 54

## C

California 229
Canada 16, 202, 230, 356, 357
carnival 167, 168
Caspian 234
Catherine the Great 113, 196, 224, 395
Catholics
   Greek Catholics 43
Cato Institute 28
   Center for Global Liberty and Prosperity 28
Caucasus 25, 81, 97
Cavusoglu, Mevlut 239
Central Europe
   societies 97
Central European Policy Institute 261

Central Spiritual Board of Muslims of Crimea 285
Chalyi, Aleksei 190
Charter of the United Nations of 1945 78
chauvinism 80, 81, 122, 134
Chechnia 195, 266
chekists 82
Chepynoha, Vitalii 155
Cherenkov, Mikhail 303, 304
Chernivtsi 332
Chernobyl 18, 389
China 71, 197, 259, 269
Christianity 93, 222
   Christian community 308
Chubarov, Refat 191, 201–203, 288–290, 292
CIA 270
civil society 18, 20, 32, 59, 97, 123, 130, 132, 163, 199, 277, 322, 327, 331, 339–344, 346, 389, 396, 399
collectivization 49, 50, 53
colonialism 214
   neo-colonialism 237
Commonwealth of Independent States 103, 191, 406
Communism (st) 47, 49, 50, 53, 72, 79, 389
compatriots (*sootechestvenniki*) 46, 59, 108, 110, 144, 191, 195
Constantinople, *see also* Tsargrad 216, 218, 220, 223–226, 384
'corpse ideology' 406, 407
corruption 15, 23, 31, 34, 85, 101, 156, 186, 199, 273, 307, 317–326, 331–339, 341–346, 353, 354, 356–358, 368, 396, 402, 404
   anti-corruption policies 32, 320, 345
   Law on Preventing Corruption (Ukraine) 367
Cossack
   Cossack Hetmanate 96
   Cossack state 126
   Don Cossacks 80
   Kuban Cossacks 304
   Zaporizhian Cossacks 165
Council of Europe 289, 361, 363, 369
Council of Muftis of Russia 291
counter-disinformation 274

Crimea  25, 27, 30, 31, 42, 54, 55, 57,
    61, 62, 70, 73–75, 79–82, 89, 104,
    115, 126, 127, 139, 141, 148, 154,
    181, 183–186, 188, 189, 191, 193,
    194, 196, 197, 200–206, 214, 221,
    229, 233, 234, 237, 238, 283–285,
    287, 288–292, 300, 303, 386, 393,
    394
    'Crimean Blockade'  203
    Crimean Field Mission for Human
        Rights  289
    Crimean Khanate  196
    Crimean oblast  200
    Crimean parliament  62
    Crimean peninsula  72, 185, 206, 213,
        214, 222, 224, 228, 229, 232, 234,
        243
    Crimeans  26, 62, 126, 287, 291
        Crimean citizens  26
        Crimean Tatar(s)  54, 141, 148,
            185, 191, 193, 196, 201–204,
            284, 287–290, 292, 309, 310
            Crimean Tatar *umma*  292, 293
        Interconfessional Council of Crimea
            285
crisis, *see also* Ukrainian crisis  27,
    28, 57, 169, 207, 228, 307, 310,
    390, 392
Croatia  357
cultural realignment  18, 19, 377, 378,
    382, 383, 385
cyber space  272
Czechoslovakia  51, 199
    Czech  80, 357
    Czech Republic  357
Czyżewski, Dmytro  166

# D

Danilevskii, Nikolai  220
Danube  224
Dardanelles  215, 224, 226, 227
Davutoğlu, Ahmet  288
decentralization  257, 342, 355, 360,
    364, 369
de-colonization  402
Dekanoidze, Khatia  359, 363–365
Denikin, Anton  112
deputies  24, 61, 189, 191, 192, 333
'discursive formation'  30, 216, 217,
    219, 223, 236, 242

disinformation  72, 121, 255, 261–
    263, 266, 272, 273, 275, 306
displacement  31, 33, 283, 297, 299,
    310, 311, 401
dissidents
    dissident movement  17
Dnipro Battalion  301
Dnipropetrovsk  127, 147, 151, 296,
    297, 301
DNR  75, 81, 149, 294
Donbas  16, 23, 31, 72–75, 79–81,
    83, 84, 89, 127, 133, 197, 200,
    206, 207, 283, 284, 309, 310, 391,
    393
Donets Basin  54
Donetsk  15, 47, 62, 75, 83, 147, 149,
    151, 154, 188, 203, 283, 294,
    297–299, 301, 303, 304, 309, 329
    Donetsk Council of Churches and
        Religious Organizations  294
Dontsov, Dmytro  122
Dostoevsky, Fiodor  220
drug trafficking  24
Dugin, Aleksandr  19, 80, 81, 133,
    222, 407
Dukhovny, Alexander  297
DUMK  285, 287–289, 291
Dzhemilev, Mustafa  201, 203, 288,
    291, 292
Dziuba, Ivan  380

# E

East Central Europe  51, 52, 56, 57
eastern Europe  19, 25, 57, 254, 378
eastern Slavs  114
Edelman, Murray  26
Egypt  224, 234
empires  91, 109, 381
    Russian (Romanov)  81, 109, 406
England, *see also* Great Britain  223
Enlightenment  22
Erdoğan, Recep Tayyip  235, 236
Estonia  17, 18, 57, 271
ethics of politics  19
ethnopsychology  379, 400
Eurasia  60, 63, 303
    Eurasian Customs Union  41, 42, 60,
        198
    Eurasianism  81, 110, 111, 133

Euromaidan, *see also* revolutions 15, 18–22, 32, 34, 62, 64, 91, 100, 101, 107, 115, 122, 123, 125, 126, 128, 133, 137, 142, 146, 151, 155, 161–163, 165, 166, 168, 176, 207, 253, 263, 293, 300, 312, 322, 324, 327, 330, 333, 337, 339, 342, 343, 345, 346, 353, 362, 385, 393, 398, 399, 405, 406
Europe 16, 17, 24, 25, 33, 41, 57, 58, 61, 71, 72, 76, 77, 84, 90, 92, 105, 114, 125, 131, 133, 164, 186, 198, 207, 218, 223, 224, 227, 229, 233, 240, 258, 293, 331, 369, 370, 382, 383, 390, 392, 406
   EU Summit Meeting (Vilnius) 42
   European Charter for Regional or Minority Languages 150
   European Union (EU) 32, 41, 57, 59, 61, 63, 84, 92, 113, 114, 183, 184, 202, 205, 213, 214, 237, 241, 258, 354
'evil empire' 18, 71
expansionism 132, 237
extremism 275, 288, 289, 292, 309, 311, 383
   Extremism Law (Russia) 383
   extremists 60, 189, 204, 290, 401
   Federal List of Extremist Materials 406
   Islamist extremism 288

## F

Fabios 187
famine 16, 49
FAPSI 257
Far East 97
fascism 26, 90, 129, 130, 132, 133, 190, 295, 309, 385
   fascist 25, 70, 121, 122, 129, 131–134, 385
federalism 105, 392, 395
Filofei 218, 219, 220
Finland 230
   Finns 270
Firtash, Dmytro 329
Foucault, Michel 216
France 77, 103, 197, 224, 256
FSB 75, 187, 188, 257, 289
FSK 257
Furman, Dmitrii 97

## G

Gainutdin, Ravil 291, 292
Galicia 51, 126
geopolitics 90, 113, 214, 224
Georgia 57, 59, 84, 195, 213, 215, 236–238, 243, 263, 271, 354, 356, 359, 362, 384
   Georgians 32, 102
Germany 56, 57, 71, 81, 132, 357
glasnost 389
Glaziev, Sergei 80
global security 19
Goebbels, Joseph 72, 81
Gorbachev, Mikhail 54, 56, 57, 64, 378, 389
Gorky, Maksim (Peshkov) 379, 382
Grand Duchy of Lithuania 96
Grand Princes of Moscow 219
Great Britain, *see also* England 16, 77
Greek 43, 54, 89, 218
GRU 257
Gulf of Mexico 229

## H

Hayden, Michael 270
'Heavenly Hundred,' *see also nebesna sotnia* 167, 187
Hitler 17, 71, 77, 78, 80, 81, 132, 407
Holocaust 130, 309
Holodomor 16, 49, 390
Holy Scriptures 166
homophobia 134
Hroch, Miroslav 45
Hroisman, Volodymyr 371
Hrushevskyi, Mykhailo 125
Hrytsak, Vasyl 163, 368
human rights 17, 285, 287, 289, 360, 364, 366, 370, 396
   Human Rights Commission (Ukraine) 365
   Human Rights Court (Strasbourg) 292
Hutsalo, Ievhen 406

## I

Ianukovych, Viktor  15, 27, 41, 42, 57, 59, 61, 62, 70, 72, 75, 100, 101, 123, 128, 151, 162, 167, 171, 172, 183–188, 190, 192, 197–200, 300, 317, 321, 333, 341, 342, 361, 368, 395–398
Iarosh, Dmytro  128
Iatseniuk, Arsenii  127, 190, 236, 325, 334, 336, 338, 354, 371
identity  20, 43, 45, 48, 49, 74, 90, 102, 103, 106, 107, 113, 114, 125, 126, 134, 141, 147, 148, 217, 222, 223, 232, 236, 242, 243, 254, 274, 284, 285, 289, 378–383, 385, 387, 390–394, 396–398, 401
   civic  385
   collective  32, 380, 387, 397, 398, 400
   cultural  393
   European  114
   individual  397
   national  45, 50, 56, 99, 102, 123, 217, 222, 241, 380, 381, 385, 387, 388, 396, 397
   political  90, 112
   Ukrainian  43, 48, 90, 104, 107, 112, 126, 385
ideology  19, 26, 80, 122, 128, 130, 139, 140, 143, 150, 157, 220, 241, 307, 386, 392, 406, 407
   ideological subversion  30, 75, 255, 256, 258, 259, 262, 387
   language ideology(ies)  139, 143, 157
   neo-Nazism  296, 310
   racist ideology  128
Iefremov, Oleksandr  75
Ieltsin, Boris  54, 55, 106, 257
   Era  54
Ierofeev, Viktor  379
Ievpatoria  289
Ilin, Ivan  406
Illarionov, Andrei  28, 82
IMF  339
Incirlik airbase (Turkey)  240
Independence Square, Kyiv  21, 58, 165, 168, 171, 172
Indian Ocean  234
industrialization  45, 50, 53
insulation  383
insurgents, *see also opolchentsy*  74, 89

intelligence  70–72, 75, 77, 200, 231, 255, 257, 275
international community  17, 30, 70, 79, 132, 201, 202, 206, 285, 383
international relations  78, 79, 258
international terrorism  79
Internet Research Agency  260, 262–264
Iraq  57, 60, 264
ISIL (*see also* ISIS)  264
Islam(ic)  207, 264, 285, 288, 290–293
Isliamov, Lenur  204
Ismailov, Said  288
isolation  203, 293, 383
ISP  274
Israel  297, 298, 301, 302
   Israel Defense Forces  301
Istanbul  218, 239, 241
Italy  71, 361
Iurkevych, Pamfil  166
Ivanov, Viacheslav  146, 220

## J

Japan  71
Jews  17, 31, 127, 128, 130, 284, 293–295, 297–302, 309, 310, 387
   Jewish  82, 127, 128, 283, 293–302, 310, 329
      *aliyah*  298, 299
      Communities and Organizations (Russia)  295
      Congress of Jewish Religious  295
      Federation of Jewish Communities of Russia  296
      population  297
   Jewish-Ukrainian relations  293
   World Forum of Russian Jewry  297
Jones, Gareth  256
journalism(sts)  24, 27, 56, 145, 167, 183, 202, 256, 261, 262, 266, 318, 335, 344, 362
   investigative  256, 262, 318, 335, 344
   journalists  24, 56, 145, 183, 202, 256, 261, 262, 266, 318, 344
Judaism  297

## K

Kalashnikov  26
Kaliningrad  97

Katechon, *see also* Russian
  messianism 222
Kazakhstan 41, 54, 198
Kennan, George 106
Kennedy, John F. 256
Kerch 192, 205
  Kerch Strait 192, 205
  Kerch Strait Bridge 205
KGB 27, 56, 57, 75, 82, 83, 253,
  255–257, 261, 265, 387, 389
Kharkiv (Kharkov) 54, 59, 74, 104,
  151, 188, 197, 297, 300, 301, 354,
  361, 393, 394
  Kharkiv Accords 59, 197
Kherson 204
  Kherson oblast 204
'*khokhly*' 76
Kholmogorov, Iegor [Egor] 109, 222
Khomiakov, Valerii 58
Khrushchev, Nikita 200
King, Martin Luther 307, 308
Kirby, John 201
Kistiakovskii, Bogdan 112
Kivalov-Kolesnichenko law 151–153
Kniazhytskyi, Mykola 362
Kobzon, Iosif 75
Kofman, Aleksandr 81, 301
Kogan, Zinovii 295
Kokh, Alfred 24, 74
Kolchugino 287
Kolesnikov, Borys 75
Kolomoiskyi, Ihor 127, 291, 301
Konchalovskii, Andrei 382
Konovalets, Ievhen 128
Konstantinov, Vladimir 189, 191
Koselleck, Reinhart 27
Kosovo 57, 60
Kostenko, Lina 148
Kostomarov, Nikolai (Mykola) 96, 99
Kozhara, Leonid 41
Kravchenko, Iurii 363
Kravchuk, Leonid 54, 106, 198, 391,
  392
Kremlin 26, 30, 49, 57, 70, 71, 80,
  89, 93, 95, 99, 101, 110, 115, 121,
  125, 130, 134, 185, 189, 190, 192,
  194, 196–205, 256, 260–262, 393,
  394
Kryvyi Rih 47
Kuban region 205

Kuchabsky, Vasyl 105
Kuchma, Leonid 94, 100, 198, 363,
  391, 392, 397
Kusturica, Emir 404
Kvit, Serhii 122, 130
Kyiv 15, 21, 24, 26, 27, 41, 44, 52,
  53, 58, 61, 62, 69, 70, 72, 82, 83,
  91, 93–95, 103, 104, 107, 111,
  115, 121–124, 127, 130, 147, 161,
  163–165, 168, 169, 171, 172,
  183–190, 192, 195, 197–199, 204,
  205, 207, 229, 293, 294, 297, 298,
  300, 303, 304, 318, 353, 356, 365,
  389, 392, 393, 395, 405
Kyiv(an) Rus 53, 93, 95, 111, 125
Kyiv-Mohyla Academy (Kyiv) 122

## L

Lane, Mark 256
Latakia 232, 235
Latin America 370
Latvia 17, 18, 57
Lazar, Berl 296
Lenin 48, 76, 107, 287, 405
liberalism 131, 144
Libya 57, 59, 234
Lithuania 17, 18, 57
'little green men' 62, 81, 185, 188,
  193
Litvinenko, Aleksandr 24
Liumanov, Ruslan 202
LNR 75, 149
London 24
Louisiana 261, 269
Luhansk 15, 62, 75, 83, 149, 151,
  154, 203, 297, 299, 301, 303–305,
  309
Lukashenka, Aleksandr 198
Lukianov, Fiodor 55
Lukin, Vladimir 55, 187
Luzhkov, Iurii 200
Lviv 353, 403
Lypynskyi, Viacheslav 96, 99, 401

## M

*madrasa* 287
Maidan 21, 23, 28, 128, 161–173, 175, 176, 184–190, 195, 197, 203, 229, 295, 305, 309, 342, 393, 399, 400, 403, 405
Makhno, Nestor 76
'*malorosy*' 76, 112
MAP 59
*Maritime Doctrine of Russian Federation 2020* 234
Mariupol 188, 299
Martens Centre for European Studies 265
Marx, Carl 28
Marzani, Carl Aldo 256
mass killings 17, 20, 164, 391
Mausoleum 405
Mazepa, Ivan 64, 125
Mediterranean Sea 226, 233, 234, 241
Mejlis 191, 193, 201, 202, 287–292
Members of the Ukrainian Parliament 403
memory 29, 98, 129, 199, 217, 222, 223, 310, 381, 389, 400
  memory politics 29, 98
mercenaries 78, 80, 304
Merezhkovskii, Dmitrii 220
Meshkov, Aleksei 235
Middle Ages 94
Middle East 25, 30, 59, 71, 77, 370
Middle Volga 96
military doctrine 24, 197
*militia, see also militsiia* 74, 149, 187–189, 332
Mitrokhin, Vasili 256
modernization 45, 49, 63, 176, 353
Moldova 84, 215, 357
Molotov, Viacheslav 176, 227, 228, 295
monasteries
  monastery of Eleazar (Pskov) 218
  Sretenskii monastery (Moscow) 221
monolingualism 139, 153, 380
Moscovite 379
Moscovy 219

Moscow 17, 23, 25, 41, 56, 57, 60, 64, 75, 81, 89, 93, 94, 101–103, 108, 110, 114, 115, 123, 124, 129, 130, 184, 188, 189, 195, 197–201, 207, 218, 220, 221, 255, 258, 260, 263, 271, 272, 311, 387, 395, 405
Moskovitz, Moishe 300
MTCR 79
Munich Agreement of 1938 71
Murmansk 233
Muscovy, *see also* Moscovy 96, 98, 113, 114, 219
Muslims 31, 284, 287, 289, 292, 293, 302, 310
  Muslim Brotherhood 286
  Spiritual Board of Muslims 285, 292
Myanmar 82
Mykolaiv 52, 151

## N

Nagorno-Karabakh 64, 215, 238
Nalyvaichenko, Valentyn 187, 368
Narochnitskaia, Nataliia 222
Naryshkin, Sergei 189
'nashi' (ours) 43
nation building 104, 110, 156, 223, 390, 393, 398, 402
national consciousness 18, 385, 387
National Police of Ukraine 353, 360
national security 71, 154, 253, 269, 359, 397
nationalism(st) 43, 46, 47, 50, 54, 89, 106, 109, 110, 121, 122, 124, 125, 128, 130, 132, 134, 142, 222, 295, 304, 383, 385, 388, 393, 396, 398
  Russian 132, 133, 236, 383
  Ukrainian 70, 105, 112, 122, 128, 388
nation-states 46, 55, 97, 253
NATO 24, 28, 56, 57, 59, 60, 63, 64, 69, 70, 72, 189, 199, 200, 202, 213, 214, 228–230, 234, 238, 239, 241, 242, 395
  NATO Membership Plan for Ukraine 395
  Parliamentary Assembly 28
*nebesna sotnia, see also* 'Heavenly Hundred' 167
Nestor-Iskander 220
Netherlands 357
New Jersey 55

New York 55, 261
Nikolai I (Russian Tsar) 223, 226
Nikolai II (Russian Tsar) 226
Novodvorskaia, Valeriia 80
Novorosiia 72
Novorossiisk 188, 190
Novosti press agency 256

# O

Obama, Barack 76, 263, 268
occupation 29, 31, 57, 78, 83, 197, 202, 206, 235, 283, 287, 291, 293, 310
   German 46
   of Abkhazia 57
   of Crimea 29, 83, 202
   Romanian 51
   Russian 31, 286, 287
Odesa 74, 104, 236, 264, 295, 305, 322, 353, 354, 405
Oman 82
*opolchentsy, see also* insurgents 74
Opuk (Crimea) 233
Orange Revolution 18, 58, 100, 194, 199
Orthodox 43, 44, 60, 81, 97, 111, 216, 219, 220, 222, 224, 239, 290, 294, 297, 397
   Church 60
   faith 216, 224
OSCE 58, 59, 289, 331
Osmanov, Aider 287
Ossetia
   South Ossetia 57, 59, 64
OUN 72, 122, 128–130, 388

# P

Pacific Ocean 225
Palmyra 231
Panarin, Igor 265
Pan-Slavism(st) 220, 392
parliamentary elections, in Ukraine 59, 183, 186, 327, 329, 403
party (ies)
   All-Union Communist Party 49
   Batkivshchyna 332, 361
   extremist parties 134
   far-right parties 133
   Nazi party 80

Novorossiia (New Russia) Party 81, 291
Party of Regions 61, 333, 342, 368, 400
Right Sector 128–130, 203
Soviet Ukraine's communist party 48
Svoboda 125, 128, 129, 296, 300, 396
Pathé, Pierre-Charles 256
Patriarch Kirill 296
patriotism 26, 84, 195, 300, 385
   'excessive patriotism' 382
perestroika 378, 389
Peter the Great 64, 397
Petliura, Symon 125
Pliushch, Leonid 17
Podillia 44
Poklonskaia, Natalia 201
Poland 17, 18, 51, 81, 105, 113, 199, 207, 357, 382
   Poles 17, 47, 387, 393
   Polish 24, 80, 81, 96, 105, 113, 126, 407
police 32, 75, 128, 184, 192, 202, 206, 294, 353–357, 359–370, 399
   business channel 24
Polish-Lithuanian Commonwealth 96, 126
political activism 184, 198, 345, 389, 394, 396
Politkovskaia, Anna 80
Poltorak, Stepan 23
Poroshenko, Petro 62, 63, 94, 125, 141, 187, 325, 329, 330, 333–335, 353, 354, 359, 371, 395, 402
Portnikov, Vitalii 206
Portugal 357
Prigozhin, Ievgenii 262
Prokhanov, Aleksandr 80
Prokhasko, Taras 166, 171, 399
propaganda *see* Russian propaganda, Ukrainian propaganda
*propiska* 26
Pskov 218
PSYOP 265, 266, 267
punitive psychiatry 17
Pushkin, Aleksandr 381
Pussy Riot 60
Putin
   administration 28
   regime 134, 381

Putin, Vladimir 19, 23–25, 28, 34, 41, 42, 56–64, 69, 71, 72, 74, 76, 78–82, 84, 93, 95, 98, 100–102, 107, 108, 111, 121–134, 144, 183–185, 187, 188, 190, 192–195, 198–200, 204, 205, 207, 221, 222, 231, 233, 234, 242, 257, 259, 264, 267, 270, 271, 275, 277, 296, 303, 379, 381, 383, 385, 405, 407

## Q

Qatar 82

## R

Radicalism
   Islamic 286
   radical movements 286
      Hizb-ut-Tahrir (Islamic Party of Liberation) 286
      Muslim Brotherhood 286
      Wahhabis 286
Red Square 75, 405
reflexive control 269, 270, 275
refugees 31, 46, 73, 284, 296, 298, 311, 312
regionalism 96, 393, 394
religion 20, 96, 105, 107, 113, 391
   religious communities 31, 283, 284, 297, 303, 310, 311
   religious policies 287
revolution 15, 18, 21, 34, 58, 91, 96, 99, 100, 101, 162, 163, 167, 168, 170–173, 176, 226, 265, 271, 317, 321, 387, 398–400, 402–406
   'postcolonial revolution' 91, 101
   Arab Spring 59–61
   Bolshevik 99
   fatigue 404
   French 28
   Orange revolution 170, 184, 342, 393, 395, 396
   Revolution of Dignity 21, 84, 101, 163, 205
   Ukrainian revolution (2013–2014), *see also* Euromaidan 22, 100, 101, 161, 163, 169, 172, 186, 229, 304, 317
      Revolution of Dignity 21, 84, 101, 163, 205
      Revolution of Values 101, 163
Ribbentrop, Joachim von 227
Rogozin, Dmitrii 61, 234

Romania 30, 51, 199, 213, 215, 232, 238, 240, 242
Roosevelt, Franklin D. 77
'Rossiia-3' (Eurasian Union of Youth) 19
Rostovtsev, Oleh 296
RSFSR 17, 102, 106
Rudnytsky, Ivan L. 96, 105
Rurikid princes 113
Russia 16, 19, 20, 23–27, 29–32, 34, 41–44, 46, 50, 52–65, 69–82, 84, 89–96, 98–105, 107–111, 113, 114, 122, 124–128, 130–133, 141, 142, 144, 145, 147, 148, 150, 151, 153, 156, 183–190, 192–195, 198–200, 202–207, 213–216, 218, 220–229, 231–238, 240, 241, 253–255, 258–260, 262–264, 266, 267, 269–271, 273–277, 283–285, 287, 290–293, 295, 296, 303–309, 311, 312, 368, 377–383, 385, 386, 390–392, 394–398, 401–403, 405, 406
   'historic' Russia 55, 92, 102, 103, 108, 113, 114
   Central Russia 44
   Great Russia (*Velikorossiia*) 105
   Little Russia 43, 44, 46, 105, 111, 112
Russian 15, 16, 19, 22–24, 26–31, 34, 41–47, 49, 50, 52–55, 57–60, 62, 63, 64, 70, 72, 74, 75, 77, 79–81, 83, 84, 90, 92–99, 101–114, 115, 121–123, 125–134, 139–156, 161, 173, 183, 185, 187–197, 199–207, 213–238, 240, 241, 243, 253–260, 262–268, 270, 271, 275, 276, 284, 286–290, 292, 293, 296, 299, 300, 303, 304, 307, 310, 311, 368, 377, 379, 380, 381, 383, 385, 386, 391, 393–398, 401, 405, 407
   'Black Hundreds' 81
   adventurism 213, 214
   army (military) 22, 62, 79, 122, 147, 185, 190, 193, 203, 214, 228, 230–232, 234–237, 242, 265, 275, 284, 384
   Black Sea Fleet (Sevastopol) 57, 194, 197
   bombers 229, 230
   channels (TV), television stations 26, 42, 62, 141, 154, 325
      RTR 221

citizens 19, 62, 81, 83, 108, 195, 213, 222, 258, 267, 394, 407
culture 49, 108, 111, 222, 382
expansion (Russia's expansion) 237
Federation 16, 24, 29, 42, 54, 55, 60, 62, 64, 81, 82, 92, 102–110, 114, 189, 193, 195, 197, 201, 202, 207, 214, 228, 233, 276, 292, 383, 385, 395, 396, 398
foreign policies
    Foreign Policy Concept of the Russian Federation 221
government 24, 41, 133, 141
Great Russian 43, 44, 105, 107, 111
history 43, 96, 108, 125, 126, 196, 217, 221, 381
identity 42, 107, 111, 216, 217, 383
invasion 42, 126, 133, 148, 173, 222, 398
language 125, 139, 144, 147, 149, 151, 154, 156, 380, 381, 395, 396
law 202, 290, 311
Little Russian 43, 44, 46, 105, 112
messianism (Katechon) 220, 222
militarism 214
military 62, 79, 122, 185, 190, 203, 214, 228, 230–237, 242, 265, 275, 284, 384
nation 50, 64, 81, 102, 104, 107, 110, 112, 132–134, 217, 219, 222, 236, 243, 378, 382, 383
national security 64, 384
nationalism 132, 133, 236, 383
nationhood 110
Navy 234
people 26, 53, 58, 95, 97, 106, 108, 111, 215, 237, 241, 290, 406
politics 221, 222
President 23, 93, 407
propaganda 23, 127, 130, 133, 200, 229, 264, 266–268, 271, 385, 387
psyche 109, 217, 219
RT news network 274
secret services (security services) 24, 75, 187, 191, 394
soldiers 23
troops 191, 224
White Russian 43
Russian Union of Evangelical Christians-Baptists 303
Russianness 109, 111

Russians 17, 27, 28, 43–45, 47, 50, 51, 53, 55, 56, 60, 63, 74, 75, 84, 94–96, 98, 99, 102, 103, 105, 107, 110–114, 123–126, 131, 132, 144, 184, 189, 192, 195, 196, 198, 200, 214, 218, 223, 225–228, 231, 232, 234, 235, 238, 239, 241, 290, 304, 305, 377, 380, 383, 384, 387, 393, 403, 405, 407
Russian-Turkish relations 231
Russian-Ukrainian relations 31, 34
Russian-Ukrainian Treaty of Friendship 54
Russification 45, 50, 139, 144, 147, 149, 150, 156
'Russkii mir' (the Russian World) 72
Russophobia 295, 310
    Russophobes 123
Russophones 152, 153, 157
Ruthenians 46
Rwanda 82

## S

Saakashvili, Mikheil 59, 322, 354, 359, 403
Saitvaliev, Ruslan 286
Sakharov, Andrei 80
Sakvarelidze, David 405
sanctions 23, 24, 64, 77, 198, 203, 205, 206, 235–237, 243, 267, 383
Sardinia 224
Saudi Arabia 269
Savchenko, Nadiia 400, 401
Sazonov, Serge 224, 226
Schmitt, Carl 132
Schwartz, Ari 298, 299
Scythians 129
Sea of Marmara 215
secret police 256
self-identification, *see also* identity 31, 121, 378
Semena, Mykola 202
separatism 43, 124, 190, 393
    separatists 22, 62, 63, 81, 142, 150, 185, 190, 192, 193, 213, 275, 294, 301, 395
Serbia 57

Sevastopol 59, 62, 79, 151, 188–190, 193, 194, 197, 200, 224, 233, 234
Shevchenko, Taras 162, 172
Shevkunov, Tikhon 221
*shistdesiatnytstvo* 388
Shoigu, Sergei 233
Sikorski, Radoslaw 187
Silantiev, Roman 288, 290, 291
Sipko, Iurii 304, 305
Skovoroda, Hryhorii 166
Skrypnyk, Mykola 125
Slavic 43, 44, 53, 93, 105, 110, 115, 216, 221, 224
  civilization 224
  people 53, 105, 110, 216
  prince 93
  Slavdom, Eastern 93
Slavophiles 224
Slovakia 357
Slovenia 357
Slutskii, Leonid 191
SNG 406
Sobor 290
social engineering 266, 269
social media 142, 146, 155, 190, 253, 258, 260–263, 268, 270–273, 276
Solzhenitsyn, Alexander 99
Soviet 15–19, 47–57, 59–61, 63, 64, 71, 74, 75, 90–92, 96–98, 101–108, 111, 112, 121, 122, 126, 129–131, 143, 144, 154, 163, 167, 172, 195, 196, 198, 199, 201, 206, 214, 222, 223, 227, 228, 234, 237, 243, 254–258, 293, 294, 299, 302, 306, 319, 353, 354, 361, 362, 365, 378, 381, 382, 384, 387–390, 392, 393, 396, 398–401, 403–405
  Bloc 255
  era 74, 91, 92, 104, 113, 172, 396
  government 50, 53, 256, 388
  paraphernalia 399
  republics 19, 143, 387
  Soviet Odesa Republics 47
  terror 16
  traditions 15
  Union (*see also* USSR) 17, 48, 51, 53, 55–57, 64, 71, 74, 97, 98, 101, 102, 103, 106–108, 126, 144, 227, 234, 256, 302, 306, 387

  collapse of the Soviet Union 18, 92, 108
Spain 357
special forces 162, 188, 206, 359
  Alfa 192
  Berkut 128, 162, 166, 187, 192, 359
  Omega 359
  Sokil 359
St. Petersburg 111, 113, 225, 233, 262, 303
Stalin 17, 49, 50–52, 56, 71, 75, 80, 81, 106, 129, 287, 388, 407
Stalinism 20, 391
Starovoitova, Galina 80
state building 379, 385, 388, 390, 392
state violence 16, 22, 32, 387
Steinmeier, Frank-Walter 187
Stoltenberg, Jens 229
Struve, Piotr 111, 112
subjugation 84, 162, 403
Sufism 286
Sürgün (1944) 287, 309
Surkov, Vladislav 187, 188, 265
SVR 257
Sweden 229
*sylovyky* (*siloviki*) 172
Symferopil 285, 287
Symonenko, Iurii 305
Syria 60, 61, 84, 213–215, 231–235, 237, 238, 266, 274

**T**

Tabachnyk, Dmytro 397
Tadjuddin, Talgat 291, 292
Tarkovskii, Andrei 33
Tartus 233, 234
Taurida (Tauridia) 285
  Tauride Directorate 285
  Tauride Muftiate 285, 286, 288–293
Tbilisi 69, 362
terrorism(sts) 79, 84, 231, 235, 239
  terrorist activities 29
theory 161, 174, 400
  of performance 174
  of society 174
Third Reich 80, 308
'Third Rome' myth 31, 216
Thucydides 89, 90, 115
Time of Troubles (*Smuta*) 98

Transcarpathia 51
Transnistria 64
Treaty of Pereiaslav 52, 53
'trolls' 29, 253–255, 258–277
'trolling' 253, 255, 260, 268, 271, 276, 277
Tsargrad, *see also* Constantinople 218, 220
Tsarist 43
Tsymburskii, Vadim 222
Turchynov, Oleksandr 61, 62, 152
Turgenev, Ivan 382
Turkey 30, 213, 215, 216, 224, 227, 228, 230, 233, 235–237, 239, 240, 288
    Turkish 31, 215, 218, 223, 225–228, 230, 233, 235, 236, 238, 241, 384
    Turkish Straits 31, 215, 218, 223, 226, 227, 233, 238, 384
    Turks 224, 226, 239
Tuzla Island conflict (2003) 71
Tymoshenko, Iuliia 41, 58, 59, 61, 198, 199, 321, 325, 361, 394, 403

## U

Ukraine 15–34, 39, 41–44, 47–49, 51–55, 57–59, 61–65, 69–77, 79–85, 89–101, 103–107, 111, 113–115, 121–127, 129, 130, 133, 137, 139–143, 145, 147, 148, 150–157, 162, 164–167, 171, 175, 176, 183, 185–193, 194, 195, 197–200, 202–207, 213–215, 218, 222, 232–234, 236–238, 243, 253, 261, 263–265, 267, 271–277, 283–285, 288, 293–299, 301, 302, 303, 305–310, 312, 315, 317–331, 333, 334, 336, 339–342, 344–346, 353, 358, 362, 368–370, 377, 378, 380, –382, 384–402, 404–406
    eastern 15, 16, 24, 27, 42, 62, 64, 72, 76, 126, 127, 139, 142, 213, 214, 223, 238, 297, 302, 394, 396, 401, 403
    western 72, 391, 392

Ukrainian 15–20, 22, 25, 27, 28, 32, 41–54, 57, 59, 62, 63, 64, 70–77, 80, 82–85, 90, 92–95, 97, 99–101, 103–107, 111–113, 121–129, 131, 139, 141–157, 161–164, 166, 167, 169, 170–174, 183–194, 196–207, 213, 228, 229, 232, 237, 254, 263, 264, 266, 267, 285, 287, 288, 292, 293, 296, 298, 299, 301, 303–305, 307–311, 317, 318, 321, 328–330, 336, 342, 345, 346, 356, 361, 367, 371, 379–381, 385–407
    conflict 77, 90, 296, 401
    consciousness 166
    crisis 27, 28
    culture 16, 50, 74, 379, 387, 392, 395
    diaspora 16
    government 25, 32, 62, 63, 65, 70, 149, 198, 207, 254, 264, 267, 298, 346, 371, 395, 397, 401
    history 20, 104, 125, 390, 392
    identity 43, 48, 90, 104, 107, 112, 126, 385
    institutions 50, 199
    intellectuals (intelligentsia) 16, 43, 49, 111, 380, 388
    language 52, 74, 122, 126, 127, 142, 144, 146–149, 151, 154–157, 380, 381, 387, 392
    nation 32, 43, 45, 48, 70, 72, 76, 90, 92, 94, 95, 99, 101, 104, 105, 112, 122, 124, 127, 128, 141–143, 172, 174, 195, 200, 380–382, 385, 387–389, 391, 394, 399, 400
    national movement 43, 45
    national project 32
    nationalism(sts) 70, 76, 105, 112, 122, 127, 128, 195, 200, 388, 391
    oligarchs 329, 346, 403
    Parliament 150
    patriotism 303
    peasants 16, 48, 387
    propaganda 71, 386
    society 20, 49, 97, 101, 122, 170, 172, 184, 342, 389, 391, 393, 394, 396–398, 403
    SSR 46–48, 51, 53, 54, 106, 107, 143, 200
    State Security Service 187
    territories (lands) 19, 22, 51, 53, 71, 73, 77, 85, 95, 228, 403
    TV channels 73
    Ukrainian military 42, 75, 84, 185, 193, 266
        military bases 185, 193

Ukrainianness 156
Ukrainian-Russian relations 91, 107, 397
Ukrainians 15, 17, 20, 41, 43, 45–48, 50–53, 59, 64, 73, 75, 76, 81, 85, 92, 94–99, 102, 104, 105, 107, 111, 112, 121, 122, 124–129, 141, 147, 148, 155, 162, 164, 176, 183, 186, 198, 199, 203, 206, 207, 264, 304, 305, 346, 377, 379–381, 386–390, 395, 396, 398–402, 404, 407
Ukrainization 139, 146, 147, 156, 206, 395
Ukrainophile 45
Umerov, Ilmi 288
United Kingdom, *see also* Great Britain, England 197, 229, 357, 367
United Nations 42, 77–79, 202, 271
    United Nations Declaration of Human Rights 271
    United Nations General Assembly Resolution (1974) 78
    United Nations Security Council 77
    United Nations' High Commissioner for Human Rights 42
United States 16, 17, 24, 42, 55, 57, 59, 76, 77, 82, 84, 113, 197, 202, 232, 237, 255, 256, 258, 382
UPA 72, 122, 128–130, 388
USSR, *see also* Soviet Union 42, 46, 50–58, 71, 75, 102, 103, 105, 106, 126, 143, 150, 189, 256, 257, 388, 389, 392
Ustrialov, Nikolai 111
Uzbeks 102

## V

Vasilii III (Grand Prince of Moscow) 218
Velychkovych, Mykola 356
Venetism 206
Venice Commission 202
Verkhovna Rada 334, 343, 357, 358, 361, 365
Vilnius 28, 42, 183, 184, 186, 198
Vishedski, Pinchas 298, 301
Vladimir (Volodymyr) the Great 93
Vladivostok 97

Volhynia 44, 51, 126
volunteer movement 84, 175, 401
Voznesenskii, Andrei 22
VPN 274

## W

war (wars, warfare)
    civil war (Ukraine) 27, 84
    Cold War 42, 56, 213, 234, 255, 270, 387, 405
    conventional warfare 29, 84, 207, 275
    Crimean War (1853–56) 196, 223
    First World War (*see also* Great War) 46, 71, 105, 112, 223
    Fourth World War 29
    German-Soviet war 130
    Great Patriotic War (1941–1944) 196
    hybrid wars 30
    ideological warfare 253, 254
    information wars 29
    language wars 380, 381
    of narratives 89, 386
    of words 89, 283, 386
    propaganda wars 386
    Russian-Ukrainian 'trade war' 205
    Russian-Ukrainian war 15, 28, 29, 31, 34, 253, 267, 385, 396
    Russo-Turkish war 225
    second Chechen War (1999–2009) 195
    Second World War 17, 51, 71–73, 106, 122, 129, 130, 134, 295
    Spanish civil war 71
    Syrian civil war 231, 268
    Third World War 71, 79, 84
    troll warfare 276
    World War 29, 46, 71
West 16, 17, 19, 25, 55, 56, 58, 60, 63, 76, 77, 80–82, 84, 90, 115, 124, 129, 130, 133, 134, 183, 185, 195, 203, 207, 215, 222, 224, 228, 230, 240, 241, 272, 276, 277, 370, 382–384, 390, 391
    Western Powers 228
    Western values 229, 277
Witte, Sergei 105
Wolf, Eric R. 397

## X

xenophobia 294, 381, 383
    xenophobic 127

## Y

Yalta 78, 188, 190
Yemen 82
Yugoslavia 234

## Z

Zabuzhko, Oksana 129
Zaharchenko, Vitalii 187, 189
Zakharov, Mark 405
Zaldostanov, Aleksandr 200
Zalizniak, Bohdan 402
Zamiliukhin, Sergei 141
Zaporizhian Sich 165
Zaporizhzhia 52, 146
Zguladze-Gluksmann, Iekateryna 354
Zhirinovskii, Vladimir 54
Zhyzhko, Serhii 385
Zimbabwe 82
Zissels, Josef 299

# SOVIET AND POST-SOVIET POLITICS AND SOCIETY

Edited by Dr. Andreas Umland

ISSN 1614-3515

1   Андреас Умланд (ред.)
    Воплощение Европейской
    конвенции по правам человека в
    России
    Философские, юридические и
    эмпирические исследования
    ISBN 3-89821-387-0

2   Christian Wipperfürth
    Russland – ein vertrauenswürdiger
    Partner?
    Grundlagen, Hintergründe und Praxis
    gegenwärtiger russischer Außenpolitik
    Mit einem Vorwort von Heinz Timmermann
    ISBN 3-89821-401-X

3   Manja Hussner
    Die Übernahme internationalen Rechts
    in die russische und deutsche
    Rechtsordnung
    Eine vergleichende Analyse zur
    Völkerrechtsfreundlichkeit der Verfassungen
    der Russländischen Föderation und der
    Bundesrepublik Deutschland
    Mit einem Vorwort von Rainer Arnold
    ISBN 3-89821-438-9

4   Matthew Tejada
    Bulgaria's Democratic Consolidation
    and the Kozloduy Nuclear Power Plant
    (KNPP)
    The Unattainability of Closure
    With a foreword by Richard J. Crampton
    ISBN 3-89821-439-7

5   Марк Григорьевич Меерович
    Квадратные метры, определяющие
    сознание
    Государственная жилищная политика в
    СССР. 1921 – 1941 гг
    ISBN 3-89821-474-5

6   Andrei P. Tsygankov, Pavel
    A.Tsygankov (Eds.)
    New Directions in Russian
    International Studies
    ISBN 3-89821-422-2

7   Марк Григорьевич Меерович
    Как власть народ к труду приучала
    Жилище в СССР – средство управления
    людьми. 1917 – 1941 гг.
    С предисловием Елены Осокиной
    ISBN 3-89821-495-8

8   David J. Galbreath
    Nation-Building and Minority Politics
    in Post-Socialist States
    Interests, Influence and Identities in Estonia
    and Latvia
    With a foreword by David J. Smith
    ISBN 3-89821-467-2

9   Алексей Юрьевич Безугольный
    Народы Кавказа в Вооруженных
    силах СССР в годы Великой
    Отечественной войны 1941-1945 гг.
    С предисловием Николая Бугая
    ISBN 3-89821-475-3

10  Вячеслав Лихачев и Владимир
    Прибыловский (ред.)
    Русское Национальное Единство,
    1990-2000. В 2-х томах
    ISBN 3-89821-523-7

11  Николай Бугай (ред.)
    Народы стран Балтии в условиях
    сталинизма (1940-е – 1950-е годы)
    Документированная история
    ISBN 3-89821-525-3

12  Ingmar Bredies (Hrsg.)
    Zur Anatomie der Orange Revolution
    in der Ukraine
    Wechsel des Elitenregimes oder Triumph des
    Parlamentarismus?
    ISBN 3-89821-524-5

13  Anastasia V. Mitrofanova
    The Politicization of Russian
    Orthodoxy
    Actors and Ideas
    With a foreword by William C. Gay
    ISBN 3-89821-481-8

14  Nathan D. Larson
Alexander Solzhenitsyn and the
Russo-Jewish Question
ISBN 3-89821-483-4

15  Guido Houben
Kulturpolitik und Ethnizität
Staatliche Kunstförderung im Russland der
neunziger Jahre
Mit einem Vorwort von Gert Weisskirchen
ISBN 3-89821-542-3

16  Leonid Luks
Der russische „Sonderweg"?
Aufsätze zur neuesten Geschichte Russlands
im europäischen Kontext
ISBN 3-89821-496-6

17  Евгений Мороз
История «Мёртвой воды» – от
страшной сказки к большой
политике
Политическое неоязычество в
постсоветской России
ISBN 3-89821-551-2

18  Александр Верховский и Галина
Кожевникова (ред.)
Этническая и религиозная
интолерантность в российских СМИ
Результаты мониторинга 2001-2004 гг.
ISBN 3-89821-569-5

19  Christian Ganzer
Sowjetisches Erbe und ukrainische
Nation
Das Museum der Geschichte des Zaporoger
Kosakentums auf der Insel Chortycja
Mit einem Vorwort von Frank Golczewski
ISBN 3-89821-504-0

20  Эльза-Баир Гучинова
Помнить нельзя забыть
Антропология депортационной травмы
калмыков
С предисловием Кэролайн Хамфри
ISBN 3-89821-506-7

21  Юлия Лидерман
Мотивы «проверки» и «испытания»
в постсоветской культуре
Советское прошлое в российском
кинематографе 1990-х годов
С предисловием Евгения Марголита
ISBN 3-89821-511-3

22  Tanya Lokshina, Ray Thomas, Mary
Mayer (Eds.)
The Imposition of a Fake Political
Settlement in the Northern Caucasus
The 2003 Chechen Presidential Election
ISBN 3-89821-436-2

23  Timothy McCajor Hall, Rosie Read
(Eds.)
Changes in the Heart of Europe
Recent Ethnographies of Czechs, Slovaks,
Roma, and Sorbs
With an afterword by Zdeněk Salzmann
ISBN 3-89821-606-3

24  Christian Autengruber
Die politischen Parteien in Bulgarien
und Rumänien
Eine vergleichende Analyse seit Beginn der
90er Jahre
Mit einem Vorwort von Dorothée de Nève
ISBN 3-89821-476-1

25  Annette Freyberg-Inan with Radu
Cristescu
The Ghosts in Our Classrooms, or:
John Dewey Meets Ceauşescu
The Promise and the Failures of Civic
Education in Romania
ISBN 3-89821-416-8

26  John B. Dunlop
The 2002 Dubrovka and 2004 Beslan
Hostage Crises
A Critique of Russian Counter-Terrorism
With a foreword by Donald N. Jensen
ISBN 3-89821-608-X

27  Peter Koller
Das touristische Potenzial von
Kam''janec'–Podil's'kyj
Eine fremdenverkehrsgeographische
Untersuchung der Zukunftsperspektiven und
Maßnahmenplanung zur
Destinationsentwicklung des „ukrainischen
Rothenburg"
Mit einem Vorwort von Kristiane Klemm
ISBN 3-89821-640-3

28  Françoise Daucé, Elisabeth Sieca-
Kozlowski (Eds.)
Dedovshchina in the Post-Soviet
Military
Hazing of Russian Army Conscripts in a
Comparative Perspective
With a foreword by Dale Herspring
ISBN 3-89821-616-0

29   *Florian Strasser*
     Zivilgesellschaftliche Einflüsse auf die Orange Revolution
     Die gewaltlose Massenbewegung und die ukrainische Wahlkrise 2004
     Mit einem Vorwort von Egbert Jahn
     ISBN 3-89821-648-9

30   *Rebecca S. Katz*
     The Georgian Regime Crisis of 2003-2004
     A Case Study in Post-Soviet Media Representation of Politics, Crime and Corruption
     ISBN 3-89821-413-3

31   *Vladimir Kantor*
     Willkür oder Freiheit
     Beiträge zur russischen Geschichtsphilosophie
     Ediert von Dagmar Herrmann sowie mit einem Vorwort versehen von Leonid Luks
     ISBN 3-89821-589-X

32   *Laura A. Victoir*
     The Russian Land Estate Today
     A Case Study of Cultural Politics in Post-Soviet Russia
     With a foreword by Priscilla Roosevelt
     ISBN 3-89821-426-5

33   *Ivan Katchanovski*
     Cleft Countries
     Regional Political Divisions and Cultures in Post-Soviet Ukraine and Moldova
     With a foreword by Francis Fukuyama
     ISBN 3-89821-558-X

34   *Florian Mühlfried*
     Postsowjetische Feiern
     Das Georgische Bankett im Wandel
     Mit einem Vorwort von Kevin Tuite
     ISBN 3-89821-601-2

35   *Roger Griffin, Werner Loh, Andreas Umland (Eds.)*
     Fascism Past and Present, West and East
     An International Debate on Concepts and Cases in the Comparative Study of the Extreme Right
     With an afterword by Walter Laqueur
     ISBN 3-89821-674-8

36   *Sebastian Schlegel*
     Der „Weiße Archipel"
     Sowjetische Atomstädte 1945-1991
     Mit einem Geleitwort von Thomas Bohn
     ISBN 3-89821-679-9

37   *Vyacheslav Likhachev*
     Political Anti-Semitism in Post-Soviet Russia
     Actors and Ideas in 1991-2003
     Edited and translated from Russian by Eugene Veklerov
     ISBN 3-89821-529-6

38   *Josette Baer (Ed.)*
     Preparing Liberty in Central Europe
     Political Texts from the Spring of Nations 1848 to the Spring of Prague 1968
     With a foreword by Zdeněk V. David
     ISBN 3-89821-546-6

39   *Михаил Лукьянов*
     Российский консерватизм и реформа, 1907-1914
     С предисловием Марка Д. Стейнберга
     ISBN 3-89821-503-2

40   *Nicola Melloni*
     Market Without Economy
     The 1998 Russian Financial Crisis
     With a foreword by Eiji Furukawa
     ISBN 3-89821-407-9

41   *Dmitrij Chmelnizki*
     Die Architektur Stalins
     Bd. 1: Studien zu Ideologie und Stil
     Bd. 2: Bilddokumentation
     Mit einem Vorwort von Bruno Flierl
     ISBN 3-89821-515-6

42   *Katja Yafimava*
     Post-Soviet Russian-Belarussian Relationships
     The Role of Gas Transit Pipelines
     With a foreword by Jonathan P. Stern
     ISBN 3-89821-655-1

43   *Boris Chavkin*
     Verflechtungen der deutschen und russischen Zeitgeschichte
     Aufsätze und Archivfunde zu den Beziehungen Deutschlands und der Sowjetunion von 1917 bis 1991
     Ediert von Markus Edlinger sowie mit einem Vorwort versehen von Leonid Luks
     ISBN 3-89821-756-5

44  *Anastasija Grynenko in Zusammenarbeit mit Claudia Dathe*
Die Terminologie des Gerichtswesens der Ukraine und Deutschlands im Vergleich
Eine übersetzungswissenschaftliche Analyse juristischer Fachbegriffe im Deutschen, Ukrainischen und Russischen
Mit einem Vorwort von Ulrich Hartmann
ISBN 3-89821-691-8

45  *Anton Burkov*
The Impact of the European Convention on Human Rights on Russian Law
Legislation and Application in 1996-2006
With a foreword by Françoise Hampson
ISBN 978-3-89821-639-5

46  *Stina Torjesen, Indra Overland (Eds.)*
International Election Observers in Post-Soviet Azerbaijan
Geopolitical Pawns or Agents of Change?
ISBN 978-3-89821-743-9

47  *Taras Kuzio*
Ukraine – Crimea – Russia
Triangle of Conflict
ISBN 978-3-89821-761-3

48  *Claudia Šabić*
"Ich erinnere mich nicht, aber L'viv!"
Zur Funktion kultureller Faktoren für die Institutionalisierung und Entwicklung einer ukrainischen Region
Mit einem Vorwort von Melanie Tatur
ISBN 978-3-89821-752-1

49  *Marlies Bilz*
Tatarstan in der Transformation
Nationaler Diskurs und Politische Praxis 1988-1994
Mit einem Vorwort von Frank Golczewski
ISBN 978-3-89821-722-4

50  *Марлен Ларюэль (ред.)*
Современные интерпретации русского национализма
ISBN 978-3-89821-795-8

51  *Sonja Schüler*
Die ethnische Dimension der Armut
Roma im postsozialistischen Rumänien
Mit einem Vorwort von Anton Sterbling
ISBN 978-3-89821-776-7

52  *Галина Кожевникова*
Радикальный национализм в России и противодействие ему
Сборник докладов Центра «Сова» за 2004-2007 гг.
С предисловием Александра Верховского
ISBN 978-3-89821-721-7

53  *Галина Кожевникова и Владимир Прибыловский*
Российская власть в биографиях I
Высшие должностные лица РФ в 2004 г.
ISBN 978-3-89821-796-5

54  *Галина Кожевникова и Владимир Прибыловский*
Российская власть в биографиях II
Члены Правительства РФ в 2004 г.
ISBN 978-3-89821-797-2

55  *Галина Кожевникова и Владимир Прибыловский*
Российская власть в биографиях III
Руководители федеральных служб и агентств РФ в 2004 г.
ISBN 978-3-89821-798-9

56  *Ileana Petroniu*
Privatisierung in Transformationsökonomien
Determinanten der Restrukturierungs-Bereitschaft am Beispiel Polens, Rumäniens und der Ukraine
Mit einem Vorwort von Rainer W. Schäfer
ISBN 978-3-89821-790-3

57  *Christian Wipperfürth*
Russland und seine GUS-Nachbarn
Hintergründe, aktuelle Entwicklungen und Konflikte in einer ressourcenreichen Region
ISBN 978-3-89821-801-6

58  *Togzhan Kassenova*
From Antagonism to Partnership
The Uneasy Path of the U.S.-Russian Cooperative Threat Reduction
With a foreword by Christoph Bluth
ISBN 978-3-89821-707-1

59  *Alexander Höllwerth*
Das sakrale eurasische Imperium des Aleksandr Dugin
Eine Diskursanalyse zum postsowjetischen russischen Rechtsextremismus
Mit einem Vorwort von Dirk Uffelmann
ISBN 978-3-89821-813-9

60 Олег Рябов
«Россия-Матушка»
Национализм, гендер и война в России XX века
С предисловием Елены Гощило
ISBN 978-3-89821-487-2

61 Ivan Maistrenko
Borot'bism
A Chapter in the History of the Ukrainian Revolution
With a new introduction by Chris Ford
Translated by George S. N. Luckyj with the assistance of Ivan L. Rudnytsky
ISBN 978-3-89821-697-5

62 Maryna Romanets
Anamorphosic Texts and Reconfigured Visions
Improvised Traditions in Contemporary Ukrainian and Irish Literature
ISBN 978-3-89821-576-3

63 Paul D'Anieri and Taras Kuzio (Eds.)
Aspects of the Orange Revolution I
Democratization and Elections in Post-Communist Ukraine
ISBN 978-3-89821-698-2

64 Bohdan Harasymiw in collaboration with Oleh S. Ilnytzkyj (Eds.)
Aspects of the Orange Revolution II
Information and Manipulation Strategies in the 2004 Ukrainian Presidential Elections
ISBN 978-3-89821-699-9

65 Ingmar Bredies, Andreas Umland and Valentin Yakushik (Eds.)
Aspects of the Orange Revolution III
The Context and Dynamics of the 2004 Ukrainian Presidential Elections
ISBN 978-3-89821-803-0

66 Ingmar Bredies, Andreas Umland and Valentin Yakushik (Eds.)
Aspects of the Orange Revolution IV
Foreign Assistance and Civic Action in the 2004 Ukrainian Presidential Elections
ISBN 978-3-89821-808-5

67 Ingmar Bredies, Andreas Umland and Valentin Yakushik (Eds.)
Aspects of the Orange Revolution V
Institutional Observation Reports on the 2004 Ukrainian Presidential Elections
ISBN 978-3-89821-809-2

68 Taras Kuzio (Ed.)
Aspects of the Orange Revolution VI
Post-Communist Democratic Revolutions in Comparative Perspective
ISBN 978-3-89821-820-7

69 Tim Bohse
Autoritarismus statt Selbstverwaltung
Die Transformation der kommunalen Politik in der Stadt Kaliningrad 1990-2005
Mit einem Geleitwort von Stefan Troebst
ISBN 978-3-89821-782-8

70 David Rupp
Die Rußländische Föderation und die russischsprachige Minderheit in Lettland
Eine Fallstudie zur Anwaltspolitik Moskaus gegenüber den russophonen Minderheiten im „Nahen Ausland" von 1991 bis 2002
Mit einem Vorwort von Helmut Wagner
ISBN 978-3-89821-778-1

71 Taras Kuzio
Theoretical and Comparative Perspectives on Nationalism
New Directions in Cross-Cultural and Post-Communist Studies
With a foreword by Paul Robert Magocsi
ISBN 978-3-89821-815-3

72 Christine Teichmann
Die Hochschultransformation im heutigen Osteuropa
Kontinuität und Wandel bei der Entwicklung des postkommunistischen Universitätswesens
Mit einem Vorwort von Oskar Anweiler
ISBN 978-3-89821-842-9

73 Julia Kusznir
Der politische Einfluss von Wirtschaftseliten in russischen Regionen
Eine Analyse am Beispiel der Erdöl- und Erdgasindustrie, 1992-2005
Mit einem Vorwort von Wolfgang Eichwede
ISBN 978-3-89821-821-4

74 Alena Vysotskaya
Russland, Belarus und die EU-Osterweiterung
Zur Minderheitenfrage und zum Problem der Freizügigkeit des Personenverkehrs
Mit einem Vorwort von Katlijn Malfliet
ISBN 978-3-89821-822-1

75  Heiko Pleines (Hrsg.)
    Corporate Governance in post-
    sozialistischen Volkswirtschaften
    ISBN 978-3-89821-766-8

76  Stefan Ihrig
    Wer sind die Moldawier?
    Rumänismus versus Moldowanismus in
    Historiographie und Schulbüchern der
    Republik Moldova, 1991-2006
    Mit einem Vorwort von Holm Sundhaussen
    ISBN 978-3-89821-466-7

77  Galina Kozhevnikova in collaboration
    with Alexander Verkhovsky and
    Eugene Veklerov
    Ultra-Nationalism and Hate Crimes in
    Contemporary Russia
    The 2004-2006 Annual Reports of Moscow's
    SOVA Center
    With a foreword by Stephen D. Shenfield
    ISBN 978-3-89821-868-9

78  Florian Küchler
    The Role of the European Union in
    Moldova's Transnistria Conflict
    With a foreword by Christopher Hill
    ISBN 978-3-89821-850-4

79  Bernd Rechel
    The Long Way Back to Europe
    Minority Protection in Bulgaria
    With a foreword by Richard Crampton
    ISBN 978-3-89821-863-4

80  Peter W. Rodgers
    Nation, Region and History in Post-
    Communist Transitions
    Identity Politics in Ukraine, 1991-2006
    With a foreword by Vera Tolz
    ISBN 978-3-89821-903-7

81  Stephanie Solywoda
    The Life and Work of
    Semen L. Frank
    A Study of Russian Religious Philosophy
    With a foreword by Philip Walters
    ISBN 978-3-89821-457-5

82  Vera Sokolova
    Cultural Politics of Ethnicity
    Discourses on Roma in Communist
    Czechoslovakia
    ISBN 978-3-89821-864-1

83  Natalya Shevchik Ketenci
    Kazakhstani Enterprises in Transition
    The Role of Historical Regional Development
    in Kazakhstan's Post-Soviet Economic
    Transformation
    ISBN 978-3-89821-831-3

84  Martin Malek, Anna Schor-
    Tschudnowskaja (Hrsg.)
    Europa im Tschetschenienkrieg
    Zwischen politischer Ohnmacht und
    Gleichgültigkeit
    Mit einem Vorwort von Lipchan Basajewa
    ISBN 978-3-89821-676-0

85  Stefan Meister
    Das postsowjetische Universitätswesen
    zwischen nationalem und
    internationalem Wandel
    Die Entwicklung der regionalen Hochschule
    in Russland als Gradmesser der
    Systemtransformation
    Mit einem Vorwort von Joan DeBardeleben
    ISBN 978-3-89821-891-7

86  Konstantin Sheiko in collaboration
    with Stephen Brown
    Nationalist Imaginings of the
    Russian Past
    Anatolii Fomenko and the Rise of Alternative
    History in Post-Communist Russia
    With a foreword by Donald Ostrowski
    ISBN 978-3-89821-915-0

87  Sabine Jenni
    Wie stark ist das „Einige Russland"?
    Zur Parteibindung der Eliten und zum
    Wahlerfolg der Machtpartei
    im Dezember 2007
    Mit einem Vorwort von Klaus Armingeon
    ISBN 978-3-89821-961-7

88  Thomas Borén
    Meeting-Places of Transformation
    Urban Identity, Spatial Representations and
    Local Politics in Post-Soviet St Petersburg
    ISBN 978-3-89821-739-2

89  Aygul Ashirova
    Stalinismus und Stalin-Kult in
    Zentralasien
    Turkmenistan 1924-1953
    Mit einem Vorwort von Leonid Luks
    ISBN 978-3-89821-987-7

90 Leonid Luks
Freiheit oder imperiale Größe?
Essays zu einem russischen Dilemma
ISBN 978-3-8382-0011-8

91 Christopher Gilley
The 'Change of Signposts' in the
Ukrainian Emigration
A Contribution to the History of
Sovietophilism in the 1920s
With a foreword by Frank Golczewski
ISBN 978-3-89821-965-5

92 Philipp Casula, Jeronim Perovic
(Eds.)
Identities and Politics
During the Putin Presidency
The Discursive Foundations of Russia's
Stability
With a foreword by Heiko Haumann
ISBN 978-3-8382-0015-6

93 Marcel Viëtor
Europa und die Frage
nach seinen Grenzen im Osten
Zur Konstruktion ‚europäischer Identität' in
Geschichte und Gegenwart
Mit einem Vorwort von Albrecht Lehmann
ISBN 978-3-8382-0045-3

94 Ben Hellman, Andrei Rogachevskii
Filming the Unfilmable
Casper Wrede's 'One Day in the Life
of Ivan Denisovich'
Second, Revised and Expanded Edition
ISBN 978-3-8382-0044-6

95 Eva Fuchslocher
Vaterland, Sprache, Glaube
Orthodoxie und Nationenbildung
am Beispiel Georgiens
Mit einem Vorwort von Christina von Braun
ISBN 978-3-89821-884-9

96 Vladimir Kantor
Das Westlertum und der Weg
Russlands
Zur Entwicklung der russischen Literatur und
Philosophie
Ediert von Dagmar Herrmann
Mit einem Beitrag von Nikolaus Lobkowicz
ISBN 978-3-8382-0102-3

97 Kamran Musayev
Die postsowjetische Transformation
im Baltikum und Südkaukasus
Eine vergleichende Untersuchung der
politischen Entwicklung Lettlands und
Aserbaidschans 1985-2009
Mit einem Vorwort von Leonid Luks
Ediert von Sandro Henschel
ISBN 978-3-8382-0103-0

98 Tatiana Zhurzhenko
Borderlands into Bordered Lands
Geopolitics of Identity in Post-Soviet Ukraine
With a foreword by Dieter Segert
ISBN 978-3-8382-0042-2

99 Кирилл Галушко, Лидия Смола
(ред.)
Пределы падения – варианты
украинского будущего
Аналитико-прогностические исследования
ISBN 978-3-8382-0148-1

100 Michael Minkenberg (ed.)
Historical Legacies and the Radical
Right in Post-Cold War Central and
Eastern Europe
With an afterword by Sabrina P. Ramet
ISBN 978-3-8382-0124-5

101 David-Emil Wickström
Rocking St. Petersburg
Transcultural Flows and Identity Politics in
the St. Petersburg Popular Music Scene
With a foreword by Yngvar B. Steinholt
Second, Revised and Expanded Edition
ISBN 978-3-8382-0100-9

102 Eva Zabka
Eine neue „Zeit der Wirren"?
Der spät- und postsowjetische Systemwandel
1985-2000 im Spiegel russischer
gesellschaftspolitischer Diskurse
Mit einem Vorwort von Margareta Mommsen
ISBN 978-3-8382-0161-0

103 Ulrike Ziemer
Ethnic Belonging, Gender and
Cultural Practices
Youth Identitites in Contemporary Russia
With a foreword by Anoop Nayak
ISBN 978-3-8382-0152-8

104 Ksenia Chepikova
‚Einiges Russland' - eine zweite KPdSU?
Aspekte der Identitätskonstruktion einer postsowjetischen „Partei der Macht"
Mit einem Vorwort von Torsten Oppelland
ISBN 978-3-8382-0311-9

105 Леонид Люкс
Западничество или евразийство? Демократия или идеократия?
Сборник статей об исторических дилеммах России
С предисловием Владимира Кантора
ISBN 978-3-8382-0211-2

106 Anna Dost
Das russische Verfassungsrecht auf dem Weg zum Föderalismus und zurück
Zum Konflikt von Rechtsnormen und -wirklichkeit in der Russländischen Föderation von 1991 bis 2009
Mit einem Vorwort von Alexander Blankenagel
ISBN 978-3-8382-0292-1

107 Philipp Herzog
Sozialistische Völkerfreundschaft, nationaler Widerstand oder harmloser Zeitvertreib?
Zur politischen Funktion der Volkskunst im sowjetischen Estland
Mit einem Vorwort von Andreas Kappeler
ISBN 978-3-8382-0216-7

108 Marlène Laruelle (ed.)
Russian Nationalism, Foreign Policy, and Identity Debates in Putin's Russia
New Ideological Patterns after the Orange Revolution
ISBN 978-3-8382-0325-6

109 Michail Logvinov
Russlands Kampf gegen den internationalen Terrorismus
Eine kritische Bestandsaufnahme des Bekämpfungsansatzes
Mit einem Geleitwort von Hans-Henning Schröder
und einem Vorwort von Eckhard Jesse
ISBN 978-3-8382-0329-4

110 John B. Dunlop
The Moscow Bombings of September 1999
Examinations of Russian Terrorist Attacks at the Onset of Vladimir Putin's Rule
Second, Revised and Expanded Edition
ISBN 978-3-8382-0388-1

111 Андрей А. Ковалёв
Свидетельство из-за кулис российской политики I
Можно ли делать добро из зла?
(Воспоминания и размышления о последних советских и первых послесоветских годах)
With a foreword by Peter Reddaway
ISBN 978-3-8382-0302-7

112 Андрей А. Ковалёв
Свидетельство из-за кулис российской политики II
Угроза для себя и окружающих
(Наблюдения и предостережения относительно происходящего после 2000 г.)
ISBN 978-3-8382-0303-4

113 Bernd Kappenberg
Zeichen setzen für Europa
Der Gebrauch europäischer lateinischer Sonderzeichen in der deutschen Öffentlichkeit
Mit einem Vorwort von Peter Schlobinski
ISBN 978-3-89821-749-1

114 Ivo Mijnssen
The Quest for an Ideal Youth in Putin's Russia I
Back to Our Future! History, Modernity, and Patriotism according to Nashi, 2005-2013
With a foreword by Jeronim Perović
Second, Revised and Expanded Edition
ISBN 978-3-8382-0368-3

115 Jussi Lassila
The Quest for an Ideal Youth in Putin's Russia II
The Search for Distinctive Conformism in the Political Communication of Nashi, 2005-2009
With a foreword by Kirill Postoutenko
Second, Revised and Expanded Edition
ISBN 978-3-8382-0415-4

116 Valerio Trabandt
Neue Nachbarn, gute Nachbarschaft?
Die EU als internationaler Akteur am Beispiel ihrer Demokratieförderung in Belarus und der Ukraine 2004-2009
Mit einem Vorwort von Jutta Joachim
ISBN 978-3-8382-0437-6

117 Fabian Pfeiffer
Estlands Außen- und Sicherheitspolitik I
Der estnische Atlantizismus nach der
wiedererlangten Unabhängigkeit 1991-2004
Mit einem Vorwort von Helmut Hubel
ISBN 978-3-8382-0127-6

118 Jana Podßuweit
Estlands Außen- und Sicherheitspolitik II
Handlungsoptionen eines Kleinstaates im
Rahmen seiner EU-Mitgliedschaft (2004-2008)
Mit einem Vorwort von Helmut Hubel
ISBN 978-3-8382-0440-6

119 Karin Pointner
Estlands Außen- und Sicherheitspolitik III
Eine gedächtnispolitische Analyse estnischer
Entwicklungskooperation 2006-2010
Mit einem Vorwort von Karin Liebhart
ISBN 978-3-8382-0435-2

120 Ruslana Vovk
Die Offenheit der ukrainischen
Verfassung für das Völkerrecht und
die europäische Integration
Mit einem Vorwort von Alexander
Blankenagel
ISBN 978-3-8382-0481-9

121 Mykhaylo Banakh
Die Relevanz der Zivilgesellschaft
bei den postkommunistischen
Transformationsprozessen in mittel-
und osteuropäischen Ländern
Das Beispiel der spät- und postsowjetischen
Ukraine 1986-2009
Mit einem Vorwort von Gerhard Simon
ISBN 978-3-8382-0499-4

122 Michael Moser
Language Policy and the Discourse on
Languages in Ukraine under President
Viktor Yanukovych (25 February
2010–28 October 2012)
ISBN 978-3-8382-0497-0 (Paperback edition)
ISBN 978-3-8382-0507-6 (Hardcover edition)

123 Nicole Krome
Russischer Netzwerkkapitalismus
Restrukturierungsprozesse in der
Russischen Föderation am Beispiel des
Luftfahrtunternehmens "Aviastar"
Mit einem Vorwort von Petra Stykow
ISBN 978-3-8382-0534-2

124 David R. Marples
'Our Glorious Past'
Lukashenka's Belarus and
the Great Patriotic War
ISBN 978-3-8382-0574-8 (Paperback edition)
ISBN 978-3-8382-0675-2 (Hardcover edition)

125 Ulf Walther
Russlands "neuer Adel"
Die Macht des Geheimdienstes von
Gorbatschow bis Putin
Mit einem Vorwort von Hans-Georg Wieck
ISBN 978-3-8382-0584-7

126 Simon Geissbühler (Hrsg.)
Kiew – Revolution 3.0
Der Euromaidan 2013/14 und die
Zukunftsperspektiven der Ukraine
ISBN 978-3-8382-0581-6 (Paperback edition)
ISBN 978-3-8382-0681-3 (Hardcover edition)

127 Andrey Makarychev
Russia and the EU
in a Multipolar World
Discourses, Identities, Norms
With a foreword by Klaus Segbers
ISBN 978-3-8382-0629-5

128 Roland Scharff
Kasachstan als postsowjetischer
Wohlfahrtsstaat
Die Transformation des sozialen
Schutzsystems
Mit einem Vorwort von Joachim Ahrens
ISBN 978-3-8382-0622-6

129 Katja Grupp
Bild Lücke Deutschland
Kaliningrader Studierende sprechen über
Deutschland
Mit einem Vorwort von Martin Schulz
ISBN 978-3-8382-0552-6

130 Konstantin Sheiko, Stephen Brown
History as Therapy
Alternative History and Nationalist
Imaginings in Russia, 1991-2014
ISBN 978-3-8382-0665-3

131 Elisa Kriza
Alexander Solzhenitsyn: Cold War
Icon, Gulag Author, Russian
Nationalist?
A Study of the Western Reception of his
Literary Writings, Historical Interpretations,
and Political Ideas
With a foreword by Andrei Rogatchevski
ISBN 978-3-8382-0589-2 (Paperback edition)
ISBN 978-3-8382-0690-5 (Hardcover edition)

132 Serghei Golunov
The Elephant in the Room
Corruption and Cheating in Russian
Universities
ISBN 978-3-8382-0570-0

133 Manja Hussner, Rainer Arnold (Hgg.)
Verfassungsgerichtsbarkeit in
Zentralasien I
Sammlung von Verfassungstexten
ISBN 978-3-8382-0595-3

134 Nikolay Mitrokhin
Die "Russische Partei"
Die Bewegung der russischen Nationalisten in der UdSSR 1953-1985
Aus dem Russischen übertragen von einem Übersetzerteam unter der Leitung von Larisa Schippel
ISBN 978-3-8382-0024-8

135 Manja Hussner, Rainer Arnold (Hgg.)
Verfassungsgerichtsbarkeit in
Zentralasien II
Sammlung von Verfassungstexten
ISBN 978-3-8382-0597-7

136 Manfred Zeller
Das sowjetische Fieber
Fußballfans im poststalinistischen Vielvölkerreich
Mit einem Vorwort von Nikolaus Katzer
ISBN 978-3-8382-0757-5

137 Kristin Schreiter
Stellung und Entwicklungspotential zivilgesellschaftlicher Gruppen in Russland
Menschenrechtsorganisationen im Vergleich
ISBN 978-3-8382-0673-8

138 David R. Marples, Frederick V. Mills (eds.)
Ukraine's Euromaidan
Analyses of a Civil Revolution
ISBN 978-3-8382-0660-8

139 Bernd Kappenberg
Setting Signs for Europe
Why Diacritics Matter for European Integration
With a foreword by Peter Schlobinski
ISBN 978-3-8382-0663-9

140 René Lenz
Internationalisierung, Kooperation und Transfer
Externe bildungspolitische Akteure in der Russischen Föderation
Mit einem Vorwort von Frank Ettrich
ISBN 978-3-8382-0751-3

141 Juri Plusnin, Yana Zausaeva, Natalia Zhidkevich, Artemy Pozanenko
Wandering Workers
Mores, Behavior, Way of Life, and Political Status of Domestic Russian Labor Migrants
Translated by Julia Kazantseva
ISBN 978-3-8382-0653-0

142 Matthew Kott, David J. Smith (eds.)
Latvia – A Work in Progress?
100 Years of State- and Nation-building
ISBN 978-3-8382-0648-6

143 Инна Чувычкина (ред.)
Экспортные нефте- и газопроводы на постсоветском пространстве
Анализ трубопроводной политики в свете теории международных отношений
ISBN 978-3-8382-0822-0

144 Johann Zajaczkowski
Russland – eine pragmatische Großmacht?
Eine rollentheoretische Untersuchung russischer Außenpolitik am Beispiel der Zusammenarbeit mit den USA nach 9/11 und des Georgienkrieges von 2008
Mit einem Vorwort von Siegfried Schieder
ISBN 978-3-8382-0837-4

145 Boris Popivanov
Changing Images of the Left in Bulgaria
The Challenge of Post-Communism in the Early 21st Century
ISBN 978-3-8382-0667-7

146 Lenka Krátká
A History of the Czechoslovak Ocean Shipping Company 1948-1989
How a Small, Landlocked Country Ran Maritime Business During the Cold War
ISBN 978-3-8382-0666-0

147 Alexander Sergunin
Explaining Russian Foreign Policy Behavior
Theory and Practice
ISBN 978-3-8382-0752-0

148　*Darya Malyutina*
　　Migrant Friendships in
　　a Super-Diverse City
　　Russian-Speakers and their Social
　　Relationships in London in the 21st Century
　　With a foreword by Claire Dwyer
　　ISBN 978-3-8382-0652-3

149　*Alexander Sergunin, Valery Konyshev*
　　Russia in the Arctic
　　Hard or Soft Power?
　　ISBN 978-3-8382-0753-7

150　*John J. Maresca*
　　Helsinki Revisited
　　A Key U.S. Negotiator's Memoirs
　　on the Development of the CSCE into the
　　OSCE
　　With a foreword by Hafiz Pashayev
　　ISBN 978-3-8382-0852-7

151　*Jardar Østbø*
　　The New Third Rome
　　Readings of a Russian Nationalist Myth
　　With a foreword by Pål Kolstø
　　ISBN 978-3-8382-0870-1

152　*Simon Kordonsky*
　　Socio-Economic Foundations of the
　　Russian Post-Soviet Regime
　　The Resource-Based Economy and Estate-
　　Based Social Structure of Contemporary
　　Russia
　　With a foreword by Svetlana Barsukova
　　ISBN 978-3-8382-0775-9

153　*Duncan Leitch*
　　Assisting Reform in Post-Communist
　　Ukraine 2000–2012
　　The Illusions of Donors and the Disillusion of
　　Beneficiaries
　　With a foreword by Kataryna Wolczuk
　　ISBN 978-3-8382-0844-2

154　*Abel Polese*
　　Limits of a Post-Soviet State
　　How Informality Replaces, Renegotiates, and
　　Reshapes Governance in Contemporary
　　Ukraine
　　With a foreword by Colin Williams
　　ISBN 978-3-8382-0845-9

155　*Mikhail Suslov (ed.)*
　　Digital Orthodoxy in the Post-Soviet
　　World
　　The Russian Orthodox Church and Web 2.0
　　With a foreword by Father Cyril Hovorum
　　ISBN 978-3-8382-0871-8

156　*Leonid Luks*
　　Zwei „Sonderwege"? Russisch-
　　deutsche Parallelen und Kontraste
　　(1917-2014)
　　Vergleichende Essays
　　ISBN 978-3-8382-0823-7

157　*Vladimir V. Karacharovskiy, Ovsey I.
　　Shkaratan, Gordey A. Yastrebov*
　　Towards a New Russian Work Culture
　　Can Western Companies and Expatriates
　　Change Russian Society?
　　With a foreword by Elena N. Danilova
　　Translated by Julia Kazantseva
　　ISBN 978-3-8382-0902-9

158　*Edmund Griffiths*
　　Aleksandr Prokhanov and Post-Soviet
　　Esotericism
　　ISBN 978-3-8382-0903-6

159　*Timm Beichelt, Susann Worschech
　　(eds.)*
　　Transnational Ukraine?
　　Networks and Ties that Influence(d)
　　Contemporary Ukraine
　　ISBN 978-3-8382-0944-9

160　*Mieste Hotopp-Riecke*
　　Die Tataren der Krim zwischen
　　Assimilation und Selbstbehauptung
　　Der Aufbau des krimtatarischen
　　Bildungswesens nach Deportation und
　　Heimkehr (1990-2005)
　　Mit einem Vorwort von Swetlana
　　Czerwonnaja
　　ISBN 978-3-89821-940-2

161　*Olga Bertelsen (ed.)*
　　Revolution and War in
　　Contemporary Ukraine
　　The Challenge of Change
　　ISBN 978-3-8382-1016-2

***ibidem**.eu*